SOUTH-WESTERN CENTURY 21 ACCOUNTING

MULTICOLUMN JOURNAL
INTRODUCTORY COURSE

ANNIVERSARY EDITION

SOUTH-WESTERN CENTURY 21 ACCOUNTING

MULTICOLUMN JOURNAL INTRODUCTORY COURSE

Kenton E. Ross, CPA
Professor Emeritus of Accounting
Texas A&M University–Commerce
Commerce, Texas

Mark W. Lehman, CPA
Associate Professor
School of Accountancy
Mississippi State University
Starkville, Mississippi

Claudia Bienias Gilbertson, CPA
Teaching Professor
North Hennepin Community College
Brooklyn Park, Minnesota

Robert D. Hanson
Late Associate Dean
College of Business Administration
Central Michigan University
Mount Pleasant, Michigan

CENTURY 21 ACCOUNTING · 100 YEARS OF EXCELLENCE

THOMSON
SOUTH-WESTERN

Australia · Canada · Mexico · Singapore · Spain · United Kingdom · United States

THOMSON
SOUTH-WESTERN

Century 21 Accounting, Multicolumn Journal, Anniversary Edition
by Kenton E. Ross, Claudia Bienias Gilbertson, Mark W. Lehman, and Robert D. Hanson

Vice President/ Executive Publisher
Dave Shaut
Team Leader
Karen Schmohe
Acquisitions Editor
Marilyn Hornsby
Project Manager
Carol Sturzenberger
Sr. Marketing Manager
Nancy A. Long
Marketing Coordinator
Yvonne Patton-Beard
Production Manager
Patricia Matthews Boies
Manufacturing Coordinator
Kevin Kluck
Editorial Assistant
Stephanie White
Production Assistant
Nancy Stamper
Design Coordinator
Tippy McIntosh
Cycle Opener Artwork
Marti Shohet
Cover Design
Tom Nikosey
Composition/Prepress
Better Graphics
Printer
R. R. Donnelley/Willard

ISBN: 0-538-43525-9
Printed in the United States of America

1 2 3 4 5 6 7 D 07 06 05 04 03 02

For more information, contact South-Western, 5191 Natorp Boulevard, Mason, OH 45040; or find us on the World Wide Web at http://www.swep.com

About the Authors

Kenton E. Ross, Ed.D., C.P.A., is Professor Emeritus, Department of Accounting, at Texas A&M University—Commerce. He formerly served as Dean of the College of Business and Technology; Director of Business and Economic Research; and Head, Department of Accounting.

Claudia Bienias Gilbertson, M.B.A., C.P.A., is an experienced high school and community college instructor. She is currently a teaching professor at North Hennepin Community College.

Mark W. Lehman, Ph.D., C.P.A., is an Associate Professor in the School of Accountancy at Mississippi State University, where he teaches in the areas of microcomputers, accounting systems, and auditing. He regularly teaches continuing education classes on microcomputers and internal control.

The late **Robert D. Hanson**, Ph.D., was Professor of Business Education and Associate Dean of the College of Business Administration at Central Michigan University.

REVIEWERS

Bruce J. (Ike) Bergeron
Business Instructor, Southeastern Vermont
Career Education Center
Brattleboro Union High School
Brattleboro, Vermont

Judith K. Berry
Business Services and Technology Consultant
Michigan Department of Education
East Lansing, Michigan

Margaret Chester
Instructor, Business Technology Department
Biloxi High School
Biloxi, Mississippi

Debbie Davidson
Accounting Instructor, Business Department
Ben Davis High School
Indianapolis, Indiana

Maurice Ellington
Chairperson, Business Education Department
John Marshall Metropolitan High School
Chicago, Illinois

Mary A. Gonzalez
Business Education Instructor
Weslaco High School
Weslaco, Texas

Cynthia A. Greene
Chairperson, Career Technology Department
Centennial High School
Fulton County Schools
Roswell, Georgia

James L. Knutson
Finance Director
City of Anoka
Anoka, Minnesota

Mary A. Lively
Business Technology Instructor
Great Oaks Institute of Technology and
Career Development
Cincinnati, Ohio

Maria Medina-Perez
Chairperson, Business Technology Education
Miami Palmetto Senior High School
Miami, Florida

Kelvin Meeks
Teacher, Business and Technology Department
Raleigh-Egypt High School
Memphis, Tennessee

Lisa Olson
Chairperson, Business Education Department
Hartford Union High School
Hartford, Wisconsin

Ronald Romano
Chairperson, Business Education Department
Ogdensburg Free Academy
Ogdensburg, New York

Judith P. Sams
Chairperson, Business Department
Fuqua School
Farmville, Virginia

Patricia Samuels
Director, Academy of Finance
Withrow High School
Cincinnati, Ohio

William Sinai
Chairperson, Computerized Accounting
West Valley Occupational Center
Woodland, California

Linda L. White
Chairperson, Business Education Department
Accounting Teacher
Waynesboro Area Senior High School
Waynesboro, Pennsylvania

Vera M. White
Chairperson, Vocational Technology
Hallandale High School
Hallandale, Florida

SOUTH-WESTERN CENTURY 21

ACCOUNTING

SEVENTH EDITION

CENTURY 21 ACCOUNTING

FAMILY OF PRODUCTS

South-Western Educational Publishing provides everything you and your students need to have a successful accounting classroom.

Wraparound Teacher's Edition provides

✷ OVERVIEW of each accounting cycle and each chapter within a cycle.

✷ TEACHING STRATEGIES loaded with hints, tips, and suggestions for reaching students with different learning styles—plus, a variety of instructional methods, such as cooperative learning, different media options, and more.

✷ CHAPTER INTERLEAF CHARTS that present concepts and skills covered in a chapter. Instructors can determine what will be new for students and what concepts and skills need reinforcement and emphasis. Also included is information about special features, technology and media, teaching strategies, and practice and assessment.

✷ EFFECTIVE TEACHING MODEL LESSON PLANS that provide step-by-step instructional support for every lesson. Each Lesson Plan includes the headings Motivate, Explain, Demonstrate, Guided Practice, Independent Practice, Reteach, Enrich, and Close.

✷ CHECK FIGURES that can be provided to students as guideposts as students complete their work or that can be used by instructors for quick and easy grading.

Working Papers contain accounting forms and rulings for completing chapter problems and Reinforcement Activities. The *Working Papers* are carefully laid out so that forms for the next problem are available while the previous problem is being graded. Plenty of extra forms are provided for any necessary rework. The Teacher's Editions of the *Working Papers* provide solutions to the problems. A separate *Study Guide and Recycling Problem Working Papers* book is also available.

Transparency Packages

An extensive array of **transparency packages** includes full-color teaching transparencies, blank accounting rulings to be used for guided practice and demonstrations, and transparencies of the solutions in the Teacher's Edition of the *Working Papers*.

Simulations

A **new simulation** is available for each accounting cycle in both manual and automated versions.

- ❑ *FOREIGN EXCHANGE TRANSLATION SERVICE* is a language translation service business organized as a sole proprietorship.
- ❑ *FITNESS JUNCTION* is an exercise equipment merchandising business organized as a partnership.
- ❑ *PUTTING GREEN GOLF SUPPLY* is a golf equipment and supply merchandising business organized as a corporation.

Technology

✷ TEMPLATE DISKS are available for use with *Automated Accounting 7.0, Windows; Automated Accounting 6.0, Windows;* and *Automated Accounting 6.0, Macintosh.* Template files are available for many problems in the textbook, the comprehensive Reinforcement Activities in each cycle, plus the three simulations. *Electronic Auditors* are also available.

✷ SPREADSHEET TEMPLATE DISKS correspond to selected textbook problems.

Assessment Binder Package Includes two separate versions of printed chapter and cycle tests, containing both objective questions and problems and a computerized testing program.

Other items available include

- ❑ **English and Spanish Dictionary**
- ❑ **Teacher's Resource Guide** in three-ring binder
- ❑ **Videotapes**
- ❑ **Multimedia CD-ROM**

CYCLE 1 Accounting for a Service Business Organized as a Proprietorship

Contents

CYCLE 2 ACCOUNTING FOR A MERCHANDISING BUSINESS ORGANIZED AS A PARTNERSHIP

Contents

SOUTH-WESTERN CENTURY 21 ACCOUNTING

INSTRUCTIONAL STRATEGIES

COMPLETE ACCOUNTING COVERAGE

Century 21 Accounting continues to provide complete coverage of three types of business—**proprietorship**, **partnership**, and **corporation**. This Introductory Course covers only proprietorships and partnerships. Each type of business is presented in a complete accounting cycle covering analyzing transactions, journalizing, posting, petty cash, financial statements, and adjusting and closing entries. Accounting concepts are introduced using a modern business with owners that students can relate to in each cycle. In Cycle 1, students study Encore Music, a business that provides music lessons. Cycle 2 features Omni Import, a retail merchandising business that purchases and sells imported gift items. Each accounting cycle opens with a two-page illustration connected to the business in the cycle.

South-Western Educational Publishing provides **two different approaches** to the study of first-year accounting. In its traditional blue cover, the Multicolumn Journal Approach lets students focus on analyzing transactions, knowing that all transactions will be entered in the same journal. In its familiar green cover, the General Journal Approach introduces special journals in Cycle 2. The focus on special journals mirrors college accounting and automated accounting approaches.

COLORFUL, ATTRACTIVE PAGES

Bright, interesting colors throughout the text draw students in and get them excited about accounting! Imagine how eager students will be about reading a bright and colorful textbook.

Scattered throughout are **eye-catching photos** that represent the featured businesses. Encore Music in Cycle 1 is represented by photos of musical instruments such as drums, maracas, and a trumpet. Omni Import in Cycle 2 by photos of imported gift items such as an elephant bowl from Africa, a mask from Asia, a jaguar figurine from Latin America, and nesting dolls from Europe.

MANAGEABLE PEDAGOGY WITH SHORT, ACCESSIBLE LESSONS

Have you ever heard a student say, "Accounting is hard"? Century 21 Accounting, Seventh Edition has the answer. Chapters are divided into **short, accessible lessons** that cover one or two concepts.

The Wraparound Teacher's Edition contains comprehensive lesson plans for each lesson to help you plan your instructional time more easily.

- ❑ **Chart of Accounts** used throughout the cycle is provided on the cycle opening pages for easy reference.
- ❑ **Terms Preview** displays all the key words introduced in the chapter.
- ❑ **Objectives** are listed at the beginning of each chapter to highlight lesson concepts and preview what students will learn.

Illustrations are consistently placed directly above the corresponding text. No more flipping pages back and forth to find an illustration that appears on a different page from the explanatory text! Plus, students can quickly find the illustration they are looking for when reviewing or working problems.

Steps and call-outs are completely integrated into the illustrations. This makes it easy to understand and then apply the procedure being taught. Clear, concise, step-by-step instructions are directly linked to the specific part of the illustration where the work is recorded.

The **concentrated supporting text** covers one specific topic and motivates students to read each page. Students are not intimidated by pages of text, but are encouraged to investigate the illustration and get further information by reading.

Many students are visual learners. First-year accounting emphasizes learning step-by-step procedures. With the combination of consistently placed, easy-to-locate illustrations, call-outs and instructions placed inside the illustrations, and step-by-step instructions, students can see how to complete accounting procedures and can refer to **easy-to-read steps** for reinforcement and clarification.

LESSON PRACTICE

Each lesson ends with an activity page that provides immediate reinforcement of the lesson material. Instructors can use the end-of-lesson activities to make sure students fully understand all concepts and procedures before moving on to the next lesson.

- **Terms Review** lists all the important new words learned in the lesson in the order they appear in the text.
- **Audit Your Understanding** asks two or more conceptual questions about the material covered in the lesson. The answers appear in Appendix D so students can check their understanding.
- **Work Together** provides guided practice through the students' first hands-on application of chapter procedures and concepts. Forms to complete the exercise are given in the Working Papers. Performing this exercise together with the instructor gives students a basis for completing similar problems later.
- **On Your Own** mirrors and builds on the Work Together problem to give the student independent practice. Forms to complete the exercise are given in the Working Papers. Students work this problem to demonstrate proficiency, giving them a real sense of accomplishment. Instructors can informally assess whether students have mastered the basic concept covered in the lesson. Accounting isn't so hard after all!
- Students get further independent practice from an end-of-chapter **Application Problem** that mirrors the end-of-lesson problems.

WORK SHEET OVERLAY

The Work Sheet Overlay is an excellent visual summary of the steps taken to prepare a work sheet. Students can see how a work sheet is prepared one section at a time, simplifying the process. The Work Sheet Overlay appears in Chapter 7: Work Sheet for a Service Business.

CHAPTER PRACTICE

Century 21 Accounting, Seventh Edition gives students **many short problems**. Students can now easily find and fix mistakes.

The **Summary** is a quick, short list of the topics covered in each lesson. Students can use the Summary to review their understanding of the material presented in the chapter. Instructors can ask questions based on the Summary as a fast way to verify student comprehension.

End-of-chapter exercises contain

- **Application problems** at least one for each lesson.
- **Mastery problems** that test overall comprehension of the entire chapter.
- **Challenge problems** that test overall comprehension of the entire chapter.

Many end-of-chapter problems can be completed using Automated Accounting software.

- **Reinforcement Activities** in each cycle.

And something new, most chapters contain one problem using real-life transaction statements.

APPENDICES

- **Appendix A: Accounting Concepts** Lists in one place all of the accounting concepts that students encounter throughout the text.
- **Appendix B: Using a Calculator and Computer Keypad** Provides important instruction in business calculator use and the ten-key touch system.
- **Appendix C: Recycling Problems** Offers additional opportunities for student practice. There is one recycling problem for each chapter, and these problems mirror the end-of-chapter mastery problems. Working papers are provided in the Study Guide and Recycling Problem Working Papers.
- **Appendix D: Answers to Audit Your Understanding** Contains brief answers to Audit Your Understanding questions that appear at the end of each lesson. Students can use the questions and answers for self study.

FEATURES

Special features provide context for accounting learning and real-life information about business. Features provide cross-curricular material for the accounting classroom.

LESSON FEATURES

❑ **Cultural Diversity** shows students that many different cultures around the world and throughout history have contributed to the development of accounting and financial record keeping.

❑ **Professional Business Ethics** presents dilemmas that can arise in day-to-day business operations.

❑ **Small Business Spotlight** features information about how to become a successful entrepreneur.

❑ **Accounting at Work** introduces real-life businesspeople who tell their stories about how accounting helps in their careers.

❑ **Technology for Business** covers the interplay between technology and business life. Topics covered include spreadsheets, the Internet, and commercial accounting software.

❑ **Global Perspective** provides insight into working with international suppliers and customers. Most students will have some global business experience in their careers. This feature introduces students to some of the issues involved in global business.

❑ **Legal Issues in Accounting** covers the legal issues involved in forming and dissolving the different forms of business organization and touches on other legal aspects of business life.

❑ **Applied Mathematics** boxes visually represent the intersection between accounting and mathematics and are strategically placed near relevant text to ensure optimum learning.

❑ **Remember** appears at the bottom of selected pages to reinforce critical accounting facts and procedures.

❑ **FYI** gives additional accounting and general business information related to the topics in a chapter.

CHAPTER FEATURES

❑ **Accounting in Your Career** features appear at the beginning of each chapter and entice students by showing how accounting is part of everyone's life. These scenarios answer the question, "Why should I learn this?" The Accounting in Your Career feature focuses your students' attention on the topics to be studied in the chapter.

❑ **Critical Thinking Questions** for Accounting in Your Career energize students with class discussions about accounting-related issues. The Critical Thinking Questions can even be used as an informal pretest and posttest to demonstrate how much students have learned after studying a chapter. Suggested answers to each question are provided in the Wraparound Teacher's Edition.

❑ **Internet Activity** provides the Web address and instructions for accessing the Internet activity for each chapter.

❑ **Applied Communication** offers exercises for strengthening communication skills, a must for all students. Employers are expecting their business and accounting new hires to be able to communicate effectively, so get started here.

❑ **Cases for Critical Thinking** require students to carefully consider one or more questions, based on the accounting scenario being presented. An excellent opportunity for in-class discussion or group work!

❑ **Explore Accounting** includes opportunities for higher-level learning with Discussion, Research, and Required exercises directly related to the material presented in the feature. Topics include GAAP, fiscal periods, cash controls, and more.

AUTOMATED ACCOUNTING

Automated Accounting sections conclude every chapter, and are a terrific opportunity for hands-on computer instruction with Automated Accounting. Now students see the connection between manual and automated accounting in every chapter.

INTRODUCTION

After studying this introduction, you will be able to:

1. Identify the many job opportunities available that require an accounting background.
2. Identify numerous careers in the accounting profession.
3. Identify the transferable skills an accounting class can strengthen.

On the first day of school, Kendra headed toward her fourth period class: accounting. She wondered what the class would be like. She had taken some other business classes, and enjoyed them. She was even thinking about pursuing a career in business. Last year, one of her teachers recommended that she take accounting. She hoped she would like it.

When she arrived at the classroom, Kendra was happy to find her friend Rob already there. "Hey, Rob, what are you doing here? I didn't know you were interested in business courses."

"Well, this is the first one I've taken. I really don't know what I want to do when I graduate in a couple of years, so I thought I should check out accounting. I'm really not sure it's for me, though."

The bell rang and the teacher came into the room. Everyone took a seat to get ready for class. Kendra sat next to Rob.

"Hi, everybody. I'm Mr. Perez, your accounting teacher for this year. And your first assignment is to come to the cafeteria with me."

Rob and Kendra looked at each other and at several of the other students. What was this?

Everyone followed Mr. Perez through the halls to the cafeteria. On the way there, Mr. Perez said, "I've assembled lots of people in the cafeteria. Professionals in all kinds of jobs. Feel free to talk to them about accounting fields, job opportunities, and more. You might be surprised at what you find out."

When they arrived at the cafeteria, they found a dozen people waiting to talk to them. They were from many companies, including accounting firms, entrepreneurial businesses, and governmental agencies. The class broke into smaller groups, and Rob and Kendra decided to walk around together. They chose to talk to an accountant first, because

When they arrived at the cafeteria, they found a dozen people waiting to talk to them. They were from many companies, including accounting firms, entrepreneurial businesses, and governmental agencies.

"I have a friend who has started her own floral shop, and she tells me she is very glad to have knowlege of accounting. It has really helped her ensure that the business succeeds."

Kendra wanted to find out more about the different fields in accounting.

"Why, there are many different specialized jobs accountants can do," said Ms. Ikeda, an employee for a large accounting firm in town. "I am a financial accountant, which means I record a business's financial activities and prepare the financial reports for my business. What I do helps creditors, investors, bankers, and auditors know the financial stability of my firm.

"The managerial accountants I work with take the financial accounting information I prepare and then analyze, measure, and interpret the information for internal use. Managers then use these interpretations to help them make the right business decisions.

"Cost accountants analyze and control the costs of an organization. They provide information that aids in decision making concerning the costs of operating the business and the costs of manufacturing goods or services.

"And, of course, there are tax accountants. They prepare tax returns and also perform tax planning responsibilities. They must stay up-to-date with changes in the law to ensure a business complies with the law.

"Systems accountants design and adapt the accounting systems that create financial, managerial, cost, and tax information reports for an organization. They also work hard to make these systems more efficient.

"An auditor's job is to review the reliability of a business's accounting records, and issue an opinion based on the information analyzed. An auditor's opinion enables those outside the business to feel confident about the stability of the business.

"Lastly, some accountants decide to become personal financial planners. They help individuals manage their personal investments, and they make suggestions about when and where money should be invested."

Rob and Kendra thanked Ms. Ikeda and then went to speak to some of the other professionals in the cafeteria. They found out about different types of employment opportunities available to people who have accounting backgrounds. Private accountants work for only one business; they may do all of the required summarizing, analyzing, and reporting, or they may specialize in one specific field of accounting. Public accountants can work independently or as a member of a public accounting firm, selling services such as preparing accounting reports or completing the tax forms for a business. Governmental/not-for-profit agencies also seem to have many opportunities for accountants. The Internal Revenue Service, hospitals, and churches all have needs for people to perform accounting duties.

Kendra thought all of the things she was learning were interesting. But Rob wasn't as excited as Kendra about possibly becoming an accountant. It just didn't seem to be for him, and he told Kendra he might decide to take a different class. He walked over to Mr. Perez and said, "Mr. Perez, maybe I shouldn't be taking this class. I don't think I want to be an accountant."

Mr. Perez smiled. "You don't have to want to be an accountant to benefit from taking this class. I'm not an accountant, but I have to know accounting to be your teacher. There are also many other accounting-related occupations that may interest you—travel agent, law clerk, manager, nurse, veterinarian. For these jobs, you'll need an understanding of accounting to make the right business decisions. I have a friend who has started her own floral shop, and she tells me she is very glad she has a knowledge of accounting. It has really helped her ensure that the business succeeds.

"Also, lots of small businesses need people to perform general accounting tasks. Businesses look for employees who can handle billing and collections, and payroll. But this is only part of the employee's job. They may also answer the phone, communicate with clients, and prepare annual reports or other documentation.

"What's more, there are many skills you will learn and strengthen by taking this class—skills that will help you regardless of what you decide you want to do. One of the most important skills you'll learn is how to communicate well, both when you write and when you speak. Accountants need to be able to communicate well because they often must relay information to people who have little or no accounting knowledge. But, being a good communicator is an invaluable tool for everyone to learn. Taking an accounting course will also help you learn to pay attention to details, improve your problem solving abilities, evaluate your own work, listen well, and interpret data. Those are all skills that will help you with any occupation you choose."

"Thanks Mr. Perez. I never realized I could learn so many important things by taking accounting," Rob said.

After finding out they could use accounting knowledge in so many different ways, Kendra, Rob, and all the other students were looking forward to studying accounting for the rest of the term.

Mr. Perez smiled. "You don't have to be an accountant to benefit from taking this class. I'm not an accountant, but I have to know accounting to be your teacher."

Accounting for a Service Business

CYCLE 1

Organized as a Proprietorship

ENCORE MUSIC CHART OF ACCOUNTS

General Ledger

Balance Sheet Accounts

(100) ASSETS
110 Cash
120 Petty Cash
130 Accounts Receivable—Kids Time
140 Accounts Receivable—Learn N Play
150 Supplies
160 Prepaid Insurance

(200) LIABILITIES
210 Accounts Payable—Ling Music Supplies
220 Accounts Payable—Sullivan Office Supplies

(300) OWNER'S EQUITY
310 Barbara Treviño, Capital
320 Barbara Treviño, Drawing
330 Income Summary

Income Statement Accounts

(400) REVENUE
410 Sales

(500) EXPENSES
510 Advertising Expense
520 Insurance Expense
530 Miscellaneous Expense
540 Rent Expense
550 Supplies Expense
560 Utilities Expense

The chart of accounts for Encore Music is illustrated above for ready reference as you study Cycle 1 of this textbook.

1 Starting a Proprietorship

AFTER STUDYING CHAPTER 1, YOU WILL BE ABLE TO:

1. Define accounting terms related to starting a service business organized as a proprietorship.
2. Identify accounting concepts and practices related to starting a service business organized as a proprietorship.
3. Classify accounts as assets, liabilities, or owner's equity and demonstrate their relationships in the accounting equation.
4. Analyze how transactions related to starting a service business organized as a proprietorship affect accounts in an accounting equation.
5. Prepare a balance sheet for a service business organized as a proprietorship from information in an accounting equation.

TERMS PREVIEW

accounting
accounting system
accounting records
service business
proprietorship
asset
equities
liability
owner's equity
accounting equation
transaction
account
account title
account balance
capital
balance sheet

WHAT IS ACCOUNTING?

Planning, recording, analyzing, and interpreting financial information is called **accounting.** A planned process for providing financial information that will be useful to management is called an **accounting system.** Organized summaries of a business's financial activities are called **accounting records.**

Accounting is the language of business. Many individuals in a business complete accounting forms and prepare accounting reports. Owners, managers, and accounting personnel use their knowledge of accounting to understand the information provided in the accounting reports. Regardless of their responsibilities within an organization, individuals can perform their jobs more efficiently if they know the language of business—accounting.

Inaccurate accounting records often contribute to business failure and bankruptcy. Failure to understand accounting information can result in poor business decisions for both businesses and nonprofit organizations. Understanding accounting helps managers and owners make better business decisions.

In addition, nearly everyone in the United States earns money and must submit income tax reports to the federal and state governments. Everyone, personally or for a business, must plan ways to keep spending within available income.

ACCOUNTING IN YOUR CAREER

THE JOB INTERVIEW

Robert Walker had a job interview today. He has just finished his first year of college but is undecided about what he should major in for the rest of his program. He cannot depend on his family to finance his college education, so he is prepared to continue his education as a part-time student and get a full-time job to pay tuition. He has been considering majoring in business, maybe even accounting, but he knows very little about the realities of the business world. Although he knows that completing college as a part-time student will take longer, he feels comfortable with his decision because of the practical experience he will gain from working.

Robert is looking for an office job as an administrative assistant. He can key 60 words per minute and has taken courses in word processing and spreadsheets.

Robert was interviewed by Paula Humphries, who operates a plumbing contractor business in town. At the end of the interview she said to Robert:

> Robert, you've got a good academic record. My company is growing rapidly, and I need people I can count on to help it grow. You don't have enough experience to be an administrative assistant, but I would like to start you as a general office assistant, which is an entry-level position. You would do some typing of bids, invoices, purchase orders, and correspondence, set appointments, file, and manage the telephones. You would be required to take an accounting course, which the company will pay for, but you will have to do it on your own time and get a good grade. I am offering you an opportunity to grow with my company. With a good performance record and the additional education, it wouldn't be too long before I could consider promoting you to administrative assistant.

Critical Thinking:

1. Why would Ms. Humphries want Robert to take an accounting course?
2. Should Robert reject this offer and hold out for an administrative assistant position?

1-1 The Accounting Equation

In 1989, Barbara Treviño started Encore Music. After several years of teaching at a local university, Barbara decided to start her own business so that she could have a more flexible schedule. After only two months, she had made all the arrangements and scheduled her first lessons. She has never looked back.

Barbara gets tremendous satisfaction from teaching music. Nothing matches the thrill of hearing a student master an instrument. She also really enjoys being her own boss. She gets a different kind of satisfaction from keeping her own accounting records and seeing that she is making money every month.

THE BUSINESS—ENCORE MUSIC

A business that performs an activity for a fee is called a **service business.** Barbara Treviño decided to start her own business, giving music lessons. A business owned by one person is called a **proprietorship.** A proprietorship is also referred to as a sole proprietorship. Ms. Treviño named her new proprietorship *Encore Music*. Encore Music will rent office space and the instruments used to teach music lessons.

Since Encore Music is a new business, Ms. Treviño must design the accounting system that will be used to keep Encore Music's accounting records. Ms. Treviño must be careful to keep Encore Music's accounting records separate from her own personal financial records. For example, Ms. Treviño owns a house and a personal car. Encore Music's financial records must *not* include information about Ms. Treviño's house, car, or other personal belongings. Ms. Treviño must use one checking account for her personal expenses and another checking account for Encore Music. The accounting concept, *Business Entity*, is applied when a business's financial information is recorded and reported separately from the owner's personal financial information. (*CONCEPT: Business Entity*)

Accounting concepts are described throughout this textbook when an application of a concept first occurs. When additional applications occur, a concept reference, such as (*CONCEPT: Business Entity*), indicates an application of a specific accounting concept. A brief description of each accounting concept used in this text is also provided in Appendix A.

Assets	=	Liabilities + Owner's Equity
Left side amount		Right side amounts
$0	=	$0 + $0

Encore Music will own items such as cash and supplies that will be used to conduct daily operations. Anything of value that is owned is called an **asset.** Assets have value because they can be used to acquire other assets or be used to operate a business. For example, Encore Music will use cash to buy supplies for the business. Encore Music will then use the asset, supplies, in the operation of the music lesson business.

Financial rights to the assets of a business are called **equities.** A business has two types of equities. (1) Equity of those to whom money is owed. For example, Encore Music may buy some supplies and agree to pay for the supplies at a later date. The business from whom supplies are bought will have a right to some of Encore Music's assets until Encore Music pays for the supplies. An amount owed by a business is called a **liability.** (2) Equity of the owner. Ms. Treviño will own Encore Music and invest in the assets of the business. Therefore, she will have a right to decide how the assets will be used. The amount remaining after the value of all liabilities is subtracted from the value of all assets is called **owner's equity.**

The relationship among assets, liabilities, and owner's equity can be written as an equation. An equation showing the relationship among assets, liabilities, and owner's equity is called the **accounting equation.** The accounting equation is most often stated as:

Assets = Liabilities + Owner's Equity

The accounting equation must be in balance to be correct. Thus, the total of the amounts on the left side of the equation must always equal the total of the amounts on the right side. Before Ms. Treviño actually starts the business, Encore Music's accounting equation would show all zeros.

Professional Business Ethics

Introduction to Business Ethics

The principles of right and wrong that guide an individual in making decisions are called *ethics.* The use of personal ethics in making business decisions is called *business ethics.*

Throughout this textbook you will have the opportunity to analyze the ethics of common business situations by using the following three-step checklist as a guide in collecting relevant information regarding an action.

1. *Is the action illegal? Does the action violate any laws?* Obeying the law is in your best interest and the best interest of your business.
2. *Does the action violate company or professional standards?* Public laws often set only minimum standards of behavior. Many businesses and professions set even higher standards of behavior. Thus, an action may be legal, yet still violate standards of the business or profession. Violating these standards may affect your job security and professional certification.
3. *Who is affected, and how, by the action?* If an action is legal and complies with business and professional standards, you must rely on your principles of right and wrong to determine if the action is ethical. Determining how the action affects individuals and groups—including business employees and owners, customers, the local community, and society—will help you decide if an action is ethical.

TERMS REVIEW

accounting
accounting system
accounting records
service business
proprietorship
asset
equities
liability
owner's equity
accounting equation

AUDIT YOUR UNDERSTANDING

1. What is accounting?
2. Give two examples of service businesses.
3. What is a proprietorship?
4. State the accounting equation.

WORK TOGETHER

Completing the accounting equation

Write the answers to the following problem in the *Working Papers*. Your instructor will guide you through the following example.

5. For each line, fill in the missing amount to complete the accounting equation:

Assets	=	Liabilities	+	Owner's Equity
?		3,000		8,000
10,000		?		6,000
63,000		35,000		?

ON YOUR OWN

Completing the accounting equation

Write the answers to the following problem in the *Working Papers*. Work this problem independently.

6. For each line, fill in the missing amount to complete the accounting equation:

Assets	=	Liabilities	+	Owner's Equity
23,000		?		13,000
?		70,000		30,000
48,000		25,000		?

1-2 How Business Activities Change the Accounting Equation

RECEIVING CASH

	Assets	=	Liabilities	+	Owner's Equity
	Cash	=			Barbara Treviño, Capital
Beginning Balances	$0		$0		$0
Received cash from owner as an investment	+10,000				+10,000
New Balances	$10,000		$0		$10,000

Business activities change the amounts in the accounting equation. A business activity that changes assets, liabilities, or owner's equity is called a **transaction.** For example, a business that pays cash for supplies is engaging in a transaction. After each transaction, the accounting equation must remain in balance.

The accounting concept, *Unit of Measurement*, is applied when business transactions are stated in numbers that have common values; that is, using a common unit of measurement. (*CONCEPT: Unit of Measurement*) For example, in the United States, business transactions are recorded in dollars. In Ghana, business transactions are recorded in *cedis*. The unit of measurement concept is followed so that the financial reports of businesses can be clearly stated and understood in numbers that have comparable values.

Received Cash from Owner as an Investment

Ms. Treviño uses $10,000.00 of her own money to invest in Encore Music. Encore Music should only be concerned with the effect of this transaction on Encore Music's records. The business should not be concerned about Ms. Treviño's personal records. (*CONCEPT: Business Entity*)

Transaction 1 ***August 1. Received cash from owner as an investment, $10,000.00.***

A record summarizing all the information pertaining to a single item in the accounting equation is called an **account.** The name given to an account is called an **account title.** Each part of the accounting equation consists of one or more accounts. For example, one of the asset accounts is titled Cash. The cash account is used to summarize information about the amount of money the business has available.

In the accounting equation shown above, the asset account, Cash, is increased by $10,000.00, the amount of cash received by the business. This increase is on the left side of the accounting equation. The amount in an account is called the **account balance.** Before the owner's investment, the account balance of Cash was zero. After the owner's investment, the account balance of Cash is $10,000.00.

The account used to summarize the owner's equity in a business is called **capital.** The capital account is an owner's equity account. Encore Music's capital account is titled Barbara Treviño, Capital. In the accounting equation shown above, the owner's equity account, Barbara Treviño, Capital, is increased by $10,000.00. This increase is on the right side of the accounting equation. Before the owner's investment, the account balance of Barbara Treviño, Capital was zero. After the owner's investment, the account balance of Barbara Treviño, Capital is $10,000.00.

The accounting equation has changed as a result of the receipt of cash as the owner's investment. However, both sides of the equation are changed by the same amount, $10,000.00. The $10,000.00 increase on the left side of the equation equals the $10,000.00 increase on the right side of the equation. Therefore, the accounting equation is still in balance.

PAYING CASH

	Assets			= Liabilities	+ Owner's Equity
	Cash	+ Supplies	+ Prepaid Insurance	=	Barbara Treviño, Capital
Balances	$10,000	$0	$0	$0	$10,000
Paid cash for supplies	−1,577	+1,577			
Balances	$8,423	$1,577	$0	$0	$10,000
Paid cash for insurance	−1,200		+1,200		
New Balances	$7,223	$1,577	$1,200	$0	$10,000

Encore Music pays cash for supplies and insurance.

Paid Cash for Supplies

Encore Music needs supplies to operate the business. Barbara Treviño uses some of Encore Music's cash to buy supplies.

Transaction 2 ***August 3. Paid cash for supplies, $1,577.00.***

In this transaction, two asset accounts are changed. One asset, cash, has been exchanged for another asset, supplies. The asset account, Cash, is decreased by $1,577.00, the amount of cash paid out. This decrease is on the left side of the accounting equation. The asset account, Supplies, is increased by $1,577.00, the amount of supplies bought. This increase is also on the left side of the accounting equation.

For this transaction, two assets are changed. Therefore, the two changes are both on the left side of the accounting equation. When changes are made on only one side of the accounting equation, the equation must still be in balance. Therefore, if one account is increased, another account on the same side of the equation must be decreased. After this transaction, the new account balance of Cash is $8,423.00. The new account balance of Supplies is $1,577.00. The sum of the amounts on the left side is $10,000.00 (Cash, $8,423.00 + Supplies, $1,577.00). The amount on the right side is also $10,000.00. Therefore, the accounting equation is still in balance.

Paid Cash for Insurance

Insurance premiums must be paid in advance. For example, Encore Music pays a $1,200.00 insurance premium for future insurance coverage.

Transaction 3 ***August 4. Paid cash for insurance, $1,200.00.***

In return for this payment, Encore Music is entitled to insurance coverage for the length of the policy. The insurance coverage is something of value owned by Encore Music. Therefore, the insurance coverage is an asset. Because insurance premiums are paid in advance, or *prepaid*, the premiums are recorded in an asset account titled Prepaid Insurance.

In this transaction, two assets are changed. One asset, cash, has been exchanged for another asset, prepaid insurance. The asset account, Cash, is decreased by $1,200.00, the amount of cash paid out. The asset account, Prepaid Insurance, is increased by $1,200.00, the amount of insurance bought.

After this transaction, the new account balance of Cash is $7,223.00. The new account balance of Prepaid Insurance is $1,200.00. The sum of the amounts on the left side is $10,000.00 (Cash, $7,223.00 + Supplies, $1,577.00 + Prepaid Insurance, $1,200.00). The amount on the right side is also $10,000.00. Therefore, the accounting equation is still in balance.

TRANSACTIONS ON ACCOUNT

	Assets			= Liabilities	+ Owner's Equity
	Cash +	Supplies +	Prepaid Insurance =	Accts. Pay.— Ling Music Supplies +	Barbara Treviño, Capital
Balances	$7,223	$1,577	$1,200	$0	$10,000
Bought supplies on account		+2,720		+2,720	
New Balances	$7,223	$4,297	$1,200	$2,720	$10,000
Paid cash on account	−1,360			−1,360	
New Balances	$5,863	$4,297	$1,200	$1,360	$10,000

Bought Supplies on Account

Encore Music needs to buy additional supplies. The supplies are obtained from Ling Music Supplies, which is located in a different city. It is a common business practice to buy items and pay for them at a future date. Another way to state this activity is to say that these items are bought *on account*.

Transaction 4 ***August 7. Bought supplies on account from Ling Music Supplies, $2,720.00.***

In this transaction, one asset and one liability are changed. The asset account, Supplies, is increased by $2,720.00, the amount of supplies bought. Ling Music Supplies will have a claim against some of Encore Music's assets until Encore Music pays for the supplies bought. Therefore, Accounts Payable—Ling Music Supplies is a liability account. The liability account, Accounts Payable—Ling Music Supplies, is increased by $2,720.00, the amount owed for the supplies.

After this transaction, the new account balance of Supplies is $4,297.00. The new account balance of Accounts Payable—Ling Music Supplies is $2,720.00. The sum of the amounts on the left side is $12,720.00 (Cash, $7,223.00 + Supplies, $4,297.00 + Prepaid Insurance, $1,200.00). The sum of the amounts on the right side is also $12,720.00 (Accounts Payable—Ling Music Supplies, $2,720.00 + Barbara Treviño, Capital, $10,000.00). Therefore, the accounting equation is still in balance.

Paid Cash on Account

Since Encore Music is a new business, Ling Music Supplies has not done business with Encore Music before. Ling Music Supplies allows Encore Music to buy supplies on account but requires Encore Music to send a check for one half of the amount immediately. Encore Music will pay the remaining liability at a later date.

Transaction 5 ***August 11. Paid cash on account to Ling Music Supplies, $1,360.00.***

In this transaction, one asset and one liability are changed. The asset account, Cash, is decreased by $1,360.00, the amount of cash paid out. After this payment, Encore Music owes less money to Ling Music Supplies. Therefore, the liability account, Accounts Payable—Ling Music Supplies, is decreased by $1,360.00, the amount paid on account.

After this transaction, the new account balance of Cash is $5,863.00. The new account balance of Accounts Payable—Ling Music Supplies is $1,360.00. The sum of the amounts on the left side is $11,360.00 (Cash, $5,863.00 + Supplies, $4,297.00 + Prepaid Insurance, $1,200.00). The sum of the amounts on the right side is also $11,360.00 (Accounts Payable—Ling Music Supplies, $1,360.00 + Barbara Treviño, Capital, $10,000.00). Therefore, the accounting equation is still in balance.

REMEMBER

The left side of the accounting equation must always equal the right side.

Terms Review

transaction
account
account title
account balance
capital

Audit Your Understanding

1. What must be done if a transaction increases the left side of the accounting equation?
2. How can a transaction affect only one side of the accounting equation?
3. To what does the phrase *on account* refer?

Work Together

Determining how transactions change an accounting equation

Write the answers to the following problem in the *Working Papers*. Your instructor will guide you through the following example.

Trans. No.	Assets	= Liabilities	+ Owner's Equity
1.			

4. For each transaction, place a plus (+) in the appropriate column if the classification is increased. Place a minus (−) in the appropriate column if the classification is decreased.

Transactions:

1. Bought supplies on account.
2. Received cash from owner as an investment.
3. Paid cash for insurance.
4. Paid cash on account.

On Your Own

Determining how transactions change an accounting equation

Write the answers to the following problem in the *Working Papers*. Work this problem independently.

Trans. No.	Assets	= Liabilities	+ Owner's Equity
1.			

5. For each transaction, place a plus (+) in the appropriate column if the classification is increased. Place a minus (−) in the appropriate column if the classification is decreased.

Transactions:

1. Received cash from owner as investment.
2. Paid cash for supplies.
3. Paid cash for insurance.
4. Bought supplies on account.
5. Paid cash on account.

1-3 Reporting Financial Information on a Balance Sheet

BALANCE SHEET

Periodically a business reports details about its assets, liabilities, and owner's equity. The financial details about assets, liabilities, and owner's equity could be found on the last line of the accounting equation. However, most businesses prepare more formal financial statements that may be copied and sent to interested persons. A financial statement that reports assets, liabilities, and owner's equity on a specific date is called a **balance sheet.**

When a business is started, it is expected that the business will continue to operate indefinitely. For example, Barbara Treviño assumes that she will own and operate Encore Music for many years. When she retires, she expects to sell Encore Music to someone else who will continue its operation. The accounting concept, *Going Concern*, is applied when financial statements are prepared with the expectation that a business will remain in operation indefinitely. (*CONCEPT: Going Concern*)

Body of a Balance Sheet

A balance sheet has three major sections. (1) *Assets* are on the left side of the accounting equation. Therefore, Encore Music lists its assets on the left side of the balance sheet. (2) *Liabilities* are on the right side of the accounting equation. Therefore, Encore Music lists its liabilities on the right side of the balance sheet. (3) *Owner's equity* is also on the right side of the accounting equation. Therefore, Encore Music lists its owner's equity on the right side of the balance sheet.

CULTURAL DIVERSITY

PROFESSIONAL ORGANIZATIONS

Professional organizations provide important social and economic benefits to their members. For example, the National Association of Black Accountants is a professional organization. Members of this association are CPAs, accountants, and accounting students. The organizational purpose is to unite accountants and accounting students who have similar interests and ideals. Members must be committed to professional and academic excellence. They must possess a sense of professional and civic responsibility. They must also be concerned with enhancing opportunities for minorities in the accounting profession.

Activities of the National Association of Black Accountants are diverse. They include free income tax preparation, student scholarships, high school and university career seminars, regional student conferences, and technical seminars and lectures. Other services of the organization include a speakers' bureau, a placement service, and publications of a journal and newsletter.

PREPARING A BALANCE SHEET

	Assets			= Liabilities	+ Owner's Equity
	Cash	+ Supplies	+ Prepaid Insurance	= Accts. Pay.—Ling Music Supplies	+ Barbara Treviño, Capital
Balances	$5,863	$4,297	$1,200	$1,360	$10,000

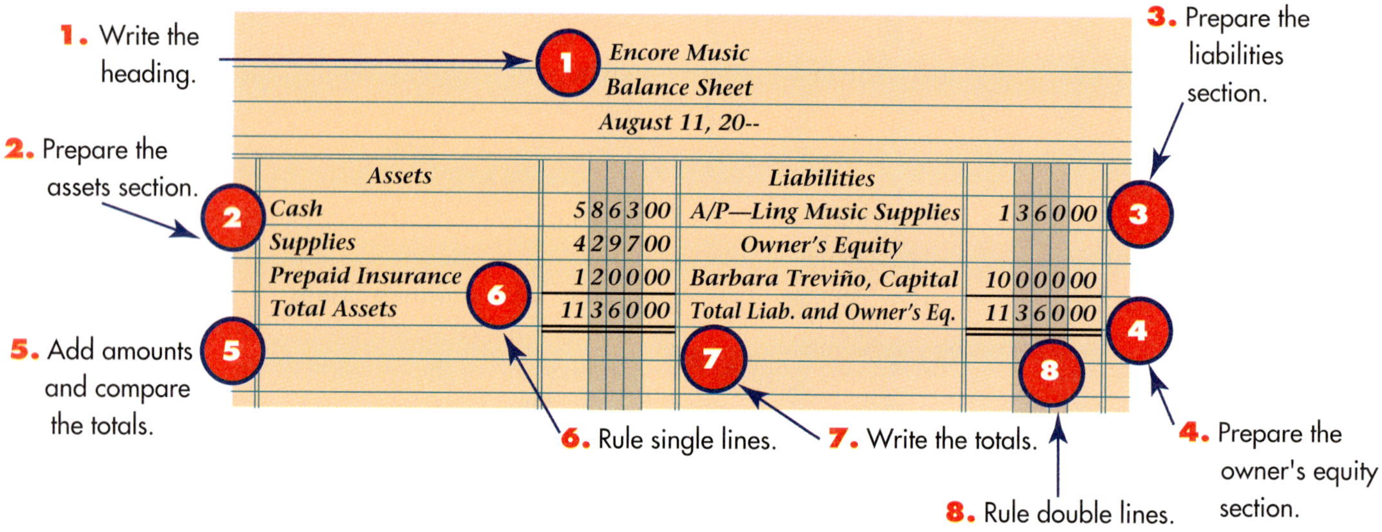

STEPS: Preparing a balance sheet

1. Write the *heading* centered on three lines at the top of the balance sheet: the name of the business, the name of the report, and the date of the report.
2. Because assets are on the LEFT side of the accounting equation, prepare the *assets section* on the LEFT side. Center the word *Assets* on the first line of the wide column. Under this heading, write each asset account title and amount.
3. Because liabilities are on the RIGHT side of the accounting equation, prepare the *liabilities section* on the RIGHT side. Center the word *Liabilities* on the first line of the wide column. Under this heading, write each liability account title and amount.
4. Because owner's equity is also on the RIGHT side of the accounting equation, prepare the *owner's equity section* on the RIGHT side. Center the words *Owner's Equity* on the next blank line. Under this heading, write the owner's equity account title and amount.
5. Add all the asset amounts. Add the liabilities and owner's equity amounts. If the totals equal, the balance sheet is *in balance*. If the totals do not equal, find the errors before completing any more work. Prepare a new balance sheet without errors.
6. Rule a single line across each amount column. A single line means that amounts are to be added or subtracted.
7. On the next line on the left side, write *Total Assets* and write the total asset amount under the single rule. On the right side, write *Total Liabilities and Owner's Equity* and write the total liabilities and owner's equity amount under the single rule.
8. Rule double lines below the amount column totals. Double rules mean that the totals have been verified as correct.

TERM REVIEW

balance sheet

AUDIT YOUR UNDERSTANDING

1. List the three sections of a balance sheet.
2. What kinds of accounts are listed on the left side of a balance sheet?
3. What kinds of accounts are listed on the right side of a balance sheet?
4. What should be done if a balance sheet is not in balance?

WORK TOGETHER

Preparing a balance sheet from information in an accounting equation

Write the answers to the following problem in the *Working Papers*. Your instructor will guide you through the following example.

On October 31 the Hess Company's accounting equation indicated the following account balances.

Trans. No.	Assets					=	Liabilities	+	Owner's Equity
	Cash	+	Supplies	+	Prepaid Insurance	=	Accts. Pay.—Hulett Company	+	Jim Hess, Capital
New Bal.	2,400		300		600		250		3,050

5. Using the October 31 balances in the accounting equation, prepare a balance sheet for the Hess Company.

ON YOUR OWN

Preparing a balance sheet from information in an accounting equation

Write the answers to the following problem in the *Working Papers*. Work this problem independently.

On July 31 the Goldstein Company's accounting equation indicated the following account balances.

Trans. No.	Assets					=	Liabilities	+	Owner's Equity
	Cash	+	Supplies	+	Prepaid Insurance	=	Accts. Pay.—Heino Company	+	Mary Goldstein, Capital
New Bal.	2,500		800		1,200		500		4,000

6. Using the July 31 balances in the accounting equation, prepare a balance sheet for the Goldstein Company.

CHAPTER 1 SUMMARY

After completing this chapter, you can

1. Define important accounting terms related to starting a service business organized as a proprietorship.
2. Identify accounting concepts and practices related to starting a service business organized as a proprietorship.
3. Classify accounts as assets, liabilities, or owner's equity and demonstrate their relationships in the accounting equation.
4. Analyze how transactions related to starting a service business organized as a proprietorship affect accounts in an accounting equation.
5. Prepare a balance sheet for a service business organized as a proprietorship from information in an accounting equation.

EXPLORE ACCOUNTING

WHAT IS GAAP?

The standards and rules that accountants follow while recording and reporting financial activities are commonly referred to as generally accepted accounting principles, or GAAP. These rules have not been developed by any one group of rule makers, but have instead evolved over time and from many sources.

By law, the Securities and Exchange Commission (SEC) has the authority to establish GAAP. The SEC, however, has allowed a series of private organizations to determine GAAP. Currently the organization that has the authority to set accounting standards is the Financial Accounting Standards Board (FASB), which was established in 1973.

The standard-setting process includes getting input and feedback from many sources. FASB listens to this feedback and considers all sides of each issue.

WHY IS GAAP NECESSARY?

Users of financial statements rely on the information those statements contain. If the preparers of financial statements were allowed to follow *any* measurement, recording, and reporting rules, the users of the statements would have no way to determine if the financial statements present fairly the financial position of the business.

By requiring the financial statement preparers to follow consistently certain standards and rules—such as GAAP—the users are able to compare the financial statements of several companies and to track the results of one company over several time periods.

Discussion: Why would a group of people disagree with a proposed accounting standard?

Research: Using your local library or the Internet, find additional information about the FASB. Write a one-page report on your findings.

1-1 APPLICATION PROBLEM
Completing the accounting equation

Instructions:
For each line, fill in the missing amount to complete the accounting equation, using your *Working Papers.*

Assets	=	Liabilities	+	Owner's Equity
90,000		49,000		?
?		68,000		30,000
3,000		?		2,000
108,000		60,000		?
19,000		?		11,000
?		4,000		12,000
25,000		13,000		?
?		113,000		49,000
4,000		?		2,000
86,000		48,000		?
12,000		?		7,000
?		5,000		14,000
47,000		24,000		?
?		29,000		13,000
38,000		?		21,000
125,000		69,000		?
11,000		?		6,000
?		1,000		3,000

1-2 APPLICATION PROBLEM
Determining how transactions change an accounting equation

Frank Mori is starting Mori Repair Shop, a small service business. Mori Repair Shop uses the accounts shown in the following accounting equation. Use the form in your *Working Papers* to complete this problem.

Trans. No.	Assets			= Liabilities		+ Owner's Equity
	Cash +	Supplies +	Prepaid Insurance	= Accts. Pay.— Swan's Supply Company +	Accts. Pay.— York Company +	Frank Mori, Capital
Beg. Bal. 1.	0 *+2,000*	0	0	0	0	0 *+2,000*
New Bal. 2.	*2,000*	*0*	*0*	*0*	*0*	*2,000*

Transactions:
1. Received cash from owner as an investment, $2,000.00.
2. Paid cash for insurance, $600.00.
3. Bought supplies on account from Swan's Supply Company, $100.00.
4. Bought supplies on account from York Company, $500.00.
5. Paid cash on account to Swan's Supply Company, $100.00.

6. Paid cash on account to York Company, $300.00.
7. Paid cash for supplies, $500.00.
8. Received cash from owner as an investment, $500.00.

Instructions:

For each transaction, complete the following. Transaction 1 is given as an example.

a. Analyze the transaction to determine which accounts in the accounting equation are affected.
b. Write the amount in the appropriate columns using a plus (+) if the account increases or a minus (−) if the account decreases.
c. Calculate the new balance for each account in the accounting equation.
d. Before going on to the next transaction, determine that the accounting equation is still in balance.

1-3 APPLICATION PROBLEM
Determining how transactions change an accounting equation

Ellie VonSpreecken is starting Ellie's Computer Repair, a small service business. Ellie's Computer Repair uses the accounts shown in the following accounting equation. Use the form in your *Working Papers* to complete this problem.

Trans. No.	Assets			= Liabilities		+ Owner's Equity
	Cash +	Supplies +	Prepaid Insurance	= Accts. Pay.— Seiler Supply	+ Accts. Pay.— Miles Company	+ Ellie Von Spreecken, Capital
Beg. Bal.	0	0	0	0	0	0
1.	*+3,000*					*+3,000*
New Bal.	*3,000*	*0*	*0*	*0*	*0*	*3,000*
2.						

Transactions:

1. The owner invested $3,000.00 cash in the business.
2. Paid $1,200.00 for insurance for the next year.
3. Purchased supplies from Seiler Supply for $800.00 on account.
4. Purchased $500.00 of supplies from Miles Company. Agreed to pay Miles next month for these supplies.
5. Paid $400.00 to Seiler Supply on account.
6. Ellie VonSpreecken invested an additional $1,000.00 in the business.

Instructions:

For each transaction, complete the following. Transaction 1 is given as an example.

a. Analyze the transaction to determine which accounts in the accounting equation are affected.
b. Write the amount in the appropriate columns using a plus (+) if the account increases or a minus (−) if the account decreases.
c. Calculate the new balance for each account in the accounting equation.
d. Before going on to the next transaction, determine that the accounting equation is still in balance.

1-4 APPLICATION PROBLEM
Determining where items are listed on a balance sheet

Use the form in your *Working Papers* to complete this problem.

1	2	3
Items	Balance Sheet	
	Left Side	Right Side
1. Cash	*Asset*	

Instructions:

Classify each item as an asset, liability, or owner's equity. Write the classification in Column 2 or 3 to show where each item is listed on a balance sheet. Item 1 is given as an example.

1. Cash
2. Michelle Sullivan, Capital
3. Supplies
4. Prepaid Insurance
5. Accounts Payable—Action Laundry
6. Anything owned
7. Any amount owed
8. Owner's capital account

1-5 APPLICATION PROBLEM
Preparing a balance sheet from information in an accounting equation

On September 30 the Steffens Company's accounting equation indicated the following account balances.

Trans. No.	Assets					=	Liabilities	+	Owner's Equity
	Cash	+	Supplies	+	Prepaid Insurance	=	Accts. Pay.—Morton Company	+	Steven Steffens, Capital
New Bal. (Sept. 30)	1,200		150		300		250		1,400

Instructions:

Using the September 30 balance in the accounting equation, prepare a balance sheet for the Steffens Company. A form is given in the *Working Papers*.

1-6 MASTERY PROBLEM
Determining how transactions change an accounting equation and preparing a balance sheet

Nancy Dirks is starting Dirks Company, a small service business. Dirks Company uses the accounts shown in the following accounting equation. Use the form in your *Working Papers* to complete this problem.

Trans. No.	Cash (Assets)	+ Supplies (Assets)	+ Prepaid Insurance (Assets)	= Accts. Pay.— Helfrey Company (Liabilities)	+ Nancy Dirks, Capital (Owner's Equity)
New Bal. 1.	0 +350	0	0	0	0 +350
New Bal. 2.	350	0	0	0	350

Transactions:

1. Received cash from owner as an investment, $350.00.
2. Bought supplies on account from Helfrey Company, $100.00.
3. Paid cash for insurance, $150.00.
4. Paid cash for supplies, $50.00.
5. Received cash from owner as an investment, $300.00.
6. Paid cash on account to Helfrey Company, $75.00.

Instructions:

1. For each transaction, complete the following. Transaction 1 is given as an example.
   a. Analyze the transaction to determine which accounts in the accounting equation are affected.
   b. Write the amount in the appropriate columns, using a plus (+) if the account increases or a minus (−) if the account decreases.
   c. Calculate the new balance for each account in the accounting equation.
   d. Before going on to the next transaction, determine that the accounting equation is still in balance.
2. Using the final balances in the accounting equation, prepare a balance sheet for Dirks Company. Use July 31 of the current year as the date of the balance sheet.

1-7 CHALLENGE PROBLEM
Applying accounting concepts to determine how transactions change the accounting equation

Morgan Delivery Service, a new business owned by Gregory Morgan, uses the accounts shown in the following accounting equation. Use the form in your *Working Papers* to complete this problem.

Trans. No.	Cash (Assets)	+ Supplies (Assets)	+ Prepaid Insurance (Assets)	= Accts. Pay.— Mutual Savings Bank (Liabilities)	+ Accts. Pay.— Nelson Supply Co. (Liabilities)	+ Gregory Morgan, Capital (Owner's Equity)
Beg. Bal. 1.	0 +1,500	0	0	0	0	0 +1,500
New Bal. 2.	1,500	0	0	0	0	1,500

Transactions:

1. Owner invested cash, $1,500.00.
2. Bought supplies for cash, $400.00.

3. Paid cash for insurance, $240.00.
4. Supplies were bought on account from Nelson Supply Company, $80.00.
5. The owner, Gregory Morgan, paid $1,000.00 of his personal cash to Mutual Savings Bank for the car payment on his personal car.
6. Wrote a check for supplies. The supplies were bought from a Canadian company. The supplies cost $120.00 in Canadian dollars, which is equivalent to $100.00 in United States dollars.
7. The owner, Gregory Morgan, used $300.00 of his personal cash to buy supplies for the business.

Instructions:

For each transaction, complete the following. Transaction 1 is given as an example.

a. Analyze the transaction to determine which business accounts in the accounting equation, if any, are affected. You will need to apply the Business Entity and Unit of Measurement concepts in this problem.
b. If business accounts are affected, determine the appropriate amount of the change. Write the amount in the appropriate columns, using a plus (+) if the account increases or a minus (−) if the account decreases.
c. Calculate the new balance for each account in the accounting equation.
d. Before going on to the next transaction, determine that the accounting equation is still in balance.

INTERNET ACTIVITY

Point your browser to

http://accounting.swpco.com

Choose **First-Year Course**, choose **Activities**, and complete the activity for Chapter 1.

Applied Communication

Since reports are valuable communication tools used to make decisions, they must be clearly written.

Instructions: The following paragraph is part of a report. Use a dictionary to check the spelling of any words you think may be misspelled. Use a thesaurus to replace the underlined words with better choices.

> Because comunication is such an important <u>device</u> in life today, ocasionnally we need to sharpen our communication skills. To be most effective, reports need to make every word count and every sentence <u>donate</u> to the <u>intention</u> of the report.

Cases for Critical Thinking

Case 1 James Patton starts a new business. Mr. Patton uses his personal car in the business with the expectation that later the business can buy a car. All expenses for operating the car, including license plates, gasoline, oil, tune-ups, and new tires, are paid for out of business funds. Is this an acceptable procedure? Explain.

Case 2 At the end of the first day of business, Quick Clean Laundry has the assets and liabilities shown below.

The owner, Susan Whiteford, wants to know the amount of her equity in Quick Clean Laundry. Determine this amount and explain what this amount represents.

Assets		Liabilities	
Cash	$3,500.00	A/P—Smith Office Supplies	$ 750.00
Supplies	950.00	A/P—Super Supplies Company	1,500.00
Prepaid Insurance	1,200.00		

AUTOMATED ACCOUNTING

COMPUTER SAFETY TIPS AND OPERATION BASICS

The following rules protect the operator of the equipment, other persons in the environment, and the equipment itself.

Electrical Equipment

1. Do not unplug equipment by pulling on the electrical cord. Instead, grasp the plug at the outlet and remove it.
2. Do not stretch electrical cords across an aisle where someone might trip over them.
3. Avoid food and beverages near equipment where a spill might result in an electrical short.
4. Do not attempt to remove the cover of equipment for any reason while the power is turned on.
5. Do not attempt to repair equipment while it is plugged in. To avoid damage, most repairs should be done by an authorized service technician.
6. Always turn the power off when finished using equipment.
7. Do not overload extension cords.
8. Follow manufacturer recommendations for safe use.
9. Replace frayed electrical cords immediately.

Computers

1. To avoid damage to the drives, do not insert pencils or other implements in floppy disk or CD-ROM drives.
2. To prevent overheating, avoid blocking air vents.
3. Position keyboards to prevent bumping or dropping them off the work surface.
4. Take care not to spill food or liquid on or in any computer component. If you do, turn off the computer immediately; unplug it; and notify your instructor before cleaning up the spill or turning on the equipment.
5. Avoid jolting or jostling your computer if it becomes necessary to move it.
6. Do NOT attempt to open or repair any part of the computer or monitor unless directed to do so by your instructor.

Monitors

1. Most manufacturers advise repair by authorized service technicians only.
2. Adjust brightness and focus for comfortable viewing.
3. Reposition computer to avoid glare on the monitor screen or use glare visors.
4. Do not leave fingerprints on the screen. Keep the screen clear of dust. Only use a soft cloth for cleaning the screen.

Printers

1. Do not let jewelry, ties, scarves, loose sleeves, or other clothing get caught in the machinery. This could result in damage to the machinery and could cause personal injury.
2. Exercise caution when using toxic chemicals such as toner in order to avoid spills.

Disks and Disk Drives

1. Do not bend disks.
2. Do not touch exposed surfaces of disks.
3. Be sure the disk drive is not running when you insert or remove a disk.
4. Keep disks away from extreme hot or cold temperatures. Do not leave disks in a car during very hot or cold weather.
5. Keep disks away from magnetic fields such as transformers and magnets.
6. Keep disks away from smoke, ashes, and dust, including chalk dust.
7. Be sure to make back-up copies.

Basic Mouse and Keyboard Operations

The installation and start-up procedures for *Automated Accounting* assume that you have a basic working knowledge of the mouse and keyboard operations. In preparation for your use of the *Automated Accounting* program, study the table on the next page. This table provides you with an opportunity to review important software functions.

AUTOMATED ACCOUNTING

BASIC MOUSE AND KEYBOARD OPERATIONS

Mouse Operation	Description
Point	Move the pointer to a specific location on the screen.
Click	Quickly press and release the left mouse button.
Drag	Press and hold down the left mouse button and move the mouse.
Point and Click	Pointing to an object on the screen and clicking on the mouse button is "clicking on the object." For example, if you are directed to "click on" Cancel, you should point to the Cancel button and click on the left mouse button.
Double-Click	Pointing to an object on the screen and clicking on the left mouse button twice, very rapidly (once to select [highlight] the item and once to choose it).

Keyboard Operation	Description
Tab	Use this key to move the focus (the current location on the display screen where the insertion point, highlight, and so on, is positioned) to the next control in the tab sequence.
Shift+Tab	Strike the Tab key while holding down the Shift key to move the focus back to the previous control in the tab sequence.
Enter	Press the Enter key to choose the action or response of the default command button or command button that currently has the focus.
Home	Use the Home key to move the insertion point to the first position within the current text box.
End	Use the End key to move the insertion point to the last position within the current text box.
Right/Down Arrow	Use the Right or Down Arrow key to move the insertion point one position to the right within the text box. Also, use these arrow keys to select option buttons within an option group.
Left/Up Arrow	Use the Left or Up Arrow key to move the insertion point one position to the left within the text box. Also, use these arrow keys to select option buttons within an option group.
Backspace	Within a text box, use this key to erase the character immediately to the left of the insertion point.
Delete	Within a text box, use the Del key to erase the character at the current insertion point position.
Esc	Use the Esc key to choose Cancel or Close within the active window.

2 Starting a Proprietorship: Changes That Affect Owner's Equity

TERMS PREVIEW

revenue

sale on account

expense

withdrawals

AFTER STUDYING CHAPTER 2, YOU WILL BE ABLE TO:

1. Define accounting terms related to changes that affect owner's equity for a service business organized as a proprietorship.
2. Identify accounting concepts and practices related to changes that affect owner's equity for a service business organized as a proprietorship.
3. Analyze changes in an accounting equation that affect owner's equity for a service business organized as a proprietorship.
4. Prepare a balance sheet for a service business organized as a proprietorship from information in an accounting equation.

TRANSACTIONS

A business activity that changes assets, liabilities, or owner's equity is known as a transaction. Chapter 1 described five transactions involved in starting Encore Music, a proprietorship. Encore Music is now ready to open for business.

In the last chapter, you studied transactions in which Encore Music received cash from the owner as an investment, paid cash for supplies, paid cash for insurance, bought supplies on account, and paid cash on account. This chapter presents more transactions that commonly occur during the daily operations of a business. In this chapter, you will study transactions in which Encore Music receives cash from sales, sells services on account, pays cash for rent and for a telephone bill, receives cash on account, and pays cash to the owner for personal use.

Many transactions involved in the daily operations of a business increase or decrease owner's equity. Detailed information about these changes in owner's equity is needed by owners and managers to make sound business decisions.

ACCOUNTING IN YOUR CAREER

A SMALL-BUSINESS OPPORTUNITY

Marcia Tran is an accounting clerk at Hader Specialties. Although she took accounting in high school, she wants to gain practical experience while planning to start her own business. Marcia has a natural artistic ability and has taken several college-level graphics courses. At the local university she earned enough income to pay for her coursework by designing logos and T-shirts for university groups. Jason Sudberry, a buyer for a national department store chain, has seen her designs and has asked her to have 3,000 T-shirts manufactured for his chain to buy. He has chosen a design from her portfolio and has stated that he thinks they'll sell quickly and that he may want to quickly reorder more, if that is the case.

Marcia has always planned to own her own business, combining her graphic arts talent with the knowledge of business she is gaining from her courses. She has worked hard to get this opportunity with the department store, and it took several appointments to convince Mr. Sudberry that her designs would be effectively used on apparel. She has also met with buyers from other department stores, and some of them have shown interest but are waiting to see how this first venture works out.

Marcia thinks this can be her big opportunity. She has prepared a business plan based on Mr. Sudberry's commitment to purchase 3,000 T-shirts. She has included price quotations from three manufacturers and an analysis showing expected profit. She is meeting this afternoon with the loan officer of Security National Bank to apply for a loan for $9,000 to manufacture the T-shirts and start her own business.

Critical Thinking:

1. What do you think of Marcia's idea to apply for a loan?
2. Do you think Marcia will get the loan?

2-1 How Transactions Change Owner's Equity in an Accounting Equation

REVENUE TRANSACTIONS

	Assets				=	Liabilities +	Owner's Equity
	Cash +	Accts. Rec.— Kids Time +	Supplies +	Prepaid Insurance	=	Accts. Pay.— Ling Music Supplies +	Barbara Treviño, Capital
Balances	$5,863	—0—	$4,297	$1,200		$1,360	$10,000
Received cash from sales	+325						+325 (revenue)
New Balances	$6,188	—0—	$4,297	$1,200		$1,360	$10,325
Sold services on account		+200					+200 (revenue)
New Balances	$6,188	$200	$4,297	$1,200		$1,360	$10,525

Total of left side:
$6,188 + $200 + $4,297 + $1,200 = $11,885

Total of right side:
$1,360 + $10,525 = $11,885

Received Cash from Sales

A transaction for the sale of goods or services results in an increase in owner's equity. An increase in owner's equity resulting from the operation of a business is called **revenue.** When cash is received from a sale, the total amount of assets and owner's equity is increased.

When Encore Music receives cash for services performed, the asset account, Cash, is increased by the amount of cash received. The owner's equity account, Barbara Treviño, Capital, is increased by the same amount.

Transaction 6 ***August 12. Received cash from sales, $325.00.***

Cash is increased by $325.00. This increase is on the left side of the equation. Barbara Treviño, Capital, is also increased by $325.00. This increase is on the right side of the equation. After this transaction is recorded, the equation is still in balance.

In this chapter, three different kinds of transactions that affect owner's equity are described. Therefore, a description of the transaction is shown in parentheses to the right of the amount in the accounting equation.

Sold Services on Account

A sale for which cash will be received at a later date is called a **sale on account,** or a charge sale. Encore Music contracts with two daycare centers to provide music lessons to the children at the centers. These centers are allowed to pay the cash to Encore Music at a later date. All other customers of Encore Music must pay cash at the time of the lessons.

When Encore Music sells services on account, the asset account, Accounts Receivable—Kids Time, is increased by the amount of cash that will be received. Regardless of when payment is made, the revenue should be recorded at the time of a sale. Therefore, the owner's equity account, Barbara Treviño, Capital, is also increased by the amount of the sale. The accounting concept, *Realization of Revenue,* is applied when revenue is recorded at the time goods or services are sold. *(CONCEPT: Realization of Revenue)*

Transaction 7 ***August 12. Sold services on account to Kids Time, $200.00.***

Accounts Receivable—Kids Time is increased by $200.00. This increase is on the left side of the equation. Barbara Treviño, Capital is also increased by $200.00. This increase is on the right side of the equation. After this transaction is recorded, the equation is still in balance.

PAID CASH FOR EXPENSES

	Assets				= Liabilities	+ Owner's Equity
	Cash +	Accts. Rec.— Kids Time +	Supplies +	Prepaid Insurance =	Accts. Pay.— Ling Music Supplies +	Barbara Treviño, Capital
Balances	$6,188	$200	$4,297	$1,200	$1,360	$10,525
Paid cash for rent	−250					−250 (expense)
New Balances	$5,938	$200	$4,297	$1,200	$1,360	$10,275
Paid cash for telephone bill	−45					−45 (expense)
New Balances	$5,893	$200	$4,297	$1,200	$1,360	$10,230

Total of left side:
$5,893 + $200 + $4,297 + $1,200 = $11,590

Total of right side:
$1,360 + $10,230 = $11,590

A transaction to pay for goods or services needed to operate a business results in a decrease in owner's equity. A decrease in owner's equity resulting from the operation of a business is called an **expense.** When cash is paid for expenses, the business has less cash. Therefore, the asset account, Cash, is decreased. The owner's equity account, Barbara Treviño, Capital, is also decreased by the same amount.

Transaction 8 ***August 12. Paid cash for rent, $250.00.***

The asset account, Cash, is decreased by $250.00, the amount of cash paid out. This decrease is on the left side of the equation. The owner's equity account, Barbara Treviño, Capital, is also decreased by $250.00. This decrease is on the right side of the equation. After this transaction is recorded, the equation is still in balance.

Transaction 9 ***August 12. Paid cash for telephone bill, $45.00.***

The asset account, Cash, is decreased by $45.00, the amount of cash paid out. This decrease is on the left side of the equation. The owner's equity account, Barbara Treviño, Capital, is also decreased by $45.00. This decrease is on the right side of the equation. After this transaction is recorded, the equation is still in balance.

Other expense transactions might be for advertising, equipment rental or repairs, charitable contributions, and other miscellaneous items. All expense transactions affect the accounting equation in the same way as Transactions 8 and 9.

CULTURAL VALUES IN THE UNITED STATES

Many of the values, norms, and roles in society come from the country's overall culture. A *value* reflects the goals a society considers important. It expresses the culture's shared ideas about what is good, right, and desirable. These are some generally accepted social values in the United States:

- *Freedom* of individuals to act as they please is a basic value.
- *Achievement and success* through honest efforts is highly valued. Achievement leads to a higher standard of living.
- The *work ethic* in the U.S. emphasizes working regularly.
- *Patriotism or nationalism* embody pride in a democratic heritage.
- Americans value *individual responsibility* and *self-fulfillment.* They try to develop themselves as individuals and are responsible for their own achievements.

CULTURAL DIVERSITY

	Assets				= Liabilities +	Owner's Equity
	Cash +	Accts. Rec.—Kids Time +	Supplies +	Prepaid Insurance =	Accts. Pay.—Ling Music Supplies +	Barbara Treviño, Capital
Balances	$5,893	$200	$4,297	$1,200	$1,360	$10,230
Received cash on account	+100	−100				
New Balances	$5,993	$100	$4,297	$1,200	$1,360	$10,230
Paid cash to owner for personal use	−100					−100 (withdrawal)
New Balances	$5,893	$100	$4,297	$1,200	$1,360	$10,130

Total of left side:
$5,893 + $100 + $4,297 + $1,200 = $11,490

Total of right side:
$1,360 + $10,130 = $11,490

Received Cash on Account

When a company receives cash from a customer for a prior sale, the transaction increases the cash account balance and decreases the accounts receivable balance.

Transaction 10 ***August 12. Received cash on account from Kids Time, $100.00.***

The asset account, Cash, is increased by $100.00. This increase is on the left side of the equation. The asset account, Accounts Receivable—Kids Time, is decreased by $100.00. This decrease is also on the left side of the equation. After this transaction is recorded, the equation is still in balance.

Paid Cash to Owner for Personal Use

Assets taken out of a business for the owner's personal use are called **withdrawals.** A withdrawal decreases owner's equity. Although an owner may withdraw any kind of asset, usually an owner withdraws cash. The withdrawal decreases the account balance of the withdrawn asset, such as Cash.

Transaction 11 ***August 12. Paid cash to owner for personal use, $100.00.***

The asset account, Cash, is decreased by $100.00. This decrease is on the left side of the accounting equation. The owner's equity account, Barbara Treviño, Capital, is also decreased by $100.00. This decrease is on the right side of the equation. After this transaction is recorded, the equation is still in balance.

A decrease in owner's equity because of a withdrawal is not a result of the normal operations of a business. Therefore, a withdrawal is not an expense.

Summary of Changes in Owner's Equity

After recording the transactions for starting Encore Music as a proprietorship, the total owner's equity was $10,000.00, which represented an investment by the owner, Barbara Treviño. In this chapter, five transactions that changed owner's equity were recorded in the accounting equation.

These transactions increased owner's equity by $130.00, from $10,000.00 to $10,130.00. Transaction 10 affects two accounts that are both on the left side of the accounting equation.

Transaction Number	Kind of Transaction	Change in Owner's Equity
6	Revenue (cash)	+325.00
7	Revenue (on account)	+200.00
8	Expense (rent)	−250.00
9	Expense (telephone)	− 45.00
11	Withdrawal	−100.00
	Net change in owner's equity	+130.00

TERMS REVIEW

revenue

sale on account

expense

withdrawals

AUDIT YOUR UNDERSTANDING

1. How is owner's equity affected when cash is received from sales?
2. How is owner's equity affected when services are sold on account?
3. How is owner's equity affected when cash is paid for expenses?

WORK TOGETHER

Determining how transactions change an accounting equation

Write the answers to the following problem in the *Working Papers.* Your instructor will guide you through the following example.

4. Place a plus (+) in the appropriate column if the account is increased. Place a minus (−) in the appropriate column if the account is decreased.

	Assets				= Liabilities	+ Owner's Equity
Trans. No.	Cash +	Accts. Rec.— Bowman Co. +	Supplies +	Prepaid Insurance =	Accts. Pay.— Maxwell Co. +	Susan Sanders, Capital
1.						

Transactions:

1. Received cash from sales.
2. Sold services on account to Bowman Company.
3. Paid cash for telephone bill.
4. Received cash on account from Bowman Company.

ON YOUR OWN

Determining how transactions change an accounting equation

Write the answers to the following problem in the *Working Papers.* Work this problem independently.

5. Place a plus (+) in the appropriate column if the account is increased. Place a minus (−) in the appropriate column if the account is decreased.

	Assets				= Liabilities	+ Owner's Equity
Trans. No.	Cash +	Accts. Rec.— O'Leary Co. +	Supplies +	Prepaid Insurance =	Accts. Pay.— Barrett Co. +	Sue Marist, Capital
1.						

Transactions:

1. Sold services on account to O'Leary Company.
2. Paid cash to owner for personal use.
3. Received cash from sales.
4. Received cash on account from O'Leary Company.

2-2 Reporting a Changed Accounting Equation on a Balance Sheet

BALANCE SHEET PREPARATION

	Assets				=	Liabilities + Owner's Equity	
	Cash +	Accts. Rec.—Kids Time +	Supplies +	Prepaid Insurance	=	Accts. Pay.—Ling Music Supplies +	Barbara Treviño, Capital
Balances	$5,893	$100	$4,297	$1,200		$1,360	$10,130

Encore Music
Balance Sheet
August 12, 20--

Assets		Liabilities	
Cash	5,893.00	A/P—Ling Music Supplies	1,360.00
Accts. Rec.—Kids Time	100.00	Owner's Equity	
Supplies	4,297.00	Barbara Treviño, Capital	10,130.00
Prepaid Insurance	1,200.00		
Total Assets	11,490.00	Total Liab. and Owner's Eq.	11,490.00

1. Write the heading.
2. Prepare the assets section.
3. Prepare the liabilities section.
4. Prepare the owner's equity section.
5. Add and compare the totals.
6. Rule single lines.
7. Write the totals.
8. Rule double lines.

A balance sheet may be prepared on any date to report information about the assets, liabilities, and owner's equity of a business. The balance sheet prepared in Chapter 1 reports Encore Music's financial condition at the end of business on August 11. The transactions recorded in Chapter 2 have changed the account balances of Cash, Accounts Receivable—Kids Time, and Barbara Treviño, Capital in the accounting equation. A revised balance sheet is prepared to report Encore Music's financial condition after recording these transactions.

The last transaction on August 12 is recorded in the accounting equation. The new account balances in the accounting equation after Transaction 11 are used to prepare the balance sheet.

The August 12 balance sheet is prepared using the same steps as described in Chapter 1.

The accounts on the left side of the accounting equation are reported on the left side of Encore Music's balance sheet. The accounts on the right side of the accounting equation are reported on the right side of Encore Music's balance sheet. The total of the left side of the balance sheet is equal to the total of the right side of the balance sheet. The balance sheet is in balance.

When one side of the balance sheet is longer than the other side, an adjustment must be made in order to have the totals of the two sides on the same line. On the August 12 balance sheet for Encore Music, one line is left blank on the right side so the the two totals are recorded on the same line.

Few businesses need to prepare a balance sheet every day. Many businesses prepare a balance sheet only on the last day of each month. Monthly balance sheets provide business owners and managers with frequent and regular information for making business decisions.

AUDIT YOUR UNDERSTANDING

1. What is the three-line heading on the top of the balance sheet?
2. What is the heading on the left side of the balance sheet?
3. What are the headings on the right side of the balance sheet?

WORK TOGETHER

Preparing a balance sheet

Write the answers to the following problem in the *Working Papers.* Your instructor will guide you through the following example.

On October 31 of the current year, the Marier Company's accounting equation indicated the following account balances.

	Assets				= Liabilities	+ Owner's Equity
	Cash +	Accts. Rec.— Poole Co. +	Supplies +	Prepaid Insurance =	Accts. Pay.— Alvarez Co. +	Joel Marier, Capital
Balances	$7,733	$5,000	$800	$2,400	$250	$15,683

4. Using the October 31 balances in the accounting equation, prepare a balance sheet for the Marier Company.

ON YOUR OWN

Preparing a balance sheet

Write the answers to the following problem in the *Working Papers.* Work this problem independently.

On December 31 of the current year, the Lynum Company's accounting equation indicated the following account balances.

	Assets				= Liabilities	+ Owner's Equity
	Cash +	Accts. Rec.— Meyer Co. +	Supplies +	Prepaid Insurance =	Accts. Pay.— Kelly Co. +	Tanya Lynum, Capital
Balances	$5,400	$600	$350	$1,800	$2,250	$5,900

5. Using the December 31 balances in the accounting equation, prepare a balance sheet for the Lynum Company.

CHAPTER 2 SUMMARY

After completing this chapter, you can

1. Define accounting terms related to changes that affect owner's equity for a service business organized as a proprietorship.
2. Identify accounting concepts and practices related to changes that affect owner's equity for a service business organized as a proprietorship.
3. Analyze changes in an accounting equation that affect owner's equity for a service business organized as a proprietorship.
4. Prepare a balance sheet for a service business organized as a proprietorship from information in an accounting equation.

EXPLORE ACCOUNTING

WHEN IS IT CALLED "REVENUE"?

Generally accepted accounting principles, GAAP, state that revenue should be counted as revenue when it is earned, regardless of when the cash is received. This means that a sale on account is counted as revenue at the time of the sale rather than when the cash is received.

What about long-term construction contracts or when a business isn't sure it will be able to collect the money on account?

For example, a construction company can contract to build a highway over a two-year period, receiving the money throughout both years or at the end of the project. When should the company include the revenue in its financial statements?

GAAP requires the use of the "percentage of completion" method for some long-term construction projects. This method requires the company to make an estimate of how much of the project is completed at the end of the first fiscal period. If the project is estimated to be 35% completed, the company is required to include 35% of the project's revenue as revenue for that period.

In another example, a company may sell services on account, allowing the customer to make six monthly payments for the services. If the seller is unsure of the ability of the customer to make the payments, GAAP requires the company to delay counting the entire sale as "revenue" even though, technically, the company has earned it. Using the "installment method" of recognizing revenue, the seller would count each installment as revenue as it is received.

Discussion:

1. Identify methods a company could use to estimate how much of a project is completed.
2. Why is it misleading to wait until a two-year contract is completed to include all the revenue from the contract in the financial statements for the second year?

2-1 APPLICATION PROBLEM

Determining how revenue, expense, and withdrawal transactions change an accounting equation

Peter Smith operates a service business called Peter's Service Company. Peter's Service Company uses the accounts shown in the following accounting equation. Use the form in your *Working Papers* to complete this problem.

Trans. No.	Assets				= Liabilities	+ Owner's Equity
	Cash +	Accts. Rec.— Lisa Lee +	Supplies +	Prepaid Insurance =	Accts. Pay.— Kline Co. +	Peter Smith, Capital
Beg. Bal.	625	—0—	375	300	200	1,100
1.	−300					−300 (expense)
New Bal.	325	—0—	375	300	200	800
2.						

Transactions:

1. Paid cash for rent, \$300.00.
2. Paid cash to owner for personal use, \$150.00.
3. Received cash from sales, \$800.00.
4. Paid cash for equipment repairs, \$100.00.
5. Sold services on account to Lisa Lee, \$400.00.
6. Received cash from sales, \$650.00.
7. Paid cash for charitable contributions, \$35.00.
8. Received cash on account from Lisa Lee, \$300.00.

Instructions:

For each transaction, complete the following. Transaction 1 is given as an example.

a. Analyze the transaction to determine which accounts in the accounting equation are affected.
b. Write the amount in the appropriate columns, using a plus (+) if the account increases or a minus (−) if the account decreases.
c. For transactions that change owner's equity, write in parentheses a description of the transaction to the right of the amount.
d. Calculate the new balance for each account in the accounting equation.
e. Before going on to the next transaction, determine that the accounting equation is still in balance.

2-2 APPLICATION PROBLEM

Determining how transactions change an accounting equation

Doris Becker operates a word processing business called QuickDoc. QuickDoc uses the accounts shown in the following accounting equation. Use the form in your *Working Papers* to complete this problem.

Trans. No.	Assets				= Liabilities	+ Owner's Equity
	Cash +	Accts. Rec.—Suburban Rental +	Supplies +	Prepaid Insurance =	Accts. Pay.—Teale Co. +	Doris Becker, Capital
Beg. Bal. 1.	500 −50	—0—	260	300	100	960 −50 (expense)
New Bal. 2.	450	—0—	260	300	100	910

Transactions:

1. Had equipment repaired and paid $50.00 cash.
2. Sold services for cash, $325.00.
3. Purchased supplies for $200.00, paying cash.
4. Bought supplies on account from Teale Company, $1,200.00.
5. Paid cash for advertising, $200.00.
6. Received cash from sales, $280.00.
7. Paid cash for water bill, $60.00.
8. Sold services to Suburban Rental on account, $320.00.
9. Owner withdrew cash for personal use, $125.00.
10. Suburban Rental sent $250.00 to pay part of the amount it owes QuickDoc.
11. Paid cash on account to Teale Company, $100.00.
12. Received cash from owner as an investment, $1,000.00.

Instructions:

For each transaction, complete the following. Transaction 1 is given as an example.

a. Analyze the transaction to determine which accounts in the accounting equation are affected.
b. Write the amount in the appropriate columns, using a plus (+) if the account increases or a minus (−) if the account decreases.
c. For transactions that change owner's equity, write in parentheses a description of the transaction to the right of the amount.
d. Calculate the new balance for each account in the accounting equation.
e. Before going on to the next transaction, determine that the accounting equation is still in balance.

2-3 APPLICATION PROBLEM
Preparing a balance sheet

On June 30, the Heil Company's accounting equation indicated the following account balances.

	Assets				= Liabilities	+ Owner's Equity
	Cash	+ Accts. Rec.—Jana Friestad	+ Supplies	+ Prepaid Insurance	= Accts. Pay.—Franco Supplies	+ Kevin Heil, Capital
Balance	8,655	942	475	750	665	10,157

Using the June 30 balances in the accounting equation, prepare a balance sheet for the Heil Company. Use the form in the *Working Papers* to complete this problem.

2-4 MASTERY PROBLEM
Determining how transactions change an accounting equation and preparing a balance sheet

Mikaela Mundt operates a service business called Mundt Company. Mundt Company uses the accounts shown in the following accounting equation. Use the form in your *Working Papers* to complete this problem.

	Assets				= Liabilities	+ Owner's Equity
Trans. No.	Cash	+ Accts. Rec.—Dorothy Romano	+ Supplies	+ Prepaid Insurance	= Accts. Pay.—Sickle Co.	+ Mikaela Mundt, Capital
Beg. Bal.	1,400	—0—	300	400	1,500	600
1.	*−100*					*−100 (expense)*
New Bal.	*1,300*	*—0—*	*300*	*400*	*1,500*	*500*
2.						

Transactions:

1. Paid cash for telephone bill, $100.00.
2. Received cash from owner as an investment, $200.00.
3. Paid cash for rent, $500.00.
4. Received cash from sales, $895.00.
5. Bought supplies on account from Sickle Company, $600.00.
6. Sold services on account to Dorothy Romano, $920.00.
7. Paid cash for supplies, $400.00.
8. Paid cash for advertising, $250.00.
9. Received cash on account from Dorothy Romano, $800.00.
10. Paid cash on account to Sickle Company, $1,500.00.
11. Paid cash for one month of insurance, $250.00.
12. Received cash from sales, $1,960.00.
13. Paid cash to owner for personal use, $1,000.00.

Instructions:

1. For each transaction, complete the following. Transaction 1 is given as an example.
   a. Analyze the transaction to determine which accounts in the accounting equation are affected.
   b. Write the amount in the appropriate columns, using a plus (+) if the account increases or a minus (−) if the account decreases.
   c. For transactions that change owner's equity, write in parentheses a description of the transaction to the right of the amount.
   d. Calculate the new balance for each account in the accounting equation.
   e. Before going on to the next transaction, determine that the accounting equation is still in balance.
2. Using the final balances in the accounting equation, prepare a balance sheet for Mundt Company. Use the date April 30 of the current year.

2-5 CHALLENGE PROBLEM

Determining how transactions change an accounting equation

Zachary Martin owns Zachary's Repair Shop. On February 1, Zachary's Repair Shop's accounting equation indicated the following account balances. Use the form in your *Working Papers* to complete this problem.

	Assets				= Liabilities	+ Owner's Equity
Trans. No.	**Cash**	**+ Accts. Rec.— Mary Lou Pier**	**+ Supplies**	**+ Prepaid Insurance**	**= Accts. Pay.— Kollasch Co.**	**+ Zachary Martin, Capital**
Beg. Bal.	8,552	1,748	1,485	615	3,145	9,255
1.						

Transactions:

1. Took $400.00 of supplies for personal use.
2. Had equipment repaired at Kollasch Company and agreed to pay Kollasch Company at a later date, $250.00.
3. Mr. Martin had some personal property which he sold for $500.00 cash.
4. Paid Kollasch Company $120.00 on account.

Instructions:

1. For each transaction, complete the following.
   a. Analyze the transaction to determine which accounts in the accounting equation are affected.
   b. Write the amount in the appropriate columns, using a plus (+) if the account increases or a minus (−) if the account decreases.
   c. For transactions that change owner's equity, write in parentheses a description of the transaction to the right of the amount.
   d. Calculate the new balance for each account in the accounting equation.
   e. Before going on to the next transaction, determine that the accounting equation is still in balance.
2. Answer the following questions:
   a. Why can the owner of a business withdraw assets from that business for personal use?
   b. Why would the owner withdraw assets other than cash?

INTERNET ACTIVITY

Point your browser to

http://accounting.swpco.com

Choose **First-Year Course**, choose **Activities**, and complete the activity for Chapter 2.

Applied Communication

A resume provides a statement of your education, experience, and qualifications for a prospective employer. Your resume should be accurate, honest, and perfect in every respect. It should include all work experience along with the companies and dates of employment. Education, activities, and interests are all important items that should be covered.

Instructions: Go to the library and research how to prepare an appropriate resume. Then prepare one that you could send to a prospective employer.

Cases for Critical Thinking

Case 1 Garcia Books received an investment from its owner, Ms. Juanita Garcia. This transaction is recorded in the following accounting equation. Is the analysis correct? Explain.

Assets			= Liabilities	+ Owner's Equity
Cash +	Supplies +	Prepaid Insurance =	Accts. Pay.—Panther Supply Company +	Juanita Garcia, Capital
$1,000 +750	$3,000	$2,000	$2,500	$3,500
$1,750	$3,000	$2,000	$2,500	$3,500

Case 2 The manager of Phillip's Department Store prepares a balance sheet at the end of each business day. Is this a satisfactory procedure?

Case 3 The supervisor of cash management at Joe's Consulting Agency wants to see how much cash was received from cash sales and sales on account. Which of the following transactions would be included in determining this amount? How do you know your analysis is correct? Explain.

Transactions:

1. Received cash from sales.
2. Sold services on account to Johnson Company.
3. Paid cash for advertising.
4. Paid cash to owner for personal use.
5. Received cash on account from Laundry Services.

AUTOMATED ACCOUNTING

LANGUAGE AND SKILLS FOR AUTOMATED ACCOUNTING

Using computer software to process accounting data can be an efficient and effective way to control the financial information of a business. In order to use the software, it is important to have a general understanding of computer and software terminology. Keyboarding skills are also essential for entering data. The more skilled you are and the greater your understanding, the better able you will be to accurately process financial information.

Automated Accounting Software

Automated Accounting 7.0 or higher software is used to teach students about computerized accounting principles. Accounting software is a set of instructions that operate the computer and enable the user to enter financial information and create reports, spreadsheets, and graphs. Specifically, *Automated Accounting* can process transactions for

- the purchase of assets, supplies, services, and the related payments.
- recording investments in the business.
- sales, cash receipts, and noncash transactions.

There are many other types of transactions that can be entered into an automated accounting system. Many of the various types of transactions will be studied in this class.

Automated Accounting versus Manual Accounting

Most students learn accounting by first processing transactions manually (by hand). It is important to learn the methods of recording transactions by hand before entering this information into an automated accounting system. Learning the principles of accounting is necessary in order to analyze how to process transactions. Once you learn accounting principles, you will be better able to understand the functions of an automated system.

Understanding automated accounting will help you in the workplace. Many businesses use computers to enter accounting data to process information more efficiently. After learning automated accounting, you will be able to more easily follow trails of information to analyze and correct errors.

Menu Bar and Drop-Down Lists versus Toolbar

The menu bar and drop-down lists enable you to communicate with the software. When a menu title is selected, a drop-down menu list appears. This drop-down list presents additional options to perform specific actions. Toolbar buttons can also be selected without using the drop-down list. Each toolbar button has a unique function that is similar to an item found on a drop-down list. The illustration shows the menu bar titles and the toolbar. *Automated Accounting 8.0* has additional menu

Menu Bar— Lists the menu titles.

Current File Name and User Name— Displays file and user name when a file is opened and loaded into memory.

Toolbar— Provides a shortcut method of accessing the most commonly used menu items by clicking a button.

Automated Accounting

options and toolbar buttons.

The following terms are elements of the *Automated Accounting 7.0* menu bar. Most of the terms will be studied again in later chapters.

File is a menu title that includes options to create a new document, open an existing document, save new or existing documents, and print. The Exit menu item is also listed under the File menu title.

Edit is a menu title that includes options to cut, copy, and paste text to separate spreadsheet and word processing documents. When processing information in the Journal Entries window, Find and Find Next can be used to locate data you wish to find.

Data is a menu title that includes options to customize accounting elements, select planning tools, maintain accounts, and create journal entries. The Other Activities option leads you to special activities such as Bank Reconciliation.

Options is a menu title that includes choices to generate depreciation adjusting entries, current payroll journal entries, employer's payroll taxes, and closing journal entries. Options also includes a calculator.

Reports is a menu title that includes options for report selection and graph selection. An important element of Reports is the run date because a report consists of accounting data up to and including the run date.

The run date is printed on reports prepared by the software. The run date can be changed on the report selection screen by changing the numbers in the Run Date field or using the calendar. If the run date is not manually changed, the run date will be the date of the last transaction entered in any of the journals.

Window is a menu title that includes an option to close all windows.

Help includes options to search and view help contents, problem instructions, and information about *Automated Accounting.*

Automated Accounting 8.0 has an additional menu item, Internet for accessing the Web Browser.

Selecting and Opening Files

When selecting and opening files, it is important to open the appropriate directory/folder in order to select the desired file. Also, it is best to save your files promptly upon completion of a problem before properly exiting the *Automated Accounting* system.

Changing Directories/Folders

When changing directories/folders, choose the disk drive that contains the file you want to open. The desired file may not always be in the folder shown when the Open command is selected. Your instructor may tell you to change folders. After selecting the directory/folder that includes the file you need, highlight the file you wish to choose and click OK.

Saving Files

Choose the Save menu item from the File menu or click on the Save toolbar button. Before using the Save menu item, be sure to check the upper right corner of the screen for the file name to which you want to save. (This information displays in the title bar in *Automated Accounting 8.0.*) The opening balance file, also called a template, includes a database of information about a particular business and can be used more than once.

Specifically, the opening balance file includes general information about the business, a chart of accounts, and account balances. If the file name has not been changed from the original opening balance file name, you must use the Save As menu item first. *Automated Accounting* will not allow you to save to the opening balance file.

Exit

After you have completed your session and saved your file, click on the Exit toolbar button to exit *Automated Accounting.*

3 Analyzing Transactions into Debit and Credit Parts

AFTER STUDYING CHAPTER 3, YOU WILL BE ABLE TO:

1. Define accounting terms related to analyzing transactions into debit and credit parts.
2. Identify accounting practices related to analyzing transactions into debit and credit parts.
3. Use T accounts to analyze transactions showing which accounts are debited or credited for each transaction.
4. Analyze how transactions to set up a business affect accounts.
5. Analyze how transactions affect owner's equity accounts.

TERMS PREVIEW

T account

debit

credit

normal balance

chart of accounts

ANALYZING THE ACCOUNTING EQUATION

Even though the effects of transactions *can* be recorded in an accounting equation, the procedure is not practical in an actual accounting system. The number of accounts used by most businesses would make the accounting equation cumbersome to use as a major financial record. Therefore, a separate record is commonly used for each account. The accounting equation can be represented as a T, as shown.

Assets	= Liabilities + Owner's Equity
Left side	Right side

The values of all things owned (assets) are on the left side of the accounting equation. The values of all equities or claims against the assets (liabilities and owner's equity) are on the right side of the accounting equation. The total of amounts on the left side of the accounting equation must always equal the total of amounts on the right side. Therefore, the total of all assets on the left side of the accounting equation must always equal the total of all liabilities and owner's equity on the right side.

ACCOUNTING IN YOUR CAREER

ADDING ACCOUNTS

John Robbin, the owner of Robbin's Auto Service, has requested a meeting with Diane Endo, his accounting assistant, to discuss changes in the business.

Diane Endo: You asked to see me, John. What's up?

John Robbin: Diane, you've been my accounting assistant for nine months, and I've been impressed with what you've learned and how well you journalize all the company's transactions.

Diane Endo: Thanks, John. It's been fun to learn and I enjoy working for this company.

John Robbin: Now I need your creative thinking. More and more people are servicing their own cars, so I've been thinking about branching out to sell auto parts.

Diane Endo: Sounds like a good idea. What do you want me to do?

John Robbin: I'd like you to recommend changes to the chart of accounts.

Diane Endo: I've got some thoughts already. What do you want to accomplish?

John Robbin: I want to be able to break sales and expenses down by departments. In addition to our existing repair business, the new department would be parts. I will also need to rent additional space next door to create a showroom area to merchandise the auto parts.

Diane Endo: When do you need this information?

John Robbin: Well, today is Monday. Can you have it ready by Wednesday? I want to move fast on this.

Critical Thinking:

1. What kinds of new accounts should Diane Endo recommend?
2. Should she recommend any changes to the numbering system of the chart of accounts?

3-1 Using T Accounts

ACCOUNTS

Assets	= Liabilities + Owner's Equity
Left side	Right side

T Account	
Left side **DEBIT SIDE**	Right side **CREDIT SIDE**

A record summarizing all the information pertaining to a single item in the accounting equation is known as an account. Transactions change the balances of accounts in the accounting equation. Accounting transactions must be analyzed to determine how account balances are changed. An accounting device used to analyze transactions is called a **T account.**

There are special names for amounts recorded on the left and right sides of a T account. An amount recorded on the left side is called a **debit.** An amount recorded on the right side is called a **credit.** The words *debit* and *credit* come from the Latin and Italian words *debere* and *credere.* Common abbreviations are *dr.* for debit and *cr.* for credit.

ACCOUNT BALANCES

Assets = **Liabilities** + **Owner's Equity**

Any Asset	
Debit **NORMAL BALANCE**	Credit

Any Liability	
Debit	Credit **NORMAL BALANCE**

Owner's Capital Account	
Debit	Credit **NORMAL BALANCE**

The side of the account that is increased is called the **normal balance.** The process of increasing or decreasing account balances is discussed on the next page. Assets are on the left side of the accounting equation, and asset accounts have normal debit balances (left side). Liabilities are on the right side of the accounting equation, and liability accounts have normal credit balances (right side). The owner's capital account is on the right side of the accounting equation and has a normal credit balance (right side).

INCREASES AND DECREASES IN ACCOUNTS

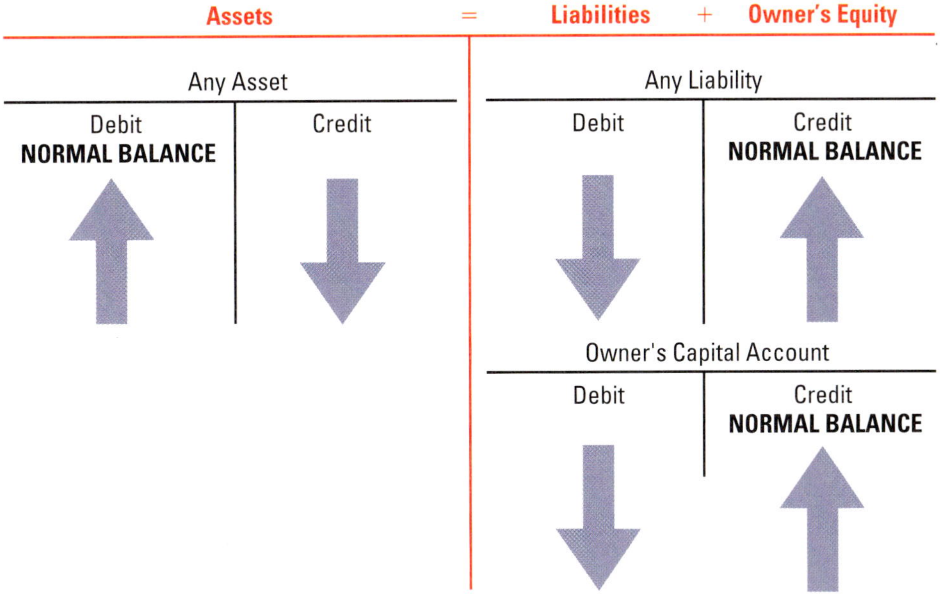

The sides of a T account are used to show increases and decreases in account balances.

Two basic accounting rules regulate increases and decreases of account balances. (1) Account balances increase on the normal balance side of an account. (2) Account balances decrease on the side opposite the normal balance side of an account.

Asset accounts have normal debit balances; therefore, asset accounts increase on the debit side and decrease on the credit side. Liability accounts have normal credit balances; therefore, liability accounts increase on the credit side and decrease on the debit side. The owner's capital account has a normal credit balance; therefore, the capital account increases on the credit side and decreases on the debit side.

Dining Out with Computers

Next time you order a taco—think technology. That's right, technology is changing the way restaurants do business. Computers are widely used to enter orders, generate guest checks, and print receipts. Computers also track the menu items that diners order—how many of each item is served each day, what time of day it is ordered, and what other items are ordered along with it.

The technology makes it possible for restaurant managers to predict how much of each food item to order, how much to prepare on a given day, and when to start cooking. Computer software programs also help managers plan their staffing needs based on trends developed from historical data.

Hand-held computers are used by servers in some restaurants to transmit information to the kitchen, where it is printed for the chef. This technology can reduce the time diners sit at a table. That translates into more diners served and more revenue for the restaurant.

Remember, technology is all around, even when you order that taco.

Technology for Business

TERMS REVIEW

T account

debit

credit

normal balance

AUDIT YOUR UNDERSTANDING

1. Draw the accounting equation on a T account.
2. What are the two accounting rules that regulate increases and decreases of account balances?

WORK TOGETHER

Determining the normal balance, increase, and decrease sides for accounts

Write the answers to the following problems in the *Working Papers*. Your instructor will guide you through the following examples.

Cash
Accounts Receivable—Christine Kelly
Supplies
Prepaid Insurance
Accounts Payable—Miller Supplies
Accounts Payable—Wayne Office Supplies
Jeff Dixon, Capital

For each of the accounts, complete the following:

3. Prepare a T account.
4. Label the debit and credit sides.
5. Label each side of the T account using the following labels:
   a. Normal balance
   b. Increase side
   c. Decrease side

ON YOUR OWN

Determining the normal balance, increase, and decrease sides for accounts

Write the answers to the following problems in the *Working Papers*. Work these problems independently.

Cash
Accounts Receivable—Brian Lee
Supplies
Prepaid Insurance
Accounts Payable—Golf Tees
Vickie Haskins, Capital

For each of the accounts, complete the following:

6. Prepare a T account.
7. Label the debit and credit sides.
8. Label each side of the T account using the following labels:
   a. Normal balance
   b. Increase side
   c. Decrease side

3-2 Analyzing How Transactions Affect Accounts

RECEIVED CASH FROM OWNER AS AN INVESTMENT

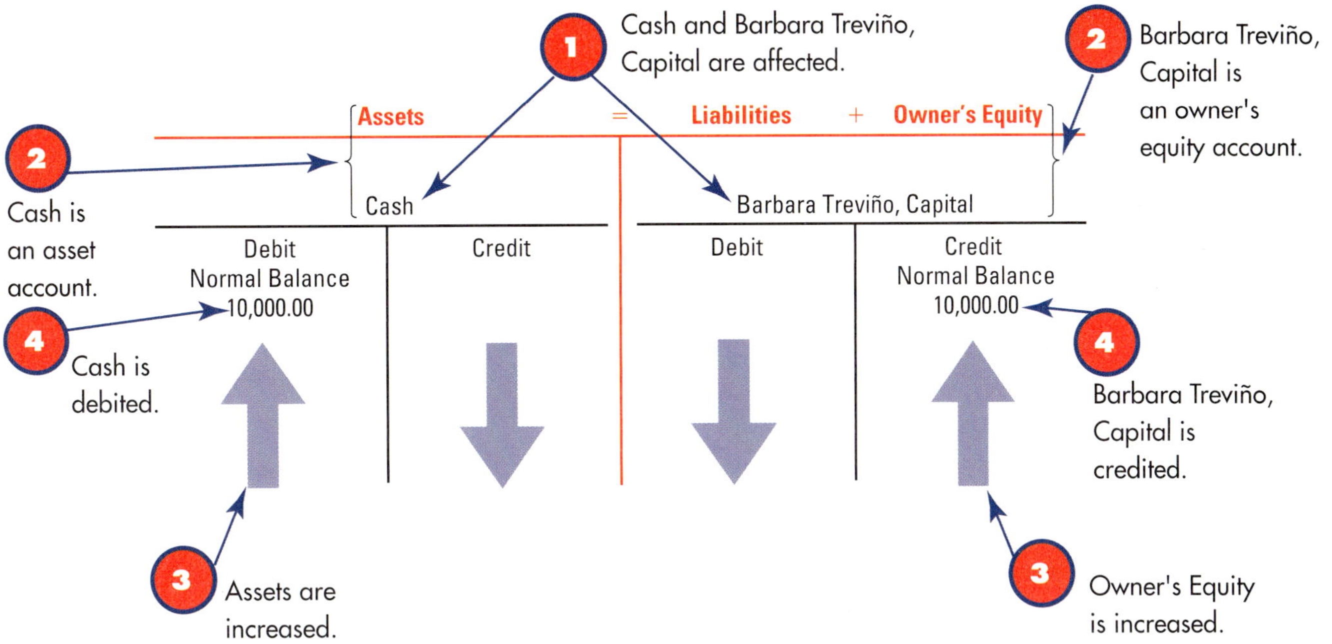

August 1. Received cash from owner as an investment, $10,000.00.

The effect of this transaction is shown in the illustration. Before a transaction is recorded in the records of a business, the information is analyzed to determine which accounts are changed and how. Each transaction changes the balances of at least two accounts. A list of accounts used by a business is called a **chart of accounts.** The chart of accounts for Encore Music is found on page 3.

Four questions are used in analyzing a transaction into its debit and credit parts. Debits equal credits for each transaction. In addition, after a transaction is recorded, total debits must equal total credits.

STEPS: Questions for analyzing a transaction into its debit and credit parts

1. Which accounts are affected?
   Cash and *Barbara Treviño, Capital*
2. How is each account classified?
   Cash is an asset account. *Barbara Treviño, Capital* is an owner's equity account.
3. How is each classification changed?
   Assets are increased. Owner's equity is increased.
4. How is each amount entered in the accounts?
   Assets increase on the debit side. Therefore, the asset account, *Cash,* is debited. Owner's equity accounts increase on the credit side. Therefore, the owner's equity account, *Barbara Treviño, Capital,* is credited.

PAID CASH FOR SUPPLIES

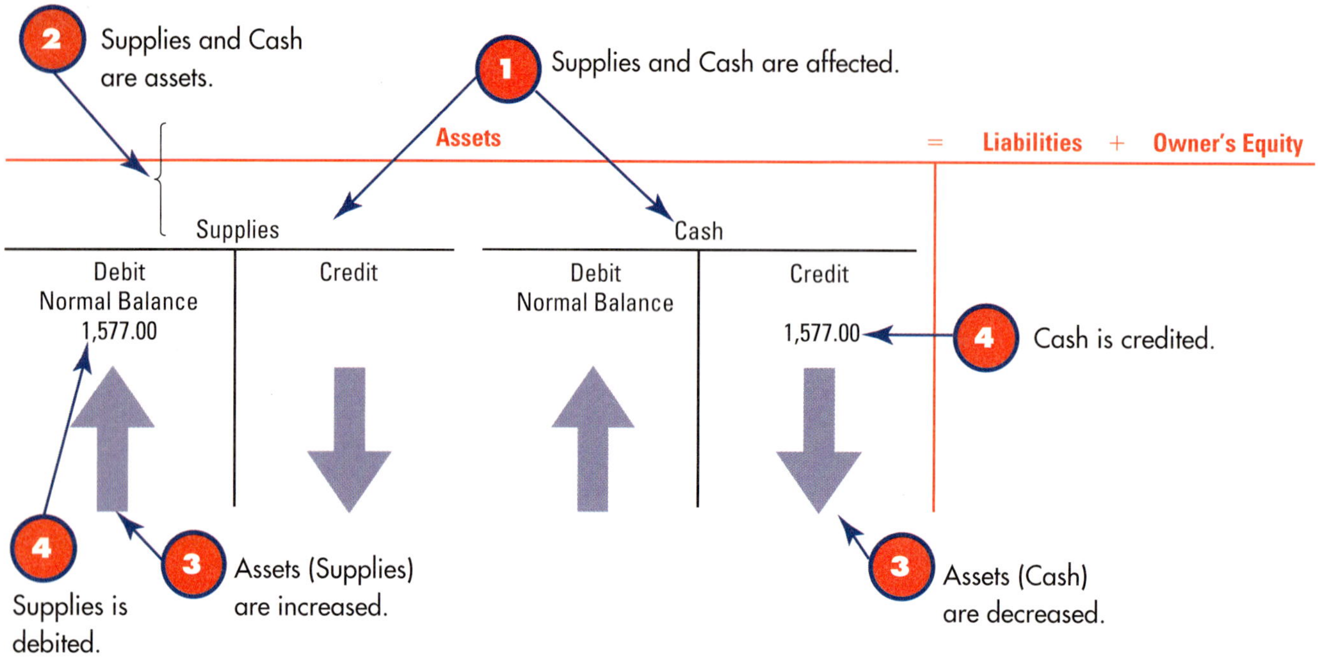

August 3. Paid cash for supplies, $1,577.00.

The effect of this transaction on the accounting equation is shown in the illustration. In this transaction, two asset accounts are changed. One asset, cash, has been exchanged for another asset, supplies. The asset account, Cash, is decreased by $1,577.00, the amount of cash paid out. This decrease is on the left side of the accounting equation. The asset account, Supplies, is increased by $1,577.00, the amount of supplies bought. This increase is also on the left side of the accounting equation.

The two changes are both on the left side of the accounting equation. When changes are made on only one side of the accounting equation, the equation must still be in balance. Therefore, if one account is increased, another account on the same side of the equation must be decreased.

As you have seen, transactions must be carefully analyzed. It must be determined if a transaction affects accounts from both sides of the accounting equation. Or a transaction may affect accounts that are on the same side of the accounting equation, as is true in this example. A common error is to assume that every transaction must affect accounts from both sides of the accounting equation.

The same four questions are used every time a transaction is analyzed.

STEPS — Questions for analyzing a transaction into its debit and credit parts

1. Which accounts are affected?
   Supplies and *Cash*
2. How is each account classified?
   Supplies is an asset account. *Cash* is an asset account.
3. How is each classification changed?
   Assets *(Supplies)* are increased and assets *(Cash)* are decreased.
4. How is each amount entered in the accounts?
   Assets increase on the debit side. Therefore, the asset account, *Supplies,* is debited. Assets decrease on the credit side. Therefore, the asset account, *Cash,* is credited.

PAID CASH FOR INSURANCE

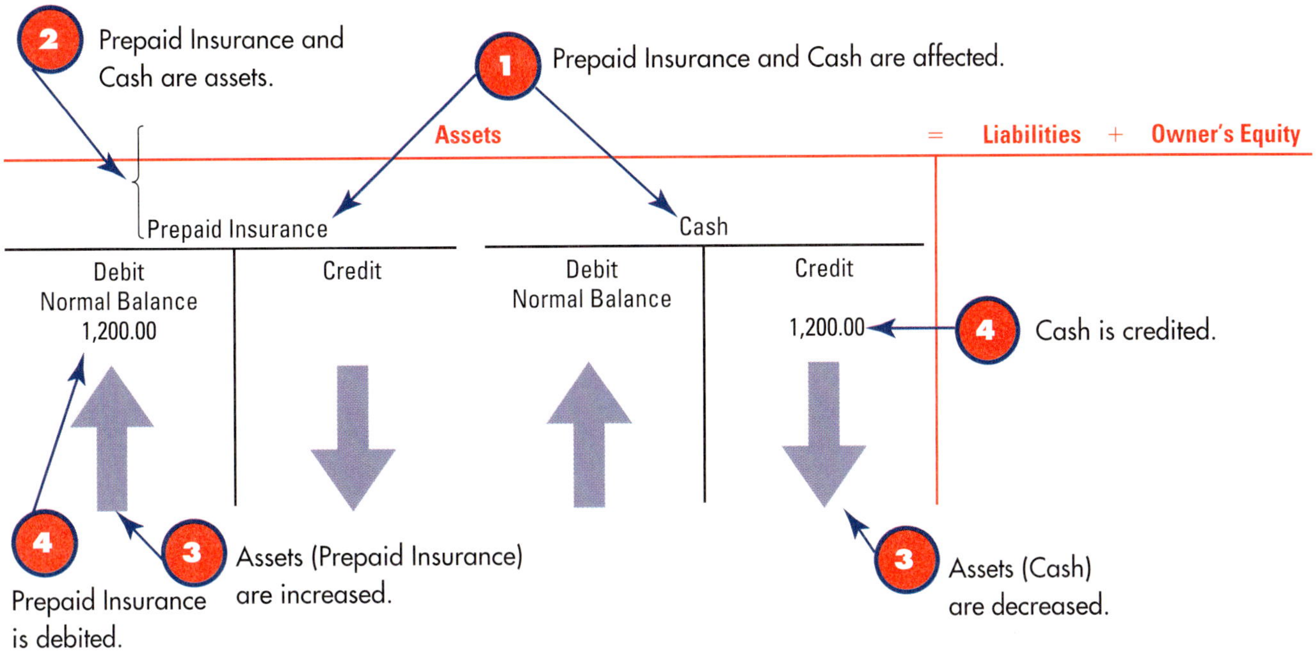

August 4. Paid cash for insurance, $1,200.00.

Paying cash for insurance is very similar to paying cash for supplies. One asset is increased and one asset is decreased.

The effect of this transaction on the accounting equation is shown in the illustration. In this transaction, two assets are changed. One asset, cash, has been exchanged for another asset, prepaid insurance. The asset account, Cash, is decreased by $1,200.00, the amount of cash paid out. This decrease is on the left side of the accounting equation. The asset account, Prepaid Insurance, is increased by $1,200.00, the amount of insurance bought. This increase is also on the left side of the accounting equation.

FYI

T accounts get their names from the arrangement of the lines making up the account. The horizontal line on top of the centered vertical line together look like a capital T.

STEPS: Questions for analyzing a transaction into its debit and credit parts

1. Which accounts are affected?
   Prepaid Insurance and *Cash*
2. How is each account classified?
   Prepaid Insurance is an asset account. *Cash* is an asset account.
3. How is each classification changed?
   Assets *(Prepaid Insurance)* are increased and assets *(Cash)* are decreased.
4. How is each amount entered in the accounts?
   Assets increase on the debit side. Therefore, the asset account, *Prepaid Insurance*, is debited. Assets decrease on the credit side. Therefore, the asset account, *Cash*, is credited.

FYI

Paying cash for insurance and buying supplies for cash are examples of transactions that affect only one side of the accounting equation. All the accounts involved in these transactions are assets.

BOUGHT SUPPLIES ON ACCOUNT

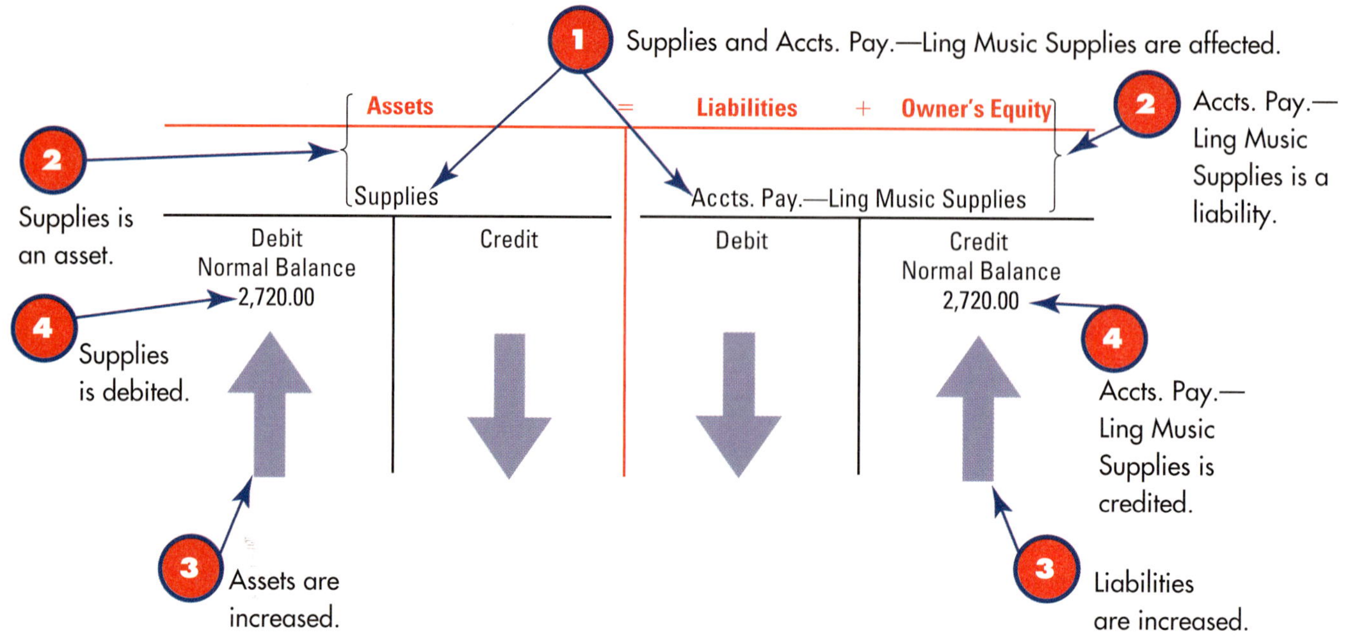

August 7. Bought supplies on account from Ling Music Supplies, $2,720.00.

The effect of this transaction on the accounting equation is shown in the illustration. In this transaction, one asset and one liability are changed. The asset account, Supplies, is increased by $2,720.00, the amount of supplies bought. This increase is on the left side of the accounting equation. Ling Music Supplies will have a claim against some of Encore Music's assets until Encore Music pays for the supplies bought. Therefore, Accounts Payable—Ling Music Supplies is a liability account. The liability account, Accounts Payable—Ling Music Supplies, is increased by $2,720.00, the amount owed for the supplies. This increase is on the right side of the accounting equation.

STEPS: Questions for analyzing a transaction into its debit and credit parts

1. Which accounts are affected?
   Supplies and *Accounts Payable—Ling Music Supplies*
2. How is each account classified?
   Supplies is an asset account. *Accounts Payable—Ling Music Supplies* is a liability account.
3. How is each classification changed?
   Assets are increased. Liabilities are increased.
4. How is each amount entered in the accounts?
   Assets increase on the debit side. Therefore, the asset account, *Supplies,* is debited. Liabilities increase on the credit side. Therefore, the liability account, *Accounts Payable—Ling Music Supplies,* is credited.

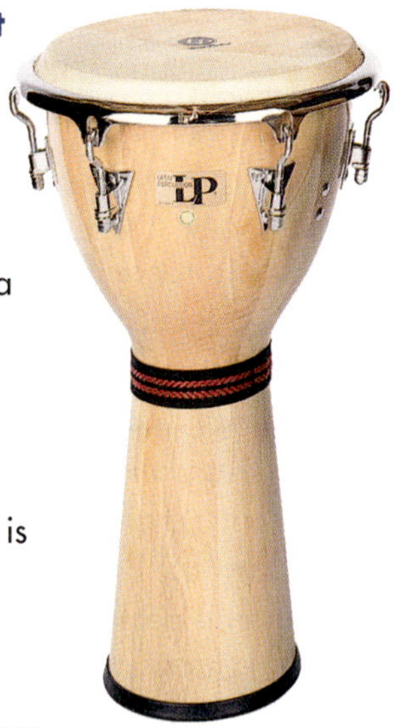

PAID CASH ON ACCOUNT

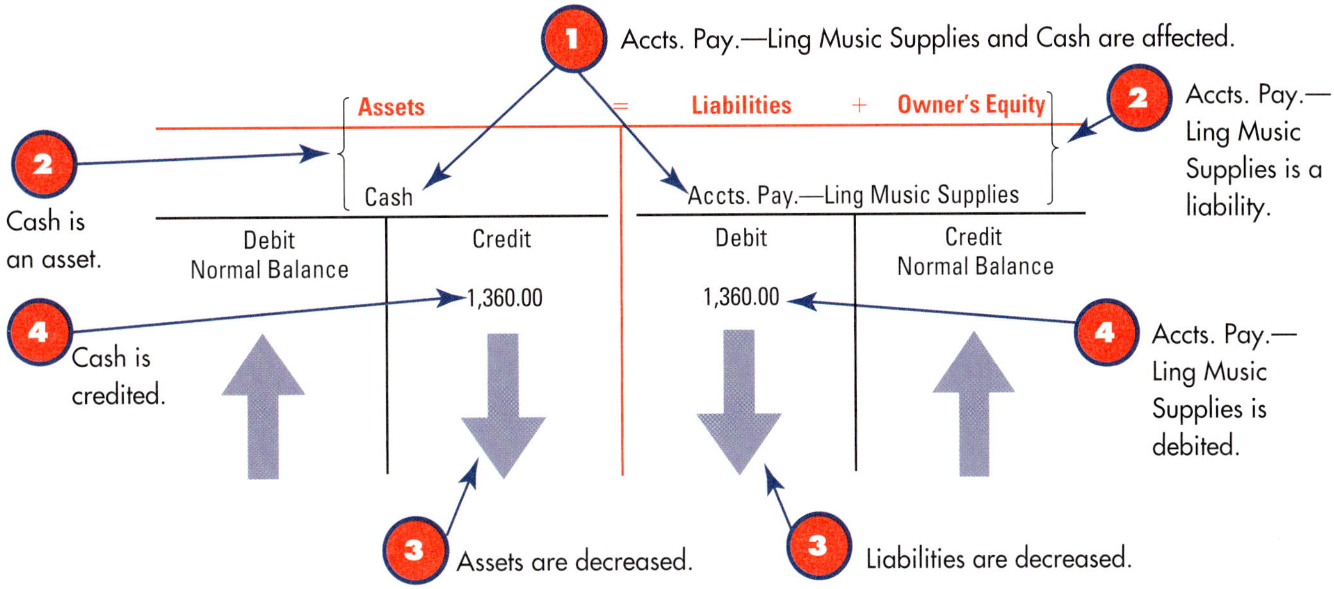

August 11. Paid cash on account to Ling Music Supplies, $1,360.00.

The effect of this transaction on the accounting equation is shown in the illustration. In this transaction, one asset and one liability are changed. The asset account, Cash, is decreased by $1,360.00, the amount of cash paid out. This decrease is on the left side of the accounting equation. After this payment, Encore Music owes less money to Ling Music Supplies. Therefore, the liability account, Accounts Payable—Ling Music Supplies, is decreased by $1,360.00, the amount paid on account. The decrease is on the right side of the accounting equation.

STEPS Questions for analyzing a transaction into its debit and credit parts

1. Which accounts are affected?
   Accounts Payable—Ling Music Supplies and *Cash*
2. How is each account classified?
   Accounts Payable—Ling Music Supplies is a liability account. *Cash* is an asset account.
3. How is each classification changed?
   Liabilities are decreased. Assets are decreased.
4. How is each amount entered in the accounts?
   Liabilities decrease on the debit side. Therefore, the liability account, *Accounts Payable—Ling Music Supplies,* is debited. Assets decrease on the credit side. Therefore, the asset account, *Cash,* is credited.

FYI

A chart of accounts is sometimes referred to by its initials COA. Many accounting terms are often abbreviated or referred to by initials. For example, accounts payable is sometimes referred to as A/P.

REMEMBER

When you decrease an account balance, record the decrease on the side opposite the normal balance side of the account. The side opposite the normal balance side can be on the left or the right depending on the type of account.

TERM REVIEW

chart of accounts

AUDIT YOUR UNDERSTANDING

1. State the four questions used to analyze a transaction.
2. What two accounts are affected when a business pays cash for supplies?

WORK TOGETHER

Analyzing a transaction into its debit and credit parts

T accounts are given in the *Working Papers.* Your instructor will guide you through the following examples. Kathy Bergum owns Bergum Services. Bergum Services uses the following accounts. Some of the accounts will be explained in Lesson 3-3.

Cash	Supplies	Kathy Bergum, Drawing	Rent Expense
Accts. Rec.—Sam Erickson	Prepaid Insurance	Sales	
Accts. Pay.—Bales Supplies	Kathy Bergum, Capital	Advertising Expense	

Transactions: Apr. 1. Received cash from owner as an investment, $5,000.00.
2. Paid cash for supplies, $50.00.
5. Paid cash for insurance, $75.00.
6. Bought supplies on account from Bales Supplies, $100.00.
9. Paid cash on account to Bales Supplies, $50.00.

3. For each transaction write on T accounts the account titles of the two accounts affected.
4. Write the debit or credit amount in each T account to show the transaction's effect.

ON YOUR OWN

Analyzing a transaction into its debit and credit parts

T accounts are given in the *Working Papers.* Work these problems independently. Jens Puckett owns Jens Accounting Service. Jens Accounting Service uses the following accounts. Some of the accounts will be explained in Lesson 3-3.

Cash	Supplies	Jens Puckett, Drawing	Utilities Expense
Accts. Rec.—King Company	Prepaid Insurance	Sales	
Accts. Pay.—Computer Supply	Jens Puckett, Capital	Miscellaneous Expense	

Transactions: Sept. 1. Received cash from owner as an investment, $3,000.00.
4. Paid cash for insurance, $100.00.
5. Paid cash for supplies, $90.00.
6. Bought supplies on account from Computer Supply, $200.00.
11. Paid cash on account to Computer Supply, $150.00.

5. For each transaction write on T accounts the account titles of the two accounts affected.
6. Write the debit or credit amount in each T account to show the transaction's effect.

3-3 Analyzing How Transactions Affect Owner's Equity Accounts

RECEIVED CASH FROM SALES

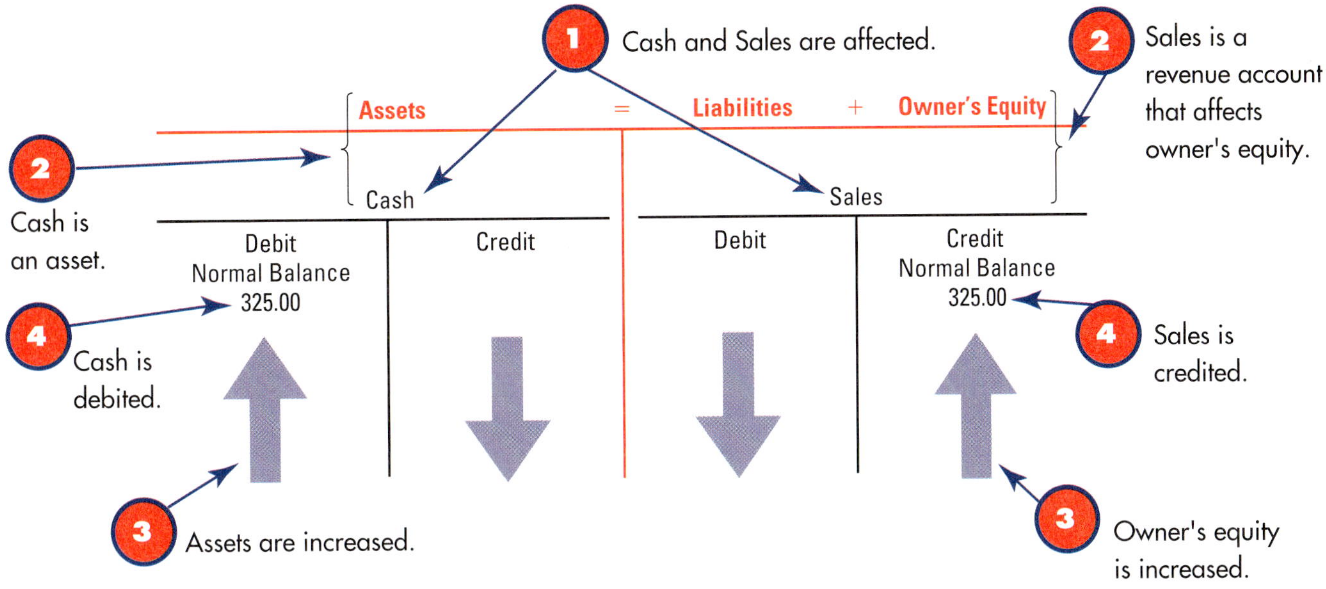

August 12. Received cash from sales, $325.00.

Revenue increases owner's equity. The increases from revenue could be recorded directly in the owner's capital account. However, to avoid a capital account with a large number of entries and to summarize revenue information separately from the other records, Encore Music uses a separate revenue account titled Sales.

The owner's capital account has a normal credit balance. Increases in the owner's capital account are shown as credits. Because revenue increases owner's equity, increases in revenue are recorded as credits. A revenue account has a normal credit balance.

FYI

The Small Business Administration (SBA) offers two major types of loans to small businesses. One type of loan is made by private lending institutions. Another type of loan is made directly by the SBA.

Questions for analyzing a transaction into its debit and credit parts

1. Which accounts are affected?
Cash and *Sales*

2. How is each account classified?
Cash is an asset account. *Sales* is a revenue account that affects owner's equity.

3. How is each classification changed?
Assets are increased. Owner's equity is increased.

4. How is each amount entered in the accounts?
Assets increase on the debit side. Therefore, the asset account, *Cash*, is debited. Owner's equity accounts increase on the credit side. Revenue increases owner's equity. Therefore, the revenue account, *Sales,* is credited.

SOLD SERVICES ON ACCOUNT

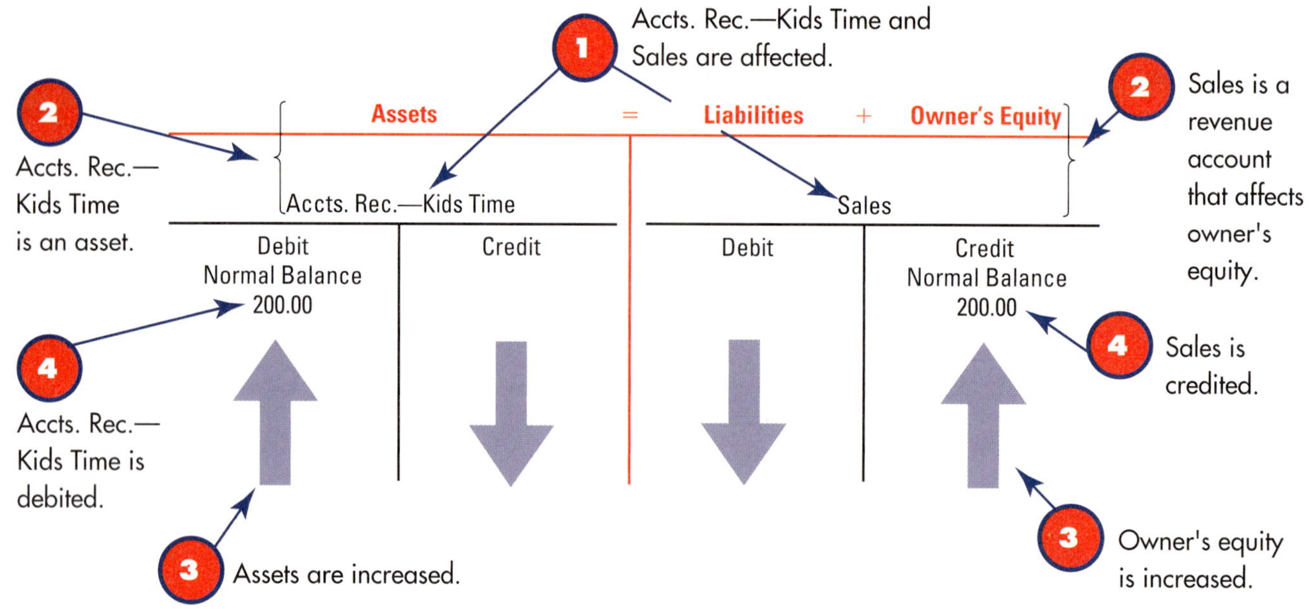

August 12. Sold services on account to Kids Time, $200.00.

The analysis for selling services on account is similar to that for selling services for cash. The only difference is that cash is not received at this time; therefore, the cash account is not affected by the transaction. Instead, this transaction increases an accounts receivable account. The same four questions are used to analyze this transaction into its debit and credit parts.

STEPS — Questions for analyzing a transaction into its debit and credit parts

1. Which accounts are affected?
   Accounts Receivable—Kids Time and *Sales*
2. How is each account classified?
   Accounts Receivable—Kids Time is an asset account. *Sales* is a revenue account that affects owner's equity.
3. How is each classification changed?
   Assets are increased. Owner's equity is increased.
4. How is each amount entered in the accounts?
   Assets increase on the debit side. Therefore, the asset account, *Accounts Receivable—Kids Time,* is debited. Owner's equity accounts increase on the credit side. Revenue increases owner's equity. Therefore, the revenue account, *Sales,* is credited.

REMEMBER

Owner's equity is recorded on the right side of the accounting equation. The right side of a T account is the credit side. Therefore, owner's equity has a normal credit balance.

PAID CASH FOR AN EXPENSE

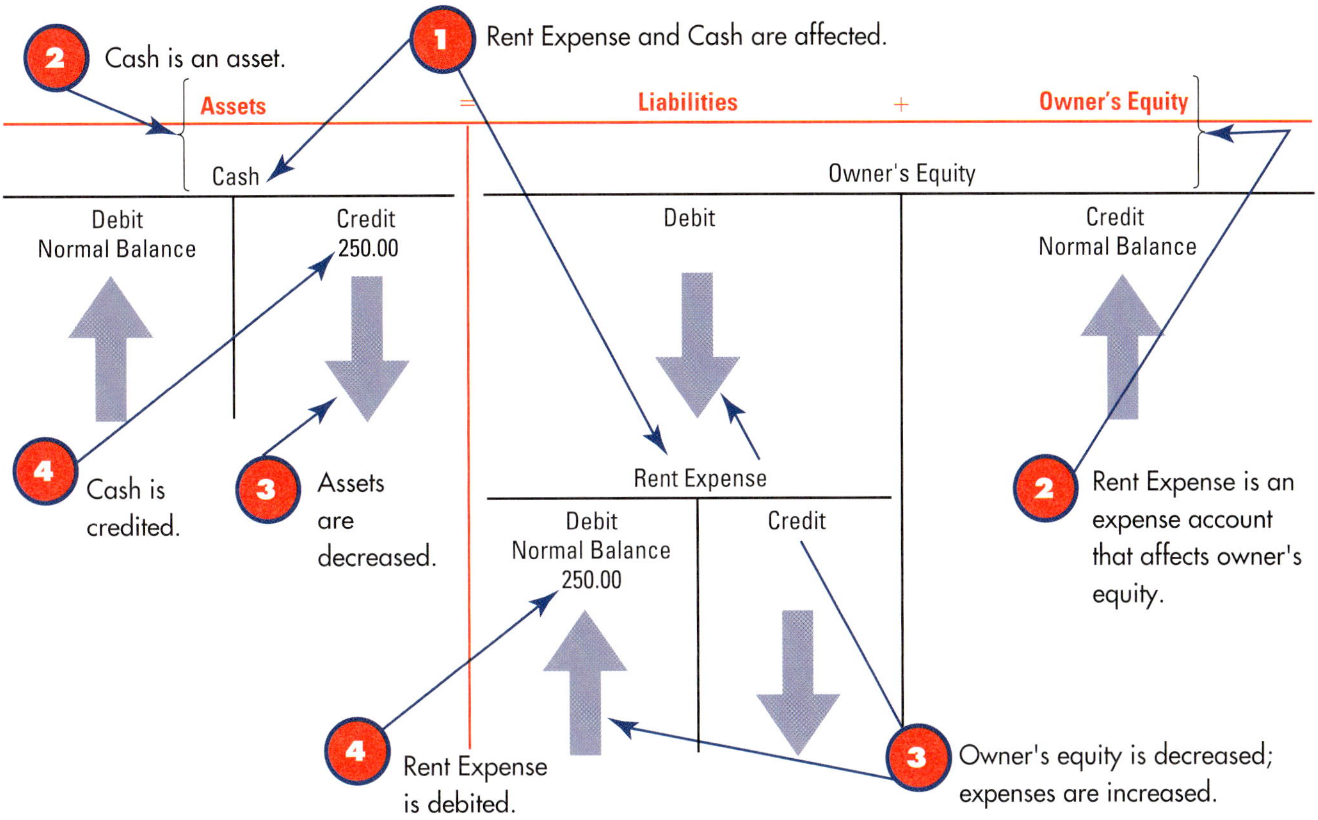

August 12. Paid cash for rent, $250.00.

Expenses decrease owner's equity. The decreases from expenses could be recorded directly in the owner's capital account. However, to avoid a capital account with a large number of entries and to summarize expense information separately from the other records, Encore Music uses separate expense accounts.

The titles of Encore Music's expense accounts are shown on its chart of accounts. The expense account, Rent Expense, is used to record all payments for rent.

The owner's capital account has a normal credit balance. Decreases in the owner's capital account are shown as debits. Therefore, an expense account has a normal debit balance. Because expenses decrease owner's equity, increases in expenses are recorded as debits.

All expense transactions are recorded in a similar manner.

STEPS Questions for analyzing a transaction into its debit and credit parts

1. Which accounts are affected?
   Rent Expense and *Cash*
2. How is each account classified?
   Rent Expense is an expense account that affects owner's equity. *Cash* is an asset account.
3. How is each classification changed?
   Owner's equity is decreased by an increase in expenses. Assets are decreased.
4. How is each amount entered in the accounts?
   Owner's equity accounts decrease on the debit side. An increase in expenses decreases owner's equity. Expense accounts have normal debit balances. Therefore, the expense account, *Rent Expense*, is debited. Assets decrease on the credit side. Therefore, the asset account, *Cash,* is credited.

RECEIVED CASH ON ACCOUNT

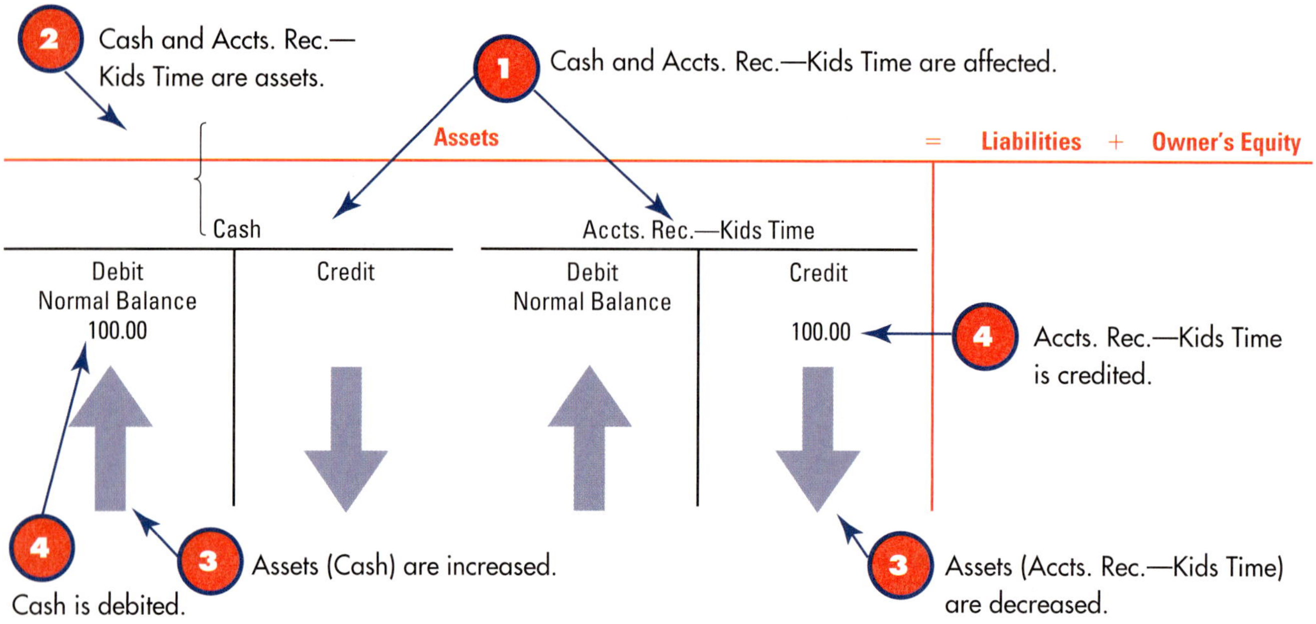

August 12. Received cash on account from Kids Time, $100.00.

STEPS Questions for analyzing a transaction into its debit and credit parts

1. Which accounts are affected?
Cash and *Accounts Receivable—Kids Time*

2. How is each account classified?
Cash is an asset account. *Accounts Receivable—Kids Time* is an asset account.

3. How is each classification changed?
Assets *(Cash)* are increased and assets *(Accounts Receivable—Kids Time)* are decreased.

4. How is each amount entered in the accounts?
Assets increase on the debit side. Therefore, the asset account, *Cash,* is debited. Assets decrease on the credit side. Therefore, the asset account, *Accounts Receivable—Kids Time,* is credited.

CULTURAL DIVERSITY

ANCIENT CHINA

By approximately 1000 B.C. the Chinese had developed one of the most sophisticated accounting systems in the world. The Chao Dynasty ruled China from 1122 to 256 B.C. During this time the dynasty oversaw territorial expansion and a Golden Age in literature and philosophy. The famous philosopher Confucius lived during this dynasty. Confucius was said to have been a government recordkeeper.

During the Chao Dynasty, the Chinese used a system of currency and had a central bank. The Office of the Superintendent of Records furnished compilations of receipts and payments. It also kept maps and records of production tools used. Many of the accounting and record keeping tasks that affect businesses and governments today can be traced back to systems established in ancient China.

PAID CASH TO OWNER FOR PERSONAL USE

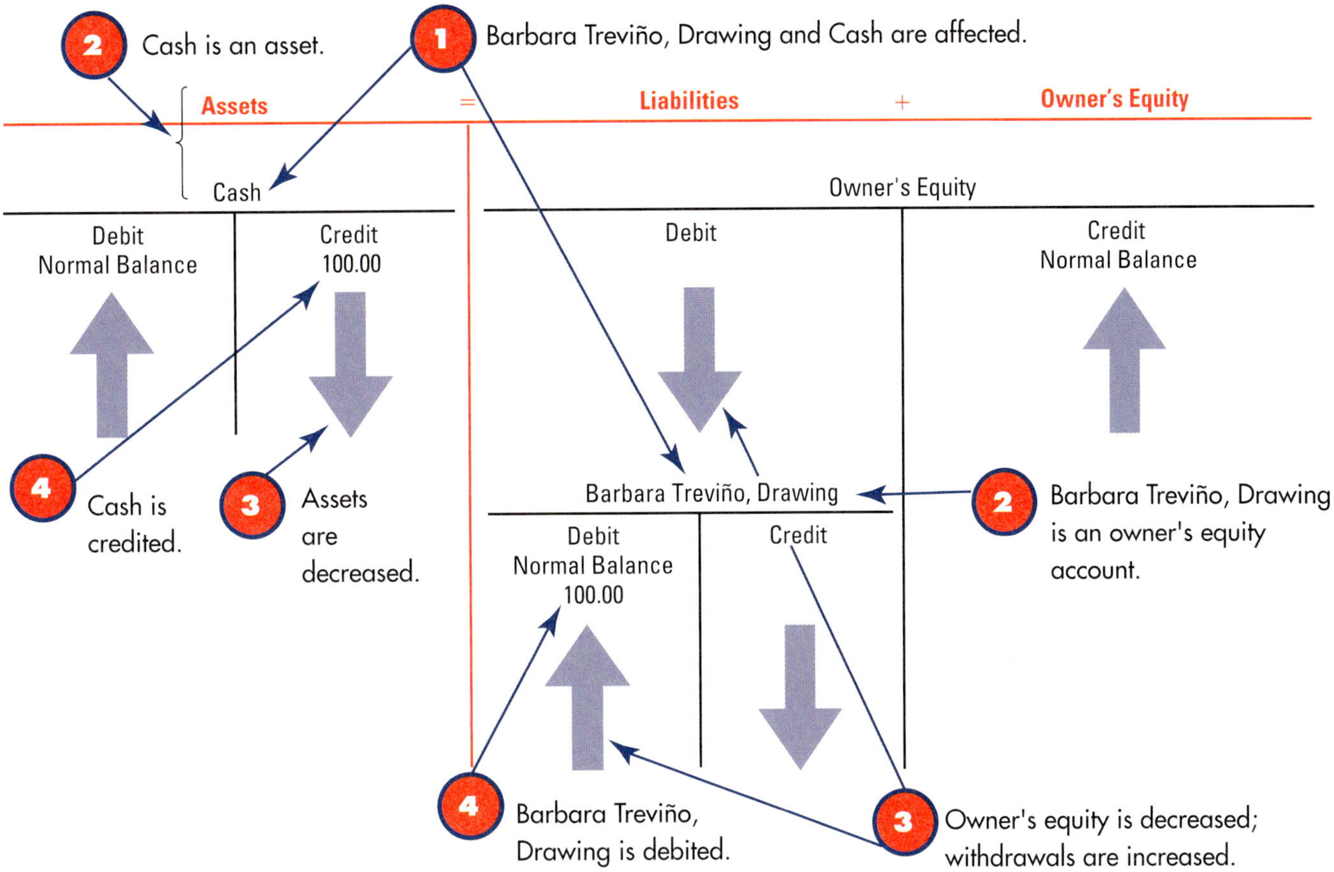

August 12. Paid cash to owner for personal use, $100.00.

Withdrawals decrease owner's equity. Withdrawals could be recorded directly in the owner's capital account. However, to avoid a capital account with a large number of entries and to summarize withdrawal information separately from the other records, Encore Music uses a separate withdrawal account titled Barbara Treviño, Drawing.

STEPS Questions for analyzing a transaction into its debit and credit parts

1. Which accounts are affected?
   Barbara Treviño, Drawing, and *Cash*
2. How is each account classified?
   Barbara Treviño, Drawing is an owner's equity account. *Cash* is an asset account.
3. How is each classification changed?
   Owner's equity is decreased by an increase in withdrawals. Assets are decreased.
4. How is each amount entered in the accounts?
   Owner's equity accounts decrease on the debit side. An increase in withdrawals decreases owner's equity. Withdrawal accounts have normal debit balances. Therefore, the owner's equity account, *Barbara Treviño, Drawing,* is debited. Assets decrease on the credit side. Therefore, the asset account, *Cash,* is credited.

FYI

When drawing T accounts to analyze transactions, stack the accounts instead of writing them horizontally. Stacking the accounts will make it easier to recognize debits and credits.

AUDIT YOUR UNDERSTANDING

1. What two accounts are affected when a business receives cash from sales?
2. What two accounts are affected when services are sold on account?
3. What two accounts are affected when a business pays cash to the owner for personal use?
4. Are revenue accounts increased on the debit side or credit side?
5. Are expense accounts increased on the debit side or credit side?

WORK TOGETHER

Analyzing revenue, expense, and withdrawal transactions into debit and credit parts

T accounts are given in the *Working Papers*. Your instructor will guide you through the following examples.

Use the chart of accounts for Bergum Services on page 50.

Transactions: Apr. 10. Received cash from sales, $600.00.
11. Sold services on account to Sam Erickson, $850.00.
14. Paid cash for rent, $250.00.
18. Received cash on account from Sam Erickson, $425.00.
20. Paid cash to owner for personal use, $300.00.

6. Prepare two T accounts for each transaction. On each T account, write the account title of one of the accounts affected by the transaction.
7. Write the debit or credit amount in each T account to show the transaction's effect.

ON YOUR OWN

Analyzing revenue, expense, and withdrawal transactions into debit and credit parts

T accounts are given in the *Working Papers*. Work these problems independently.

Use the chart of accounts for Jens Accounting Service on page 50.

Transactions: Sept. 13. Received cash from sales, $1,000.00.
15. Sold services on account to King Company, $1,500.00.
16. Paid cash for utilities, $500.00.
18. Received cash on account from King Company, $750.00.
21. Paid cash to owner for personal use, $650.00.

8. Prepare two T accounts for each transaction. On each T account, write the account title of one of the accounts affected by the transaction.
9. Write the debit or credit amount in each T account to show the transaction's effect.

CHAPTER 3 SUMMARY

After completing this chapter, you can

1. Define important accounting terms related to analyzing transactions into debit and credit parts.
2. Identify accounting practices related to analyzing transactions into debit and credit parts.
3. Use T accounts to analyze transactions showing which accounts are debited or credited for each transaction.
4. Analyze how transactions to set up a business affect accounts.
5. Analyze how transactions affect owner's equity accounts.

EXPLORE ACCOUNTING

OWNER WITHDRAWALS

Employee salaries are considered an expense that reduces the net income of a company. When the owner withdraws cash from the company, this withdrawal is *not* considered an expense. The income of a business is calculated by subtracting total expenses from total revenue. Since withdrawals are not considered to be an expense, they do not affect the business's income.

A business owned by one person is called a proprietorship. The Internal Revenue Service does not require the proprietorship, itself, to pay taxes. However, the owner of the proprietorship must include the net income of the proprietorship in his or her own taxable income.

Because the net income of a proprietorship is not affected by owner withdrawals, the income tax paid by the owner is not affected by how much cash the owner withdraws from the business. If Wang Accounting Services has revenues of $2,500.00 and expenses of $1,100.00, its net income is $1,400.00 ($2,500.00 – $1,100.00). Wang Accounting Services will have net income of $1,100.00 regardless of whether the owner withdraws $100.00 or $1,000.00 from the business during that period.

Discussion:

1. Ed Westing owns ESW Party Service. He is considering giving his employees a raise that would increase salaries by $15,000.00 per year. What effect would this raise have on Mr. Westing's income tax?
2. Mr. Westing is also considering withdrawing $5,000.00 from ESW Party Service for his personal use. What effect would this withdrawal have on the income tax Mr. Westing must pay this year?

3-1 APPLICATION PROBLEM

Determining the normal balance, increase, and decrease sides for accounts

Write the answers for the following problem in the *Working Papers.*

Cash
Accounts Receivable—Laurie Menz
Supplies
Prepaid Insurance
Accounts Payable—Gerald B's
Accounts Payable—VanDyke Company
Vivian Marx, Capital

1	2	3	4	5	6	7	8
Account	Account Classification	Account's Normal Balance		Increase Side		Decrease Side	
		Debit	Credit	Debit	Credit	Debit	Credit
Cash	*Asset*	√		√			√

Instructions:

Do the following for each account. The cash account is given as an example.

1. Write the account title in Column 1.
2. Write the account classification in Column 2.
3. Place a check mark in either Column 3 or 4 to indicate the normal balance of the account.
4. Place a check mark in either Column 5 or 6 to indicate the increase side of the account.
5. Place a check mark in either Column 7 or 8 to indicate the decrease side of the account.

3-2 APPLICATION PROBLEM

Analyzing transactions into debit and credit parts

John Burke owns John's Marketing Services, which uses the following accounts:

Cash
Supplies
Prepaid Insurance
Accounts Receivable—Orv Grant
Accounts Payable—D & S Company
John Burke, Capital
John Burke, Drawing
Sales
Advertising Expense
Rent Expense

Transactions:

Mar. 1. Received cash from owner as an investment, $1,500.00.
1. Paid cash for insurance, $600.00.
3. Bought supplies on account from D & S Company, $800.00
5. Paid cash for supplies, $200.00.
8. Paid cash on account to D & S Company, $400.00.

Instructions:

1. Prepare two T accounts for each transaction. On each T account, write the account title of one of the accounts affected by the transaction. Use the forms in your *Working Papers.*

2. Write the debit or credit amount in each T account to show how the transaction affected that account. T accounts for the first transaction are given as an example.

MARCH 1.

Cash	
1,500.00	

John Burke, Capital	
	1,500.00

3-3 APPLICATION PROBLEM
Analyzing revenue, expense, and withdrawal transactions into debit and credit parts

Use the chart of accounts for John's Marketing Services given in Application Problem 3-2.

Transactions:

Mar. 11. Received cash from sales, $2,200.00.
12. Paid cash for advertising, $150.00.
14. Sold services on account to Orv Grant, $1,700.00.
18. Paid cash to owner for personal use, $500.00.
19. Received cash on account from Orv Grant, $1,000.00.

Instructions:

1. Prepare two T accounts for each transaction. On each T account, write the account title of one of the accounts affected by the transaction. Use the forms in your *Working Papers*.
2. Write the debit or credit amount in each T account to show how the transaction affected that account.

3-4 APPLICATION PROBLEM
Analyzing revenue, expense, and withdrawal transactions into debit and credit parts

Use the chart of accounts for John's Marketing Services given in Application Problem 3-2.

Transactions:

Mar. 25. Sold services for cash, $900.00.
26. Performed $750.00 of services for Orv Grant on account.
27. Ran an ad in the local newspaper. Paid $25.00 cash.
28. John Burke withdrew $450.00 for his personal use.
29. Received a $375.00 check from Orv Grant on account.

Instructions:

1. Prepare two T accounts for each transaction. On each T account, write the account title of one of the accounts affected by the transaction. Use the forms in your *Working Papers*.
2. Write the debit or credit amount in each T account to show how the transaction affected that account.

3-5 MASTERY PROBLEM
Analyzing transactions into debit and credit parts

Mark Lands owns a business called LandScape. LandScape uses the following accounts.

Cash
Accounts Receivable—Joseph Corbett
Accounts Receivable—Vera Rice
Supplies
Prepaid Insurance
Accounts Payable—Derner Office Supplies
Accounts Payable—Janitor Supplies
Mark Lands, Capital
Mark Lands, Drawing
Sales
Advertising Expense
Miscellaneous Expense
Rent Expense
Repair Expense
Utilities Expense

Instructions:

1. Prepare a T account for each account. Use the forms in your *Working Papers.*
2. Analyze each transaction into its debit and credit parts. Write the debit and credit amounts in the proper T accounts to show how each transaction changes account balances. Write the date of the transaction in parentheses before each amount.

Transactions:

June 1. Received cash from owner as an investment, $3,000.00.
2. Paid cash for supplies, $60.00.
4. Paid cash for rent, $200.00.
4. Received cash from sales, $350.00.
5. Paid cash for repairs, $10.00.
8. Sold services on account to Joseph Corbett, $200.00.
9. Bought supplies on account from Janitor Supplies, $500.00.
10. Paid cash for insurance, $100.00.
11. Received cash from owner as an investment, $900.00.
11. Received cash from sales, $300.00.
12. Bought supplies on account from Derner Office Supplies, $50.00.
13. Received cash on account from Joseph Corbett, $125.00.
15. Paid cash for miscellaneous expense, $5.00.
16. Paid cash on account to Janitor Supplies, $50.00.
22. Paid cash for electric bill (utilities expense), $35.00.
23. Paid cash for advertising, $30.00.
25. Sold services on account to Vera Rice, $220.00.
26. Paid cash to owner for personal use, $600.00.
30. Received cash on account from Vera Rice, $100.00.

3-6 CHALLENGE PROBLEM

Analyzing transactions recorded in T accounts

Carol Burns owns a business for which the following T accounts show the current financial situation. Write the answers for the following problem in the *Working Papers.*

Cash

(1)	5,000.00	(2)	80.00
(6)	475.00	(4)	15.00
(8)	350.00	(5)	16.00
(9)	400.00	(7)	900.00
		(10)	150.00
		(11)	95.00
		(12)	50.00

Sales

		(6)	475.00
		(8)	350.00
		(9)	400.00
		(13)	225.00

Accts. Rec.—David Gotch

(13)	225.00		

Advertising Expense

(5)	16.00		

Supplies

(3)	300.00		
(11)	95.00		

Miscellaneous Expense

(4)	15.00		

Accts. Pay.—Midwest Supplies

(10)	150.00	(3)	300.00

Rent Expense

(7)	900.00		

Carol Burns, Capital

		(1)	5,000.00

Utilities Expense

(12)	50.00		

Carol Burns, Drawing

(2)	80.00		

1	2	3	4	5	6
Trans. No.	Accounts Affected	Account Classification	Entered in Account as a		Description of Transaction
			Debit	Credit	
1.	*Cash* *Carol Burns, Capital*	*Asset* *Owner's Equity*	√	 √	*Received cash from owner as an investment*

Instructions:

1. Analyze each numbered transaction in the T accounts. Write the titles of accounts affected in Column 2. For each account, write the classification of the account in Column 3.
2. For each account, place a check mark in either Column 4 or 5 to indicate if the account is affected by a debit or a credit.
3. For each transaction, write a brief statement in Column 6 describing the transaction. Information for Transaction 1 is given as an example.

INTERNET ACTIVITY

Point your browser to

http://accounting.swpco.com

Choose **First-Year Course**, choose **Activities**, and complete the activity for Chapter 3.

Applied Communication

An entrepreneur is a person who attempts to earn a profit by taking the risk of operating a business. You have expressed an interest in starting your own business after graduation. Your family has agreed to help finance your new business if you can convince them that you would be successful.

Instructions: Develop a plan outlining the details of the business you would operate. Describe the type of business, the equipment or resources needed, and financial information, such as start-up costs and expenses. Write clear and persuasive sentences.

Cases for Critical Thinking

Case 1 Sharon Morris records all cash receipts as revenue and all cash payments as expenses. Is Ms. Morris recording her cash receipts and cash payments correctly? Explain your answer.

Case 2 Thomas Bueler records all investments, revenue, expenses, and withdrawals in his capital account. At the end of each month, Mr. Bueler sorts the information to prepare a summary of what has caused the changes in his capital account balance. To help Mr. Bueler prepare this summary in the future, what changes would you suggest he make in his records?

AUTOMATED ACCOUNTING

SETTING UP THE AUTOMATED ACCOUNTING SOFTWARE DATABASE

The *Automated Accounting* software includes company information, a classification of all the accounts to be used, and required accounts necessary for a business. Also, a general ledger database needs to be created containing a chart of accounts that will be used to enter all transactions.

General Ledger Database

The General Ledger Database consists of a collection of accounts and the related account numbers needed to prepare financial statements. The general ledger specifically lists accounts for assets, liabilities, owner's equity, expenses, and revenue.

Database

A prearranged file in which data can be entered and retrieved is a database. An example of a database in Automated Accounting is the general ledger. It contains general information about the business, a chart of accounts, and a list of the financial activities for each account. The database is designed so that when you enter information it updates the account balances and also stores data in a designated area for creating reports. The general ledger databases to be used for various problems are stored as templates.

Ledger and General Ledger

A *ledger* is a group of accounts. A ledger that contains all accounts needed to prepare financial statements is called a *general ledger.* The name given to an account is known as an account title.

Chart of Accounts Numbering System

A chart of accounts numbering system includes the account numbers that will be used to process transactions for various accounts. This numbering system is generally the same for manual and automated systems. There are procedures designed to set up the chart of accounts. The process includes arranging accounts in the general ledger, assigning the numbers, and keeping records current. This is called *file maintenance.*

Account Number

The number assigned to an account is called an *account number.* The first digit of an account number describes the account type. The number of digits in an account number can vary. This book presents three- or four-digit account numbers.

File Maintenance

File maintenance includes adding and changing accounts in the chart of accounts. The process of file maintenance can be done in three steps:

1. Create an account number or modify an existing number.
2. Enter the account number in the chart of accounts.
3. Check for accuracy by creating a revised chart of accounts list.

Adding an Account Within a Ledger

Adding a new account within a ledger may be necessary when an asset is purchased, a liability is incurred, and for additional expense categories. When adding an account within a ledger, an unused middle number is used. The new account number for Insurance Expense is 525.

520 Gasoline Expense
525 Insurance Expense
530 Supplies Expense

Adding an Account at the End of a Ledger

The new account number is the next sequence of 10 from the last account number used so that new numbers can be added easily. There are nine unused numbers between each account when initially set up. New numbers can be assigned between existing account numbers without renumbering all existing accounts.

4 Journalizing Transactions

AFTER STUDYING CHAPTER 4, YOU WILL BE ABLE TO:

1. Define accounting terms related to journalizing transactions.
2. Identify accounting concepts and practices related to journalizing transactions.
3. Record in a five-column journal transactions to set up a business.
4. Record in a five-column journal transactions to buy insurance for cash and supplies on account.
5. Record in a five-column journal transactions that affect owner's equity and receiving cash on account.
6. Prove and rule a five-column journal and prove cash.

TERMS PREVIEW

journal
journalizing
special amount column
general amount column
entry
double-entry accounting
source document
check
invoice
sales invoice
receipt
memorandum
proving cash

JOURNALS AND JOURNALIZING

As described in Chapter 3, transactions are analyzed into debit and credit parts before information is recorded. A form for recording transactions in chronological order is called a **journal.** Recording transactions in a journal is called **journalizing.**

Transactions could be recorded in the accounting equation. However, most companies wish to create a more permanent record by recording transactions in a journal.

Each business uses the kind of journal that best fits the needs of that business. The nature of a business and the number of transactions to be recorded determine the kind of journal to be used.

The word *journal* comes from the Latin *diurnalis,* meaning daily. Most businesses conduct transactions every day. To keep from getting overloaded, the businesses will make entries in their accounting journals every day.

FYI

The Small Business Administration (SBA) has programs that offer free management and accounting advice to small business owners. The SBA sponsors various workshops and publishes a variety of booklets for small business owners.

ACCOUNTING IN YOUR CAREER

HIGH STANDARDS FOR JOURNALIZING

Sandra Huffman has worked for Marquesa Advertising for 30 days as an accounting clerk, a position for which the company owner, Ramona Marquesa, hired her. She journalizes all transactions, about 50 per day, handles all incoming and outgoing mail, prepares and files all source documents, and performs other duties as assigned.

One day Ramona asked to see the journal. Sandra handed the journal to Ramona, who scanned a few pages while Sandra fidgeted in her chair. Sandra didn't know exactly what to expect, but she knew she had not done as good a job with journalizing transactions as she should have.

Ramona then sighed and said, "I'm concerned about this journal, Sandra. You have recorded all transactions in pencil, and I notice numerous erasures. I don't know if the debits equal the credits, but I can see right away that this one transaction for $20,000 should have been for $2,000. Some of the dates are missing and some are out of order. What do you suggest we do to turn this situation around?"

After apologizing, Sandra thanked Ramona for giving her the chance to improve her work. She explained that she realized she had not been giving the journal the priority it required and went on to describe how she would improve her performance in the future.

Critical Thinking:

1. What do you think Sandra should say about the journal to demonstrate that she knows it is important?
2. What specific improvements do you think Sandra should make?

4-1 Journals, Source Documents, and Recording Entries in a Journal

A FIVE-COLUMN JOURNAL

JOURNAL PAGE

	DATE	ACCOUNT TITLE	DOC. NO.	POST. REF.	1 GENERAL DEBIT	2 GENERAL CREDIT	3 SALES CREDIT	4 CASH DEBIT	5 CASH CREDIT	
1										1
2										2
3										3

Using a Journal

Encore Music uses a journal that has five amount columns: General Debit, General Credit, Sales Credit, Cash Debit, and Cash Credit. A journal amount column headed with an account title is called a **special amount column.** These columns are used for frequently occurring transactions. For example, most of Encore Music's transactions involve receipt or payment of cash. A large number of the transactions involve receipt of cash from sales. Therefore, Encore Music uses three special amount columns in its journal: Sales Credit, Cash Debit, and Cash Credit. Using special amount columns eliminates writing an account title in the Account Title column and saves time.

A journal amount column that is not headed with an account title is called a **general amount column.** In Encore Music's journal, the General Debit and General Credit columns are general amount columns.

Accuracy

Information recorded in a journal includes the debit and credit parts of each transaction recorded in one place. The information can be verified by comparing the data in the journal with the transaction data.

Chronological Record

Transactions are recorded in a journal in order by date. All information about a transaction is recorded in one place, making the information for a specific transaction easy to locate.

Double-Entry Accounting

Information for each transaction recorded in a journal is called an **entry.** The recording of debit and credit parts of a transaction is called **double-entry accounting.** In double-entry accounting, each transaction affects at least two accounts. Both the debit and the credit parts are recorded, reflecting the dual effect of each transaction on the business's records. Double-entry accounting assures that debits equal credits.

Source Documents

A business paper from which information is obtained for a journal entry is called a **source document.** Each transaction is described by a source document that proves that the transaction did occur. For example, Encore Music prepares a check stub for each cash payment made. The check stub describes information about the cash payment transaction for which the check is prepared. The accounting concept, *Objective Evidence,* is applied when a source document is prepared for each transaction. *(CONCEPT: Objective Evidence)*

A transaction should be journalized only if it actually occurs. The amounts recorded must be accurate and true. Nearly all transactions result in the preparation of a source document. Encore Music uses five source documents: checks, sales invoices, receipts, calculator tapes, and memorandums.

CHECKS

NO. 1	$ 1,577.00	
Date August 3	20 --	
To Quick Clean Supplies Co.		
For Supplies		
BAL. BRO'T. FOR'D.	0	00
AMT. DEPOSITED (Date 8/1/--)	10,000	00
SUBTOTAL	10,000	00
OTHER:		
SUBTOTAL	10,000	00
AMT. THIS CHECK	1,577	00
BAL. CAR'D. FOR'D.	8,423	00

Encore Music
530 Anoka Avenue
Tampa, FL 33601

NO. 1 63-109/631

August 3, 20 --

PAY TO THE ORDER OF Quick Clean Supplies Co. $ 1,577.00

One thousand five hundred seventy-seven and no/100 DOLLARS

For Classroom Use Only

Peoples national bank
Tampa, FL 33602

FOR Supplies Barbara Treviño

⑆063101098⑆ 431⑈452119⑈

A business form ordering a bank to pay cash from a bank account is called a **check.** The source document for cash payments is a check. Encore Music makes all cash payments by check. The checks are prenumbered to help Encore Music account for all checks. Encore Music's record of information on a check is the check stub prepared at the same time as the check. A check and check stub prepared by Encore Music are shown in the illustration above.

Procedures for preparing checks and check stubs are described in Chapter 6.

SALES INVOICES

Encore Music
530 Anoka Avenue
Tampa, FL 33601

Sold to: Kids Time
405 Michigan Avenue
Tampa, FL 33619

No. 1
Date 8/12/--
Terms 30 days

Description	Amount
Individual lessons on Aug. 12	$200.00
Total	$200.00

When services are sold on account, the seller prepares a form showing information about the sale. A form describing the goods or services sold, the quantity, and the price is called an **invoice.** An invoice used as a source document for recording a sale on account is called a **sales invoice.** A sales invoice is also referred to as a sales ticket or a sales slip.

A sales invoice is prepared in duplicate. The original copy is given to the customer. The copy is used as the source document for the sale on account transaction. *(CONCEPT: Objective Evidence)* Sales invoices are numbered in sequence.

OTHER SOURCE DOCUMENTS

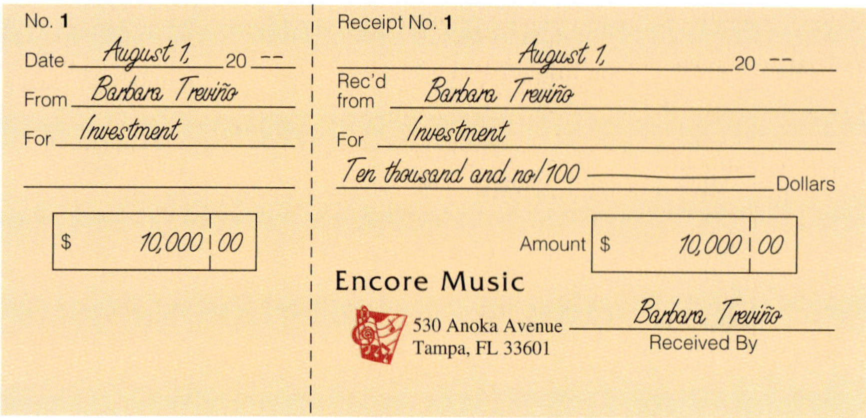
No. 1
Date August 1, 20 --
From Barbara Treviño
For Investment
$ 10,000 00

Receipt No. 1
August 1, 20 --
Rec'd from Barbara Treviño
For Investment
Ten thousand and no/100 Dollars
Amount $ 10,000 00
Encore Music
530 Anoka Avenue
Tampa, FL 33601
Barbara Treviño
Received By

Receipts

A business form giving written acknowledgement for cash received is called a **receipt.** When cash is received from sources other than sales, Encore Music prepares a receipt. The receipts are prenumbered to help account for all of the receipts. A receipt is the source document for cash received from transactions other than sales. *(CONCEPT: Objective Evidence)*

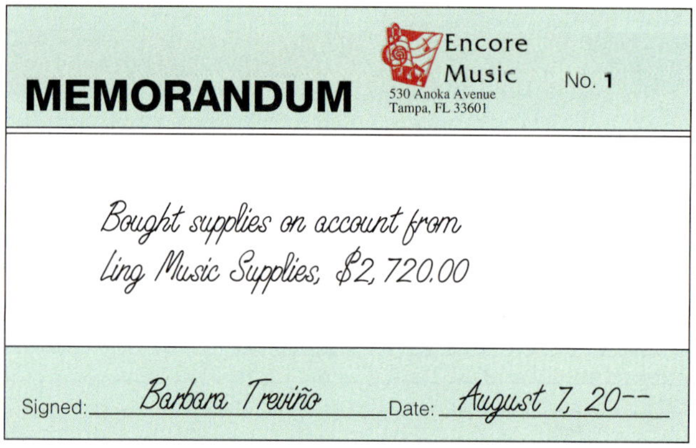
MEMORANDUM
Encore Music
530 Anoka Avenue
Tampa, FL 33601
No. 1

Bought supplies on account from Ling Music Supplies, $2,720.00

Signed: Barbara Treviño Date: August 7, 20--

Memorandums

A form on which a brief message is written describing a transaction is called a **memorandum.** When no other source document is prepared for a transaction, or when an additional explanation is needed about a transaction, Encore Music prepares a memorandum. *(CONCEPT: Objective Evidence)* Encore Music's memorandums are prenumbered to help account for all of the memorandums. A brief note is written on the memorandum to describe the transaction.

Calculator Tapes

Encore Music collects cash at the time services are rendered to customers. At the end of each day, Encore Music uses a printing electronic calculator to total the amount of cash received from sales for that day. By totaling all the individual sales, a single source document is produced for the total sales of the day. Thus, time and space are saved by recording only one entry for all of a day's sales. The calculator tape is the source document for daily sales. *(CONCEPT: Objective Evidence)* A calculator tape used as a source document is shown.

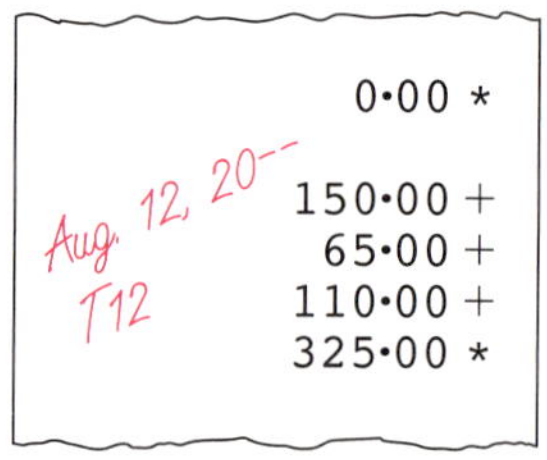
0•00 *
Aug. 12, 20--
T12
150•00 +
65•00 +
110•00 +
325•00 *

Encore Music dates and numbers each calculator tape. For example, in the illustration, the number, *T12*, indicates that the tape is for the twelfth day of the month.

RECEIVED CASH FROM OWNER AS AN INVESTMENT

1 Date · 4 Source Document · 2 Debit · 3 Credit

JOURNAL — PAGE *1*

					1	2	3	4	5	
	DATE	ACCOUNT TITLE	DOC. NO.	POST. REF.	GENERAL DEBIT	GENERAL CREDIT	SALES CREDIT	CASH DEBIT	CASH CREDIT	
1	20-- Aug. 1	*Barbara Treviño, Capital*	*R1*			*10 000 00*		*10 000 00*		1

Information for each transaction recorded in a journal is known as an entry. An entry consists of four parts: (1) date, (2) debit, (3) credit, and (4) source document. Before a transaction is recorded in a journal, the transaction is analyzed into its debit and credit parts.

August 1. Received cash from owner as an investment, $10,000.00. Receipt No. 1.

Cash	
10,000.00	

Barbara Treviño, Capital	
	10,000.00

The source document for this transaction is Receipt No. 1. *(CONCEPT: Objective Evidence)* The analysis of this transaction is shown in the T accounts.

The asset account, Cash, is increased by a debit, $10,000.00. The owner's capital account, Barbara Treviño, Capital, is increased by a credit, $10,000.00.

FYI

Dollars and cents signs and decimal points are not used when writing amounts on ruled accounting paper. Sometimes a color tint or a heavy vertical rule is used on printed accounting paper to separate the dollars and cents columns.

STEPS

Journalizing cash received from owner as an investment

1. **Date.** Write the date, *20—, Aug. 1,* in the Date column. This entry is the first one on this journal page. Therefore, the year and month are both written for this entry. Neither the year nor the month are written again on the same page.
2. **Debit.** The journal has a special amount column for debits to Cash. Write the debit amount, *$10,000.00,* in the Cash Debit column. The title of the account is in the column heading. Therefore, the account title does not need to be written in the Account Title column.
3. **Credit.** There is no special amount column with the title of the account credited, Barbara Treviño, Capital, in its heading. Therefore, the credit amount, *$10,000.00,* is recorded in the General Credit column. In order to indicate what account is to be credited for this amount, write the title of the account, *Barbara Treviño, Capital,* in the Account Title column. (All amounts recorded in the General Debit or General Credit amount columns must have an account title written in the Account Title column.)
4. **Source document.** Write the source document number, *R1,* in the Doc. No. column. The source document number, R1, indicates that this is Receipt No. 1. (The source document number is a cross reference from the journal to the source document. If more details are needed about this transaction, a person can refer to Receipt No. 1.)

PAID CASH FOR SUPPLIES

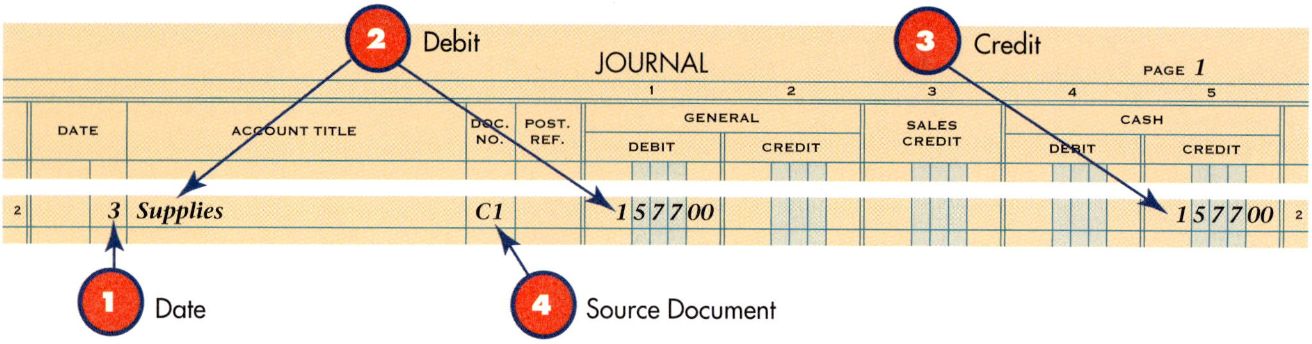

August 3. Paid cash for supplies, $1,577.00. Check No. 1.

Supplies

Debit	Credit
1,577.00	

Cash

Debit	Credit
	1,577.00

The source document for this transaction is Check No. 1. *(CONCEPT: Objective Evidence)* The analysis of this transaction is shown in the T accounts.

The asset account, Supplies, is increased by a debit, $1,577.00. The asset account, Cash, is decreased by a credit, $1,577.00.

FYI

If you draw T accounts for analyzing transactions, it will make journalizing easier.

STEPS Journalizing cash paid for supplies

1. **Date.** Write the date, *3*, in the Date column. This is not the first entry on the journal page. Therefore, the year and month are not written for this entry.
2. **Debit.** There is no special amount column with the title of the account debited, Supplies, in its heading. Therefore, the debit amount, *$1,577.00*, is recorded in the General Debit column. In order to indicate what account is to be debited for this amount, write the title of the account, *Supplies*, in the Account Title column.
3. **Credit.** The journal has a special amount column for credits to Cash. Write the credit amount, *$1,577.00*, in the Cash Credit column. The title of the account is in the column heading. Therefore, the account title does not need to be written in the Account Title column.
4. **Source document.** Write the source document number, *C1*, in the Doc. No. column. The source document number, C1, indicates that this is Check No. 1.

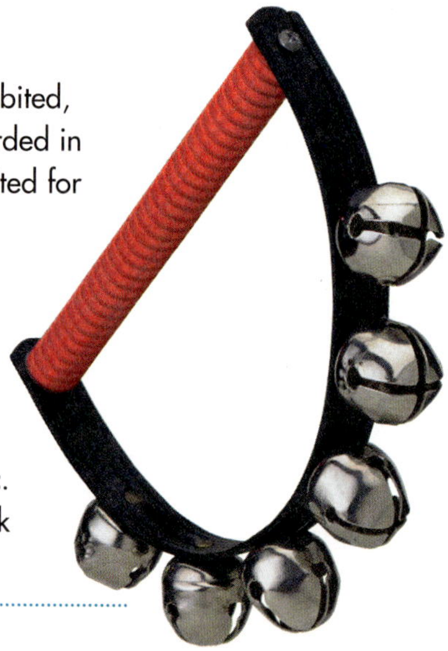

REMEMBER

When an account such as Cash is used frequently, it can be time-consuming to write the account title over and over. Using a special amount column for a frequently used account saves time.

Terms Review

journal
journalizing
special amount column
general amount column
entry
double-entry accounting
source document
check
invoice
sales invoice
receipt
memorandum

Audit Your Understanding

1. In what order are transactions recorded in a journal?
2. Why are source documents important?
3. List the four parts of a journal entry.

Work Together

Journalizing entries into a five-column journal

A journal is given in the *Working Papers.* Your instructor will guide you through the following example.

Ruth Muldoon owns Muldoon Copy Center, which uses the following accounts:

Cash	Prepaid Insurance	Ruth Muldoon, Drawing	Rent Expense
Accts. Rec.—Lester Dodge	Accts. Pay.—Ron's Supplies	Sales	Utilities Expense
Supplies	Ruth Muldoon, Capital	Miscellaneous Expense	

Transactions: Apr. 1. Received cash from owner as an investment, $7,000.00. R1.
2. Paid cash for supplies, $425.00. C1.

4. Journalize each transaction completed during April of the current year. Use page 1 of the journal. Source documents are abbreviated as follows: check, C; memorandum, M; receipt, R; sales invoice, S; calculator tape, T. Save your work to complete Work Together on page 75.

On Your Own

Journalizing entries into a five-column journal

A journal is given in the *Working Papers.* Work this problem independently.

Gale Klein owns Klein's Service Center, which uses the following accounts:

Cash	Prepaid Insurance	Gale Klein, Drawing	Miscellaneous Expense
Accts. Rec.—Connie Vaughn	Accts. Pay.—Osamu Supply Co.	Sales	Rent Expense
Supplies	Gale Klein, Capital	Advertising Expense	

Transactions: June 2 Received cash from owner as an investment, $1,500.00. R1.
3. Paid cash for supplies, $35.00. C1.

5. Jounalize each transaction completed during June of the current year. Use page 1 of the journal. Source documents are abbreviated as follows: check, C; memorandum, M; receipt, R; sales invoice, S; calculator tape, T. Save your work to complete On Your Own on page 75.

4-2 Journalizing Buying Insurance, Buying on Account, and Paying on Account

PAID CASH FOR INSURANCE

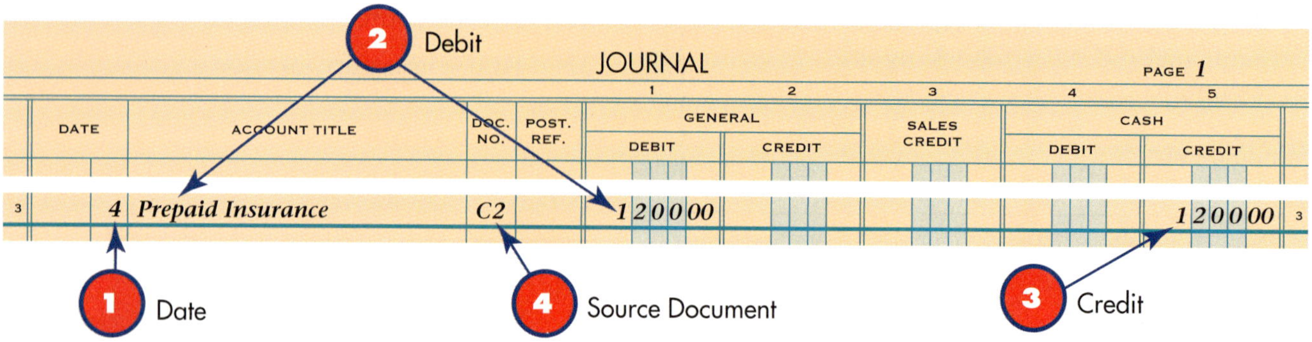

JOURNAL PAGE 1

	DATE	ACCOUNT TITLE	DOC. NO.	POST. REF.	1 GENERAL DEBIT	2 GENERAL CREDIT	3 SALES CREDIT	4 CASH DEBIT	5 CASH CREDIT	
3	4	*Prepaid Insurance*	*C2*		*1 200 00*				*1 200 00*	3

August 4. Paid cash for insurance, $1,200.00. Check No. 2.

Prepaid Insurance	
1,200.00	

Cash	
	1,200.00

The source document for this transaction is Check No. 2. *(CONCEPT: Objective Evidence)* The analysis of this transaction is shown in the T accounts.

The asset account, Prepaid Insurance, is increased by a debit, $1,200.00. The asset account, Cash, is decreased by a credit, $1,200.00.

STEPS: Journalizing cash paid for insurance

1. **Date.** Write the date, *4*, in the Date column.
2. **Debit.** There is no special amount column with the title of the account debited, Prepaid Insurance, in its heading. Therefore, the debit amount, *$1,200.00*, is recorded in the General Debit column. In order to indicate what account is to be debited for this amount, write the title of the account, *Prepaid Insurance*, in the Account Title column.
3. **Credit.** The journal has a special amount column for credits to Cash. Write the credit amount, *$1,200.00*, in the Cash Credit column. The title of the account is in the column heading. Therefore, the account title does not need to be written in the Account Title column.
4. **Source document.** Write the source document number, *C2*, in the Doc. No. column.

REMEMBER

All amounts recorded in the General Debit or General Credit amount columns must have an account title written in the Account Title column.

BOUGHT SUPPLIES ON ACCOUNT

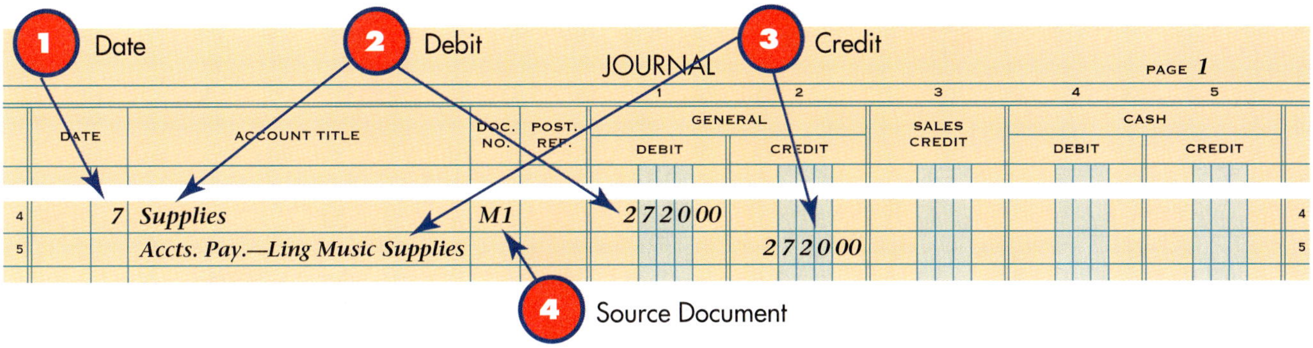

August 7. Bought supplies on account from Ling Music Supplies, $2,720.00. Memorandum No. 1.

Supplies	
2,720.00	

Accts. Pay.—Ling Music Supplies	
	2,720.00

Encore Music ordered these supplies by telephone. Encore Music wishes to record this transaction immediately. Therefore, a memorandum is prepared that shows supplies received on account.

The source document for this transaction is Memorandum No. 1. *(CONCEPT: Objective Evidence)* The analysis of this transaction is shown in the T accounts.

The asset account, Supplies, is increased by a debit, $2,720.00. The liability account, Accounts Payable—Ling Music Supplies, is increased by a credit, $2,720.00

FYI

Of all service businesses in the United States, only 4 percent employ 50 or more people and 80 percent have fewer than 10 employees.

STEPS: Journalizing supplies bought on account

1. **Date.** Write the date, *7*, in the Date column.
2. **Debit.** There is no special amount column with the title of the account debited, Supplies, in its heading. Therefore, the debit amount, *$2,720.00*, is recorded in the General Debit column. In order to indicate what account is to be debited for this amount, write the title of the account, *Supplies*, in the Account Title column.
3. **Credit.** Again, there is no special amount column with the title of the account credited, Accounts Payable—Ling Music Supplies, in its heading. Therefore, the credit amount, *$2,720.00*, is recorded on the next journal line in the General Credit column. In order to indicate what account is to be credited for this amount, write the title of the account, *Accounts Payable—Ling Music Supplies*, in the Account Title column on the same line as the credit amount.

   This entry requires two lines in the journal because account titles for both the debit and credit amounts must be written in the Account Title column.
4. **Source document.** Write the source document number, *M1*, in the Doc. No. column on the first line of the entry.

PAID CASH ON ACCOUNT

2 Debit

JOURNAL PAGE *1*

	DATE	ACCOUNT TITLE	DOC. NO.	POST. REF.	1 GENERAL DEBIT	2 GENERAL CREDIT	3 SALES CREDIT	4 CASH DEBIT	5 CASH CREDIT	
6	*11*	*Accts. Pay.—Ling Music Supplies*	*C3*		*1360 00*				*1360 00*	6

1 Date

4 Source Document

3 Credit

August 11. Paid cash on account to Ling Music Supplies, $1,360.00. Check No. 3.

Accts. Pay.—Ling Music Supplies	
1,360.00	

Cash	
	1,360.00

The source document for this transaction is Check No. 3. *(CONCEPT: Objective Evidence)* The analysis of this transaction is shown in the T accounts.

The liability account, Accounts Payable—Ling Music Supplies, is decreased by a debit, $1,360.00. The asset account, Cash, is decreased by a credit, $1,360.00.

ACCOUNTING AT WORK

MARY WITHERSPOON

In high school, Mary M. Witherspoon considered pursuing a degree in accounting. Her career choice was confirmed by ACCUMATION, a career education program for high school students sponsored by the Dallas Chapter of the Texas Society of CPAs. Students participate in this week-long summer program, which includes visits to an international accounting firm and the chance to sit in on university accounting classes.

Mary graduated with a BBA in Accounting and works for Oryx Energy Company, a large independent producer of oil and gas in Dallas. Currently in gas balancing accounting, she reconciles records of jointly owned properties to ensure Oryx receives their entitled gas volumes. Working in the corporate environment has allowed Mary to change job responsibilities over her career to gain additional experience.

Mary believes that exceptional people skills coupled with technical experience is the formula for business success. People skills include written and verbal communication, respecting diversity, and the ability to work in teams.

Mary also serves as a district vice-president of the American Business Women's Association (ABWA). ABWA promotes the advancement of women in business by sponsoring continuing education, providing leadership training, and offering encouragement.

"High school students can contact their state or local society of certified public accountants for accounting career information," says Mary. "We CPAs support programs to encourage student interest in our field."

AUDIT YOUR UNDERSTANDING

1. Which journal columns are used to record paying cash for insurance?
2. Which journal columns are used to record buying supplies on account?
3. Which journal columns are used to record paying cash on account?

WORK TOGETHER

Journalizing entries into a five-column journal

Use the journal that you started for Work Together on page 71. Your instructor will guide you through the following example.

Ruth Muldoon owns Muldoon Copy Center, which uses the following accounts:

Cash	Prepaid Insurance	Ruth Muldoon, Drawing	Rent Expense
Accts. Rec.—Lester Dodge	Accts. Pay.—Ron's Supplies	Sales	Utilities Expense
Supplies	Ruth Muldoon, Capital	Miscellaneous Expense	

Transactions: Apr. 5. Bought supplies on account from Ron's Supplies, $300.00. M1.
7. Paid cash for insurance, $600.00. C2.
9. Paid cash on account to Ron's Supplies, $300.00. C3.

4. Journalize the transactions continuing on the next blank line of page 1 of the journal. Save your work to complete Work Together on page 81.

ON YOUR OWN

Journalizing entries into a five-column journal

Use the chart of accounts above and the journal that you started for On Your Own on page 71. Work this problem independently.

Gale Klein owns Klein's Service Center, which uses the following accounts:

Cash	Prepaid Insurance	Gale Klein, Drawing	Miscellaneous Expense
Accts. Rec.—Connie Vaughn	Accts. Pay.—Osamu Supply Co.	Sales	Rent Expense
Supplies	Gale Klein, Capital	Advertising Expense	

Transactions: June 5. Paid cash for insurance, $100.00. C2.
9. Bought supplies on account from Osamu Supply Co., $155.00. M1.
10. Paid cash on account to Osamu Supply Co., $155.00. C3.

5. Journalize the transactions continuing on the next blank line of page 1 of the journal. Save your work to complete On Your Own on page 81.

4-3 Journalizing Transactions That Affect Owner's Equity and Receiving Cash on Account

RECEIVED CASH FROM SALES

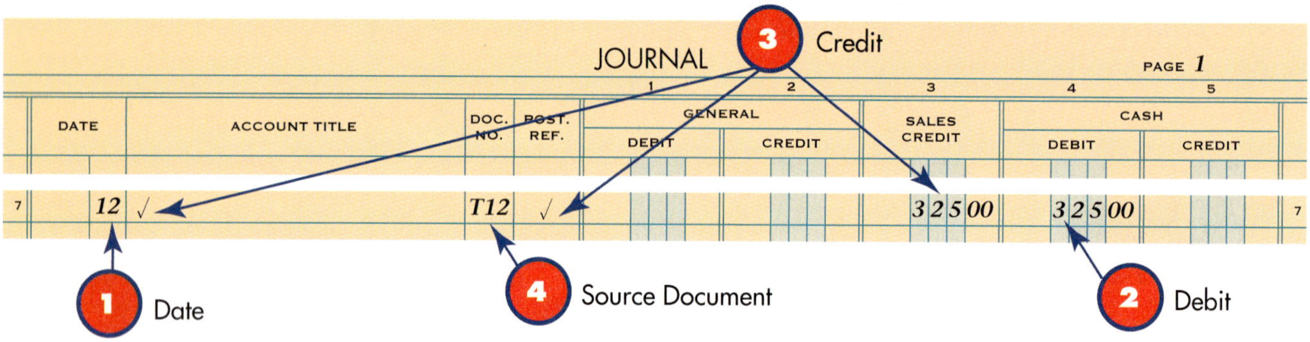

August 12. Received cash from sales, $325.00. Tape No. 12.

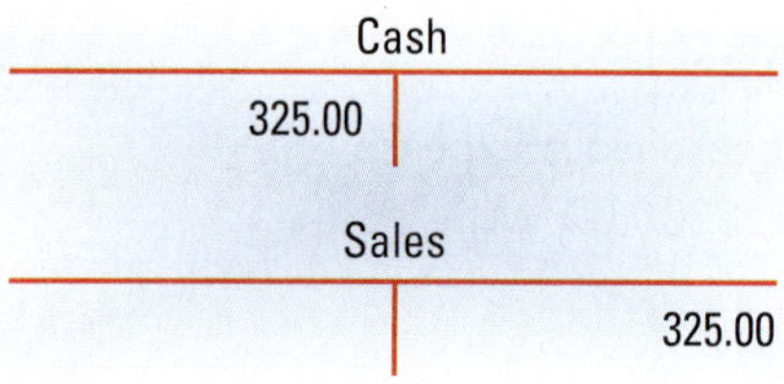

The source document for this transaction is Calculator Tape No. 12. *(CONCEPT: Objective Evidence)* The analysis of this transaction is shown in the T accounts.

The asset account, Cash, is increased by a debit, $325.00. The revenue account, Sales, is increased by a credit, $325.00.

The reason that Sales is increased by a credit is discussed in the previous chapter. The owner's capital account has a normal credit balance. Increases in the owner's capital account are shown as credits. Because revenue increases owner's equity, increases in revenue are recorded as credits. A revenue account, therefore, has a normal credit balance.

STEPS: Journalizing cash received from sales

1. **Date.** Write the date, *12*, in the Date column.
2. **Debit.** The journal has a special amount column for debits to Cash. Write the debit amount, *$325.00*, in the Cash Debit column. The title of the account is in the column heading. Therefore, the account title does not need to be written in the Account Title column.
3. **Credit.** The journal also has a special amount column for credits to Sales. Write the credit amount, *$325.00*, in the Sales Credit column. The title of the account is in the column heading. Therefore, the account title does not need to be written in the Account Title column.

   Because both amounts for this entry are recorded in special amount columns, no account titles are written in the Account Title column. Therefore, a check mark is placed in the Account Title column to show that no account titles need to be written for this transaction. A check mark is also placed in the Post. Ref. column.

   The use of the Post. Ref. column is described in Chapter 5.
4. **Source document.** Write the source document number, *T12*, in the Doc. No. column.

REMEMBER

In double-entry accounting, each transaction affects at least two accounts. At least one account will be debited and at least one account will be credited.

SOLD SERVICES ON ACCOUNT

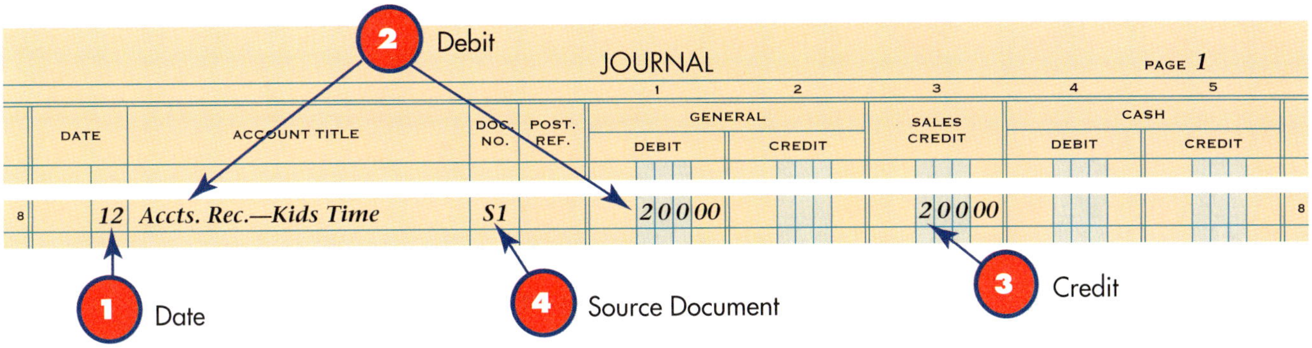

August 12. Sold services on account to Kids Time, $200.00. Sales Invoice No. 1.

Accts. Rec.—Kids Time	
200.00	

Sales	
	200.00

The source document for this transaction is Sales Invoice No. 1. *(CONCEPT: Objective Evidence)* The analysis of this transaction is shown in the T accounts.

The asset account, Accounts Receivable—Kids Time, is increased by a debit, $200.00. The revenue account, Sales, is increased by a credit, $200.00.

STEPS: Journalizing services sold on account

1. **Date.** Write the date, *12*, in the Date column.
2. **Debit.** There is no special amount column with the title of the account debited, Accounts Receivable—Kids Time, in its heading. Therefore, the debit amount, *$200.00*, is recorded in the General Debit column. In order to indicate what account is to be debited for this amount, write the title of the account, *Accounts Receivable—Kids Time*, in the Account Title column.
3. **Credit.** The journal has a special amount column for credits to Sales. Write the credit amount, *$200.00*, in the Sales Credit column. The title of the account is in the column heading. Therefore, the account title does not need to be written in the Account Title column.
4. **Source document.** Write the source document number, *S1*, in the Doc. No. column.

F.Y.I.

Accounting is not just for accountants. For example, a performing artist earns revenue from providing a service. Financial decisions must be made such as the cost of doing a performance, the percentage of revenue paid to a manager, travel expenses, and the cost of rehearsal space.

PAID CASH FOR AN EXPENSE

JOURNAL PAGE 1

	DATE		ACCOUNT TITLE	DOC. NO.	POST. REF.	1 GENERAL DEBIT	2 GENERAL CREDIT	3 SALES CREDIT	4 CASH DEBIT	5 CASH CREDIT	
9		12	Rent Expense	C4		250 00				250 00	9
10		12	Utilities Expense	C5		45 00				45 00	10

1 Date
2 Debit
3 Credit
4 Source Document

August 12. Paid cash for rent, $250.00. Check No. 4.

Rent Expense

Debit	Credit
250.00	

Cash

Debit	Credit
	250.00

The source document for this transaction is Check No. 4. *(CONCEPT: Objective Evidence)* The analysis of this transaction is shown in the T accounts.

The expense account, Rent Expense, is increased by a debit, $250.00. The asset account, Cash, is decreased by a credit, $250.00.

The reason that Rent Expense is increased by a debit is discussed in the previous chapter. The owner's capital account has a normal credit balance. Decreases in the owner's capital account are shown as debits.

Because expenses decrease owner's equity, increases in expenses are recorded as debits. An expense account, therefore, has a normal debit balance.

STEPS

Journalizing cash paid for an expense

1. **Date.** Write the date, *12*, in the Date column.
2. **Debit.** There is no special amount column with the title of the account debited, Rent Expense, in its heading. Therefore, the debit amount, *$250.00*, is recorded in the General Debit column. In order to indicate what account is to be debited for this amount, write the title of the account, *Rent Expense*, in the Account Title column.
3. **Credit.** The journal has a special amount column for credits to Cash. Write the credit amount, *$250.00*, in the Cash Credit column. The title of the account is in the column heading. Therefore, the account title does not need to be written in the Account Title column.
4. **Source document.** Write the source document number, *C4*, in the Doc. No. column.

Whenever cash is paid for an expense, the journal entry is similar to the entry discussed above. Therefore, the journal entry to record paying cash for utilities is also illustrated.

FYI

Source documents can be critically important in tracking down errors. Businesses file their source documents so they can be referred to if it is necessary to verify information entered into their journals.

RECEIVED CASH ON ACCOUNT

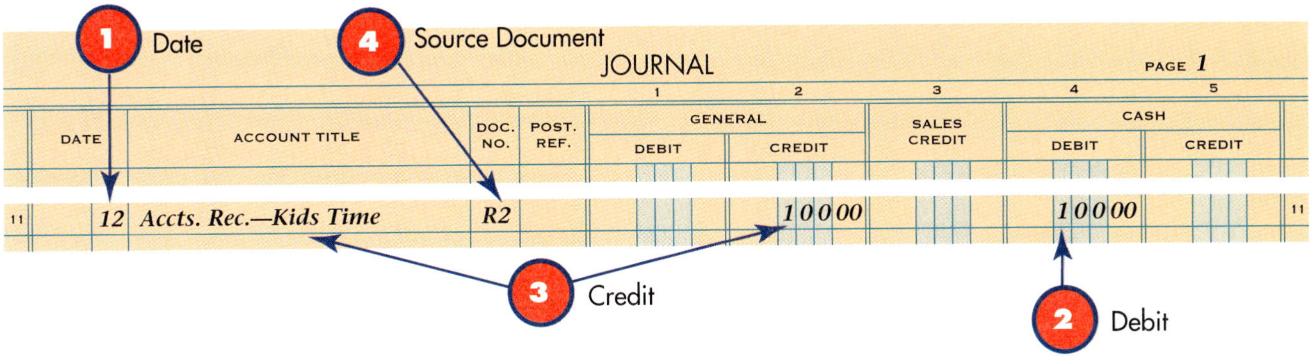

August 12. Received cash on account from Kids Time, $100.00. Receipt No. 2.

Cash	
100.00	

Accts. Rec.—Kids Time	
	100.00

The source document for this transaction is Receipt No. 2. *(CONCEPT: Objective Evidence)* The analysis of this transaction is shown in the T accounts.

The asset account, Cash, is increased by a debit, $100.00. The asset account, Accounts Receivable—Kids Time, is decreased by a credit, $100.00.

STEPS: Journalizing cash received on account

1. **Date.** Write the date, *12*, in the Date column.
2. **Debit.** The journal has a special amount column for debits to Cash. Write the debit amount, *$100.00*, in the Cash Debit column. The title of the account is in the column heading. Therefore, the account title does not need to be written in the Account Title column.
3. **Credit.** There is no special amount column with the title of the account credited, Accounts Receivable—Kids Time, in its heading. Therefore, the credit amount, *$100.00*, is recorded in the General Credit column. In order to indicate what account is to be credited for this amount, write the title of the account, *Accounts Receivable—Kids Time*, in the Account Title column.
4. **Source document.** Write the source document number, *R2*, in the Doc. No. column.

REMEMBER

If you misspell words in your written communications, people may mistrust the quality of your accounting skills. Note that in the word receipt the "e" comes before the "i" and there is a silent "p" before the "t" at the end of the word.

PAID CASH TO OWNER FOR PERSONAL USE

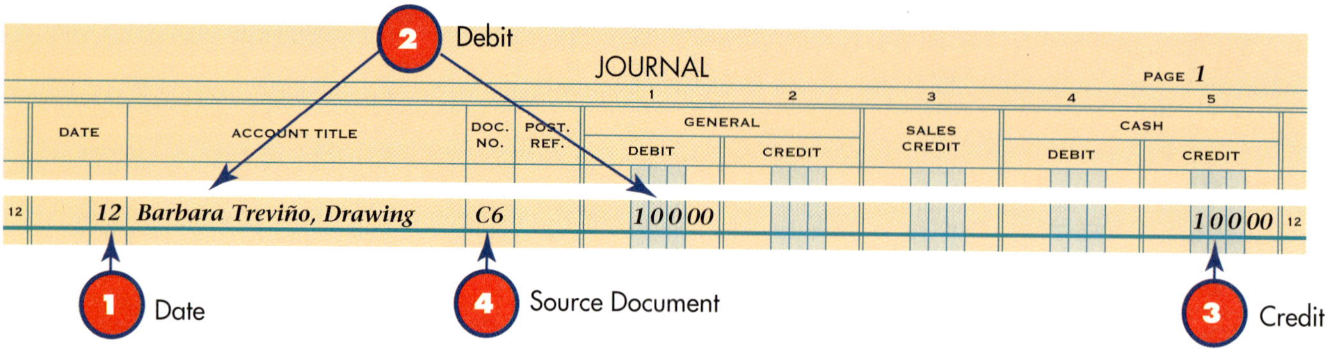

August 12. Paid cash to owner for personal use, $100.00. Check No. 6.

Barbara Treviño, Drawing

Debit	Credit
100.00	

Cash

Debit	Credit
	100.00

The source document for this transaction is Check No. 6. *(CONCEPT: Objective Evidence)* The analysis of this transaction is shown in the T accounts.

The reason that Barbara Treviño, Drawing is increased by a debit is discussed in the previous chapter. Decreases in the owner's capital account are shown as debits. Because withdrawals decrease owner's equity, increases in withdrawals are recorded as debits. A withdrawal account, therefore, has a normal debit balance.

LEGAL ISSUES IN ACCOUNTING

FORMING AND DISSOLVING A PROPRIETORSHIP

A proprietorship is a business owned and controlled by one person. The advantages of a proprietorship include:

- Ease of formation.
- Total control by the owner.
- Profits that are not shared.

However, there are some disadvantages of organizing a proprietorship:

- Limited resources. The owner is the only person who can invest cash and other assets in the business.
- Unlimited liability. The owner is totally responsible for the liabilities of the business. Personal assets, such as a car, can be claimed by creditors to pay the business's liabilities.
- Limited expertise. Limited time, energy, and experience can be put into the business by the owner.
- Limited life. A proprietorship must be dissolved when the owner dies or decides to stop doing business.

The owner is required to follow the laws of both the federal government and the state and city in which the business is formed. Most cities and states have few, if any, legal procedures to follow. Once any legal requirements are met, the proprietorship can begin business.

Should the owner decide to dissolve the proprietorship, he or she merely needs to stop doing business. Noncash assets can be sold, with the cash used to pay any creditors.

AUDIT YOUR UNDERSTANDING

1. Which journal columns are used to record receiving cash from sales?
2. Which journal columns are used to record sales on account?
3. Which journal columns are used to record paying cash for an expense?
4. Which journal columns are used to record receiving cash on account?
5. Which journal columns are used to record paying cash to owner for personal use?

WORK TOGETHER

Journalizing transactions that affect owner's equity into a five-column journal

Use the chart of accounts and journal from Work Together on page 75. Your instructor will guide you through the following example.

Transactions: Apr.
12. Paid cash for rent, $950.00. C4.
13. Received cash from sales, $2,200.00. T13.
14. Sold services on account to Lester Dodge, $625.00. S1.
19. Paid cash for electric bill, $157.00. C5.
20. Received cash on account from Lester Dodge, $300.00. R2.
21. Paid cash to owner for personal use, $1,400.00. C6.

6. Journalize the transactions continuing on the next blank line of page 1 of the journal. Save your work to complete Work Together on page 87.

ON YOUR OWN

Journalizing transactions that affect owner's equity into a five-column journal

Use the chart of accounts and journal from On Your Own on page 75. Work this problem independently.

Transactions: June
11. Paid cash for rent, $200.00. C4.
12. Sold services on account to Connie Vaughn, $200.00. S1.
16. Received cash from sales, $1,050.00. T16.
17. Paid cash for postage (Miscellaneous Expense), $32.00. C5.
19. Received cash on account from Connie Vaughn, $100.00. R2.
20. Paid cash to owner for personal use, $250.00. C6.

7. Journalize the transactions continuing on the next blank line of page 1 of the journal. Save your work to complete On Your Own on page 87.

4-4 Proving and Ruling a Journal

PROVING A JOURNAL PAGE

1 Add each amount column

2 Add debit totals and credit totals

Column	Debit Column Totals	Credit Column Totals
General	$ 7,960.00	$12,840.00
Sales		2,439.00
Cash	12,319.00	5,000.00
Totals	$20,279.00	$20,279.00

3 Totals equal

After Encore Music uses all but the last line on a journal page, columns are proved and ruled before totals are carried forward to the next page.

To prove a journal page, Encore Music verifies that the total debits on the page equal the total credits. Three steps are followed in proving a journal page.

If the total debits do not equal the total credits, the errors must be found and corrected before any more work is completed.

STEPS

Proving a journal page

1. Add each of the amount columns. Use a calculator if one is available.
2. Add the debit column totals, and then add the credit column totals as shown.
3. Verify that the total debits and total credits are equal. Because the total debits equal the total credits, page 1 of Encore Music's journal is proved.

GLOBAL PERSPECTIVE

FOREIGN CURRENCY

As our world becomes smaller and global trade increases, U.S. businesses become more involved in transactions with foreign businesses. These transactions can be stated in terms of U.S. dollars or in the currency of the other country. If the transaction involves foreign currency, a U.S. business must convert the foreign currency into U.S. dollars before the transaction can be recorded. *(CONCEPT: Unit of Measurement)*

The value of foreign currency may change daily. In the United States, the *exchange rate* is the value of foreign currency in relation to the U.S. dollar. Current exchange rates can be found in many daily newspapers, on-line services, or banks.

The exchange rate is stated in terms of one unit of foreign currency. Using Germany as an example, presume that one German *mark* is worth 0.5789 U.S. dollars (or about 58 U.S. cents). This rate would be used when exchanging German marks for U.S. dollars.

A *conversion formula* can be used to find out how many foreign currency units can be purchased with one U.S. dollar. The formula is:

1/exchange rate = foreign currency per U.S. dollar

1 dollar/0.5789 = 1.7272 marks per dollar

RULING A JOURNAL PAGE

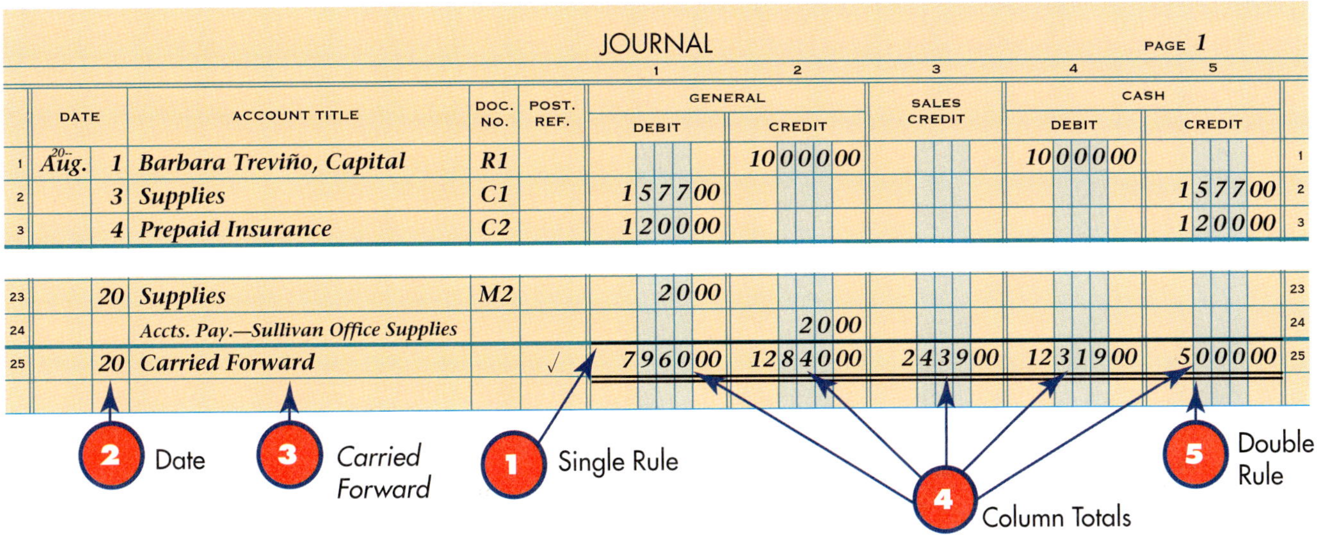

JOURNAL — PAGE 1

	DATE		ACCOUNT TITLE	DOC. NO.	POST. REF.	1 GENERAL DEBIT	2 GENERAL CREDIT	3 SALES CREDIT	4 CASH DEBIT	5 CASH CREDIT	
1	20-- Aug.	1	Barbara Treviño, Capital	R1			10000 00		10000 00		1
2		3	Supplies	C1		1577 00				1577 00	2
3		4	Prepaid Insurance	C2		1200 00				1200 00	3
23		20	Supplies	M2		20 00					23
24			Accts. Pay.—Sullivan Office Supplies				20 00				24
25		20	Carried Forward		√	7960 00	12840 00	2439 00	12319 00	5000 00	25

After a journal page is proved, it is ruled. Five steps are followed in ruling a journal page.

STEPS

Ruling a journal page

1. Rule a single line across all amount columns directly below the last entry.
2. On the next line, write the date, *20*, in the Date column.
3. Write the words *Carried Forward* in the Account Title column. A check mark is also placed in the Post. Ref. column. The use of the Post. Ref. column is described in Chapter 5.
4. Write each column total below the single line.
5. Rule double lines below the column totals across all amount columns.

SMALL BUSINESS SPOTLIGHT

Successful small business owners typically have the following characteristics: confidence to make decisions, determination to keep trying during hard times for the business, willingness to take risks, creativity to surpass the competition, and an inner need to achieve.

STARTING A NEW JOURNAL PAGE

JOURNAL — PAGE 2

	DATE		ACCOUNT TITLE	DOC. NO.	POST. REF.	GENERAL DEBIT (1)	GENERAL CREDIT (2)	SALES CREDIT (3)	CASH DEBIT (4)	CASH CREDIT (5)	
1	20-- Aug.	20	*Brought Forward*		√	7960 00	12840 00	2439 00	12319 00	5000 00	1
2											2

1 Page
2 Date
3 Brought Forward
4 Column Totals

The column totals from the previous page are carried forward to a new page. The totals are recorded on the first line of the new page, using the following four steps.

STEPS — Starting a new journal page

1. Write the page number, *2*, at the top of the journal.
2. Write the date, *20—, Aug. 20*, in the Date column. Because this is the first time that a date is written on page 2, the year, month, and day are all written in the Date column.
3. Write *Brought Forward* in the Account Title column. A check mark is also placed in the Post. Ref. column.
4. Record the column totals brought forward from the previous page.

PROVING AND RULING A JOURNAL AT THE END OF A MONTH

JOURNAL — PAGE 2

	DATE		ACCOUNT TITLE	DOC. NO.	POST. REF.	GENERAL DEBIT (1)	GENERAL CREDIT (2)	SALES CREDIT (3)	CASH DEBIT (4)	CASH CREDIT (5)	
1	20-- Aug.	20	*Brought Forward*		√	7960 00	12840 00	2439 00	12319 00	5000 00	1
2		21	√	T21	√			270 00	270 00		2
13		31	√	T31	√			290 00	290 00		13
14		31	*Miscellaneous Expense*	M3	530	3 00				3 00	14
15		31	*Totals*			8979 00	12840 00	4411 00	14291 00	6019 00	15

1 Single Rule
2 Date
3 Totals
4 Column Totals
5 Double Rule

Encore Music always proves and rules a journal at the end of each month even if the last page for the month is not full.

The last page of a journal for a month is proved using the same steps previously described. Then, cash is proved and the journal is ruled. The proof of page 2 of Encore Music's journal is completed as shown. Proving cash is discussed on the next page.

Column	Debit Column Totals	Credit Column Totals
General	$ 8,979.00	$12,840.00
Sales		4,411.00
Cash	14,291.00	6,019.00
Totals	$23,270.00	$23,270.00

Page 2 of Encore Music's journal is proved because the total debits are equal to the total credits, $23,270.00.

Proving Cash

Determining that the amount of cash agrees with the accounting records is called **proving cash.** Cash can be proved at any time Encore Music wishes to verify the accuracy of the cash records. However, Encore Music *always* proves cash at the end of a month when the journal is proved. Encore Music uses two steps to prove cash.

1. Calculate the cash balance.

Cash on hand at the beginning of the month	$ 0.00
Encore Music began the month with no cash balance. Ms. Treviño invested the initial cash on August 1.	
Plus total cash received during the month	+14,291.00
This amount is the total of the journal's Cash Debit column.	
Equals total	$14,291.00
Less total cash paid during the month	− 6,019.00
This amount is the total of the journal's Cash Credit column.	
Equals cash balance at the end of the month	$ 8,272.00
Checkbook balance on the next unused check stub	$ 8,272.00

2. Verify that the cash balance equals the checkbook balance on the next unused check stub in the checkbook. Because the cash balance calculated using the journal and the checkbook balance are the same, $8,272.00, cash is proved.

Ruling a Journal at the End of a Month

A journal is ruled at the end of each month even if the last journal page is not full. The procedures for ruling a journal at the end of a month are similar to those for ruling a journal page to carry the totals forward.

Encore Music uses five steps in ruling a journal at the end of each month, as shown on the previous page.

STEPS

Ruling a journal at the end of a month (these steps are illustrated on the previous page)

1. Rule a single line across all amount columns directly below the last entry to indicate that the columns are to be added.
2. On the next line, write the date, *31*, in the Date column.
3. Write the word *Totals* in the Account Title column.
   A check mark is not placed in the Post. Ref. column for this line. More information about the Totals line will be provided in Chapter 5.
4. Write each column total below the single line.
5. Rule double lines below the column totals across all amount columns. The double lines mean that the totals have been verified as correct.

STANDARD ACCOUNTING PRACTICES

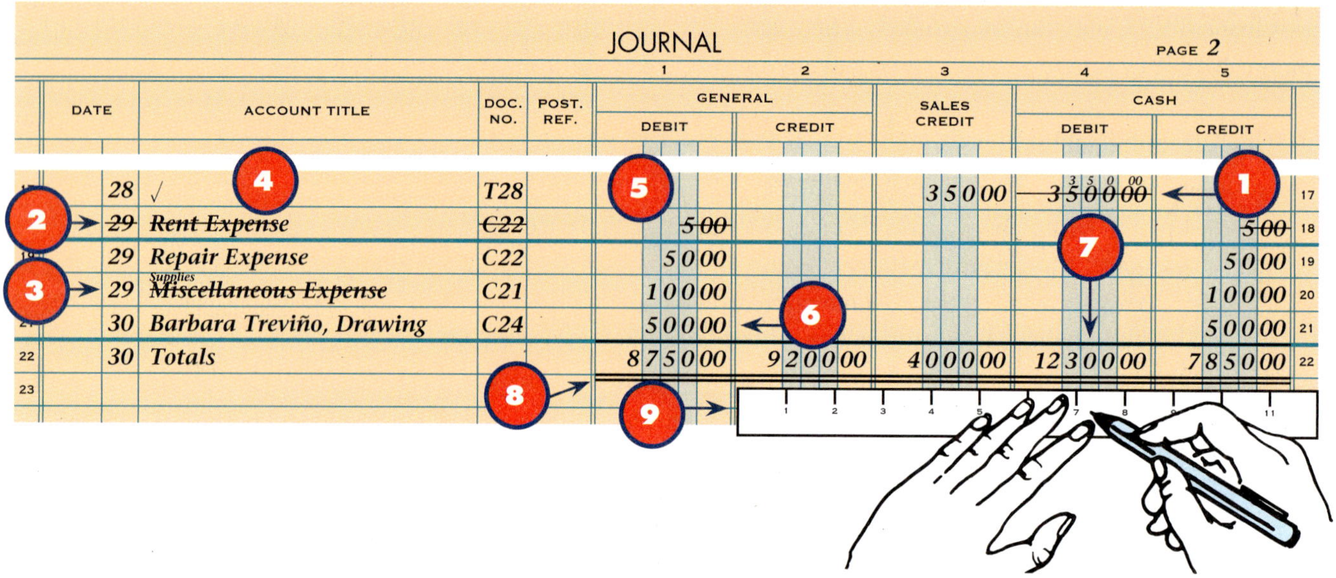

JOURNAL — PAGE 2

	DATE	ACCOUNT TITLE	DOC. NO.	POST. REF.	1 GENERAL DEBIT	2 GENERAL CREDIT	3 SALES CREDIT	4 CASH DEBIT	5 CASH CREDIT	
17	28	√	T28				350 00	350 00 ~~3500 00~~		17
18	~~29~~	~~Rent Expense~~	~~C22~~		~~5 00~~				~~5 00~~	18
19	29	Repair Expense	C22		50 00				50 00	19
20	29	Supplies ~~Miscellaneous Expense~~	C21		100 00				100 00	20
21	30	Barbara Treviño, Drawing	C24		500 00				500 00	21
22	30	Totals			8750 00	9200 00	4000 00	12300 00	7850 00	22
23										

In completing accounting work, Encore Music follows standard accounting practices. These practices include procedures for error corrections, abbreviating words, writing dollar and cents signs, and rulings.

1. Errors are corrected in a way that does not cause doubts about what the correct information is. If an error is recorded, cancel the error by neatly drawing a line through the incorrect item. Write the correct item immediately above the canceled item.
2. Sometimes an entire entry is incorrect and is discovered before the next entry is journalized. Draw neat lines through all parts of the incorrect entry. Journalize the entry correctly on the next blank line.
3. Sometimes several correct entries are recorded after an incorrect entry is made. The next blank lines are several entries later. Draw neat lines through all incorrect parts of the entry. Record the correct items on the same lines as the incorrect items, directly above the canceled parts.
4. Words in accounting records are written in full when space permits. Words may be abbreviated only when space is limited. All items are written legibly.
5. Dollars and cents signs and decimal points are not used when writing amounts on ruled accounting paper. Sometimes a color tint or a heavy vertical rule is used on printed accounting paper to separate the dollars and cents columns.
6. Two zeros are written in the cents column when an amount is in even dollars, such as $500.00. If the cents column is left blank, doubts may arise later about the correct amount.
7. A single line is ruled across amount columns to indicate addition or subtraction.
8. A double line is ruled across amount columns to indicate that the totals have been verified as correct.
9. Neatness is very important in accounting records so that there is never any doubt about what information has been recorded. A ruler is used to make single and double lines.

REMEMBER

Double lines ruled below totals mean the totals have been verified as correct.

TERM REVIEW

proving cash

AUDIT YOUR UNDERSTANDING

1. List the three steps for proving a journal.
2. State the formula for proving cash.
3. List the five steps to rule a journal at the end of a month.

WORK TOGETHER

Proving and ruling a journal

Use the journal from Work Together on page 81. Your instructor will guide you through the following examples.

Transactions: Apr. 23. Sold services on account to Lester Dodge, $317.00. S2.
27. Paid cash to owner for personal use, $750.00. C7.
29. Received cash on account from Lester Dodge, $75.00. R3.
30. Received cash from sales, $743.00. T30.

4. Journalize the transactions for April 23 and 27.
5. Prove and rule page 1 of the journal. Carry the column totals forward to page 2 of the journal.
6. Use page 2 of the journal to journalize the rest of the transactions for April.
7. Prove page 2 of the journal.
8. Prove cash. The beginning cash balance on April 1 is zero. The balance on the next unused check stub is $5,736.00.
9. Rule page 2 of the journal.

ON YOUR OWN

Proving and ruling a journal.

Use the journal from On Your Own on page 81. Work these problems independently.

Transactions: June 23. Sold services on account to Connie Vaughn, $135.00. S2.
26. Paid cash for delivery charges (Miscellaneous Expense), $17.00. C7.
27. Received cash on account from Connie Vaughn, $100.00. R3.
30. Received cash from sales, $235.00. T30.

10. Journalize the transactions for June 23 and 26.
11. Prove and rule page 1 of the journal. Carry the column totals forward to page 2 of the journal.
12. Use page 2 of the journal to journalize the rest of the transactions for June.
13. Prove page 2 of the journal.
14. Prove cash. The beginning cash balance on June 1 is zero. The balance on the next unused check stub is $2,196.00.
15. Rule page 2 of the journal.

CHAPTER 4 SUMMARY

After completing this chapter, you can

1. Define important accounting terms related to journalizing transactions.
2. Identify accounting concepts and practices related to journalizing transactions.
3. Record in a five-column journal transactions to set up a business.
4. Record in a five-column journal transactions to buy insurance for cash and supplies on account.
5. Record in a five-column journal transactions that affect owner's equity and receiving cash on account.
6. Prove and rule a five-column journal and prove cash.

EXPLORE ACCOUNTING

PRENUMBERED DOCUMENTS

As one way to control the operations of the business, a company often will use prenumbered documents. Such a document is one that has the form number printed on it in advance. The most common example in everyday life is the personal check.

Businesses use several prenumbered documents. Examples include business checks, sales invoices, purchase orders, receipts, and memorandums.

The use of prenumbered documents allows a simple way to ensure that all documents are recorded. For example, when a business records the checks written during a period of time, all check numbers should be accounted for in numeric order. The person recording the checks must watch to see that no numbers are skipped. In this way, the business is more confident that all checks are recorded.

By using several types of prenumbered documents, the business helps ensure that all transactions are properly recorded.

Another way a business tries to control operations is through the use of batch totals. When many (sometimes hundreds) of documents are being recorded, the total amount can be used to help ensure that all documents are recorded.

For example, when sales invoices are recorded, the total of all the invoices is calculated prior to the invoices being recorded. Once all invoices are recorded, another total can be calculated. If the two totals are equal, it can be assumed that all invoices have been recorded. If the totals *do not equal*, it may indicate that a document was skipped.

Research: Contact a local business and ask what prenumbered documents are used there. Determine how the business uses the documents to ensure that all documents are recorded properly.

4-1 APPLICATION PROBLEM
Journalizing transactions into a five-column journal

Dennis Gilbert owns a service business called D & G Company, which uses the following accounts:

Cash	Accts. Pay.—Ronken Supplies	Miscellaneous Expense
Accts. Rec.—Hetland Company	Dennis Gilbert, Capital	Rent Expense
Supplies	Dennis Gilbert, Drawing	Utilities Expense
Prepaid Insurance	Sales	

Transactions:

Feb. 1. Received cash from owner as an investment, $10,000.00. R1.
4. Paid cash for supplies, $1,000.00. C1.
5. Paid cash for supplies, $50.00. C2.

Instructions:

Journalize the transactions completed during February of the current year. Use page 1 of the journal given in the *Working Papers*. Source documents are abbreviated as follows: check, C; memorandum, M; receipt, R; sales invoice, S; calculator tape, T.

Save your work to complete Application Problem 4-2.

4-2 APPLICATION PROBLEM
Journalizing buying insurance, buying on account, and paying on account into a five-column journal

Use the chart of accounts and journal from Application Problem 4-1.

Transactions:

Feb. 6. Paid cash for insurance, $1,200.00. C3.
7. Bought supplies on account from Ronken Supplies, $1,400.00 M1.
8. Paid cash on account to Ronken Supplies, $700.00. C4.
12. Paid cash on account to Ronken Supplies, $700.00. C5.

Instructions:

Journalize the transactions. Source documents use the same abbreviations as stated in Application Problem 4-1. Save your work to complete Application Problem 4-3.

4-3 APPLICATION PROBLEM
Journalizing transactions that affect owner's equity and receiving cash on account into a five-column journal

Use the chart of accounts given in Application Problem 4-1 and the journal from Application Problem 4-2.

Transactions:

Feb. 12. Paid cash for rent, $600.00. C6.
13. Received cash from sales, $500.00. T13.
14. Sold services on account to Hetland Company, $450.00. S1.
15. Paid cash for telephone bill, $225.00. C7.
15. Paid cash to owner for personal use, $1,800.00. C8.

Feb. 18. Received cash from sales, $278.00. T18.
19. Paid cash for postage (Miscellaneous Expense), $64.00. C9.
21. Received cash an account from Hetland Company, $250.00. R2.
22. Received cash from sales, $342.00. T22.
22. Paid cash for heating fuel bill, $329.00. C10.
25. Bought supplies on account from Ronken Supplies, $76.00. M2.

Instructions:

Journalize the transactions. Source documents use the same abbreviations as stated in Application Problem 4-1. Save your work to complete Application Problem 4-4.

4-4 APPLICATION PROBLEM
Proving and ruling a journal

Use the chart of accounts given in Application Problem 4-1 and the journal from Application Problem 4-3.

Transactions:

Feb. 25. Received cash on account from Hetland Company, $200.00. R3.
25. Paid cash for a delivery (Miscellaneous Expense), $18.00. C11.
26. Sold services on account to Hetland Company, $136.00. S2.
26. Paid cash for supplies, $44.00. C12.
27. Paid cash for rent, $600.00. C13.
27. Paid cash for postage (Miscellaneous Expense), $10.00. C14.
28. Received cash from sales, $1,365.00. T28.
28. Paid cash to owner for personal use, $1,000.00. C15.

Instructions:

1. Journalize the transactions for February 25 and 26. Source documents use the same abbreviations as stated in Application Problem 4-1.
2. Prove and rule page 1 of the journal. Carry the column totals forward to page 2 of the journal.
3. Use page 2 of the journal to journalize the transactions for February 27 and 28.
4. Prove page 2 of the journal.
5. Prove cash. The beginning cash balance on February 1 is zero. The balance on the next unused check stub is $4,595.00.
6. Rule page 2 of the journal.

4-5 APPLICATION PROBLEM
Journalizing transactions

Nick Bonnocotti owns a service business called The Lawn Doctor, which uses the following accounts:

Cash	Accts. Pay.—Western Supplies	Advertising Expense
Accts. Rec.—Leon Quarve	Nick Bonnocotti, Capital	Utilities Expense
Supplies	Nick Bonnocotti, Drawing	
Prepaid Insurance	Sales	

Transactions:

Apr. 1. Nick Bonnocotti invested $2,000.00 of his own money in the business. Receipt No. 1.
3. Used business cash to purchase supplies costing $37.00. Wrote Check No. 1.

Apr. 4. Wrote Check No. 2 for insurance, $120.00.

5. Purchased supplies for $50.00 over the phone from Western Supplies, promising to send the check next week. Memo. No. 1.

11. Sent Check No. 3 to Western Supplies, $50.00.

12. Sent a check for the electricity bill, $65.00. Check No. 4.

15. Wrote a $850.00 check to Mr. Bonnocotti for personal use. Used Check No. 5.

16. Sold services for $259.00 to Leon Quarve, who agreed to pay for them within 10 days. Sales Invoice No. 1.

17. Recorded cash sales of $1,668.00.

18. Paid $50.00 for advertising. Wrote Check No. 6.

25. Received $259.00 from Leon Quarve for the services performed last week. Wrote Receipt No. 2.

Instructions:

Journalize the transactions completed during April of the current year. Use page 1 of the journal given in the *Working Papers*. Remember to enter source document numbers as necessary.

4-6 MASTERY PROBLEM

Journalizing transactions and proving and ruling a journal

Jill Statsholt owns a service business called Jill's Car Wash, which uses the following accounts:

Cash
Accts. Rec.—David's Limos
Supplies
Prepaid Insurance
Accts. Pay.—Akita Supplies
Accts. Pay.—Long Supplies
Jill Statsholt, Capital
Jill Statsholt, Drawing
Sales
Advertising Expense
Miscellaneous Expense
Rent Expense
Repair Expense
Utilities Expense

Transactions:

June 1. Received cash from owner as an investment, $17,500.00. R1.

2. Paid cash for rent, $400.00. C1.

3. Paid cash for supplies, $1,200.00. C2.

4. Bought supplies on account from Akita Supplies, $2,000.00. M1.

5. Paid cash for insurance, $4,500.00. C3.

8. Paid cash on account to Akita Supplies, $1,500.00. C4.

8. Received cash from sales, $750.00. T8.

8. Sold services on account to David's Limos, $200.00. S1.

9. Paid cash for electric bill, $75.00. C5.

10. Paid cash for miscellaneous expense, $7.00. C6.

10. Received cash from sales, $750.00. T10.

11. Paid cash for repairs, $100.00. C7.

11. Received cash from sales, $850.00. T11.

12. Received cash from sales, $700.00. T12.

15. Paid cash to owner for personal use, $350.00. C8.

15. Received cash from sales, $750.00. T15.

16. Paid cash for supplies, $1,500.00. C9.

17. Received cash on account from David's Limos, $200.00. R2.

17. Bought supplies on account from Long Supplies, $750.00. M2.

June 17. Received cash from sales, $600.00. T17.
18. Received cash from sales, $800.00. T18.
19. Received cash from sales, $750.00. T19.
22. Bought supplies on account from Long Supplies, $80.00. M3.
22. Received cash from sales, $700.00. T22.
23. Paid cash for advertising, $130.00. C10.
23. Sold services on account to David's Limos, $650.00. S2.
24. Paid cash for telephone bill, $60.00. C11.
24. Received cash from sales, $600.00. T24.
25. Received cash from sales, $550.00. T25.
26. Paid cash for supplies, $70.00. C12.
26. Received cash from sales, $600.00. T26.
29. Received cash on account from David's Limos, $650.00. R3.
30. Paid cash to owner for personal use, $375.00. C13.
30. Received cash from sales, $800.00. T30.

Instructions:

1. The journals for Jill's Car Wash are given in the *Working Papers*. Use page 1 of the journal to journalize the transactions for June 1 through June 19. Source documents are abbreviated as follows: check, C; memorandum, M; receipt, R; sales invoice, S; calculator tape, T.
2. Prove and rule page 1 of the journal. Carry the column totals forward to page 2 of the journal.
3. Use page 2 of the journal to journalize the transactions for the remainder of June.
4. Prove page 2 of the journal.
5. Prove cash. The beginning cash balance on June 1 is zero. The balance on the next unused check stub is $17,283.00.
6. Rule page 2 of the journal.

4-7 CHALLENGE PROBLEM

Journalizing transactions using a variation of the five-column journal

Tony Wirth owns a service business called Wirth's Tailors, which uses the following accounts:

Cash
Accts. Rec.—Amy's Uniforms
Supplies
Prepaid Insurance
Accts. Pay.—Marker Supplies
Tony Wirth, Capital
Tony Wirth, Drawing
Sales
Rent Expense
Utilities Expense

Transactions:

June 1. Received cash from owner as an investment, $17,000.00. R1.
2. Paid cash for insurance, $3,000.00. C1.
3. Bought supplies on account from Marker Supplies, $2,500.00. M1.
4. Paid cash for supplies, $1,400.00. C2.
8. Paid cash on account to Marker Supplies, $1,300.00. C3.
9. Paid cash for rent, $800.00. C4.
12. Received cash from sales, $550.00. T12.
15. Sold services on account to Amy's Uniforms, $300.00. S1.
16. Paid cash for telephone bill, $70.00. C5.
22. Received cash on account from Amy's Uniforms, $300.00. R2.
25. Paid cash to owner for personal use, $900.00. C6.

Instructions:

The journal for Wirth's Tailors is given in the *Working Papers*. Wirth's Tailors uses a journal that is slightly different from the journal used in this chapter. Use page 1 of the journal to journalize the transactions. Source documents are abbreviated as follows: check, C; memorandum, M; receipt, R; sales invoice, S; calculator tape, T.

INTERNET ACTIVITY

Point your browser to

http://accounting.swpco.com

Choose **First-Year Course**, choose **Activities**, and complete the activity for Chapter 4.

Applied Communication

Careful research about careers will help prepare you for making career choices. There are several U.S. government publications that provide detailed descriptions of many job titles. Two that are available in most public libraries are the *Dictionary of Occupational Titles (DOT)* and the *Occupational Outlook Handbook*.

Instructions: Go to the library and, using one of the two publications listed or any other appropriate resource, find the description for any accounting-related job. Record information you find, such as qualifications needed, job outlook, and earnings. Write one paragraph describing the pros and cons of working in such a job. Be sure to write a topic sentence and a conclusion.

Cases for Critical Thinking

Case 1 During the summer, Willard Kelly does odd jobs to earn money. Mr. Kelly keeps all his money in a single checking account. He writes checks to pay for personal items and for business expenses. These payments include personal clothing, school supplies, gasoline for his car, and recreation. Mr. Kelly uses his check stubs as his accounting records. Are Mr. Kelly's accounting procedures and records correct? Explain your answer.

Case 2 In his business, Michael Rock uses a journal with the following columns: Date, Account Title, Check No., Cash Debit, and Cash Credit. Mr. Rock's wife, Jennifer, suggests that he needs three additional amount columns: General Debit, General Credit, and Sales Credit. Mr. Rock states that all his business transactions are for cash, and he never buys on account. Therefore, he doesn't see the need for more than the Cash Debit and Cash Credit special amount columns. Who is correct, Mr. or Mrs. Rock? Explain your answer.

AUTOMATED ACCOUNTING

RECORDING TRANSACTIONS

General Journal

A journal with two amount columns in which all kinds of entries can be recorded is called a *general journal.* General journal entries are entered in the automated accounting system through the General Journal tab. In a later chapter, special journals will be discussed to instruct you on how to use the other journals on the Journal Entries screen for specific types of transactions. The other tabs on the Journal Entries screen are used for entering purchases, cash payments, cash receipts, and sales.

In an automated accounting system, the transactions that are entered and posted in the general journal update ledger account balances immediately. For verification purposes, a general ledger report can be displayed or printed to prove account balances.

Recording Transactions in the General Journal Screen

Entering general journal entries can be done in five steps.

1. Enter the date of the transaction, then press the Tab key.
2. Enter the source document number in the Reference column, then press the Tab key.
3. Enter the account number to be debited, then press the Tab key. The account title will be displayed at the bottom of the general journal, just above the command buttons. (In *Automated Accounting 8.0*, the account title is displayed next to the account number after tabbing to the next column.
4. Enter the debit amount, then press the Tab key twice. The cursor will automaticaly position itself in the Account Number field on the next line of the journal. Enter the account number to be credited, press the Tab key twice, then enter the credit amount.

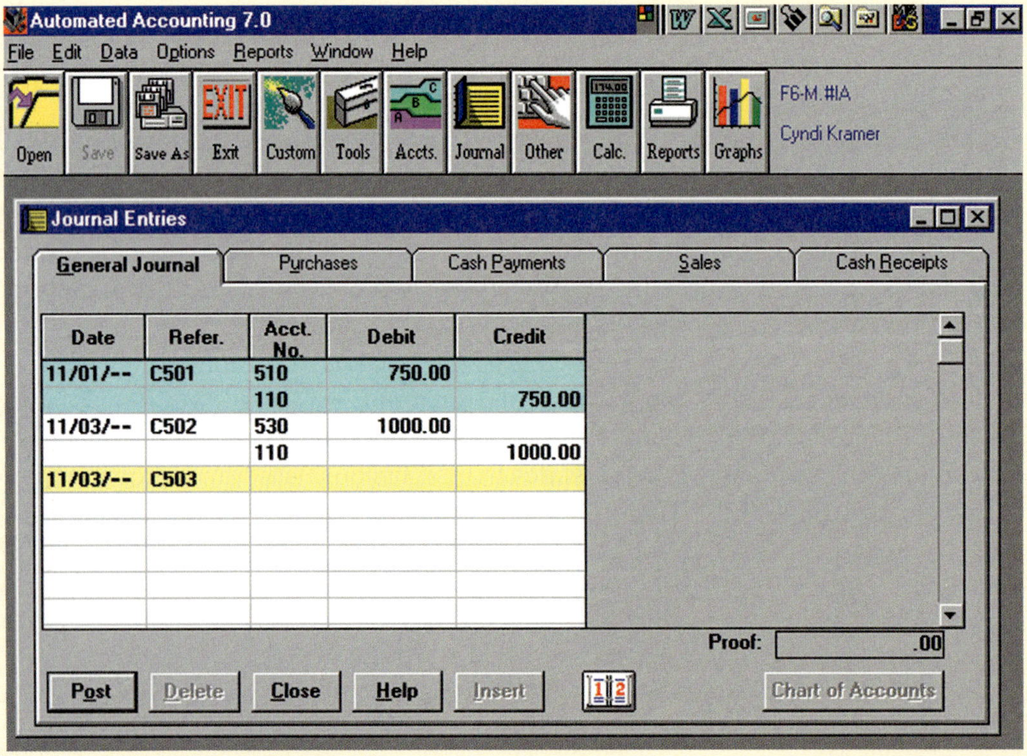

AUTOMATED ACCOUNTING

5. When the transaction is complete, click the Post button. Posting will be discussed in Chapter 5.

General Journal Transaction Additions, Changes, and Deletions

If you wish to add a part of a transaction, select the journal entry transaction to which you want to add a debit or credit. Click on the Insert button. When the blank line appears, enter the additional transaction debit or credit and click the Post button.

When changing or deleting general journal transactions, you need to select any portion of the desired transaction. Make corrections to the entry, then click the Post button. If you wish to delete the transaction, click the Delete button.

General Journal Report

In this section you will learn how to generate journal reports and specify which journal entries are to appear in the journal report. The general journal report will display or print the general journal entries that were posted for a specified period. Reports are useful in detecting errors and verifying that debits and credits are equal.

A general journal report can be generated in three steps:

1. Choose the Report Selection menu item from the Reports menu or click the Reports toolbar button.
2. When the Report Selection window appears, choose the Journals option. To change the run date, shown in the upper right corner of the screen, enter the desired date or use the + key to increase and the − key to decrease the date. You may also click on the calendar.
3. Select the General Journal report, then click the OK button. You can choose to include all general journal entries or to customize your report.

AUTOMATING APPLICATION PROBLEM 4-5: Journalizing transactions

Instructions:

1. Load *Automated Accounting 7.0* or higher software.
2. Select database F04-1 from the appropriate directory/folder.
3. Select File from the menu bar and choose the Save As menu command. Key the path to the drive and directory that contains your data files. Save the database with a file name of XXX041 (where XXX are your initials). (*Automated Accounting 8.0* allows long file names. Your instructor may direct you to use your full name when saving your files.)
4. Access Problem Instructions through the Help menu. Read the Problem Instructions screen. (In *Automated Accounting 8.0*, Problem Instructions are accessed by clicking the Browser toolbar button.)
5. Key the transactions listed on pages 90–91.
6. Exit the *Automated Accounting* software.

AUTOMATING MASTERY PROBLEM 4-6: Journalizing transactions and proving and ruling a journal

Instructions:

1. Load *Automated Accounting 7.0* or higher software.
2. Select database F04-2 from the appropriate directory/folder.
3. Select File from the menu bar and choose the Save As menu command. Key the path to the drive and directory that contains your data files. Save the database with a file name of XXX042 (where XXX are your initials). (*Automated Accounting 8.0* allows long file names. Your instructor may direct you to use your full name when saving your files.)
4. Access Problem Instructions through the Help menu. Read the Problem Instructions screen. (In *Automated Accounting 8.0*, Problem Instructions are accessed by clicking the Browser toolbar button.)
5. Key the transactions listed on pages 91–92.
6. Exit the *Automated Accounting* software.

5 Posting to a General Ledger

AFTER STUDYING CHAPTER 5, YOU WILL BE ABLE TO:

1. Define accounting terms related to posting from a journal to a general ledger.
2. Identify accounting concepts and practices related to posting from a journal to a general ledger.
3. Prepare a chart of accounts for a service business organized as a proprietorship.
4. Post separate amounts from a journal to a general ledger.
5. Post column totals from a journal to a general ledger.
6. Analyze and journalize correcting entries.

TERMS PREVIEW

ledger

general ledger

account number

file maintenance

opening an account

posting

correcting entry

ACCOUNT FORM

Encore Music records transactions in a journal as described in Chapter 4. A journal is a permanent record of the debit and credit parts of each transaction with transactions recorded in chronological order. A journal does not show, in one place, all the changes in a single account.

If only a journal is used, a business must search through all journal pages to find items affecting a single account balance. For this reason, a form is used to summarize in one place all the changes to a single account. A separate form is used for each account.

ACCOUNTING IN YOUR CAREER

TIME FOR POSTING

Shayla Graham is the bookkeeper at Hammonds Marketing Services. Tony Hammonds, who started the business, hired her to take full charge of accounting, but has never shown a great deal of interest in her daily work. Tony is now talking with Shayla to discuss ways to free up some time for her to take on additional responsibilities in the rapidly growing business.

Tony begins, "Shayla, you've done a great job with the accounting system here at Hammonds Marketing. I have come to rely on you totally for everything related to accounts. But now I need to see if we can find some ways for you to do your work in less time so you can help me with some other projects."

"Thank you for the vote of confidence, Tony," Shayla says, "I'd be happy to work with you on other projects if we can find a way for me to do so."

"Well, it looks like there's a lot of duplication in your work. You look at all the documents and then prepare some additional ones. Then you record them in the journal, and then you record them all again when you post them. You're doing the same thing three times."

"Tony," Shayla replies, "I promise you I am not creating unnecessary work. Each one of these steps is an important part of what we call the accounting cycle. And the accounting firm that audits our books has assured both you and me that I am following the correct procedures. Let me explain why each of these steps is important."

Critical Thinking:

1. How should Shayla explain the care she takes examining and preparing source documents?
2. What would be a good way to explain why both journalizing and posting are important?

5-1 Preparing a Chart of Accounts

RELATIONSHIP OF A T ACCOUNT TO AN ACCOUNT FORM

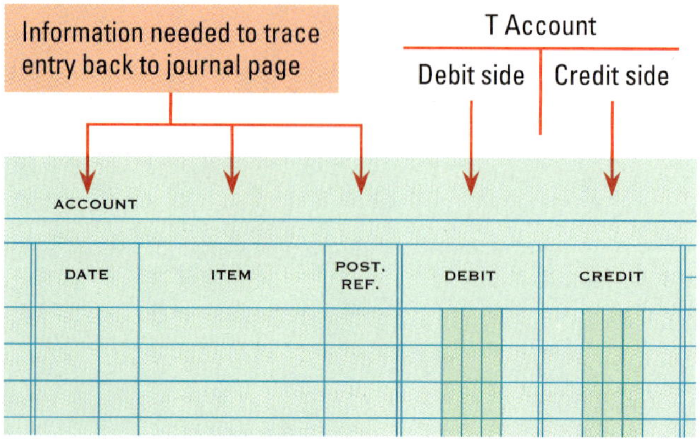

An account form is based on and includes the debit and credit sides of a T account. In addition to debit and credit columns, space is provided in the account form for recording the transaction date and journal page number. This information can be used to trace a specific entry back to where a transaction is recorded in a journal.

The major disadvantage of the account form shown is that no current, up-to-date account balance is shown. If this form is used, an up-to-date balance must be calculated each time the account is examined. When an account has a large number of entries, the balance is difficult and time consuming to calculate. Therefore, a more commonly used account form has Debit and Credit Balance columns as shown below.

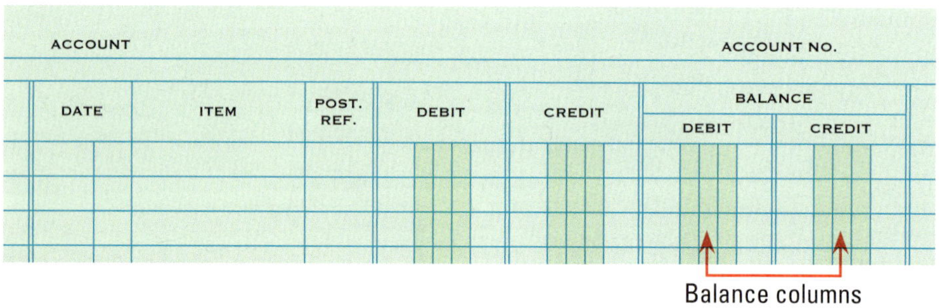

Because the form has columns for the debit and credit balance, it is often referred to as the balance-ruled account form.

The account balance is calculated and recorded as each entry is recorded in the account. Recording information in an account is described later in this chapter. The T account is a useful device for analyzing transactions into debit and credit parts. However, the balance-ruled account form is more useful as a permanent record of changes to account balances than is the T account. Encore Music uses the balance-ruled account form.

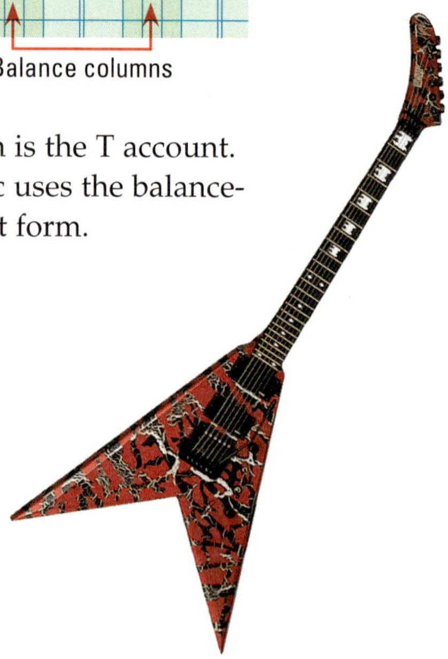

CHART OF ACCOUNTS

Encore Music

CHART OF ACCOUNTS

Balance Sheet Accounts		Income Statement Accounts	
	(100) ASSETS		(400) REVENUE
110	Cash	410	Sales
120	Petty Cash		(500) EXPENSES
130	Accounts Receivable—Kids Time	510	Advertising Expense
140	Accounts Receivable—Learn N Play	520	Insurance Expense
150	Supplies	530	Miscellaneous Expense
160	Prepaid Insurance	540	Rent Expense
	(200) LIABILITIES	550	Supplies Expense
210	Accounts Payable—Ling Music Supplies	560	Utilities Expense
220	Accounts Payable—Sullivan Office Supplies		
	(300) OWNER'S EQUITY		
310	Barbara Treviño, Capital		
320	Barbara Treviño, Drawing		
330	Income Summary		

A group of accounts is called a **ledger.** A ledger that contains all accounts needed to prepare financial statements is called a **general ledger.** The name given to an account is known as an account title. The number assigned to an account is called an **account number.**

Preparing a Chart of Accounts

A list of account titles and numbers showing the location of each account in a ledger is known as a chart of accounts. Encore Music's chart of accounts is shown above.

For ease of use while studying Cycle 1, Encore Music's chart of accounts is also shown on page 3.

Accounts in a general ledger are arranged in the same order as they appear on financial statements. Encore Music's chart of accounts shows five general ledger divisions: (1) Assets, (2) Liabilities, (3) Owner's Equity, (4) Revenue, and (5) Expenses.

ACCOUNT NUMBERS

1 5 0 **Supplies**

1 — General ledger division; 50 — Location within general ledger division

Encore Music assigns a three-digit account number to each account. For example, Supplies is assigned the number 150, as shown.

The first digit of each account number shows the general ledger division in which the account is located. For example, the asset division accounts are numbered in the 100s. Therefore, the number for the asset account, Supplies, begins with a 1.

The second two digits indicate the location of each account within a general ledger division. The 50 in the account number for Supplies indicates that the account is located between account number 140 and account number 160.

Encore Music initially assigns account numbers by 10s so that new accounts can be added easily. Nine numbers are unused between each account on Encore Music's chart of accounts. For example, numbers 111 to 119 are unused between accounts numbered 110 and 120. New numbers can be assigned between existing account numbers without renumbering all existing accounts. The procedure for arranging accounts in a general ledger, assigning account numbers, and keeping records current is called **file maintenance.**

Unused account numbers are assigned to new accounts. Encore Music records payments for gasoline in Miscellaneous Expense. If Ms. Treviño found that the amount paid each month for gasoline had become a major expense, she might decide to use a separate account. The account might be titled Gasoline Expense. Encore Music arranges expense accounts in alphabetic order in its general ledger. Therefore, the new account would be inserted between Advertising Expense and Insurance Expense.

510	Advertising Expense	(Existing account)
	Gasoline Expense	**(New Account)**
520	Insurance Expense	(Existing account)

The number selected for the new account should leave some unused numbers on either side of it for other accounts that might need to be added. The middle, unused account number between existing numbers 510 and 520 is 515. Therefore, 515 is assigned as the account number for the new account.

510	Advertising Expense	(Existing account)
515	**Gasoline Expense**	**(New Account)**
520	Insurance Expense	(Existing account)

When an account is no longer needed, it is removed from the general ledger and the chart of accounts. For example, if Encore Music were to buy its own equipment and building, there would be no need for the rent expense account. The account numbered 540 would be removed, and that number would become unused and available to assign to another account if the need should arise.

When a new account is added at the end of a ledger division, the next number in a sequence of 10s is used. For example, suppose Encore Music needs to add another expense account, Water Expense, to show more detail about one of the utility expenses. The expense accounts are arranged in alphabetic order. Therefore, the new account would be added at the end of the expense section of the chart of accounts. The last used expense account number is 560, as shown on the chart of accounts. The next number in the sequence of 10s is 570, which is assigned as the number of the new account.

550	Supplies Expense	(Existing account)
560	Utilities Expense	(Existing account)
570	**Water Expense**	**(New Account)**

Encore Music has relatively few accounts in its general ledger and does not anticipate adding many new accounts in the future. Therefore, a three-digit account number adequately provides for the few account numbers that might be added. However, as the number of general ledger accounts increases, a business may change to four or more digits.

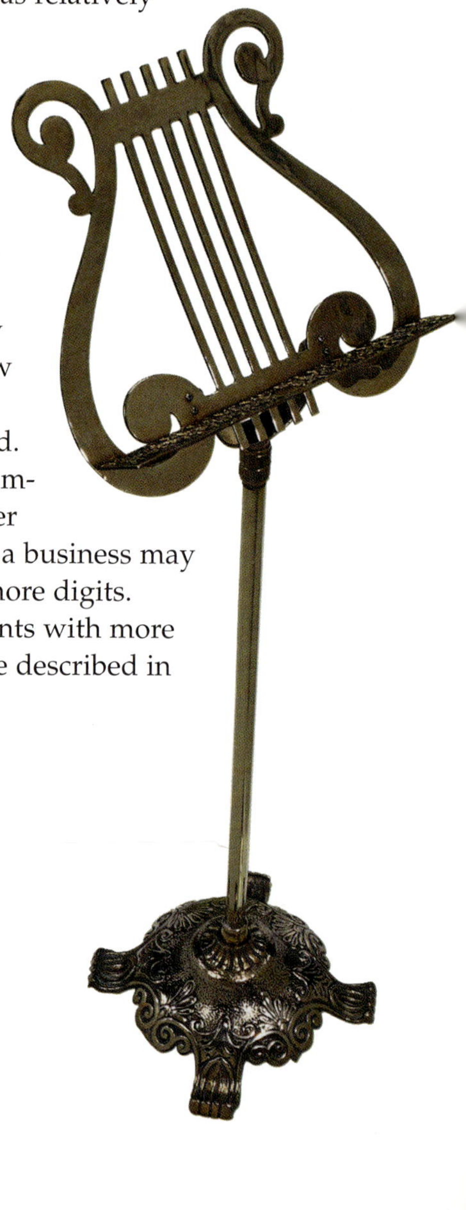

Charts of accounts with more than three digits are described in later chapters.

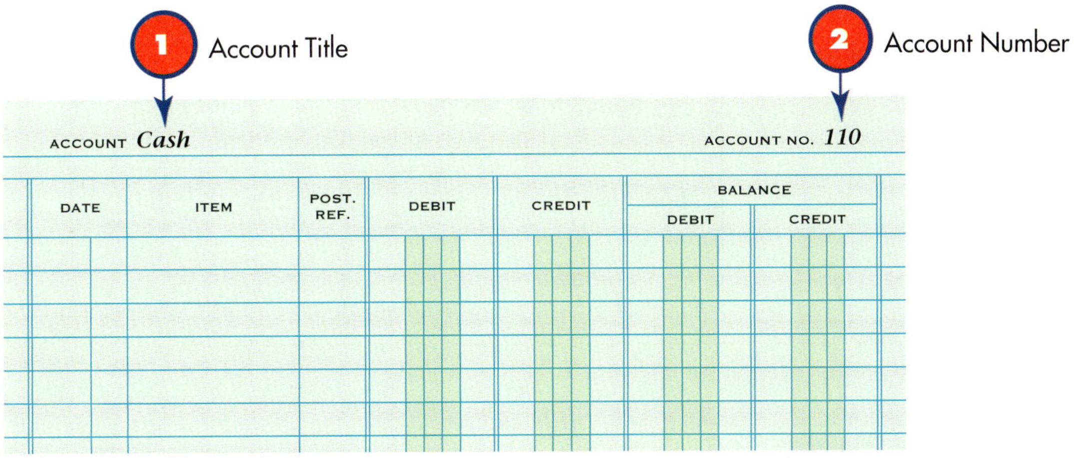

Writing an account title and number on the heading of an account is called **opening an account.** A general ledger account is opened for each account listed on a chart of accounts. Accounts are opened and arranged in a general ledger in the same order as on the chart of accounts.

Cash, account number 110, is the first account on Encore Music's chart of accounts. The cash account is opened using the following steps.

The same procedure is used to open all accounts listed on Encore Music's chart of accounts.

STEPS: Opening an account in a general ledger

1. Write the account title, *Cash*, after the word *Account* in the heading.
2. Write the account number, *110*, after the words *Account No.* in the heading.

PROFESSIONAL BUSINESS ETHICS

Can I Say This on My Resume?

Kendra Wheeler applied for a payroll clerk job with the Hampton Group, a market research firm. To improve her chances, she exaggerated her work experience on her resume.

Based on this resume, Kendra was hired. After one year, she received above-average ratings during her annual review. Shortly thereafter, her boss met Kendra's former supervisor and learned the truth.

Instructions

Use the three-step checklist to help determine whether or not each action demonstrated ethical behavior. (Suggested answers are provided for this case.)

1. *Is the action illegal?* No. Overstating qualifications is not illegal, but the employer could terminate your employment.
2. *Does the action violate company or professional standards?* No. Kendra was neither an employee of the company nor a member of any profession.
3. *Who is affected, and how, by the action?* Kendra: She obtained employment, but now she could be terminated. If retained, she could have difficulty being promoted. Other applicants: More highly qualified applicants lost an opportunity for employment. The Hampton Group: Managers may lose trust in employees.

Based on the above analysis, Kendra's actions were unethical.

TERMS REVIEW

ledger

general ledger

account number

file maintenance

opening an account

AUDIT YOUR UNDERSTANDING

1. Describe the two parts of an account number.
2. List the two steps for opening an account.

WORK TOGETHER

Preparing a chart of accounts and opening an account

Forms are given in the *Working Papers.* Your instructor will guide you through the following examples.

Clara Roseman owns a service business called Roseman's Services, which uses these accounts:

Accts. Pay.—Kammerer Supplies	Miscellaneous Expense	Cash	Automobile Expense
Accts. Rec.—Tyler Cobb	Insurance Expense	Sales	Accts. Pay.—Campbell Office Supplies
Prepaid Insurance	Rent Expense	Supplies	Accts. Rec.—Amber Jorgenson
Clara Roseman, Drawing	Clara Roseman, Capital		

3. Prepare a chart of accounts. Arrange expense accounts in alphabetical order. Use 3-digit account numbers and number the accounts within a division by 10s.
4. Two new accounts, Gasoline Expense and Utilities Expense, are to be added to the chart of accounts prepared in Instruction 3. Assign account numbers to the two new accounts.
5. Using the account form in the *Working Papers,* open Cash.

ON YOUR OWN

Preparing a chart of accounts and opening an account

Forms are given in the *Working Papers.* Work these problems independently.

Eric Yunger owns a service business called Yunger's Hair Care, which uses these accounts:

Accts. Pay.—Otgen Company	Supplies Expense	Cash	Delivery Expense
Accts. Rec.—Sarych Supplies	Insurance Expense	Sales	Accts. Pay.—North Star
Prepaid Insurance	Telephone Expense	Supplies	Accts. Rec.—Jaeson Keene
Eric Yunger, Drawing	Eric Yunger, Capital		

6. Prepare a chart of accounts. Arrange expense accounts in alphabetical order. Use 3-digit account numbers and number the accounts within a division by 10s.
7. Two new accounts, Rent Expense and Water Expense, are to be added to the chart of accounts prepared in Instruction 6. Assign account numbers to the two new accounts.
8. Using the account form in the *Working Papers,* open Delivery Expense.

5-2 Posting Separate Amounts from a Journal to a General Ledger

POSTING AN AMOUNT FROM A GENERAL DEBIT COLUMN

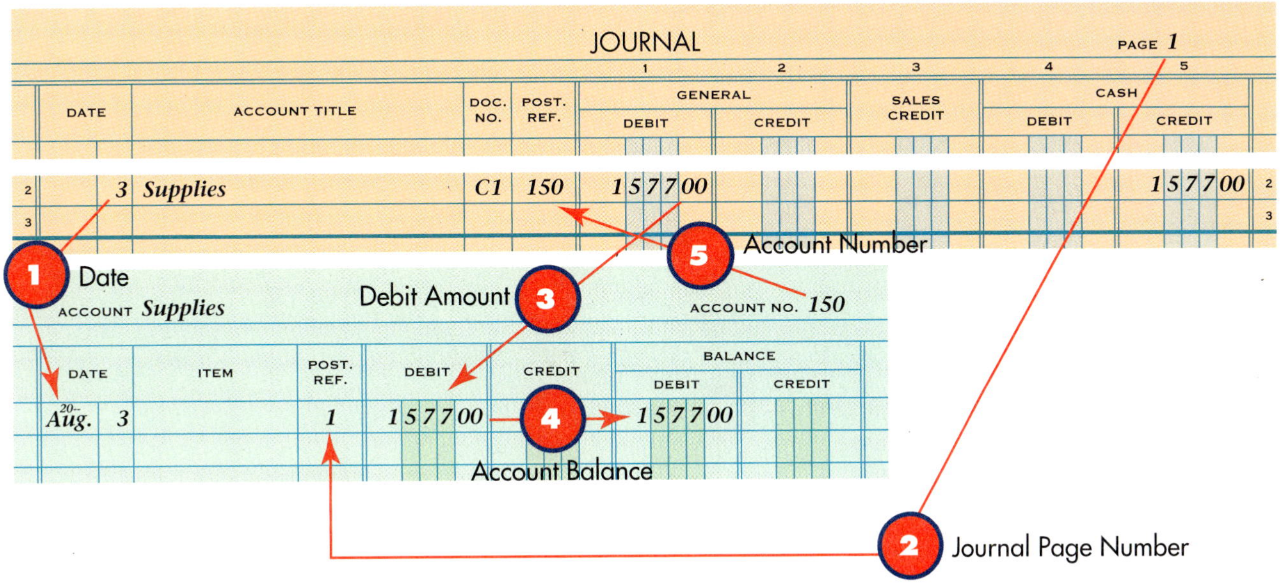

Transferring information from a journal entry to a ledger account is called **posting.** Posting sorts journal entries so that all debits and credits affecting each account are brought together. For example, all changes to Cash are brought together in the cash account.

Amounts in journal entries are recorded in either general amount columns or special amount columns. There are two rules for posting amounts from a journal. (1) Separate amounts in a journal's general amount columns are posted individually to the account written in the Account Title column. (2) Separate amounts in a journal's special amount columns are not posted individually. Instead, the special amount column totals are posted to the account named in the heading of the special amount column.

Posting a Separate Amount from a General Debit Column

For most journal entries, at least one separate amount is posted individually to a general ledger account. When an entry in a journal includes an amount in a general amount column, the amount is posted individually.

Each separate amount in the General Debit and General Credit columns of a journal is posted to the account written in the Account Title column.

STEPS: Posting an amount from a General Debit column

1. Write the date, *20—, Aug. 3,* in the Date column of the account, *Supplies.*
2. Write the journal page number, *1,* in the Post. Ref. column of the account. Post. Ref. is an abbreviation for Posting Reference.
3. Write the debit amount, *$1,577.00,* in the Debit amount column.
4. Write the new account balance, *$1,577.00,* in the Balance Debit column. Because this entry is the first in the Supplies account, the previous balance is zero.

Previous Balance	+	Debit Column Amount	=	New Debit Balance
$0.00	+	$1,577.00	=	$1,577.00

5. Return to the journal and write the account number, *150,* in the Post. Ref. column of the journal.

POSTING A SECOND AMOUNT TO AN ACCOUNT

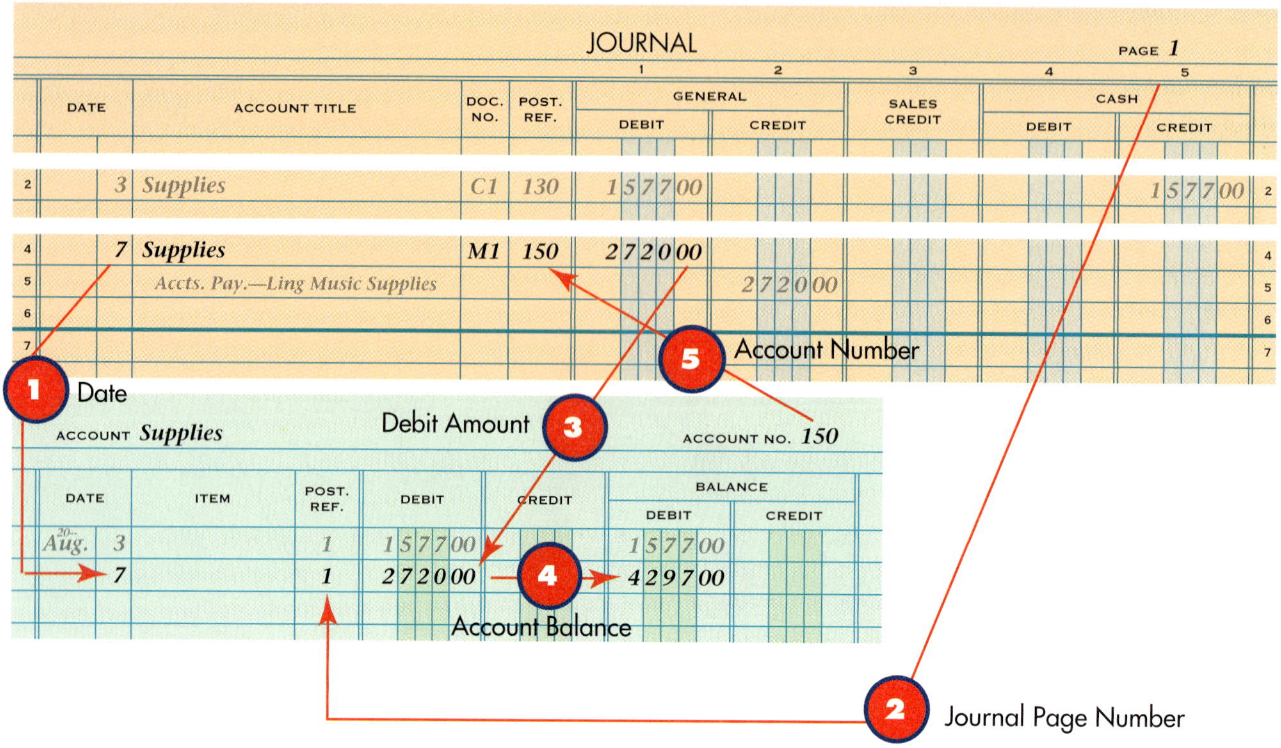

The numbers in the Post. Ref. columns of the general ledger account and the journal serve three purposes. (1) An entry in an account can be traced to its source in a journal. (2) An entry in a journal can be traced to where it was posted in an account. (3) If posting is interrupted, the accounting personnel can easily see which entries in the journal still need to be posted. A blank in the Post. Ref. column of the journal indicates that posting for that line still needs to be completed. *Therefore, the posting reference is always recorded in the journal as the last step in the posting procedure.*

The same five steps are followed when a second amount is posted to an account.

STEPS Posting a second amount to an account

1. Write the date, *7*, in the Date column of the account. The month and year are written only once on a page of a ledger account unless the month or year changes.
2. Write the journal page number, *1*, in the Post. Ref. column of the account.
3. Write the debit amount, *$2,720.00*, in the Debit amount column.
4. Write the new account balance, *$4,297.00*, in the Balance Debit column.
5. Return to the journal and write the account number, *150*, in the Post. Ref. column of the journal.

Previous Debit Balance	+	Debit Column Amount	=	New Debit Balance
$1,577.00	+	$2,720.00	=	$4,297.00

REMEMBER

Each separate amount in the General Debit and Credit columns of a journal is posted individually. The totals of these columns are not posted.

POSTING AN AMOUNT FROM A GENERAL CREDIT COLUMN

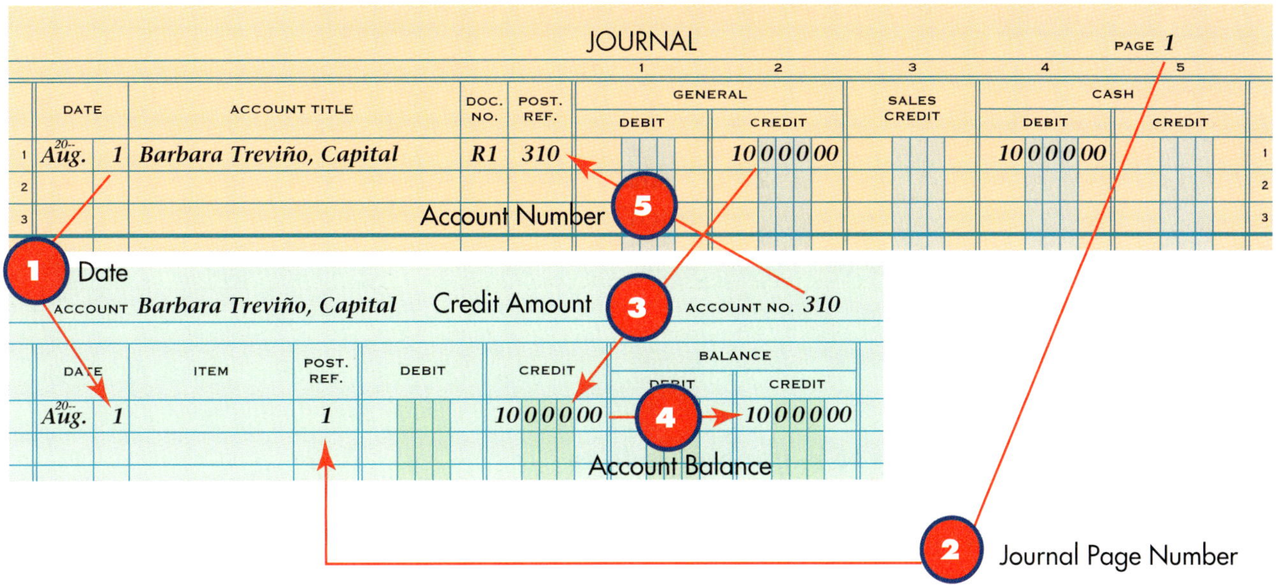

An amount in the General Credit column is posted separately. Five steps are followed when posting an amount from the General Credit column.

STEPS: Posting an amount from a General Credit column

1. Write the date, *20—, Aug. 1,* in the Date column of the account.
2. Write the journal page number, *1,* in the Post. Ref. column of the account.
3. Write the credit amount, *$10,000.00,* in the Credit amount column.
4. Write the new account balance, *$10,000.00,* in the Balance Credit column.
5. Return to the journal and write the account number, *310,* in the Post. Ref. column of the journal.

Previous Balance	+	Credit Column Amount	=	New Credit Balance
$0.00	+	$10,000.00	=	$10,000.00

CULTURAL DIVERSITY

Accounting in Ancient Civilizations

In the ancient civilizations of Asia Minor and northern Africa, most citizens were illiterate. The scribe, who could read and write, became a very important person in the society. Of ancient Hebrew origin, the scribe has been called the forerunner of today's accountant.

Public scribes often recorded transactions as citizens arrived to do business. Most scribes recorded transactions on moist clay tablets that were then dried in the sun. Therefore, permanent records of transactions were not possible until there was someone able to write them down—the scribe—and a medium on which to record them—clay tablets.

Another important contribution to accounting was made by the Greeks around 630 B.C. The Greeks invented coined money, which facilitated assigning values to transactions.

The Babylonians in Asia Minor used an early form of banking. They transferred funds with a system resembling our modern-day checking accounts. This is believed to be one of the first uses of business documents.

These early practices provided the foundation for today's financial system and recordkeeping methods.

TERM REVIEW

posting

AUDIT YOUR UNDERSTANDING

1. List the five steps of posting from the journal to the general ledger.
2. Are the totals of the General Debit and Credit columns posted? Why or why not?

WORK TOGETHER

Posting separate amounts to a general ledger

A completed journal and general ledger accounts are given in the *Working Papers*. Your instructor will guide you through the following example.

Leonard Witkowski owns a service business that uses the following accounts:

Assets		Owner's Equity	
110	Cash	310	Leonard Witkowski, Capital
120	Accounts Receivable—Danielle Braastad	320	Leonard Witkowski, Drawing
130	Supplies		**Revenue**
140	Prepaid Insurance	410	Sales
	Liabilities		**Expenses**
210	Accounts Payable—Joshua's Supplies	510	Rent Expense

3. Post the separate amounts on each line of the journal that need to be posted individually. Save your work to complete Work Together on page 111.

ON YOUR OWN

Posting separate amounts to a general ledger

A completed journal and general ledger accounts are given in the *Working Papers*. Work this problem independently.

Melanie Komoko owns a service business which uses the following accounts:

Assets		Owner's Equity	
110	Cash	310	Melanie Komoko, Capital
120	Accounts Receivable—Brenden Otto	320	Melanie Komoko, Drawing
130	Supplies		**Revenue**
140	Prepaid Insurance	410	Sales
	Liabilities		**Expenses**
210	Accounts Payable—Signs Plus	510	Utilities Expense

4. Post the separate amounts on each line of the journal that need to be posted individually. Save your work to complete On Your Own on page 111.

5-3 Posting Column Totals from a Journal to a General Ledger

CHECK MARKS SHOW THAT AMOUNTS ARE NOT POSTED

JOURNAL — PAGE 2

	DATE		ACCOUNT TITLE	DOC. NO.	POST. REF.	1 GENERAL DEBIT	2 GENERAL CREDIT	3 SALES CREDIT	4 CASH DEBIT	5 CASH CREDIT	
1	20-- Aug.	20	Brought Forward		√	7960 00	12840 00	2439 00	12319 00	5000 00	1
13		31	√	T31	√			290 00	290 00		13
14		31	Miscellaneous Expense	M3		3 00				3 00	14
15		31	Totals			8979 00	12840 00	4411 00	14291 00	6019 00	15
16						(√)	(√)				16
17											17

Check mark indicates that amounts ARE NOT posted individually.

Check marks indicate that general amount column totals ARE NOT posted.

Journal Entries That Are Not Posted Individually

Several lines in Encore Music's journal contain amounts that are not to be posted individually. These include forwarding totals and amounts recorded in special amount columns.

The totals brought forward from page 1 are shown on line 1 of the journal. None of these separate total amounts on line 1 are posted individually to general ledger accounts. To assure that no postings are overlooked, no blank posting reference spaces should be left in the Post. Ref. column of the journal. Therefore, when the totals were forwarded to page 2 of the journal, a check mark was placed in the Post. Ref. column of line 1 to show that no separate amounts are posted individually.

Separate amounts in the special amount columns, Sales Credit, Cash Debit, and Cash Credit, are not posted individually. For example, on line 13 of the journal, two separate $290.00 amounts are recorded in two special amount columns, Sales Credit and Cash Debit.

A check mark was placed in the Post. Ref. column on line 13 when the entry was journalized. The check mark indicates that no separate amounts are posted individually from this line. Instead, the totals of the special amount columns are posted.

Totals of General Debit and General Credit Amount Columns

The General Debit and General Credit columns are not special amount columns because the column headings do not contain the name of an account. All of the separate amounts in the General Debit and General Credit amount columns are posted individually.

Therefore, the column totals *are not* posted. A check mark in parentheses is placed below each general amount column total as shown. The check mark indicates that the total of the General Debit column is not posted.

A check mark in the Post. Ref. column indicates that *no amounts on that line* are posted individually. On the totals line, the amounts in the special amount columns *are* posted. Therefore, a check mark is *not* placed in the Post. Ref. column for the totals line.

POSTING THE TOTAL OF THE SALES CREDIT COLUMN

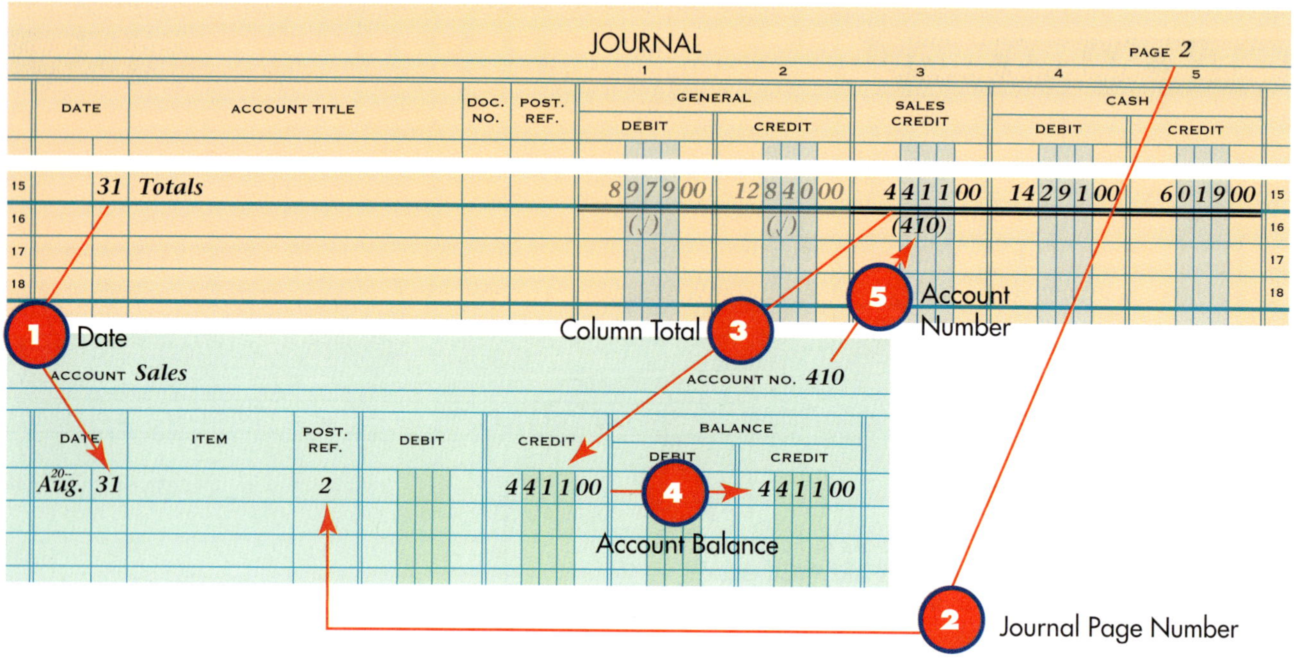

Separate amounts in special amount columns *are not* posted individually. The separate amounts are part of the special amount column totals. Only the *totals* of special amount columns are posted.

Encore Music's journal has three special amount columns for which only totals are posted: Sales Credit, Cash Debit, and Cash Credit.

The Sales Credit column of a journal is a special amount column with the account title Sales in the heading. Each separate amount in a special amount column could be posted individually. However, all of the separate amounts are debits or credits to the same account. Therefore, an advantage of a special amount column is that only the *column total* needs to be posted. For example, 14 separate sales transactions are recorded in the Sales Credit column of Encore Music's August journal. Instead of making 14 separate credit postings to Sales, only the column total is posted. As a result, only one posting is needed, which saves 13 postings. The smaller number of postings means 13 fewer opportunities to make a posting error. Posting special amount column totals saves time and results in greater accuracy.

The total of Encore Music's Sales Credit column is posted as shown.

STEPS

Posting the total of the Sales Credit column

1. Write the date, *20—, Aug. 31*, in the Date column of the account, Sales.
2. Write the journal page number, *2*, in the Post. Ref. column of the account.
3. Write the column total, *$4,411.00*, in the Credit amount column.
4. Write the new account balance, *$4,411.00*, in the Balance Credit column.
5. Return to the journal and write the account number in parentheses, *(410)*, below the Sales Credit column total.

Previous Balance	+	Credit Column Amount	=	New Credit Balance
$0.00	+	$4,411.00	=	$4,411.00

POSTING THE TOTAL OF THE CASH DEBIT COLUMN

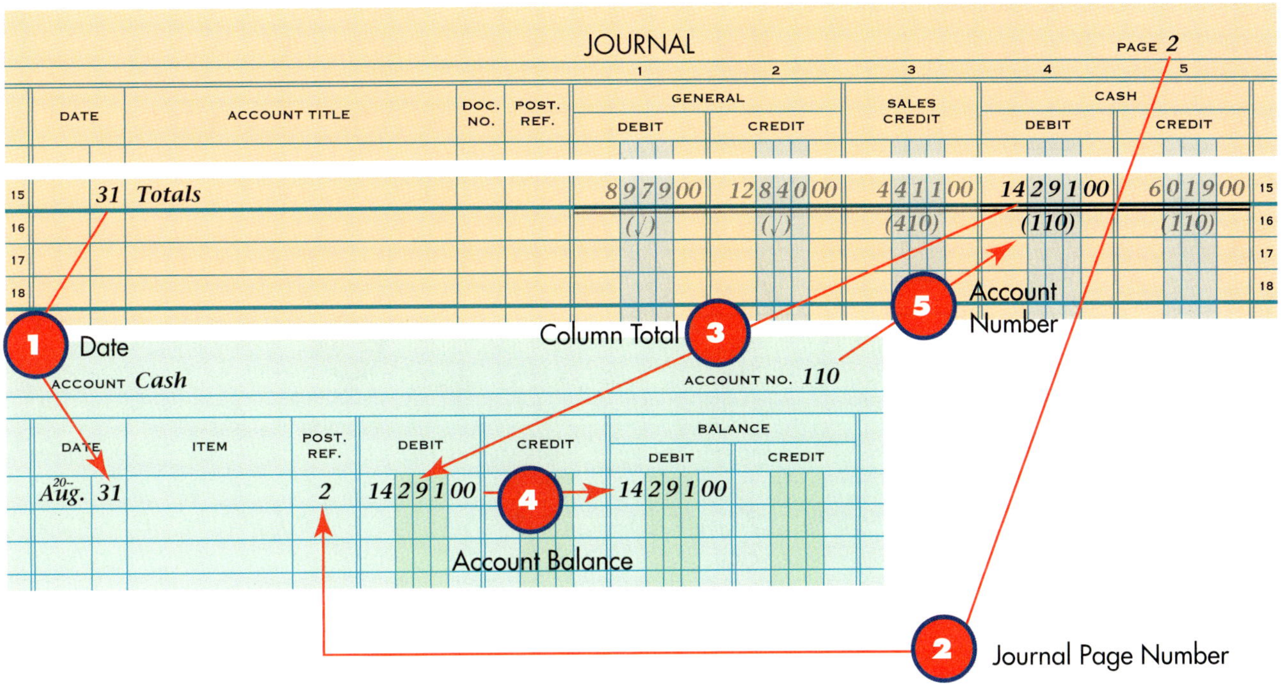

The Cash Debit column of a journal is a special amount column with the account title Cash in the heading. The Cash Debit column is posted using the following steps.

STEPS Posting the total of the Cash Debit column

1. Write the date, *20—, Aug. 31*, in the Date column of the account, Cash.
2. Write the journal page number, *2*, in the Post. Ref. column of the account.
3. Write the column total, *$14,291.00*, in the Debit amount column.
4. Write the new account balance, *$14,291.00*, in the Balance Debit column.

Previous Balance	+	Debit Column Amount	=	New Debit Balance
$0.00	+	$14,291.00	=	$14,291.00

5. Return to the journal and write the account number in parentheses, *(110)*, below the Cash Debit column total.

REMEMBER

Errors are corrected in a way that does not cause doubts about what the correct information is. If an error is recorded, cancel the error by neatly drawing a line through the incorrect item. Write the correct items immediately above the canceled item.

POSTING THE TOTAL OF THE CASH CREDIT COLUMN

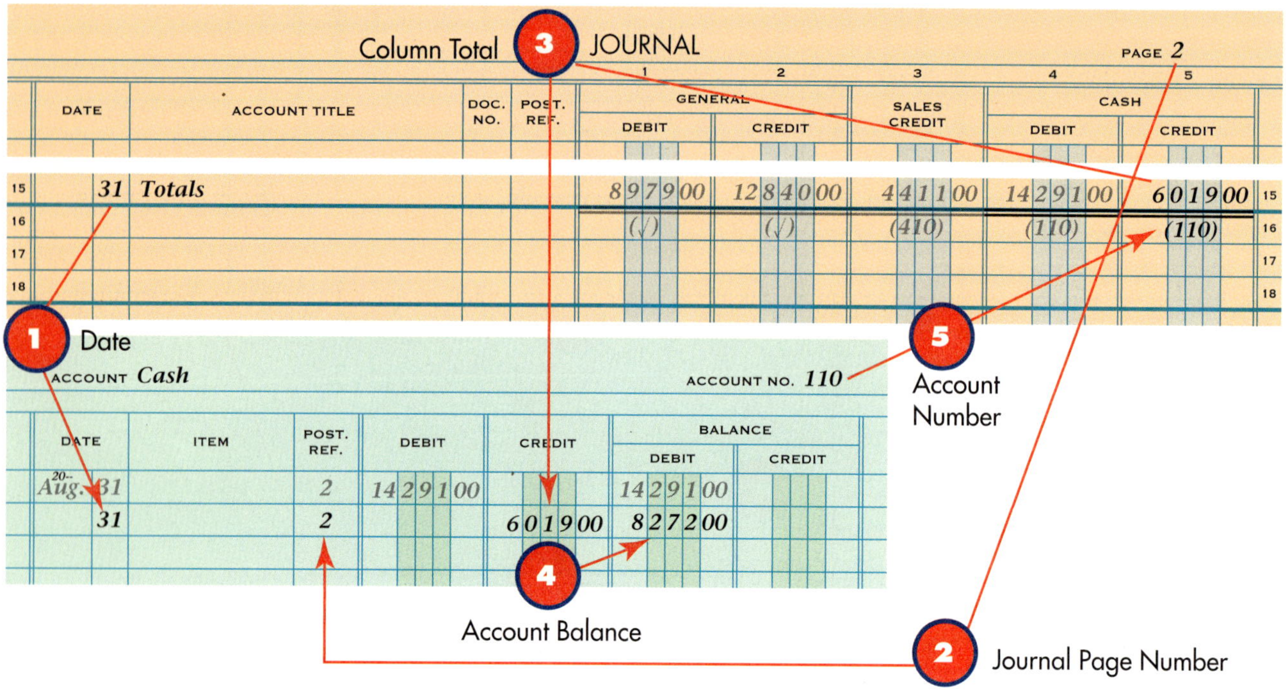

The Cash Credit column of a journal is a special amount column with the account title Cash in the heading. The Cash Credit column is posted using the following steps.

STEPS

Posting the total of the Cash Credit column

1. Write the date, *31*, in the Date column of the account, Cash.
2. Write the journal page number, *2*, in the Post. Ref. column of the account.
3. Write the column total, *$6,019.00*, in the Credit amount column.
4. Write the new account balance, *$8,272.00*, in the Balance Debit column.

Previous Debit Balance	−	Credit Column Amount	=	New Debit Balance
$14,291.00	−	$6,019.00	=	$8,272.00

5. Return to the journal and write the account number in parentheses, *(110)*, below the Cash Credit column total.

REMEMBER

Whenever the debits in an account exceed the credits, the account balance is a debit. Whenever the credits in an account exceed the debits, the account balance is a credit.

AUDIT YOUR UNDERSTANDING

1. Which column totals of a journal are posted?
2. Under what conditions will an account balance be a debit?
3. Under what conditions will an account balance be a credit?

WORK TOGETHER

Posting column totals to a general ledger

Use the journal and general ledger accounts from Work Together on page 106. Your instructor will guide you through the following example.

Leonard Witkowski owns a service business that uses the following accounts:

Assets

110 Cash
120 Accounts Receivable—Danielle Braastad
130 Supplies
140 Prepaid Insurance

Liabilities

210 Accounts Payable—Joshua's Supplies

Owner's Equity

310 Leonard Witkowski, Capital
320 Leonard Witkowski, Drawing

Revenue

410 Sales

Expenses

510 Rent Expense

4. Post the journal's special amount column totals.

ON YOUR OWN

Posting column totals to a general ledger

Use the journal and general ledger accounts from On Your Own on page 106. Work this problem independently.

Melanie Komoko owns a service business that uses the following accounts:

Assets

110 Cash
120 Accounts Receivable—Brenden Otto
130 Supplies
140 Prepaid Insurance

Liabilities

210 Accounts Payable—Signs Plus

Owner's Equity

310 Melanie Komoko, Capital
320 Melanie Komoko, Drawing

Revenue

410 Sales

Expenses

510 Utilities Expense

5. Post the journal's special amount column totals.

5-4 Completed Accounting Forms and Making Correcting Entries

JOURNAL PAGE WITH POSTING COMPLETED

JOURNAL — PAGE 2

	DATE		ACCOUNT TITLE	DOC. NO.	POST. REF.	1 GENERAL DEBIT	2 GENERAL CREDIT	3 SALES CREDIT	4 CASH DEBIT	5 CASH CREDIT	
1	20-- Aug.	20	*Brought Forward*		✓	7960 00	12840 00	2439 00	12319 00	5000 00	1
2		21	✓	T21	✓			270 00	270 00		2
3		24	✓	T24	✓			300 00	300 00		3
4		25	✓	T25	✓			310 00	310 00		4
5		26	✓	T26	✓			245 00	245 00		5
6		27	*Utilities Expense*	C10	560	70 00				70 00	6
7		27	✓	T27	✓			290 00	290 00		7
8		28	*Supplies*	C11	150	434 00				434 00	8
9		28	✓	T28	✓			267 00	267 00		9
10		31	*Miscellaneous Expense*	C12	530	7 00				12 00	10
11			*Advertising Expense*		510	5 00					11
12		31	*Barbara Treviño, Drawing*	C13	320	500 00				500 00	12
13		31	✓	T31	✓			290 00	290 00		13
14		31	*Miscellaneous Expense*	M3	530	3 00				3 00	14
15		31	*Totals*			8979 00	12840 00	4411 00	14291 00	6019 00	15
16						(✓)	(✓)	(410)	(110)	(110)	16
17											17

Page 2 of Encore Music's August journal is shown after all posting has been completed. With the exception of the Totals line, notice that the Post Ref. column is completely filled in with either an account number or a check mark.

GENERAL LEDGER WITH POSTING COMPLETED

ACCOUNT *Cash* — ACCOUNT NO. *110*

DATE		ITEM	POST. REF.	DEBIT	CREDIT	BALANCE DEBIT	BALANCE CREDIT
20-- Aug.	31		2	14291 00		14291 00	
	31		2		6019 00	8272 00	

After all posting from the August journal is completed, Encore Music's general ledger is shown here and on the next several pages.

The use of the accounts Income Summary, Insurance Expense, and Supplies Expense is described in Chapter 7.

ACCOUNT *Petty Cash* ACCOUNT NO. *120*

DATE		ITEM	POST. REF.	DEBIT	CREDIT	BALANCE DEBIT	BALANCE CREDIT
20-- Aug.	17		1	200 00		200 00	

ACCOUNT *Accounts Receivable—Kids Time* ACCOUNT NO. *130*

DATE		ITEM	POST. REF.	DEBIT	CREDIT	BALANCE DEBIT	BALANCE CREDIT
20-- Aug.	12		1	200 00		200 00	
	12		1		100 00	100 00	

ACCOUNT *Accounts Receivable—Learn N Play* ACCOUNT NO. *140*

DATE		ITEM	POST. REF.	DEBIT	CREDIT	BALANCE DEBIT	BALANCE CREDIT
20-- Aug.	13		1	20 00		20 00	

ACCOUNT *Supplies* ACCOUNT NO. *150*

DATE		ITEM	POST. REF.	DEBIT	CREDIT	BALANCE DEBIT	BALANCE CREDIT
20-- Aug.	3		1	1 577 00		1 577 00	
	7		1	2 720 00		4 297 00	
	20		1	20 00		4 317 00	
	28		2	434 00		4 751 00	

ACCOUNT *Prepaid Insurance* ACCOUNT NO. *160*

DATE		ITEM	POST. REF.	DEBIT	CREDIT	BALANCE DEBIT	BALANCE CREDIT
20-- Aug.	4		1	1 200 00		1 200 00	

ACCOUNT *Accounts Payable—Ling Music Supplies* ACCOUNT NO. *210*

DATE		ITEM	POST. REF.	DEBIT	CREDIT	BALANCE DEBIT	BALANCE CREDIT
20-- Aug.	7		1		2 720 00		2 720 00
	11		1	1 360 00			1 360 00

ACCOUNT *Accounts Payable—Sullivan Office Supplies* ACCOUNT NO. *220*

DATE		ITEM	POST. REF.	DEBIT	CREDIT	BALANCE DEBIT	BALANCE CREDIT
20-- Aug.	20		1		20 00		20 00

A General Ledger after Posting Has Been Completed *(continued)*

ACCOUNT *Barbara Treviño, Capital* ACCOUNT NO. *310*

DATE		ITEM	POST. REF.	DEBIT	CREDIT	BALANCE DEBIT	BALANCE CREDIT
20-- Aug.	1		1		10,000.00		10,000.00

ACCOUNT *Barbara Treviño, Drawing* ACCOUNT NO. *320*

DATE		ITEM	POST. REF.	DEBIT	CREDIT	BALANCE DEBIT	BALANCE CREDIT
20-- Aug.	12		1	100.00		100.00	
	31		2	500.00		600.00	

ACCOUNT *Income Summary* ACCOUNT NO. *330*

DATE		ITEM	POST. REF.	DEBIT	CREDIT	BALANCE DEBIT	BALANCE CREDIT

ACCOUNT *Sales* ACCOUNT NO. *410*

DATE		ITEM	POST. REF.	DEBIT	CREDIT	BALANCE DEBIT	BALANCE CREDIT
20-- Aug.	31		2		4,411.00		4,411.00

ACCOUNT *Advertising Expense* ACCOUNT NO. *510*

DATE		ITEM	POST. REF.	DEBIT	CREDIT	BALANCE DEBIT	BALANCE CREDIT
20-- Aug.	14		1	68.00		68.00	
	18		1	200.00		268.00	
	31		2	5.00		273.00	

A General Ledger after Posting Has Been Completed *(continued)*

ACCOUNT *Insurance Expense* **ACCOUNT NO.** *520*

DATE		ITEM	POST. REF.	DEBIT	CREDIT	BALANCE DEBIT	BALANCE CREDIT

ACCOUNT *Miscellaneous Expense* **ACCOUNT NO.** *530*

DATE		ITEM	POST. REF.	DEBIT	CREDIT	BALANCE DEBIT	BALANCE CREDIT
20-- Aug.	31		2	7 00		7 00	
	31		2	3 00		10 00	

ACCOUNT *Rent Expense* **ACCOUNT NO.** *540*

DATE		ITEM	POST. REF.	DEBIT	CREDIT	BALANCE DEBIT	BALANCE CREDIT
20-- Aug.	12		1	250 00		250 00	

ACCOUNT *Supplies Expense* **ACCOUNT NO.** *550*

DATE		ITEM	POST. REF.	DEBIT	CREDIT	BALANCE DEBIT	BALANCE CREDIT

ACCOUNT *Utilities Expense* **ACCOUNT NO.** *560*

DATE		ITEM	POST. REF.	DEBIT	CREDIT	BALANCE DEBIT	BALANCE CREDIT
20-- Aug.	12		1	45 00		45 00	
	27		2	70 00		115 00	

A General Ledger after Posting Has Been Completed *(concluded)*

MEMORANDUM FOR A CORRECTING ENTRY

MEMORANDUM — Encore Music, 530 Anoka Avenue, Tampa, FL 33601 — No. **45**

A cash payment of $120.00 for advertising, October 30, 20--, was debited in error to Miscellaneous Expense.

Signed: *Barbara Treviño* Date: *November 13, 20--*

Simple errors may be corrected by ruling through the item, as described in Chapter 4. However, a transaction may have been improperly journalized and posted to the ledger. In such a case, the incorrect journal entry should be corrected with an additional journal entry, called a **correcting entry.**

If an accounting error is discovered, a memorandum is prepared as the source document describing the correction to be made.

JOURNAL ENTRY TO RECORD A CORRECTING ENTRY

1 Date 2 Debit 3 Credit 4 Source Document

JOURNAL PAGE 7

	DATE		ACCOUNT TITLE	DOC. NO.	POST. REF.	GENERAL DEBIT (1)	GENERAL CREDIT (2)	SALES CREDIT (3)	CASH DEBIT (4)	CASH CREDIT (5)	
22		13	*Advertising Expense*	*M45*		*120 00*					22
23			*Miscellaneous Expense*				*120 00*				23
24											24

November 13. Discovered that a payment of cash for advertising in October was journalized and posted in error as a debit to Miscellaneous Expense instead of Advertising Expense, $120.00. Memorandum No. 45.

Advertising Expense	
120.00	

Miscellaneous Expense	
	120.00

To correct the error, an entry is made to add $120.00 to the advertising expense account. The entry must also deduct $120.00 from the miscellaneous expense account.

Because the advertising expense account has a normal debit balance, Advertising Expense is debited for $120.00 to show the increase in this expense account. The miscellaneous expense account also has a normal debit balance. Therefore, Miscellaneous Expense is credited for $120.00 to show the decrease in this expense account.

TERM REVIEW

correcting entry

AUDIT YOUR UNDERSTANDING

1. What is a correcting entry?
2. When is a correcting entry necessary?
3. When an amount is journalized and posted as a debit to an incorrect expense account, why is the amount of the correcting entry debited to the correct expense account?
4. When an amount is journalized and posted as a debit to an incorrect expense account, why is the amount of the correcting entry credited to the incorrect expense account?

WORK TOGETHER

Journalizing correcting entries

A journal is given in the *Working Papers*. Your instructor will guide you through the following example.

Transactions: Nov. 1. Discovered that a transaction for office supplies bought last month was journalized and posted in error as a debit to Prepaid Insurance instead of Supplies, $60.00. M15.

1. Discovered that a transaction for rent expense for last month was journalized and posted in error as a debit to Repair Expense instead of Rent Expense, $550.00. M16.

5. Journalize each correcting entry discovered during November of the current year. Use page 21 of the journal.

ON YOUR OWN

Journalizing correcting entries

A journal is given in the *Working Papers*. Work this problem independently.

Transactions: June 1. Discovered that a transaction for office supplies bought last month was journalized and posted in error as a debit to Supplies—Store instead of Supplies—Office, $45.00. M23.

1. Discovered that a transaction for utilities expense for last month was journalized and posted in error as a debit to Miscellaneous Expense instead of Utilities Expense, $550.00. M24.

6. Journalize each correcting entry discovered during June of the current year. Use page 11 of the journal.

CHAPTER 5 SUMMARY

After completing this chapter, you can

1. Define important accounting terms related to posting from a journal to a general ledger.
2. Identify accounting concepts and practices related to posting from a journal to a general ledger.
3. Prepare a chart of accounts for a service business organized as a proprietorship.
4. Post separate amounts from a journal to a general ledger.
5. Post column totals from a journal to a general ledger.
6. Analyze and journalize correcting entries.

EXPLORE ACCOUNTING

Each company designs its chart of accounts to meet the needs of that company. Encore Music, the company described in this section of the textbook, has a relatively simple chart of accounts, with a small number of accounts. Therefore, Encore Music can use a three-digit account number for each account. A company with more accounts may need to use a four- or five-digit account number for each account. The numbering system used by the company should ensure that each account can be assigned a unique number.

When setting up a chart of accounts, a company does not have to use a straight series of numbers. If a company has several departments, it may choose to use account numbers such as 12-150. The first two digits (12) can be used to designate a specific department. The last three digits (150) identify a unique account within that department. If this company has many departments or many accounts within each department, it may have to increase the number of digits in the account, such as 123-4567.

A large corporation made up of smaller companies may have one chart of accounts for the entire corporation. If the managers of the corporation also want to be able to separate out the accounts for each company, they may choose to set up the account numbers in an xx-yyy-zzzz format. The first two digits (xx) would be a unique number for each company, the second set of numbers (yyy) refer to a department number, and the third set of numbers (zzzz) is a unique account.

Another example would be a company that manufactures goods for its customers. Such a company may want to include the job order number in each account number, so that it can easily trace the cost of each job.

As you can see, there is an infinite number of possible systems that can be followed when assigning account numbers. A company should consider future growth when first setting up a system so that it can avoid having to renumber accounts at a later date.

Group Activity:
Develop a chart of accounts for an imaginary business. Write a detailed description of the company and a rationale for the account numbering system you have developed.

5-1 APPLICATION PROBLEM
Preparing a chart of accounts and opening an account

Lillian Deters owns a service business called Deters Duplicating, which uses the following accounts:

Accounts Receivable—Teegan Walters	Lillian Deters, Capital	Postage Expense	Supplies
Accounts Receivable—Austin Kirnyczuk	Lillian Deters, Drawing	Charitable Expense	Sales
Accounts Payable—Dakota Company	Prepaid Insurance	Rent Expense	Cash
Accounts Payable—Falls Supply	Advertising Expense		

Instructions:

1. Prepare a chart of accounts similar to the one described in this chapter. Arrange expense accounts in alphabetical order. Use 3-digit account numbers and number the accounts within a division by 10s.
2. Two new accounts, Delivery Expense and Telephone Expense, are to be added to the chart of accounts prepared in Instruction 1. Assign account numbers to the two new accounts.
3. Using the forms in the *Working Papers,* open the Prepaid Insurance and the Postage Expense accounts.

5-2 APPLICATION PROBLEM
Posting separate amounts to a general ledger

A completed journal and general ledger accounts are given in the *Working Papers.*
Michael Byrum owns a service business which uses the accounts given in the *Working Papers.*

Instructions:

Post the separate amounts on each line of the journal that need to be posted individually. Save your work to complete Application Problem 5-3.

5-3 APPLICATION PROBLEM
Posting column totals to a general ledger

Use the journal and general ledger from Application Problem 5-2.

Instructions:

Post the journal's special amount column totals.

5-4 APPLICATION PROBLEM
Journalizing correcting entries

The following errors were discovered after the incorrect entries were already journalized and posted.

Transactions:

Feb. 1. Discovered that a transaction for advertising expense was journalized and posted in error as a debit to Miscellaneous Expense instead of Advertising Expense, $135.00. M87.

5. Discovered that a cash withdrawal by Gregg Moen, owner, was journalized and posted in error as a credit to Sales instead of Cash, $550.00. M88.

Instructions:

Journalize each correcting entry discovered during February of the current year. Use page 3 of the journal given in the *Working Papers.*

5-5 MASTERY PROBLEM

Journalizing transactions and posting to a general ledger

Allan Derner owns a service business called Derner Cleaning. Derner Cleaning's general ledger accounts are given in the *Working Papers.*

Transactions:

Nov. 1. Received cash from owner as an investment, $7,000.00. R1.
3. Paid cash for rent, $300.00. C1.
5. Sold services on account to Alphonse Gutenberg, $180.00. S1.
6. Received cash from sales, $750.00. T6.
9. Paid cash for miscellaneous expense, $5.00. C2.
11. Paid cash for supplies, $500.00. C3.
13. Bought supplies on account from Major Supplies, $600.00. M1.
13. Received cash from sales, $700.00. T13.
16. Paid cash for electric bill, $40.00. C4.
18. Paid cash on account to Major Supplies, $300.00. C5.
20. Paid cash for advertising, $30.00. C6.
20. Received cash on account from Alphonse Gutenberg, $90.00. R2.
25. Paid cash for supplies, $150.00. C7.
27. Paid cash for supplies, $100.00. C8.
27. Received cash from sales, $1,800.00. T27.
30. Paid cash to owner for personal use, $300.00. C9.
30. Received cash from sales, $410.00. T30.

Instructions:

1. Open an account for Utilities Expense. Use the 3-digit numbering system described in the chapter.
2. Journalize the transactions completed during November of the current year. Use page 1 of a journal. Source documents are abbreviated as follows: check, C; memorandum, M; receipt, R; sales invoice, S; calculator tape, T.
3. Prove the journal.
4. Prove cash. The beginning cash balance on November 1 is zero. The balance on the next unused check stub is $9,025.00.
5. Rule the journal.
6. Post from the journal to the general ledger.

5-6 CHALLENGE PROBLEM

Posting using a variation of the five-column journal

Nathan Jackson owns a service business called HouseCare. HouseCare uses a five-column journal that is different from the journal used in this chapter. HouseCare's March journal and general ledger accounts (before posting) are given in the *Working Papers.*

Instructions:

1. Post the separate amounts on each line of the journal that need to be posted individually.
2. Post the journal's special amount column totals.

INTERNET ACTIVITY

Point your browser to

http://accounting.swpco.com

Choose **First-Year Course**, choose **Activities**, and complete the activity for Chapter 5.

Applied Communication

A fax machine allows a business to send documents anywhere in a matter of minutes using a telephone line. Most fax machines in offices are located in one or more central locations and used by a number of different workers for both sending and receiving documents. To facilitate directing the document to the intended receiver, it is usual practice to include a cover sheet in the fax transmission. The cover sheet should include the information below:

1. Names of the person sending the message and the person to receive the message.
2. Phone number of both sending and receiving fax machines.
3. Total number of pages being transmitted, including the cover sheet.

Instructions:

1. Write a memorandum responding to the following scenario: Barbara Treviño is at the bank, applying for a business loan. Ms. Treviño has just called you and asked that you fax her with the following information: Encore Music's asset, liability, owner's equity, sales, and expense accounts, and their current balances. In your memorandum, include an introductory sentence or paragraph and end with a concluding statement.
2. Prepare a cover sheet for transmitting a fax message. The bank's fax machine telephone number is 800-555-3333. Use your own name and personal telephone number or school telephone number.

Cases for Critical Thinking

Case 1 Janna Sturm does not use a journal in her business records. She records the debits and credits for each transaction directly in the general ledger accounts. Is Ms. Sturm using the correct procedure? Explain your answer.

Case 2 Trent Marvets does the accounting work for his business. When posting, he first transfers all of the information to the general ledger accounts. Then he returns to the journal and, all at one time, writes the account numbers in the Post. Ref. column of the journal. Diana Young also does the accounting work for her business. When posting, she writes all the account numbers in the Post. Ref. column of the journal before she transfers any information to the accounts. Is Mr. Marvets or Ms. Young following the correct procedure? Explain your answer.

AUTOMATED ACCOUNTING

AUTOMATED GENERAL LEDGER ACCOUNTING

A group of accounts is called a ledger. A ledger that contains all accounts needed to prepare financial statements is called a general ledger. Each account is assigned a title and a number to be used in a manual as well as an automated accounting system.

Creating a Chart of Accounts

The automated accounting system includes a chart of accounts, which includes a list of account titles and numbers showing the location of each account in a ledger. The chart of accounts can be created or changed by clicking the Accts. toolbar button. Next, click on the Accounts tab to access the Chart of Accounts maintenance screen. Accounts can be added or deleted on this screen. Adding a new account would be considered opening an account, just as deleting an account would be considered removing an account.

Chart of Accounts Maintenance

It is important to keep a business's chart of accounts up to date. This process of adding new accounts, changing titles of existing accounts, and deleting accounts is called file maintenance or account maintenance. The Account Maintenance screen will appear when you choose the Maintain Accounts menu item from the Data drop-down list or click on the Accts. toolbar button.

Adding a New Account

1. Enter the account number in the Account column at the end of the list, then hit the Tab key.
2. Enter the title for the new account.
3. For a departmentalized business, enter the department number.
4. Click the Add Account button.
5. Click the Close button to exit the Accounts window.

Changing an Account Title

1. Select the account that you wish to change.
2. Enter the correct account title or department number.
3. Click the Change button when the account title has been changed.

The account number cannot be changed. If an account number needs to be changed because of an incorrect account number, the account must be deleted, then added as a new account number.

Deleting an Account

1. Select the account that you wish to delete.
2. Click the Delete button. General ledger accounts cannot be deleted unless the account has a zero balance.
3. Click the OK button.

General Ledger Account Numbers

As described in Chapter 5, general ledger accounts are assigned a number based on a division. The first digit of each account number shows the general ledger division in which the account is located. The other digits indicate the location of each account within a general ledger division. Every business sets up its general ledger differently, but the concept is generally the same.

Posting Amounts to the General Ledger

Posting journal entries to the general ledger is done automatically in automated accounting. For example, all changes in cash are brought together into the cash account. When transactions are entered into a journal, the debit and credit amounts are automatically transferred to the general ledger accounts. Accounts with debit balances are increased by debit entries to the account, and accounts with credit balances are increased by credit entries to the account.

Every entry that is made to the journal includes the date, reference, account number, and the debit or credit entry. This is the information that is transferred to the general and subsidiary ledgers, updating the accounts immediately. See the illustration of a general

AUTOMATED ACCOUNTING

ledger report with the posting completed.

AUTOMATING APPLICATION PROBLEM 5-1: Preparing a chart of accounts and opening an account

Instructions:

1. Load *Automated Accounting 7.0* or higher software.
2. Select database F05-1 from the appropriate directory/ folder.
3. Select File from the menu bar and choose the Save As menu command. Key the path to the drive and directory that contains your data files. Save the database with a file name of XXX051 (where XXX are your initials).
4. Access Problem Instructions through the Help menu (7.0) or Browser tool (8.0). Read the Problem Instructions screen.
5. Refer to page 119 for data used in this problem.
6. Exit the *Automated Accounting* software.

AUTOMATING MASTERY PROBLEM 5-5: Journalizing transactions and posting to a general ledger

Instructions:

1. Load *Automated Accounting 7.0* or higher software.
2. Select database F05-2 from the appropriate directory/ folder.
3. Select File from the menu bar and choose the Save As menu command. Key the path to the drive and directory that contains your data files. Save the database with a file name of XXX052 (where XXX are your initials).
4. Access Problem Instructions through the Help menu (7.0) or Browser tool (8.0). Read the Problem Instructions screen.
5. Key the transactions listed on page 120.
6. Exit the *Automated Accounting* software.

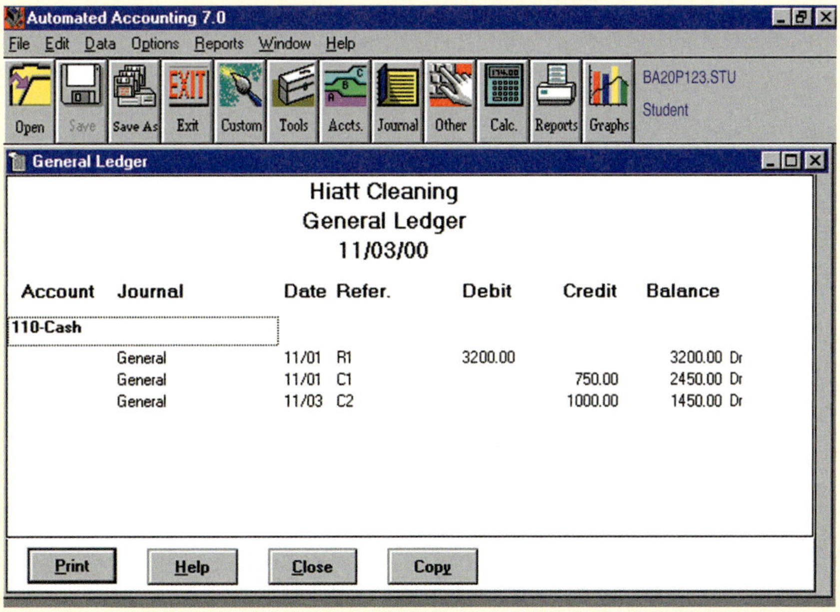

6 Cash Control Systems

AFTER STUDYING CHAPTER 6, YOU WILL BE ABLE TO:

1. Define accounting terms related to using a checking account and a petty cash fund.
2. Identify accounting concepts and practices related to using a checking account.
3. Prepare business papers related to using a checking account.
4. Reconcile a bank statement.
5. Journalize dishonored checks and electronic banking transactions.
6. Establish and replenish a petty cash fund.

TERMS PREVIEW

- checking account
- endorsement
- blank endorsement
- special endorsement
- restrictive endorsement
- postdated check
- bank statement
- dishonored check
- electronic funds transfer
- debit card
- petty cash
- petty cash slip

HOW BUSINESSES USE CASH

In accounting, money is usually referred to as cash. Most businesses make major cash payments by check. However, small cash payments for items such as postage and some supplies may be made from a cash fund kept at the place of business.

Because cash transactions occur more frequently than other types of transactions, more chances occur to make recording errors affecting cash. Cash can be transferred from one person to another without any question about ownership. Also, cash may be lost as it is moved from one place to another.

As a safety measure, Encore Music keeps most of its cash in a bank. Because all cash receipts are placed in a bank, Encore Music has written evidence to support its accounting records. Encore Music can compare its record of checks written with the bank's record of checks paid. Greater control of Encore Music's cash and greater accuracy of its cash records result from these procedures.

ACCOUNTING IN YOUR CAREER

MANAGING CASH AND THE CHECKING ACCOUNT

Raymond Gutierrez owns Gutierrez Employment Agency. Raymond started this business a year ago and operated it alone until two months ago. He hired Shanelle Gibson as an administrative assistant to handle the accounting for the business and to assist him in other responsibilities when needed. Shanelle has reorganized the record keeping for the agency, and by filling in on other tasks has freed Raymond to spend more time building contacts with employers and placing clients. The business is growing rapidly.

In their regular weekly meeting to review their goals, Shanelle says, "Raymond, I enjoy working here, and I think I have really helped you be more successful. I'd like to make two proposals that will give you more time to devote to your activities." Shanelle proceeds to outline the proposals.

She recommends establishing a petty cash fund for making small cash payments, such as urgent office supplies and postage and delivery fees. She has already arranged to have overnight delivery services billed to the firm, so only small delivery fees will be paid from petty cash. She thinks $100.00 would be a sufficient balance to avoid replenishing petty cash too frequently.

Her second recommendation is to take over writing and signing all checks, receiving and depositing all cash receipts, and reconciling the bank statement—tasks that Raymond currently performs.

Raymond tells Shanelle that he will consider her proposals and that he appreciates her good work and concern for making the business more efficient.

Critical Thinking:

1. Is the proposal to establish a petty cash fund a good idea?
2. What is your opinion of Shanelle's proposal to take over managing cash and the checking account?

6-1 Checking Accounts

DEPOSITING CASH

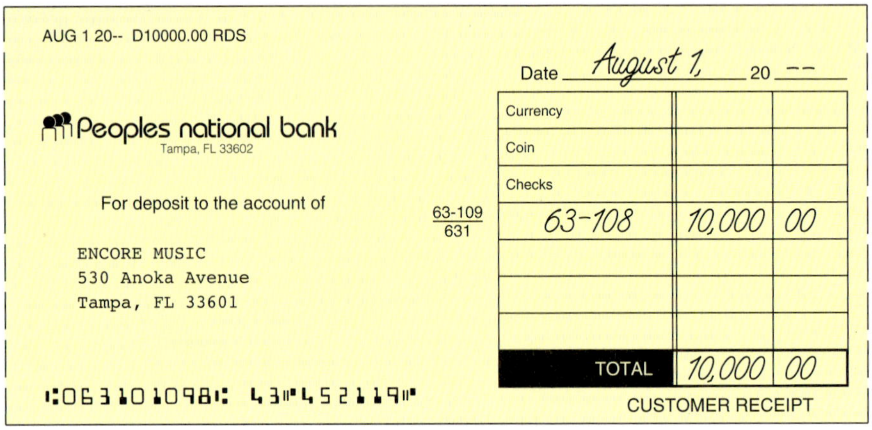

AUG 1 20-- D10000.00 RDS

Peoples national bank
Tampa, FL 33602

For deposit to the account of

ENCORE MUSIC
530 Anoka Avenue
Tampa, FL 33601

63-109
631

Date August 1, 20 --

Currency		
Coin		
Checks		
63-108	10,000	00
TOTAL	10,000	00

⑆063101098⑆ 43⑈4521191⑈

CUSTOMER RECEIPT

A business form ordering a bank to pay cash from a bank account is known as a check. A bank account from which payments can be ordered by a depositor is called a **checking account.**

When a checking account is opened, the bank customer must provide a signature on a signature card for the bank records. If several persons are authorized to sign checks, each person's signature must be on the signature card.

A bank customer prepares a deposit slip each time cash or checks are placed in a bank account. Deposit slips may differ slightly from one bank to another. Each bank designs its own deposit slips to fit the bank's recording machines. However, all deposit slips contain the same basic information.

Checks are listed on a deposit slip according to the bank number on each check. For example, the number *63-108* identifies the bank on which the $10,000.00 check is written.

When a deposit is made, a bank gives the depositor a receipt. Many banks use a copy of the deposit slip with a printed or stamped verification as the receipt. The printed verification, *Aug 1 20— D10000.00 RDS,* is printed along the top left edge of the deposit slip. This printed verification means that a total of $10,000.00 was deposited on August 1. The initials *RDS* next to the amount are those of the bank employee who accepted the deposit.

DEPOSIT RECORDED ON A CHECK STUB

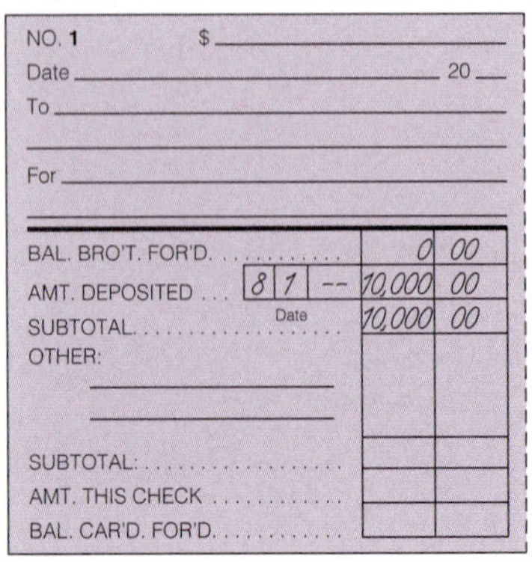

NO. 1 $

Date 20

To

For

BAL. BRO'T. FOR'D.	0	00
AMT. DEPOSITED 8 1 -- (Date)	10,000	00
SUBTOTAL	10,000	00
OTHER:		
SUBTOTAL:		
AMT. THIS CHECK		
BAL. CAR'D. FOR'D.		

After the deposit is recorded on the check stub, a checkbook subtotal is calculated. The balance brought forward on Check Stub No. 1 is zero. The previous balance, $0.00, *plus* the deposit, $10,000.00, *equals* the subtotal, $10,000.00.

Cash receipts are journalized at the time cash is received. Later, the cash receipts are deposited in the checking account. Therefore, no journal entry is needed for deposits because the cash receipts have already been journalized.

BLANK ENDORSEMENT, SPECIAL ENDORSEMENT, AND RESTRICTIVE ENDORSEMENT

[Blank Endorsement]

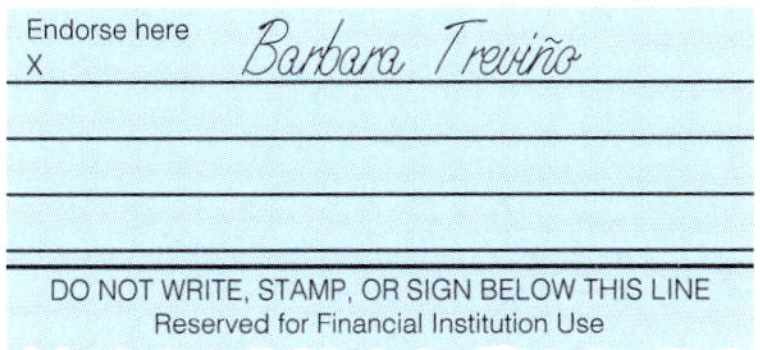

[Special Endorsement]

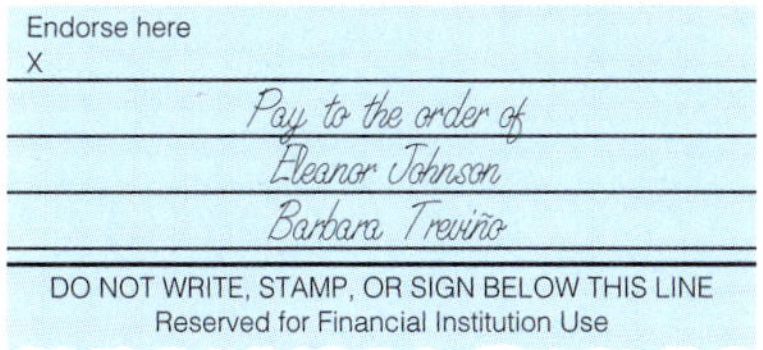

[Restrictive Endorsement]

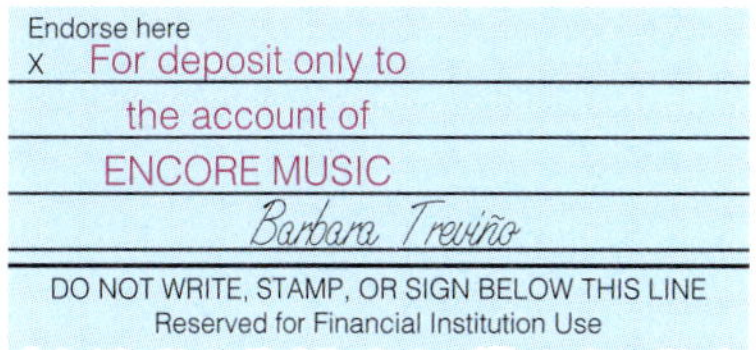

Ownership of a check can be transferred. The name of the first owner is stated on a check following the words *Pay to the order of.* Therefore, the person to whom payment is to be made must indicate that ownership of the check is being transferred. One person transfers ownership to another person by signing on the back of a check. A signature or stamp on the back of a check transferring ownership is called an **endorsement.** Federal regulations require that an endorsement be confined to a limited amount of space that is indicated on the back of a check.

An endorsement should be signed exactly as the person's name appears on the front of the check. For example, a check made payable to B. A. Treviño is endorsed on the back as *B. A. Treviño.* Immediately below that endorsement, Ms. Treviño writes her official signature, *Barbara Treviño.*

Ownership of a check might be transferred several times, resulting in several endorsements. Each endorser guarantees payment of the check. If a bank does not receive payment from the person who signed the check, each endorser is individually liable for payment.

Three types of endorsements are commonly used, each having a specific use in transferring ownership.

Blank Endorsement

An endorsement consisting only of the endorser's signature is called a **blank endorsement.** A blank endorsement indicates that the subsequent owner is whoever has the check.

If a check with a blank endorsement is lost or stolen, the check can be cashed by anyone who has possession of it. Ownership may be transferred without further endorsement. A blank endorsement should be used *only* when a person is at the bank ready to cash or deposit a check.

Special Endorsement

An endorsement indicating a new owner of a check is called a **special endorsement.** Special endorsements are sometimes known as endorsements in full.

Special endorsements include the words *Pay to the order of* and the name of the new check owner. Only the person or business named in a special endorsement can cash, deposit, or further transfer ownership of the check.

Restrictive Endorsement

An endorsement restricting further transfer of a check's ownership is called a **restrictive endorsement.** A restrictive endorsement limits use of the check to whatever purpose is stated in the endorsement.

Many businesses have a stamp prepared with a restrictive endorsement. When a check is received, it is immediately stamped with the restrictive endorsement. This prevents unauthorized persons from cashing the check if it is lost or stolen.

FYI

The Federal Deposit Insurance Corporation (FDIC) protects depositors from banks that fail. Bank deposits are generally covered up to $100,000 per depositor.

COMPLETED CHECK STUB AND CHECK

NO. 1 $ 1,577.00
Date August 3, 20 --
To Quick Clean Supplies Co.
For Supplies
BAL. BRO'T. FOR'D. 0 00
AMT. DEPOSITED 8/1/-- 10,000 00
SUBTOTAL 10,000 00
OTHER:
SUBTOTAL 10,000 00
AMT. THIS CHECK 1,577 00
BAL. CAR'D. FOR'D. 8,423 00

Encore Music
530 Anoka Avenue
Tampa, FL 33601
NO. 1
63-109
631
August 3, 20 --
PAY TO THE ORDER OF Quick Clean Supplies Co. $1,577.00
One thousand five hundred seventy-seven and no/100 DOLLARS
For Classroom Use Only
Peoples national bank
Tampa, FL 33602
FOR Supplies
Barbara Treviño
⑆063101098⑆ 43⑈452119⑈

Encore Music uses printed checks with check stubs attached. Consecutive numbers are preprinted on Encore Music's checks. Consecutive numbers on checks provide an easy way of identifying each check. Also, the numbers help keep track of all checks to assure that none are lost or misplaced.

A check stub is a business's record of each check written for a cash payment transaction. *(CONCEPT: Objective Evidence)* To avoid forgetting to prepare a check stub, the check stub is prepared before the check is written.

After the check stub is completed, the check is written.

STEPS

Preparing check stubs

1. Write the amount of the check, *$1,577.00*, in the space after the dollar sign at the top of the stub.
2. Write the date of the check, *August 3, 20—*, on the Date line at the top of the stub.
3. Write to whom the check is to be paid, *Quick Clean Supplies Co.*, on the To line at the top of the stub.
4. Record the purpose of the check, *Supplies*, on the For line.
5. Write the amount of the check, *$1,577.00*, in the amount column at the bottom of the stub on the line with the words *Amt. This Check*.
6. Calculate the new checking account balance, *$8,423.00*, and record the new balance in the amount column on the last line of the stub. The new balance is calculated as shown below.

Subtotal	–	Amount of This Check	=	New Balance
$10,000.00	–	$1,577.00	=	$8,423.00

Preparing checks

7. Write the date, *August 3, 20—*, in the space provided. The date should be the month, day, and year on which the check is issued. A check with a future date on it is called a **postdated check.** Most banks will not accept postdated checks because money cannot be withdrawn from a depositor's account until the date on the check.
8. Write to whom the check is to be paid, *Quick Clean Supplies Co.*, following the words *Pay to the order of.* If the person to whom a check is to be paid is a business, use the business's name rather than the owner's name. (*CONCEPT: Business Entity*) If the person to whom the check is to be paid is an individual, use that person's name.
9. Write the amount in figures, *$1,577.00*, following the dollar sign. Write the figures close to the printed dollar sign. This practice prevents anyone from writing another digit in front of the amount to change the amount of the check.

10. Write the amount in words, *One thousand five hundred seventy-seven and no/100*, on the line with the word *Dollars*. This written amount verifies the amount written in figures after the dollar sign. Begin the words at the extreme left. Draw a line through the unused space up to the word *Dollars*. This line prevents anyone from writing in additional words to change the amount. If the amounts in words and in figures are not the same, a bank may pay only the amount in words. Often, when the amounts do not agree, a bank will refuse to pay the check.
11. Write the purpose of the check, *Supplies*, on the line labeled For. (On some checks this space is labeled Memo.) Some checks do not have a line for writing the purpose of the check.
12. Sign the check. A check should not be signed until each item on the check and its stub has been verified for accuracy.

RECORDING A VOIDED CHECK

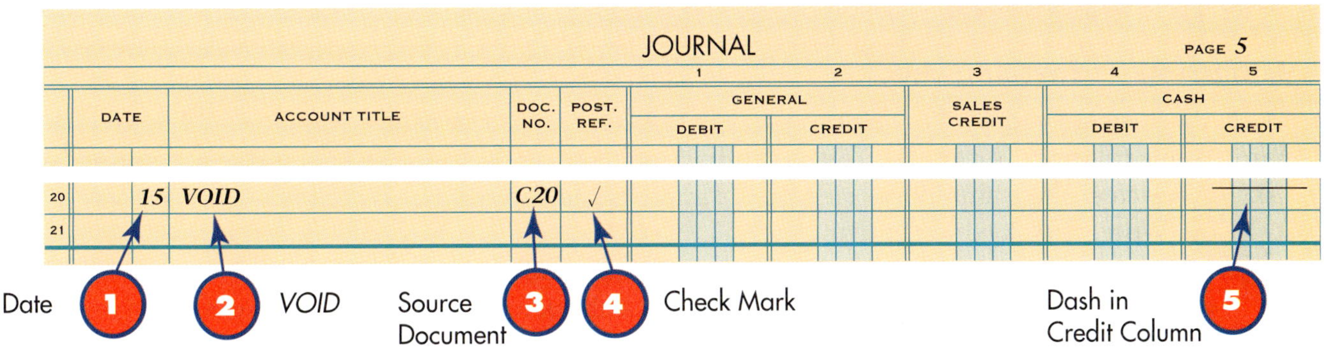

Banks usually refuse to accept altered checks. If any kind of error is made in preparing a check, a new check should be prepared. Because checks are prenumbered, all checks not used should be retained for the records. This practice helps account for all checks and assures that no checks have been lost or stolen.

A check that contains errors must be marked so that others will know that it is not to be used. The word *VOID* is written in large letters across both the check and its stub.

When Encore Music records a check in its journal, the check number is placed in the journal's Doc. No. column. If a check number is missing from the Doc. No. column, there is a question whether all checks have been journalized. To assure that all check numbers are listed in the journal, Encore Music records voided checks in the journal.

STEPS: Recording a voided check in the journal

1. Record the date, *15*, in the Date column.
2. Write the word *VOID* in the Account Title column.
3. Write the check number, *C20*, in the Doc. No. column.
4. Place a check mark in the Post. Ref. column.
5. Place a dash in the Cash Credit column.

REMEMBER

Always complete the check stub before writing the check. Otherwise you may forget to record the amount of the check on the check stub.

TERMS REVIEW

- checking account
- endorsement
- blank endorsement
- special endorsement
- restrictive endorsement
- postdated check

AUDIT YOUR UNDERSTANDING

1. List the three types of endorsements.
2. List the steps for preparing a check stub.
3. List the steps for preparing a check.

WORK TOGETHER

Endorsing and writing checks

Write the answers to the following problems in the *Working Papers.* Your instructor will guide you through the following examples. You are authorized to sign checks for Balsam Lake Accounting.

4. For each of these situations, prepare the appropriate endorsement.
   - **a.** Write a blank endorsement.
   - **b.** Write a special endorsement to transfer a check to Kelsey Sather.
   - **c.** Write a restrictive endorsement to deposit a check in the account of Balsam Lake Accounting.
5. Record the balance brought forward on Check Stub No. 78, $1,805.75.
6. Record a deposit of $489.00 made on October 30 of the current year on Check Stub No. 78.
7. Prepare check stubs and write the following checks. Use October 30 of the current year as the date.
   - **a.** Check No. 78 to Corner Garage for repairs, $162.00.
   - **b.** Check No. 79 to St. Croix Supply for supplies, $92.00.

ON YOUR OWN

Endorsing and writing checks

Write the answers to the following problems in the *Working Papers.* Work these problems independently. You are authorized to sign checks for Dresser Hair Care.

8. For each of these situations, prepare the appropriate endorsement.
   - **a.** Write a special endorsement to transfer a check to Kent Benson.
   - **b.** Write a restrictive endorsement to deposit a check in the account of Dresser Hair Care.
9. Record the balance brought forward on Check Stub No. 345, $3,054.55.
10. Record a deposit of $587.00 made on May 31 of the current year on Check Stub No. 345.
11. Prepare check stubs and write the following checks. Use May 31 of the current year as the date.
    - **a.** Check No. 345 to Uniforms Plus for uniform rental, $275.00.
    - **b.** Check No. 346 to HairWorld for supplies, $593.00.

6-2 Bank Reconciliation

BANK STATEMENT

Peoples national bank
Tampa, FL 33602

STATEMENT OF ACCOUNT FOR
ENCORE MUSIC
530 Anoka Avenue
Tampa, FL 33601

ACCOUNT NUMBER: 43-452-119

STATEMENT DATE: August 30, 20--

BALANCE FROM PREVIOUS STATEMENT	NO. OF CHECKS	AMOUNT OF CHECKS	NO. OF DEPOSITS	AMOUNT OF DEPOSITS	SERVICE CHARGES	STATEMENT BALANCE
0.00	11	5,504.00	14	14,001.00	3.00	8,494.00

DATE	CHECK	AMOUNT	CHECK	AMOUNT	DEPOSIT	BALANCE
08/01/--						0.00
08/01/--					10,000.00	10,000.00
08/04/--	1	1,577.00				8,423.00
08/07/--	2	1,200.00				7,223.00
08/12/--					425.00	7,648.00
08/13/--	4	250.00	6	100.00		7,298.00
08/14/--	3	1,360.00				5,938.00
08/15/--					120.00	6,058.00
08/16/--					416.00	6,474.00
08/17/--	5	45.00			409.00	6,838.00
08/18/--	7	68.00			295.00	7,065.00
08/19/--	8	200.00			354.00	7,219.00
08/20/--	9	200.00			300.00	7,319.00
08/21/--					270.00	7,589.00
08/24/--					300.00	7,889.00
08/25/--					310.00	8,199.00
08/26/--					245.00	8,444.00
08/27/--					290.00	8,734.00
08/28/--					267.00	9,001.00
08/29/--	10	70.00				8,931.00
08/30/--	11	434.00				8,497.00
	SC	3.00				8,494.00

PLEASE EXAMINE AT ONCE - IF NO ERRORS ARE REPORTED WITHIN 10 DAYS THE ACCOUNT WILL BE CONSIDERED CORRECT. REFER ANY DISCREPANCY TO OUR ACCOUNTING DEPARTMENT IMMEDIATELY.

A report of deposits, withdrawals, and bank balances sent to a depositor by a bank is called a **bank statement.**

When a bank receives checks, the amount of each check is deducted from the depositor's account. The bank stamps the checks to indicate that the checks are canceled and are not to be transferred further. Canceled checks are returned to a depositor with a bank statement. Outstanding checks are those checks issued by a depositor but not yet reported on a bank statement. Outstanding deposits are those deposits made at a bank but not yet shown on a bank statement. Account service charges are also listed on a bank statement.

Although banks seldom make mistakes, occasionally a check or deposit might be recorded in a wrong account. When a bank statement is received, a depositor should verify its accuracy. If errors are discovered, the bank should be notified at once. However, a bank's records and a depositor's records may differ while the bank's records are still correct. The difference may exist for several reasons.

1. A service charge may not have been recorded in the depositor's business records.
2. Outstanding deposits may be recorded in the depositor's records but not on a bank statement.
3. Outstanding checks may be recorded in the depositor's records but not on a bank statement.
4. A depositor may have made math or recording errors.

BANK STATEMENT RECONCILIATION

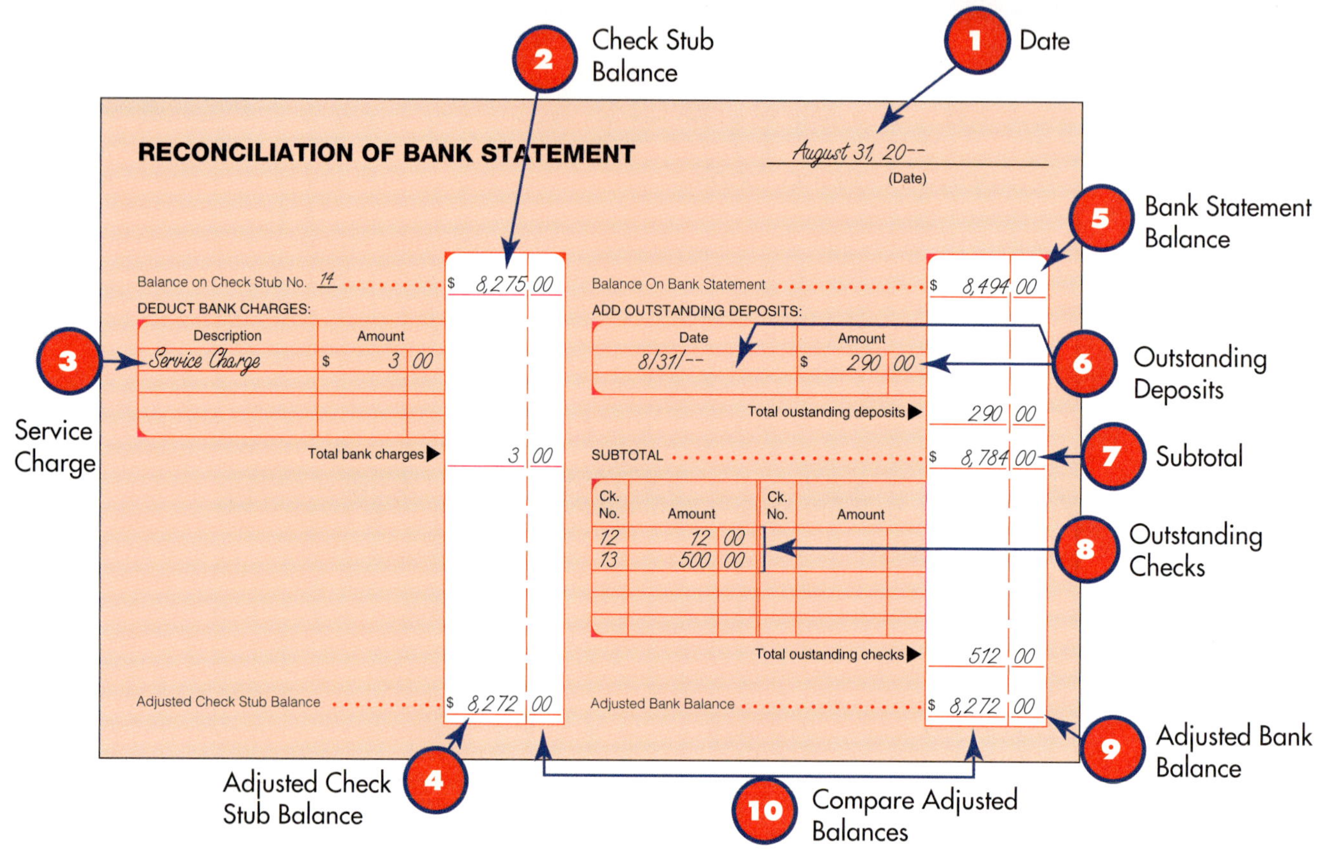

A bank statement is reconciled by verifying that information on a bank statement and a checkbook are in agreement. Reconciling immediately is an important aspect of cash control.

Encore Music's canceled checks are received with the bank statement. The returned checks are arranged in numeric order. For each canceled check, a check mark is placed on the corresponding check stub. A check stub with no check mark indicates an outstanding check.

Encore Music receives a bank statement dated August 30 on August 31. Encore Music uses a reconciliation form printed on the back of the bank statement.

STEPS: Reconciling a bank statement

1. Write the date on which the reconciliation is prepared, *August 31, 20—*.
2. In the left amount column, list the balance brought forward on Check Stub No. 14, the next unused check stub, *$8,275.00*.
3. In the space for bank charges, list any charges. The only such charge for Encore Music is the bank service charge, *$3.00*. The bank service charge is labeled *SC* on the bank statement.
4. Write the adjusted check stub balance, *$8,272.00*, in the space provided at the bottom of the left amount column. The balance on the check stub, $8,275.00, *minus* the bank's service charge, $3.00, *equals* the adjusted check stub balance, $8,272.00.
5. Write the ending balance shown on the bank statement, *$8,494.00*, in the right amount column.
6. Write the date, *8/31/—*, and the amount, *$290.00*, of any outstanding deposits in the space provided. Add the outstanding deposits. Write the total outstanding deposits, *$290.00*, in the right amount column.
7. Add the ending bank statement balance to the total outstanding deposits. Write the total, *$8,784.00*, in the space for the Subtotal.

8. List the outstanding checks, Nos. *12* and *13*, and their amounts, *$12.00* and *$500.00*, in the space provided. Add the amounts of the outstanding checks, and write the total, *$512.00*, in the right amount column.
9. Calculate the adjusted bank balance, and write the amount, *$8,272.00*, in the space provided at the bottom of the right amount column. The subtotal, $8,784.00, *minus* the total outstanding checks, $512.00, *equals* the adjusted bank balance, $8,272.00.
10. Compare adjusted balances. The adjusted balances must be the same. The adjusted check stub balance is the same as the adjusted bank balance. Because the two amounts are the same, the bank statement is reconciled. The completed reconciliation form is filed for future reference. If the two adjusted balances are not the same, the error must be found and corrected before any more work is done.

RECORDING A BANK SERVICE CHARGE ON A CHECK STUB

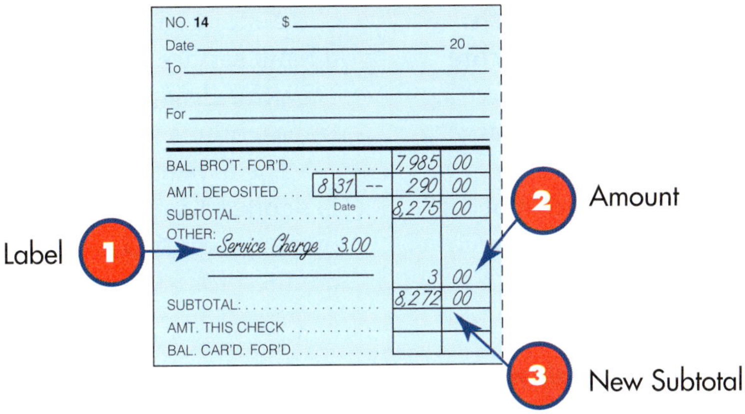

The bank deducts the service charge from Encore Music's checking account each month. Although Encore Music did not write a check for the bank service charge, this cash payment must be recorded in Encore Music's accounting records as a cash payment. First, Encore Music makes a record of a bank service charge on a check stub.

STEPS: Recording a bank service charge on a check stub

1. Write *Service Charge $3.00* on the check stub under the heading Other.
2. Write the amount of the service charge, *$3.00*, in the amount column.
3. Calculate and record the new subtotal, *$8,272.00*, on the Subtotal line. A new Balance Carried Forward is not calculated until after Check No. 14 is written.

JOURNALIZING A BANK SERVICE CHARGE

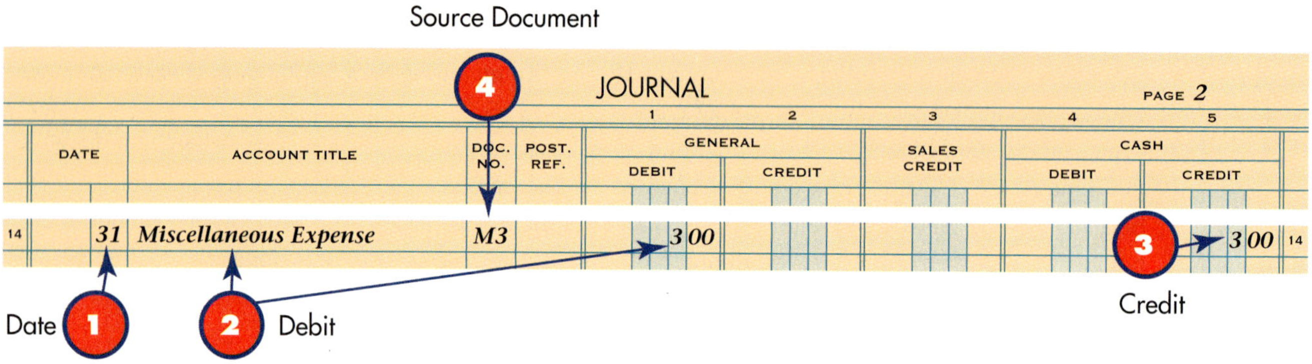

Because the bank service charge is a cash payment for which no check is written, Encore Music prepares a memorandum as the source document. Encore Music's bank service charges are relatively small and occur only once a month. Therefore, a separate ledger account for the expense is not used. Instead, Encore Music records the bank service charge as a miscellaneous expense.

August 31. Received bank statement showing August bank service charge, $3.00. Memorandum No. 3.

Miscellaneous Expense	
3.00	

Cash	
	3.00

A memorandum is the source document for a bank service charge transaction. *(CONCEPT: Objective Evidence)* The analysis of this transaction is shown in the T accounts.

The expense account, Miscellaneous Expense, is debited for $3.00 to show the decrease in owner's equity. The asset account, Cash, is credited for $3.00 to show the decrease in assets.

STEPS

Journalizing a bank service charge

1. **Date.** Write the date, *31*, in the Date column.
2. **Debit.** Write the title of the account to be debited, *Miscellaneous Expense,* in the Account Title column. Record the amount debited, *$3.00,* in the General Debit column.
3. **Credit.** Record the amount credited, *$3.00,* in the Cash Credit column.
4. **Source document.** Write the source document number, *M3,* in the Doc. No. column.

SMALL BUSINESS SPOTLIGHT

Three factors generally motivate people to start a new business: the desire to control their own destinies, the desire to work more closely with customers, and the desire to achieve substantial profits.

TERM REVIEW

bank statement

AUDIT YOUR UNDERSTANDING

1. List four reasons why a depositor's records and a bank's records may differ.
2. If a check mark is placed on the check stub of each canceled check, what does a check stub with no check mark indicate?

WORK TOGETHER

Reconciling a bank statement and recording a bank service charge

Forms are given in the *Working Papers.* Your instructor will guide you through the following examples.

On July 29 of the current year, DeepClean received a bank statement dated July 28. The following information is obtained from the bank statement and from the records of the business.

Bank statement balance	$1,528.00	Outstanding checks:	
Bank service charge	2.00	No. 103	$ 70.00
Outstanding deposit, July 28	150.00	No. 105	35.00
		Checkbook balance on Check Stub No. 106	1,575.00

3. Prepare a bank statement reconciliation. Use July 29 of the current year as the date.
4. Record the service charge on Check Stub No. 106.
5. Record the service charge on journal page 14. Use Memo. No. 44 as the source document.

ON YOUR OWN

Reconciling a bank statement and recording a bank service charge

Forms are given in the *Working Papers.* Work these problems independently.

On Sept. 30 of the current year, Ajax Service Co. received a bank statement dated Sept. 29. The following information is obtained from the bank statement and from the records of the business.

Bank statement balance	$3,208.00	Outstanding checks:	
Bank service charge	5.00	No. 214	$ 90.00
Outstanding deposits:		No. 215	135.00
September 29	310.00	No. 217	50.00
September 30	330.00	Checkbook balance on Check Stub No. 218	3,578.00

6. Prepare a bank statement reconciliation. Use Sept. 30 of the current year as the date.
7. Record the service charge on Check Stub No. 218.
8. Record the service charge on journal page 28. Use Memo. No. 74 as the source document.

6-3 Dishonored Checks and Electronic Banking

RECORDING A DISHONORED CHECK ON A CHECK STUB

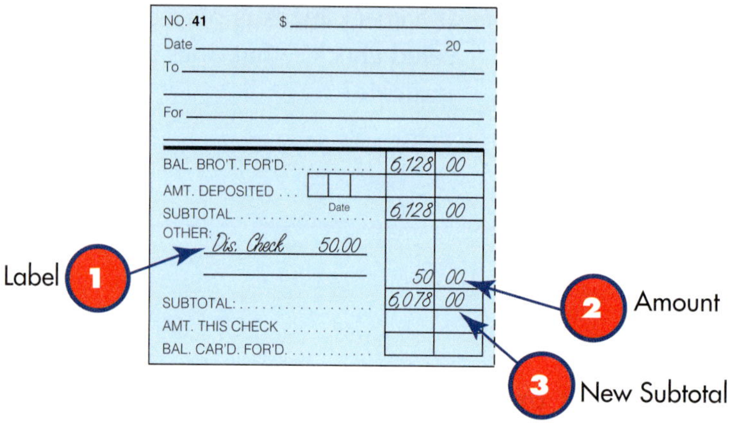

A check that a bank refuses to pay is called a **dishonored check.** Banks may dishonor a check for a number of reasons. (1) The check appears to be altered. (2) The signature of the person who signed the check does not match the one on the signature card at the bank. (3) The amounts written in figures and in words do not agree. (4) The check is postdated. (5) The person who wrote the check has stopped payment on the check. (6) The account of the person who wrote the check has insufficient funds to pay the check.

Issuing a check on an account with insufficient funds is illegal in most states. Altering or forging a check is illegal in all states. A dishonored check may affect the credit rating of the person or business who issued the check. Checking accounts and records should be maintained in such a way that all checks will be honored when presented to the bank.

Sometimes money for a dishonored check can be collected directly from the person or business who wrote the check. Often, however, the value of a dishonored check cannot be recovered and becomes an expense to the business.

Most banks charge a fee for handling dishonored checks that have been previously accepted for deposit. This fee is an expense of the business receiving a dishonored check. Encore Music's bank charges a $15.00 fee for handling dishonored checks. Encore Music attempts to collect the $15.00 fee in addition to the amount of the dishonored check.

When Encore Music receives a check, it records the check as a cash debit and deposits the check in the bank. When a check is dishonored, the bank deducts the amount of the check plus the fee, $15.00, from Encore Music's checking account. Therefore, Encore Music records a dishonored check as a cash payment transaction.

STEPS: Recording a dishonored check on a check stub

1. Write *Dishonored check $50.00* on the line under the heading Other. The amount is the total of the dishonored check, $35.00, *plus* the service fee of $15.00.
2. Write the total of the dishonored check, *$50.00,* in the amount column.
3. Calculate and record the new subtotal, *$6,078.00,* on the Subtotal line. A new Balance Carried Forward is not calculated until after Check No. 41 is written.

JOURNALIZING A DISHONORED CHECK

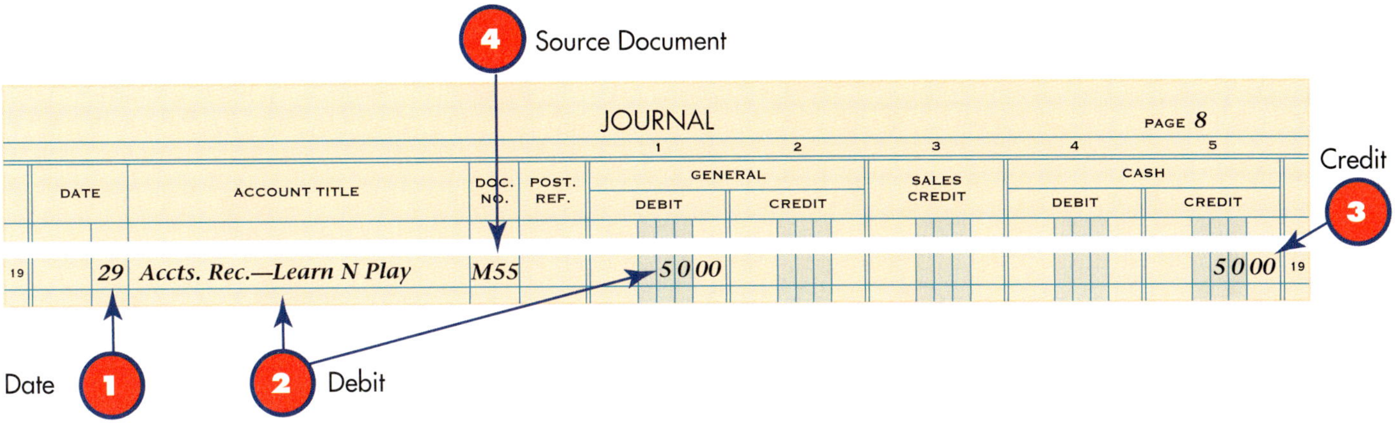

During August, Encore Music received no checks that were subsequently dishonored. However, in November Encore Music did receive a check from Learn N Play that was eventually dishonored.

November 29. Received notice from the bank of a dishonored check from Learn N Play, $35.00, plus $15.00 fee; total, $50.00. Memorandum No. 55.

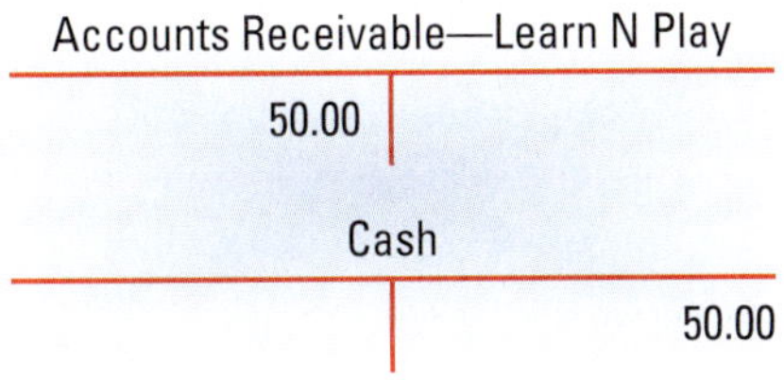

Because Encore Music did not write a check for this payment, a memorandum is prepared as the source document. *(CONCEPT: Objective Evidence)* The analysis of this transaction is shown in the T accounts.

All checks received are deposited in Encore Music's checking account. The entry for each cash receipts transaction includes a debit to Cash. If a check is subsequently returned as dishonored, the previous cash debit for the amount of the check must be offset by a cash credit. The asset account, Cash, is credited for $50.00 to show the decrease in assets.

When Encore Music originally received the check from Learn N Play, Accounts Receivable—Learn N Play was credited to reduce the balance of the account. When Encore Music finds out that the check was not accepted by the bank, the account, Accounts Receivable—Learn N Play, must be increased to show that this amount, plus the bank charge, is still owed to Encore Music. The asset account, Accounts Receivable—Learn N Play, is debited for $50.00 to show the increase in assets.

STEPS: Journalizing a dishonored check

1. **Date.** Write the date, *29,* in the Date column.
2. **Debit.** Write the title of the account to be debited, *Accounts Receivable—Learn N Play,* in the Account Title column. Record the amount debited, *$50.00,* in the General Debit column.
3. **Credit.** Write the amount credited, *$50.00,* in the Cash Credit column.
4. **Source document.** Write the source document number, *M55,* in the Doc. No. column.

REMEMBER

Checking accounts and records should be maintained in such a way that all checks will be honored when presented to the bank.

JOURNALIZING AN ELECTRONIC FUNDS TRANSFER

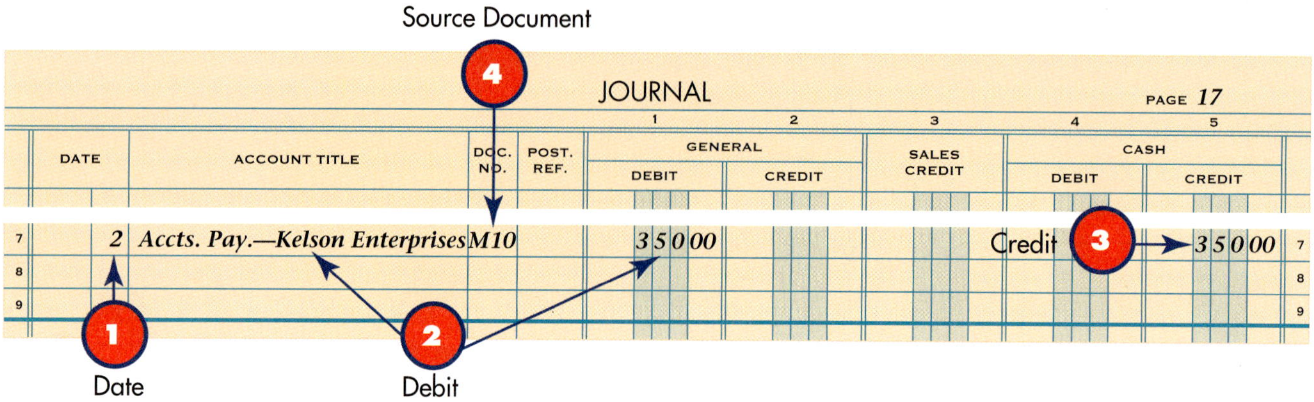

A computerized cash payments system that uses electronic impulses to transfer funds is called **electronic funds transfer.** Many businesses use electronic funds transfer (EFT) to pay vendors. To use EFT, a business makes arrangements with its bank to process EFT transactions. Arrangements are also made with vendors to accept EFT payments on account. After arranging for EFT payments on account, a telephone call is all that is needed to transfer funds from the business's account to the vendor's account.

To control cash payments through EFT, the person responsible for requesting transfers should be given a password. The bank should not accept EFT requests from any person unable to provide an established password.

Superior Cleaning Service uses electronic funds transfer to make payments on account to vendors. The journal entry for making payments on account through EFT is the same as when a check is written. The only change is the source document used to prove that the transaction did occur. Superior Cleaning Service uses a memorandum as the source document for an EFT. A note is written on the memorandum to describe the transaction.

September 2. Paid cash on account to Kelson Enterprises, $350.00, using EFT. Memorandum No. 10.

Accounts Payable—Kelson Enterprises	
350.00	

Cash	
	350.00

The source document for this transaction is Memorandum No. 10. (*CONCEPT: Objective Evidence*) The analysis of this transaction is shown in the T accounts.

The liability account, Accounts Payable—Kelson Enterprises, is decreased by a debit, $350.00. The asset account, Cash, is decreased by a credit, $350.00.

A cash payment made by EFT is recorded on the check stub as Other. This procedure keeps the checkbook in balance during the time lag from when the EFT is made until receipt of the bank statement. The EFT payments are verified as part of the regular bank statement reconciliation process. EFT payments are identified in the Check column of the bank statement by the notation EFT, rather than by a check number.

STEPS: Journalizing an electronic funds transfer

1. **Date.** Write the date, *2,* in the Date column.
2. **Debit.** Write the title of the account to be debited, *Accounts Payable—Kelson Enterprises,* in the Account Title column. Record the amount debited, *$350.00,* in the General Debit column.
3. **Credit.** Record the amount credited, *$350.00,* in the Cash Credit column.
4. **Source document.** Write the source document number, *M10,* in the Doc. No. column.

JOURNALIZING A DEBIT CARD TRANSACTION

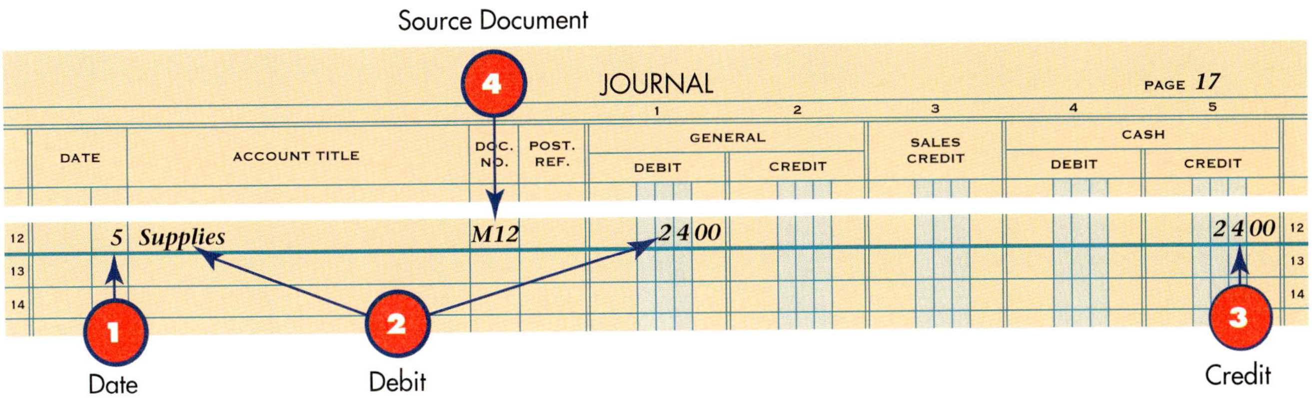

A bank card that, when making purchases, automatically deducts the amount of the purchase from the checking account of the cardholder is called a **debit card.** There is one major difference between a debit card and a credit card. When a purchase is made with a debit card, the amount of the purchase is automatically withdrawn from the checking account of the cardholder. A debit card eliminates the need to actually write out a check for the purchase. However, the effect is the same. The checking account balance is reduced by the amount of the purchase. A debit card also eliminates the need to carry a checkbook.

When using a debit card, it is important to remember to record all withdrawals to avoid errors in the checking account.

Superior Cleaning Service uses a debit card to make some purchases. Recording a cash payment made by a debit card is similar to recording a cash payment made by electronic funds transfer.

Superior Cleaning Service uses a memorandum as the source document for a debit card purchase. A note is written on the memorandum to describe the transaction.

September 5. Purchased supplies, $24.00, using debit card. Memorandum No. 12.

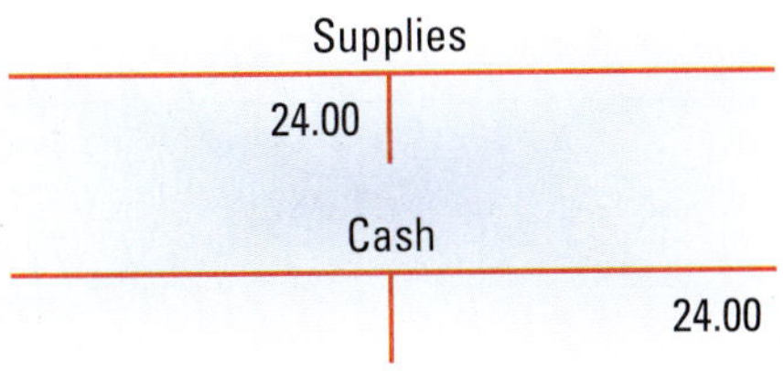

The source document for this transaction is Memorandum No. 12. *(CONCEPT: Objective Evidence)* The analysis of this transaction is shown in the T accounts.

The asset account, Supplies, is increased by a debit, $24.00. The asset account, Cash, is decreased by a credit, $24.00.

A cash payment made with a debit card is recorded on the check stub as Other. This procedure keeps the checkbook in balance during the time lag from when the debit card payment is made until receipt of the bank statement. The debit card payments are verified as part of the regular bank statement reconciliation process. Debit card payments are identified as a Purchase on the bank statement, with the date, time, location, and the amount of the debit card transaction stated.

STEPS

Journalizing a debit card purchase

1. **Date.** Write the date, *5,* in the Date column.
2. **Debit.** Write the title of the account to be debited, *Supplies,* in the Account Title column. Record the amount debited, *$24.00,* in the General Debit column.
3. **Credit.** Record the amount credited, *$24.00,* in the Cash Credit column.
4. **Source document.** Write the source document number, *M12,* in the Doc. No. column.

TERMS REVIEW

dishonored check

electronic funds transfer

debit card

AUDIT YOUR UNDERSTANDING

1. List six reasons why a bank may dishonor a check.
2. What account is credited when electronic funds transfer is used to pay cash on account?
3. What account is credited when a debit card is used to purchase supplies?

WORK TOGETHER

Recording dishonored checks, electronic funds transfers, and debit card purchases

Write the answers to this problem in the *Working Papers.* Your instructor will guide you through the following example.

4. Enter the following transactions on page 6 of a journal.

Transactions:

March 15. Received notice from the bank of a dishonored check from Christopher Ikola, $63.00, plus $10.00 fee; total, $73.00. Memorandum No. 121.

16. Paid cash on account to Laura Spinoza, $135.00, using EFT. Memorandum No. 122.

17. Purchased supplies, $31.00, using debit card. Memorandum No. 123.

ON YOUR OWN

Recording dishonored checks, electronic funds transfers, and debit card purchases

Write the answers to this problem in the *Working Papers.* Work this problem independently.

5. Enter the following transactions on page 12 of a journal.

Transactions:

June 12. Received notice from the bank of a dishonored check from Tina Horasky, $55.00, plus $15.00 fee; total, $70.00. Memorandum No. 76.

13. Paid cash on account to Paul Mancini, $112.00, using EFT. Memorandum No. 77.

14. Purchased supplies, $79.00, using debit card. Memorandum No. 78.

6-4 Petty Cash

ESTABLISHING A PETTY CASH FUND

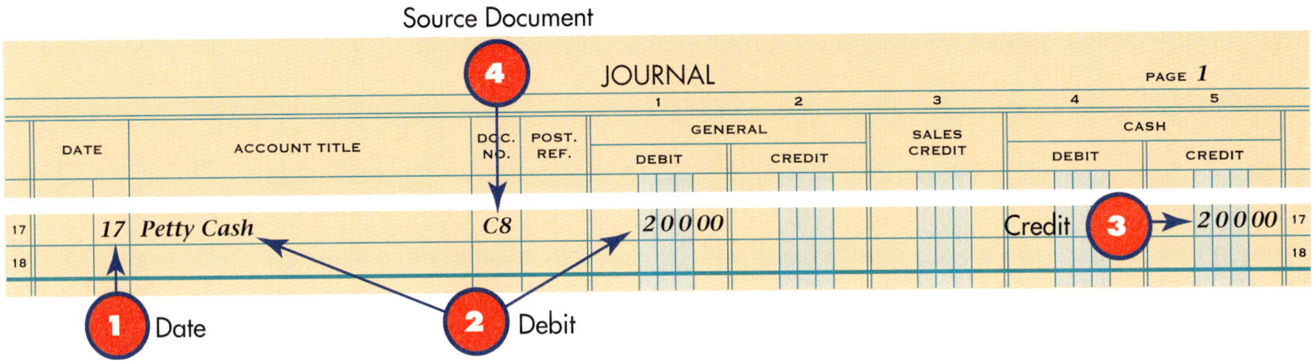

An amount of cash kept on hand and used for making small payments is called **petty cash.** A business usually has some small payments for which writing a check is not time or cost effective. Therefore, a business may maintain a separate cash fund for making small cash payments. The actual dollar amount considered to be a small payment differs from one business to another. Ms. Treviño has set $20.00 as the maximum amount to be paid at any one time from the petty cash fund.

The petty cash account is an asset with a normal debit balance. The balance of the petty cash account increases on the debit side and decreases on the credit side.

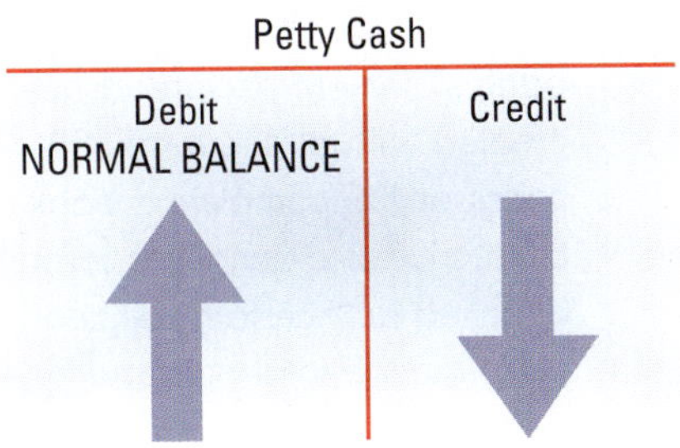

On August 17, Ms. Treviño decided that Encore Music needed a petty cash fund of $200.00. This amount should provide for small cash payments during a month.

August 17. Paid cash to establish a petty cash fund, $200.00. Check No. 8.

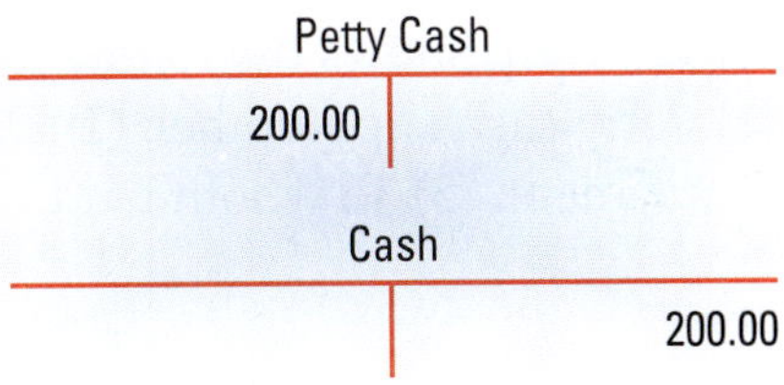

The source document for this transaction is Check No. 8. *(CONCEPT: Objective Evidence)* The analysis is shown in the T accounts. Petty Cash is debited for $200.00 to show the increase in this asset account balance. Cash is credited for $200.00 to show the decrease in this asset account balance.

Ms. Treviño cashed the check and placed the $200.00 in a locked petty cash box at her place of business. Only she is authorized to make these payments.

STEPS: Establishing a petty cash fund

1. **Date.** Write the date, *17,* in the Date column.
2. **Debit.** Write the title of the account to be debited, *Petty Cash,* in the Account Title column. Record the amount debited, *$200.00,* in the General Debit column.
3. **Credit.** Record the amount credited, *$200.00,* in the Cash Credit column.
4. **Source document.** Write the source document number, *C8,* in the Doc. No. column.

MAKING PAYMENTS FROM A PETTY CASH FUND WITH A PETTY CASH SLIP

PETTY CASH SLIP No. 1

Date: *August 18, 20--*

Paid to: *Tribune*

For: *Newspaper Ad* $ *5.00*

Account: *Advertising Expense*

Approved: *Barbara Treviño*

Each time a small payment is made from the petty cash fund, Ms. Treviño prepares a form showing the purpose and amount of the payment. A form showing proof of a petty cash payment is called a **petty cash slip.**

A petty cash slip shows the following information. (1) Petty cash slip number. (2) Date of petty cash payment. (3) To whom paid. (4) Reason for the payment. (5) Amount paid. (6) Account in which amount is to be recorded. (7) Signature of person approving the petty cash payment.

The petty cash slips are kept in the petty cash box until the fund is replenished. No entries are made in the journal for the individual petty cash payments.

TECHNOLOGY FOR BUSINESS

ELECTRONIC SPREADSHEETS AND BANK RECONCILIATION

Businesses often use forms to prepare accounting reports. Electronic spreadsheet software is a useful tool for preparing such accounting reports. Unlike paper forms, however, electronic spreadsheets contain formulas that automatically perform calculations.

An *electronic spreadsheet* displayed on a computer monitor consists of a group of rows and columns. Such spreadsheets can be extremely large, having hundreds of columns and thousands of rows. The space where a column intersects with a row is a *cell.* For example, cell A17 is located at the intersection of column A and row 17. This is known as the *cell address.*

The power of an electronic spreadsheet comes from the ability to let the software make calculations. This is accomplished by attaching formulas to different cells.

A bank reconciliation form increases the efficiency of verifying a bank statement. A spreadsheet can be created with all the formulas necessary to complete a bank reconciliation. For example, a formula attached to a certain cell can calculate the total outstanding deposits.

After the bank reconciliation is printed, the same spreadsheet can be used to reconcile other bank statements. Preparing a bank reconciliation using an electronic spreadsheet can help assure that the calculations are accurate.

REPLENISHING PETTY CASH

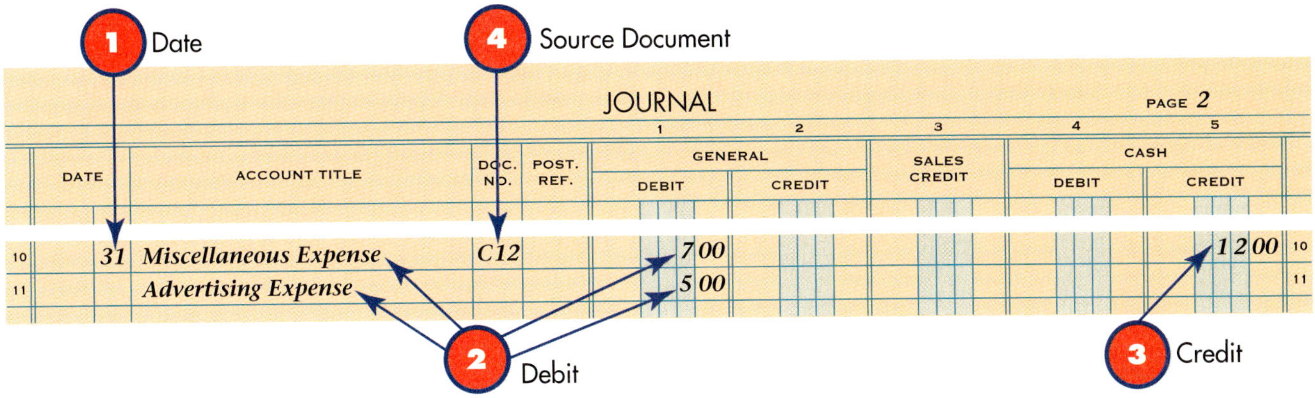

As petty cash is paid out, the amount in the petty cash box decreases. Eventually, the petty cash fund must be replenished and the petty cash payments recorded. Encore Music replenishes its petty cash fund whenever the amount on hand is reduced to $75.00. Also, the petty cash fund is always replenished at the end of each month so that all of the expenses are recorded in the month they are incurred.

Before petty cash is replenished, a proof of the fund must be completed.

Petty cash remaining in the petty cash fund	$188.00
Plus total of petty cash slips	+ 12.00
Equals petty cash fund	$200.00

The last line of the proof must show the same total as the original balance of the petty cash fund, $200.00. If petty cash does not prove, the errors must be found and corrected before any more work is done.

The proof shows that a total of $12.00 has been paid out of petty cash. An inspection of the petty cash slips shows that $7.00 has been paid for miscellaneous expenses and $5.00 has been paid for advertising. Therefore, an additional $12.00 must be placed in the fund. Encore Music will write a check to replenish the fund.

August 31. Paid cash to replenish the petty cash fund, $12.00: miscellaneous expense, $7.00; advertising, $5.00. Check No. 12.

Unless the petty cash fund is permanently increased or decreased, the balance of the account is always the original amount of the fund. The check issued to replenish petty cash is a credit to Cash and does not affect Petty Cash. When the check is cashed, the money is placed in the petty cash box. The amount in the petty cash box changes as shown below.

Amount in petty cash box before fund is replenished	$188.00
Amount from check issued to replenish petty cash	+ 12.00
Amount in petty cash box after fund is replenished	$200.00

The total amount in the petty cash box, $200.00, is again the same as the balance of the petty cash account.

STEPS: Journalizing the entry to replenish petty cash

1. **Date.** Write the date, *31*, in the Date column.
2. **Debit.** Write the title of the first account to be debited, *Miscellaneous Expense*, in the Account Title column. Write the amount to be debited to Miscellaneous Expense, *$7.00*, in the General Debit column on the same line as the account title. Write the title of the second account to be debited, *Advertising Expense*, on the next line in the Account Title column. Record the amount to be debited to Advertising Expense, *$5.00*, in the General Debit column on the same line as the account title.
3. **Credit.** Record the amount to be credited, *$12.00*, in the Cash Credit column on the first line of this entry.
4. **Source document.** Write the source document number, *C12*, in the Doc. No. column on the first line of the entry.

TERMS REVIEW

petty cash

petty cash slip

AUDIT YOUR UNDERSTANDING

1. Why do businesses use petty cash funds?
2. Why is Cash and not Petty Cash credited when a petty cash fund is replenished?

WORK TOGETHER

Establishing and replenishing a petty cash fund

Write the answers to this problem in the *Working Papers.* Your instructor will guide you through the following example.

3. Journalize the following transactions completed during July of the current year. Use page 13 of a journal. The abbreviation for check is C.

Transactions:

July 3. Paid cash to establish a petty cash fund, $250.00. C57.

31. Paid cash to replenish the petty cash fund, $78.00: supplies, $25.00; miscellaneous expense, $8.00; repairs, $45.00. C97.

ON YOUR OWN

Establishing and replenishing a petty cash fund

Write the answers to this problem in the *Working Papers.* Work this problem independently.

4. Journalize the following transactions completed during August of the current year. Use page 14 of a journal. The abbreviation for check is C.

Transactions:

Aug. 1. Paid cash to establish a petty cash fund, $500.00. C145.

31. Paid cash to replenish the petty cash fund, $134.00: supplies, $33.00; miscellaneous expense, $70.00; advertising, $31.00. C177.

CHAPTER 6 SUMMARY

After completing this chapter, you can

1. Define accounting terms related to using a checking account and a petty cash fund.
2. Identify accounting concepts and practices related to using a checking account.
3. Prepare business papers related to using a checking account.
4. Reconcile a bank statement.
5. Journalize dishonored checks and electronic banking transactions.
6. Establish and replenish a petty cash fund.

EXPLORE ACCOUNTING

CASH CONTROLS

Cash transactions occur more frequently than other types of transactions. Because cash is easily transferred from one person to another, a business must try to safeguard its cash to protect it and other assets from errors.

An unintentional error occurs when someone mistakenly records an incorrect amount or forgets to record a transaction. An intentional error occurs when someone intentionally records an incorrect amount or purposely forgets to record a transaction in order to cover up fraud or theft. Good cash control procedures should guard against both types of errors.

One common method of controlling cash is to insist that all cash payments over a certain amount be paid by check. In addition, checks should be prenumbered so that it is easy to account for each check. The document number column of a journal can be used to ensure that all checks issued are recorded in the journal. Other cash controls are to have one person responsible for authorizing all checks, and requiring a source document in support of each cash payment.

One of the best ways to safeguard assets is to separate duties so that one employee does not have total control of an entire set of processes. For example, one employee could receive and record the receipt of cash on account; a second employee could make and record deposits; and a third employee could reconcile the bank statement. By separating the duties, it is less likely that errors will be made.

A company that does not have enough employees to institute the separation of duties concept may hire a certified public accountant (CPA) to perform some of these duties on a regular basis.

Research Assignment: Talk to a business person to determine what kind of controls are in place to safeguard cash. Schools, hospitals, charitable organizations, and government offices as well as retail, wholesale, and service businesses should have established controls that are being followed. Summarize and present your findings to your class.

6-1 APPLICATION PROBLEM
Endorsing and writing checks

You are authorized to sign checks for Accounting Tutors. Forms are given in the *Working Papers.*

Instructions:

1. For each of the following situations, prepare the appropriate endorsement.
   a. Write a blank endorsement.
   b. Write a special endorsement to transfer a check to Bryan Astrup.
   c. Write a restrictive endorsement to deposit a check in the account of Accounting Tutors.
2. Record the balance brought forward on Check Stub No. 608, $9,811.71.
3. Record a deposit of $1,359.00 made on September 30 of the current year on Check Stub No. 608.
4. Prepare check stubs and write the following checks. Use September 30 of the current year as the date.
   a. Check No. 608 to Oak Street Supplies for supplies, $1,050.00.
   b. Check No. 609 to Blaine Tribune for advertising, $92.00.
   c. Check No. 610 to Bryce Kassola for rent, $750.00.

6-2 APPLICATION PROBLEM
Reconciling a bank statement and recording a bank service charge

Forms are given in the *Working Papers.* On May 31 of the current year, Parties Plus received a bank statement dated May 30. The following information is obtained from the bank statement and from the records of the business.

Bank statement balance	$2,482.00
Bank service charge	10.00
Outstanding deposit, May 30	756.25
Outstanding checks:	
No. 310	421.76
No. 311	150.50
Checkbook balance on Check Stub No. 312	2,675.99

Instructions:

1. Prepare a statement reconciliation. Use May 31 of the current year as the date.
2. Record the service charge on Check Stub No. 312.
3. Record the service charge on journal page 10. Use Memorandum No. 58 as the source document.

6-3 APPLICATION PROBLEM
Recording dishonored checks, electronic funds transfers, and debit card purchases

Enter the following transactions on page 3 of the journal given in the *Working Papers.*

Transactions:

Feb. 15. Received notice from the bank of a dishonored check from Patricia Dubay, $125.00, plus $20.00 fee; total, $145.00. Memorandum No. 217.

16. Paid cash on account to Alec Hongo, $354.00, using EFT. Memorandum No. 218.

17. Purchased supplies, $89.00, using debit card. Memorandum No. 219.

6-4 APPLICATION PROBLEM
Establishing and replenishing a petty cash fund

Journalize the following transactions completed during November of the current year. Use page 22 of the journal given in the *Working Papers*. The abbreviation for check is C.

Transactions:

Nov. 5. Paid cash to establish a petty cash fund, $300.00. C527.

30. Paid cash to replenish the petty cash fund, $165.00: supplies, $57.00; miscellaneous expense, $58.00; repairs, $40.00; postage (Postage Expense), $10.00. C555.

6-5 MASTERY PROBLEM
Reconciling a bank statement; journalizing a bank service charge, a dishonored check, and petty cash transactions

Joseph Cruz owns a business called LawnMow. Selected general ledger accounts are given below.

110	Cash	140	Prepaid Insurance	535	Repair Expense
115	Petty Cash	320	Joseph Cruz, Drawing	540	Supplies Expense
120	Accts. Rec.—Stacey Griffith	520	Miscellaneous Expense	550	Utilities Expense
130	Supplies	530	Rent Expense		

Instructions:

1. Journalize the following transactions completed during August of the current year. Use page 20 of the journal given in the *Working Papers*. Source documents are abbreviated as follows: check, C; memorandum, M.

Transactions:

Aug. 21. Paid cash to establish a petty cash fund, $200.00. C61.

24. Paid cash for repairs, $235.00. C62.

26. Paid cash for supplies, $40.00. C63.

27. Received notice from the bank of a dishonored check from Stacey Griffith, $35.00, plus $15.00 fee; total, $50.00. M22.

28. Paid cash for miscellaneous expense, $12.00. C64.

31. Paid cash to owner for personal use, $300.00. C65.

31. Paid cash to replenish the petty cash fund, $55.00: supplies, $35.00; miscellaneous expense, $20.00. C66.

2. On August 31 of the current year, LawnMow received a bank statement dated August 30. Prepare a bank statement reconciliation. Use August 31 of the current year as the date. The following information is obtained from the August 30 bank statement and from the records of the business.

Bank statement balance	$1,521.00
Bank service charge	5.00
Outstanding deposit, August 31	430.00
Outstanding checks, Nos. 65 and 66	
Checkbook balance on Check Stub No. 67	1,601.00

3. Continue using the journal and journalize the following transaction.

Transaction:

Aug. 31. Received bank statement showing August bank service charge, $5.00. M23.

6-6 CHALLENGE PROBLEM
Reconciling a bank statement and recording a bank service charge

Use the bank statement, canceled checks, and check stubs given in the *Working Papers.*

Instructions:

1. Compare the canceled checks with the check stubs. For each canceled check, place a check mark next to the appropriate check stub number. For each deposit shown on the bank statement, place a check mark next to the deposit amount on the appropriate check stub.
2. Prepare a bank statement reconciliation. Use August 29 of the current year as the date.
3. Record the following transactions on page 8 of a journal. The abbreviation for memorandum is M.

Transactions:

Sept. 1. Received bank statement showing August bank service charge, $5.00. M25.

1. Received notice from the bank of a dishonored check from Sheldon Martindale, $170.00, plus $5.00 fee; total, $175.00. M26.

4. Record the bank service charge and dishonored check on Check Stub No. 165.

INTERNET ACTIVITY

Point your browser to

http://accounting.swpco.com

Choose **First-Year Course**, choose **Activities**, and complete the activity for Chapter 6.

Applied Communication

All businesses are affected to some degree by issues and events that occur in the areas in which the businesses are located. For example, a city may gain an industry that will employ many people for a long time. Or, a town might build new roads or schools.

Instructions: Collect three to five newspaper or magazine articles about issues in your area that you think will affect local businesses. For each article, prepare a written list of consequences that a business might encounter.

Cases for Critical Thinking

Case 1

Iris Velez has a personal checking account for which she receives a bank statement every three months. She does not prepare a reconciliation. Sueanne Merker also has a personal checking account for which she receives bank statements once a month. She prepares a bank statement reconciliation for each bank statement received. Is Ms. Velez or Ms. Merker following the better procedure? Explain.

Case 2

Dorset Company decides to establish a petty cash fund. The owner, Edna Dorset, wants to establish a $100.00 petty cash fund and limit payments to $20.00 or less. The manager, Roy Evans, suggests a petty cash fund of $3,000.00 limited to payments of $50.00 or less. Mr. Evans claims this limit will help him avoid writing so many checks. Do you agree with Ms. Dorset or Mr. Evans? Explain.

AUTOMATED ACCOUNTING

AUTOMATED CASH CONTROL SYSTEMS

Cash transactions include those involving both cash in the bank and cash on hand. Because cash transactions occur so frequently, there are more chances to make recording errors. In each accounting period, cash account balances should be verified.

Cash kept on hand and used for making small payments is called *petty cash*. Each business must decide the appropriate dollar limit for payments from the petty cash fund. A check is written and cashed to transfer money to the petty cash account. Each time a payment is made from the petty cash fund, a form called a *petty cash slip* is prepared. A petty cash report is prepared, summarizing the petty cash slips, whenever the petty cash fund needs to be replenished. At that time the petty cash fund balance is verified, and journal entries are made to record the expenses paid from the fund.

In addition, completing a bank reconciliation verifies that the cash account balance in the bank equals the checkbook balance. Checkbook transactions should be compared to the bank statement each month. At that time, bank charges such as service charges and dishonored checks should be recorded.

The automated accounting system may be used to prepare the monthly bank reconciliation. Information maintained by the software, such as the checkbook balance and checks that were written during the period, will be automatically provided to make the reconciliation process simpler and more accurate.

While the *Automated Accounting 7.0* Help system contains detailed instructions, the bank statement can be reconciled to the checkbook balance in the following steps:

1. Choose the Other Activities menu item from the Data menu, or click on the Other toolbar button.
2. When the Reconciliation window appears, click on the Clear button to erase any previous data.
3. Enter the bank credit, bank charge, bank statement balance, and outstanding deposit amounts.
4. Checks written during the period are displayed in the Checks from the Journals list box. Select the outstanding checks by pointing and double-clicking. Each selected check will appear in the Outstanding Checks list and the Adjusted Bank Balance will automatically be updated.
5. Click the Report command button in the Reconciliation window to see the completed reconciliation.
6. Click the Close command button to dismiss the report window.
7. When the Bank Reconciliation reappears, click the OK command button to record your data and end the Bank Reconciliation process.

AUTOMATING APPLICATION PROBLEM 6-2: Reconciling a bank statement and recording a bank service charge

1. Load *Automated Accounting 7.0* or higher software.
2. Select database F06-1 from

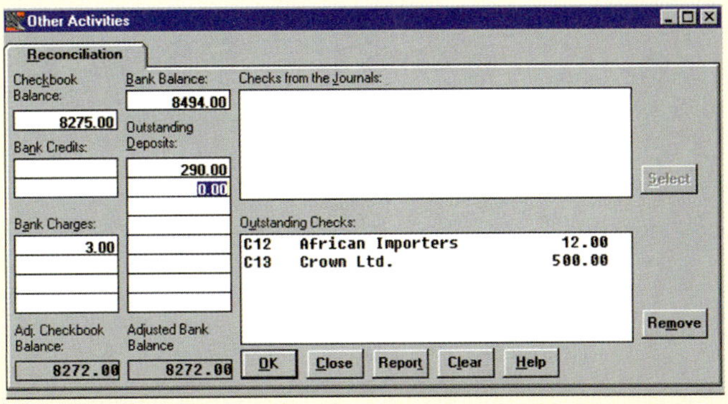

AUTOMATED ACCOUNTING

the appropriate directory/ folder.

3. Select File from the menu bar and choose the Save As menu command. Key the path to the drive and directory that contains your data files. Save the database with a file name of XXX061 (where XXX are your initials).
4. Access Problem Instructions through the Help menu (7.0) or Browser tool (8.0). Read the Problem Instructions screen.
5. Refer to page 146 for data used in this template.
6. Exit the *Automated Accounting* software.

AUTOMATING MASTERY PROBLEM 6-5: Reconciling a bank statement; journalizing a bank service charge, a dishonored check, and petty cash transactions

1. Load *Automated Accounting 7.0* or higher software.
2. Select database F06-2 from the appropriate directory/ folder.
3. Select File from the menu bar and choose the Save As menu command. Key the path to the drive and directory that contains your data files. Save the database with a file name of XXX062 (where XXX are your initials).
4. Access Problem Instructions through the Help menu (7.0) or Browser tool (8.0). Read the Problem Instructions screen.
5. Key the data listed on page 147.
6. Exit the *Automated Accounting* software.

Kellerman Services
Bank Reconciliation
11/01/--

Checkbook Balance			8275.00
Less Bank Charges:			
		3.00	
			3.00
Adjusted Checkbook Balance			8272.00
Bank Statement Balance			8494.00
Plus Outstanding Deposits:			
		290.00	
			290.00
Less Outstanding Checks:			
	C12	12.00	
	C13	500.00	
			512.00
Adjusted Bank Balance			8272.00

An Accounting Cycle for a Proprietorship: Journalizing and Posting Transactions

Reinforcement activities strengthen the learning of accounting concepts and procedures. Reinforcement Activity 1 is a single problem divided into two parts. Part A includes learnings from Chapters 1 through 6. Part B includes learnings from Chapters 7 through 9. An accounting cycle is completed in Parts A and B for a single business—The Fitness Center.

THE FITNESS CENTER

In May of the current year, Caleb Christianson starts a service business called The Fitness Center. The business provides exercise facilities for its clients. In addition, Mr. Christianson, a professional dietician, offers diet and exercise counseling for clients who request his assistance. The business rents the facilities in which it operates, pays the utilities, and is responsible for maintenance. The Fitness Center charges clients for each visit. Most of The Fitness Center's sales are for cash. However, two private schools use The Fitness Center for some physical education classes. These schools have an account with The Fitness Center.

CHART OF ACCOUNTS

The Fitness Center uses the following chart of accounts.

CHART OF ACCOUNTS

Balance Sheet Accounts

(100) ASSETS
110 Cash
120 Petty Cash
130 Accts. Rec.—Breck School
140 Accts. Rec.—Lincoln School
150 Supplies
160 Prepaid Insurance

(200) LIABILITIES
210 Accts. Pay.—Dunnel Supplies
220 Accts. Pay.—Voiles Office Supplies

(300) OWNER'S EQUITY
310 Caleb Christianson, Capital
320 Caleb Christianson, Drawing
330 Income Summary

Income Statement Accounts

(400) REVENUE
410 Sales

(500) EXPENSES
510 Advertising Expense
520 Insurance Expense
530 Miscellaneous Expense
540 Rent Expense
550 Repair Expense
560 Supplies Expense
570 Utilities Expense

RECORDING TRANSACTIONS

Instructions:

1. Journalize the following transactions completed during May of the current year. Use page 1 of the journal given in the *Working Papers.* Source documents are abbreviated as follows: check stub, C; memorandum, M; receipt, R; sales invoice, S; calculator tape, T.

May 1. Received cash from owner as an investment, $17,000.00. R1.
1. Paid cash for rent, $1,200.00. C1.
2. Paid cash for electric bill, $45.00. C2.
4. Paid cash for supplies, $400.00. C3.
4. Paid cash for insurance, $960.00. C4.
7. Bought supplies on account from Dunnel Supplies, $800.00. M1.
11. Paid cash to establish a petty cash fund, $200.00. C5.
12. Received cash from sales, $400.00. T12.
13. Paid cash for repairs, $25.00. C6.
13. Paid cash for miscellaneous expense, $35.00. C7.
13. Received cash from sales, $185.00. T13.
13. Sold services on account to Lincoln School, $150.00. S1.
14. Paid cash for advertising, $100.00. C8.
15. Paid cash to owner for personal use, $250.00. C9.
15. Paid cash on account to Dunnel Supplies, $300.00. C10.
15. Received cash from sales, $325.00. T15.
15. Sold services on account to Breck School, $335.00. S2.
18. Paid cash for miscellaneous expense, $100.00. C11.
18. Received cash on account from Lincoln School, $100.00. R2.
19. Received cash from sales, $155.00. T19.
20. Paid cash for repairs, $125.00. C12.
20. Bought supplies on account from Voiles Office Supplies, $150.00. M2.

2. Prove and rule page 1 of the journal. Carry the column totals forward to page 2 of the journal.

3. Post the separate amounts on each line of page 1 of the journal that need to be posted individually.

4. Use page 2 of the journal. Journalize the following transactions.

May 21. Paid cash for water bill, $110.00. C13.
21. Received cash from sales, $235.00. T21.
25. Paid cash for supplies, $50.00. C14.
25. Received cash from sales, $295.00. T25.
26. Paid cash for miscellaneous expense, $25.00. C15.
26. Received cash on account from Breck School, $200.00. R3.
27. Received cash from sales, $195.00. T27.
28. Paid cash for telephone bill, $210.00. C16.
28. Received cash from sales, $275.00. T28.

5. The Fitness Center received a bank statement dated May 27. The following information is obtained from the bank statement and from the records of the business. Prepare a bank statement reconciliation. Use May 29 as the date.

Bank statement balance	$15,227.00
Bank service charge	13.00
Outstanding deposit, May 28	275.00
Outstanding checks:	
No. 14	50.00
No. 15	25.00
No. 16	210.00
Checkbook balance on Check Stub No. 17	15,230.00

6. Continue using page 2 of the journal, and journalize the following transactions.

May 29. Received bank statement showing May bank service charge, $13.00. M3.
29. Paid cash for supplies, $60.00. C17.
29. Received cash from sales, $740.00. T29.
31. Paid cash to replenish the petty cash fund, $17.00: miscellaneous expense, $10.00; repairs, $7.00. C18.
31. Paid cash to owner for personal use, $250.00. C19.
31. Received cash from sales, $780.00. T31.

7. Prove page 2 of the journal.

8. Prove cash. The beginning cash balance on May 1 is zero. The balance on the next unused check stub is $16,410.00.

9. Rule page 2 of the journal.

10. Post the separate amounts on each line of page 2 of the journal that need to be posted individually.

11. Post the column totals on page 2 of the journal.

The general ledger prepared in Reinforcement Activity 1—Part A is needed to complete Reinforcement Activity 1—Part B.

7 Work Sheet for a Service Business

AFTER STUDYING CHAPTER 7, YOU WILL BE ABLE TO:

1. Define accounting terms related to a work sheet for a service business organized as a proprietorship.
2. Identify accounting concepts and practices related to a work sheet for a service business organized as a proprietorship.
3. Prepare a heading and a trial balance on a work sheet.
4. Plan adjustments for supplies and prepaid insurance.
5. Complete a work sheet for a service business organized as a proprietorship.
6. Identify selected procedures for finding and correcting errors in accounting records.

TERMS PREVIEW

fiscal period
work sheet
trial balance
adjustments
income statement
net income
net loss

CONSISTENT REPORTING

General ledger accounts contain information needed by managers and owners. Before the information can be used, however, it must be analyzed, summarized, and reported in a meaningful way. The accounting concept, *Consistent Reporting,* is applied when the same accounting procedures are followed in the same way in each accounting period. *(CONCEPT: Consistent Reporting)* For example, in one year a delivery business might report the number of deliveries made. The next year the same business reports the amount of revenue received for the deliveries made. The information for the two years cannot be compared because the business has not been consistent in reporting information about deliveries.

A summary of preparing a work sheet is shown on the Work Sheet Overlay within this chapter.

ACCOUNTING IN YOUR CAREER

NETWORKING ON WORK SHEETS

Darnell Gleason, an administrative assistant at Micelli Tailoring, has been having a good time at the five-year reunion of his high school class. He has caught up with old friends and is surprised to find some familiar careers represented at the reunion today. He has been talking with Rebecca Fong, an employee at Watson Associates, a small marketing consulting company in town. Charles King, accounting assistant with Kovell Advertising, joins them.

Darnell tells Charles that he and Rebecca have been discussing their accounting procedures and had just started talking about preparing work sheets. He says that he does a standard work sheet on 8-column paper with columns for trial balance, adjustments, income statement, and balance sheet. Rebecca immediately says, "Darnell, you still use paper and pencil? I've designed a computer spreadsheet so that whenever I want to do a work sheet, all I have to do is plug in the numbers and all the calculations are done automatically. And if I change one of the numbers, the calculations are updated immediately."

Charles smiles and says, "My company has only one adjustment to make each month, so I don't do a work sheet at all. I run a trial balance, calculate my new adjustment, journalize it and post it, then do another trial balance just to be sure the debits and credits are still equal. Then I'm ready to do the financial statements."

Darnell has never considered other ways of preparing a work sheet. "You two have given me some ideas I think I can use," he tells Rebecca and Charles. "I guess we're networking. What would you think about getting together regularly to share ideas?"

Critical Thinking:

1. Is it ethical for employees to share information about their companies this way?
2. What are the advantages and disadvantages of using a computer to perform accounting procedures?

7-1 Creating a Work Sheet

FISCAL PERIODS

The length of time for which a business summarizes and reports financial information is called a **fiscal period** (also known as an accounting period). Businesses usually select a period of time for which to summarize and report financial information. The accounting concept, *Accounting Period Cycle,* is applied when changes in financial information are reported for a specific period of time in the form of financial statements. *(CONCEPT: Accounting Period Cycle)* Each business chooses a fiscal period length that meets its needs. Because federal and state tax reports are based on one year, most businesses use a one-year fiscal period. However, because Encore Music is a new business, Ms. Treviño wishes to have financial information reported frequently to help her make decisions. For this reason, Encore Music uses a one-month fiscal period.

A fiscal period can begin on any date. However, most businesses begin their fiscal periods on the first day of a month. Encore Music started business on August 1. Therefore, Encore Music's monthly fiscal period is for the period from August 1 through August 31, inclusive. Businesses often choose a one-year fiscal period that ends during a period of low business activity. In this way, the end-of-year accounting work comes at a time when other business activities are the lightest.

Financial information may be analyzed, summarized, and reported on any date a business needs the information. However, financial information is always summarized and reported at the end of a fiscal period.

WORK SHEET

A columnar accounting form used to summarize the general ledger information needed to prepare financial statements is called a **work sheet.**

Accountants use a work sheet for four reasons. (1) To summarize general ledger account balances to prove that debits equal credits. (2) To plan needed changes to general ledger accounts to bring account balances up to date. (3) To separate general ledger account balances according to the financial statements to be prepared. (4) To calculate the amount of net income or net loss for a fiscal period.

Journals and ledgers are permanent records of a business and are usually prepared in ink or printed by a computer. However, a work sheet is a planning tool and is not considered a permanent accounting record. Therefore, a work sheet is prepared in pencil.

PREPARING THE HEADING OF A WORK SHEET

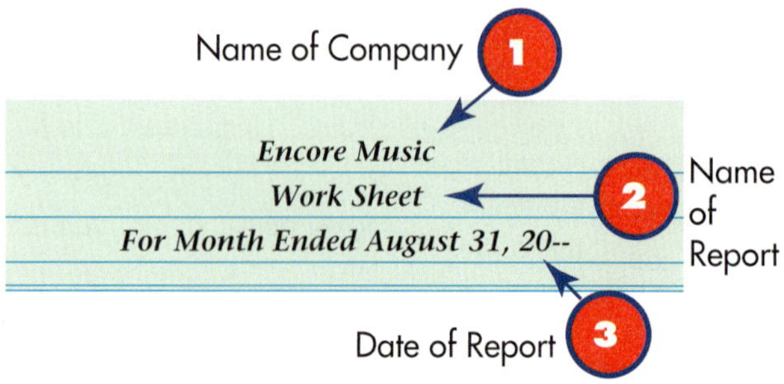

The heading on a work sheet consists of three lines and contains the name of the business, the name of the report, and the date of the report.

The date on Encore Music's work sheet indicates that the work sheet covers the 31 days from August 1 through and including August 31. If a work sheet were for a calendar year fiscal period, it might have a date stated as *For Year Ended December 31, 20—.*

PREPARING A TRIAL BALANCE ON A WORK SHEET

Encore Music
Work Sheet
For Month Ended August 31, 20--

	ACCOUNT TITLE	1 TRIAL BALANCE DEBIT	2 TRIAL BALANCE CREDIT
1	*Cash*	8272 00	
2	*Petty Cash*	200 00	
3	*Accounts Receivable—Kids Time*	100 00	
4	*Accounts Receivable—Learn N Play*	20 00	
5	*Supplies*	4751 00	
6	*Prepaid Insurance*	1200 00	
7	*Accounts Payable—Ling Music Supplies*		1360 00
8	*Accounts Payable—Sullivan Office Supplies*		20 00
9	*Barbara Treviño, Capital*		10000 00
10	*Barbara Treviño, Drawing*	600 00	
11	*Income Summary*		
12	*Sales*		4411 00
13	*Advertising Expense*	273 00	
14	*Insurance Expense*		
15	*Miscellaneous Expense*	10 00	
16	*Rent Expense*	250 00	
17	*Supplies Expense*		
18	*Utilities Expense*	115 00	
19	Add Totals	15791 00	15791 00
20			

1 Account Titles
2 Account Balances
3 Single Rule
4 Add Totals
5 Write Totals
6 Double Rule

The total of all debit account balances must equal the total of all credit account balances. A proof of the equality of debits and credits in a general ledger is called a **trial balance.**

Information for the trial balance is taken from the general ledger. General ledger account titles are listed on a trial balance in the same order as listed on the chart of accounts. All the account titles are listed, even if some accounts do not have balances.

STEPS Preparing a trial balance on a work sheet

1. Write the general ledger account titles in the work sheet's Account Title column.
2. Write the general ledger debit account balances in the Trial Balance Debit column. Write the general ledger credit account balances in the Trial Balance Credit column. If an account does not have a balance, the space in the Trial Balance columns is left blank.
3. Rule a single line across the two Trial Balance columns below the last line on which an account title is written. This single line shows that each column is to be added.
4. Add both the Trial Balance Debit and Credit columns. Use a calculator if one is available. If the two column totals are the same, then debits equal credits in the general ledger accounts. If the two column totals are not the same, recheck the Trial Balance columns to find the error. Other parts of a work sheet are not completed until the Trial Balance columns are proved. Suggestions for locating errors are described later in this chapter.
5. Write each column's total below the single line.
6. Rule double lines across both Trial Balance columns. The double lines mean that the Trial Balance column totals have been verified as correct.

TERMS REVIEW

fiscal period
work sheet
trial balance

AUDIT YOUR UNDERSTANDING

1. What is written on the three-line heading on a work sheet?
2. What general ledger accounts are listed in the Trial Balance columns of a work sheet?

WORK TOGETHER

Recording the trial balance on a work sheet

Use the work sheet given in the *Working Papers*. Your instructor will guide you through the following example.

On February 28 of the current year, Golden Tan has the following general ledger accounts and balances. The business uses a monthly fiscal period.

Account Titles	Account Balances	
	Debit	Credit
Cash	$9,800.00	
Petty Cash	150.00	
Accounts Receivable—Ruby Prince	2,795.00	
Supplies	456.00	
Prepaid Insurance	750.00	
Accounts Payable—Richard Navarro		$ 555.00
Gary Baldwin, Capital		14,885.00
Gary Baldwin, Drawing	3,400.00	
Income Summary	—	—
Sales		4,320.00
Advertising Expense	931.00	
Insurance Expense	—	
Miscellaneous Expense	378.00	
Supplies Expense	—	
Utilities Expense	1,100.00	

3. Prepare the heading and trial balance on a work sheet. Total and rule the Trial Balance columns. Save your work to complete Work Together on page 164.

ON YOUR OWN

Recording the trial balance on a work sheet

Use the work sheet given in the *Working Papers.* Work this problem independently.

On December 31 of the current year, Cragan's Copies has the following general ledger accounts and balances. The business uses a monthly fiscal period.

Account Titles	Account Balances	
	Debit	Credit
Cash	$6,900.00	
Petty Cash	75.00	
Accounts Receivable—Ross Kim	1,398.00	
Supplies	228.00	
Prepaid Insurance	375.00	
Accounts Payable—Renee Elk		$ 278.00
Lana Arola, Capital		7,443.00
Lana Arola, Drawing	1,700.00	
Income Summary	—	—
Sales		4,160.00
Advertising Expense	466.00	
Insurance Expense	—	
Miscellaneous Expense	189.00	
Supplies Expense	—	
Utilities Expense	550.00	

4. Prepare the heading and trial balance on a work sheet. Total and rule the Trial Balance columns. Save your work to complete On Your Own on page 164.

7-2 Planning Adjusting Entries on a Work Sheet

PLANNING ADJUSTMENTS ON A WORK SHEET

Sometimes a business will pay cash for an expense in one fiscal period, but the expense is not used until a later period. The expense should be reported in the same fiscal period that it is used to produce revenue. The accounting concept, *Matching Expenses with Revenue,* is applied when revenue from business activities and expenses associated with earning that revenue are recorded in the same accounting period. For example, Encore Music buys supplies in quantity in August, but some of the supplies are not used until September. Only the value of the supplies used in August should be reported as expenses in August. In this way, August revenue and the supplies expense associated with earning the August revenue are recorded in the same accounting period. *(CONCEPT: Matching Expenses with Revenue)*

In order to give accurate information on financial statements, some general ledger accounts must be brought up to date at the end of a fiscal period. For example, Encore Music debits an asset account, Supplies, each time supplies are bought. Supplies on hand are items of value owned by a business until the supplies are used. The value of supplies that are used becomes an expense to the business. However, recording an expense each time an individual supply, such as a pencil, is used would be impractical. Therefore, on August 31 the balance of the asset account, Supplies, is the value of all supplies bought rather than the value of only the supplies that have not yet been used. The amount of supplies that have been used must be deducted from the asset account, Supplies, and recorded in the expense account, Supplies Expense.

Likewise, the amount of insurance that has been used during the fiscal period is also an expense of the business. When the insurance premium for a year of insurance coverage is paid, the entire amount is debited to an asset account, Prepaid Insurance. Recording each day's amount of insurance used during August is impractical. Therefore, at the end of a fiscal period, the amount of the insurance coverage used must be deducted from the asset account, Prepaid Insurance, and recorded in the expense account, Insurance Expense.

Changes recorded on a work sheet to update general ledger accounts at the end of a fiscal period are called **adjustments.** The assets of a business, such as supplies and prepaid insurance, are used to earn revenue. The portions of the assets consumed in order to earn revenue become expenses of the business. The portions consumed are no longer assets but are now expenses. Therefore, adjustments must be made to both the asset and expense accounts for supplies and insurance. After the adjustments are made, the expenses incurred to earn revenue are reported in the same fiscal period as the revenue is earned and reported. *(CONCEPT: Matching Expenses with Revenue)*

A work sheet is used to plan adjustments. Changes are not made in general ledger accounts until adjustments are journalized and posted. The accuracy of the planning for adjustments is checked on a work sheet before adjustments are actually journalized.

Procedures for journalizing Encore Music's adjustments are described in Chapter 9.

REMEMBER

The ending balance of the asset account, Supplies, should represent the amount of supplies remaining on hand at the end of the fiscal period. The amount of supplies used during the period should be recorded in the expense account, Supplies Expense.

SUMMARY OF PREPARATION OF A WORK SHEET FOR A SERVICE BUSINESS

The following overlay summarizes the preparation of a work sheet. Follow the directions below in using the overlay.

1. Before using the overlay, be sure the pages and transparent overlays are arranged correctly. The correct arrangement is shown below.

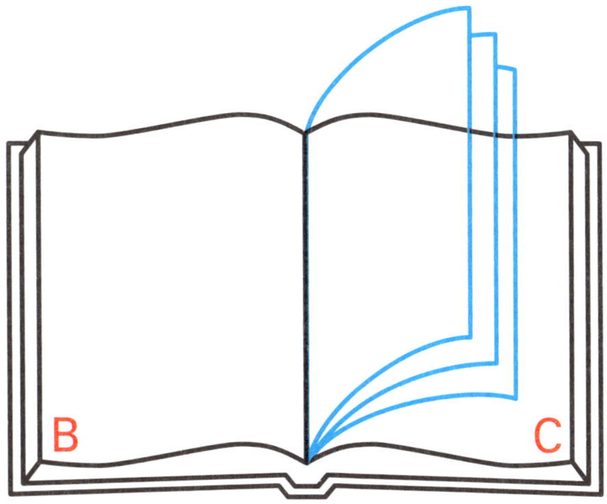

2. Place your book in a horizontal position. Study the steps on page C in preparing the work sheet. You will be able to read the text through the transparent overlays. When directed, carefully lift the transparent overlays and lay them over the work sheet as shown below.

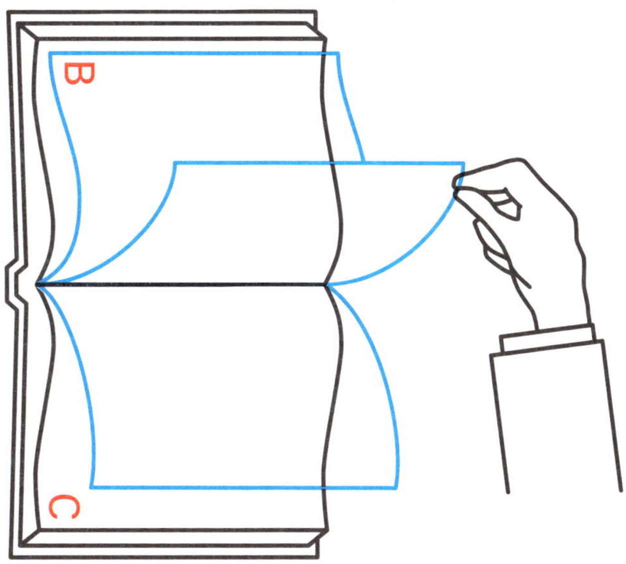

PREPARING A WORK SHEET

To correctly use the insert, read the steps on page C. Apply the transparent overlays when directed to do so in the steps.

Encore Music
Work Sheet
For Month Ended August 31, 20--

(1) → heading; (2) → account title

	ACCOUNT TITLE	1 TRIAL BALANCE DEBIT	2 TRIAL BALANCE CREDIT	3 ADJUSTMENTS DEBIT	4 ADJUSTMENTS CREDIT	5 INCOME STATEMENT DEBIT	6 INCOME STATEMENT CREDIT	7 BALANCE SHEET DEBIT	8 BALANCE SHEET CREDIT	
1	Cash	8,272 00								1
2	Petty Cash	200 00								2
3	Accounts Receivable—Kids Time	100 00								3
4	Accounts Receivable—Learn N Play	20 00								4
5	Supplies	4,751 00								5
6	Prepaid Insurance	1,200 00								6
7	Accounts Payable—Ling Music Supplies		1,360 00							7
8	Accounts Payable—Sullivan Office Supplies		20 00							8
9	Barbara Treviño, Capital		10,000 00							9
10	Barbara Treviño, Drawing	600 00								10
11	Income Summary									11
12	Sales		4,411 00							12
13	Advertising Expense	273 00								13
14	Insurance Expense									14
15	Miscellaneous Expense	10 00								15
16	Rent Expense	250 00								16
17	Supplies Expense									17
18	Utilities Expense	115 00								18
19		15,791 00	15,791 00							19
20										20
21										21
22										22
23										23
24										24
25										25

PREPARING A WORK SHEET

1. Write the heading.

2. Record the trial balance.

- Write the general ledger account titles in the Account Title column.
- Write the account balances in either the Trial Balance Debit or Credit column.
- Rule a single line across the Trial Balance columns.
- Add the Trial Balance columns and compare the totals.
- Rule double lines across both Trial Balance columns.
- *Carefully apply the first overlay.*

3. Record the supplies adjustment.

- Write the debit amount in the Adjustments Debit column on the line with the account title Supplies Expense.
- Write the credit amount in the Adjustments Credit column on the line with the account title Supplies.
- Label this adjustment *(a)*.

4. Record the prepaid insurance adjustment.

- Write the debit amount in the Adjustments Debit column on the line with the account title Insurance Expense.
- Write the credit amount in the Adjustments Credit column on the line with the account title Prepaid Insurance.
- Label this adjustment *(b)*.

5. Prove the Adjustments columns.

- Rule a single line across the Adjustments columns.
- Add the Adjustments columns and compare the totals to ensure that they are equal.
- Write the proving totals below the single line.
- Rule double lines across both Adjustments columns.
- *Carefully apply the second overlay.*

6. Extend all balance sheet account balances.

- Extend the up-to-date asset account balances to the Balance Sheet Debit column.
- Extend the up-to-date liability account balances to the Balance Sheet Credit column.
- Extend the owner's capital and drawing account balances to the Balance Sheet columns.

7. Extend all income statement account balances.

- Extend the up-to-date revenue account balance to the Income Statement Credit column.
- Extend the up-to-date expense account balances to the Income Statement Debit column.
- *Carefully apply the third overlay.*

8. Calculate and record the net income (or net loss).

- Rule a single line across the Income Statement and Balance Sheet columns.
- Add the columns and write the totals below the single line.
- Calculate the net income or net loss amount.
- Write the amount of net income (or net loss) below the smaller of the two Income Statement column totals. Write the words *Net Income* or *Net Loss* in the Account Title column.
- Extend the amount of net income (or net loss) to the Balance Sheet columns. Write the amount under the smaller of the two column totals. Write the amount on the same line as the words *Net Income* (or *Net Loss*).

9. Total and rule the Income Statement and Balance Sheet columns.

- Rule a single line across the Income Statement and Balance Sheet columns immediately below the net income (or net loss) amounts.
- Add the net income (or net loss) to the previous column totals. Compare the column totals to ensure that totals for each pair of columns are in balance.
- Write the proving totals for each column below the single line.
- Rule double lines across the Income Statement and Balance Sheet columns immediately below the proving totals.

Legal Issues in Accounting

Malpractice Liability of Accountants

Accountants are subject to the legal consequences of malpractice. They can be held financially liable for misconduct or improper practice in their profession.

Most lawsuits against public accountants involve audits of financial statements. Consider the following example. Best & Farrish, CPAs, audited the financial statements of Richmond, Inc. Relying on these statements, American Bank loaned $1,000,000 to Richmond. Unknown to the accountants, however, Richmond's president was involved in a scheme to steal cash. Richmond experienced financial difficulties and was unable to repay the loan to American Bank. The bank sued Best & Farrish for $1,000,000, claiming it was negligent for not detecting the president's fraud.

Should Best & Farrish be required to pay $1,000,000 to American Bank? Over many years the courts have established four guidelines for determining whether accountants are liable for the financial losses of third parties.

1. *Financial loss.* Did the third party incur a financial loss? Answering this question is typically an easy task. American Bank lost $1,000,000 when Richmond did not repay its loan.
2. *Reliance on financial statements.* Did the third party actually rely on the financial statements for making its decision? Accountants should not be held liable unless the third party used the financial statements in making its decision. If American Bank received a copy of the financial statements but relied solely on other information obtained from Richmond's managers, then Best & Farrish should not be held liable for American Bank's loss.
3. *Level of negligence.* Accountants who fail to exhibit a reasonable level of care are guilty of ordinary negligence. Gross negligence occurs when an accountant's actions represent a flagrant violation of professional standards.

   Professional standards recognize that accountants are not able to detect all frauds. Whether Best & Farrish were negligent in not detecting the president's fraud would depend on the facts of the case.
4. *Accountant-third party relationship.* Accountants have a contract with their clients; a client can sue the accountant for breach of contract. However, third parties do not have a contract with the accountant. Whether a third party can sue the accountant depends on whether the accountant specifically knew the third party intended to use the financial statements.

   If Best & Farrish knew American Bank would use the audited financial statements to grant a loan, then American Bank could sue Best & Farrish for ordinary negligence. However, if Best & Farrish did not know Richmond even intended to obtain a bank loan, then gross negligence or fraud would need to be proven for American Bank to win its case.

Accountants must take great care in performing their professional services. Accountants who can prove the audit was performed in accordance with professional accounting standards will prevail against negligence lawsuits.

SUPPLIES ADJUSTMENT ON A WORK SHEET

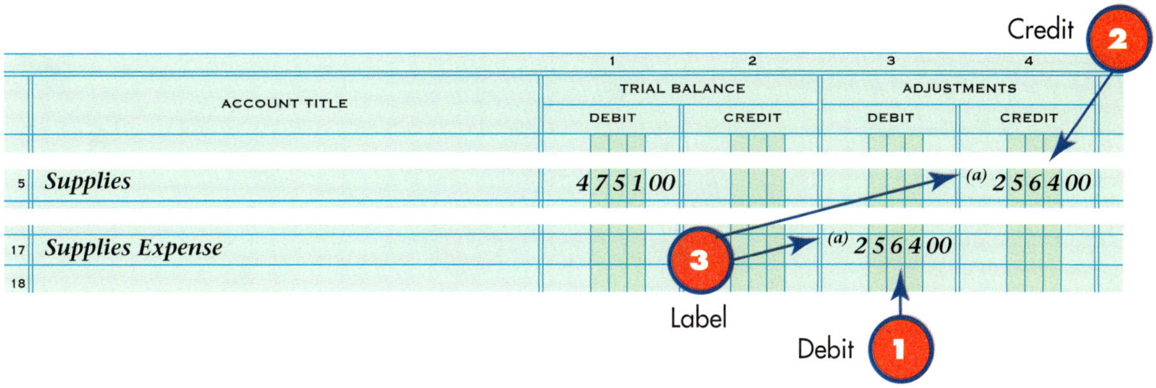

On August 31, before adjustments, the balance of Supplies is $4,751.00, and the balance of Supplies Expense is zero, as shown in the T accounts.

BEFORE ADJUSTMENT

Supplies Expense

Supplies

Aug. 31 Bal. 4,751.00	

On August 31, Ms. Treviño counted the supplies on hand and found that the value of supplies still unused on that date was $2,187.00. The value of the supplies used is calculated as follows.

Supplies Account Balance, August 31	–	Supplies on Hand, August 31	=	Supplies Used During August
$4,751.00	–	$2,187.00	=	$2,564.00

Four questions are asked in analyzing the adjustment for the asset account, Supplies.

1. **What is the balance of** Supplies? *$4,751.00*
2. **What should the balance be for this account?** *$2,187.00*
3. **What must be done to correct the account balance?** *Decrease $2,564.00*
4. **What adjustment is made?**
   Debit Supplies Expense, *$2,564.00*
   Credit Supplies, *$2,564.00*

The expense account, Supplies Expense, is increased by a debit, $2,564.00, the value of supplies used. The balance of Supplies Expense, $2,564.00, is the value of supplies used during the fiscal period from August 1 to August 31. *(CONCEPT: Matching Expenses with Revenue)*

AFTER ADJUSTMENT

Supplies Expense

Adj. (a) 2,564.00	

Supplies

Aug. 31 Bal. 4,751.00 *(New Bal. 2,187.00)*	Adj. (a) 2,564.00

The asset account, Supplies, is decreased by a credit, $2,564.00, the value of supplies used. The debit balance, $4,751.00, *less* the credit adjustment, $2,564.00, *equals* the new balance, $2,187.00. The new balance of Supplies is the same as the value of supplies on hand on August 31.

STEPS: Recording the supplies adjustment on a work sheet

1. Write the debit amount, *$2,564.00,* in the work sheet's Adjustments Debit column on the line with the account title Supplies Expense.
2. Write the credit amount, *$2,564.00,* in the Adjustments Credit column on the line with the account title Supplies.
3. Label the two parts of this adjustment with a small letter *a* in parentheses, *(a)*. The letter *a* identifies the debit and credit amounts as part of the same adjustment.

PREPAID INSURANCE ADJUSTMENT ON A WORK SHEET

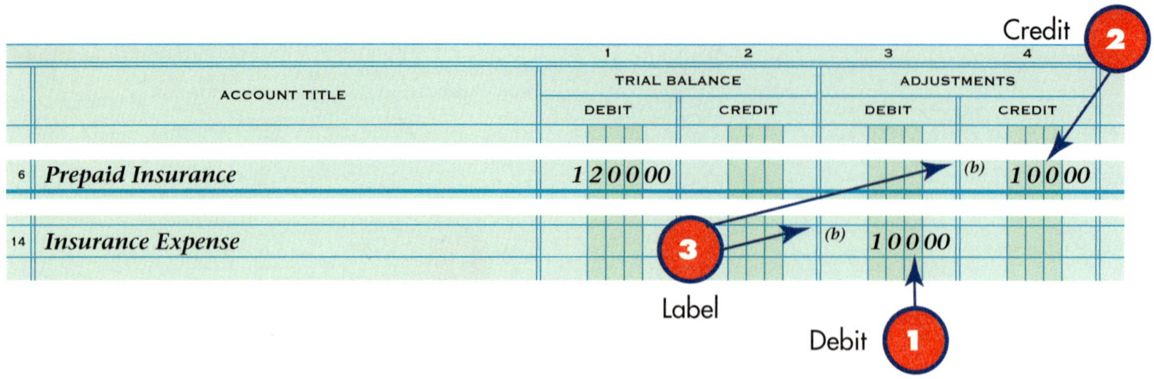

On August 31, before adjustments, the balance of Prepaid Insurance is $1,200.00 and the balance of Insurance Expense is zero.

BEFORE ADJUSTMENT

Insurance Expense	

Prepaid Insurance	
Aug. 31 Bal. 1,200.00	

On August 31, Ms. Treviño checked the insurance records and found that the value of insurance coverage remaining was $1,100.00. The value of the insurance coverage used during the fiscal period is calculated as follows.

Prepaid Insurance Balance, August 31	–	Insurance Coverage Remaining Unused, August 31	=	Insurance Coverage Used During August
$1,200.00	–	$1,100.00	=	$100.00

Four questions are asked in analyzing the adjustment for the asset account, Prepaid Insurance.

1. **What is the balance of** Prepaid Insurance**?** *$1,200.00*
2. **What should the balance be for this account?** *$1,100.00*
3. **What must be done to correct the account balance?** *Decrease $100.00*
4. **What adjustment is made?**
   Debit Insurance Expense, *$100.00*
   Credit Prepaid Insurance, *$100.00*

The expense account, Insurance Expense, is increased by a debit, $100.00, the value of insurance used. The balance of Insurance Expense, $100.00, is the value of insurance coverage used from August 1 to August 31. *(CONCEPT: Matching Expenses with Revenue)*

AFTER ADJUSTMENT

Insurance Expense	
Adj. (b) 100.00	

Prepaid Insurance	
Aug. 31 Bal. 1,200.00	Adj. (b) 100.00
(New Bal. 1,100.00)	

The asset account, Prepaid Insurance, is decreased by a credit, $100.00, the value of insurance used. The debit balance, $1,200.00, *less* the credit adjustment, $100.00, *equals* the new balance, $1,100.00. The new balance of Prepaid Insurance is the same as the amount of insurance coverage unused on August 31.

STEPS: Recording the prepaid insurance adjustment on a work sheet

1. Write the debit amount, *$100.00,* in the work sheet's Adjustments Debit column on the line with the account title Insurance Expense.
2. Write the credit amount, *$100.00,* in the Adjustments Credit column on the line with the account title Prepaid Insurance.
3. Label the two parts of this adjustment with a small letter *b* in parentheses, *(b)*. The letter *b* identifies the debit and credit amounts as part of the same adjustment.

PROVING THE ADJUSTMENTS COLUMNS OF A WORK SHEET

Encore Music
Work Sheet
For Month Ended August 31, 20--

	ACCOUNT TITLE	1 TRIAL BALANCE DEBIT	2 TRIAL BALANCE CREDIT	3 ADJUSTMENTS DEBIT	4 ADJUSTMENTS CREDIT
5	Supplies	4751 00			(a) 2564 00
6	Prepaid Insurance	1200 00			(b) 100 00
14	Insurance Expense			(b) 100 00	
15	Miscellaneous Expense	10 00			
16	Rent Expense	250 00			
17	Supplies Expense			(a) 2564 00	
18	Utilities Expense	115 00			
19		15791 00	15791 00	2664 00	2664 00

1 Single Rule

2 Totals

3 Double Rule

After all adjustments are recorded in a work sheet's Adjustments columns, the equality of debits and credits for the two columns is proved by totaling and ruling the two columns.

STEPS: Proving the Adjustments columns of a work sheet

1. Rule a single line across the two Adjustments columns on the same line as the single line for the Trial Balance columns.
2. Add both the Adjustments Debit and Credit columns. If the two column totals are the same, then debits equal credits for these two columns, and the work sheet's Adjustments columns are in balance. Write each column's total below the single line. If the two Adjustments column totals are not the same, the Adjustments columns are rechecked and errors corrected before completing the work sheet.
3. Rule double lines across both Adjustments columns. The double lines mean that the totals have been verified as correct.

GLOBAL PERSPECTIVE

INTERNATIONAL WEIGHTS AND MEASURES

The primary system of measurement in the United States is the *customary system.* Among the units of measurement in the customary system are inches, feet, and quarts. The United States is one of the few major industrial countries that does not use the *metric system* exclusively. Among the units of measurement in the metric system are centimeters, meters, and liters. The metric system is based on a decimal system—like our currency. Some U.S. industries have converted to the metric system. Others specify measurements in both customary and metric systems.

To conduct international business, the U.S. has recognized the need to convert customary units to the metric system. For example, beverages are routinely packaged in liter containers. Automobile mechanics frequently need two sets of socket wrenches—one in the customary system and an additional set in the metric system. Although the U.S. is a global business leader, it has had to adjust to meet the needs of the rest of the world.

TERMS REVIEW

adjustments

vitz

AUDIT YOUR UNDERSTANDING

1. Explain how the concept of Matching Expenses with Revenue relates to adjustments.
2. List the four questions asked in analyzing an adjustment on a work sheet.

WORK TOGETHER

Planning adjustments on a work sheet

Use the work sheet from Work Together on page 158. Your instructor will guide you through the following examples.

3. Analyze the following adjustment information into debit and credit parts. Record the adjustments on the work sheet.

Adjustment Information, February 28

Supplies on hand	$325.00
Value of prepaid insurance	500.00

4. Total and rule the Adjustments columns. Save your work sheet to complete Work Together on page 169.

ON YOUR OWN

Planning adjustments on a work sheet

Use the work sheet from On Your Own on page 159. Work these problems independently.

5. Analyze the following adjustment information into debit and credit parts. Record the adjustments on the work sheet.

Adjustment Information, December 31

Supplies on hand	$130.00
Value of prepaid insurance	250.00

6. Total and rule the Adjustments columns. Save your work sheet to complete On Your Own on page 169.

7-3 Extending Financial Statement Information on a Work Sheet

EXTENDING BALANCE SHEET ACCOUNT BALANCES ON A WORK SHEET

Encore Music
Work Sheet
For Month Ended August 31, 20--

	ACCOUNT TITLE	1 TRIAL BALANCE DEBIT	2 TRIAL BALANCE CREDIT	3 ADJUSTMENTS DEBIT	4 ADJUSTMENTS CREDIT	5 INCOME STATEMENT DEBIT	6 INCOME STATEMENT CREDIT	7 BALANCE SHEET DEBIT	8 BALANCE SHEET CREDIT	
1	Cash	8272 00						8272 00		1
2	Petty Cash	200 00						200 00		2
3	Accts. Rec.—Kids Time	100 00						100 00		3
4	Accts. Rec.—Learn N Play	20 00						20 00		4
5	Supplies	4751 00			(a) 2564 00			2187 00		5
6	Prepaid Insurance	1200 00			(b) 100 00			1100 00		6
7	Accts. Pay.—Ling Music Sup.		1360 00						1360 00	7
8	Accts. Pay.—Sullivan Off. Sup.		20 00						20 00	8
9	Barbara Treviño, Capital		10000 00						10000 00	9
10	Barbara Treviño, Drawing	600 00						600 00		10

1 Debit Balances without Adjustments

2 Debit Balances with Adjustments

3 Credit Balances without Adjustments

At the end of each fiscal period, Encore Music prepares two financial statements from information on a work sheet. *(CONCEPT: Accounting Period Cycle)* The up-to-date account balances on a work sheet are extended to columns for the two financial statements.

A financial statement that reports assets, liabilities, and owner's equity on a specific date is known as a balance sheet. The balance sheet accounts are the asset, liability, and owner's equity accounts. Up-to-date balance sheet account balances are extended to the Balance Sheet Debit and Credit columns of the work sheet.

STEPS: Extending balance sheet account balances on a work sheet

1. Extend the balance of Cash, *$8,272.00,* to the Balance Sheet Debit column. The balance of Cash in the Trial Balance Debit column is up to date because no adjustment affects this account. Extend to the Balance Sheet Debit column the balances of all accounts with debit balances, which are not affected by adjustments.
2. Calculate the up-to-date adjusted balance of Supplies. The balance of Supplies in the Trial Balance Debit column is not up to date because it is affected by an adjustment. The debit balance, $4,751.00, *minus* the credit adjustment, $2,564.00, *equals* the up-to-date adjusted balance, $2,187.00. Extend the up-to-date balance, *$2,187.00,* to the Balance Sheet Debit column. Using the same procedure, calculate and extend the up-to-date adjusted balance of the other asset account affected by an adjustment, Prepaid Insurance.
3. Extend the up-to-date balance of Accounts Payable—Ling Music Supplies, *$1,360.00,* to the Balance Sheet Credit column. The balance of Accounts Payable—Ling Music Supplies in the Trial Balance Credit column is up to date because no adjustment affects this account. Extend to the Balance Sheet Credit column the balances of all accounts with credit balances, which are not affected by adjustments.

EXTENDING INCOME STATEMENT ACCOUNT BALANCES ON A WORK SHEET

Expense Balances without Adjustments **2** **1** Sales Balance

Encore Music
Work Sheet
For Month Ended August 31, 20--

	ACCOUNT TITLE	1 TRIAL BALANCE DEBIT	2 TRIAL BALANCE CREDIT	3 ADJUSTMENTS DEBIT	4 ADJUSTMENTS CREDIT	5 INCOME STATEMENT DEBIT	6 INCOME STATEMENT CREDIT	7 BALANCE SHEET DEBIT	8 BALANCE SHEET CREDIT	
11	*Income Summary*									11
12	*Sales*		4411 00				4411 00			12
13	*Advertising Expense*	273 00				273 00				13
14	*Insurance Expense*			(b) 100 00		100 00				14
15	*Miscellaneous Expense*	10 00				10 00				15
16	*Rent Expense*	250 00				250 00				16
17	*Supplies Expense*			(a) 2564 00		2564 00				17
18	*Utilities Expense*	115 00				115 00				18
19		15791 00	15791 00	2664 00	2664 00					19
20										20

Expense Balances with Adjustments **3**

A financial statement showing the revenue and expenses for a fiscal period is called an **income statement.** Encore Music's income statement accounts are the revenue and expense accounts. Up-to-date income statement account balances are extended to the Income Statement Debit and Credit columns of the work sheet.

F Y I

Use a ruler when extending amounts on a work sheet to keep track of the line you are on.

STEPS

Extending income statement account balances on a work sheet

1. Extend the balance of Sales, *$4,411.00,* to the Income Statement Credit column. The balance of Sales in the Trial Balance Credit column is up to date because no adjustment affects this account.
2. Extend the balance of Advertising Expense, *$273.00,* to the Income Statement Debit column. The balance of Advertising Expense is up to date because no adjustment affects this account. Extend the balances of all expense accounts not affected by adjustments to the Income Statement Debit column.
3. Calculate the up-to-date adjusted balance of Insurance Expense. The balance of Insurance Expense in the Trial Balance Debit column is zero. This zero balance is not up to date because this account is affected by an adjustment. The debit balance, $0.00, *plus* the debit adjustment, $100.00, *equals* the adjusted balance, $100.00. Extend the up-to-date adjusted debit balance, *$100.00,* to the Income Statement Debit column. Using the same procedure, calculate and extend the up-to-date adjusted balance of each expense account affected by an adjustment.

F Y I

A work sheet is prepared in manual accounting to adjust the accounts and sort amounts needed to prepare financial statements. However, in automated accounting, adjustments are prepared from the trial balance and the software automatically generates the financial statements with no need for a work sheet.

RECORDING NET INCOME, AND TOTALING AND RULING A WORK SHEET

Encore Music
Work Sheet
For Month Ended August 31, 20--

	ACCOUNT TITLE	1 TRIAL BALANCE DEBIT	2 TRIAL BALANCE CREDIT	3 ADJUSTMENTS DEBIT	4 ADJUSTMENTS CREDIT	5 INCOME STATEMENT DEBIT	6 INCOME STATEMENT CREDIT	7 BALANCE SHEET DEBIT	8 BALANCE SHEET CREDIT	
1	Cash	8,272.00						8,272.00		1
2	Petty Cash	200.00						200.00		2
3	Accts. Rec.—Kids Time	100.00						100.00		3
4	Accts. Rec.—Learn N Play	20.00						20.00		4
5	Supplies	4,751.00			(a) 2,564.00			2,187.00		5
6	Prepaid Insurance	1,200.00			(b) 100.00			1,100.00		6
7	Accts. Pay.—Ling Music Sup.		1,360.00						1,360.00	7
8	Accts. Pay.—Sullivan Off. Sup.		20.00						20.00	8
9	Barbara Treviño, Capital		10,000.00						10,000.00	9
10	Barbara Treviño, Drawing	600.00						600.00		10
11	Income Summary									11
12	Sales		4,411.00				4,411.00			12
13	Advertising Expense	273.00				273.00				13
14	Insurance Expense			(b) 100.00		100.00				14
15	Miscellaneous Expense	10.00				10.00				15
16	Rent Expense	250.00				250.00				16
17	Supplies Expense			(a) 2,564.00		2,564.00				17
18	Utilities Expense	115.00				115.00				18
19		15,791.00	15,791.00	2,664.00	2,664.00	3,312.00	4,411.00	12,479.00	11,380.00	19
20	Net Income					1,099.00			1,099.00	20
21						4,411.00	4,411.00	12,479.00	12,479.00	21

1 Single Rule; 2 Totals; 3 Net Income; 4 Extend Net Income; 5 Single Rule; 6 Totals; 7 Double Rule

The difference between total revenue and total expenses when total revenue is greater is called **net income.** Before the work sheet is complete, net income must be calculated and the work sheet must be totaled and ruled. A summary of preparing a work sheet is shown on the Work Sheet Overlay.

STEPS Calculating and recording net income on a work sheet; totaling and ruling a work sheet

1. Rule a single line across the four Income Statement and Balance Sheet columns.
2. Add both the Income Statement and Balance Sheet columns. Write the totals below the single line.
3. Calculate the net income. The Income Statement Credit column total, $4,411.00, *minus* the Income Statement Debit column total, $3,312.00, *equals* net income, $1,099.00. Write the amount of net income, *$1,099.00,* below the Income Statement Debit column total. Write the words *Net Income* on the same line in the Account Title column.
4. Extend the amount of net income, *$1,099.00,* to the Balance Sheet Credit column on the same line as the words *Net Income.* The owner's equity account, Barbara Treviño, Capital, is increased by a credit. Therefore, the net income amount is extended to the Balance Sheet Credit column.
5. Rule a single line across the four Income Statement and Balance Sheet columns just below the net income amounts.
6. Add the subtotal and net income amount for each column to get proving totals for the Income Statement and Balance Sheet columns. Write the proving totals below the single line. Check the equality of the proving totals for each pair of columns.
7. Rule double lines across the Income Statement and Balance Sheet columns. The double lines mean that the totals have been verified as correct.

CALCULATING AND RECORDING A NET LOSS ON A WORK SHEET

	ACCOUNT TITLE	5 INCOME STATEMENT DEBIT	6 INCOME STATEMENT CREDIT	7 BALANCE SHEET DEBIT	8 BALANCE SHEET CREDIT	
19		2 2 0 0 00	1 8 0 0 00	5 1 0 0 00	5 5 0 0 00	
20	*Net Loss*		4 0 0 00	4 0 0 00		20
21		2 2 0 0 00	2 2 0 0 00	5 5 0 0 00	5 5 0 0 00	21
22						22
23						23

1 Single Rule
2 Totals
3 Net Loss
4 Extend Net Loss

Encore Music's completed work sheet shows a net income. However, a business might have a net loss to report. The difference between total revenue and total expenses when total expenses is greater is called a **net loss.**

STEPS: Calculating and recording a net loss on a work sheet

1. Rule a single line across the four Income Statement and Balance Sheet columns.
2. Add both the Income Statement and Balance Sheet columns. Write the totals below the single line.
3. Calculate the net loss. The Income Statement Debit column total, $2,200.00, *minus* the Income Statement Credit column total, $1,800.00, *equals* net loss, $400.00. The Income Statement Debit column total (expenses) is greater than the Income Statement Credit column total (revenue). Therefore, because expenses exceed revenue, there is a net loss. Write the amount of net loss, *$400.00,* below the Income Statement Credit column total. Write the words *Net Loss* on the same line in the Account Title column.
4. Extend the amount of net loss, *$400.00,* to the Balance Sheet Debit column on the same line as the words *Net Loss.* The owner's equity account, Barbara Treviño, Capital, is decreased by a debit. Therefore, a net loss is extended to the Balance Sheet Debit column.

ACCOUNTING AT WORK

DARYL STANTON

Daryl Stanton works for John Hancock Mutual Life Insurance Company as a Senior Financial Accountant and highly recommends accounting as a field full of opportunities for those who are dedicated to their work.

Daryl studied accounting in high school and later graduated from Suffolk University with a BSBA, majoring in accounting. At Suffolk, Daryl participated in an internship program, during which he interned at John Hancock. Each year he had a different set of responsibilities. This internship confirmed for Daryl that accounting was the career he wanted.

Daryl highly recommends seeking out an internship program in accounting. He says that it is the best way to discover what working in the accounting field is really like and whether you want to pursue it as a career. An internship program can also help you get your foot in the door of a particular company. In addition to acquiring accounting knowledge and skills, Daryl believes in the importance of developing strong communication skills so you can present yourself and your ideas well.

TERMS REVIEW

income statement

net income

net loss

AUDIT YOUR UNDERSTANDING

1. Which accounts are extended into the Balance Sheet columns of the work sheet?
2. Which accounts are extended into the Income Statement columns of the work sheet?
3. In which Balance Sheet column do you record net income on the work sheet?
4. In which Balance Sheet column do you record net loss on the work sheet?

WORK TOGETHER

Completing a work sheet

Use the work sheet from Work Together on page 164. Your instructor will guide you through the following examples.

5. Extend the up-to-date balances to the Balance Sheet and Income Statement columns.
6. Rule a single line across the Income Statement and Balance Sheet columns. Total each column. Calculate and record the net income or net loss. Label the amount in the Account Title column.
7. Total and rule the Income Statement and Balance Sheet columns.

ON YOUR OWN

Completing a work sheet

Use the work sheet from On Your Own on page 164. Work these problems independently.

8. Extend the up-to-date balances to the Balance Sheet or Income Statement columns.
9. Rule a single line across the Income Statement and Balance Sheet columns. Total each column. Calculate and record the net income or net loss. Label the amount in the Account Title column.
10. Total and rule the Income Statement and Balance Sheet columns.

7-4 Finding and Correcting Errors on the Work Sheet

CORRECTING ACCOUNTING ERRORS ON THE WORK SHEET

Some errors in accounting records are not discovered until a work sheet is prepared. For example, a debit to Supplies may not have been posted from a journal to the general ledger supplies account. The omission may not be discovered until the work sheet's trial balance does not balance. Also, information may be transferred incorrectly from general ledger accounts to the work sheet's trial balance. Additional errors may be made, such as recording adjustment information incorrectly or adding columns incorrectly. In addition, errors may be made in extending amounts to the Income Statement and Balance Sheet columns.

Any errors found on a work sheet must be corrected before any further work is completed. If an incorrect amount is found on a work sheet, erase the error and replace it with the correct amount. If an amount is written in an incorrect column, erase the amount and record it in the correct column.

CHECKING FOR TYPICAL CALCULATION ERRORS

When two column totals are not in balance, subtract the smaller total from the larger total to find the difference. Check the difference between the two amounts against the following guides.

1. **The difference is 1, such as $.01, $.10, $1.00, or $10.00.** For example, if the totals of the two columns are Debit, $14,657.00, and Credit, $14,658.00, the difference between the two columns is $1.00. The error is most likely in addition. Add the columns again.
2. **The difference can be divided evenly by 2.** For example, the difference between two column totals is $48.00, which can be divided by 2 with no remainder. Look for a $24.00 amount in the Trial Balance columns of the work sheet. If the amount is found, check to make sure it has been recorded in the correct Debit or Credit column. A $24.00 debit amount recorded in a credit column results in a difference between column totals of $48.00. If the error is not found on the work sheet, check the general ledger accounts and journal entries. An entry for $24.00 may have been recorded in an incorrect column in the journal or in an account.
3. **The difference can be divided evenly by 9.** For example, the difference between two columns is $45.00, which can be divided by 9 with no remainder. When the difference can be divided equally by 9, look for transposed numbers such as 54 written as 45 or 19 written as 91. Also, check for a "slide." A "slide" occurs when numbers are moved to the right or left in an amount column. For example, $12.00 is recorded as $120.00 or $350.00 is recorded as $35.00.
4. **The difference is an omitted amount.** Look for an amount equal to the difference. If the difference is $50.00, look for an account balance of $50.00 that has not been extended. Look for any $50.00 amount on the work sheet and determine if it has been handled correctly. Look in the accounts and journals for a $50.00 amount, and check if that amount has been handled correctly. Failure to record a $50.00 account balance will make a work sheet's column totals differ by $50.00.

CHECKING FOR ERRORS IN THE WORK SHEET

Check for Errors in the Trial Balance Column

1. Have all general ledger account balances been copied in the Trial Balance column correctly?
2. Have all general ledger account balances been recorded in the correct Trial Balance column?

Check for Errors in the Adjustments Columns

1. Do the debits equal the credits for each adjustment? Use the small letters that label each part of an adjustment to help check accuracy and equality of debits and credits.
2. Is the amount for each adjustment correct?

Check for Errors in the Income Statement and Balance Sheet Columns

1. Has each amount been copied correctly when extended to the Income Statement or Balance Sheet column?
2. Has each account balance been extended to the correct Income Statement or Balance Sheet column?
3. Has the net income or net loss been calculated correctly?
4. Has the net income or net loss been recorded in the correct Income Statement or Balance Sheet column?

For all three of these cases, correct any errors found and add the columns again.

CORRECTING AN ERROR IN POSTING TO THE WRONG ACCOUNT

ACCOUNT *Supplies* ACCOUNT NO. *130*

DATE		ITEM	POST. REF.	DEBIT	CREDIT	BALANCE DEBIT	BALANCE CREDIT
20-- Feb.	1		1	400 00		400 00	
	25		2	90 00		490 00	
	12		1	50 00		540 00	

2 Correct Entry

ACCOUNT *Prepaid Insurance* ACCOUNT NO. *140*

DATE		ITEM	POST. REF.	DEBIT	CREDIT	BALANCE DEBIT	BALANCE CREDIT
20-- Feb.	9		1	600 00		600 00	
	~~12~~		~~1~~	~~50 00~~		~~650 00~~	

1 Incorrect Entry

If a pair of work sheet columns do not balance and an error cannot be found on the work sheet, look for an error in posting from the journal to the general ledger accounts.

As each item in an account or a journal entry is verified, a check mark should be placed next to it. The check mark indicates that the item has been checked for accuracy.

1. Have all amounts that need to be posted actually been posted from the journal? To correct, complete the posting to the correct account. When posting is corrected, recalculate the account balance and correct it on the work sheet.
2. Have all amounts been posted to the correct accounts? To correct, follow these steps.

STEPS: Correcting an error in posting to the wrong account

1. Draw a line through the entire incorrect entry. Recalculate the account balance and correct the work sheet.

2. Record the posting in the correct account. Recalculate the account balance, and correct the work sheet.

CORRECTING AN INCORRECT AMOUNT AND AN AMOUNT POSTED TO THE WRONG COLUMN

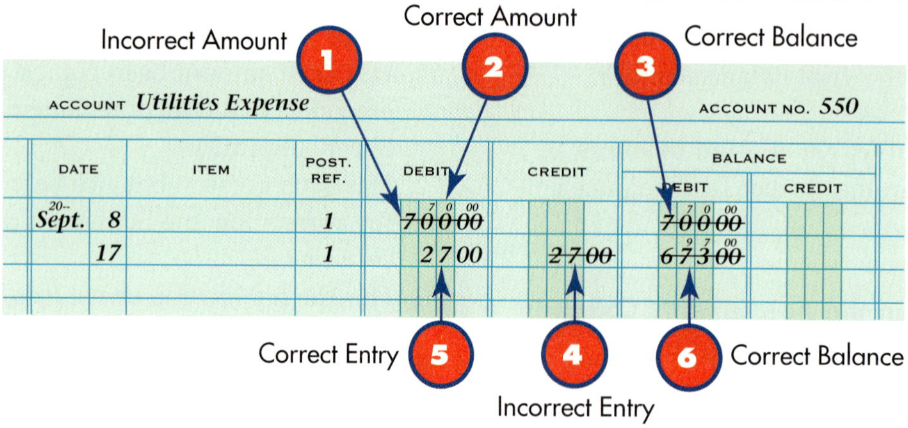

Errors may be made in writing amounts in general ledger accounts. Errors in permanent records should *never* be erased. Erasures in permanent records raise questions about whether important financial information has been altered.

STEPS

Correcting an incorrect amount

1. Draw a line through the incorrect amount.
2. Write the correct amount just above the correction in the same space.
3. Recalculate the account balance, and correct the account balance on the work sheet.

Correcting an amount posted to the wrong column

4. Draw a line through the incorrect item in the account.
5. Record the posting in the correct amount column.
6. Recalculate the account balance, and correct the work sheet.

CHECKING FOR ERRORS IN JOURNAL ENTRIES

1. Do debits equal credits in each journal entry?
2. Is each journal entry amount recorded in the correct journal column?
3. Is information in the Account Title column correct for each journal entry?
4. Are all of the journal amount column totals correct?
5. Does the sum of debit column totals equal the sum of credit column totals in the journal?
6. Have all transactions been recorded?

Some suggestions for correcting errors in journal entries are described in Chapter 4.

PREVENTING ERRORS

The best way to prevent errors is to work carefully. Check the work at each step in an accounting procedure. Most errors occur in doing arithmetic, especially in adding columns. When possible, use a calculator. When an error is discovered, do no more work until the cause of the error is found and corrections are made.

AUDIT YOUR UNDERSTANDING

1. What is the first step in checking for arithmetic errors when two column totals are not in balance?
2. What is one way to check for an error caused by transposed numbers?
3. What term is used to describe an error that occurs when numbers are moved to the right or left in an amount column?

WORK TOGETHER

Finding and correcting errors in accounting records

Paul Coty has completed the September monthly work sheet for his business, LeafyLift. The work sheet and general ledger accounts are given in the *Working Papers.* Mr. Coty believes that he has made one or more errors in preparing the work sheet. He asks you to help him verify the work sheet. Your instructor will guide you through the following examples.

4. Examine the work sheet and the general ledger accounts. Make a list of the errors you find.
5. Correct any errors you find in the general ledger accounts.
6. Prepare a corrected work sheet.

ON YOUR OWN

Finding and correcting errors in accounting records

Marlene Lewis has completed the November monthly work sheet for her business, Internet Access. The work sheet and general ledger accounts are given in the *Working Papers.* Ms. Lewis believes that she has made one or more errors in preparing the work sheet. She asks you to help her verify the work sheet. Work these problems independently.

7. Examine the work sheet and the general ledger accounts. Make a list of the errors you find.
8. Correct any errors you find in the general ledger accounts.
9. Prepare a corrected work sheet.

CHAPTER 7 SUMMARY

After completing this chapter, you can

1. Define important accounting terms related to a work sheet for a service business organized as a proprietorship.
2. Identify accounting concepts and practices related to a work sheet for a service business organized as a proprietorship.
3. Prepare a heading and a trial balance on a work sheet.
4. Plan adjustments for supplies and prepaid insurance.
5. Complete a work sheet for a service business organized as a proprietorship.
6. Identify selected procedures for finding and correcting errors in accounting records.

EXPLORE ACCOUNTING

FISCAL PERIODS

A fiscal period is the length of time for which a business summarizes and reports financial information. Since many companies are required to publish yearly annual reports, these companies choose a year for the fiscal period. In such a case, a company will prepare financial statements every year.

A fiscal year can be any consecutive 12-month period. The Internal Revenue Service (IRS) requires many companies to report taxable income for the fiscal year January 1 through December 31. A fiscal year beginning January 1 can also be called a *calendar year.* Because they use a calendar year for reporting taxable income, many companies choose to use the calendar year for issuing financial statements also.

However, there is no requirement to begin a fiscal year on January 1. Companies often choose a fiscal year that ends during a period of low business activity. Twelve consecutive months which end when business activities have reached the lowest point in their annual cycle are called a *natural business year.*

The following survey conducted on 600 businesses shows the number of companies that chose a fiscal year ending at the end of a specific month.

Fiscal Year End	No. of Companies
January	23
February	11
March	15
April	8
May	16
June	58
July	14
August	15
September	35
October	23
November	17
December	365

Activity: Assume you work for a company that makes snowmobiles. You must determine what fiscal year should be used. Make a written recommendation to the owner. Explain why your recommendation is preferable.

Source: *Accounting Trends and Techniques,* 1996, published by the American Institute of Certified Public Accountants.

7-1 APPLICATION PROBLEM
Recording the trial balance on a work sheet

Use the work sheet given in the *Working Papers*. On June 30 of the current year, Renville Rental has the following general ledger accounts and balances. The business uses a monthly fiscal period.

Account Titles	Account Balances	
	Debit	Credit
Cash	$10,610.00	
Petty Cash	100.00	
Accounts Receivable—Noah Felsen	805.00	
Supplies	750.00	
Prepaid Insurance	800.00	
Accounts Payable—Faith Meltman		$ 555.00
Rebecca Chin, Capital		11,926.00
Rebecca Chin, Drawing	700.00	
Income Summary	—	—
Sales		2,220.00
Advertising Expense	480.00	
Insurance Expense	—	
Miscellaneous Expense	144.00	
Supplies Expense	—	
Utilities Expense	312.00	

Instructions:

Prepare the heading and trial balance on a work sheet. Total and rule the Trial Balance columns. Save your work to complete Application Problem 7-2.

7-2 APPLICATION PROBLEM
Planning adjustments on a work sheet

Use the work sheet from Application Problem 7-1.

Instructions:

1. Analyze the following adjustment information into debit and credit parts. Record the adjustments on the work sheet.

Adjustment Information, June 30	
Supplies on hand	$600.00
Value of prepaid insurance	700.00

2. Total and rule the Adjustments columns. Save your work to complete Application Problem 7-3.

7-3 APPLICATION PROBLEM
Completing a work sheet

Use the work sheet from Application Problem 7-2.

Instructions:

1. Extend the up-to-date balances to the Balance Sheet or Income Statement columns.
2. Rule a single line across the Income Statement and Balance Sheet columns. Total each column. Calculate and record the net income or net loss. Label the amount in the Account Title column.
3. Total and rule the Income Statement and Balance Sheet columns.

7-4 APPLICATION PROBLEM
Finding and correcting errors in accounting records

Ervin Watkins has completed the April monthly work sheet for his business, EverClean. The work sheet and general ledger accounts are given in the *Working Papers*. Mr. Watkins believes that he has made one or more errors in preparing the work sheet. He asks you to help him verify the work sheet.

Instructions:

1. Examine the work sheet and the general ledger accounts. Make a list of the errors you find.
2. Correct any errors you find in the general ledger accounts.
3. Prepare a corrected work sheet.

7-5 MASTERY PROBLEM
Completing a work sheet

On April 30 of the current year, EasyGlo has the following general ledger accounts and balances. The business uses a monthly fiscal period. A work sheet is given in the *Working Papers*.

Account Titles	**Account Balances**	
	Debit	**Credit**
Cash	$1,729.00	
Petty Cash	200.00	
Accounts Receivable—Lois Mabry	561.00	
Supplies	895.00	
Prepaid Insurance	1,000.00	
Accounts Payable—Amery Supplies		$ 500.00
Natasha Kabila, Capital		3,500.00
Natasha Kabila, Drawing	400.00	
Income Summary	—	—
Sales		2,300.00
Advertising Expense	425.00	
Insurance Expense	—	
Miscellaneous Expense	240.00	
Rent Expense	400.00	
Supplies Expense	—	
Utilities Expense	450.00	

Instructions:

1. Prepare the heading and trial balance on a work sheet. Total and rule the Trial Balance columns.
2. Analyze the following adjustment information into debit and credit parts. Record the adjustments on the work sheet.

Adjustment Information, April 30	
Supplies inventory	$200.00
Value of prepaid insurance	750.00

3. Total and rule the Adjustments columns.
4. Extend the up-to-date balances to the Balance Sheet or Income Statement columns.
5. Rule a single line across the Income Statement and Balance Sheet columns. Total each column. Calculate and record the net income or net loss. Label the amount in the Account Title column.
6. Total and rule the Income Statement and Balance Sheet columns.

7-6 CHALLENGE PROBLEM
Completing a work sheet

Green Grass Company had a small fire in its office. The fire destroyed some of the accounting records. On November 30 of the current year, the end of a monthly fiscal period, the following information was constructed from the remaining records and other sources. A work sheet is given in the *Working Papers*.

Remains of the general ledger:

Account Titles	**Account Balances**
Accounts Receivable—J. Kjeseth	$ 350.00
Supplies	1,700.00
Donna Arnold, Drawing	170.00
Sales	4,200.00
Advertising Expense	400.00
Rent Expense	700.00
Utilities Expense	490.00
Information from the business's checkbook:	
Cash balance on last unused check stub	$3,400.00
Total payments for miscellaneous expense	60.00
Total payments for insurance	325.00
Information obtained through inquiries to other businesses:	
Owed to Outdoor Supplies	$1,800.00
Value of prepaid insurance, November 30	225.00
Information obtained by counting supplies on hand after the fire:	
Supplies on hand	$1,100.00

Instructions:

1. From the information given, prepare a heading and reconstruct a trial balance on a work sheet. The owner's capital account balance is the difference between the total of all debit account balances minus the total of all credit account balances.
2. Complete the work sheet.

INTERNET ACTIVITY

Point your browser to

http://accounting.swpco.com

Choose **First-Year Course**, choose **Activities**, and complete the activity for Chapter 7.

Applied Communication

Accounting information is used by managers to make business decisions. But exactly what kind of decisions does the owner of a local business make? How does accounting information enable the manager to make better decisions?

Instructions: Identify a local business of personal interest to you. Write five questions you would ask the manager to learn how that person uses accounting information to make decisions. Interview the manager and write a one- or two-page summary of the interview.

Cases for Critical Thinking

Case 1 Peter Dowther owns a small business. At the end of a fiscal period, he does not make an adjustment for supplies. Are Mr. Dowther's accounting procedures correct? What effect will Mr. Dowther's procedures have on the business's financial reporting? Explain your answer.

Case 2 When posting amounts from a journal to general ledger accounts, a $10.00 debit to Supplies is mistakenly posted as a credit to Utilities Expense. Will this error be discovered when the work sheet is prepared? Explain.

Case 3 Accuracy is of critical importance in accounting. Most employees who are responsible for maintaining accounting records value accuracy and completeness. Accounting employees work very hard to avoid errors and to correct any errors that do get made. Other employees within a business and other people who have contact with a business also value accurate accounting records. Other than accounting employees, who are some of the other people who expect and require accurate accounting records? Why is accounting accuracy important to these people? How tolerant should people be of mistakes? Are a small number of mistakes acceptable? Are mistakes involving small amounts—for example, just a few cents—acceptable? Or should it be expected that accounting records are completely accurate?

AUTOMATED ACCOUNTING

MANUAL ACCOUNTING CYCLE VS. AUTOMATED ACCOUNTING CYCLE

The series of accounting activities included in recording financial information for a fiscal period is called an *accounting cycle.* Large businesses prepare financial statements each month and therefore complete the accounting cycle each month. Smaller businesses without a full-time accounting staff may complete the accounting cycle only quarterly, or annually when the year-end tax returns are due. Regardless of the size of the business, the steps in the accounting cycle are generally the same:

1. Source documents are checked for accuracy, and transactions are analyzed into debit and credit parts.
2. Transactions are recorded in a journal.
3. Journal entries are posted to the general ledger, and a trial balance is prepared.
4. Adjusting entries are journalized and posted.
5. Financial statements are prepared.
6. Closing entries are journalized and posted, and a post-closing trial balance is prepared.

Manual Accounting

In a manual accounting system, all the steps are completed by hand, and a work sheet may be used to summarize information about the adjusting and closing entries and to complete the trial balance. Many of the steps are repetitive and time-consuming, particularly posting and the preparation of the various trial balances. However, all of the steps are important to ensure that accurate financial statements are available to management at the end of each period. Managers use these financial statements to make decisions, and must be able to rely on them.

Automated Accounting

In automated accounting, the emphasis is on the analysis of the source documents and the preparation of timely and accurate journal entries and adjusting entries. These are the parts of the accounting cycle that require accounting personnel to apply the matching concept to ensure that revenues and expenses are recorded in the proper periods. The automated accounting system is programmed to post journal entries and to prepare trial balances, closing entries, and financial statements as needed. The accounting staff is freed from the more repetitive tasks associated with the accounting cycle and can concentrate on the analysis functions.

Automated accounting software may include additional features to integrate applications within the accounting cycle. Options within the software may aid in the reconciliation of bank accounts and in the processing of accounts payable and accounts receivable. Automated accounting may be used to track inventory and plant assets, and to process sales orders and payroll. Budgeting, graphing, and printing capabilities are also included in automated accounting systems. Advanced accounting systems also have options that allow the user to import or export data to and from spreadsheet and word processing software.

Since control over assets and transactions is one of the most important parts of any accounting system, automated systems include controls such as passwords and audit trails to ensure the integrity of the financial statements. Using the computer as a tool to process accounting data allows accountants and managers to work together to plan, operate, and control the business.

8 Financial Statements for a Proprietorship

AFTER STUDYING CHAPTER 8, YOU WILL BE ABLE TO:

1. Define an accounting term related to financial statements for a service business organized as a proprietorship.
2. Identify accounting concepts and practices related to preparation of financial statements for a service business organized as a proprietorship.
3. Prepare an income statement for a service business organized as a proprietorship and analyze an income statement using component percentages.
4. Prepare a balance sheet for a service business organized as a proprietorship.

TERM PREVIEW

component percentage

REPORTING FINANCIAL INFORMATION

The financial information needed by managers and owners to make good business decisions can be found in the general ledger accounts. However, the information in the general ledger is very detailed. Therefore, to make this general ledger information more usable, the information is summarized, organized, and reported to the owners and managers.

Also, *all* financial information *must* be reported if good business decisions are to be made. A financial statement with incomplete information is similar to a book with missing pages. The complete story is not told. If a business has both rent and utilities expenses but reports only the rent expense, managers will have incomplete information on which to base decisions. The accounting concept, *Adequate Disclosure,* is applied when financial statements contain all information necessary to understand a business's financial condition. *(CONCEPT: Adequate Disclosure)*

Encore Music prepares two financial statements: an income statement and a balance sheet. Encore Music always prepares financial statements at the end of each monthly fiscal period. *(CONCEPT: Accounting Period Cycle)*

ACCOUNTING IN YOUR CAREER

ENHANCING FINANCIAL REPORTING

Tanya Allen works for Marci Stettner, who owns and operates Marci's Delivery Service, a proprietorship. Tanya is the office manager and does most of the clerical work, accounting, and appointment scheduling for the business. At the end of each month, Tanya prepares an income statement and a balance sheet for the business. Marci reviews the statements briefly and then files them away for future reference. In actual practice, Marci rarely looks at the statements again. The company's fiscal year ends on December 31. On December 31, Tanya prepares an income statement for the entire fiscal year, but not one for the month of December.

Tanya has not received much training in the preparation of financial statements. Each month she spends a number of hours keying each statement from scratch and arranging the columns in an attractive layout. Sometimes the appearance of the statements is inconsistent from that of the previous month.

Recently Marci has realized that the business is in trouble. She has been finding it difficult to pay the company's bills and also withdraw sufficient cash for her personal living expenses. Because she doesn't truly understand the financial statements, she spends little time reviewing them.

The company rarely shows more than $500.00 in cash on the balance sheet; total liabilities and owner's equity averages $25,000.00, but the owner's equity is usually around $5,000.00. The income statement rarely shows more than $1,000.00 in net income each month.

Critical Thinking:

1. What is your opinion of the financial condition of Marci's Delivery Service?
2. What recommendations would you make to Tanya Allen about her method of preparing the financial statements?

8-1 Preparing an Income Statement

INCOME STATEMENT INFORMATION ON A WORK SHEET

	ACCOUNT TITLE	5 INCOME STATEMENT DEBIT	6 INCOME STATEMENT CREDIT	7 BALANCE SHEET DEBIT	8 BALANCE SHEET CREDIT	
12	*Sales*		4411 00			12
13	*Advertising Expense*	273 00				13
14	*Insurance Expense*	100 00				14
15	*Miscellaneous Expense*	10 00				15
16	*Rent Expense*	250 00				16
17	*Supplies Expense*	2564 00				17
18	*Utilities Expense*	115 00				18
19		3312 00	4411 00			19
20	*Net Income*	1099 00				20
21		4411 00	4411 00			21
22						22

An income statement reports financial information over a *specific period of time,* indicating the financial *progress* of a business in earning a net income or a net loss.

Revenue is the earnings of a business from business activities. Expenses are the amounts a business pays to operate the business and earn the revenue. The revenue earned and the expenses incurred to earn that revenue are reported in the same fiscal period. *(CONCEPT: Matching Expenses with Revenue)*

Information needed to prepare financial statements could be obtained from the general ledger accounts. However, a work sheet is prepared to assist in planning the financial statements.

Information needed to prepare Encore Music's income statement is obtained from two places on the work sheet. Account titles are obtained from the work sheet's Account Title column. Account balances are obtained from the work sheet's Income Statement columns.

The income statement for a service business has four sections: (1) heading, (2) revenue, (3) expenses, and (4) net income or net loss.

HEADING OF AN INCOME STATEMENT

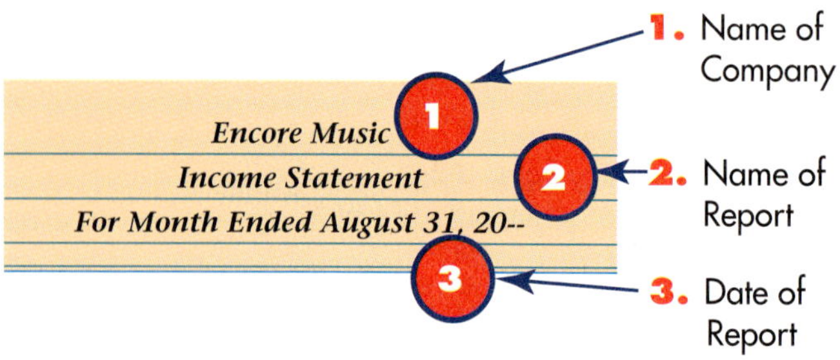

The income statement's date shows that this income statement reports information for the one-month period from August 1 through August 31.

STEPS Preparing the heading of an income statement

1. Center the name of the company, *Encore Music,* on the first line.
2. Center the name of the report, *Income Statement,* on the second line.
3. Center the date of the report, *For Month Ended August 31, 20—,* on the third line.

REVENUE, EXPENSES, AND NET INCOME SECTIONS OF AN INCOME STATEMENT

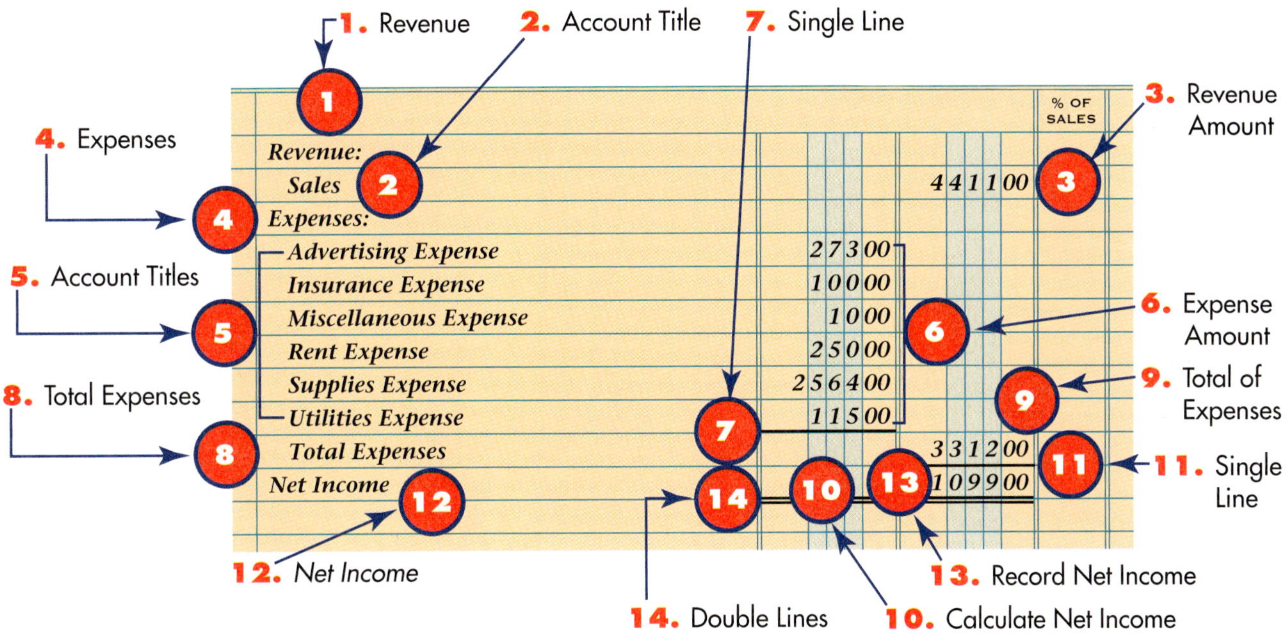

Information from the work sheet's Account Title column and Income Statement Credit column is used to prepare the revenue section.

Information from the work sheet's Account Title column and Income Statement Debit column is used to prepare the expenses section.

STEPS: Preparing the revenue, expenses, and net income sections of an income statement

1. Write the name of the first section, *Revenue:*, at the extreme left of the wide column on the first line.
2. Write the title of the revenue account, *Sales,* on the next line, indented about one centimeter.
3. Record the balance of the account, *$4,411.00,* on the same line in the second amount column.
4. Write the name of the second section, *Expenses:*, on the next line at the extreme left of the wide column.
5. Write the title of each expense account in the wide column, indented about one centimeter.
6. Record the balance of each expense account in the first amount column on the same line as the account title.
7. Rule a single line across the first amount column under the last expense account balance to indicate addition.
8. Write the words *Total Expenses* on the next blank line in the wide column, indented about one centimeter.
9. Record the amount of total expenses, *$3,312.00,* on the same line in the second amount column.
10. Calculate and verify the amount of net income using two methods:
    a. Calculate net income from information on the income statement, as shown.

Total Revenue	–	Total Expenses	=	Net Income
$4,411.00	–	$3,312.00	=	$1,099.00

    b. Compare the amount of net income, *$1,099.00,* with the net income shown on the work sheet. The two net income amounts must be the same. (If the two amounts are not the same, an error has been made.)
11. Rule a single line across the second amount column just below the amount of total expenses.
12. Write the words *Net Income* on the next line at the extreme left of the wide column.
13. On the same line, record the amount of net income, *$1,099.00,* in the second amount column.
14. Rule double lines across both amount columns below the amount of net income to show that the amount has been verified as correct.

COMPONENT PERCENTAGE ANALYSIS OF AN INCOME STATEMENT

Encore Music			
Income Statement			
For Month Ended August 31, 20--			
			% OF SALES
Revenue:			
Sales		4,411.00	100.0
Expenses:			
Advertising Expense	273.00		
Insurance Expense	100.00		
Miscellaneous Expense	10.00		
Rent Expense	250.00		
Supplies Expense	2,564.00		
Utilities Expense	115.00		
Total Expenses		3,312.00	75.1
Net Income		1,099.00	24.9

For a service business, the revenue reported on an income statement includes two components: (1) total expenses and (2) net income. To make decisions about future operations, a manager analyzes relationships between these two income statement components and the total sales. The percentage relationship between one financial statement item and the total that includes that item is called a **component percentage.** On an income statement, component percentages are calculated by dividing the amount of each component by the total amount of sales. Encore Music calculates a component percentage for total expenses and net income. The relationship between each component and total sales is shown in a separate column on the income statement at the right of the amount columns.

Acceptable Component Percentages

For a component percentage to be useful, Ms. Treviño needs to know what component percentages are acceptable for businesses similar to Encore Music. Various industry organizations publish average percentages for similar businesses. In the future, Ms. Treviño could also compare Encore Music's component percentages from one fiscal period with the percentages of previous fiscal periods.

Total Expenses Component Percentage

The total expenses component percentage, based on information from the August income statement, is calculated as shown. For businesses similar to Encore Music, an acceptable total expenses component percentage is not more than 80.0%. Therefore, Encore Music's percentage, 75.1%, is less than 80.0% and is acceptable.

Total Expenses	÷	Total Sales	=	Total Expenses Component Percentage
$3,312.00	÷	$4,411.00	=	75.1%

Net Income Component Percentage

The net income component percentage, based on information from the August income statement, is calculated as shown. For businesses similar to Encore Music, an acceptable net income component percentage is not less than 20.0%. Therefore Encore Music's percentage, 24.9%, is greater than 20.0% and is acceptable.

Net Income	÷	Total Sales	=	Net Income Component Percentage
$1,099.00	÷	$4,411.00	=	24.9%

INCOME STATEMENT WITH TWO SOURCES OF REVENUE AND A NET LOSS

5. *Total Sales*

1. Revenue

2. Account Titles

3. Revenue Amounts

4. Total of Sales

HighNote Income Statement For Month Ended August 31, 20--			
			% OF SALES
Revenue:			
Sales—Lessons	2,360.00		
Sales—Repairs	1,250.00		
Total Revenue		3,610.00	100.0
Expenses:			
Advertising Expense	1,100.00		
Insurance Expense	341.00		
Rent Expense	1,450.00		
Supplies Expense	1,575.00		
Total Expenses		4,466.00	123.7
Net Loss		(856.00)	(23.7)

6. *Net Loss*

7. Record *Net Loss*

Encore Music receives revenue from only one source, the sale of services for music lessons. HighNote receives revenue from two sources, the sale of services for music lessons and the sale of services to repair musical instruments. The business's owner wants to know how much revenue is earned from each source. Therefore, the business uses two revenue accounts: Sales—Lessons and Sales—Repairs.

When an income statement is prepared for HighNote, both revenue accounts are listed. The revenue section of HighNote differs from the income statement prepared by Encore Music.

If total expenses exceed total revenue, a net loss is reported on an income statement. HighNote reported a net loss on its August income statement.

STEPS

Preparing the revenue section of an income statement with two sources of revenue

1. Write the section heading, *Revenue:*, at the left of the wide column.
2. Write the titles of both revenue accounts in the wide column, indented about one centimeter.
3. Record the balance of each account in the first amount column on the same line as the account title.
4. Total the two revenue account balances. Write the total amount on the next line in the second amount column.
5. Write the words *Total Revenue* in the wide column, indented about one centimeter on the same line as the total revenue amount.

Preparing the net loss section of an income statement

6. Write the words *Net Loss* at the extreme left of the wide column.
7. Subtract the total expenses from the revenue to calculate the net loss. Record the amount of net loss in the second amount column in parentheses. An amount written in parentheses on a financial statement indicates a negative amount.

TERM REVIEW

component percentage

AUDIT YOUR UNDERSTANDING

1. List the four sections of an income statement.
2. What is the formula for calculating the total expenses component percentage?
3. What is the formula for calculating the net income component percentage?

WORK TOGETHER

Preparing an income statement

A partial work sheet of Darlene's Delivery Service for the month ended July 31 of the current year is given in the *Working Papers*. Also given is a blank form for completing an income statement. Your instructor will guide you through the following example.

4. Prepare an income statement for the month ended July 31 of the current year. Calculate and record the component percentages for total expenses and net income. Round percentage calculations to the nearest 0.1%.

ON YOUR OWN

Preparing an income statement

A partial work sheet of Keith's Copies for the month ended February 28 of the current year is given in the *Working Papers*. Also given is a blank form for completing an income statement. Work this problem independently.

5. Prepare an income statement for the month ended February 28 of the current year. Calculate and record the component percentages for total expenses and net income. Round percentage calculations to the nearest 0.1%.

8-2 Balance Sheet Information on a Work Sheet

BALANCE SHEET

	ACCOUNT TITLE	7 BALANCE SHEET DEBIT	8 BALANCE SHEET CREDIT	
1	*Cash*	8272 00		1
2	*Petty Cash*	200 00		2
3	*Accounts Receivable—Kids Time*	100 00		3
4	*Accounts Receivable—Learn N Play*	20 00		4
5	*Supplies*	2187 00		5
6	*Prepaid Insurance*	1100 00		6
7	*Accounts Payable—Ling Music Supplies*		1360 00	7
8	*Accounts Payable—Sullivan Office Supplies*		20 00	8
9	*Barbara Treviño, Capital*		10000 00	9
10	*Barbara Treviño, Drawing*	600 00		10
19		12479 00	11380 00	19
20	*Net Income*		1099 00	20
21		12479 00	12479 00	21

A balance sheet reports financial information on a *specific date,* indicating the financial *condition* of a business. The financial condition of a business refers to its financial strength. If a business has adequate available assets and few liabilities, that business is financially strong. If the business's financial condition is not strong, adverse changes in the economy might cause the business to fail.

Information about assets, liabilities, and owner's equity might be obtained from the general ledger accounts or from a work sheet. However, the information is easier to use if reported in an organized manner such as on a balance sheet.

Information needed to prepare Encore Music's balance sheet is obtained from two places on the work sheet. Account titles are obtained from the work sheet's Account Title column. Account balances are obtained from the work sheet's Balance Sheet columns.

A balance sheet has four sections: (1) heading, (2) assets, (3) liabilities, and (4) owner's equity.

HEADING OF A BALANCE SHEET

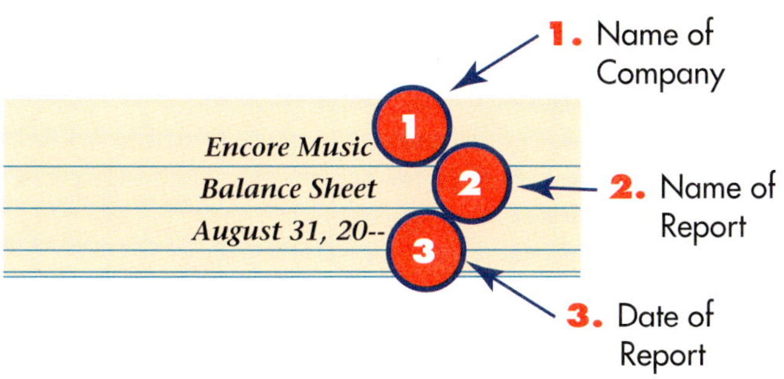

STEPS

Preparing the heading of a balance sheet

1. Center the name of the company, *Encore Music,* on the first line.
2. Center the name of the report, *Balance Sheet,* on the second line.
3. Center the date of the report, *August 31, 20—,* on the third line.

ASSETS AND LIABILITIES SECTIONS OF A BALANCE SHEET

1. *Assets* **2.** Account Titles **3.** Asset Amounts **4.** *Liabilities* **5.** Account Titles **6.** Liability Amounts **7.** Single Line **8.** *Total Liabilities* **9.** Total of Liabilities

Assets		*Liabilities*	
Cash	8272 00	*Accts. Pay.—Ling Music Supplies*	1360 00
Petty Cash	200 00	*Accts. Pay.—Sullivan Off. Supplies*	20 00
Accts. Rec.—Kids Time	100 00	*Total Liabilities*	1380 00
Accts. Rec.—Learn N Play	20 00		
Supplies	2187 00		
Prepaid Insurance	1100 00		

A balance sheet reports information about the elements of the accounting equation.

Assets = Liabilities + Owner's Equity

The assets are on the LEFT side of the accounting equation and on the LEFT side of Encore Music's balance sheet.

Two kinds of equities are reported on a balance sheet: (1) liabilities and (2) owner's equity. Liabilities and owner's equity are on the RIGHT side of the accounting equation and on the RIGHT side of Encore Music's balance sheet.

The information needed to prepare the assets section is obtained from the work sheet's Account Title column and the Balance Sheet Debit column. The information needed to prepare the liabilities section is obtained from the work sheet's Account Title column and the Balance Sheet Credit column.

STEPS: Preparing the assets and liabilities sections of a balance sheet

1. Write the title of the first section, *Assets,* in the middle of the left wide column.
2. Write the titles of all asset accounts under the heading.
3. Record the balance of each asset account in the left amount column on the same line as the account title.
4. Write the title of the next section, *Liabilities,* in the middle of the right wide column.
5. Write the titles of all liability accounts under the heading.
6. Record the balance of each liability account in the right amount column on the same line as the account title.
7. Rule a single line across the right amount column under the last amount, to indicate addition.
8. Write the words *Total Liabilities* in the right wide column on the next blank line, indented about 1 centimeter.
9. Record the total of all liabilities, *$1,380.00,* in the right amount column.

CULTURAL DIVERSITY

Feng Shui

In the U.S., culture has been influenced by the cultures of its foreign business partners. For example, the Chinese philosophy of *feng shui* (pronounced "fung shway") is having an influence on the design of homes and office buildings in America.

This philosophy reflects Chinese beliefs in luck. The goal is to maintain a flow of positive energies throughout a building and to find the most favorable places to live and work. *Feng shui* dictates how a room or house should be set up. Each angle in the building corresponds to a sphere of life—including health, love, and money. Some U.S. companies are using the *feng shui* philosophy in designing their facilities.

OWNER'S EQUITY SECTION OF A BALANCE SHEET

Encore Music			
Balance Sheet			
August 31, 20--			
Assets		**Liabilities**	
Cash	8 272 00	Accts. Pay.—Ling Music Supplies	1 360 00
Petty Cash	200 00	Accts. Pay—Sullivan Off. Supplies	20 00
Accts. Rec.—Kids Time	100 00	Total Liabilities	1 380 00
Accts. Rec.—Learn N Play	20 00	Owner's Equity	
Supplies	2 187 00	Barbara Treviño, Capital	10 499 00
Prepaid Insurance	1 100 00		
Total Assets	11 879 00	Total Liab. and Owner's Eq.	11 879 00

1. Owner's Equity
2. Account Title
3. Capital Amount
4. Single Line
5. Total Assets
6. Total of Assets
7. Total Liabilities and Owner's Equity
8. Total of Liabilities and Owner's Equity
9. Compare Totals
10. Double Lines

Only the amount of current capital is reported on Encore Music's balance sheet. The amounts needed to calculate the current capital are found in the work sheet's Balance Sheet Debit and Credit columns. The amount of current capital is calculated as shown.

Capital Account Balance	+	Net Income	−	Drawing Account Balance	=	Current Capital
$10,000.00	+	$1,099.00	−	$600.00	=	$10,499.00

The title of the owner's capital account is obtained from the work sheet's Account Title column. Encore Music's balance sheet prepared on August 31 is shown in the illustration.

When a business has a net loss, current capital is calculated as shown. The current capital is reported on the balance sheet in the same way as when the business has a net income.

Capital Account Balance	−	Net Loss	−	Drawing Account Balance	=	Current Capital
$12,000.00	−	$200.00	−	$500.00	=	$11,300.00

STEPS: Preparing the owner's equity section of a balance sheet

1. Write the title of the section, *Owner's Equity,* in the middle of the right wide column on the next line below Total Liabilities.
2. Write the title of the owner's capital account, *Barbara Treviño, Capital,* on the next line.
3. Record the current amount of owner's equity, *$10,499.00,* in the right amount column.
4. Determine which amount column is longer. For Encore Music, the longer column is the left amount column. Rule a single line under the last amount in the left amount column: Prepaid Insurance, $1,100.00. Rule a single line in the right amount column on the same line as in the left amount column.
5. Write the words *Total Assets* on the next line, in the left wide column.
6. Record the amount of total assets, *$11,879.00,* in the left amount column.
7. Write the words *Total Liab. and Owner's Eq.* in the right wide column on the same line as *Total Assets.*
8. Record the amount of total liabilities and owner's equity, *$11,879.00,* in the right amount column.
9. Compare the totals of the two amount columns. Because the totals are the same on both sides of Encore Music's balance sheet, $11,879.00, the balance sheet is in balance.
10. Rule double lines across both the left and right amount columns just below the column totals to show that the totals have been verified as correct.

OWNER'S EQUITY REPORTED IN DETAIL ON A BALANCE SHEET

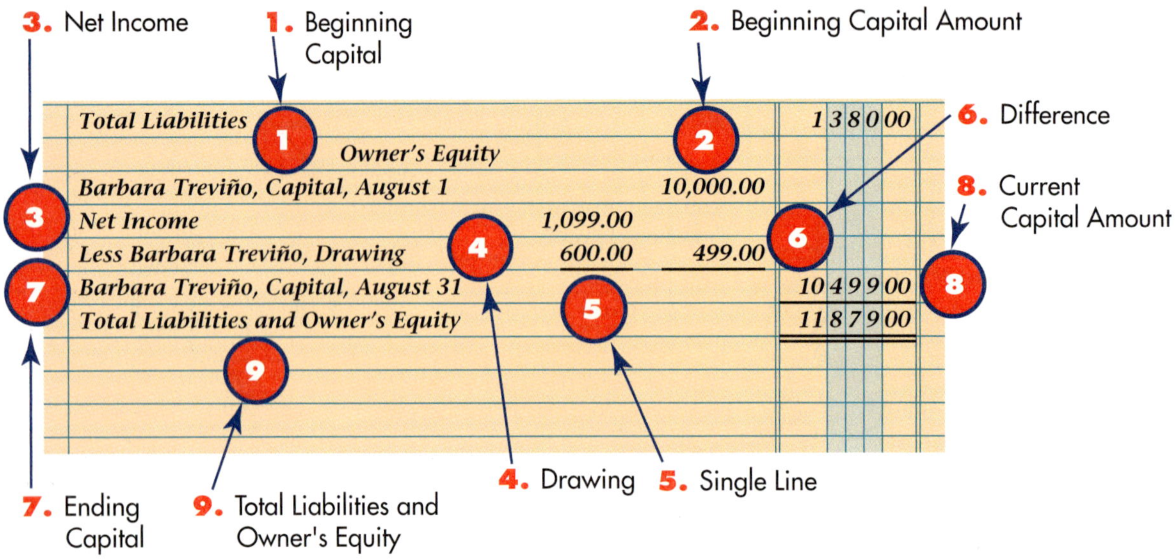

Encore Music's balance sheet reports the current capital on August 31 but does not show how this amount was calculated. Encore Music is a small business with relatively few changes in owner's equity to report. Therefore, Barbara Treviño decided that the business does not need to report all the details in the owner's equity section. However, some businesses prefer to report the details about how owner's equity is calculated.

If Encore Music were to report details about owner's equity, the owner's equity section of the balance sheet would be prepared as shown in the illustration.

STEPS: Preparing the owner's equity section reported in detail on a balance sheet

1. Write the words *Barbara Treviño, Capital, August 1* on the first line under the words *Owner's Equity.*
2. Record the owner's capital account balance on August 1, *$10,000.00,* in the wide column.
3. Write the words *Net Income* on the next line. Record the net income, *$1,099.00,* in the wide column to the left of the capital account balance.
4. Write the words *Less Barbara Treviño, Drawing* on the next line. Record the balance of the drawing account, *$600.00,* in the wide column.
5. Rule a single line under the amount.
6. Subtract the balance of the drawing account from the net income. Record the difference, *$499.00,* in the wide column to the right of the drawing account balance.
7. Write the words *Barbara Treviño, Capital, August 31* on the next line.
8. Add the August 1 capital amount, *$10,000.00,* and the difference between the net income and the drawing account, *$499.00.* Record the sum, *$10,499.00,* in the right amount column.
9. Write the words *Total Liabilities and Owner's Equity* on the next line. Record the amount of total liabilities and owner's equity, *$11,879.00,* in the right amount column.

REMEMBER

Capital is not copied from the work sheet to the balance sheet. Capital is calculated using beginning capital, plus net income or minus net loss, minus drawing.

AUDIT YOUR UNDERSTANDING

1. List the four sections on a balance sheet.
2. What is the formula for calculating current capital?

WORK TOGETHER

Preparing a balance sheet

A partial work sheet of Ken's Carpet Cleaning for the month ended April 30 of the current year is given in the *Working Papers*. Also given is a blank form for completing a balance sheet. Your instructor will guide you through the following example.

3. Prepare a balance sheet for April 30 of the current year.

ON YOUR OWN

Preparing a balance sheet

A partial work sheet of Jane's Sewing Machine Repair for the month ended October 31 of the current year is given in the *Working Papers*. Also given is a blank form for completing a balance sheet. Work this problem independently.

4. Prepare a balance sheet for October 31 of the current year.

CHAPTER 8 SUMMARY

After completing this chapter, you can

1. Define an important accounting term related to financial statements for a service business organized as a proprietorship.
2. Identify accounting concepts and practices related to preparation of financial statements for a service business organized as a proprietorship.
3. Prepare an income statement for a service business organized as a proprietorship and analyze an income statement using component percentages.
4. Prepare a balance sheet for a service business organized as a proprietorship.

EXPLORE ACCOUNTING

COMPARATIVE AND INTERIM FINANCIAL STATEMENTS

A corporation that trades its stock on a U.S. stock exchange must submit an annual report to the Securities and Exchange Commission (SEC). The SEC has specific requirements as to what must be included in the financial statements.

One requirement is that the financial statements included in the annual report must show amounts for more than one year. The balance sheet must show ending balances for the current and the previous year. The income statement and statement of stockholder's equity must show amounts for the current year and the two previous years. Financial statements providing information for multiple fiscal periods are called *comparative financial statements.*

These statements make it possible for a user to compare performance from year to year. For example, the net income for the current year can be compared to the net income for the two previous years. In this way, the user can determine if there is a positive or negative trend occuring in net income. On the balance sheet, the ending cash balance for the current year can be compared to the ending cash balance from the previous year to determine if the amount of cash on hand is increasing or decreasing.

Businesses that are required to submit an annual report to the SEC must also submit a quarterly report. This report is not as detailed as the annual report, but it must include the financial statements for the quarter. Financial statements providing information for a time period shorter than the fiscal year are called *interim financial statements.* Users of financial information are able to evaluate the progress of the firm every three months rather than waiting an entire year. The importance of interim financial statements can be verified by the fact that the results reported in these statements are often summarized and reported in financial news sources, such as the *Wall Street Journal* and CNBC.

Activity: Contact a corporation near you. Ask if the business prepares interim financial statements and, if it does, find out how often these statements are prepared.

8-1 APPLICATION PROBLEM
Preparing an income statement

A form is given in the *Working Papers.* The following information is obtained from the work sheet of Robbie's Rugcare for the month ended August 31 of the current year.

		5	6	7	8	
	ACCOUNT TITLE	INCOME STATEMENT		BALANCE SHEET		
		DEBIT	CREDIT	DEBIT	CREDIT	
11	*Sales*		5707 00			11
12	*Advertising Expense*	900 00				12
13	*Insurance Expense*	20 00				13
14	*Miscellaneous Expense*	267 00				14
15	*Supplies Expense*	500 00				15
16	*Utilities Expense*	1542 00				16
17		3229 00	5707 00	11547 00	9069 00	17
18	*Net Income*	2478 00			2478 00	18
19		5707 00	5707 00	11547 00	11547 00	19
20						20

Instructions:

1. Prepare an income statement for the month ended August 31 of the current year.
2. Calculate and record the component percentages for total expenses and net income. Round percentage calculations to the nearest 0.1%.

8-2 APPLICATION PROBLEM
Preparing a balance sheet

A form is given in the *Working Papers.* The following information is obtained from the work sheet of Robbie's Rugcare for the month ended August 31 of the current year.

		7	8	
	ACCOUNT TITLE	BALANCE SHEET		
		DEBIT	CREDIT	
1	*Cash*	8752 00		1
2	*Accts. Rec.—Crystal Thompson*	200 00		2
3	*Accts. Rec.—Robert Boje*	175 00		3
4	*Supplies*	400 00		4
5	*Prepaid Insurance*	220 00		5
6	*Accts. Pay.—Daniel Supplies*		442 00	6
7	*Accts. Pay.—Irene's Irons*		676 00	7
8	*Roberta Greenstein, Capital*		7951 00	8
9	*Roberta Greenstein, Drawing*	1800 00		9
10	*Income Summary*			10
17		11547 00	9069 00	17
18	*Net Income*		2478 00	18
19		11547 00	11547 00	19
20				20

Instructions:

Prepare a balance sheet for August 31 of the current year.

8-3 MASTERY PROBLEM
Preparing financial statements with a net loss

Forms are given in the *Working Papers.* The following information is obtained from the work sheet of Mancini Hair Care for the month ended September 30 of the current year.

		5	6	7	8	
	ACCOUNT TITLE	INCOME STATEMENT		BALANCE SHEET		
		DEBIT	CREDIT	DEBIT	CREDIT	
1	*Cash*			7678 00		1
2	*Petty Cash*			100 00		2
3	*Accts. Rec.—Jennifer Balsa*			164 00		3
4	*Supplies*			690 00		4
5	*Prepaid Insurance*			700 00		5
6	*Accts. Pay.—Alto Supplies*				733 00	6
7	*Jon Mancini, Capital*				9500 00	7
8	*Jon Mancini, Drawing*			500 00		8
9	*Income Summary*					9
10	*Sales*		4596 00			10
11	*Advertising Expense*	550 00				11
12	*Insurance Expense*	175 00				12
13	*Miscellaneous Expense*	58 00				13
14	*Supplies Expense*	1500 00				14
15	*Utilities Expense*	2714 00				15
16		4997 00	4596 00	9832 00	10233 00	16
17	*Net Loss*		401 00	401 00		17
18		4997 00	4997 00	10233 00	10233 00	18
19						19
20						20

Instructions:

1. Prepare an income statement for the month ended September 30 of the current year.
2. Calculate and record the component percentages for total expenses and net loss. Place the percentage for net loss in parentheses to show that it is for a net loss. Round percentage calculations to the nearest 0.1%.
3. Prepare a balance sheet for September 30 of the current year.

8-4 CHALLENGE PROBLEM
Preparing financial statements with two sources of revenue and a net loss

Forms are given in the *Working Papers.* The information on the next page is obtained from the work sheet of LawnMow for the month ended October 31 of the current year.

Instructions:

1. Prepare an income statement for the month ended October 31 of the current year.
2. Calculate and record the component percentages for total expenses and net loss. Place the percentage for net loss in parentheses to show that it is for a net loss. Round percentage calculations to the nearest 0.1%.
3. Prepare a balance sheet for October 31 of the current year.

	ACCOUNT TITLE	5 INCOME STATEMENT DEBIT	6 INCOME STATEMENT CREDIT	7 BALANCE SHEET DEBIT	8 BALANCE SHEET CREDIT	
1	*Cash*			1898 00		1
2	*Accts. Rec.—Sandra Rohe*			95 00		2
3	*Supplies*			650 00		3
4	*Prepaid Insurance*			1200 00		4
5	*Accts. Pay.—Corner Garage*				58 00	5
6	*Accts. Pay.—Broadway Gas*				110 00	6
7	*Accts. Pay.—Esko Repair*				215 00	7
8	*Ryo Morrison, Capital*				4000 00	8
9	*Ryo Morrison, Drawing*			100 00		9
10	*Income Summary*					10
11	*Sales—Lawn Care*		4900 00			11
12	*Sales—Shrub Care*		2500 00			12
13	*Advertising Expense*	390 00				13
14	*Insurance Expense*	400 00				14
15	*Miscellaneous Expense*	550 00				15
16	*Rent Expense*	3300 00				16
17	*Supplies Expense*	3200 00				17
18		7840 00	7400 00	3943 00	4383 00	18
19	*Net Loss*		440 00	440 00		19
20		7840 00	7840 00	4383 00	4383 00	20
21						21

INTERNET ACTIVITY

Point your browser to

http://accounting.swpco.com

Choose **First-Year Course**, choose **Activities**, and complete the activity for Chapter 8.

Applied Communication

Assume that you are the owner of a proprietorship, and you have just hired a new assistant. In the past, your assistants have had difficulty understanding the importance of financial statements to your business.

Instructions: Write down what you would say to your assistant about the importance of income statements and balance sheets in making financial decisions. Your statements should be no longer than one or two paragraphs.

Cases for Critical Thinking

Case 1 Romelle Woods and Ahti Indihar each own small businesses. Ms. Woods prepares an income statement and balance sheet at the end of each day for her business, in order to make business decisions. Mr. Indihar prepares an income statement and balance sheet for his business only at the end of each one-year fiscal period, when preparing tax reports. Which owner is using the better procedure? Explain your answer.

AUTOMATED ACCOUNTING

FINANCIAL STATEMENTS GENERATED FROM AUTOMATED ACCOUNTING

Financial information needed by managers and owners of a business to make decisions is recorded in the journals and the ledgers. While this information may be helpful in analyzing the activity in a particular account, it is too detailed to be useful in decision making. When information from the ledgers is summarized and organized, the reports that are prepared are referred to as *financial statements*. The most commonly presented financial statements for a business organized as a sole proprietorship are the balance sheet and the income statement.

To display financial statements:

1. Click the Reports toolbar button, or choose the Report Selection menu item from the Report menu.
2. When the Report Selection dialog appears, choose the Financial Statements option from the Select a Report Group list.
3. Choose the financial statement report you would like to display from the Choose a Report to Display list.
4. Click the OK button.

The up-to-date account balances stored by the software are used to calculate and display the current financial statements.

Income Statement

An income statement shows the revenue and expenses for a fiscal period. Revenues are the amounts earned from business activities. Expenses are the amounts paid to operate a business. The software will display net income or loss (the difference between revenues earned and expenses incurred) in one of two formats:

1. *Report by Fiscal Period:* This format shows the profitability of the business from the beginning of the fiscal year to the date the income statement is displayed.
2. *Report by Month and Year:* This format includes columns for the current month and for the year to date.

A component percentage is included for each dollar amount. A component percentage shows the percentage relationship between one financial statement item and the total that includes that item. Component percentages calculated on the income statement show the relationship of items to total sales.

Balance Sheet

The balance sheet is the financial statement that reports assets, liabilities, and owner's equity on a specific date, usually the end of the fiscal period. It is used to help evaluate the financial strength of the business. Additional information about owner's equity is shown on the Statement of Owner's Equity. This statement shows changes to the capital account during the period.

AUTOMATING MASTERY PROBLEM 8-3: Preparing financial statements with a net loss

Instructions:

1. Load *Automated Accounting 7.0* or higher software.

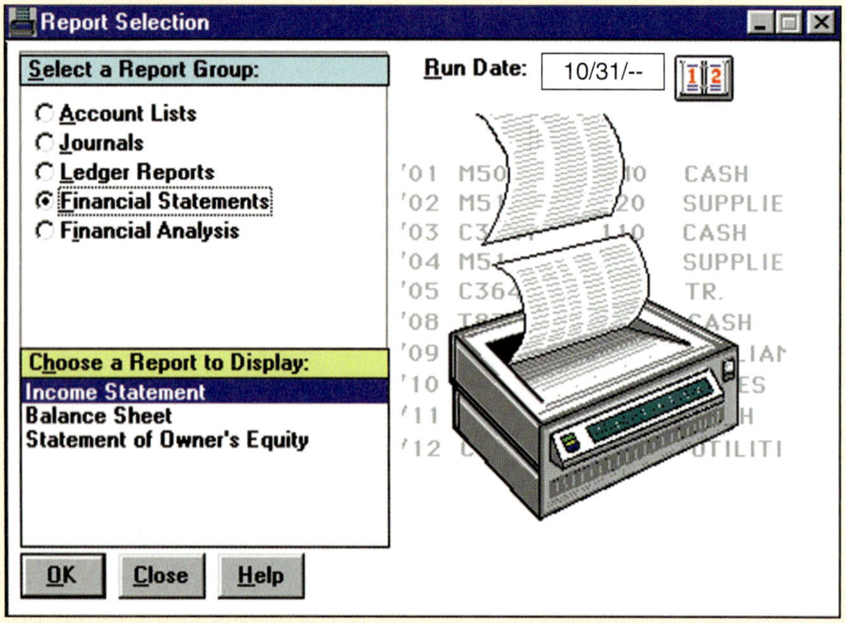

AUTOMATED ACCOUNTING

2. Select problem F08-1 from the appropriate directory/folder.
3. Select File from the menu bar and choose the Save As menu command. Key the path to the drive and directory that contains your data files. Save the database with a file name of XXX081 (where XXX are your initials).
4. Access Problem Instructions through the Help menu (7.0) or Browser tool (8.0). Read the Problem Instructions screen.
5. Refer to page 194 for data used in this template.
6. Exit the *Automated Accounting* software.

AUTOMATING CHALLENGE PROBLEM 8-4: Preparing financial statements with two sources of revenue and a net loss

Instructions:

1. Load *Automated Accounting 7.0* or higher software.
2. Select problem F08-2 from the appropriate directory/folder.
3. Select File from the menu bar and choose the Save As menu command. Key the path to the drive and directory that contains your data files. Save the database with a file name of XXX082 (where XXX are your initials).
4. Access Problem Instructions through the Help menu (7.0) or Browser tool (8.0). Read the Problem Instruc-tions screen.
5. Refer to page 194 for data used in this template.
6. Exit the *Automated Accounting* software.

Pittman Consulting
Income Statement
For Period Ended 10/31/--

Operating Revenue		
Fees	12751.45	100.00
Total Operating Revenue	12751.45	100.00
Operating Expenses		
Advertising Expense	595.00	4.67
Charitable Contrib. Exp.	190.00	1.49
Dues & Subscriptions Exp.	155.65	1.22
Miscellaneous Expense	285.00	2.24
Rent Expense	950.00	7.45
Telephone Expense	263.45	2.07
Travel & Entertain. Exp.	173.73	1.36
Utilities Expense	493.34	3.87
Total Operating Expenses	3106.17	24.36
Net Income	9645.28	75.64

9 Recording Adjusting and Closing Entries for a Service Business

AFTER STUDYING CHAPTER 9, YOU WILL BE ABLE TO:

1. Define accounting terms related to adjusting and closing entries for a service business organized as a proprietorship.
2. Identify accounting concepts and practices related to adjusting and closing entries for a service business organized as a proprietorship.
3. Record adjusting entries for a service business organized as a proprietorship.
4. Record closing entries for a service business organized as a proprietorship.
5. Prepare a post-closing trial balance for a service business organized as a proprietorship.

TERMS PREVIEW

adjusting entries

permanent accounts

temporary accounts

closing entries

post-closing trial balance

accounting cycle

ADJUSTING ENTRIES

Encore Music prepares a work sheet at the end of each fiscal period to summarize the general ledger information needed to prepare financial statements. *(CONCEPT: Accounting Period Cycle)* Financial statements are prepared from information on the work sheet. *(CONCEPT: Adequate Disclosure)*

Encore Music's adjustments are analyzed and planned on a work sheet. However, these adjustments must be journalized so they can be posted to the general ledger accounts. Journal entries recorded to update general ledger accounts at the end of a fiscal period are called **adjusting entries.**

Adjusting entries are recorded on the next journal page following the page on which the last daily transactions for the month are recorded. The adjusting entries are entered in the General Debit and General Credit columns of a journal.

Encore Music records two adjusting entries: (1) an adjusting entry to bring the supplies account up to date and (2) an adjusting entry to bring the prepaid insurance account up to date.

ACCOUNTING IN YOUR CAREER

REPLACE YOURSELF WITH A COMPUTER

"I want you to replace yourself with a computer, Dani," said Stephen Moy, as Dani Tobler entered his office. Dani had worked at Moy Enterprises for two years as an office/accounting assistant. She thought she had been doing a good job, and she knew she frequently took the initiative to do more than her job required. She was startled by Stephen's statement about replacing her.

"Let me explain what I mean, Dani," Stephen continued. "You've been an outstanding resource for me as the business has grown. But now I need to promote you and give you more responsibilities. Therefore, I'd like to convert the accounting system to a computerized system to run more efficiently and give you more time to take on additional projects and responsibilities. I know you took several computer classes in high school. I want you to research the accounting software available and make a recommendation on which package to buy. Do you think you can make a recommendation by the end of the month?"

Dani immediately went to several computer stores and got prices and specifications for a number of accounting software packages. At the end of the day, she was feeling overwhelmed by the large number of accounting packages from which to choose.

Critical Thinking:

1. Assuming that the computer is equipped to handle any popular brand, what should Dani consider in making her decision?
2. An advantage of computer software for accounting is that the computer can take care of the repetitive tasks quickly and accurately. What are some of the repetitive tasks Dani might want to be sure the selected software will do?

ADJUSTING ENTRY FOR SUPPLIES

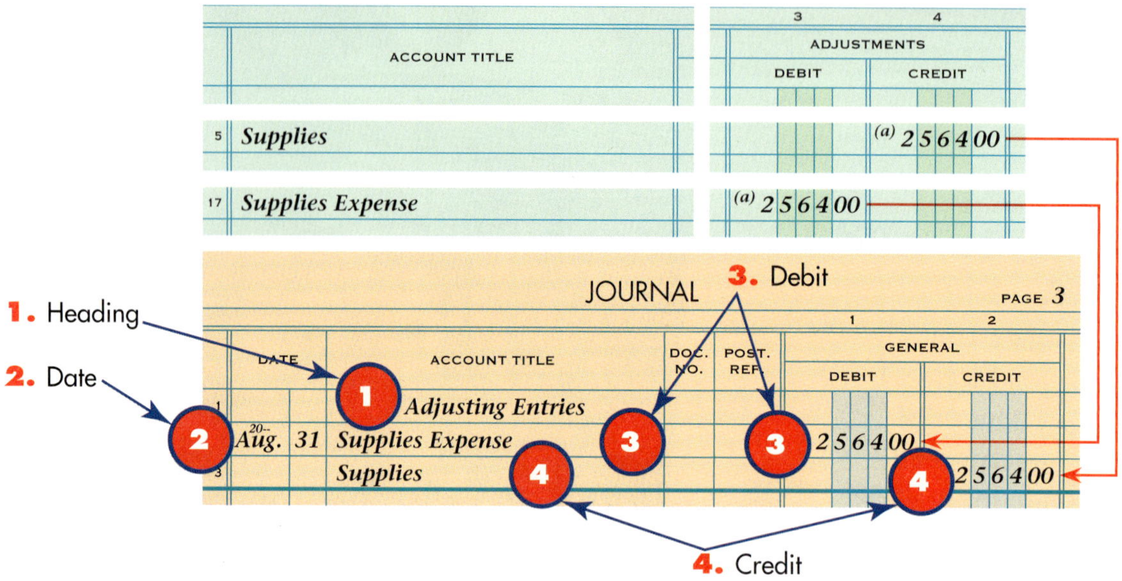

The information needed to journalize the adjusting entry for supplies is obtained from lines 5 and 17 of the work sheet, as shown in the illustration. The entry must be recorded in a journal and posted to the general ledger accounts affected by the entry.

The effect of posting the adjusting entry for supplies to the general ledger accounts is shown in the T accounts.

Supplies Expense has an up-to-date balance of $2,564.00, which is the value of the supplies used during the fiscal period. *(CONCEPT: Matching Expenses with Revenue)* Supplies has a new balance of $2,187.00, which is the cost of the supplies on hand at the end of the fiscal period.

Supplies Expense

Adj. (a)	2,564.00		

Supplies

Bal.	4,751.00	Adj. (a)	2,564.00
(New Bal.	*2,187.00)*		

STEPS: Adjusting entry for supplies

1. Write the heading, *Adjusting Entries,* in the middle of the Account Title column of the journal. Because no source document is prepared for adjusting entries, the entries are identified with a heading in the journal. This heading explains all of the adjusting entries that follow. Therefore, the heading is written only once for all adjusting entries.
2. Write the date, *20—, Aug. 31,* in the Date column.
3. Write the title of the account debited, *Supplies Expense,* in the Account Title column. Record the debit amount, *$2,564.00,* in the General Debit column on the same line as the account title.
4. Write the title of the account credited, *Supplies,* on the next line in the Account Title column. Record the credit amount, *$2,564.00,* in the General Credit column on the same line as the account title.

ADJUSTING ENTRY FOR PREPAID INSURANCE

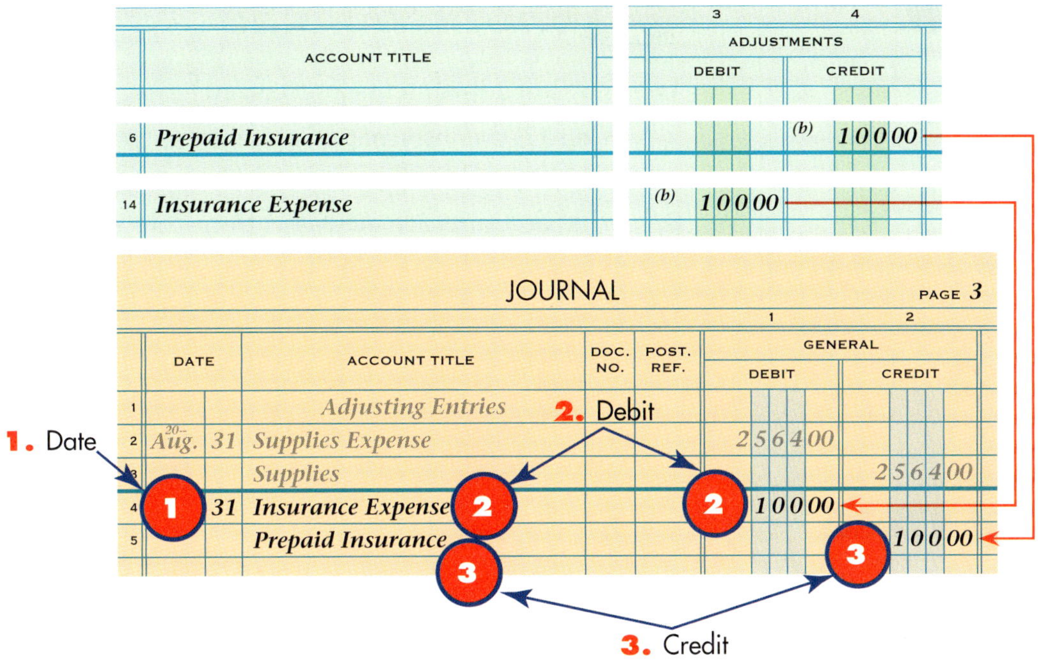

The information needed to journalize the adjusting entry for prepaid insurance is obtained from lines 6 and 14 of the work sheet. The entry must be recorded in a journal and posted to the general ledger accounts affected by the entry.

The effect of posting the adjusting entry for prepaid insurance to the general ledger accounts is shown in the T accounts.

Insurance Expense

Adj. (b)	100.00		

Prepaid Insurance

Bal.	1,200.00	Adj. (b)	100.00
(New Bal.	*1,100.00)*		

PROFESSIONAL BUSINESS ETHICS

IS IT DISCRIMINATION OR POOR JUDGMENT?

CyberMarket provides market research for companies that sell products and services on the Internet.

Instructions

Use the three-step checklist to help determine whether or not the following situation demonstrates ethical behavior.

Your group at CyberMarket has an opening for a research analyst. You are on the search committee to pick candidates to be interviewed. Committee members give the following reasons for wanting to eliminate various candidates.

a. "She graduated from college before I was born. She can't possibly know anything about our business."
b. "The ad said two to five years of experience, but we really need someone with more than two years of experience."
c. "This guy went to the same college I did. Let's give him a shot."

TERM REVIEW

adjusting entries

AUDIT YOUR UNDERSTANDING

1. Why are adjustments journalized?
2. Where is the information obtained to journalize adjusting entries?
3. What accounts are increased from zero balances after adjusting entries for supplies and prepaid insurance are journalized and posted?

WORK TOGETHER

Journalizing and posting adjusting entries

A partial work sheet of Darlene's Delivery Service for the month ended July 31 of the current year is given in the *Working Papers*. Also given are a journal and general ledger accounts. The general ledger accounts do not show all details for the fiscal period. The Balance shown in each account is the account's balance before adjusting entries are posted. Your instructor will guide you through the following example.

4. Use page 4 of a journal. Journalize and post the adjusting entries. Save your work to complete Work Together on page 209.

ON YOUR OWN

Journalizing and posting adjusting entries

A partial work sheet of Keith's Copies for the month ended February 28 of the current year is given in the *Working Papers*. Also given are a journal and general ledger accounts. The general ledger accounts do not show all details for the fiscal period. The Balance shown in each account is the account's balance before adjusting entries are posted. Work this problem independently.

5. Use page 8 of a journal. Journalize and post the adjusting entries. Save your work to complete On Your Own on page 209.

9-2 Recording Closing Entries

NEED FOR PERMANENT AND TEMPORARY ACCOUNTS

Accounts used to accumulate information from one fiscal period to the next are called **permanent accounts.** Permanent accounts are also referred to as real accounts. Permanent accounts include the asset and liability accounts and the owner's capital account. The ending account balances of permanent accounts for one fiscal period are the beginning account balances for the next fiscal period.

Accounts used to accumulate information until it is transferred to the owner's capital account are called **temporary accounts.** Temporary accounts are also referred to as nominal accounts. Temporary accounts include the revenue, expense, and owner's drawing accounts plus the income summary account. Temporary accounts show changes in the owner's capital for a single fiscal period. Therefore, at the end of a fiscal period, the balances of temporary accounts are summarized and transferred to the owner's capital account. The temporary accounts begin a new fiscal period with zero balances.

NEED FOR CLOSING TEMPORARY ACCOUNTS

Journal entries used to prepare temporary accounts for a new fiscal period are called **closing entries.** The temporary account balances must be reduced to zero at the end of each fiscal period. This procedure prepares the temporary accounts for recording information about the next fiscal period. Otherwise, the amounts for the next fiscal period would be added to amounts for previous fiscal periods. *(CONCEPT: Matching Expenses with Revenue)* The net income for the next fiscal period would be difficult to calculate because amounts from several fiscal periods remain in the accounts. Therefore, the temporary accounts must start each new fiscal period with zero balances.

To close a temporary account, an amount equal to its balance is recorded in the account on the side opposite to its balance. For example, if an account has a credit balance of $4,411.00, a debit of $4,411.00 is recorded to close the account.

NEED FOR THE INCOME SUMMARY ACCOUNT

Whenever a temporary account is closed, the closing entry must have equal debits and credits. If an account is debited for $3,000.00 to close the account, some other account must be credited for the same amount. A temporary account titled Income Summary is used to summarize the closing entries for the revenue and expense accounts.

The income summary account is unique because it does not have a normal balance side. The balance of this account is determined by the amounts posted to the account at the end of a fiscal period. When revenue is greater than total expenses, resulting in a net income, the income summary account has a credit balance, as shown in the T account.

Income Summary

Debit	Credit
Total expenses	Revenue (greater than expenses) (Credit balance is the net income.)

When total expenses are greater than revenue, resulting in a net loss, the income summary account has a debit balance, as shown in the T account.

Income Summary

Debit	Credit
Total expenses (greater than revenue) (Debit balance is the net loss.)	Revenue

Thus, whether the balance of the income summary account is a credit or a debit depends upon whether the business earns a net income or incurs a net loss. Because Income Summary is a temporary account, the account is also closed at the end of a fiscal period when the net income or net loss is recorded.

Encore Music records four closing entries: (1) an entry to close income statement accounts with credit balances; (2) an entry to close income statement accounts with debit balances; (3) an entry to record net income or net loss and close Income Summary; and (4) an entry to close the owner's drawing account.

Information needed to record the four closing entries is found in the Income Statement and Balance Sheet columns of the work sheet.

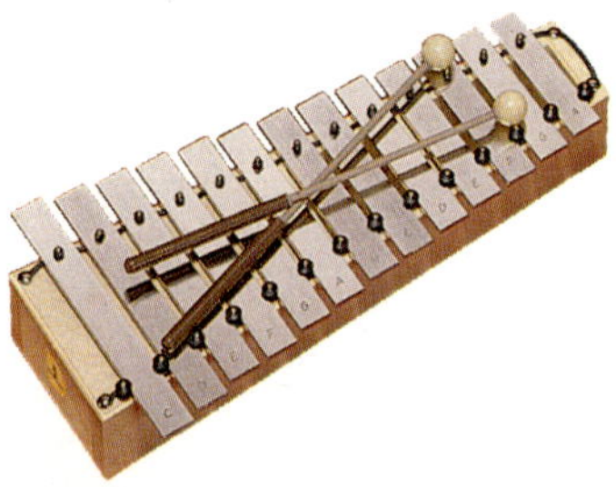

FYI

Most small businesses use the calendar year as their fiscal year because it matches the way in which the owners have to file their personal income tax returns.

REMEMBER

Encore Music makes four closing entries: (1) Close income statement accounts with credit balances. (2) Close income statement accounts with debit balances. (3) Record net income or loss in the owner's capital account and close Income Summary. (4) Close the owner's drawing account.

CLOSING ENTRY FOR AN INCOME STATEMENT ACCOUNT WITH A CREDIT BALANCE

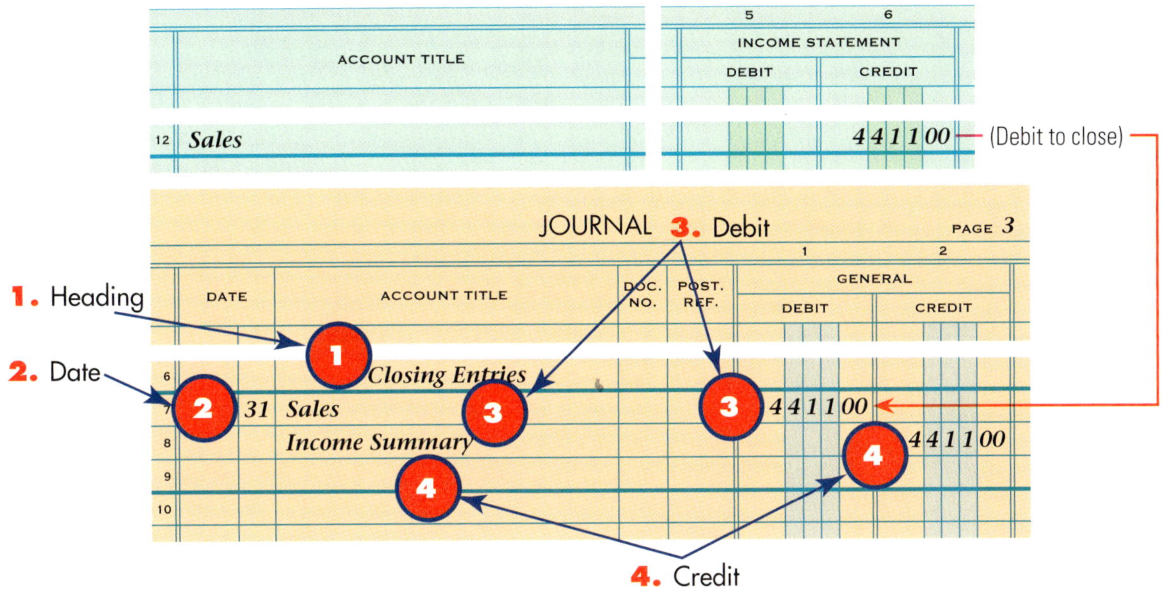

Encore Music has one income statement account with a credit balance, Sales. This credit balance must be reduced to zero to prepare the account for the next fiscal period. To reduce the balance to zero, Sales is debited for the amount of the balance. Because debits must equal credits for each journal entry, some other account must be credited. The account used for the credit part of this closing entry is Income Summary.

The effect of this closing entry on the general ledger accounts is shown in the T accounts.

Sales

Debit		Credit	
Closing	4,411.00	Bal.	4,411.00
		(New Bal. zero)	

Income Summary

Debit		Credit	
		Closing (revenue)	4,411.00

The balance of Sales is now zero, and the account is ready for the next fiscal period. The credit balance of Sales is transferred to Income Summary.

STEPS: Closing entry for an income statement account with a credit balance

1. Write the heading, *Closing Entries,* in the middle of the Account Title column of the journal. For Encore Music, this heading is placed in the journal on the first blank line after the last adjusting entry.
2. Write the date, *31,* on the next line in the Date column.
3. Write the title of the account debited, *Sales,* in the Account Title column. Record the debit amount, *$4,411.00,* in the General Debit column on the same line as the account title.
4. Write the title of the account credited, *Income Summary,* on the next line in the Account Title column. Record the credit amount, *$4,411.00,* in the General Credit column on the same line as the account title.

FYI

The reasons for recording closing entries can be compared to a trip odometer. Closing entries are recorded to prepare the temporary accounts for the next fiscal period by reducing their balances to zero. Likewise, a trip odometer must be reset to zero to begin recording the miles for the next trip.

CLOSING ENTRY FOR INCOME STATEMENT ACCOUNTS WITH DEBIT BALANCES

	ACCOUNT TITLE	5 INCOME STATEMENT DEBIT	6 INCOME STATEMENT CREDIT
13	*Advertising Expense*	273 00	
14	*Insurance Expense*	100 00	
15	*Miscellaneous Expense*	10 00	
16	*Rent Expense*	250 00	
17	*Supplies Expense*	2,564 00	
18	*Utilities Expense*	115 00	

(Credit to close)

JOURNAL **2.** Income Summary PAGE *3*

	DATE	ACCOUNT TITLE	DOC. NO.	POST. REF.	1 GENERAL DEBIT	2 GENERAL CREDIT
9	31	*Income Summary*			3,312 00	
10		*Advertising Expense*				273 00
11		*Insurance Expense*				100 00
12		*Miscellaneous Expense*				10 00
13		*Rent Expense*				250 00
14		*Supplies Expense*				2,564 00
15		*Utilities Expense*				115 00

1. Date

2. Income Summary

3. Credit

4. Debit Amount

Encore Music has six income statement accounts with debit balances. The six expense accounts have normal debit balances at the end of a fiscal period. The balances of the expense accounts must be reduced to zero to prepare the accounts for the next fiscal period. Each expense account is credited for an amount equal to its balance. Income Summary is debited for the total of all the expense account balances. The amount debited to Income Summary is not entered in the amount column until all expenses have been journalized and the total amount calculated.

The effect of this closing entry on the general ledger accounts is shown in the T accounts. The balance of each expense account is returned to zero, and the accounts are ready for the next fiscal period. The balance of Income Summary is the net income for the fiscal period, $1,099.00.

Income Summary

Debit		Credit	
Closing (expenses)	3,312.00	Closing (revenue)	4,411.00
		(New Bal.	*1,099.00)*

Advertising Expense

Debit		Credit	
Bal.	273.00	Closing	273.00
(New Bal. zero)			

Rent Expense

Debit		Credit	
Bal.	250.00	Closing	250.00
(New Bal. zero)			

Insurance Expense

Debit		Credit	
Bal.	100.00	Closing	100.00
(New Bal. zero)			

Supplies Expense

Debit		Credit	
Bal.	2,564.00	Closing	2,564.00
(New Bal. zero)			

Miscellaneous Expense

Debit		Credit	
Bal.	10.00	Closing	10.00
(New Bal. zero)			

Utilities Expense

Debit		Credit	
Bal.	115.00	Closing	115.00
(New Bal. zero)			

CLOSING ENTRY TO RECORD NET INCOME OR LOSS AND CLOSE THE INCOME SUMMARY ACCOUNT

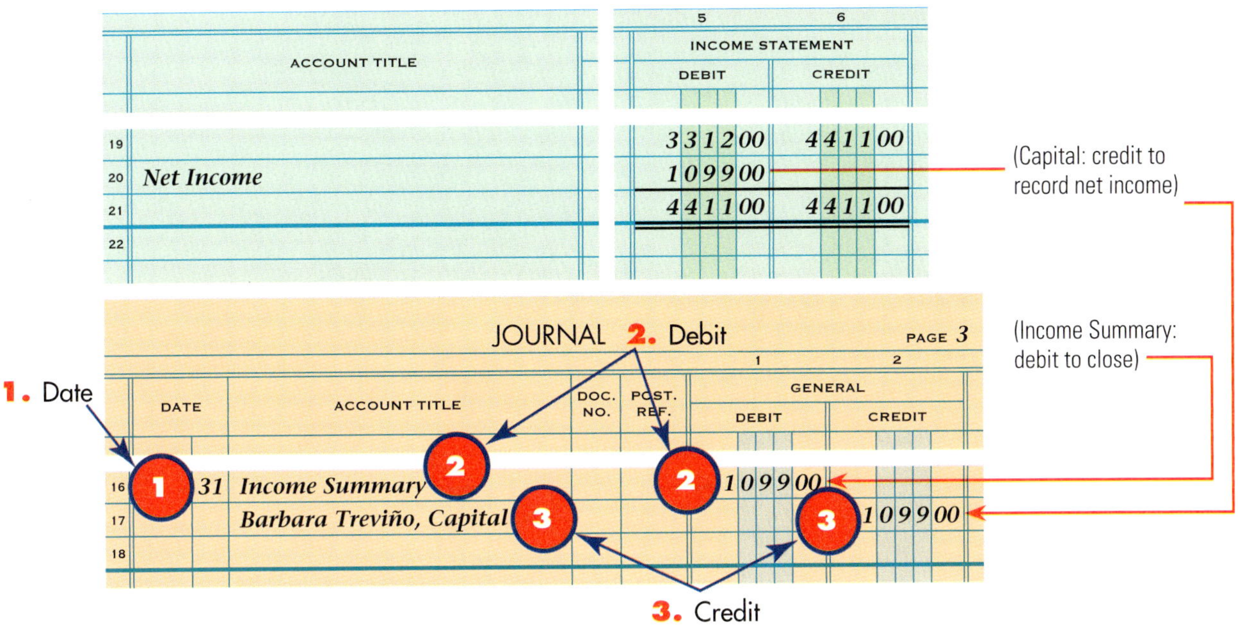

Encore Music's net income appears on line 20 of the work sheet. The amount of net income increases the owner's capital and, therefore, must be credited to the owner's capital account. The balance of the temporary account, Income Summary, must be reduced to zero to prepare the account for the next fiscal period.

The effect of this closing entry on the general ledger accounts is shown in the T accounts.

The debit to the income summary account, $1,099.00, reduces the account balance to zero and prepares the account for the next fiscal period. The credit, $1,099.00, increases the balance of the owner's capital account, Barbara Treviño, Capital.

Income Summary			
Closing (expenses)	3,312.00	Closing (revenue)	4,411.00
Closing	1,099.00	*(New Bal. zero)*	

Barbara Treviño, Capital			
		Bal.	10,000.00
		Closing (net inc.)	1,099.00
		(New Bal.	*11,099.00)*

If a business incurs a net loss, the closing entry is a debit to the owner's capital account and a credit to the income summary account.

STEPS: Closing entry to record net income or loss and close the income summary account

1. Write the date, *31*, on the next line in the Date column.
2. Write the title of the account debited, *Income Summary*, in the Account Title column. Record the debit amount, *$1,099.00*, in the General Debit column on the same line as the account title.
3. Write the title of the account credited, *Barbara Treviño, Capital*, on the next line in the Account Title column. Record the credit amount, *$1,099.00*, in the General Credit column on the same line as the account title.

REMEMBER

Amounts for closing entries are taken from the Income Statement and Balance Sheet columns of the work sheet.

CLOSING ENTRY FOR THE OWNER'S DRAWING ACCOUNT

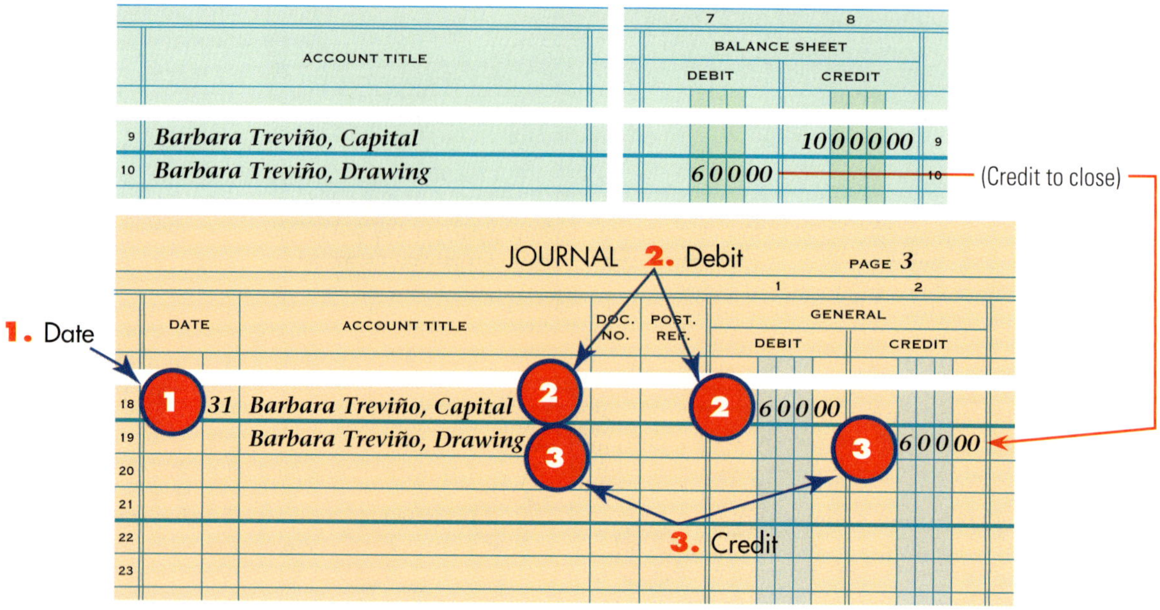

Withdrawals are assets that the owner takes out of a business and which decrease the amount of the owner's equity. The drawing account is a temporary account that accumulates information separately for each fiscal period. Therefore, the drawing account balance is reduced to zero at the end of one fiscal period to prepare the account for the next fiscal period.

The drawing account is neither a revenue nor an expense account. Therefore, the drawing account is not closed through Income Summary. The drawing account balance is closed directly to the owner's capital account.

The effect of the entry to close the drawing account is shown in the T accounts.

The drawing account has a zero balance and is ready for the next fiscal period. The capital account's new balance, $10,499.00, is verified by comparing the balance to the amount of capital shown on the balance sheet prepared at the end of the fiscal period. The capital account balance shown on Encore Music's balance sheet in Chapter 8 is $10,499.00. The two amounts are the same, and the capital account balance is verified.

Barbara Treviño, Capital

Closing (drawing)	600.00	Bal.	10,000.00
		Net Income	1,099.00
		(New Bal.	*10,499.00)*

Barbara Treviño, Drawing

Bal.	600.00	Closing	600.00
(New Bal. zero)			

STEPS: Closing entry for the owner's drawing account

1. Write the date, *31,* in the Date column.
2. Write the title of the account debited, *Barbara Treviño, Capital,* in the Account Title column. Record the debit amount, *$600.00,* in the General Debit column on the same line as the account title.
3. Write the title of the account credited, *Barbara Treviño, Drawing,* in the Account Title column. Record the credit amount, *$600.00,* in the General Credit column on the same line as the account title.

Terms Review

permanent accounts

temporary accounts

closing entries

Audit Your Understanding

1. What do the ending balances of permanent accounts for one fiscal period represent at the beginning of the next fiscal period?
2. What do the balances of temporary accounts show?
3. List the four closing entries.

Work Together

Journalizing and posting closing entries

Use the journal and general ledger accounts from Work Together on page 202. A partial work sheet for the month ended July 31 of the current year is given in the *Working Papers*. Your instructor will guide you through the following example.

4. Continue on the same journal page. Journalize and post the closing entries. Save your work to complete Work Together on page 215.

On Your Own

Journalizing and posting closing entries

Use the journal and general ledger accounts from On Your Own on page 202. A partial work sheet for the month ended February 28 of the current year is given in the *Working Papers*. Work this problem independently.

5. Continue on the same journal page. Journalize and post the closing entries. Save your work to complete On Your Own on page 215.

9-3 Preparing a Post-Closing Trial Balance

GENERAL LEDGER ACCOUNTS AFTER ADJUSTING AND CLOSING ENTRIES ARE POSTED

ACCOUNT *Cash* ACCOUNT NO. *110*

DATE		ITEM	POST. REF.	DEBIT	CREDIT	BALANCE DEBIT	BALANCE CREDIT
20-- Aug.	31		2	14,291.00		14,291.00	
	31		2		6,019.00	8,272.00	

ACCOUNT *Petty Cash* ACCOUNT NO. *120*

DATE		ITEM	POST. REF.	DEBIT	CREDIT	BALANCE DEBIT	BALANCE CREDIT
20-- Aug.	17		1	200.00		200.00	

ACCOUNT *Accounts Receivable—Kids Time* ACCOUNT NO. *130*

DATE		ITEM	POST. REF.	DEBIT	CREDIT	BALANCE DEBIT	BALANCE CREDIT
20-- Aug.	12		1	200.00		200.00	
	12		1		100.00	100.00	

ACCOUNT *Accounts Receivable—Learn N Play* ACCOUNT NO. *140*

DATE		ITEM	POST. REF.	DEBIT	CREDIT	BALANCE DEBIT	BALANCE CREDIT
20-- Aug.	13		1	20.00		20.00	

ACCOUNT *Supplies* ACCOUNT NO. *150*

DATE		ITEM	POST. REF.	DEBIT	CREDIT	BALANCE DEBIT	BALANCE CREDIT
20-- Aug.	3		1	1,577.00		1,577.00	
	7		1	2,720.00		4,297.00	
	20		1	20.00		4,317.00	
	28		2	434.00		4,751.00	
	31		3		2,564.00	2,187.00	

Encore Music's general ledger, after the adjusting and closing entries are posted, is shown here and on the next several pages. When an account has a zero balance, lines are drawn in both the Balance Debit and Balance Credit columns. The lines assure a reader that a balance has not been omitted.

ACCOUNT *Prepaid Insurance* ACCOUNT NO. *160*

DATE		ITEM	POST. REF.	DEBIT	CREDIT	BALANCE DEBIT	BALANCE CREDIT
20-- Aug.	4		1	1200 00		1200 00	
	31		3		100 00	1100 00	

ACCOUNT *Accounts Payable—Ling Music Supplies* ACCOUNT NO. *210*

DATE		ITEM	POST. REF.	DEBIT	CREDIT	BALANCE DEBIT	BALANCE CREDIT
20-- Aug.	7		1		2720 00		2720 00
	11		1	1360 00			1360 00

ACCOUNT *Accounts Payable—Sullivan Office Supplies* ACCOUNT NO. *220*

DATE		ITEM	POST. REF.	DEBIT	CREDIT	BALANCE DEBIT	BALANCE CREDIT
20-- Aug.	20		1		20 00		20 00

ACCOUNT *Barbara Treviño, Capital* ACCOUNT NO. *310*

DATE		ITEM	POST. REF.	DEBIT	CREDIT	BALANCE DEBIT	BALANCE CREDIT
20-- Aug.	1		1		10000 00		10000 00
	31		3		1099 00		11099 00
	31		3	600 00			10499 00

ACCOUNT *Barbara Treviño, Drawing* ACCOUNT NO. *320*

DATE		ITEM	POST. REF.	DEBIT	CREDIT	BALANCE DEBIT	BALANCE CREDIT
20-- Aug.	12		1	100 00		100 00	
	31		2	500 00		600 00	
	31		3		600 00	—	—

ACCOUNT *Income Summary* ACCOUNT NO. *330*

DATE		ITEM	POST. REF.	DEBIT	CREDIT	BALANCE DEBIT	BALANCE CREDIT
20-- Aug.	31		3		4411 00		4411 00
	31		3	3312 00			1099 00
	31		3	1099 00		—	—

ACCOUNT *Sales* ACCOUNT NO. *410*

DATE		ITEM	POST. REF.	DEBIT	CREDIT	BALANCE DEBIT	BALANCE CREDIT
20-- Aug.	31		2		4411 00		4411 00
	31		3	4411 00		—	—

A General Ledger after Adjusting and Closing Entries Are Posted *(continued)*

ACCOUNT *Advertising Expense* ACCOUNT NO. *510*

DATE		ITEM	POST. REF.	DEBIT	CREDIT	BALANCE DEBIT	BALANCE CREDIT
20-- Aug.	14		1	68 00		68 00	
	18		1	200 00		268 00	
	31		2	5 00		273 00	
	31		3		273 00	—	—

ACCOUNT *Insurance Expense* ACCOUNT NO. *520*

DATE		ITEM	POST. REF.	DEBIT	CREDIT	BALANCE DEBIT	BALANCE CREDIT
20-- Aug.	31		3	100 00		100 00	
	31		3		100 00	—	—

ACCOUNT *Miscellaneous Expense* ACCOUNT NO. *530*

DATE		ITEM	POST. REF.	DEBIT	CREDIT	BALANCE DEBIT	BALANCE CREDIT
20-- Aug.	31		2	7 00		7 00	
	31		2	3 00		10 00	
	31		3		10 00	—	—

ACCOUNT *Rent Expense* ACCOUNT NO. *540*

DATE		ITEM	POST. REF.	DEBIT	CREDIT	BALANCE DEBIT	BALANCE CREDIT
20-- Aug.	12		1	250 00		250 00	
	31		3		250 00	—	—

ACCOUNT *Supplies Expense* ACCOUNT NO. *550*

DATE		ITEM	POST. REF.	DEBIT	CREDIT	BALANCE DEBIT	BALANCE CREDIT
20-- Aug.	31		3	2564 00		2564 00	
	31		3		2564 00	—	—

ACCOUNT *Utilities Expense* ACCOUNT NO. *560*

DATE		ITEM	POST. REF.	DEBIT	CREDIT	BALANCE DEBIT	BALANCE CREDIT
20-- Aug.	12		1	45 00		45 00	
	27		2	70 00		115 00	
	31		3		115 00	—	—

A General Ledger after Adjusting and Closing Entries Are Posted *(concluded)*

POST-CLOSING TRIAL BALANCE

2. Account Titles

1. Heading

Encore Music		
Post-Closing Trial Balance		
August 31, 20--		
ACCOUNT TITLE	DEBIT	CREDIT
Cash	8,272.00	
Petty Cash	200.00	
Accounts Receivable—Kids Time	100.00	
Accounts Receivable—Learn N Play	20.00	
Supplies	2,187.00	
Prepaid Insurance	1,100.00	
Accounts Payable—Ling Music Supplies		1,360.00
Accounts Payable—Sullivan Office Supplies		20.00
Barbara Treviño, Capital		10,499.00
Totals	11,879.00	11,879.00

3. Account Balances

4. Single Rule

6. *Totals*

8. Double Rule

5. Compare Totals

7. Record Totals

After the closing entries are posted, Encore Music verifies that debits equal credits in the general ledger accounts by preparing a trial balance. A trial balance prepared after the closing entries are posted is called a **post-closing trial balance.**

Only general ledger accounts with balances are included on a post-closing trial balance. The permanent accounts (assets, liabilities, and owner's capital) have balances and do appear on a post-closing trial balance. Because the temporary accounts (income summary, revenue, expense, and drawing) are closed and have zero balances, they do not appear on a post-closing trial balance.

The total of all debits must equal the total of all credits in a general ledger. The totals of both columns on Encore Music's post-closing trial balance are the same, \$11,879.00. Encore Music's post-closing trial balance shows that the general ledger account balances are in balance and ready for the new fiscal period.

STEPS: Preparing a post-closing trial balance

1. Write the heading on three lines.
2. Write the titles of all general ledger accounts with balances in the Account Title column.
3. On the same line with each account title, write each account's balance in either the Debit or Credit column.
4. Rule a single line across both amount columns below the last amount, and add each amount column.
5. Compare the two column totals. The two column totals must be the same. If the two column totals are not the same, the errors must be found and corrected before any more work is completed.
6. Write the word *Totals* on the line below the last account title.
7. Write the column totals, *\$11,879.00,* below the single line.
8. Rule double lines across both amount columns to show that the totals have been verified as correct.

ACCOUNTING CYCLE FOR A SERVICE BUSINESS

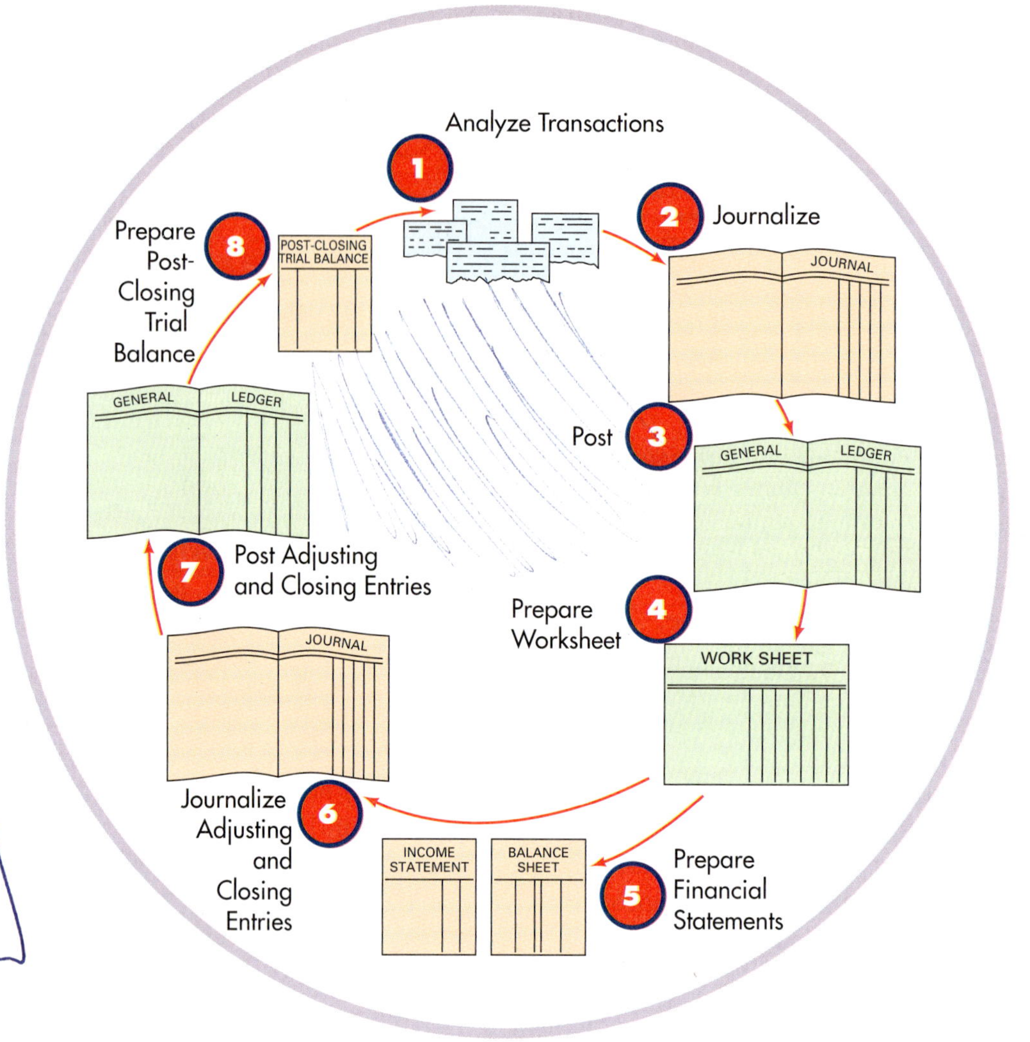

Chapters 1 through 9 describe Encore Music's accounting activities for a one-month fiscal period. The series of accounting activities included in recording financial information for a fiscal period is called an **accounting cycle.** *(CONCEPT: Accounting Period Cycle)*

For the next fiscal period, the cycle begins again at Step 1.

STEPS — Steps in an accounting cycle

1. Source documents are checked for accuracy, and transactions are analyzed into debit and credit parts.
2. Transactions, from information on source documents, are recorded in a journal.
3. Journal entries are posted to the general ledger.
4. A work sheet, including a trial balance, is prepared from the general ledger.
5. Financial statements are prepared from the work sheet.
6. Adjusting and closing entries are journalized from the work sheet.
7. Adjusting and closing entries are posted to the general ledger.
8. A post-closing trial balance of the general ledger is prepared.

FYI

The word post *means* after. *The Post-Closing Trial Balance is prepared after closing entries.*

TERMS REVIEW

post-closing trial balance

accounting cycle

AUDIT YOUR UNDERSTANDING

1. Why are lines drawn in both the Balance Debit and Balance Credit columns when an account has a zero balance?
2. Which accounts go on the post-closing trial balance?
3. Why are temporary accounts omitted from a post-closing trial balance?

WORK TOGETHER

Preparing a post-closing trial balance

Use the general ledger accounts from Work Together on page 209. Your instructor will guide you through the following example. A form to complete a post-closing trial balance is given in the *Working Papers.*

4. Prepare a post-closing trial balance for Darlene's Delivery Service on July 31 of the current year.

ON YOUR OWN

Preparing a post-closing trial balance

Use the general ledger accounts from On Your Own on page 209. Work this problem independently. A form to complete a post-closing trial balance is given in the *Working Papers.*

5. Prepare a post-closing trial balance for Keith's Copies on February 28 of the current year.

CHAPTER 9 SUMMARY

After completing this chapter, you can

1. Define accounting terms related to adjusting and closing entries for a service business organized as a proprietorship.
2. Identify accounting concepts and practices related to adjusting and closing entries for a service business organized as a proprietorship.
3. Record adjusting entries for a service business organized as a proprietorship.
4. Record closing entries for a service business organized as a proprietorship.
5. Prepare a post-closing trial balance for a service business organized as a proprietorship.

EXPLORE ACCOUNTING

PUBLIC ACCOUNTING FIRMS

A business that helps other businesses with accounting issues is known as a public accounting firm.

The independent reviewing and issuing of an opinion on the reliability of accounting records is known as *auditing*.

When performing an audit for a client, the accounting firm looks closely at the client's financial statements and the way the client records transactions. The auditor's job is to determine if the financial statements fairly present the financial position of the client. The auditor issues an opinion, which is a statement as to whether the financial statements follow standard accounting rules (GAAP). This "opinion" is used by bankers deciding to lend money to the company. It is also used by investors when making investment decisions.

Auditing, however, is just one of many services provided by public accounting firms. Other services include tax preparation, tax advice, payroll services, bookkeeping services, financial statement preparation, and consulting services. These other services often make up a higher percentage of business for the accounting firm than performing audits.

Many accounting firms report that they are getting more requests for consulting services than for other services they can provide. In many cases, consulting is also the area that produces the largest profit margin for the public accounting firm.

Therefore, some firms are actively advertising their ability to provide management consulting services for clients.

Activity: Contact a public accounting firm in your area. Research what services the firm provides and which service area (if any) is growing. Present your findings to your class.

9-1 APPLICATION PROBLEM
Journalizing and posting adjusting entries

A journal and general ledger accounts are given in the *Working Papers*. A partial work sheet for the month ended April 30 of the current year is shown below.

	ACCOUNT TITLE	3 ADJUSTMENTS DEBIT	4 ADJUSTMENTS CREDIT
5	*Supplies*		(a) 180 00
6	*Prepaid Insurance*		(b) 160 00
14	*Insurance Expense*	(b) 160 00	
15	*Miscellaneous Expense*		
16	*Supplies Expense*	(a) 180 00	

Use page 12 of a journal. Journalize and post the adjusting entries. Save your work to complete Application Problem 9-2.

9-2 APPLICATION PROBLEM
Journalizing and posting closing entries

Use the journal and general ledger accounts from Application Problem 9-1. A partial work sheet for the month ended April 30 of the current year is shown below.

	ACCOUNT TITLE	5 INCOME STATEMENT DEBIT	6 INCOME STATEMENT CREDIT	7 BALANCE SHEET DEBIT	8 BALANCE SHEET CREDIT	
1	*Cash*			9500 00		1
2	*Petty Cash*			100 00		2
3	*Accounts Receivable—Betsy Russell*			1650 00		3
4	*Accounts Receivable—Charles Healy*			1403 00		4
5	*Supplies*			220 00		5
6	*Prepaid Insurance*			640 00		6
7	*Accounts Payable—Lindgren Supply*				548 00	7
8	*Accounts Payable—Taxes By Thomas*				111 00	8
9	*Ken Cherniak, Capital*				11810 00	9
10	*Ken Cherniak, Drawing*			855 00		10
11	*Income Summary*					11
12	*Sales*		4400 00			12
13	*Advertising Expense*	800 00				13
14	*Insurance Expense*	160 00				14
15	*Miscellaneous Expense*	351 00				15
16	*Supplies Expense*	180 00				16
17	*Utilities Expense*	1010 00				17
18		2501 00	4400 00	14368 00	12469 00	18
19	*Net Income*	1899 00			1899 00	19
20		4400 00	4400 00	14368 00	14368 00	20
21						21

Continue on the same journal page. Journalize and post the closing entries. Save your work to complete Application Problem 9-3.

9-3 APPLICATION PROBLEM
Preparing a post-closing trial balance

Use the general ledger accounts from Application Problem 9-2. A form to complete a post-closing trial balance is given in the *Working Papers*.

Prepare a post-closing trial balance for Ken's Carpet Cleaning on April 30 of the current year.

9-4 MASTERY PROBLEM
Journalizing and posting adjusting and closing entries; preparing a post-closing trial balance

Jane's Sewing Machine Repair's partial work sheet for the month ended October 31 of the current year is given below. The general ledger accounts are given in the *Working Papers*. The general ledger accounts do not show all details for the fiscal period. The Balance shown in each account is the account's balance before adjusting and closing entries are posted.

		3	4	5	6	7	8	
	ACCOUNT TITLE	ADJUSTMENTS		INCOME STATEMENT		BALANCE SHEET		
		DEBIT	CREDIT	DEBIT	CREDIT	DEBIT	CREDIT	
1	*Cash*					6400 00		1
2	*Petty Cash*					100 00		2
3	*Accts. Rec.—Debbie McDonald*					657 00		3
4	*Accts. Rec.—Howard Kikles*					599 00		4
5	*Supplies*		(a) 120 00			155 00		5
6	*Prepaid Insurance*		(b) 150 00			300 00		6
7	*Accts. Pay.—Bailey's Supply*						187 00	7
8	*Accts. Pay.—Freida's on Fulton*						126 00	8
9	*Jane Wisen, Capital*						6430 00	9
10	*Jane Wisen, Drawing*					1500 00		10
11	*Income Summary*							11
12	*Sales*				4238 00			12
13	*Advertising Expense*			382 00				13
14	*Insurance Expense*	(b) 150 00		150 00				14
15	*Supplies Expense*	(a) 120 00		120 00				15
16	*Utilities Expense*			618 00				16
17		270 00	270 00	1270 00	4238 00	9711 00	6743 00	17
18	*Net Income*			2968 00			2968 00	18
19				4238 00	4238 00	9711 00	9711 00	19
20								20

Instructions:

1. Use page 20 of a journal. Journalize and post the adjusting entries.
2. Continue to use page 20 of the journal. Journalize and post the closing entries.
3. Prepare a post-closing trial balance.

9-5 CHALLENGE PROBLEM

Journalizing and posting adjusting and closing entries with a net loss; preparing a post-closing trial balance

Mancini Hair Care's partial work sheet for the month ended September 30 of the current year is given below. The general ledger accounts are given in the *Working Papers*. The general ledger accounts do not show all details for the fiscal period. The Balance shown in each account is the account's balance before adjusting and closing entries are posted.

		3	4	5	6	7	8	
	ACCOUNT TITLE	ADJUSTMENTS		INCOME STATEMENT		BALANCE SHEET		
		DEBIT	CREDIT	DEBIT	CREDIT	DEBIT	CREDIT	
1	*Cash*					7678 00		1
2	*Petty Cash*					100 00		2
3	*Accts. Rec.—Jennifer Balsa*					164 00		3
4	*Supplies*		(a) 1500 00			690 00		4
5	*Prepaid Insurance*		(b) 175 00			700 00		5
6	*Accts. Pay.—Alto Supplies*						733 00	6
7	*Jon Mancini, Capital*						9500 00	7
8	*Jon Mancini, Drawing*					500 00		8
9	*Income Summary*							9
10	*Sales*				4596 00			10
11	*Advertising Expense*			550 00				11
12	*Insurance Expense*	(b) 175 00		175 00				12
13	*Miscellaneous Expense*			58 00				13
14	*Supplies Expense*	(a) 1500 00		1500 00				14
15	*Utilities Expense*			2714 00				15
16		1675 00	1675 00	4997 00	4596 00	9832 00	10233 00	16
17	*Net Loss*				401 00	401 00		17
18				4997 00	4997 00	10233 00	10233 00	18

4997 4596

Instructions:

1. Use page 18 of a journal. Journalize and post the adjusting entries.
2. Continue to use page 18 of the journal. Journalize and post the closing entries.
3. Prepare a post-closing trial balance.
4. Jon Mancini, owner of Mancini Hair Care, is disappointed that his business incurred a net loss for September of the current year. Mr. Mancini would have preferred not to have to reduce his capital by $401.00. He knows that you are studying accounting, so Mr. Mancini asks you to analyze his work sheet for September. Based on your analysis of the work sheet, what would you suggest may have caused the net loss for Mancini Hair Care? What steps would you suggest so that Mr. Mancini can avoid a net loss in future months?

Too many expenses caused the net loss. Mr. Mancini should cut down his supplies and advertising expenses.

4997
- 4596
401

INTERNET ACTIVITY

Point your browser to

http://accounting.swpco.com

Choose **First-Year Course**, choose **Activities**, and complete the activity for Chapter 9.

Applied Communication

Service businesses are the fastest growing part of our business world. Social and economic changes create needs for new and different kinds of service businesses to satisfy customer demands.

For example, the growing popularity of the World Wide Web led to the creation of service businesses that design Web pages. These businesses create text, graphics, animation, and links for business and private clients. Another example of a new type of service business is a personal services business that runs errands or stands in long lines for clients. As lifestyles become busier and busier, some people do not have the time to take care of all their personal errands. Service businesses have appeared to fill this need.

Instructions: Using library, online, or other information resources, write a one-page report on a new or unusual service business that you would be interested in working for or owning.

Cases for Critical Thinking

Case 1 Gretel Bakken forgot to journalize and post the adjusting entry for prepaid insurance at the end of the June fiscal period. What effect will this omission have on the records of Ms. Bakken's business as of June 30? Explain your answer.

Case 2 Miles Reed states that his business is so small that he just records supplies and insurance as expenses when he pays for them. Thus, at the end of a fiscal period, Mr. Reed does not record adjusting and closing entries for his business. Do you agree with his accounting procedures? Explain your answer.

Case 3 As you have learned, accounting procedures can be complicated and time-consuming. However, completing accounting work in a timely fashion is very important to business operations and decision making. Business owners rely upon accounting information in order to make good plans for the future. Knowing whether sales are increasing or decreasing or whether the business is earning net income or incurring a net loss is critical information for the owner and other people interested in the financial results of a business.

Completing a work sheet, preparing financial statements, and journalizing and posting adjusting and closing entries are sometimes referred to as end-of-fiscal-period activities. How important is it for end-of-fiscal-period activities to be completed soon after a fiscal period ends? Why do accounting employees often work long hours and weekends just before and just after a fiscal period ends? Explain your answers.

AUTOMATED ACCOUNTING

AUTOMATED ADJUSTING AND CLOSING ENTRIES FOR PROPRIETORSHIPS

During the fiscal period, numerous transactions are analyzed, journalized, and posted. When a transaction affects more than one accounting period, an adjusting entry may be needed to match revenues and expenses with the appropriate accounting period. To complete the accounting cycle, adjusting entries are recorded, entered into the computer, and verified for accuracy. The financial statements are generated, and then closing entries are generated and posted by the software.

Adjusting Entries

After all the usual transactions of the business are entered as journal entries, a preliminary trial balance is generated. This trial balance and period-end adjustment data are used as the basis for the adjusting entries. Usually this will include entries for assets that have been consumed or sold during the period and have become expenses, such as supplies and insurance policies. For most asset accounts, such as Supplies and Insurance, the adjustment is made to the related expense account. The General Journal tab within the Journal Entries window is used to enter and post the adjusting entries. All of the adjusting entries are dated the last day of the fiscal period, and use Adj. Ent. as the reference.

Period-End Closing for a Proprietorship

In an automated accounting system, closing entries are generated and posted by the software. The software automatically closes net income to the owner's capital account after closing the revenue and expense accounts. The drawing account is closed as well.

To perform a period-end closing:

1. Choose Generate Closing Journal Entries from the Options menu.
2. Click Yes to generate the closing entries.
3. The general journal will appear, containing the journal entries.
4. Click the Post button.

AUTOMATING MASTERY PROBLEM 9-4: Journalizing and posting adjusting and closing entries; preparing a post-closing trial balance

Instructions:

1. Load *Automated Accounting 7.0* or higher software.
2. Select database F09-1 from the appropriate directory/folder.
3. Select File from the menu bar and choose the Save As menu command. Key the path to the drive and directory that contains your data files. Save the database with a file name of XXX091 (where XXX are your initials).
4. Access Problem Instructions through the Help menu (7.0) or Browser tool (8.0). Read the Problem Instructions screen.
5. Refer to page 212 for data used in this template.
6. Exit the *Automated Accounting* software.

AUTOMATING CHALLENGE PROBLEM 9-5: Journalizing and posting adjusting and closing entries with a net loss; preparing a post-closing trial balance

Instructions:

1. Load *Automated Accounting 7.0* or higher software.
2. Select database F09-2 from the appropriate directory/folder.
3. Select File from the menu bar and choose the Save As menu command. Key the path to the drive and directory that contains your data files. Save the database with a file name of XXX092 (where XXX are your initials).
4. Access Problem Instructions through the Help menu (7.0) or Browser tool (8.0). Read the Problem Instructions screen.
5. Refer to page 213 for data used in this template.
6. Exit the *Automated Accounting* software.

REINFORCEMENT ACTIVITY 1—PART B

An Accounting Cycle for a Proprietorship: End-of-Fiscal-Period Work

The general ledger prepared in Reinforcement Activity 1—Part A is needed to complete Reinforcement Activity 1—Part B.

Reinforcement Activity 1—Part B includes end-of-fiscal-period activities studied in Chapters 7 through 9.

WORK SHEET

Instructions:

12. Prepare a trial balance on the work sheet given in the *Working Papers*. Use a one-month fiscal period ended May 31 of the current year.
13. Analyze the following adjustment information into debit and credit parts. Record the adjustments on the work sheet.

Adjustment Information, May 31

Supplies on hand	$520.00
Value of prepaid insurance	800.00

14. Total and rule the Adjustments columns.
15. Extend the up-to-date account balances to the Balance Sheet and Income Statement columns.
16. Complete the work sheet.

FINANCIAL STATEMENTS

Instructions:

17. Prepare an income statement. Figure and record the component percentages for sales, total expenses, and net income. Round percentage calculations to the nearest 0.1%.
18. Prepare a balance sheet.

ADJUSTING ENTRIES

Instructions:

19. Use page 3 of the journal. Journalize and post the adjusting entries.

CLOSING ENTRIES

Instructions:

20. Continue using page 3 of the journal. Journalize and post the closing entries.

POST-CLOSING TRIAL BALANCE

Instructions:

21. Prepare a post-closing trial balance.

The following activities are included in this simulation:

1. Journalizing transactions in a journal.
2. Forwarding column totals to a new page.
3. Preparing a bank statement reconciliation and recording a bank service charge.
4. Proving cash.
5. Proving and ruling a journal.
6. Posting from a journal to a general ledger.
7. Preparing a trial balance on a work sheet.
8. Recording adjustments on a work sheet.
9. Completing a work sheet.
10. Preparing financial statements (income statement and balance sheet).
11. Journalizing and posting adjusting entries.
12. Journalizing and posting closing entries.
13. Preparing a post-closing trial balance.

This simulation covers the transactions completed by Foreign Exchange Translation Service, a service business organized as a proprietorship. On September 1 of the current year, Foreign Exchange begins business. The business specializes in translating items such as web pages, books, speeches, and reports into other languages.

The activities included in the accounting cycle for Foreign Exchange are listed at the left. The company uses a journal and a general ledger similar to those described for Encore Music in Cycle 1.

This simulation is available in manual and in automated versions, for use with *Automated Accounting* software.

Accounting for a Merchandising

CYCLE 2

Business Organized as a Partnership

OMNI IMPORT CHART OF ACCOUNTS

General Ledger

Balance Sheet Accounts

(1000) ASSETS
1110 Cash
1120 Petty Cash
1130 Accounts Receivable
1140 Merchandise Inventory
1145 Supplies—Office
1150 Supplies—Store
1160 Prepaid Insurance

(2000) LIABILITIES
2110 Accounts Payable
2120 Employee Income Tax Payable
2130 Social Security Tax Payable
2135 Medicare Tax Payable
2140 Sales Tax Payable
2150 Unemployment Tax Payable—Federal
2160 Unemployment Tax Payable—State
2170 Health Insurance Premiums Payable
2180 U.S. Savings Bonds Payable
2190 United Way Donations Payable

(3000) OWNERS' EQUITY
3110 Karl Koehn, Capital
3120 Karl Koehn, Drawing
3130 Michelle Wu, Capital
3140 Michelle Wu, Drawing
3150 Income Summary

Income Statement Accounts

(4000) OPERATING REVENUE
4110 Sales

(5000) COST OF MERCHANDISE
5110 Purchases

(6000) OPERATING EXPENSES
6110 Advertising Expense
6120 Credit Card Fee Expense
6130 Insurance Expense
6140 Miscellaneous Expense
6150 Payroll Taxes Expense
6160 Rent Expense
6170 Salary Expense
6175 Supplies Expense—Office
6180 Supplies Expense—Store
6190 Utilities Expense

Subsidiary Ledgers

Accounts Receivable Ledger

110 Ashton Jaycees
120 Children's Paradise
130 Fiesta Costumes
140 Keystone Corner
150 Parties Unlimited
160 Quality Fashions

Accounts Payable Ledger

210 Accent Importers
220 African Importers
230 Crown Ltd.
240 Embassy Office Supplies
250 Foxfire Supply
260 Pacific Imports

The charts of accounts for Omni Import are illustrated above for ready reference as you study Cycle 2 of this textbook.

10 Journalizing Purchases and Cash Payments

AFTER STUDYING CHAPTER 10, YOU WILL BE ABLE TO:

1. Define accounting terms related to purchases and cash payments for a merchandising business.
2. Identify accounting concepts and practices related to purchases and cash payments for a merchandising business.
3. Journalize purchases of merchandise for cash.
4. Journalize purchases of merchandise on account and buying supplies.
5. Journalize cash payments and other transactions.

TERMS PREVIEW

partnership
partner
merchandising business
retail merchandising business
merchandise
wholesale merchandising business
cost of merchandise
markup
vendor
purchase invoice
terms of sale

PARTNERSHIPS

Many businesses start small. An individual has an idea for a business, develops a plan, secures financial capital, and starts a business. Encore Music, the business described in Cycle 1, is a small business owned by one person. A business owned by one person is known as a proprietorship.

Businesses often require the skills of more than one person. As they grow, many businesses also need more capital than one owner can provide. Therefore, some businesses are owned by two or more persons. A business in which two or more persons combine their assets and skills is called a **partnership.** Each member of a partnership is called a **partner.** Partners must agree on how each partner will share the business's profit or loss. As in proprietorships, reports and financial records of the business are kept separate from the personal records of the partners. *(CONCEPT: Business Entity)*

ACCOUNTING IN YOUR CAREER

UNTANGLING CASH PAYMENTS

Denise Klein and Martin Nadler are partners in an office supply business called OfficeTown. Their store is located next to a complex of office towers, ensuring frequent purchases by nearby companies.

The partners are considering a major expansion to include more emphasis on computer supplies, both hardware and software, and they believe they can also profit from adding copying and packing and delivery services. They have just hired David Bradford as office manager because he has a degree in accounting and extensive experience with computers. David has discovered the following problems related to cash payments.

- Both partners withdraw a set amount of cash each month, paid by check. During the week, however, both Denise and Martin take cash from the cash register for their daily personal expenses.
- Both partners regularly take office and computer supplies home for personal use.
- Incidental small payments, such as delivery charges and postage stamps, are paid for by removing cash from the cash register.
- When office supplies are needed for the operation of the business, they are removed from the stock of the store. No journal entry is made.
- At the end of the day, the cash in the cash register is counted and the cash register tape shows the total sales for the day. The cash count is subtracted from the total of the beginning cash plus total sales, and the difference is posted as Miscellaneous Expense.

Critical Thinking:

1. How could each problem area be corrected and what journal entries should be recorded?
2. Describe for each of the five identified problems which accounts are affected and whether they will be overstated or understated on the financial statements.

10-1 Journalizing Purchases of Merchandise for Cash

When Michelle Wu and Karl Koehn were exchange students in Thailand, they talked about someday going into business together. After each gained a variety of international business experience, Michelle and Karl started Omni Import five years ago. They both enjoy applying their knowledge about other countries and cultures to the operation of their business.

Michelle is especially good at traveling and finding merchandise that people want to buy. Karl has a knack for displaying the merchandise in the most attractive way. These compatible skills make Michelle and Karl more successful as partners than if each ran a business alone. Both partners are convinced, moreover, that keeping accurate and complete accounting records is essential to the success of their business.

THE BUSINESS—OMNI IMPORT

Encore Music, the business described in Cycle 1, sells services for a fee. A business that sells a service for a fee is known as a service business. However, many other businesses purchase goods to sell. A business that purchases and sells goods is called a **merchandising business.** A merchandising business that sells to those who use or consume the goods is called a **retail merchandising business.** Goods that a merchandising business purchases to sell are called **merchandise.** The selling of merchandise rather than a service is what makes the activities of a merchandising business different from those of a service business.

Omni Import, the business described in this cycle, is a retail merchandising business organized as a partnership. The business is owned by Michelle Wu and Karl Koehn. The business purchases and sells imported novelty and gift items such as Russian nesting dolls, African masks, and Irish woolens. Because of the complexities of importing merchandise from numerous foreign countries, Omni purchases its merchandise from other domestic businesses that import foreign merchandise and resell to other businesses. A business that buys and resells merchandise to retail merchandising businesses is called a **wholesale merchandising business.** Omni rents the building in which the business is located as well as the equipment used for operation. Omni expects to make money and continue in business indefinitely. *(CONCEPT: Going Concern)*

EXPANDED JOURNAL

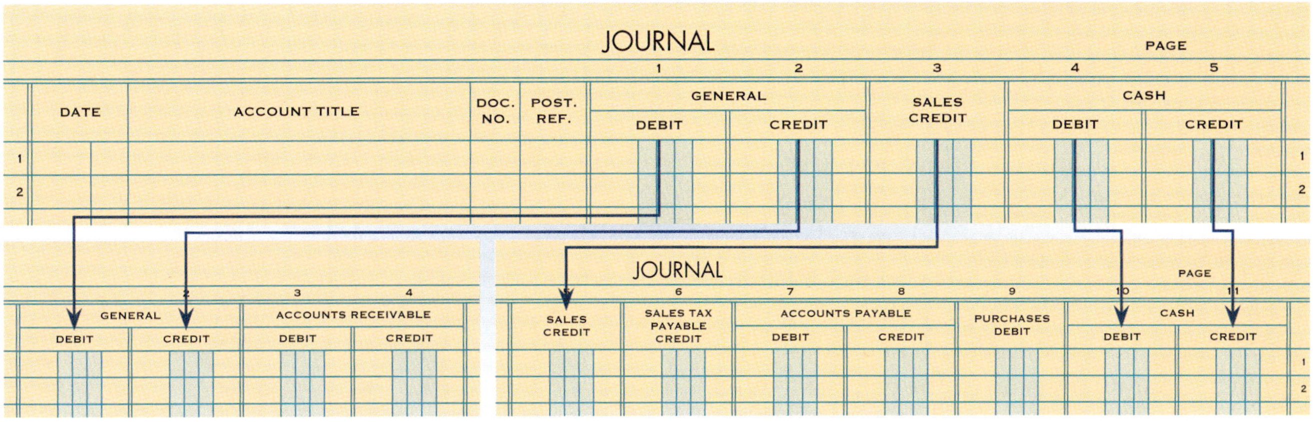

Omni Import, a merchandising business, has many noncash and other frequently occurring transactions that affect single accounts. Omni could use the 5-column journal used by Encore Music. However, without adding more special amount columns to the journal, the large number of transactions would require many entries in the General Debit and Credit columns.

To save time and space in journalizing transactions, Omni uses an expanded 11-column journal. The journal includes additional special amount columns for recording frequently occurring transactions that affect single accounts.

An expanded journal is commonly used by small merchandising businesses in which only one person records transactions. Karl Koehn records all transactions for Omni.

Omni's journal has special amount columns for the recording of frequently occurring transactions related to the purchasing and selling of merchandise. The columns are arranged to make accurate journalizing and posting easier. Debit and credit columns for cash, accounts receivable, and accounts payable are arranged in pairs. This arrangement helps avoid errors in recording amounts in the wrong columns. All columns are placed to the right of the Account Title column. The General Debit and Credit amount columns are placed first so that amounts in these columns will be close to the titles in the Account Title column.

FYI

The number and arrangement of columns in a journal is determined by the type and frequency of transactions.

PURCHASING MERCHANDISE

The price a business pays for goods it purchases to sell is called **cost of merchandise.** The selling price of merchandise must be greater than the cost of merchandise for a business to make a profit. The amount added to the cost of merchandise to establish the selling price is called **markup.** Revenue earned from the sale of merchandise includes both the cost of merchandise and markup. Only the markup increases capital. Accounts for the cost of merchandise are kept in a separate division of the general ledger. The cost of merchandise division is shown in Omni's chart of accounts on page 225.

In addition to purchasing merchandise to sell, a merchandising business also buys supplies and other assets for use in the business. A business from which merchandise is purchased or supplies or other assets are bought is called a **vendor.**

The account used for recording the cost of merchandise is titled Purchases. Purchases is classified as a cost account because it is in the cost of merchandise division in the chart of accounts. Purchases is a temporary account. Because the cost of merchandise reduces capital when the merchandise is purchased, Purchases has a normal debit balance. Therefore, the purchases account is increased by a debit and decreased by a credit, as shown in the T account.

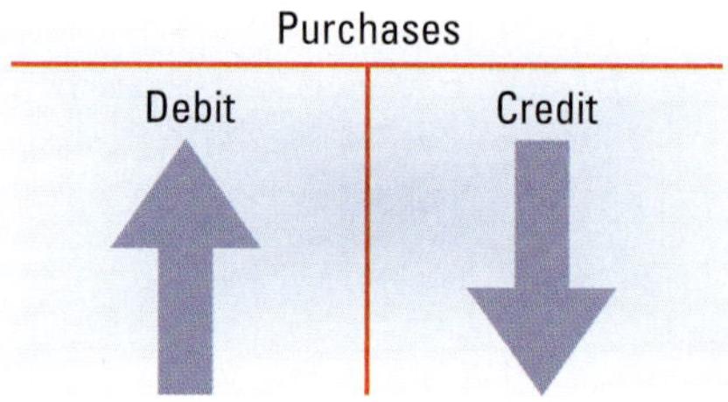

Purchases is used only to record the cost of merchandise purchased. Therefore, only purchases of merchandise are recorded in the Purchases Debit column of the journal. All other items bought, such as supplies, are recorded in the General Debit column of the journal. Merchandise and other items bought are recorded and reported at the price agreed upon at the time the transactions occur. The accounting concept, *Historical Cost,* is applied when the actual amount paid for merchandise or other items bought is recorded. *(CONCEPT: Historical Cost)*

ACCOUNTING AT WORK

JOHN CHUANG

With two partners, John Chuang started MacTemps, a temporary employment agency for workers skilled in using Macintosh computers. Today, John Chuang is the sole shareholder and chairman and chief executive officer. MacTemps has 2,300 temporary workers on assignment on an average day and more than 40 offices worldwide.

John earned his MBA from Harvard and says that his cost accounting course was one of the most useful. It is important to know what each division is earning and what it costs to earn it. "Cost accounting is critical to success," John says.

In the early years of MacTemps, cash flow was difficult to manage because temporary workers had to be paid weekly, but clients often didn't pay for 40 days. Managing cash is essential to the ongoing operations of any business enterprise.

Understanding an income statement and balance sheet are important skills for a business owner, too. John says, "It is surprising how many business owners make terrible decisions because they don't understand their financial statements. Accounting is like reading a box score at a baseball game. It is how we measure ourselves in business. It is the language of business. Furthermore, if you plan to invest, you will need to understand accounting to read an annual report intelligently."

In two years, his company's revenue doubled to $100 million. John Chuang knows what he's talking about.

PURCHASING MERCHANDISE FOR CASH

1. Date **2.** Check Mark **3.** Check Number **4.** Check Mark **5.** Debit **6.** Credit

PAGE 21 JOURNAL PAGE 21

	DATE		ACCOUNT TITLE	DOC. NO.	POST. REF.	9 PURCHASES DEBIT	10 CASH DEBIT	11 CASH CREDIT	
1	20-- Nov.	1	√	C290	√	575 00		575 00	1
2									2

November 1. Purchased merchandise for cash, $575.00. Check No. 290.

Purchases

Debit	Credit
575.00	

Cash

Debit	Credit
	575.00

Omni pays cash for some purchases. All cash payments are made by check.

A cash purchase transaction increases the purchases account balance and decreases the cash account balance.

Because the purchases account has a normal debit balance, Purchases is debited for $575.00 to show the increase in this cost account. The cash account also has a normal debit balance. Therefore, Cash is credited for $575.00 to show the decrease in this asset account.

STEPS Journalizing a purchase of merchandise for cash

1. Write the date, *20—, Nov. 1,* in the Date column.
2. Place a check mark in the Account Title column to show that no account title needs to be written. Both the debit and credit amounts will be recorded in special amount columns.
3. Write the check number, *C290,* in the Doc. No. column.
4. Place a check mark in the Post. Ref. column to show that amounts on this line are not to be posted individually. Both the debit and credit amounts will be posted as part of special amount column totals.
5. Write the debit amount, *$575.00,* in the Purchases Debit column.
6. Write the credit amount, *$575.00,* in the Cash Credit column.

REMEMBER

A check mark in the Account Title column means that all accounts in the transaction have their own special amount columns. A check mark in the Post. Ref. column means don't post.

TERMS REVIEW

partnership
partner
merchandising business
retail merchandising business
merchandise
wholesale merchandising business
cost of merchandise
markup
vendor

AUDIT YOUR UNDERSTANDING

1. Why would two or more persons want to own a single business?
2. What makes the activities of a merchandising business different from those of a service business?
3. What are the special amount columns of an expanded journal?

WORK TOGETHER

Journalizing purchases of merchandise for cash

The journal for Elite Draperies is given in the *Working Papers*. Your instructor will guide you through the following example.

4. Using the current year, journalize the following transactions on page 10 of the journal. Save your work to complete On Your Own below. Source document for check, C.

Transactions:

Oct. 1. Purchased merchandise for cash, $810.00. C317.
2. Purchased merchandise for cash, $1,530.00. C318.

ON YOUR OWN

Journalizing purchases of merchandise for cash

Use the journal for Elite Draperies you started above in Work Together. Work this problem independently.

5. Using the current year, journalize the following transactions, continuing on the next blank line of page 10 of the journal. Save your work to complete Work Together on page 237.

Transactions:

Oct. 3. Purchased merchandise for cash, $345.00. C319.
4. Purchased merchandise for cash, $295.00. C320.

10-2 Journalizing Purchases of Merchandise on Account and Buying Supplies

PURCHASE INVOICE

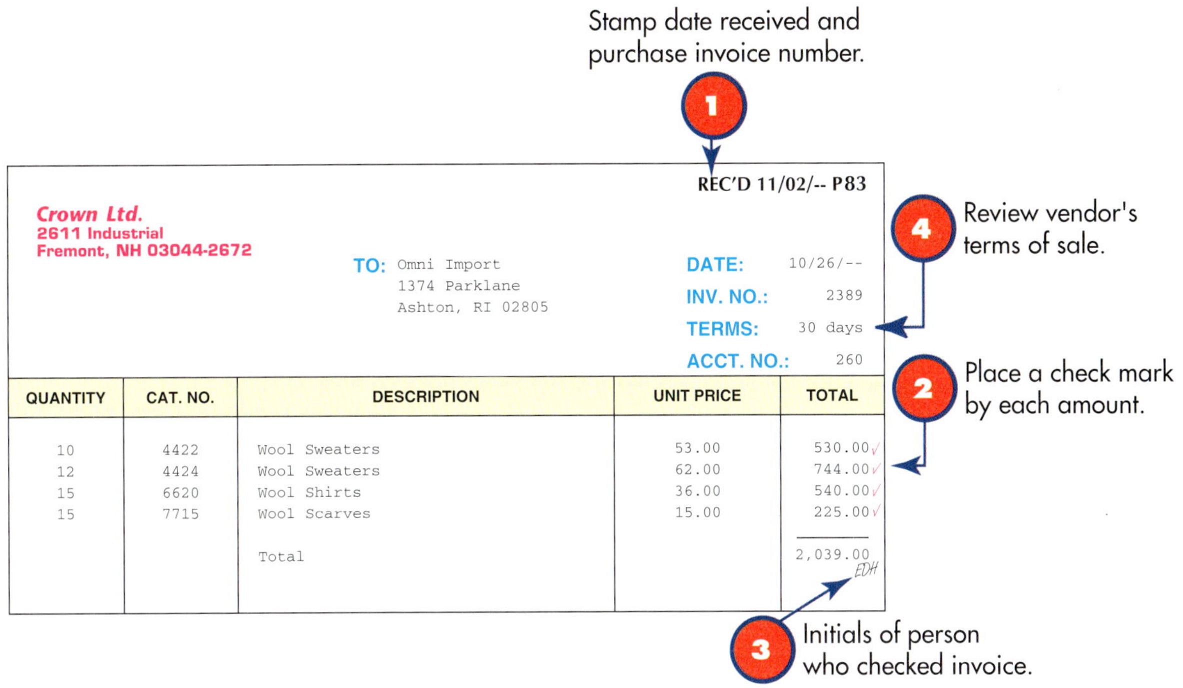

A transaction in which the merchandise purchased is to be paid for later is known as a purchase on account.

When a vendor sells merchandise to a buyer, the vendor prepares a form showing what has been sold. A form describing the goods sold, the quantity, and the price is known as an invoice. An invoice used as a source document for recording a purchase on account transaction is called a **purchase invoice.** *(CONCEPT: Objective Evidence)*

STEPS

Receiving a purchase invoice

1. Stamp the date received, *11/02/—*, and Omni's purchase invoice number, *P83*, in the upper right corner.
   This date should not be confused with the vendor's date on the invoice, 10/26. Omni assigns numbers in sequence to easily identify all purchase invoices. The number stamped on the invoice, P83, is the number assigned by Omni to this purchase invoice. This number should not be confused with the invoice number, 2389, assigned by the vendor. Each vendor uses a different numbering system. Therefore, vendor invoice numbers could not be recorded in sequence, which would make it impossible to detect a missing invoice.
2. Place a check mark by each of the amounts in the Total column to show that the items have been received and that amounts have been checked and are correct.
3. The person who checked the invoice should initial below the total amount in the Total column.
4. Review the vendor's terms. An agreement between a buyer and a seller about payment for merchandise is called the **terms of sale.** The terms of sale on the invoice are 30 days. These terms mean that payment is due within 30 days from the vendor's date of the invoice. The invoice is dated October 26. Therefore, payment must be made by November 25.

PURCHASING MERCHANDISE ON ACCOUNT

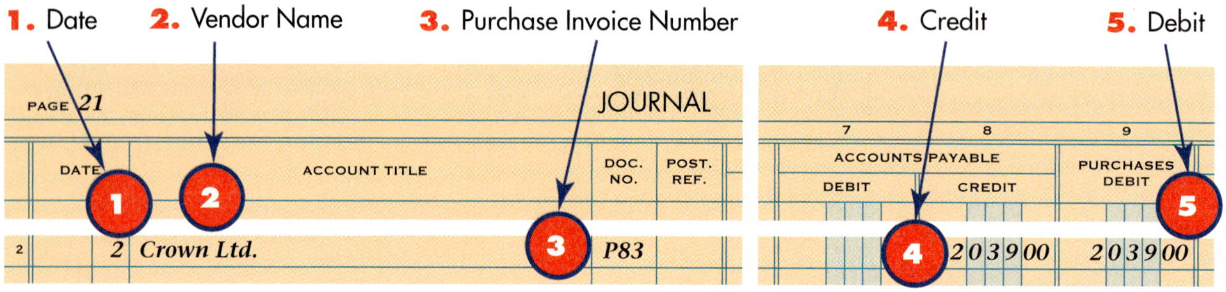

Some businesses that purchase on account from only a few vendors keep a separate general ledger account for each vendor to whom money is owed. Businesses that purchase on account from many vendors will have many accounts for vendors. To avoid a bulky general ledger, the total amount owed to all vendors can be summarized in a single general ledger account. A liability account that summarizes the amounts owed to all vendors is titled Accounts Payable. Omni uses an accounts payable account.

The liability account, Accounts Payable, has a normal credit balance. Therefore, the accounts payable account is increased by a credit and decreased by a debit, as shown in the T account.

November 2. Purchased merchandise on account from Crown Ltd., $2,039.00. Purchase Invoice No. 83.

A purchase on account transaction increases the amount owed to a vendor. This transaction increases the purchases account balance and increases the accounts payable account balance.

Because the purchases account has a normal debit balance, Purchases is debited for $2,039.00 to show the increase in this cost account. The accounts payable account has a normal credit balance. Therefore, Accounts Payable is credited for $2,039.00 to show the increase in this liability account.

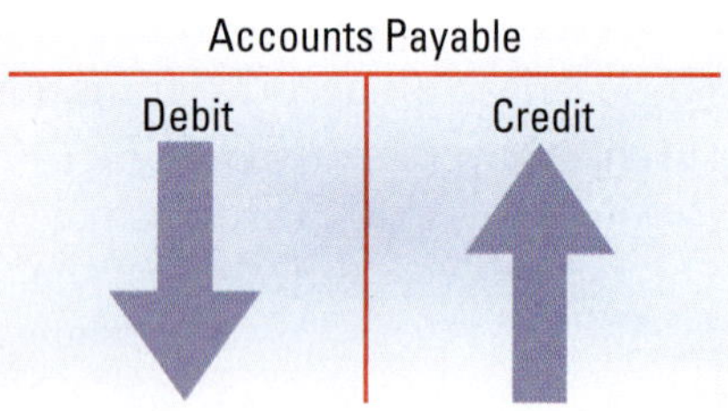

Purchases	
2,039.00	

Accounts Payable	
	2,039.00

STEPS: Journalizing a purchase of merchandise on account

1. Write the date, *2*, in the Date column.
2. Write the vendor name, *Crown Ltd.*, in the Account Title column. The debit to Purchases and the credit to Accounts Payable are recorded in special amount columns. Therefore, it is not necessary to write the title of either general ledger account in the Account Title column. However, the name of the vendor is written in the Account Title column to show to whom the amount is owed. The way Omni keeps records of the amount owed to each vendor is described in Chapter 12.
3. Write the purchase invoice number, *P83*, in the Doc. No. column.
4. Write the credit amount, *$2,039.00*, in the Accounts Payable Credit column.
5. Write the debit amount, *$2,039.00*, in the Purchases Debit column.

REMEMBER

The cost account, Purchases, is used only to record the cost of merchandise purchased. All other items bought, such as supplies, are recorded in the appropriate asset account.

BUYING SUPPLIES FOR CASH

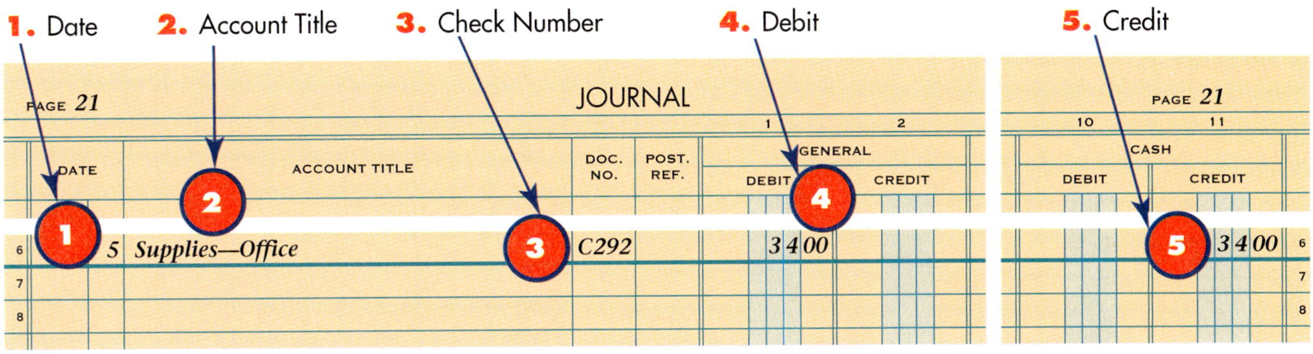

November 5. Paid cash for office supplies, $34.00. Check No. 292.

Supplies—Office	
34.00	

Cash	
	34.00

Omni buys supplies for use in the business. Supplies are not recorded in the purchases account because supplies are not intended for sale. Cash register tapes and price tags are examples of supplies used in a merchandising business. Omni buys most of its supplies for cash.

Because the office supplies account has a normal debit balance, Supplies—Office is debited for $34.00 to show the increase in this asset account. The cash account also has a normal debit balance. Therefore, Cash is credited for $34.00 to show the decrease in this asset account.

STEPS: Journalizing buying supplies for cash

1. Write the date, *5*, in the Date column.
2. Write the account title, *Supplies—Office*, in the Account Title column.
3. Write the check number, *C292*, in the Doc. No. column.
4. Write the debit amount to Supplies—Office, *$34.00*, in the General Debit column.
5. Write the credit amount, *$34.00*, in the Cash Credit column.

MEMORANDUM FOR BUYING SUPPLIES ON ACCOUNT

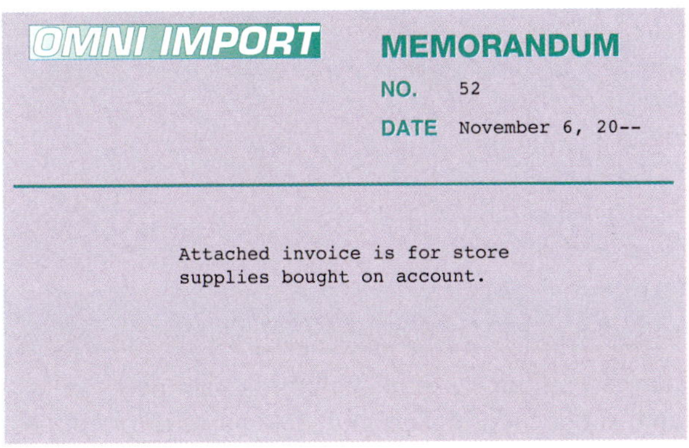
OMNI IMPORT
MEMORANDUM
NO. 52
DATE November 6, 20--

Attached invoice is for store supplies bought on account.

Omni usually buys supplies for cash. Occasionally, however, Omni buys some supplies on account.

When Omni buys supplies on account, an invoice is received from the vendor. This invoice is similar to the purchase invoice received when merchandise is purchased. To assure that no mistake is made, a memorandum is attached to the invoice, noting that the invoice is for supplies and not for purchases.

BUYING SUPPLIES ON ACCOUNT

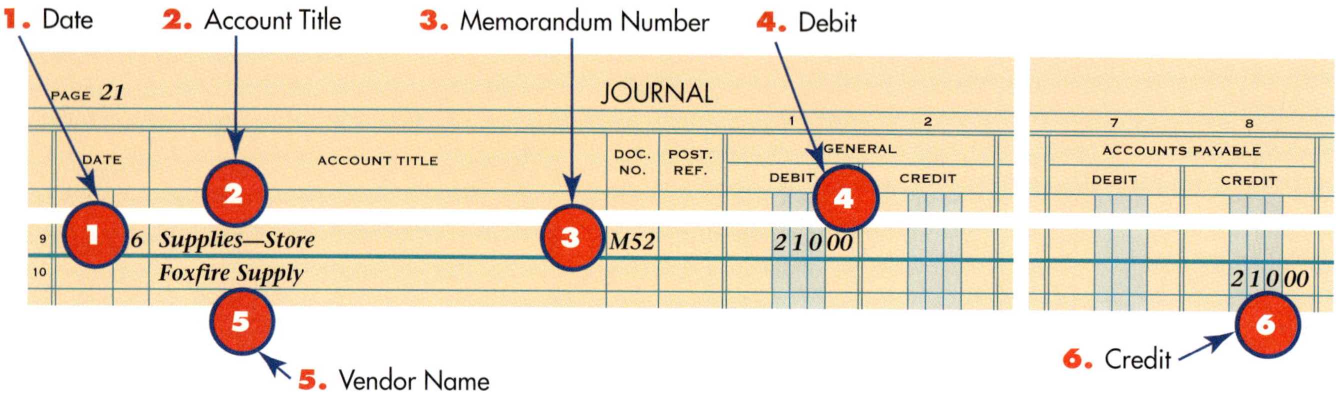

November 6. Bought store supplies on account from Foxfire Supply, $210.00. Memorandum No. 52.

Supplies—Store	
210.00	

Accounts Payable	
	210.00

This transaction increases the store supplies account balance and increases the accounts payable account balance.

Because the store supplies account has a normal debit balance, Supplies—Store is debited for $210.00 to show the increase in this asset account. The accounts payable account has a normal credit balance. Therefore, Accounts Payable is credited for $210.00 to show the increase in this liability account.

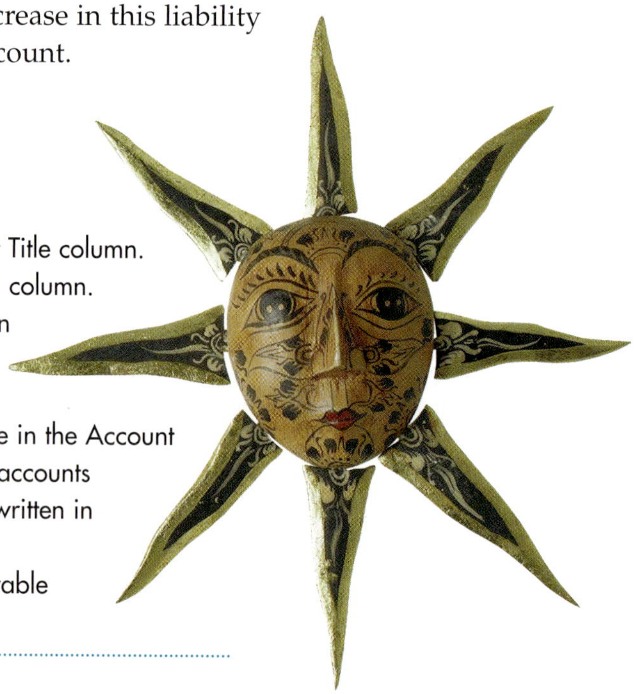

STEPS: Journalizing buying supplies on account

1. Write the date, *6*, in the Date column.
2. Write the account title, *Supplies—Store*, in the Account Title column.
3. Write the memorandum number, *M52*, in the Doc. No. column.
4. Write the debit amount to Supplies—Store, *$210.00*, in the General Debit column on the same line as the account title.
5. Write the vendor name, *Foxfire Supply*, on the next line in the Account Title column. A special amount column is provided for accounts payable. Therefore, this general ledger account is not written in the Account Title column.
6. Write the credit amount, *$210.00*, in the Accounts Payable Credit column.

REMEMBER

When supplies are bought on account, an invoice is received from the vendor. To avoid confusion with purchase invoices received when merchandise is purchased, a memorandum is attached, noting that the invoice is for supplies and not for purchases.

TERMS REVIEW

purchase invoice
terms of sale

AUDIT YOUR UNDERSTANDING

1. In what amount columns would the debit amount and credit amount be written for a purchase of merchandise on account?
2. What account titles would be written in the Account Title column for buying supplies on account?

WORK TOGETHER

Journalizing purchases of merchandise on account and buying supplies

Use the journal for Elite Draperies from On Your Own on page 232. Your instructor will guide you through the following example.

3. Using the current year, journalize the following transactions on page 10 of the journal. Source documents are abbreviated as follows: check, C; memorandum, M; purchase invoice, P. Save your work to complete On Your Own below.

Transactions:

Oct. 5. Purchased merchandise on account from Fabric Outlet, $1,230.00. P116.
6. Paid cash for office supplies, $52.00. C321.
7. Bought store supplies on account from Designer Supplies, $180.00. M62.

ON YOUR OWN

Journalizing purchases of merchandise on account and buying supplies

Use the journal for Elite Draperies from Work Together above. Work this problem independently.

4. Using the current year, journalize the following transactions, continuing on the next blank line of page 10 of the journal. Source documents are abbreviated as follows: check, C; memorandum, M; purchase invoice, P. Save your work to complete Work Together on page 243.

Transactions:

Oct. 8. Purchased merchandise on account from Drapery Hardware, Inc., $480.00. P117.
10. Paid cash for store supplies, $76.00. C322.
11. Bought office supplies on account from Office Express, $240.00. M63.

10-3 Journalizing Cash Payments and Other Transactions

CASH PAYMENT ON ACCOUNT

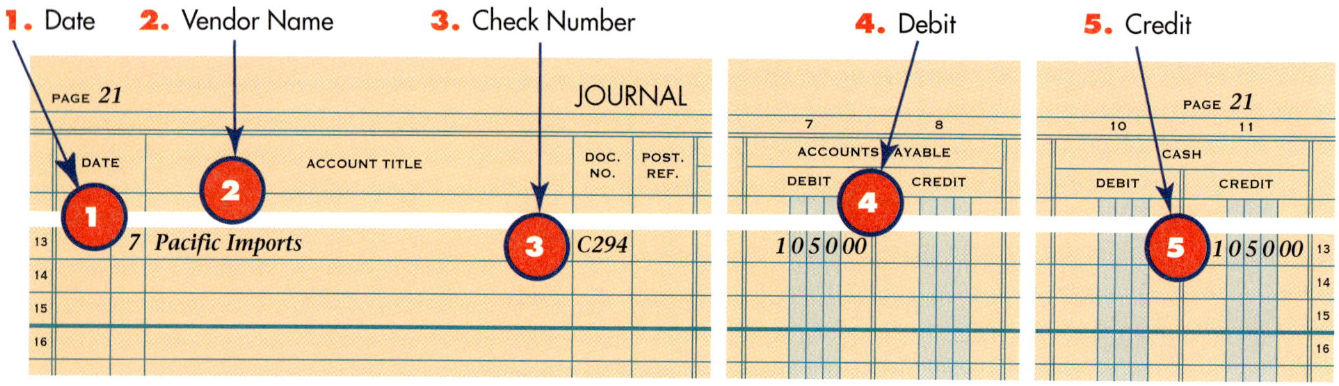

November 7. Paid cash on account to Pacific Imports, $1,050.00, covering Purchase Invoice No. 81. Check No. 294.

Accounts Payable	
1,050.00	

Cash	
	1,050.00

Payments to vendors are made according to the terms of sale on the purchase invoices. Payment for an expense is usually made at the time the expense occurs.

Omni pays by check for all cash purchases and for payments on account.

The cash payment on account transaction shown decreases the amount owed to a vendor. This transaction decreases the accounts payable account balance and decreases the cash account balance.

Because the accounts payable account has a normal credit balance, Accounts Payable is debited for $1,050.00 to show the decrease in this liability account. The cash account has a normal debit balance. Therefore, Cash is credited for $1,050.00 to show the decrease in this asset account.

FYI

CFO stands for Chief Financial Officer.

STEPS: Journalizing a cash payment on account

1. Write the date, *7*, in the Date column.
2. Write the vendor name, *Pacific Imports*, in the Account Title column.
3. Write the check number, *C294*, in the Doc. No. column.
4. Write the debit amount, *$1,050.00*, in the Accounts Payable Debit column.
5. Write the credit amount, *$1,050.00*, in the Cash Credit column.

REMEMBER

The name of the vendor must be written in the Account Title column to show to whom the payment is made.

CASH PAYMENT OF AN EXPENSE

1. Date **2.** Account Title **3.** Check Number **4.** Debit **5.** Credit

PAGE 21 JOURNAL PAGE 21

				1	2	10	11	
				GENERAL		CASH		
DATE	ACCOUNT TITLE	DOC. NO.	POST. REF.	DEBIT	CREDIT	DEBIT	CREDIT	
17 9	Advertising Expense	C296		150 00			150 00	17

November 9. Paid cash for advertising, $150.00. Check No. 296.

Advertising Expense	
150.00	

Cash	
	150.00

Omni usually pays for an expense at the time the transaction occurs.

This cash payment increases the advertising expense account balance and decreases the cash account balance. Because the advertising expense account has a normal debit balance, Advertising Expense is debited for $150.00 to show the increase in this expense account. The cash account also has a normal debit balance. Therefore, Cash is credited for $150.00 to show the decrease in this asset account.

STEPS Journalizing a cash payment of an expense

1. Write the date, *9*, in the Date column.
2. Write the account title, *Advertising Expense*, in the Account Title column.
3. Write the check number, *C296*, in the Doc. No. column.
4. Write the debit amount to Advertising Expense, *$150.00*, in the General Debit column.
5. Write the credit amount, *$150.00*, in the Cash Credit column.

FYI

Gross Domestic Product (GDP) is the total dollar value of all final goods and services produced by resources located in the United States (regardless of who owns the resources) during one year's time.

SMALL BUSINESS SPOTLIGHT

A business plan is required by most banks before they will consider lending money to hopeful small business owners. A typical business plan includes goals and objectives, marketing plans, management and operations plans, estimated financial statements, and budgets.

CASH PAYMENT TO REPLENISH PETTY CASH

1. Date **2.** Account Titles **3.** Check Number **4.** Debit **5.** Credit

PAGE 21 JOURNAL PAGE 21

	DATE	ACCOUNT TITLE	DOC. NO.	POST. REF.	1 GENERAL DEBIT	2 GENERAL CREDIT	10 CASH DEBIT	11 CASH CREDIT	
18	9	*Supplies—Office*	*C297*		*35 00*			*205 00*	18
19		*Supplies—Store*			*47 00*				19
20		*Advertising Expense*			*92 00*				20
21		*Miscellaneous Expense*			*31 00*				21

November 9. Paid cash to replenish the petty cash fund, $205.00: office supplies, $35.00; store supplies, $47.00; advertising, $92.00; miscellaneous, $31.00. Check No. 297.

Supplies—Office	
35.00	

Supplies—Store	
47.00	

Advertising Expense	
92.00	

Miscellaneous Expense	
31.00	

Cash	
	205.00

Omni deposits all cash in a bank. Some cash, however, is kept in a petty cash fund for making change at the cash register and for making small cash payments. Omni has a petty cash fund of $300.00, which is replenished whenever the petty cash on hand drops below $100.00.

This cash payment increases the balances of the supplies accounts and several expense accounts and decreases the cash account balance.

The supplies accounts have normal debit balances. Therefore, Supplies—Office is debited for $35.00 and Supplies—Store is debited for $47.00 to show the increases in these two asset accounts. The expense accounts also have normal debit balances. Therefore, Advertising Expense is debited for $92.00 and Miscellaneous Expense is debited for $31.00 to show the increases in these expense accounts. The cash account has a normal debit balance. Therefore, Cash is credited for $205.00, the total amount needed to replenish the petty cash fund, to show the decrease in this asset account.

STEPS Journalizing a cash payment to replenish petty cash

1. Write the date, *9*, in the Date column.
2. Write the titles of the accounts for which the petty cash fund was used on separate lines in the Account Title column since there are no special amount columns for these accounts.
3. Write the check number, *C297*, in the Doc. No. column.
4. Write the debit amounts for the various accounts in the General Debit column.
5. Write the credit amount, *$205.00*, in the Cash Credit column on the first line of the entry.

REMEMBER

The account title Petty Cash is used only when establishing the petty cash account.

CASH WITHDRAWALS BY PARTNERS

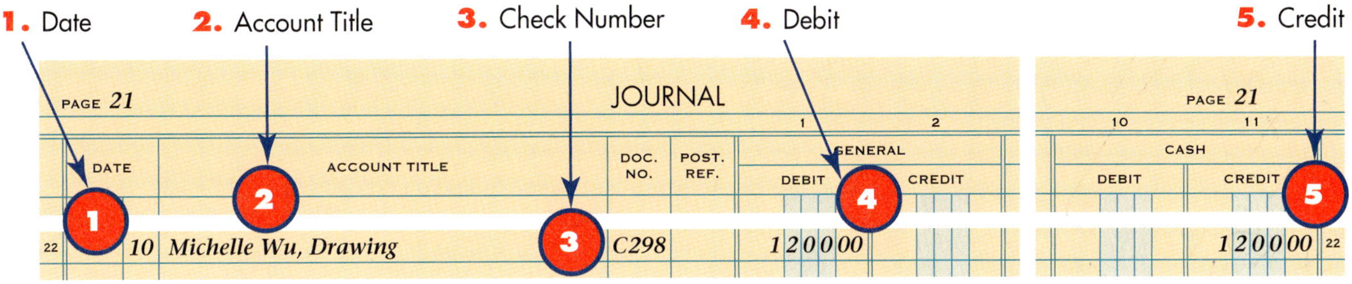

Assets taken out of a business for the personal use of an owner are known as withdrawals. The two assets generally taken out of a merchandising business are cash and merchandise. Withdrawals reduce the amount of a business's capital. The account titles of the partners' drawing accounts are Michelle Wu, Drawing and Karl Koehn, Drawing. Since capital accounts have credit balances, partners' drawing accounts have normal debit balances. Therefore, the drawing accounts are increased by a debit and decreased by a credit, as shown in the T accounts.

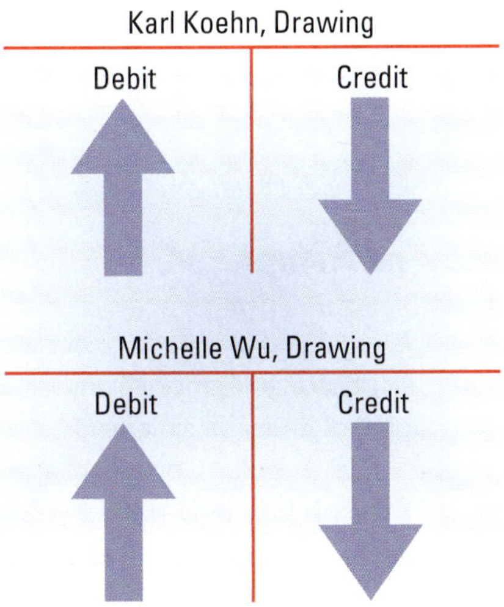

Withdrawals could be recorded as debits directly to the partners' capital accounts. However, withdrawals are normally recorded in separate accounts so that the total amounts are easily determined for each accounting period.

When either Michelle Wu or Karl Koehn withdraws cash from Omni, a check is written for the payment.

November 10. Michelle Wu, partner, withdrew cash for personal use, $1,200.00. Check No. 298.

This cash withdrawal increases Michelle Wu's drawing account balance and decreases the cash account balance.

Because the drawing account has a normal debit balance, Michelle Wu, Drawing is debited for $1,200.00 to show the increase in this account. The cash account also has a normal debit balance. Therefore, Cash is credited for $1,200.00 to show the decrease in this asset account.

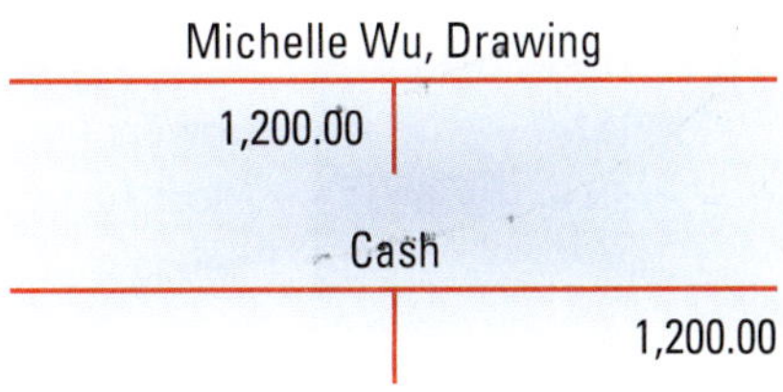

STEPS: Journalizing cash withdrawals by partners

1. Write the date, *10*, in the Date column.
2. Write the account title, *Michelle Wu, Drawing*, in the Account Title column.
3. Write the check number, *C298*, in the Doc. No. column.
4. Write the debit amount to Michelle Wu, Drawing, *$1,200.00*, in the General Debit column.
5. Write the credit amount, *$1,200.00*, in the Cash Credit column.

MERCHANDISE WITHDRAWALS BY PARTNERS

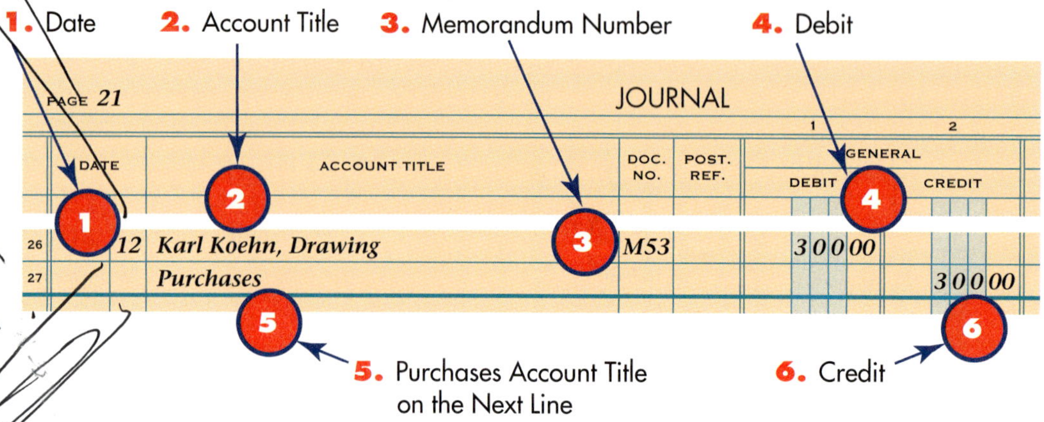

November 12. Karl Koehn, partner, withdrew merchandise for personal use, $300.00. Memorandum No. 53.

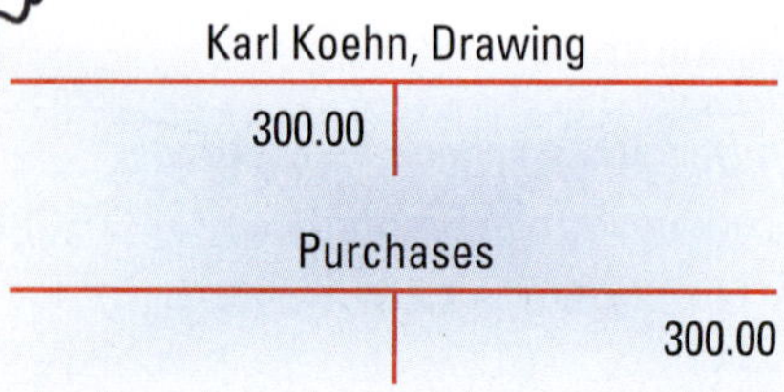

A partner usually withdraws cash for personal use. However, a partner may also withdraw merchandise for personal use.

This merchandise withdrawal increases Karl Koehn's drawing account balance and decreases the purchases account balance.

Because the drawing account has a normal debit balance, Karl Koehn, Drawing is debited for $300.00 to show the increase in this account. The purchases account also has a normal debit balance. Therefore, Purchases is credited for $300.00 to show the decrease in this cost account.

GLOBAL PERSPECTIVE

ACCOUNTANCY IN AFRICA

The accounting profession in Africa has been influenced by the European colonial powers who formerly governed there. Most African nations gained independence in the mid-twentieth century.

In Nigeria, Kenya, Ghana, and Zimbabwe (formerly under British rule), accounting is seen as a tool for financial management and is oriented toward the needs of the enterprise. Tax authorities are concerned with account items that can be valued in different ways, like fixed assets, inventories, and depreciation.

In Togo, Rwanda, and Gambia (formerly ruled by France), accountancy is regulated by *charts of accounts* that standardize financial transactions and annual financial statements.

In Angola, Cape Verde, and Principe (formerly ruled by Portugal), the accounting system also is based on charts of accounts that provide rules and regulations for companies. There are no professional accounting organizations in these countries.

In the expanding economies of many developing African countries, the belief is that it is important to have well-qualified and experienced accountants and a sound accounting framework to sustain economic growth.

AUDIT YOUR UNDERSTANDING

1. In what amount columns would the debit amount and credit amount be written for a cash payment on account?
2. What account title, if any, would be written in the Account Title column for paying cash for advertising expense?
3. What is the purpose of using a petty cash fund?
4. What account title would be written in the Account Title column for a partner's withdrawal of cash?
5. In what amount columns would the debit amount and credit amount be written for a partner's withdrawal of merchandise?

WORK TOGETHER

Journalizing cash payments and other transactions

Use the journal from On Your Own on page 237. Your instructor will guide you through the following example.

6. Using the current year, journalize the following transactions, continuing on the next blank line of page 10 of the journal. Save your work to complete On Your Own below.

Transactions:

Oct. 12. Paid cash on account to Design Fabrics, $563.00. C323.
13. Paid cash for telephone bill, $85.00. C324.
14. Paid cash to replenish petty cash fund, $309.00: office supplies, $82.00; store supplies, $43.00; advertising, $94.00; miscellaneous, $90.00. C325.
15. Steven Cafaro, partner, withdrew cash for personal use, $400.00. C326.
15. Consuela Martinez, partner, withdrew merchandise for personal use, $225.00. M66.

ON YOUR OWN

Journalizing cash payments and other transactions

Use the journal that you used above in Work Together. Work this problem independently.

7. Using the current year, journalize the following transactions, continuing on the next blank line of page 10 of the journal.

Transactions:

Oct. 16. Paid cash for advertising, $140.00. C327.
18. Paid cash on account to Fabric Outlet, $1,150.00. C328.
18. Steven Cafaro, partner, withdrew merchandise for personal use, $200.00. M69.
20. Paid cash to replenish petty cash fund, $305.00: office supplies, $62.00; store supplies, $116.00; advertising, $38.00; miscellaneous, $89.00. C329.
22. Consuela Martinez, partner, withdrew cash for personal use, $500.00. C330.

CHAPTER 10 SUMMARY

After completing this chapter, you can

1. Define accounting terms related to purchases and cash payments for a merchandising business.
2. Identify accounting concepts and practices related to purchases and cash payments for a merchandising business.
3. Journalize purchases of merchandise for cash.
4. Journalize purchases of merchandise on account and buying supplies.
5. Journalize cash payments and other transactions.

EXPLORE ACCOUNTING

FREIGHT CHARGES

When a business purchases merchandise from a vendor, ordinarily a third-party freight company is used to deliver the merchandise from the seller (vendor) to the buyer (purchasing business). As part of the terms of sale, the buyer and seller must agree who is responsible for the freight charges. Those terms will be listed on the seller's sales invoice as either FOB shipping point or FOB destination. FOB is an abbreviation for the phrase "Free on Board." FOB shipping point means that the buyer is responsible for the freight charges. FOB destination means that the seller is responsible for the freight charges. Shipping point is the location where the freight company receives the merchandise from the seller. Destination refers to the receiving point of the buyer.

The accounting entries for freight charges can be complicated when one business is responsible for the freight charges according to the terms of sale, but the other business pays the freight company. For example, terms of sale may be FOB shipping point, meaning that the buyer is responsible for the freight charges. However, the freight company may require payment in advance. Therefore, the seller pays the freight company for the freight charges.

Four different situations may occur:

1. FOB shipping point, seller pays freight company.
2. FOB shipping point, buyer pays freight company.
3. FOB destination, seller pays freight company.
4. FOB destination, buyer pays freight company.

Research: Investigate this issue by reviewing collegiate Principles of Accounting or Intermediate Accounting textbooks. Also, you might interview a merchandising business manager to determine how the business accounts for freight charges.

After completing your research, write a report on the issue of freight charges that would clearly explain the correct accounting procedures to a new accounting department employee.

10-1 APPLICATION PROBLEM
Journalizing purchases of merchandise for cash

Ralph Bridges and Olivia Herron, partners, own a small appliance store.

Instructions:

Journalize the following transactions completed during August of the current year. Use page 17 of the journal given in the *Working Papers*. Source documents are abbreviated as follows: check, C; memorandum, M; purchase invoice, P.

Transactions:

Aug. 1. Purchased merchandise for cash, $300.00. C210.
10. Purchased merchandise for cash, $817.00. C211.
22. Purchased merchandise for cash, $184.00. C212.

10-2 APPLICATION PROBLEM
Journalizing purchases of merchandise on account and buying supplies

Ralph Benitez and Tina Chirfo, partners, own a small music store.

Instructions:

Journalize the following transactions completed during September of the current year. Use page 17 of the journal given in the *Working Papers*. Source documents are abbreviated as follows: check, C; memorandum, M; purchase invoice, P.

Transactions:

Sept. 4. Purchased merchandise on account from Woodland Music, $2,600.00. P54.
7. Paid cash for office supplies, $75.00. C211.
10. Purchased merchandise on account from Quality Wholesalers, $1,460.00. P55.
15. Bought store supplies on account from Displays Warehouse, $275.00. M39.

10-3 APPLICATION PROBLEM
Journalizing cash payments and other transactions

Mary Caesar and Glen Kelly, partners, own an auto parts store.

Instructions:

Journalize the following transactions completed during October of the current year. Use page 19 of the journal given in the *Working Papers*. Source documents are abbreviated as follows: check, C; memorandum, M; purchase invoice, P.

Transactions:

Oct. 2. Paid cash for telephone bill, $96.00. C241.
6. Mary Caesar, partner, withdrew cash for personal use, $1,000.00. C242.
6. Glen Kelly, partner, withdrew cash for personal use, $1,200.00. C243.
12. Paid cash on account to East Gate Auto Parts, $1,250.00, covering P67. C244.
16. Paid cash for advertising, $75.00. C245.
24. Paid cash on account to Auto Center, $925.00, covering P68. C246.
26. Mary Caesar, partner, withdrew merchandise for personal use, $120.00. M51.
30. Paid cash to replenish the petty cash fund, $211.00: office supplies, $41.00; store supplies, $29.00; advertising, $63.00; miscellaneous, $78.00. C247.

10-4 APPLICATION PROBLEM
Journalizing purchases, cash payments, and other transactions

Michael Deaton and Pamela Parks, partners, own a bridal shop.

Instructions:

Journalize the following transactions completed during November of the current year. Use page 22 of the journal given in the *Working Papers*. Source documents are abbreviated as follows: check, C; memorandum, M; purchase invoice, P.

Transactions:

Nov. 1. Purchased merchandise on account from Formal Wear, $1,850.00. P71.
5. Bought store supplies on account from Classic Fixtures, $180.00. M48.
10. Purchased merchandise for cash, $330.00. C240.
12. Paid cash for office supplies, $50.00. C241.
18. Purchased merchandise on account from Bridal Designs, $2,300.00. P72.
22. Paid cash on account to Formal Wear, $1,850.00, covering P71. C242.
25. Paid cash for advertising, $110.00. C243.
26. Michael Deaton, partner, withdrew merchandise for personal use, $140.00. M49.
29. Michael Deaton, partner, withdrew cash for personal use, $1,110.00. C244.
29. Pamela Parks, partner, withdrew cash for personal use, $1,250.00. C245.
30. Paid cash to replenish the petty cash fund, $261.00: office supplies, $52.00; store supplies, $40.00; advertising, $77.00; miscellaneous, $92.00. C246.

10-5 MASTERY PROBLEM
Journalizing purchases, cash payments, and other transactions

Jimmie Chang and Susan Shirey, partners, own a gift shop.

Instructions:

Journalize the following transactions completed during October of the current year. Use page 19 of the journal given in the *Working Papers*. Source documents are abbreviated as follows: check, C; memorandum, M; purchase invoice, P.

Transactions:

Oct. 1. Paid cash for rent, $1,500.00. C361.
2. Purchased merchandise on account from Marion's Collectibles, $1,115.00. P108.
3. Paid cash for office supplies, $74.00. C362.
5. Paid cash on account to Gift Supplies, Inc., $548.00, covering P105. C363.
6. Purchased merchandise for cash, $155.00. C364.
9. Purchased merchandise on account from Jarvis Fabrics, $850.00. P109.
9. Bought store supplies on account from Creative Store Supplies, $150.00. M50.
10. Purchased merchandise for cash, $103.00. C365.
12. Paid cash on account to Contemporary Gifts, $885.00, covering P106. C366.
12. Bought office supplies on account from A to Z Supplies, $80.00. M51.
16. Jimmie Chang, partner, withdrew cash for personal use, $1,000.00. C367.
16. Susan Shirey, partner, withdrew cash for personal use, $1,000.00. C368.
17. Paid cash for advertising, $100.00. C369.
19. Paid cash on account to Classic Gifts, $490.00, covering P107. C370.
19. Purchased merchandise on account from Jarvis Fabrics, $625.00. P110.

Oct. 20. Susan Shirey, partner, withdrew merchandise for personal use, $120.00. M52.
22. Purchased merchandise for cash, $60.00. C371.
24. Paid cash on account to Marion's Collectibles, $1,115.00, covering P108. C372.
25. Jimmie Chang, partner, withdrew merchandise for personal use, $225.00. M53.
27. Paid cash for store supplies, $92.00. C373.
30. Paid cash to replenish the petty cash fund, $201.00: office supplies, $53.00; store supplies, $27.00; advertising, $100.00; miscellaneous, $21.00. C374.
30. Paid cash on account to Jarvis Fabrics, $850.00, covering P109. C375.

10-6 CHALLENGE PROBLEM
Journalizing purchases, cash payments, and other transactions

Jack Armstrong and Barbara Kirk, partners, own an exercise equipment store.

Instructions:

1. Journalize the following transactions completed during November of the current year. Use page 26 of the journal given in the *Working Papers*. Record the appropriate source document for each transaction.

Transactions:

Nov. 1. Wrote Check No. 361 for the monthly rent of $1,300.00.
2. Wrote Checks No. 362 and 363 for $1,250.00 each to partners, Jack Armstrong and Barbara Kirk, for their personal use.
4. Paid $150.00 with Check No. 364 for merchandise.
6. Wrote Check No. 365 for $1,020.00 to Pacer Equipment for Purchase Invoice 82's payment on account.
9. Purchased $2,900.00 of merchandise on account from Trackmaster on Purchase Invoice 85.
10. Paid $52.00 for office supplies with Check No. 366.
12. Wrote Check No. 367 for $90.00 to pay the monthly insurance premium.
15. Bought $120.00 worth of store supplies on account from Mecca Store Supplies and recorded on Memo 43.
19. Jack Armstrong took $75.00 worth of merchandise for his personal use and recorded it on Memo 44.
24. Wrote Check No. 368 for $2,900.00 to pay Trackmaster amount owed on Purchase Invoice 85.
30. Wrote Check No. 369 for $206.00 to the employee who maintains the petty cash fund for the purpose of replenishing the fund. Receipts were submitted for the following: office supplies, $48.00; store supplies $24.00; advertising, $68.00; and miscellaneous, $66.00.

2. Evaluate and then write a response to the following questions.
   a. The expanded journal used in this problem has nine special amount columns. Under what circumstances would you recommend additional special amount columns be added or existing amount columns be deleted from an expanded journal?
   b. Jack Armstrong has asked why he could not be paid a salary rather than making withdrawals from his ownership in the partnership. How would you respond to him?
   c. When insurance premiums are paid, should the debit entry be to the asset account, Prepaid Insurance, or to the expense account, Insurance Expense? Are there circumstances where either entry could be correct? Explain.

INTERNET ACTIVITY

Point your browser to

http://accounting.swpco.com

Choose **First-Year Course**, choose **Activities**, and complete the activity for Chapter 10.

Applied Communication

When you purchase merchandise for your business, you are considered a customer. Sometimes a customer might have a problem or complaint about the product. There are several ways to go about resolving the problem. One suggestion is to write to the person or company selling the product.

Instructions: Assume that you bought stereo speakers for your consumer electronics store last week. Write a business-like letter of complaint to the company selling the merchandise because the speakers make a strange static noise. Be specific about the problem and provide factual information about the purchase. Request a refund or a new set of speakers.

Cases for Critical Thinking

Case 1 Sophia Perez is a high school student who works part time in a local sports equipment store. As part of her duties, she records daily transactions in a journal. One day she asks the owner, "You use the purchase invoice as your source document for recording purchases of merchandise on account. You use a memorandum as your source document for recording the entry when supplies are bought on account. Why don't you use the invoice for both entries?" How would you respond to this question?

Case 2 Charles Davis owns and operates an antique shop in a downtown shopping area. Because of a shopping mall that has opened in one of the suburbs, the antique shop's business has been declining. Mr. Davis has an opportunity to move the business to the shopping mall. Additional capital, however, is required to move and operate the business in a new location. The local bank has agreed to lend the money needed. The business hours would be extended at the new location. The business would also be open seven days a week. The extended hours plus the expected increase in business would require the hiring of one additional employee. Mr. Davis has been contacted by Kathryn Harless, a person with similar merchandising experience, who would like to become a partner. As an alternative to borrowing cash, Ms. Harless would provide the capital necessary to move the business to the new location. For the capital provided, Ms. Harless would share equally in the net income or loss of the business. Ms. Harless would also share equally in the operation of the business. Should Mr. Davis (1) borrow the money from the bank or (2) bring in a partner? Explain your answer.

AUTOMATED ACCOUNTING

AUTOMATED ENTRIES FOR PURCHASES AND CASH PAYMENTS USING SPECIAL JOURNALS

A merchandising business is a business that purchases and resells goods. The merchandise inventory account shows the value of the goods on hand for sale to customers. The cost of merchandise purchased for resale is recorded in an account called Purchases.

A merchandising business has many frequently occurring transactions that would require many entries in the general journal. Therefore, special journals are used to simplify the recording of these repetitive transactions. All transactions involving the payment of cash are recorded in a special journal called the *Cash Payments Journal*. The purchase of merchandise on account is recorded in the *Purchases Journal*.

A business from which merchandise, supplies, or other assets are bought is called a *vendor*. Businesses that use many vendors maintain a separate vendor file. The total owed to all vendors maintained in a vendor file is summarized in a single general ledger liability account called Accounts Payable. Vendor accounts may be added, changed, or deleted from the accounting system in the same way as general ledger account maintenance.

To maintain the Vendors list:

1. Click the Accounts toolbar button.
2. Select the Vendors tab.
3. To add a vendor, key in the new vendor name. Press Enter or click the Add Vendor command button. The new vendor will be arranged alphabetically with existing vendors.
4. To change a vendor, highlight the vendor name. Key the correct vendor name. Press Enter or click the Add Vendor command button.
5. To delete a vendor, highlight the vendor name. Click the Delete command button. A vendor must have a zero balance to be deleted.
6. Click the Close command button.

Purchases

A transaction recording a merchandise purchase that will be paid for at a later date is called a *purchase on account.* Only merchandise that is purchased on account is recorded in the purchases journal. Purchase transactions may be entered directly into the computer from the invoice (source document). When the debit portion of a purchase transaction is entered, the computer will automatically make the credit to Accounts Payable.

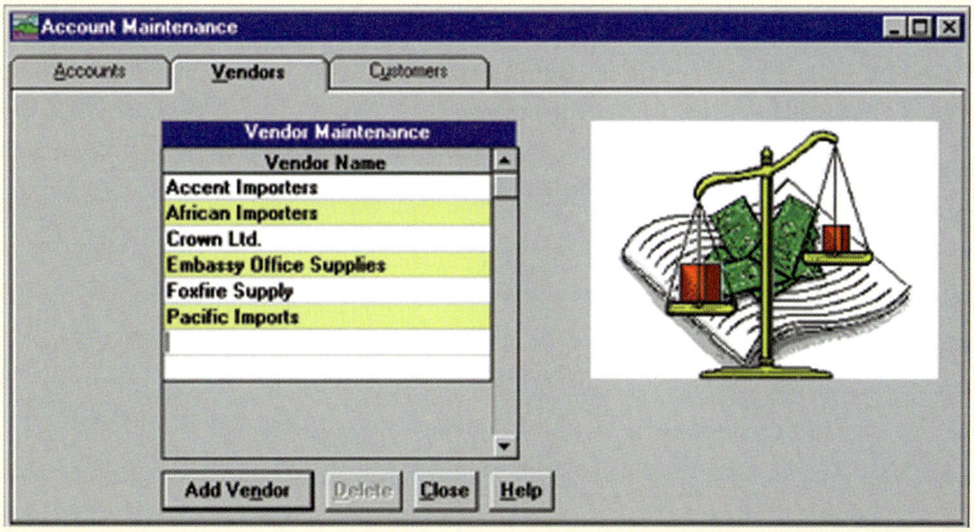

AUTOMATED ACCOUNTING

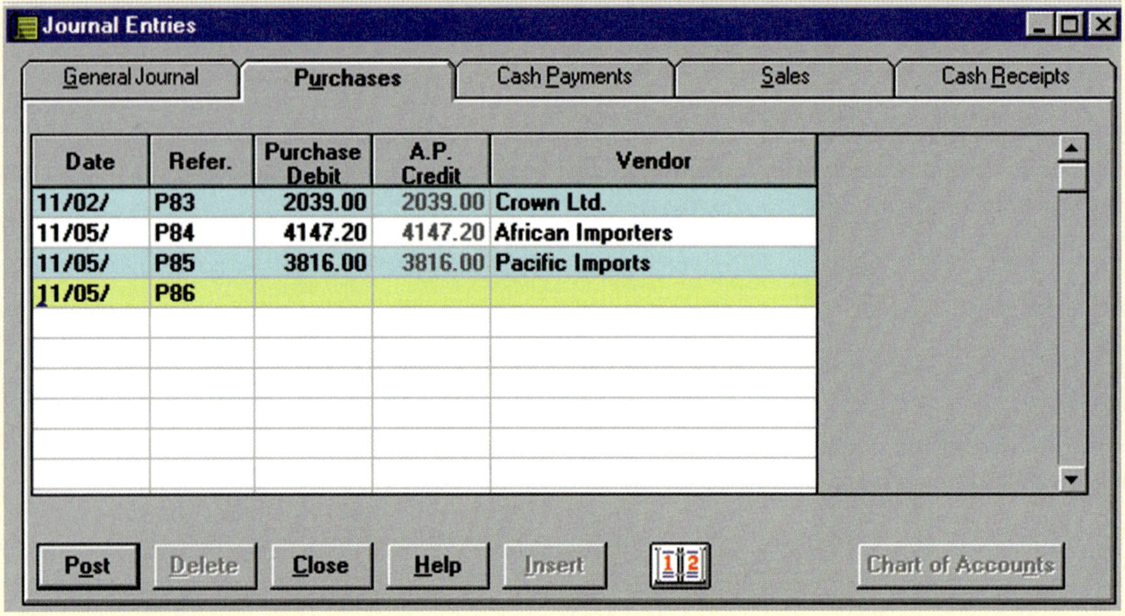

To record transactions in the purchases journal:

1. Choose the Journal Entries menu item from the Data menu or click the Journal toolbar button.
2. Click the Purchases tab.
3. Enter the transaction date and press Tab.
4. Enter the invoice number in the Refer. column and press Tab.
5. Enter the amount of the invoice in the Purchases Debit column and press Tab. The Accounts Payable credit amount is calculated and displayed automatically.
6. Choose a vendor name from the drop-down list.
7. Click the Post button.

Cash Payments

The cash payments journal is used to enter all cash payments transactions.

Examples of cash payment transactions are:

- vendor payments
- payments of expenses
- cash purchases of merchandise
- cash purchases of supplies

The credit to cash is automatically calculated and displayed by the computer. There are two types of cash payments:

1. Direct payments are made for assets or expenses that *do not* affect Accounts Payable.
2. Payments on account are made for cash transactions that *do* affect Accounts Payable.

AUTOMATED ACCOUNTING

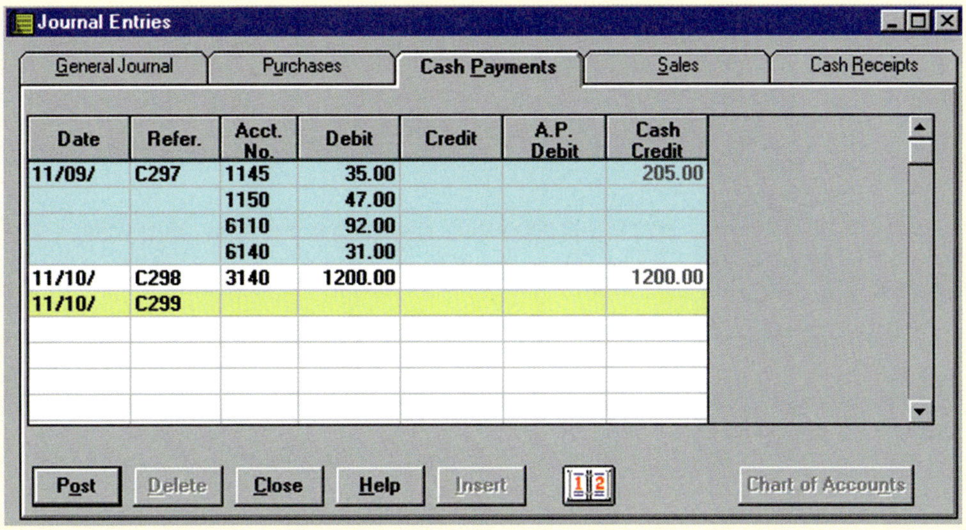

Date	Refer.	Acct. No.	Debit	Credit	A.P. Debit	Cash Credit
11/09/	C297	1145	35.00			205.00
		1150	47.00			
		6110	92.00			
		6140	31.00			
11/10/	C298	3140	1200.00			1200.00
11/10/	C299					

To record transactions in the cash payments journal:

1. Choose the Journal Entries menu item from the Data menu or click the Journal toolbar button.
2. Click the Cash Payments tab.
3. Enter the transaction date and press Tab.
4. Enter the check number in the Refer. column and press Tab.
5. If making a direct payment, enter the account number and amounts to debit or credit and press Tab. If more than one account is debited or credited in the transaction, enter the first account number and the corresponding debit or credit. Press Tab until the cursor appears in the Acct. No. column on the next line. Then enter the next account number and its corresponding debit or credit. Continue this procedure for all accounts involved in the transaction.The cash credit is automatically calculated and displayed by the computer.
6. If making a payment on account, enter the accounts payable debit amount and choose the vendor from the drop-down vendor list. The cash credit is automatically calculated and displayed by the computer.
7. If the transaction is correct, click the Post button.

AUTOMATING MASTERY PROBLEM 10-5: Journalizing purchases, cash payments, and other transactions

Instructions:

1. Load *Automated Accounting 7.0* or higher software.
2. Select database F10-1 from the appropriate directory/folder.
3. Select File from the menu bar and choose the Save As menu command. Key the path to the drive and directory that contains your data files. Save the database with a file name of XXX101 (where XXX are your initials).
4. Access Problem Instructions through the Help menu. Read the Problem Instructions screen.
5. Key the data listed on page 246.
6. Exit the *Automated Accounting* software.

11 Journalizing Sales and Cash Receipts

AFTER STUDYING CHAPTER 11, YOU WILL BE ABLE TO:

1. Define accounting terms related to sales and cash receipts for a merchandising business.
2. Identify accounting concepts and practices related to sales and cash receipts for a merchandising business.
3. Journalize sales and cash receipts transactions for a merchandising business.
4. Prove and rule a journal.

TERMS PREVIEW

customer

sales tax

cash sale

credit card sale

SALES TAX

Purchases and sales of merchandise are the two major activities of a merchandising business. A person or business to whom merchandise or services are sold is called a **customer.** Omni Import sells merchandise.

Laws of most states and some cities require that a tax be collected from customers for each sale made. A tax on a sale of merchandise or services is called a **sales tax.** Sales tax rates are usually stated as a percentage of sales. Regardless of the tax rates used, accounting procedures are the same.

Businesses must file reports with the proper government unit and pay the amount of sales tax collected. Every business collecting a sales tax needs accurate records of the amount of (1) total sales and (2) total sales tax collected. The amount of sales tax collected is a business liability until paid to the state government. Therefore, the sales tax amount is recorded in a separate liability account titled Sales Tax Payable, which has a normal credit balance.

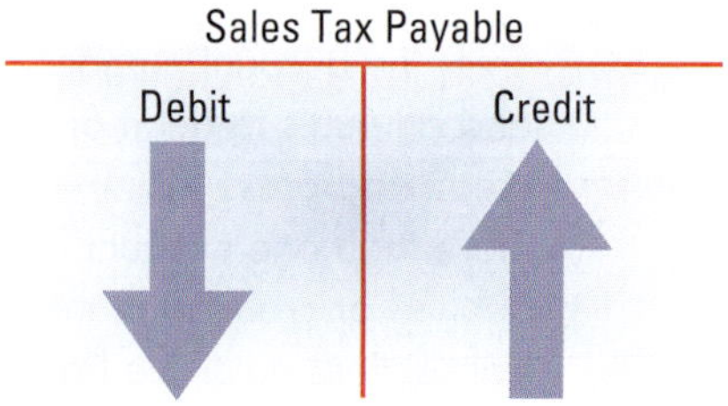

Omni operates in a state with a 6% sales tax rate. The total amount of a sale of merchandise priced at $300.00 is calculated as follows.

Price of Goods	×	Sales Tax Rate	=	Sales Tax
$300.00	×	6%	=	$18.00
Price of Goods	**+**	**Sales Tax**	**=**	**Total Amount Received**
$300.00	+	$18.00	=	$318.00

A customer must pay $318.00 for the merchandise. Omni records the price of goods sold, the sales tax, and the total amount received.

ACCOUNTING IN YOUR CAREER

GROWING THE BUSINESS

David Bradford, the office manager of OfficeTown, has been asked by the owners, Denise Klein and Martin Nadler, to help plan a business expansion into computer supplies and office services.

"David," says Denise, "Martin and I need to make this expansion. Our location is so good that if we don't do it, someone else will. We may not be able to survive with increased competition."

"Yes, that's true," adds Martin, "but I don't think we have the cash to make this expansion. The store is very successful, and we make a good living. But I don't know what happens to all the money we make. That's what we need your help with. Please investigate and give us some ideas."

David recognizes that this is a great opportunity to make a contribution to the business. He begins immediately and discovers:

- Twenty percent of the accounts receivable, including several with large outstanding balances, are over one month overdue.
- There is nearly a three-month supply of most inventory items.
- The partners do not withdraw extraordinary amounts of cash each month.
- The company has not borrowed from a bank in ten years, but has good credit.
- An investor with computer retailing experience is interested in joining the partnership.

Critical Thinking:

1. What kinds of recommendations should David make regarding accounts receivable?
2. What are some possible solutions to the problem of overstocked inventory?
3. Besides generating more cash from the business, what are some other options for financing an expansion of the business? What are some advantages and disadvantages of these options?

11-1 Journalizing Sales and Cash Receipts from Sales

SALES OF MERCHANDISE

A sale of merchandise may be (1) for cash or (2) on account. A sale of merchandise increases the revenue of a business. Regardless of when payment is made, revenue is recorded at the time of a sale, not on the date cash is received. *(CONCEPT: Realization of Revenue)* For example, on June 15 Omni sells merchandise on account to a customer. The customer pays Omni for the merchandise on July 12. Omni records the revenue on June 15, the date of the sale.

Omni sells most of its merchandise for cash. A sale in which cash is received for the total amount of the sale at the time of the transaction is called a **cash sale.** Omni also sells merchandise to customers who have a bank-approved credit card. A sale in which a credit card is used for the total amount of the sale at the time of the transaction is called a **credit card sale.** Major bank-approved credit cards include VISA, MasterCard, and Discover Card. Omni accepts all major bank-approved credit cards from customers. A customer who uses a credit card promises to pay the amount due for the credit card transaction to the bank issuing the credit card.

Omni prepares a credit card slip for each credit card sale. At the end of each week, these credit card slips are included with Omni's bank deposit. Omni's bank accepts the credit card slips the same way it accepts checks and cash for deposit. If a credit card was issued by another bank, Omni's bank sends the credit card slips to the issuing bank. The issuing bank then bills the customer and collects the amount owed. The bank that accepts and processes the credit card slips for a business charges a fee for this service. This fee is included on Omni's monthly bank statement.

LEGAL ISSUES IN ACCOUNTING

FORMING A PARTNERSHIP

Two or more persons may form a partnership. This form of organization has several advantages:

- More assets such as cash that can be invested in the business.
- More time, energy, and experience brought to the new business.

However, there are also some disadvantages to a partnership:

- Shared decision making. Business decisions must be discussed and agreements reached by both partners. Disagreements among partners must be resolved.
- Unlimited liability. Each partner is responsible for the liabilities of the business, even those incurred by the other partner. Either partner's personal assets may be claimed by creditors to pay the partnership's liabilities.
- Shared profits. Any profits earned must be divided between the partners. Losses also must be shared.

In most states, the minimum legal requirement to form a partnership is to file a document to register the business name. A document called a *partnership agreement* also should be created by the partners. This is a written agreement setting forth the conditions under which the partnership is to operate. It includes the name and description of the business, capital investments of each partner, distribution of profits and losses, duties and responsibilities of each partner, and provisions for dissolving the partnership. A partnership agreement is not required by law, but it is in the best interest of both partners.

CASH AND CREDIT CARD SALES

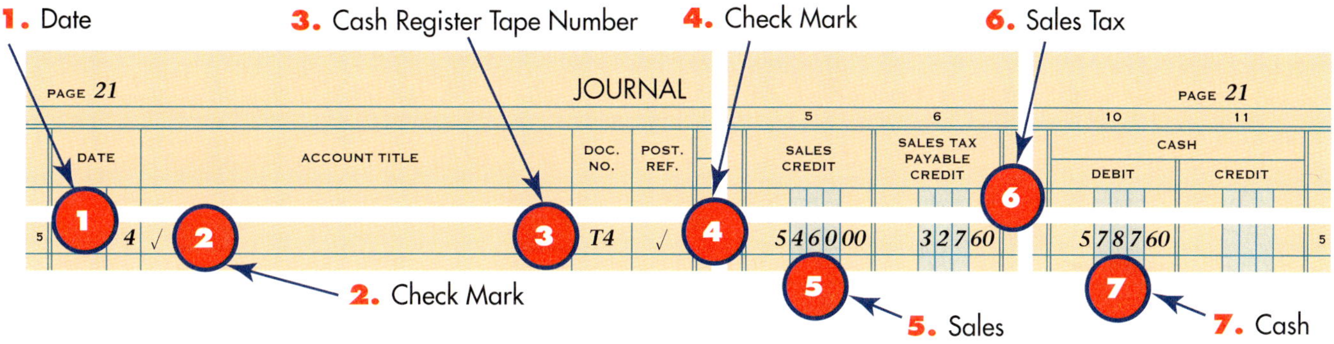

Omni's bank accepts credit card slips the same way it accepts cash. Therefore, Omni combines all cash and credit card sales and records the two revenue items as a single cash sales transaction.

November 4. Recorded cash and credit card sales, $5,460.00, plus sales tax, $327.60; total, $5,787.60. Cash Register Tape No. 4.

Cash	
5,787.60	

Sales	
	5,460.00

Sales Tax Payable	
	327.60

Omni uses a cash register to list all cash and credit card sales. When a transaction is entered on the cash register, a paper tape is printed as a receipt for the customer. The cash register also internally accumulates data about total cash and credit card sales.

At the end of each week, a cash register tape is printed showing total cash and credit card sales. The tape is removed from the cash register and marked with a T and the date (T4). The cash register tape is used by Omni as the source document for weekly cash and credit card sales transactions. *(CONCEPT: Objective Evidence)* Cash sales are also totaled at the end of each month so Omni can analyze monthly sales. Because October of the current year ended on Tuesday, the first weekend of November is November 4. Thus, there are only four days' sales recorded on this tape.

Because the asset account, Cash, has a normal debit balance, Cash is debited for the total sales and sales tax, $5,787.60, to show the increase in this asset account. The sales account has a normal credit balance. Therefore, Sales is credited for the total price of all goods sold, $5,460.00, to show the increase in this revenue account. The sales tax payable account also has a normal credit balance. Therefore, Sales Tax Payable is credited for the total sales tax, $327.60, to show the increase in this liability account.

STEPS: Journalizing cash and credit card sales

1. Write the date, *4,* in the Date column.
2. Place a check mark in the Account Title column to show that no account title needs to be written. The debit and credit amounts will be recorded in special amount columns.
3. Write the cash register tape number, *T4,* in the Doc. No. column.
4. Place a check mark in the Post. Ref. column to show that amounts on this line are not to be posted individually.
5. Write the sales amount, *$5,460.00,* in the Sales Credit column.
6. Write the sales tax amount, *$327.60,* in the Sales Tax Payable Credit column.
7. Write the cash amount, *$5,787.60,* in the Cash Debit column.

SALES INVOICE

OMNI IMPORT
1374 Parklane
Ashton, RI 02805

Sold to: Children's Paradise
430 Main Street
Alton, RI 02803-1163

Cust. No. 120

No. 76
Date 11/3/--
Terms 30 days

Stock No.	Description	Quantity	Unit Price	Amount
4422	African masks	25	18.00	450.00
7710	Russian nesting dolls	30	12.20	366.00
			Subtotal	816.00
Customer's Signature		Salesclerk	Sales Tax	48.96
Max Schindler		S. A.	Total	864.96

A sale for which cash will be received at a later date is known as a sale on account. A sale on account is also referred to as a charge sale.

When merchandise is sold on account, the seller prepares a form showing what has been sold. A form describing the goods or services sold, the quantity, and the price is known as an invoice. An invoice used as a source document for recording a sale on account is known as a sales invoice. *(CONCEPT: Objective Evidence)* A sales invoice is also referred to as a sales ticket or a sales slip.

The seller considers an invoice for a sale on account to be a sales invoice. The same invoice is considered by the customer to be a purchase invoice.

Three copies of a sales invoice are prepared. The original copy is given to the customer. The second copy goes to Omni's shipping department. The third copy is used as the source document for the sale on account transaction. *(CONCEPT: Objective Evidence)* Sales invoices are numbered in sequence. The number 76 is the number of the sales invoice issued to Children's Paradise.

FYI

The bank that accepts and processes credit card slips for a business charges a fee for this service. Businesses may choose not to accept credit cards in order to avoid such fees.

SALE ON ACCOUNT

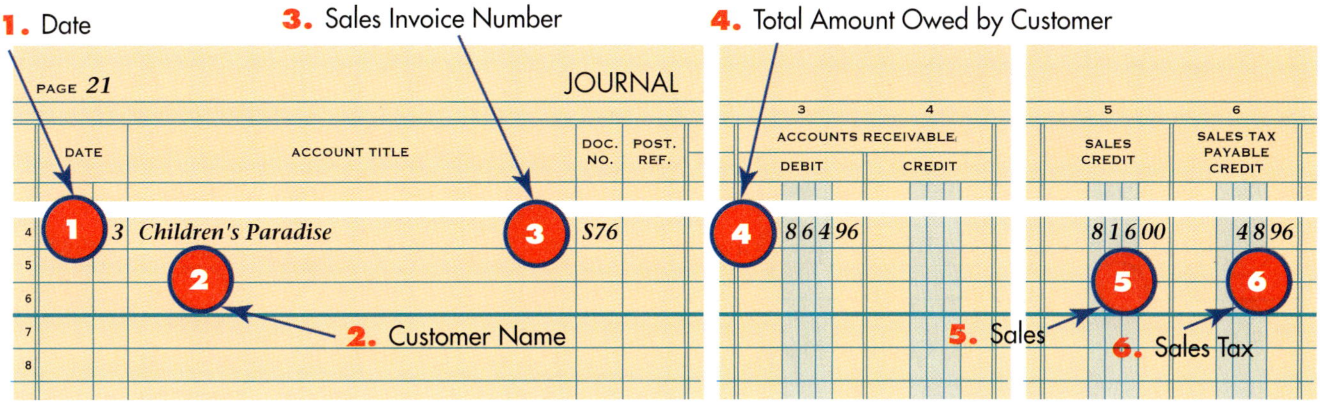

Omni sells on account only to businesses. Other customers must either pay cash or use a credit card.

Omni summarizes the total due from all charge customers in a general ledger account titled Accounts Receivable. Accounts Receivable is an asset account with a normal debit balance. Therefore, the accounts receivable account is increased by a debit and decreased by a credit.

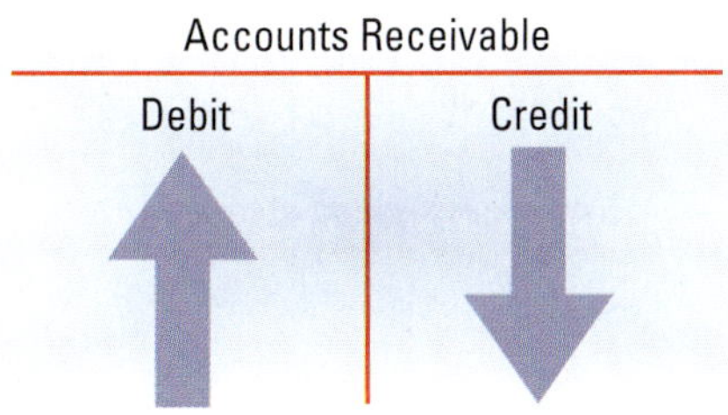

November 3. Sold merchandise on account to Children's Paradise, $816.00, plus sales tax, $48.96; total, $864.96. Sales Invoice No. 76.

A sale on account transaction increases the amount to be collected later from a customer. Payment for this sale will be received at a later date. However, the sale is recorded at the time the sale is made. *(CONCEPT: Realization of Revenue)*

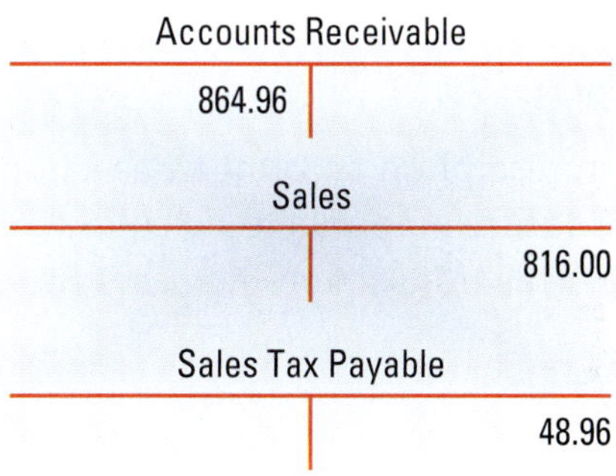

STEPS: Journalizing a sale on account

1. Write the date, *3*, in the Date column.
2. Write the customer name, *Children's Paradise*, in the Account Title column. The debit and credit amounts are recorded in special amount columns. Therefore, writing the titles of the general ledger accounts in the Account Title column is not necessary. However, the name of the customer is written in the Account Title column to show from whom the amount is due. Omni's procedures for keeping records of the amounts to be collected from each customer are described in Chapter 12.
3. Write the sales invoice number, *S76*, in the Doc. No. column.
4. Write the total amount owed by the customer, *$864.96*, in the Accounts Receivable Debit column.
5. Write the sales amount, *$816.00*, in the Sales Credit column.
6. Write the sales tax amount, *$48.96*, in the Sales Tax Payable Credit column.

CASH RECEIPTS ON ACCOUNT

1. Date **2.** Customer Name **3.** Receipt Number **4.** Credit **5.** Debit

PAGE 21 JOURNAL PAGE 21

	DATE		ACCOUNT TITLE	DOC. NO.	POST. REF.	3 ACCOUNTS RECEIVABLE DEBIT	4 ACCOUNTS RECEIVABLE CREDIT	10 CASH DEBIT	11 CASH CREDIT	
11		6	Fiesta Costumes	R90			2 1 6 2 40	2 1 6 2 40		11
12										12

When cash is received on account from a customer, Omni prepares a receipt. The receipts are prenumbered so that all receipts can be accounted for. Receipts are prepared in duplicate. The original copy of the receipt is given to the customer. The copy of the receipt is used as the source document for the cash receipt on account transaction. *(CONCEPT: Objective Evidence)*

November 6. Received cash on account from Fiesta Costumes, $2,162.40, covering S69. Receipt No. 90.

A cash receipt on account transaction decreases future amounts to be collected from a customer. This transaction increases the cash account balance and decreases the accounts receivable account balance. Because the cash account has a normal debit balance, Cash is debited for the amount of cash received, $2,162.40, to show the increase in this asset account. The accounts receivable account also has a normal debit balance. Therefore, Accounts Receivable is credited for $2,162.40 to show the decrease in this asset account.

Cash	
2,162.40	

Accounts Receivable	
	2,162.40

STEPS: Journalizing cash receipts on account

1. Write the date, *6*, in the Date column.
2. Write only the customer's name, *Fiesta Costumes*, in the Account Title column.
3. Write the receipt number, *R90*, in the Doc. No. column.
4. Write the credit amount, *$2,162.40*, in the Accounts Receivable Credit column.
5. Write the debit amount, *$2,162.40*, in the Cash Debit column.

TERMS REVIEW

customer

sales tax

cash sale

credit card sale

AUDIT YOUR UNDERSTANDING

1. How do merchandising and service businesses differ?
2. How are sales tax rates usually stated?
3. Why is sales tax collected considered a liability?
4. Which accounting concept is being applied when revenue is recorded at the time a sale is made, regardless of when payment is made?
5. What is the title of the general ledger account used to summarize the total amount due from all charge customers?

WORK TOGETHER

Journalizing sales and cash receipts

The journal for Distinctive Appliances is given in the *Working Papers*. Your instructor will guide you through the following example.

6. Using the current year, journalize the following transactions on page 9 of the journal. Source documents are abbreviated as follows: receipt, R; sales invoice; S; cash register tape, T. Save your work to complete On Your Own below.

Transactions:

Sept. 1. Sold merchandise on account to Adrian Makowski, $800.00, plus sales tax, $48.00; total, $848.00. S104.

4. Received cash on account from Jessica Oakley, $371.00, covering S96. R144.

6. Recorded cash and credit card sales, $5,840.00, plus sales tax, $350.40; total, $6,190.40. T6.

ON YOUR OWN

Journalizing sales and cash receipts

Use the journal for Distinctive Appliances you started above in Work Together. Work this problem independently.

7. Journalize the following transactions continuing on the next blank line of page 9 of the journal. Source documents are abbreviated as follows: receipt, R; sales invoice, S; cash register tape, T.

Transactions:

Sept. 8. Received cash on account from Marcia Hakala, $265.00, covering S98. R145.

10. Sold merchandise on account to Perry Rajan, $1,050.00, plus sales tax, $63.00; total, $1,113.00. S105.

13. Recorded cash and credit card sales, $6,200.00, plus sales tax, $372.00; total, $6,57 T13.

11-2 Proving and Ruling an Expanded Journal

CARRYING TOTALS FORWARD ON THE LEFT PAGE

PAGE 21 — JOURNAL

	DATE		ACCOUNT TITLE	DOC. NO.	POST. REF.	1 GENERAL DEBIT	2 GENERAL CREDIT	3 ACCOUNTS RECEIVABLE DEBIT	4 ACCOUNTS RECEIVABLE CREDIT	
1	20-- Nov.	1	✓	C290	✓					1
2		2	Crown Ltd.	P83						2
32		15	Ashton Jaycees	R93					381 60	32
33		15	✓	T15	✓					33
34		15	Carried Forward		✓	5151 60	384 00	4070 40	4770 00	34

2. Write the date. **3.** Write the words *Carried Forward.* **4.** Place a check mark.

A journal is proved and ruled whenever a journal page is filled and always at the end of a month.

After all November 15 entries are recorded, page 21 of Omni's journal is filled. Page 21 is totaled and proved before column totals are forwarded to page 22. The proof that Omni's debit totals equal the credit totals on page 21 of the journal is shown below.

After a journal page has been proved, the journal must be prepared for forwarding.

Col. No.	Column Title	Debit Totals	Credit Totals
1	General Debit	$ 5,151.60	
2	General Credit		$ 384.00
3	Accounts Receivable Debit	4,070.40	
4	Accounts Receivable Credit		4,770.00
5	Sales Credit		17,700.00
6	Sales Tax Payable Credit		1,062.00
7	Accounts Payable Debit	6,432.00	
8	Accounts Payable Credit		14,028.00
9	Purchases Debit	14,415.60	
10	Cash Debit	19,461.60	
11	Cash Credit		11,587.20
	Totals	$49,531.20	$49,531.20

CARRYING TOTALS FORWARD ON THE RIGHT PAGE

PAGE 21

	5	6	7	8	9	10	11	
	SALES CREDIT	SALES TAX PAYABLE CREDIT	ACCOUNTS PAYABLE DEBIT	ACCOUNTS PAYABLE CREDIT	PURCHASES DEBIT	CASH DEBIT	CASH CREDIT	
1					575 00		575 00	1
2				2 039 00	2 039 00			2
32						381 60		32
33	6 120 00	367 20				6 487 20		33
34	17 700 00	1 062 00	6 432 00	14 028 00	14 415 60	19 461 60	11 587 20	34

1. Rule a single line.

5. Write each column total.

6. Rule double lines.

STEPS: Ruling an expanded journal to carry totals forward

1. Rule a single line across all amount columns directly below the last entry to indicate that all the columns are to be added. Be sure to rule the single line on both the left and right pages.
2. On the next line write the date, *15*, in the Date column.
3. Write the words *Carried Forward* in the Account Title column.
4. Place a check mark in the Post. Ref. column to show that nothing on this line needs to be posted.
5. For both the left and right pages, write each column total below the single line.
6. Rule double lines below the column totals across all amount columns to show that the totals have been verified as correct. Be sure to rule the double line on both the left and right pages.

REMEMBER

Double lines below totals show that the totals have been verified as correct.

STARTING A NEW EXPANDED JOURNAL LEFT PAGE

1. Write journal page number.

PAGE 22 — JOURNAL

	DATE		ACCOUNT TITLE	DOC. NO.	POST. REF.	1 GENERAL DEBIT	2 GENERAL CREDIT	3 ACCOUNTS RECEIVABLE DEBIT	4 ACCOUNTS RECEIVABLE CREDIT	
1	20-- Nov.	15	Brought Forward		√	5151 60	384 00	4070 40	4770 00	1
2										2
3										3
4										4

2. Write the date. **3.** Write the words *Brought Forward.* **4.** Place check mark.

The totals from the previous journal page are carried forward to the next journal page. The totals are recorded on the first line of the new page.

STEPS: Forwarding totals to a new journal page

1. Write the journal page number, *22,* at the top of the journal on both the left and right pages.
2. Write the date, *20—, Nov. 15,* in the Date column.
3. Write the words *Brought Forward* in the Account Title column.
4. Place a check mark in the Post. Ref. column to show that nothing on this line needs to be posted.
5. For both the left and right pages, record the column totals brought forward from page 21 of the journal.

1. Write journal page number.

PAGE 22

	5	6	7	8	9	10	11	
	SALES CREDIT	SALES TAX PAYABLE CREDIT	ACCOUNTS PAYABLE		PURCHASES DEBIT	CASH		
			DEBIT	CREDIT		DEBIT	CREDIT	
1	17,700.00	1,062.00	6,432.00	14,028.00	14,415.60	19,461.60	11,587.20	1
2								2
3								3
4								4

5. Record column totals brought forward.

Is Anyone Listening?

Riverside Payroll enjoys a reputation as a good place to work. The company strives to provide quality services for clients. In addition, Riverside is committed to a diverse workforce and is a drug-free workplace.

As an account manager, you are participating in a management retreat focused on ethics. During the retreat you are asked to analyze the situations described below.

Instructions

Use the three-step checklist to help determine whether or not each of the following situations demonstrates ethical behavior.

Situation 1. Seamus Ryan likes to be the first to know what is going on in the office. One of the reasons he is so well informed is that he looks through the papers on other employees' desks.

Situation 2. To improve customer service quality, employees' telephone calls are monitored. Monitoring is random, and employees do not know when a quality manager is listening to a call. Customer service representative Ricki Bassett made a personal phone call while Lillian Issacs was monitoring the line. During the call, Ricki made plans for her weekend activities.

Situation 3. Lynnette Tillar and Bob Rebold are co-workers and good friends. Their supervisor, George Parton, has previously reprimanded them for spending too much time chatting on the phone and visiting. George has decided to access their e-mail to see if they are wasting company time with personal online communications as well.

Situation 4. Ann Xiao used her office computer to prepare her resume and some cover letters. Ann worked on these documents after hours and provided her own paper for printing. She later learned that her supervisor knew about her job search. The supervisor, Kathy Martz, found the computer files while looking for a report that Ann prepared.

PROFESSIONAL BUSINESS ETHICS

PROVING AND RULING THE LEFT PAGE OF AN EXPANDED JOURNAL AT THE END OF THE MONTH

PAGE *23* JOURNAL

	DATE		ACCOUNT TITLE	DOC. NO.	POST. REF.	1 GENERAL DEBIT	2 GENERAL CREDIT	3 ACCOUNTS RECEIVABLE DEBIT	4 ACCOUNTS RECEIVABLE CREDIT	
15		*30*	✓	*T30*	✓					15
16		*30*	*Totals*			*18823 54*	*2434 82*	*11066 40*	*9540 00*	16
17										17
18										18
19										19
20										20

2. Write the date. **3.** Write the word *Totals*. **1.** Rule a single line.

Equality of debits and credits in a journal is proved at the end of each month. Compare the sum of the debit totals to the sum of the credit totals for Omni at the end of November. Use the same steps that were completed to prove a journal whenever a journal page is filled. The two totals, $99,270.34, are equal. Equality of debits and credits in Omni's journal for November is proved.

The accuracy of the cash account is also proved at the end of each month. Omni's cash proof at the end of November is shown below.

Since the balance on the next unused check stub is the same as the cash proof, cash is proved.

Cash on hand at the beginning of the month (November 1 balance of cash account in general ledger)	$17,647.44
Plus total cash received during the month (Cash Debit column total, line 16, Journal page 23)	38,668.80
Equals total	$56,316.24
Less total cash paid during the month (Cash Credit column total, line 16, Journal page 23)	28,056.24
Equals cash balance on hand at end of the month . . .	$28,260.00
Checkbook balance on the next unused check stub . .	$28,260.00

REMEMBER

When cash is proved, it must always equal the amount on the next unused check stub.

PROVING AND RULING THE RIGHT PAGE OF AN EXPANDED JOURNAL AT THE END OF THE MONTH

PAGE *23*

	5	6	7	8	9	10	11	
	SALES CREDIT	SALES TAX PAYABLE CREDIT	ACCOUNTS PAYABLE		PURCHASES DEBIT	CASH		
			DEBIT	CREDIT		DEBIT	CREDIT	
15	*1380 00*	*82 80*				*1462 80*		15
16	*37920 00*	*2275 20*	*12984 00*	*19044 08*	*17727 60*	*38668 80*	*28056 24*	16
17								17
18								18
19								19
20								20

4. Write each column total.

5. Rule double lines.

After Omni's journal and cash are proved at the end of the month, the journal is ruled.

Some of the column totals will be posted as described in Chapter 12. Therefore, a check mark is not placed in the Post. Ref. column for this line.

STEPS: Ruling an expanded journal at the end of the month

1. Rule a single line across all amount columns directly below the last entry to indicate that all the columns are to be added. Be sure to rule the single line on both the left and right pages.
2. On the next line write the date, *30*, in the Date column.
3. Write the word *Totals* in the Account Title column.
4. For both the left and right pages, write each column total below the single line.
5. Rule double lines across all amount columns to show that the totals have been verified as correct. Be sure to rule the double line on both the left and right pages.

FYI

To prove a journal page, use a calculator to verify that total debit amounts equal total credit amounts.

Audit Your Understanding

1. What is the purpose of proving a journal?
2. How often should a journal be proved?
3. What is the purpose of ruling double lines below amount columns of a journal?
4. Describe how to prove cash.

Work Together

Proving and ruling an expanded journal

Partial journal pages 15 and 16 for Graphics Co. are given in the *Working Papers*. Your instructor will guide you through the following examples.

5. October 18 column totals to be carried forward have been entered on line 32 of journal page 15. Prove the equality of debits and credits and rule page 15 of the journal.
6. Record the totals brought forward from journal page 15 to line 1 of page 16 of the journal. Prove the equality of debits and credits again.
7. October 31 column totals have been entered on line 30 of journal page 16. Prove the equality of debits and credits of journal page 16.
8. Prove cash. The October 1 cash account balance in the general ledger was $11,764.96. On October 31 the balance on the next unused check stub was $18,840.00.
9. Rule page 16 of the journal.

On Your Own

Proving and ruling an expanded journal

Partial journal pages 17 and 18 for Graphics Co. are given in the *Working Papers*. Work these problems independently.

10. November 16 column totals to be carried forward have been entered on line 32 of journal page 17. Prove the equality of debits and credits and rule page 17 of the journal.
11. Record the totals brought forward from journal page 17 to line 1 of page 18 of the journal. Prove the equality of debits and credits again.
12. November 30 column totals have been entered on line 28 of journal page 18. Prove the equality of debits and credits of journal page 18.
13. Prove cash. The November cash account balance in the general ledger was $18,840.00. On November 30 the balance on the next unused check stub was $26,799.42.
14. Rule page 18 of the journal.

CHAPTER 11 SUMMARY

After completing this chapter, you can

1. Define accounting terms related to sales and cash receipts for a merchandising business.
2. Identify accounting concepts and practices related to sales and cash receipts for a merchandising business.
3. Journalize sales and cash receipts transactions for a merchandising business.
4. Prove and rule a journal.

EXPLORE ACCOUNTING

BUSINESS FORMS

Properly designed business forms can provide several important functions for a company. Business forms may (1) initiate action, (2) exercise control, (3) provide essential accounting information, and (4) provide information to multiple users.

Review Omni Import's sales invoice on page 256 to identify how these various functions have been or can be achieved.

1. *Initiate action.* The major action initiated is the collection of the amount owed by a customer for merchandise received. Information needed to accomplish this action is the customer's name and address; stock number, description, quantity, unit price, and total amounts owed for items purchased; Omni's name and address; date of the invoice; and terms of sale (due in 30 days).

2. *Exercise control.* Omni needs to insure that all merchandise shipped is properly invoiced to the customer and the information on the invoice is correct. Omni's invoices are sequentially numbered, which permits Omni to insure that all invoices are accounted for. The invoice date and terms permit Omni to file the invoice by the due date so that the company can follow up if payment is not received.

The sales clerk's initials show who made the sale so that person can be consulted if there are any questions. If the merchandise is delivered in person, the customer's signature confirms the delivery. If the merchandise is delivered by a freight company, the freight company normally requires a signature to verify delivery.

3. *Provide essential accounting information.* To account for the merchandise sold, the accounting department needs the description, unit price and total amounts of merchandise, name, address, customer number, and invoice date and terms of sale.

4. *Provide information to multiple users.* Several individuals or departments need some or all of the information on a business form. Omni has color-coded multiple copies of its sales invoice. The first copy (white) goes to the customer, Children's Paradise. The second copy (yellow) goes to Omni's shipping department. The third copy (salmon) goes to Omni's accounts receivable department. Although different businesses may use different colors, the use of color coding insures that the appropriate copy goes to the correct user.

Required: Visit a local business and request a copy of one of their business forms. Identify the items on the form that achieve the important functions for the company.

11-1 APPLICATION PROBLEM
Journalizing sales and cash receipts

James Edwards and Mildred Edwards, partners, own a boot store.

Instructions:

Journalize the following transactions completed during August of the current year on page 15 of the expanded journal given in the *Working Papers*. Source documents are abbreviated as follows: receipt, R; sales invoice, S; cash register tape, T.

Transactions:

Aug. 1. Sold merchandise on account to Frieda Leno, $137.50, plus sales tax, $8.25; total, $145.75. S62.
4. Sold merchandise on account to Alfredo Guiterrez, $95.00, plus sales tax, $5.70; total, $100.70. S63.
5 Received cash on account from Dorothy Reader, $153.70, covering S57. R88.
6. Recorded cash and credit card sales, $2,596.00, plus sales tax, $155.76; total, $2,751.76. T6.
9. Received cash on account from Denise Thibodeau, $222.60, covering S58. R89.
11. Sold merchandise on account to Rick Wisener, $126.00, plus sales tax, $7.56; total, $133.56. S64.
13. Recorded cash and credit card sales, $3,180.00, plus sales tax, $190.80; total, $3,370.80. T13.

11-2 APPLICATION PROBLEM
Journalizing sales and cash receipts

Susan Gaines and Lee Kemp, partners, own a camera and film shop.

Instructions:

Journalize the following transactions completed during September of the current year on page 16 of the expanded journal given in the *Working Papers*. Sales tax rate is 8%. Source documents are abbreviated as follows: receipt, R; sales invoice, S; cash register tape, T.

Transactions:

Sept. 2. We received a check from Charles Brittain for $111.30 as payment in full on his account covering S84. R115.
5. Jessica Gilcrease bought $126.00 worth of merchandise on account from us. Sales tax was $10.08 for a total of $136.08. S90.
7. Weekly cash and credit card sales were $3,372.00 plus sales tax of $269.76 for a total amount collected of $3,641.76. T7.
10. Sold $90.00 worth of merchandise on account to Penelope Horwitz. Sales tax was $7.20 for a total of $97.20. S91.
12. Sharon Kelly paid us $168.48 on her account covering S87. R116.
14. Weekly cash and credit card sales were $3,180.00 plus sales tax of $254.40 for a total collected of $3,434.40. T14.

11-3 APPLICATION PROBLEM
Proving and ruling an expanded journal

John Nye and Donna Kirton, partners, own a novelty store.

Partial journal pages 13 and 14 for Novelties Galore are given in the *Working Papers.*

Instructions:

1. The July 20 column totals to be carried forward have been entered on line 32 of journal page 13. Prove the equality of debits and credits and rule the column totals of journal page 13.
2. Record the totals brought forward from journal page 13 to line 1 of page 14 of the journal. Prove the equality of debits and credits again.

11-4 APPLICATION PROBLEM
Proving and ruling an expanded journal

Wanda Hagan and Art Kline, partners, own a trophies store.

A partial journal page 16 for Elegant Trophies is given in the *Working Papers.*

Instructions:

1. August 31 column totals have been entered on line 22 of journal page 16. Prove the equality of debits and credits of journal page 16.
2. Prove cash. The August 1 cash account balance in the general ledger was $7,346.50. On August 31 the balance on the next unused check stub was $18,218.86.
3. Rule page 16 of the journal.

11-5 MASTERY PROBLEM
Journalizing sales and cash receipts transactions; proving and ruling a journal

Jose Manuel and Beth Rose, partners, own Neat Look, a clothing accessories boutique.

Partial journal pages 19 and 20 for Neat Look are given in the *Working Papers.*

Instructions:

1. October 24 column totals to be carried forward have been entered on line 32 of journal page 19. Prove the equality of debits and credits and rule the column totals of journal page 19.
2. Record the totals brought forward from journal page 19 to line 1 of page 20 of the journal. Prove the equality of debits and credits again.
3. Journalize the following transactions completed during the remainder of October on journal page 20. Sales tax rate is 4%. Source documents are abbreviated as follows: receipt, R; sales invoice, S; cash register tape, T.

Transactions:

Oct. 25. Received cash on account from Bertha Libby, $143.00, covering S77. R104.
26. Sold merchandise on account to Bertha Libby, $192.50, plus sales tax, $7.70; total, $200.20. S81.
27. Recorded cash and credit card sales, $2,915.00, plus sales tax, $116.60; total, $3,031.60. T27.
29. Received cash on account from Jack Olson, $97.24, covering S78. R105.
30. Sold merchandise on account to Lisa Gardiner, $104.50, plus sales tax, $4.18; total, $108.68. S82.
31. Recorded cash and credit card sales, $1,694.00, plus sales tax, $67.76; total, $1,761.76. T31.

4. Total the journal. Prove the equality of debits and credits.
5. Rule the journal.

11-6 CHALLENGE PROBLEM
Journalizing transactions; proving and ruling a journal

Cynthia Lincoln and Mike McGinty, partners, own Always Green, a lawn and garden store.

Instructions:

1. Journalize the following transactions completed during May of the current year. Use page 19 of the journal given in the *Working Papers*. Sales tax rate is 8%. Compute and add the appropriate sales tax amount to each sale. Source documents are abbreviated as follows: check, C; memorandum, M; purchase invoice, P; receipt, R; sales invoice, S; cash register tape, T.

Transactions:

May 1. Paid cash for rent, $1,500.00. C224.
2. Cynthia Lincoln, partner, withdrew cash for personal use, $720.00. C225.
2. Mike McGinty, partner, withdrew cash for personal use, $720.00. C226.
3. Paid cash for electric bill, $156.00. C227.
3. Purchased merchandise on account from Accent Lawn Supplies, $2,730.00. P50.
4. Paid cash on account to Garden World, $1,632.00, covering P48. C228.
4. Sold merchandise on account to Colette Buckner, $1,356.00, plus sales tax. S57.
5. Bought office supplies for cash, $74.40. C229.
5. Paid cash for some merchandise, $198.00. C230.
5. Recorded cash and credit card sales, $7,020.00, plus sales tax. T5.
7. Charles Chuang bought merchandise on account, $430.00, plus sales tax. S58.
8. Felipe Garza paid cash on his account, $2,170.80, covering S53. R106.
9. Bought office supplies on account from Office Mart, $81.60. M41.
10. Purchased merchandise for cash, $216.00. C231.
10. Leonard Houston paid $1,218.24 on his account, covering S54. R107.
11. Paid cash on account to Magic Lawn and Garden, $1,638.00, covering P49. C232.
12. Mike McGinty, partner, withdrew merchandise for personal use with a cost of $462.00. M42.
12. Cash and credit card sales for the week were $3,216.00, plus sales tax. T12.
15. Cynthia Lincoln, partner, withdrew $720.00 cash for personal use. C233.
15. Mike McGinty, partner, withdrew $720.00 cash for personal use. C234.
16. Purchased merchandise on account from Lawn Doctor, $990.00. P51.
17. Paid $235.20 cash for some merchandise. C235.
17. Bought store supplies on account from McKinney Supply, $110.40. M43.
18. Paid cash on account to Office Mart, $81.60, covering M41. C236.
19. Cash and credit card sales for the week were $2,920.00, plus sales tax. T19.
21. Paid $52.80 cash for office supplies. C237.
21. Sheila Macy paid $771.12 cash on her account, covering S55. R108.
22. Nicole Oman bought merchandise on account for $390.00 plus sales tax. S59.

2. Prepare page 19 of the journal for forwarding. Total the amount columns. Prove the equality of debits and credits, and record the totals to be carried forward on line 32. Rule the column totals.
3. Record the totals brought forward on line 1 of page 20 of the journal. Prove the equality of debits and credits again.
4. Journalize the following transactions on page 20 of the journal.

Transactions:

May 23. Purchased merchandise on account from Lawn Scapes, Inc., $1,488.00. P52.
25. Paid $102.00 cash for advertising. C238.
26. Cash and credit card sales for the week were $3,216.00, plus sales tax. T26.
28. Jeffery Reagan paid $1,574.64 on his account, covering S56. R109.

May 29. Derek Sims bought merchandise on account for $174.00, plus sales tax. S60.

30. Paid cash to replenish the petty cash fund, $360.40: office supplies, $74.40; store supplies, $85.00; advertising, $105.00; miscellaneous, $96.00. C239.

30. Recorded cash and credit card sales, $768.00, plus sales tax. T30.

5. Total page 20 of the journal. Prove the equality of debits and credits.
6. Prove cash. The May 1 cash account balance in the general ledger was $7,314.50. On May 31 the balance on the next unused check stub was $22,434.10.
7. Rule page 20 of the journal.

INTERNET ACTIVITY

Point your browser to **http://accounting.swpco.com** Choose **First-Year Course**, choose **Activities**, and complete the activity for Chapter 11.

Applied Communication

The tendency for prices to increase over time is referred to as inflation. Increasing prices reduce what an individual or company can purchase with the same amount of money.

Instructions: The following table represents the prices for selected consumer goods in 1990. Copy the table and add a column for the current year and a column for the percent of change. Use the newspaper and identify current prices for the products listed. Determine the percentage change in the price of each item. If an item decreased in price, can you explain the reason for the decrease?

COMPARISON OF PRICES FOR SELECTED CONSUMER ITEMS

Item	**1990 Price**
19-inch color television	$149.00
Cassette tape	13.50
Milk (gallon)	1.99
Ground beef (pound)	1.69
Eggs, medium (dozen)	.99
Raisin bran	1.99
Film, 24 exposures	3.88
Theater ticket	6.50
Motor oil (quart)	.84
Refrigerator (19.1 cu. ft.)	790.00

Cases for Critical Thinking

Case 1 Linda Tyner, an accountant for an office supplies store, has noted a major increase in overdue amounts from charge customers. All invoice amounts from sales on account are due within 30 days. The amounts due have reduced the amount of cash available for the day-to-day operation of the business. Ms. Tyner recommends that the business (1) stop all sales on account and (2) begin accepting bank credit cards. The owner is reluctant to accept the recommendations because the business might lose some reliable customers who do not have credit cards. Also, the business will have increased expenses because of the credit card fee. How would you respond to Ms. Tyner's recommendations? What alternatives might the owner consider?

AUTOMATED ACCOUNTING

AUTOMATED ENTRIES FOR SALES AND CASH RECEIPTS USING SPECIAL JOURNALS

A merchandising business is a business that purchases and resells goods. All transactions involving the receipt of cash are recorded in a special journal called the *Cash Receipts Journal.* The sale of merchandise on account is recorded in the *Sales Journal.*

A business or individual to whom merchandise or services are sold is called a *customer.* Businesses that have many customers maintain a separate customer file. The total owed by all customers maintained in a customer file is summarized in a single general ledger asset account called Accounts Receivable. Customer accounts may be added, changed, or deleted from the accounting system just as general ledger accounts are.

Sales

A transaction in which merchandise or services are sold in exchange for another asset is called a *sales transaction.* A sales transaction may be on account or for cash. The sales journal is used to enter sales on account transactions. Sales transactions may be entered directly into the computer from the invoice (source document). When the credit portion of a sales transaction is entered, the computer will automatically make the debit to Accounts Receivable.

To record transactions in the sales journal:

1. Click the Journal toolbar button.
2. Click the Sales tab.
3. Enter the transaction date and press Tab.
4. Enter the invoice number in the Refer. column and press Tab.
5. Enter the amount of the invoice in the Sales Credit column and press Tab. The Accounts Receivable debit amount is calculated and displayed automatically.
6. If the transaction involves sales tax, enter the amount in the Sales Tax Credit column and press Tab. If there is no sales tax, press Tab to bypass the Sales Tax Credit column.
7. Press Tab as necessary to position the cursor in the Customer column. Choose a customer name from the Customer drop-down list.
8. Click the Post button.

Cash Receipts

The cash receipts journal is used to enter all cash receipt transactions. The debit to cash is automatically calculated and displayed by the computer. There are two types of cash receipts:

1. *Cash and credit card sales* are cash receipts that *do not* affect Accounts Receivable.
2. *Receipts on account* are cash receipts that *do* affect Accounts Receivable.

To record transactions in the cash receipts journal:

1. Click the Journal toolbar button.
2. Click the Cash Receipts tab.
3. Enter the transaction date and press Tab.
4. Enter the transaction reference and press Tab.
5. Enter the account number to debit or credit.
6. If recording a cash or credit card sale, press Tab until the cursor appears in the Sales Credit column. Enter the sales amount of the merchandise sold and press Tab. Enter the amount of sales tax in the Sales Tax Payable Credit column. The debit to Cash is auto-

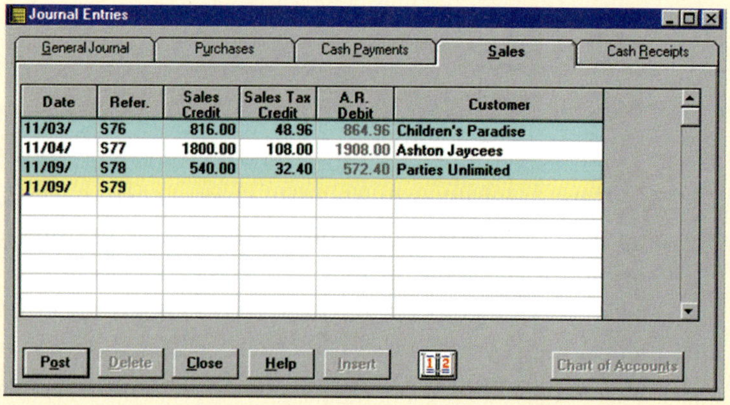

AUTOMATED ACCOUNTING

matically calculated and displayed.

7. If recording a receipt on account, press Tab until the cursor appears in the A.R. Credit column. Enter the amount. The debit to Cash is automatically calculated and displayed. Press Tab until the cursor appears in the Customer column. Choose the customer from the Customer drop-down list.
8. Click the Post button.

AUTOMATING MASTERY PROBLEM 11-5: Journalizing sales and cash receipts transactions; proving and ruling a journal

Instructions:

1. Load *Automated Accounting 7.0* or higher software.
2. Select database F11-1 from the appropriate directory/folder.
3. Select File from the menu bar and choose the Save As menu command. Key the path to the drive and directory that contains your data files. Save the database with a file name of XXX111 (where XXX are your initials).
4. Access Problem Instructions through the Help menu. Read the Problem Instructions screen.
5. Key the data listed on page 269.
6. Exit the *Automated Accounting* software.

AUTOMATING CHALLENGE PROBLEM 11-6: Journalizing transactions; proving and ruling a journal

Instructions:

1. Load *Automated Accounting 7.0* or higher software.
2. Select database F11-2 from the appropriate directory/folder.
3. Select File from the menu bar and choose the Save As menu command. Key the path to the drive and directory that contains your data files. Save the database with a file name of XXX112 (where XXX are your initials).
4. Access Problem Instructions through the Help menu. Read the Problem Instructions screen.
5. Key the data listed on pages 270–271.
6. Exit the *Automated Accounting* software.

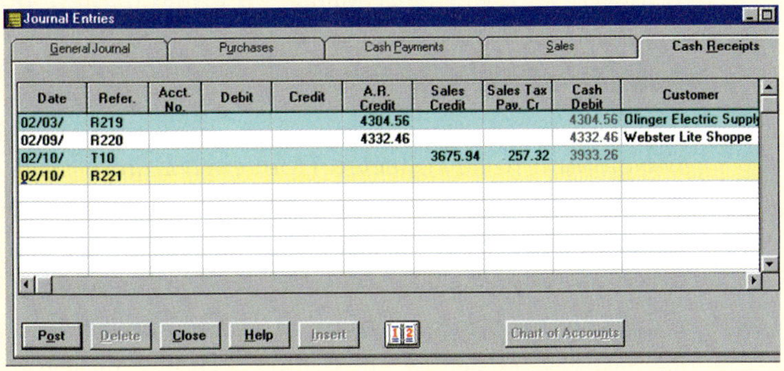

12 Posting to General and Subsidiary Ledgers

AFTER STUDYING CHAPTER 12, YOU WILL BE ABLE TO:

1. Define accounting terms related to posting to ledgers.
2. Identify accounting practices related to posting to ledgers.
3. Post to a general ledger from a journal.
4. Post to an accounts payable ledger.
5. Post to an accounts receivable ledger.
6. Verify the accuracy of accounting records.

TERMS PREVIEW

- subsidiary ledger
- accounts payable ledger
- accounts receivable ledger
- controlling account
- schedule of accounts payable
- schedule of accounts receivable

LEDGERS AND CONTROLLING ACCOUNTS

A business's size, number of transactions, and type of transactions determine the number of ledgers used in an accounting system.

General Ledger

Omni Import's general ledger chart of accounts is on page 225. However, because of the business's size and the number and type of transactions, Omni also uses additional ledgers in its accounting system.

Subsidiary Ledgers

A business needs to know the amount owed each vendor as well as the amount to be collected from each charge customer. Therefore, a separate account is needed for each vendor and each customer. Omni keeps a separate ledger for vendors and a separate ledger for customers. Each separate ledger is summarized in a single general ledger account. A ledger that is summarized in a single general ledger account is called a **subsidiary ledger.** A subsidiary ledger containing only accounts for vendors from whom items are purchased or bought on account is called an **accounts payable ledger.** A subsidiary ledger containing only accounts for charge customers is called an **accounts receivable ledger.** Total amounts are summarized in single general ledger accounts: Accounts Payable for vendors and Accounts Receivable for charge customers. An account in a general ledger that summarizes all accounts in a subsidiary ledger is called a **controlling account.** The balance of a controlling account equals the total of all account balances in its related subsidiary ledger.

ACCOUNTING IN YOUR CAREER

HOW TO KEEP YOUR JOB

Ramon Suarez is the new manager of the accounting department at Toys-for-Kids, a retail toy shop with stores in 20 locations within the state. The business has grown rapidly over the last three years, and Ramon was hired because of his expertise in automated accounting systems.

Up to now, the accounting work has all been done manually. The accounting department has two accounting clerks, Celia Johnson and Thomas Vinton. Both employees have received good performance ratings and are valued employees. However, with the increase in the business, the increased number of accounting transactions can no longer be handled by two clerks efficiently. Ramon has announced that the accounting system will soon be automated.

Meeting privately, Ramon tells Celia that she will operate the new automated accounting system. "You have always done more than your job requires, and you have taken additional accounting and computer courses. I like that kind of initiative. You'll start training on the new system next week." He explains that Thomas will be reassigned to another department, where he will be responsible for maintaining inventory records.

"Ramon, from what I already know about automated accounting, I'm not ever going to have to post again, am I?" asks Celia.

"No, you're right about that," he says with a smile on his face. "The routine parts of the accounting cycle will be handled by the software. Of course, you'll still have to get the transactions analyzed and entered into the computer. But I'm looking at ways to automate some of that also."

Critical Thinking:

1. Celia will receive a new work assignment as a result of the new automated accounting system. What can employees do to increase their chances of receiving similar opportunities?
2. Ramon referred to automating some kinds of data entry in the accounting system. What are some of the kinds of data that can be entered automatically, and how can it be done?

12-1 Posting to a General Ledger

POSTING A JOURNAL'S GENERAL AMOUNT COLUMNS

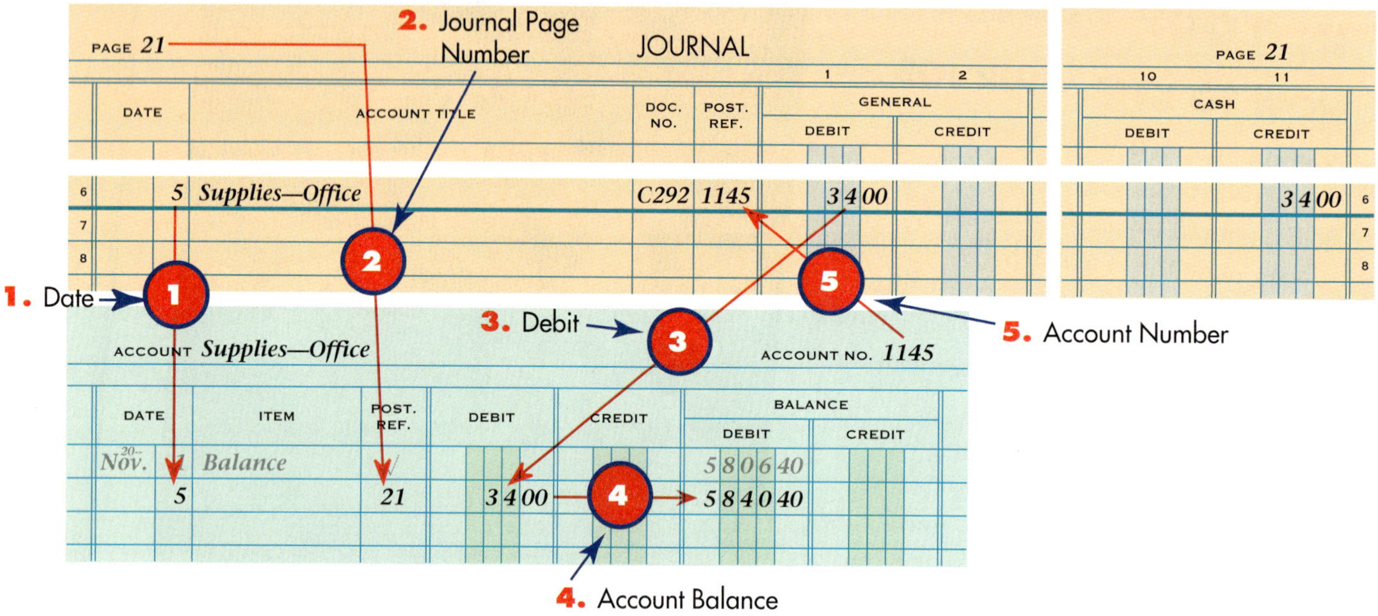

Daily general ledger account balances are usually not necessary. Balances of general ledger accounts are needed only when financial statements are prepared. Posting from a journal to a general ledger can be done periodically throughout a month. The number of transactions determines how often to post to a general ledger. A business with many transactions would normally post more often than a business with few transactions. Posting often helps keep the work load evenly distributed throughout a month. However, posting must always be done at the end of a month.

Amounts recorded in a journal's general amount columns are amounts for which no special amount columns are provided. Therefore, separate amounts in a journal's General Debit and General Credit columns *are* posted individually to the accounts written in the journal's Account Title column.

STEPS

Posting a debit entry to the general ledger

1. Write the date, *5,* in the Date column of the account.
2. Write the journal page number, *21,* in the Post. Ref. column of the account.
3. Write the debit amount, *$34.00,* in the account's Debit amount column.
4. Add the amount in the Debit column to the previous balance in the Balance Debit column ($5,806.40 + $34.00 = $5,840.40). Write the new account balance, *$5,840.40,* in the Balance Debit column.
5. Write the general ledger account number, *1145,* in the Post. Ref. column of the journal.

REMEMBER

Separate amounts in a journal's general amount columns are posted individually.

POSTING A JOURNAL'S SPECIAL AMOUNT COLUMNS

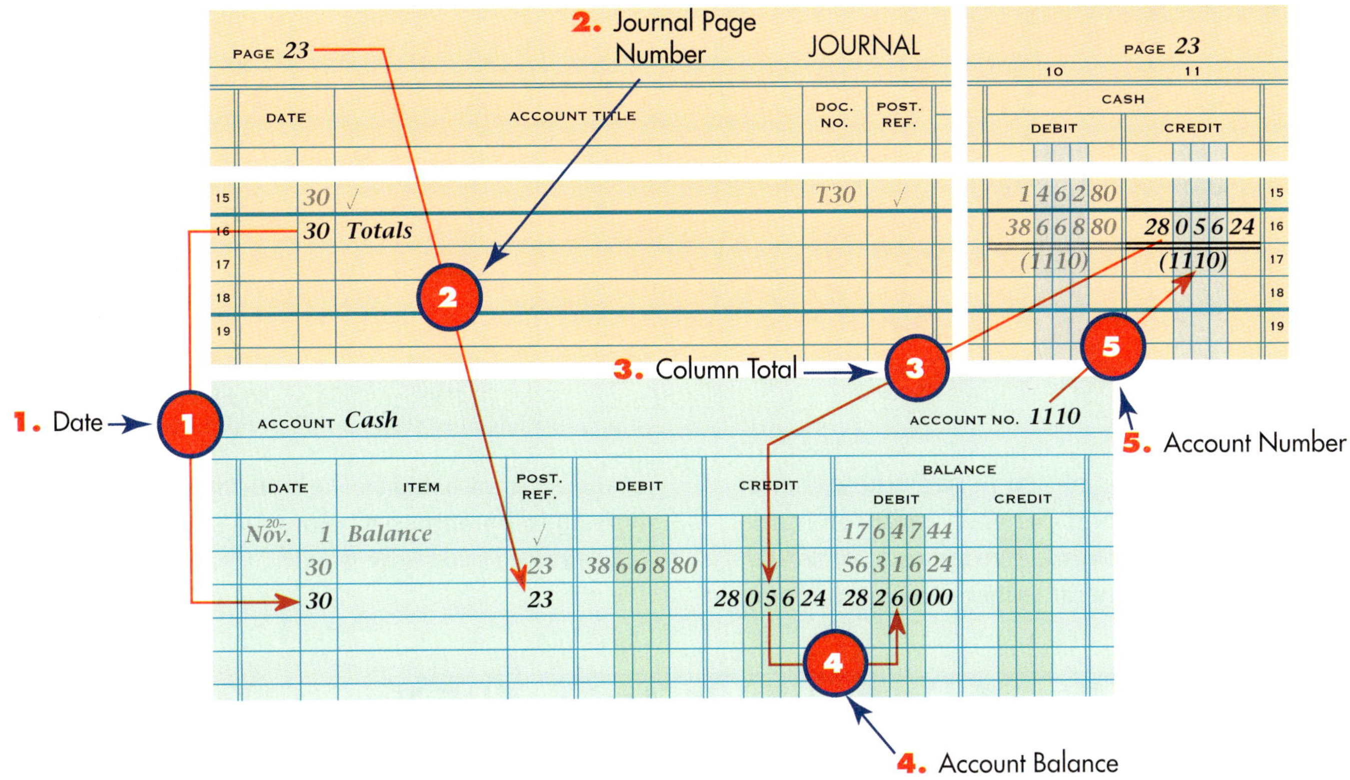

Omni's journal has nine special amount columns. Separate amounts written in these special amount columns are *not* posted individually to the general ledger. Separate amounts in a special amount column all affect the same general ledger account. Therefore, only the totals of special amount columns *are* posted to the general ledger. Each special amount column total is posted to the general ledger account listed in the column heading.

STEPS: Posting the Cash Credit column total to the general ledger

1. Write the date, *30,* in the Date column of the account.
2. Write the journal page number, *23,* in the Post. Ref. column of the account.
3. Write the Cash Credit column total, *$28,056.24,* in the account's Credit column.
4. Subtract the amount in the Credit column from the previous balance in the Balance Debit column ($56,316.24 – $28,056.24 = $28,260.00). Write the new account balance, *$28,260.00,* in the Balance Debit column.
5. Return to the journal and write the general ledger account number, *1110,* in parentheses below the Cash Credit column total.

RULES FOR POSTING A JOURNAL'S COLUMN TOTALS

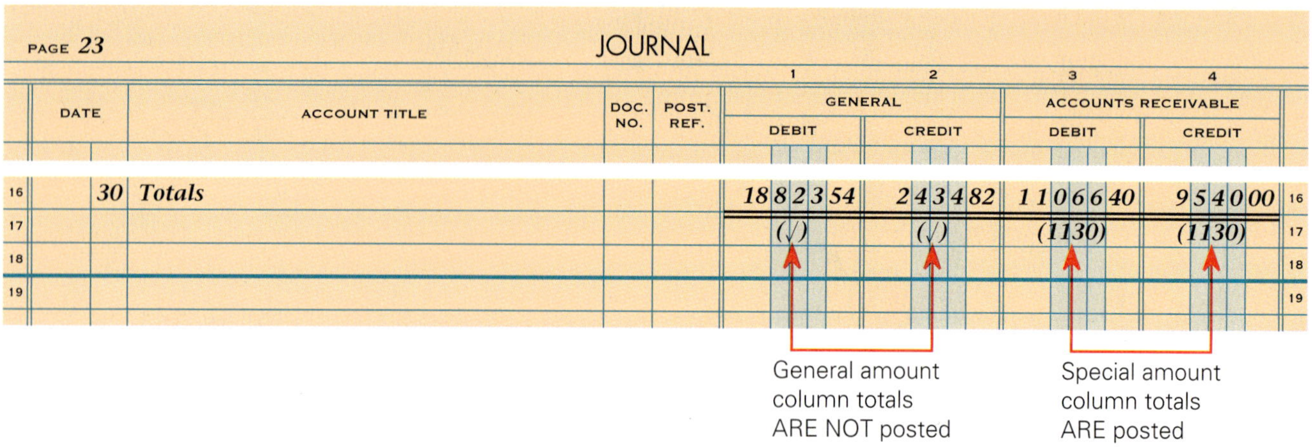

A check mark is placed in parentheses below the General Debit and General Credit column totals to indicate that the two column totals are *not* posted. The general ledger account number of the account listed in the column heading is written in parentheses below the special amount column totals to show that the totals *are* posted.

STARTING A NEW PAGE FOR AN ACCOUNT IN A GENERAL LEDGER

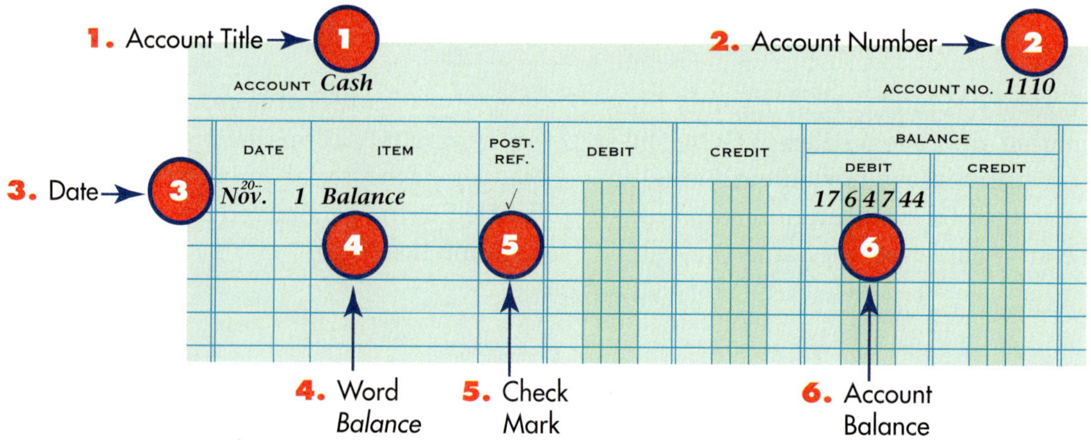

When all lines of a general ledger account form have been used, a new page is prepared.

On November 1 Omni prepared a new page for Cash in the general ledger because the existing page was full.

STEPS: Starting a new page for a general ledger account

1. Write the account title, *Cash,* at the top of the page.
2. Write the account number, *1110,* at the top of the page.
3. Write the date, *20 —, Nov. 1,* in the Date column.
4. Write the word *Balance* in the Item column.
5. Place a check mark in the Post. Ref. column to show that the entry has been carried forward from a previous page rather than posted from a journal.
6. Write the account balance, *$17,647.44,* in the Balance Debit column.

Terms Review

subsidiary ledger

accounts payable ledger

accounts receivable ledger

controlling account

Audit Your Understanding

1. What is a controlling account?
2. What is the relationship between a controlling account and a subsidiary ledger?
3. What are the four amount columns of the general ledger account form?
4. What are the rules for posting a journal's column totals?

Work Together

Posting to a general ledger

Partial journal page 16 for Graphics, Inc. is given in the *Working Papers.* Also given in the *Working Papers* are two general ledger account forms: one for Cash and a blank form. Your instructor will guide you through the following examples.

5. Start a new page for a general ledger account for Supplies—Office. The account number is 1145, and the balance for October 1 of the current year is $3,824.00.
6. Post the General Debit entry on line 2, page 16 of the journal to the Supplies—Office account.
7. Post the Cash Debit column total on line 30, page 16 of the journal to Cash.
8. Record the appropriate entry under the General Debit and Cash Debit column totals on line 31, page 16 of the journal. Save your work to complete Work Together on page 285.

On Your Own

Posting to a general ledger

Partial journal page 18 for Graphics, Inc. is given in the *Working Papers.* Also given in the *Working Papers* are two general ledger account forms: one for Cash and a blank form. Work these problems independently.

9. Start a new page for a general ledger account for Supplies—Store. The account number is 1150, and the balance for November 1 of the current year is $4,302.00.
10. Post the General Debit entry on line 2, page 18 of the journal to the Supplies—Store account.
11. Post the Cash Credit column total on line 28, page 18 of the journal to Cash.
12. Record the appropriate entry under the General Debit and Cash Credit column totals on line 29, page 18 of the journal. Save your work to complete On Your Own on page 285.

12-2 Posting to an Accounts Payable Ledger

ACCOUNTS PAYABLE LEDGER AND GENERAL LEDGER CONTROLLING ACCOUNT

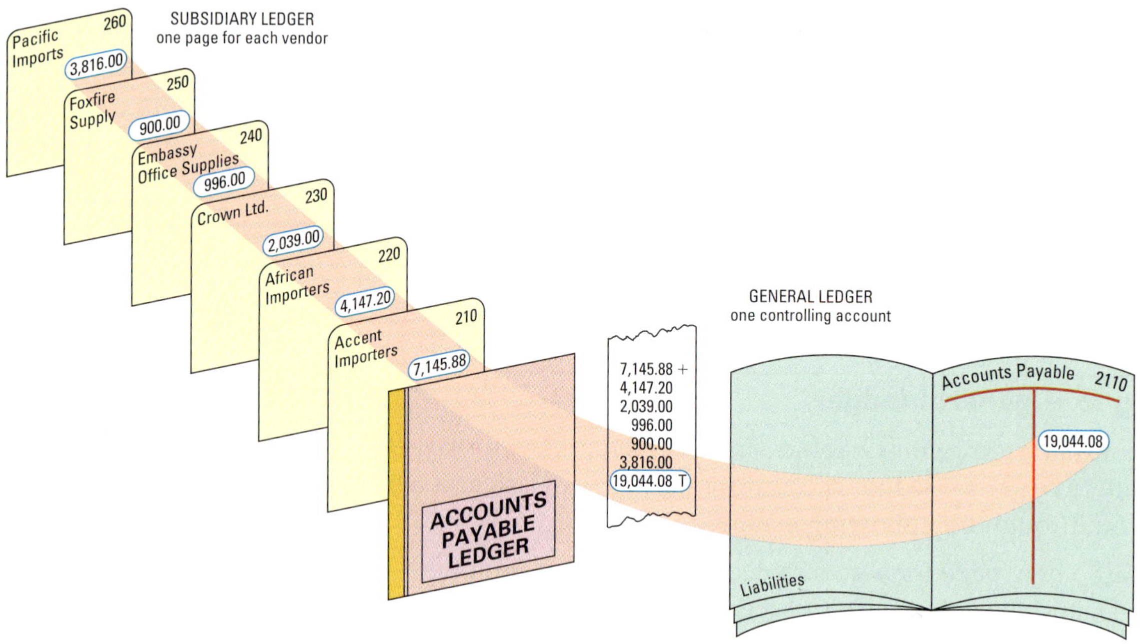

Omni assigns a vendor number to each account in the accounts payable ledger. A three-digit number is used. The first digit identifies the division in which the controlling account appears in the general ledger. The second two digits show each account's location within a subsidiary ledger. Accounts are assigned by 10s beginning with the second digit. Accounts in the subsidiary ledgers can be located by either number or name.

The vendor number for Accent Importers is 210. The first digit, *2,* shows that the controlling account is a liability, Accounts Payable. The second and third digits, *10,* show the vendor number assigned to Accent Importers.

The procedure for adding new accounts to subsidiary ledgers is the same as described for Encore Music's general ledger in Chapter 5. Accounts are arranged in alphabetical order within the subsidiary ledgers. New accounts are assigned the unused middle number. If the proper alphabetical order places a new account as the last account, the next number in the sequence of 10s is assigned. Omni's chart of accounts for the subsidiary ledgers is on page 225.

When the balance of a vendor account in an accounts payable ledger is changed, the balance of the controlling account, Accounts Payable, is also changed. The total of all vendor account balances in the accounts payable ledger equals the balance of the controlling account, Accounts Payable.

OPENING ACCOUNTS PAYABLE LEDGER FORMS

1. Vendor Name → (1)   **2.** Vendor Number → (2)

VENDOR *Crown Ltd.*   VENDOR NO. *230*

DATE		ITEM	POST. REF.	DEBIT	CREDIT	CREDIT BALANCE

Omni Import uses a 3-column accounts payable subsidiary account form. Information to be recorded in the accounts payable ledger includes the date, posting reference, debit or credit amount, and new account balance. Accounts payable are liabilities, and liabilities have normal credit balances. Therefore, the Debit Balance column is usually not needed for the accounts payable ledger accounts.

Each new account is opened by:

1. Writing the vendor name on the heading of the ledger account.
2. Writing the vendor number on the heading of the ledger account.

The vendor name is obtained from the first purchase invoice received. The vendor number is assigned using the three-digit numbering system previously described. The correct alphabetical order for Crown Ltd. places the account as the third account in the accounts payable subsidiary ledger. Vendor number 230 is assigned to Crown Ltd.

Some businesses record both the vendor name and vendor address on the ledger form. However, the address information is usually kept in a separate name and address file. This practice eliminates having to record the vendor address on the ledger form each time a new ledger page is started or the address changes.

GLOBAL PERSPECTIVE

THE INTERNATIONAL BUSINESS DAY

American business offices normally operate Monday through Friday, eight hours a day, with a 30- to 45-minute lunch break. This is not necessarily true in other countries, however. In the People's Republic of China, for example, employees usually work Monday through Saturday, eight hours a day, with lunch from 1:00 P.M. to 2:00 P.M.

When doing business internationally, both time zone differences and cultural factors affecting the business day must be taken into consideration. For example, in Spain, many businesses close at 2:00 P.M. so that employees may eat lunch with their families. The office reopens at 5:00 P.M. and stays open until about 8:00 P.M. Spain is in a time zone that is five hours ahead of *Eastern Standard Time (EST),* the time zone along the eastern coast of the United States. If doing business with a company in Spain, it would not be a good idea to try to call at 9:00 A.M. EST because the business may just be closing for lunch. A better time to call Spain from the EST time zone would be between noon and 3:00 P.M.

POSTING A CREDIT TO AN ACCOUNTS PAYABLE LEDGER

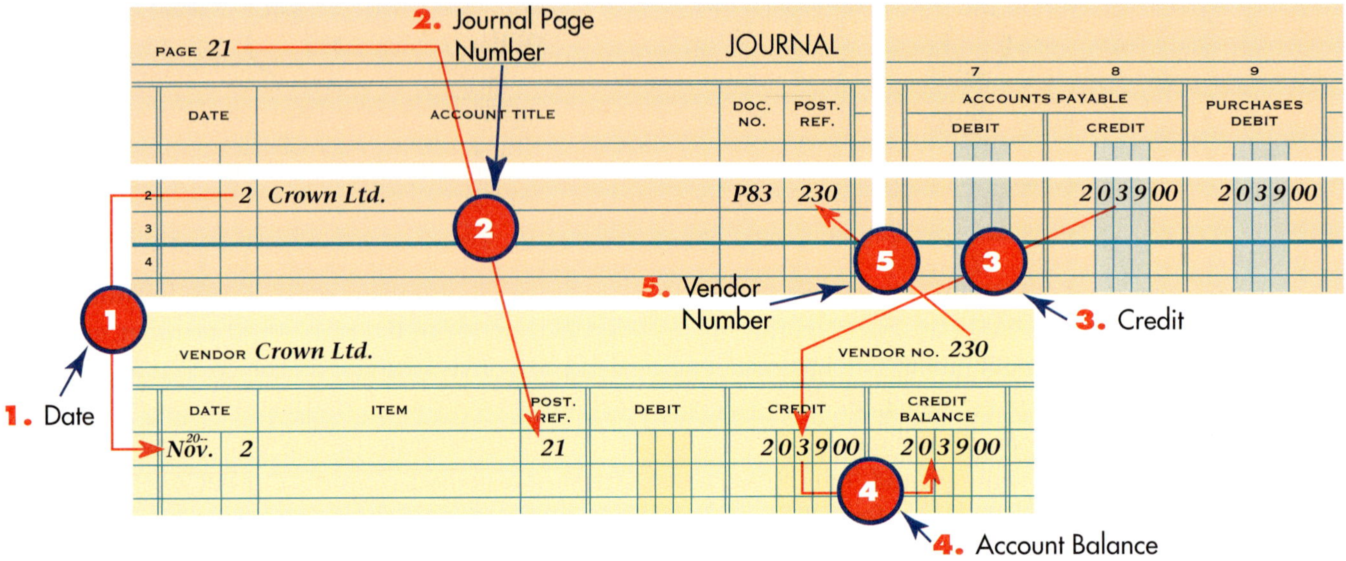

Each entry in the Accounts Payable columns of a journal affects the vendor named in the Account Title column. Omni posts each amount in these two columns often. Posting often keeps each vendor account balance up to date. Totals of Accounts Payable special amount columns are posted to the general ledger at the end of each month.

The controlling account in the general ledger, Accounts Payable, is also increased by this entry. At the end of the month, the journal's Accounts Payable Credit column total is posted to the controlling account, Accounts Payable.

FYI *When an account that is no longer used is removed from the accounts payable ledger, that vendor number is available for assignment to a new vendor.*

STEPS

Posting a credit entry to an accounts payable ledger

1. Write the current date, *20—, Nov. 2,* in the Date column of the account.
2. Write the journal page number, *21,* in the Post. Ref. column of the account.
3. Write the credit amount, *$2,039.00,* in the Credit column of the account for Crown Ltd.
4. Add the amount in the Credit column to the previous balance in the Credit Balance column. Crown Ltd. has no previous balance; therefore, $0 + $2,039.00 = $2,039.00. Write the new account balance, *$2,039.00,* in the Credit Balance column.
5. Write the vendor number, *230,* in the Post. Ref. column of the journal. The vendor number recorded in the journal shows that the posting for this entry is complete.

POSTING A DEBIT TO AN ACCOUNTS PAYABLE LEDGER

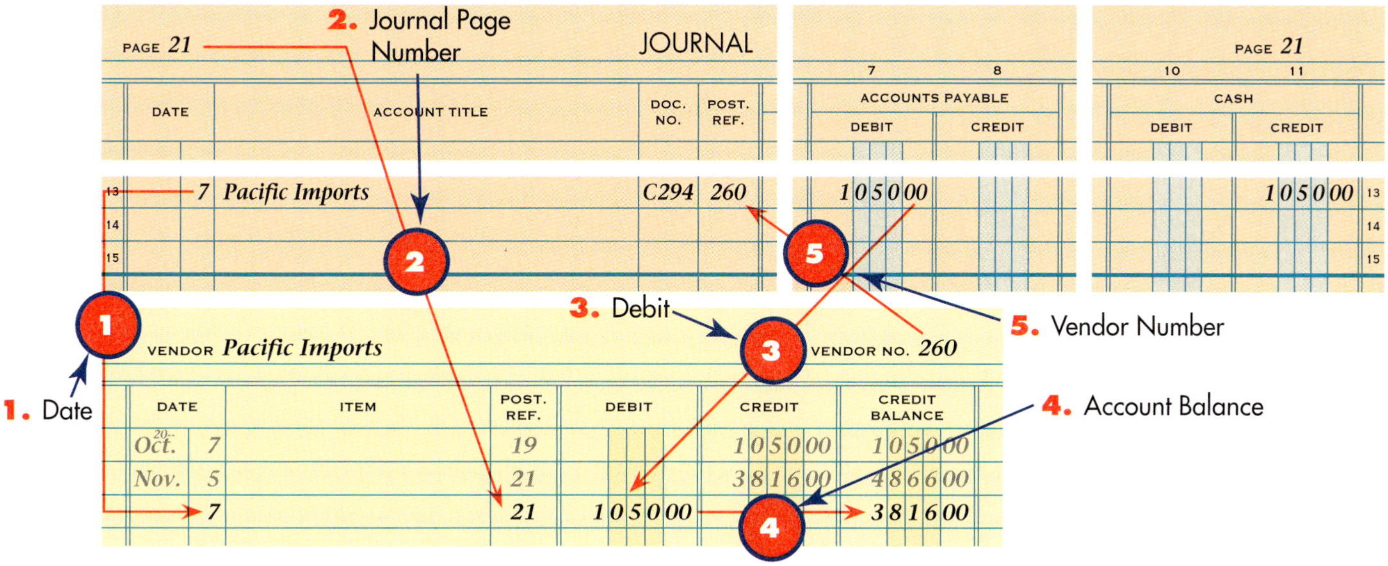

Similar steps are followed to post a debit to a vendor account as are used to post a credit. However, the debit amount is entered in the Debit column of the vendor account. The debit amount is subtracted from the previous credit balance. The controlling account in the general ledger, Accounts Payable, is decreased by this entry. At the end of the month, the journal's Accounts Payable Debit column total is posted to the controlling account, Accounts Payable.

STARTING A NEW PAGE FOR A VENDOR IN AN ACCOUNTS PAYABLE LEDGER

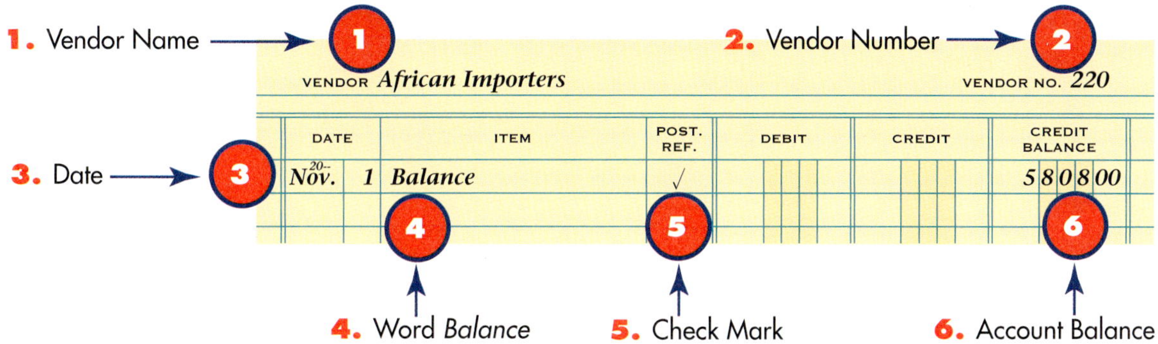

When all lines have been used, a new page is prepared. The vendor name, vendor number, and account balance are recorded on the new page.

STEPS Starting a new page in the accounts payable ledger

1. Write the vendor name, *African Importers,* on the Vendor line.
2. Write the vendor number, *220,* on the Vendor No. line.
3. Write the date, *20—, Nov. 1,* in the Date column.
4. Write the word *Balance* in the Item column.
5. Place a check mark in the Post. Ref. column to show that the amount has been carried forward from a previous page rather than posted from a journal.
6. Write the account balance, *$5,808.00,* in the Credit Balance column.

COMPLETED ACCOUNTS PAYABLE LEDGER

VENDOR *Accent Importers* VENDOR NO. *210*

DATE		ITEM	POST. REF.	DEBIT	CREDIT	CREDIT BALANCE
20-- Nov.	1	Balance	✓			4,752.00
	6		21	4,752.00		—
	13		21		3,768.00	3,768.00
	20		22		3,377.88	7,145.88

VENDOR *African Importers* VENDOR NO. *220*

DATE		ITEM	POST. REF.	DEBIT	CREDIT	CREDIT BALANCE
20-- Nov.	1	Balance	✓			5,808.00
	5		21		4,147.20	9,955.20
	20		22	5,808.00		4,147.20

VENDOR *Crown Ltd.* VENDOR NO. *230*

DATE		ITEM	POST. REF.	DEBIT	CREDIT	CREDIT BALANCE
20-- Nov.	2		21		2,039.00	2,039.00

VENDOR *Embassy Office Supplies* VENDOR NO. *240*

DATE		ITEM	POST. REF.	DEBIT	CREDIT	CREDIT BALANCE
20-- Oct.	23		20		744.00	744.00
Nov.	23		22	744.00		—
	24		22		996.00	996.00

VENDOR *Foxfire Supply* VENDOR NO. *250*

DATE		ITEM	POST. REF.	DEBIT	CREDIT	CREDIT BALANCE
20-- Oct.	12		19		498.00	498.00
Nov.	6		21		210.00	708.00
	11		21	498.00		210.00
	23		22		690.00	900.00

VENDOR *Pacific Imports* VENDOR NO. *260*

DATE		ITEM	POST. REF.	DEBIT	CREDIT	CREDIT BALANCE
20-- Oct.	7		19		1,050.00	1,050.00
Nov.	5		21		3,816.00	4,866.00
	7		21	1,050.00		3,816.00

Omni's accounts payable ledger has been posted for the month of November.

AUDIT YOUR UNDERSTANDING

1. What is the title of the balance amount column of the accounts payable ledger form? Why is that title used?
2. How is a new vendor account opened?
3. List the five steps for posting to an accounts payable ledger.

WORK TOGETHER

Posting to an accounts payable ledger

Use the partial journal page 16 for Graphics, Inc. from Work Together on page 279. Also given in the *Working Papers* are two accounts payable ledger account forms: one for Electro-Graphic Supply and a blank form. Your instructor will guide you through the following examples.

4. Start a new page for an accounts payable ledger account for Regal Designs. The account number is 240, and the balance for October 1 of the current year is $877.00.
5. Post the Accounts Payable Credit entry on line 3, page 16 of the journal to the accounts payable account for Regal Designs.
6. Post the Accounts Payable Debit entry on line 4, page 16 of the journal to the accounts payable account for Electro-Graphic Supply. Save your work to complete Work Together on page 291.

ON YOUR OWN

Posting to an accounts payable ledger

Use the partial journal page 18 for Graphics, Inc. from On Your Own on page 279. Also given in the *Working Papers* are two accounts payable ledger account forms: one for Art and Things and a blank form. Work these problems independently.

7. Start a new page for an accounts payable ledger account for Can Do Graphics. The account number is 220, and the balance for November 1 of the current year is $986.00.
8. Post the Accounts Payable Credit entry on line 3, page 18 of the journal to the accounts payable account for Can Do Graphics.
9. Post the Accounts Payable Debit entry on line 4, page 18 of the journal to the accounts payable account for Art and Things. Save your work to complete On Your Own on page 291.

12-3 Posting to an Accounts Receivable Ledger

ACCOUNTS RECEIVABLE LEDGER AND GENERAL LEDGER CONTROLLING ACCOUNT

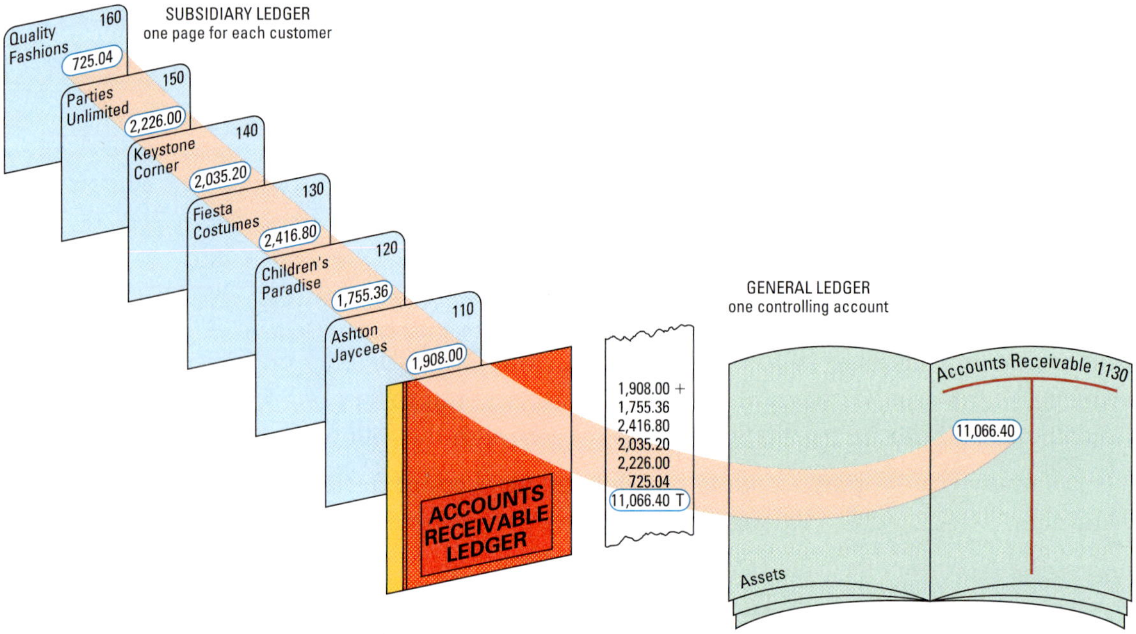

Omni assigns a customer number to each account in the accounts receivable ledger. A three-digit number is used.

The customer number for Ashton Jaycees is 110. The first digit, *1,* shows that the controlling account is an asset, Accounts Receivable. The second and third digits, *10,* show the customer number assigned to Ashton Jaycees.

When the balance of a customer account in an accounts receivable ledger is changed, the balance of the controlling account, Accounts Receivable, is also changed. The total of all customer account balances in the accounts receivable ledger equals the balance of the controlling account, Accounts Receivable.

SMALL BUSINESS SPOTLIGHT

The major ways of starting a new small business are:
1. Buy an existing business.
2. Buy a franchise.
3. Start a business from scratch.

OPENING ACCOUNTS RECEIVABLE LEDGER FORMS

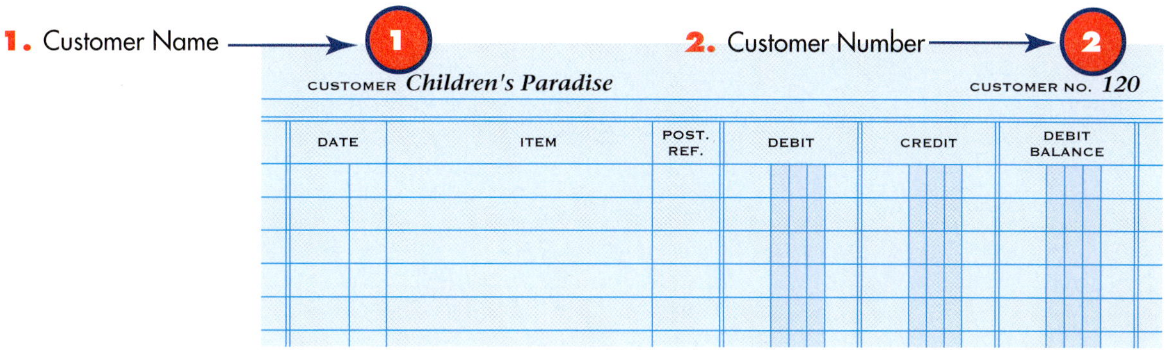

Omni Import uses a 3-column accounts receivable subsidiary account form. The accounts receivable account form is similar to the one used for the accounts payable ledger. Accounts receivable are assets, and assets have normal debit balances. Therefore, the form used in the accounts receivable ledger has a Debit Balance column instead of a Credit Balance column.

Procedures for opening customer accounts are similar to those used for opening vendor accounts. Each new account is opened by:

1. Writing the customer name on the heading of the ledger account.
2. Writing the customer number on the heading of the ledger account.

The customer name is obtained from the first sales invoice prepared for a customer. The customer number is assigned using the three-digit numbering system previously described.

Some businesses record both the customer name and customer address on the ledger form. However, the address information is usually kept in a separate name and address file. This practice eliminates having to record the customer address on the ledger form each time a new ledger page is started or the address changes.

F.Y.I.

When an account that is no longer used is removed from the accounts receivable ledger, that customer number is available for assignment to a new customer.

POSTING A DEBIT TO AN ACCOUNTS RECEIVABLE LEDGER

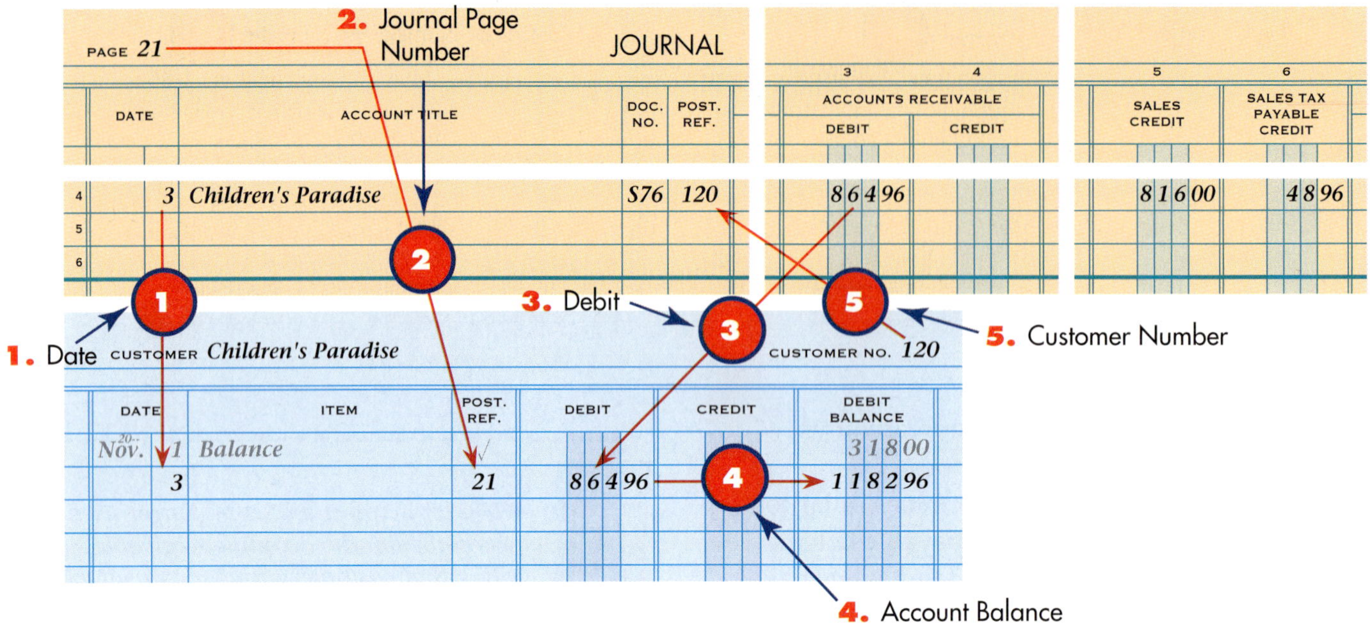

Each entry in the Accounts Receivable columns of a journal affects the customer named in the Account Title column. Each amount listed in these two columns is posted to a customer account in the accounts receivable ledger often. Posting often keeps each customer account balance up to date. Totals of Accounts Receivable special amount columns are posted to the general ledger at the end of each month.

The controlling account in the general ledger, Accounts Receivable, is also increased by this entry. At the end of the month, the journal's Accounts Receivable Debit column total is posted to the controlling account, Accounts Receivable.

STEPS: Posting a debit entry to an accounts receivable ledger

1. Write the date, *3,* in the Date column of the account.
2. Write the journal page number, *21,* in the Post. Ref. column of the account.
3. Write the debit amount, *$864.96,* in the Debit column of the account for Children's Paradise.
4. Add the amount in the Debit column to the previous balance in the Debit Balance column ($318.00 + $864.96 = $1,182.96). Write the new account balance, *$1,182.96,* in the Debit Balance column.
5. Write the customer number, *120,* in the Post. Ref. column of the journal. The customer number shows that the posting for this entry is complete.

FYI

An error in posting may cause a business to overcharge or undercharge its customers.

POSTING A CREDIT TO AN ACCOUNTS RECEIVABLE LEDGER

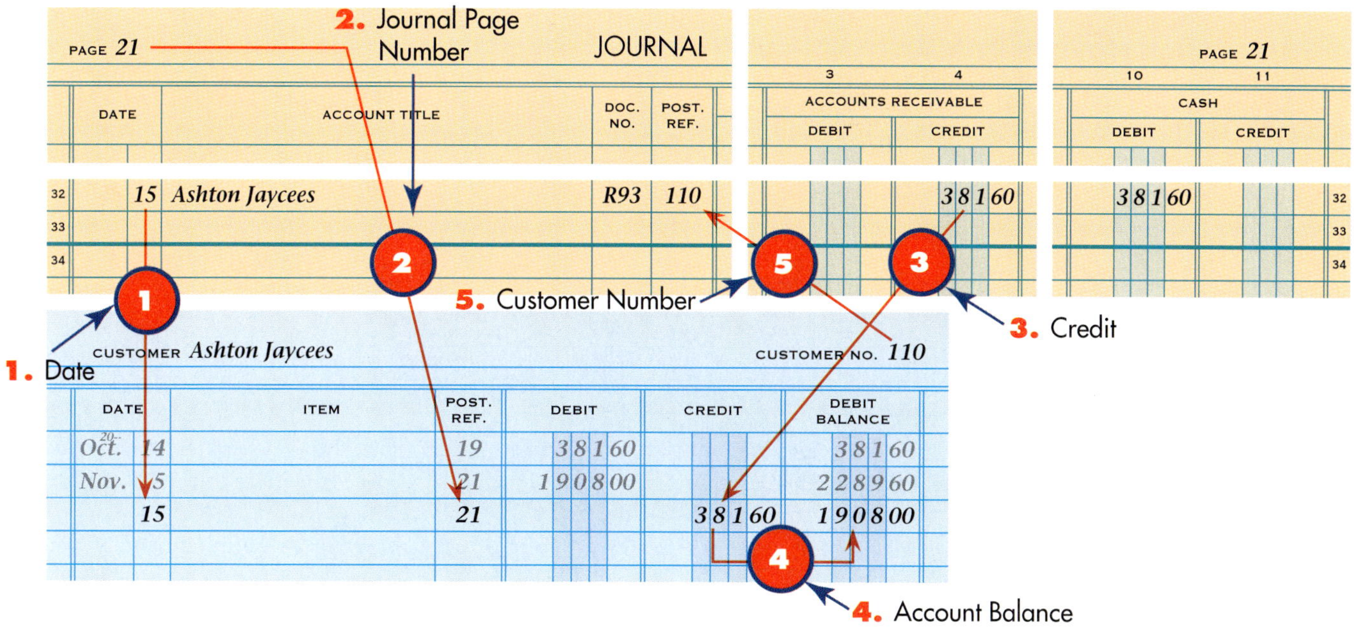

Similar steps are followed to post a credit to a customer account as are used to post a debit. However, the credit amount is written in the Credit column of the customer account. The credit amount is subtracted from the previous debit balance to determine the new balance. The new balance is written in the Debit Balance column.

The controlling account in the general ledger, Accounts Receivable, is decreased by this entry. However, the amount is not posted individually to the accounts receivable account. At the end of the month, the amount, $381.60, is posted as part of the special amount column total to Accounts Receivable.

STARTING A NEW PAGE FOR A CUSTOMER IN AN ACCOUNTS RECEIVABLE LEDGER

Procedures for starting a new page in an accounts receivable ledger are similar to those used for starting new pages for vendor accounts.

The vendor name and number are written in the heading of the account. The date is written in the Date column. The word *Balance* is written in the Item column, and a check mark is placed in the Post. Ref. column. The balance is written in the Debit Balance column.

COMPLETED ACCOUNTS RECEIVABLE LEDGER

CUSTOMER *Ashton Jaycees* CUSTOMER NO. *110*

DATE		ITEM	POST. REF.	DEBIT	CREDIT	DEBIT BALANCE
20-- Oct.	14		19	381 60		381 60
Nov.	5		21	1 908 00		2 289 60
	15		21		381 60	1 908 00

CUSTOMER *Children' Paradise* CUSTOMER NO. *120*

DATE		ITEM	POST. REF.	DEBIT	CREDIT	DEBIT BALANCE
20-- Nov.	1	Balance	✓			318 00
	3		21	864 96		1 182 96
	24		22	890 40		2 073 36
	25		22		318 00	1 755 36

CUSTOMER *Fiesta Costumes* CUSTOMER NO. *130*

DATE		ITEM	POST. REF.	DEBIT	CREDIT	DEBIT BALANCE
20-- Nov.	1	Balance	✓			2 162 40
	6		21		2 162 40	—
	18		22	2 416 80		2 416 80

CUSTOMER *Keystone Corner* CUSTOMER NO. *140*

DATE		ITEM	POST. REF.	DEBIT	CREDIT	DEBIT BALANCE
20-- Oct.	10		19	1 144 80		1 144 80
Nov.	10		21		1 144 80	—
	24		22	381 60		381 60
	29		22	1 653 60		2 035 20

CUSTOMER *Parties Unlimited* CUSTOMER NO. *150*

DATE		ITEM	POST. REF.	DEBIT	CREDIT	DEBIT BALANCE
20-- Nov.	1	Balance	✓			2 989 20
	9		21	572 40		3 561 60
	16		22	1 653 60		5 215 20
	17		22		2 989 20	2 226 00

CUSTOMER *Quality Fashions* CUSTOMER NO. *160*

DATE		ITEM	POST. REF.	DEBIT	CREDIT	DEBIT BALANCE
20-- Nov.	1	Balance	✓			2 544 00
	11		21	725 04		3 269 04
	13		21		1 081 20	2 187 84
	20		22		1 462 80	725 04

Omni Import's accounts receivable ledger has been posted for the month of November.

Audit Your Understanding

1. Why does the 3-column account form used in an accounts receivable ledger have a Debit Balance column?
2. List the five steps for posting to an accounts receivable ledger.

Work Together

Posting to an accounts receivable ledger

Use the partial journal page 16 for Graphics, Inc., from Work Together on page 285. Also given in the *Working Papers* are two accounts receivable ledger account forms: one for Alfredo Lopez and a blank form. Your instructor will guide you through the following examples.

3. Start a new page for an accounts receivable ledger account for Maria Farrell. The account number is 120, and the balance for October 1 of the current year is $212.00.
4. Post the Accounts Receivable Debit entry on line 5, page 16 of the journal to the accounts receivable account for Maria Farrell.
5. Post the Accounts Receivable Credit entry on line 6, page 16 of the journal to the accounts receivable account for Alfredo Lopez.

On Your Own

Posting to an accounts receivable ledger

Use the partial journal page 18 for Graphics, Inc., from On Your Own on page 285. Also given in the *Working Papers* are two accounts receivable ledger account forms: one for Brandee Sparks and a blank form. Work these problems independently.

6. Start a new page for an accounts receivable ledger account for David Bishop. The account number is 110, and the balance for November 1 of the current year is $238.50.
7. Post the Accounts Receivable Debit entry on line 5, page 18 of the journal to the accounts receivable account for David Bishop.
8. Post the Accounts Receivable Credit entry on line 6, page 18 of the journal to the accounts receivable account for Brandee Sparks.

12-4 Accuracy of Accounting Records

PROVING THE ACCURACY OF POSTING

A single error in posting to a ledger account may cause the trial balance to be out of balance. An error in posting may cause the cash account balance to disagree with the actual cash on hand. An error in posting may cause the income to be understated or overstated on an income statement. An error in posting may cause a business to overpay or underpay its vendors. Posting must be accurate to assure correct account balances. Therefore, to prove the accuracy of posting, three things are done. (1) Cash is proved. (2) Subsidiary schedules are prepared to prove that the total of the balances in the subsidiary ledgers equals the balance of the controlling account in the general ledger. (3) A trial balance is prepared to prove that debits equal credits in the general ledger.

Preparation of a trial balance is described in Chapter 15.

Proving Cash

The method used to prove cash is described in Chapter 11. The cash proof total is compared with the balance on the next unused check stub in the checkbook.

PROVING THE ACCOUNTS PAYABLE LEDGER

Omni Import
Schedule of Accounts Payable
November 30, 20--

Accent Importers	7,145.88
African Importers	4,147.20
Crown Ltd.	2,039.00
Embassy Office Supplies	996.00
Foxfire Supply	900.00
Pacific Imports	3,816.00
Total Accounts Payable	19,044.08

A controlling account balance in a general ledger must equal the sum of all account balances in a subsidiary ledger. Omni Import proves subsidiary ledgers at the end of each month.

A listing of vendor accounts, account balances, and total amount due all vendors is called a **schedule of accounts payable.** A schedule of accounts payable is prepared after all entries in a journal are posted. The balance of Accounts Payable in the general ledger is $19,044.08. The total of the schedule of accounts payable is $19,044.08. Because the two amounts are the same, the accounts payable ledger is proved.

PROVING THE ACCOUNTS RECEIVABLE LEDGER

Omni Import		
Schedule of Accounts Receivable		
November 30, 20--		
Ashton Jaycees	1908	00
Children's Paradise	1755	36
Fiesta Costumes	2416	80
Keystone Corner	2035	20
Parties Unlimited	2226	00
Quality Fashions	725	04
Total Accounts Receivable	11066	40

A listing of customer accounts, account balances, and total amount due from all customers is called a **schedule of accounts receivable.** A schedule of accounts receivable is prepared after all entries in a journal are posted. The balance of Accounts Receivable in the general ledger is $11,066.40. The total of the schedule of accounts receivable is $11,066.40. Because the two amounts are the same, the accounts receivable ledger is proved.

Communication Overload

Electronic mail or *e-mail* is intended to make an employee's job easier. E-mail is a convenient way to communicate with other workers within a company. Through the use of the Internet, e-mail also provides a way to communicate with colleagues, suppliers, and clients in other locations.

The volume of e-mail is growing. In the past, more than 700 billion messages passed through U.S.-based computer networks. Currently, that number exceeds 6.6 trillion.

In the case of e-mail, is more better? Who sends all the messages? Who receives them? What do the messages say?

Some managers and executives may receive more than 200 messages per day. Many of these messages are *CCs*—copies of messages sent to others. (CC originally meant carbon copy.) This kind of e-mail overload eats into productivity as workers spend time reading and managing messages.

It's important to remember that e-mail is not a private communication. Some companies routinely review e-mail communications. Others check e-mail when they suspect a problem. Many companies back up their computer systems and save all data including e-mail files. You might have deleted an e-mail message from your computer, but there is a good chance it is still lurking somewhere in the system.

Technology for Business

TERMS REVIEW

schedule of accounts payable

schedule of accounts receivable

AUDIT YOUR UNDERSTANDING

1. Why is accuracy in posting important?
2. How are subsidiary ledgers proved at the end of the month?
3. What accounts are listed on a schedule of accounts payable?
4. What does it mean when the total of the schedule of accounts receivable is the same as the balance of Accounts Receivable in the general ledger?

WORK TOGETHER

Proving an accounts payable ledger

Given in the *Working Papers* is a blank form for preparation of a schedule of accounts payable. Your instructor will guide you through the following example.

5. One step in proving the accuracy of posting for Graphics, Inc., is proving accounts payable. Prepare a schedule of accounts payable for Graphics, Inc. on October 31 of the current year. October 31 balances are: Art and Things, $873.00; Can Do Graphics, $986.00; Electro-Graphic Supply, $2,544.00; and Regal Designs, $2,280.20. Accounts Payable balance in the general ledger on October 31 is $6,683.20.

ON YOUR OWN

Proving an accounts receivable ledger

Given in the *Working Papers* is a blank form for preparation of a schedule of accounts receivable. Work this problem independently.

6. Prepare a schedule of accounts receivable for Graphics, Inc., on November 30 of the current year. November 30 balances are: David Bishop, $887.22; Maria Farrell, $788.64; Alfredo Lopez, $1,272.00; and Brandee Sparks, $1,431.00. Accounts Receivable balance in the general ledger on November 30 is $4,378.86.

CHAPTER 12 SUMMARY

After completing this chapter, you can

1. Define important accounting terms related to posting to ledgers.
2. Identify accounting practices related to posting to ledgers.
3. Post to a general ledger from a journal.
4. Post to an accounts payable ledger.
5. Post to an accounts receivable ledger.
6. Verify the accuracy of accounting records.

EXPLORE ACCOUNTING

CATEGORIES OF INTERNAL CONTROL

Posting transactions from a journal to both the general ledger and subsidiary ledgers presents opportunities for errors. Omni Import is a small company with few employees. Generally, the same person at Omni posts to both the general ledger and subsidiary ledgers. Larger businesses with more employees generally split up duties among several employees to reduce the chances of error.

To avoid errors and their resulting losses, businesses should institute effective internal controls. Internal controls may be categorized in three phases: (1) preventive, (2) detective, and (3) corrective.

A preventive control prevents the individual from making the error. Establishing and following consistent procedures for posting transactions is a preventive control. A detective control detects or finds the error. Preparing a trial balance is a detective control. A corrective control restores the business back to normal if an error occurs. Insurance, such as a fidelity bond on a cashier, is a corrective control.

Discussion: Describe internal control procedures that you have observed either as an employee or as a customer. Identify each procedure as (1) preventive, (2) detective, or (3) corrective.

12-1 APPLICATION PROBLEM
Posting to a general ledger

Selected entries from the journal for Healthy Nutrition, a health food store, are given in the *Working Papers.*

Instructions:

1. Start new pages for the following accounts in the general ledger. Record the balances as of August 1 of the current year.

General Ledger

Account No.	Account Title	Balance
1110	Cash	$ 21,960.00
1150	Supplies—Office	4,416.00
1170	Prepaid Insurance	1,870.00
2120	Sales Tax Payable	1,778.00
4110	Sales	206,904.00
6110	Advertising Expense	2,230.00
6160	Rent Expense	8,400.00

2. Post the separate items recorded in the journal's General Debit column.
3. Post the totals of the special columns of the journal.

12-2 APPLICATION PROBLEM
Posting to an accounts payable ledger

Selected entries from the journal for Healthy Nutrition, a health food store, are given in the *Working Papers.*

Instructions:

1. Start new pages for the following accounts in the general ledger. Record the balances as of September 1 of the current year.

General Ledger

Account No.	Account Title	Balance
1110	Cash	$ 40,650.20
2110	Accounts Payable	12,666.00
5110	Purchases	115,800.00

2. Start new pages for the following vendor accounts in the accounts payable ledger. Record the balances as of September 1 of the current year.

Vendor No.	Vendor Name	Account Balance
210	Cornucopia, Inc.	$3,090.00
220	Healthy Foods	5,064.00
230	Nutrition Center	—
240	Sports Nutrition	4,512.00

3. Post the separate items recorded in the Accounts Payable Debit and Credit columns of the journal.
4. Post the totals of the special columns of the journal. Save your work to complete Application Problem 12-4.

12-3 APPLICATION PROBLEM
Posting to an accounts receivable ledger

Selected entries from the journal for Healthy Nutrition are given in the *Working Papers.*

Instructions:

1. Start new pages for the following accounts in the general ledger. Record the balances as of October 1 of the current year.

General Ledger

Account No.	**Account Title**	**Balance**
1110	Cash	$ 18,300.00
1130	Accounts Receivable	10,164.00
2120	Sales Tax Payable	1,235.00
4110	Sales	172,420.00

2. Start new pages for the following customer accounts in the accounts receivable ledger. Record the balances as of October 1 of the current year.

Customer No.	**Customer Name**	**Account Balance**
110	Children's Center	$4,416.00
120	Eastman Sports Arena	2,220.00
130	Maple Tree Club	3,528.00
140	Southwest Community Club	—

3. Post the separate items recorded in the Accounts Receivable Debit and Credit columns of the journal.
4. Post the totals of the special columns of the journal. Save your work to complete Application Problem 12-4.

12-4 APPLICATION PROBLEM
Proving subsidiary ledgers

Use the general ledger and vendor accounts from Application Problem 12-2. Also use the general ledger and customer accounts from Application Problem 12-3. Blank forms for preparation of a schedule of accounts payable and a schedule of accounts receivable are given in the *Working Papers.*

Instructions:

1. Prepare a schedule of accounts payable as of September 30 of the current year. Compare the total of the schedule with the balance of the controlling account, Accounts Payable, in the general ledger. If the totals are not the same, find and correct the errors.
2. Prepare a schedule of accounts receivable as of October 31 of the current year. Compare the total of the schedule with the balance of the controlling account, Accounts Receivable, in the general ledger. If the totals are not the same, find and correct the errors.

12-5 MASTERY PROBLEM
Posting to ledgers from a journal

The journal and ledgers for Aqua Pools, a swimming pool supply company, are given in the *Working Papers*.

Instructions:

1. Post the separate items recorded in the following columns of the journal. (a) General Debit and Credit. (b) Accounts Receivable Debit and Credit. (c) Accounts Payable Debit and Credit.
2. Post the totals of the special columns of the journal.
3. Using the current year, prepare a schedule of accounts payable and a schedule of accounts receivable. Prove the accuracy of the subsidiary ledgers by comparing the schedule totals with the balances of the controlling accounts in the general ledger. If the totals are not the same, find and correct the errors.

12-6 CHALLENGE PROBLEM
Journalizing and posting business transactions

The general, accounts payable, and accounts receivable ledgers for Custom Golf Land are given in the *Working Papers*.

Instructions:

1. Journalize the following transactions completed during October of the current year. Use page 21 of a journal similar to the one described in this chapter. Add an 8% sales tax to all sales transactions. Source documents are abbreviated as follows: check, C; memorandum, M; purchase invoice, P; receipt, R; sales invoice, S; cash register tape, T.

Transactions:

Oct. 2. Wrote a check for rent, $1,150.00. C263.
3. Received an invoice from Vista Golf Co. for merchandise purchased on account, $1,950.00. P71.
4. Paid for merchandise, $142.80. C264.
6. A check was received in payment on account from Viola Davis, $829.44, covering S45. R43.
7. Eagle Golf Equipment was paid on account, $2,358.00, covering P67. C265.
7. Cash and credit card sales, $5,676.00. T7.
Posting. Post the items that are to be posted individually.
9. Julie Freed, partner, withdrew merchandise for personal use, $200.00. M33.
11. Merchandise was sold on account to Doris McCarley, $306.00. S49.
13. Store supplies were bought on account from Golf Source, $258.00. M34.
14. Cash and credit card sales, $5,808.00. T14.
Posting. Post the items that are to be posted individually.
16. Cash was withdrawn by Julie Freed, partner, for personal use, $1,500.00. C266.
16. Cash was withdrawn by Troy Nordstrom, partner, for personal use, $1,500.00. C267.
17. Wrote a check for electric bill, $220.20. C268.
20. Wrote a check to Vista Golf Co. on account, $3,216.00, covering P68. C269.
21. Recorded cash and credit card sales, $5,376.00. T21.
Posting. Post the items that are to be posted individually.
23. Design Golf was paid on account, $2,916.00, covering P69. C270.
24. Barry Fuller bought merchandise on account, $1,315.00. S50.
24. Received payment on account from Leona Silva, $285.12, covering S46. R44.

Oct. 25. Merchandise was purchased on account from Pro Golf Supply, $1,542.00. P72.
27. A check was received in payment on account from David Bench, $972.00, covering S47. R45.
28. Received an invoice on account from Design Golf for merchandise purchased on account, $2,790.00. P73.
28. Merchandise was sold on account to Leona Silva, $1,314.00. S51.
28. Recorded cash and credit card sales, $5,556.00. T28.
Posting. Post the items that are to be posted individually.
31. Replenish the petty cash fund, $251.00: office supplies, $40.00; store supplies, $51.00; advertising, $62.00; miscellaneous, $98.00. C271.
31. Recorded cash and credit card sales, $1,680.00. T31.
Posting. Post the items that are to be posted individually.

2. Total the journal. Prove the equality of debits and credits.
3. Prove cash. The balance on the next unused check stub is $35,076.24.
4. Rule the journal.
5. Post the totals of the special columns of the journal.
6. Prepare a schedule of accounts payable and a schedule of accounts receivable. Prove the accuracy of the subsidiary ledgers by comparing the schedule totals with the balances of the controlling accounts in the general ledger. If the totals are not the same, find and correct the errors.

In states that have sales taxes, businesses are required to collect taxes on their sales and submit the taxes to the state. This additional activity requires considerable extra effort: keeping a separate record of the taxes collected at the time of sale, maintaining a separate account for the sales taxes collected, Sales Taxes Payable, and recording the collection and payment of the sales taxes in the account. These additional activities place an additional administrative burden on businesses, especially small businesses with few employees.

Can you think of a procedure that would not require the separate record for collecting and accounting for sales taxes, yet comply with a state's requirement to collect and submit sales taxes based on sale of merchandise sold? Write a brief response, providing an alternative approach to collecting and paying sales taxes.

INTERNET ACTIVITY

Point your browser to
http://accounting.swpco.com
Choose **First-Year Course**, choose **Activities**, and complete the activity for Chapter 12.

Applied Communication

Write a letter to the Cute and Cuddly Corporation explaining you are returning an order of stuffed toys because of poor workmanship. You would like to receive a refund for the full amount of the order, $350.25. Explain that you are providing a copy of the invoice, and ask for written confirmation of the processing of the refund. Include information that will allow the Cute and Cuddly Corp. to comply with your request.

Cases for Critical Thinking

Case 1 Heritage House purchased merchandise on account six weeks ago for $600.00 from Pegasus Supply. A check for $600.00 was sent three weeks ago in payment of the account. Although no additional purchases have been made, Heritage House recently received a bill from Pegasus Supply that listed the balance due as $1,200.00. What probably caused this error? When would the error probably be discovered?

Case 2 Larry Hayes observes his accountant at work and says, "You post each individual accounts receivable entry in the journal. Then you post the totals of the Accounts Receivable columns. You are posting these entries twice, which will make the records wrong." The accountant does not agree that the posting procedure is incorrect. Is Mr. Hayes or his accountant correct? Why?

Case 3 The accounting method presented in this textbook is double-entry accounting. Each transaction has debit and credit parts. Each transaction affects at least two accounts. For example, paying the rent requires a debit to Rent Expense and a credit to Cash. The accounting equation remains in balance after each transaction is posted. Verifying that the accounting equation remains balanced is one way of ensuring accuracy in maintaining accounting records.

Increasingly used by many small businesses, some financial management software programs are based on a different accounting method. These programs use *single-entry accounting*. Debits and credits are not used. Many transactions are recorded to only one account. For example, paying the rent is accounted for by increasing the balance in Rent Expense. The software deducts the amount of the rent from the checkbook balance, but does not use a cash account. Accuracy is verified when financial statements are created. The amount of cash shown on the balance sheet should equal the checkbook balance.

Compared to double-entry accounting, what are the advantages of using a single-entry accounting system? Are there any disadvantages?

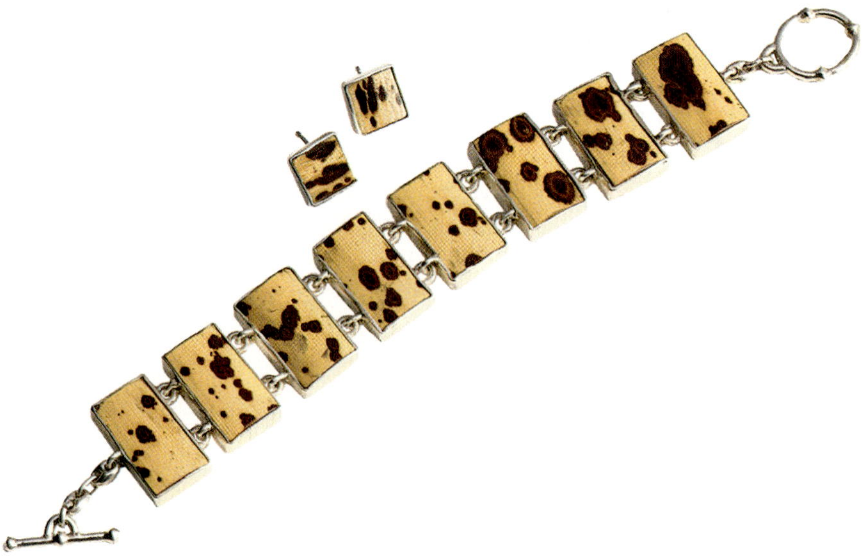

AUTOMATED ACCOUNTING

CORRECTION OF ERRORS

In manual accounting, errors can be made even though care is taken in recording transactions. Likewise in automated accounting, an incorrect entry can be journalized or posted. Account numbers or dollar amounts can be transposed, or the wrong customer, vendor, or general ledger account selected. If an error has been made, it is necessary to locate and correct the inaccurate journal entry.

Decision makers in business base their decisions on the various types of reports they receive. That is why it is important to detect incorrect entries early in order to eliminate reports that may be generated with incorrect amounts. Therefore, finding and correcting errors is very important in order to create accurate, reliable financial reports as well as to make decisions based on correct information.

The procedures for locating and correcting journal entries are identical for all journals.

Finding a Journal Entry

1. Click the desired journal tab: General, Purchases, Sales, Cash Payments, or Cash Receipts.
2. Choose Find from the Edit menu bar.
3. Enter the date, reference, name, or amount you want to find in the Find What text box. Click OK.
4. If a matching transaction is found, it will be highlighted in the journal.

Changing or Deleting Journal Transactions

1. Select (highlight) the specific transaction text box that you wish to change or delete.
2. To change the transaction, enter the correction and click the Post command button. To delete the entire transaction, choose the Delete command button.

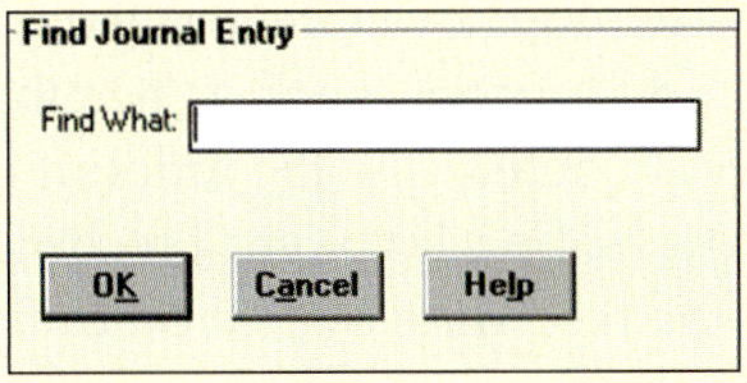

AUTOMATING CHALLENGE PROBLEM 12-6: Journalizing and posting business transactions

Instructions:

1. Load *Automated Accounting 7.0* or higher software.
2. Select database F12-1 from the appropriate directory/folder.
3. Select File from the menu bar and choose the Save As menu command. Key the path to the drive and directory that contains your data files. Save the database with a file name of XXX121 (where XXX are your initials).
4. Access Problem Instructions through the Help menu. Read the Problem Instructions screen.
5. Refer to the data listed on pages 298–299.
6. Exit the *Automated Accounting* software.

13 Preparing Payroll Records

AFTER STUDYING CHAPTER 13, YOU WILL BE ABLE TO:

1. Define accounting terms related to payroll records.
2. Identify accounting practices related to payroll records.
3. Complete a payroll time card.
4. Calculate payroll taxes.
5. Complete a payroll register and an employee earnings record.
6. Prepare payroll checks.

TERMS PREVIEW

salary
pay period
payroll
total earnings
payroll taxes
withholding allowance
social security tax
Medicare tax
tax base
payroll register
net pay
employee earnings record

PAYING EMPLOYEES

Omni Import employs several people to work in the business. These employees record the time they work for Omni each day. Periodically Omni pays its employees for the number of hours each employee has worked. The money paid for employee services is called a **salary.** The period covered by a salary payment is called a **pay period.** A business may decide to pay employee salaries every week, every two weeks, twice a month, or once a month. Omni uses a semimonthly pay period. Employees are paid twice a month, on the 15th and last day of each month.

The total amount earned by all employees for a pay period is called a **payroll.** The payroll is reduced by state and federal taxes and other deductions, such as health insurance, to determine the amount paid to all employees. Special payroll records support the recording of payroll transactions in a journal. The business also uses these records to inform employees of their annual earnings and to prepare payroll reports for the government.

F Y I

Salaries are usually stated as a fixed amount on a weekly, biweekly, semimonthly, or monthly basis. Salaried workers do not normally receive overtime pay.

ACCOUNTING IN YOUR CAREER

WHY COMPANIES OFFER BENEFITS

MaryAnn Spargo directs the recruiting program for Computex Publishing Company. The company has prospered by publishing books on computer topics. Computex needs to increase its editorial, marketing, and sales staff, and MaryAnn has been recruiting new employees at college campuses.

On her first day back from a three-week recruiting trip, she meets her friend Donald Hawkins, who works in the payroll department, for lunch in the cafeteria. "How was the trip, MaryAnn?" asks Donald. "Did you find us some new talent?"

"No, Don," replies MaryAnn. "I talked to over 50 candidates. Of course they weren't all qualified, but I offered positions to 15 of them and only one has accepted. I know unemployment is very low and so there are more jobs being offered than there are skilled workers to fill them. But what am I doing wrong?"

"I don't know, MaryAnn," says Don. "What kind of salaries are you offering?"

"Oh, Don, we've studied that. Our salaries are competitive with the other publishers in the market. I've thought about this a lot, and I wonder if it's our benefits program."

"That could be it, MaryAnn. You know, I belong to an accounting association, and I remember that there are surveys available on benefits packages. Would you like me to try to get that information for you?"

MaryAnn replies, "Yes, Don, that might help. If I can show management that our benefits need to be improved to attract skilled workers, it might help us all."

Critical Thinking:

1. Do you think most employees consider the benefits offered when they look for a job?
2. What are some kinds of benefits offered by companies today?
3. If Computex wanted to get creative with its benefit package to attract new employees, what kinds of benefits might they offer?

13-1 Preparing Payroll Time Cards

ANALYZING A PAYROLL TIME CARD

Omni Import

EMPLOYEE NO. 3

NAME Rick E. Selby

PAY PERIOD ENDED December 15, 20--

MORNING		AFTERNOON		OVERTIME		HOURS	
IN	OUT	IN	OUT	IN	OUT	REG	OT
7 58	12 02	12 59	5 06				

A payroll system must include an accurate record of the time each employee has worked. Several methods are used for keeping time records. One of the more frequently used methods is a time card. Time cards are used as the basic source of information to prepare a payroll.

Some time cards require employees to record only the total hours worked each day. Employees who record the total hours worked each day usually complete time cards by hand.

A business may use a time card that requires employees to record their arrival and departure times. Omni uses a time clock to record the daily arrival and departure times of its employees.

The time card shown here is for Rick E. Selby. Mr. Selby's employee number is at the top of the card. Below the employee number are the employee name and the ending date of the pay period.

Omni's time cards have three sections (Morning, Afternoon, and Overtime), with In and Out columns under each section. When Mr. Selby reported for work on December 1, he inserted the card in the time clock. The clock recorded his time of arrival, 7:58, on the first line of the time card. The other entries on this line indicate that he left for lunch at 12:02. He returned at 12:59 and left for the day at 5:06.

Omni calculates overtime pay for each employee who works more than 8 hours in one day. No employee works more than 5 days in any one week.

FYI

Using a time card system provides internal control for accurate reporting of time worked.

CALCULATING EMPLOYEE HOURS WORKED

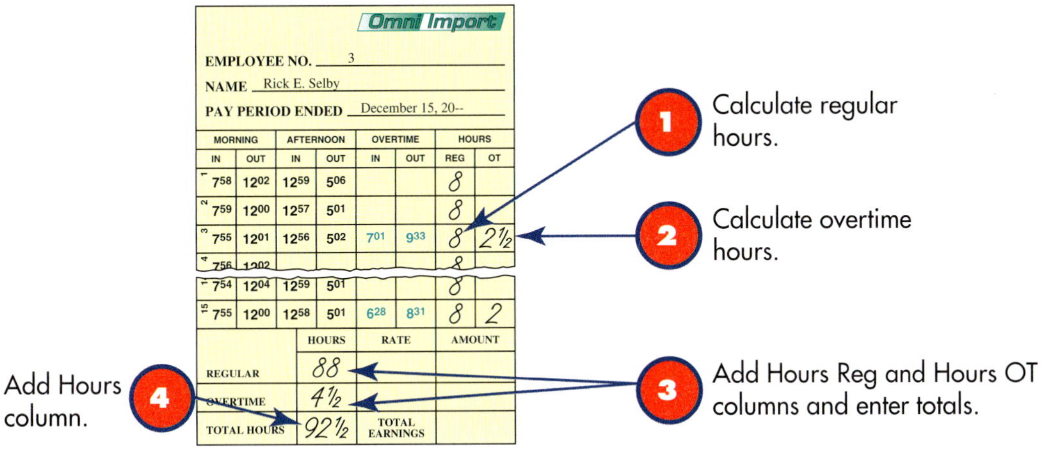

The first task in preparing a payroll is to calculate the number of hours worked by each employee.

STEPS Calculating employee hours worked

1. Calculate the number of regular hours for each day and enter the amounts in the Hours Reg column. Mr. Selby works 8 hours during a normal day. The hours worked on December 3, the third line of the time card, are calculated using the arrival and departure times imprinted on the time card. Times are rounded to the nearest quarter hour to calculate the hours worked.

The hours worked in the morning and afternoon are calculated separately. The morning departure time of 12:01 is rounded to the nearest quarter hour, 12:00. The rounded arrival time, 8:00, subtracted from the departure time,

	Departure Time	–	Arrival Time	=	Hours Worked
Morning:					
Time card	12:01		7:55		
Nearest quarter hour	12:00	–	8:00	=	4:00
Afternoon:					
Time card	5:02		12:56		
Nearest quarter hour	5:00	–	1:00	=	4:00
Total regular hours worked on December 3					8:00

12:00, equals the morning hours worked. Hours worked of 4:00 means that Mr. Selby worked 4 hours and no (00) minutes. The total regular hours worked, 8, is recorded in the Hours Reg column.

2. Calculate the number of overtime hours for each day and enter the amounts in the Hours OT column. Overtime hours for December 3 are calculated using the same procedure as for regular hours.

	Departure Time	–	Arrival Time	=	Hours Worked
Time card	9:33		7:01		
Nearest quarter hour	9:30	–	7:00	=	2:30

The hours worked of 2:30 means that Mr. Selby worked 2 hours and 30 minutes ($\frac{1}{2}$ hour) of overtime.

3. Add the hours worked in the Hours Reg and Hours OT columns and enter the totals in the spaces provided at the bottom of the time card. Mr. Selby worked 88 regular hours (8 hours × 11 days) and $4\frac{1}{2}$ overtime hours during the semimonthly pay period.

4. Add the Hours column to calculate the total hours. Enter the total in the Hours column at the bottom of the time card. Mr. Selby worked 88 regular hours and $4\frac{1}{2}$ overtime hours for a total of $92\frac{1}{2}$ hours.

CALCULATING EMPLOYEE TOTAL EARNINGS

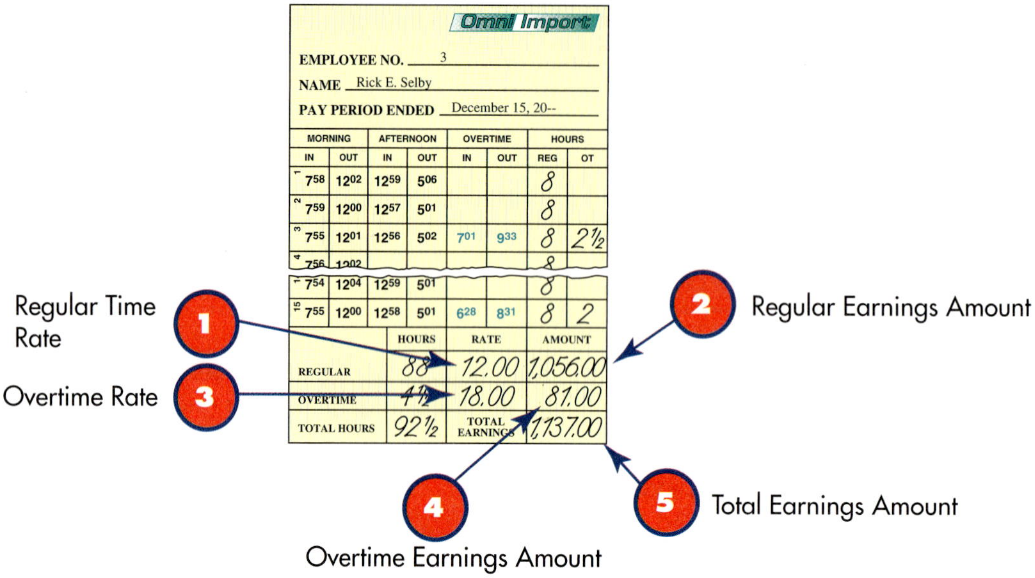

Omni Import

EMPLOYEE NO. 3
NAME Rick E. Selby
PAY PERIOD ENDED December 15, 20--

	MORNING IN	MORNING OUT	AFTERNOON IN	AFTERNOON OUT	OVERTIME IN	OVERTIME OUT	HOURS REG	HOURS OT
1	758	1202	1259	506			8	
2	759	1200	1257	501			8	
3	755	1201	1256	502	701	933	8	2½
4	756	1202					8	
14	754	1204	1259	501			8	
15	755	1200	1258	501	628	831	8	2

	HOURS	RATE	AMOUNT
REGULAR	88	12.00	1,056.00
OVERTIME	4½	18.00	81.00
TOTAL HOURS	92½	TOTAL EARNINGS	1,137.00

Once the total regular and overtime hours are determined, employee earnings can be calculated. The total pay due for a pay period before deductions is called **total earnings.** Total earnings are sometimes referred to as gross pay or gross earnings.

Omni owes Mr. Selby $1,137.00 for his work during the pay period ending December 15. However, taxes and other deductions must be subtracted from total earnings to determine the actual amount Omni will pay Mr. Selby.

STEPS: Calculating an employee's total earnings

1. Enter the rate for regular time in the Rate column. Mr. Selby's regular hourly rate is *$12.00*.
2. Calculate the regular earnings by multiplying regular hours times the regular rate. Enter the amount of regular earnings, *$1,056.00*, in the Regular Amount space.
3. Enter the rate for overtime, *$18.00*, in the Rate column. Mr. Selby is paid $1\frac{1}{2}$ times his regular rate for overtime work.
4. Calculate the overtime earnings by multiplying overtime hours times the overtime rate. Enter the amount of overtime earnings, *$81.00*, in the Overtime Amount space.
5. Add the Amount column to calculate the total earnings. Enter the amount of total earnings, *$1,137,00*, in the Total Earnings space.

Regular Hours	×	Regular Rate	=	Regular Earnings
88	×	$12.00	=	$1,056.00

Regular Rate	×	$1\frac{1}{2}$	=	Overtime Rate
$12.00	×	$1\frac{1}{2}$	=	$18.00

Overtime Hours	×	Overtime Rate	=	Overtime Earnings
$4\frac{1}{2}$	×	$18.00	=	$81.00

TERMS REVIEW

salary
pay period
payroll
total earnings

AUDIT YOUR UNDERSTANDING

1. What is a payroll?
2. How many hours were worked by an employee who arrived at 8:29 and departed at 12:02?
3. How does Omni calculate overtime earnings?
4. What are the total earnings of an employee who worked 40 hours and earned $11.00 per hour?

WORK TOGETHER

Preparing payroll time cards

Information taken from employee time cards is provided in the *Working Papers.* Your instructor will guide you through the following example.

5. For each employee, calculate the amount of regular, overtime, and total earnings. Overtime hours are paid at $1\frac{1}{2}$ times the regular rate.

ON YOUR OWN

Preparing payroll time cards

Information taken from employee time cards is provided in the *Working Papers.* Work this problem independently.

6. For each employee, calculate the amount of regular, overtime, and total earnings. Overtime hours are paid at $1\frac{1}{2}$ times the regular rate.

13-2 Determining Payroll Tax Withholding

PAYROLL TAXES

Taxes based on the payroll of a business are called **payroll taxes.** A business is required by law to withhold certain payroll taxes from employee salaries. All payroll taxes are based on employee total earnings. Therefore, accurate and detailed payroll records must be maintained. Errors in payroll records could cause incorrect payroll tax payments. Federal and state governments may charge a business a penalty for failure to pay correct payroll taxes when they are due. Payroll taxes withheld represent a liability for the employer until payment is made to the government.

Employee Income Tax

A business must withhold federal income taxes from employee total earnings. Federal income taxes withheld must be forwarded periodically to the federal government. Federal income tax is withheld from employee earnings in all 50 states. Employers in many states also are required to withhold state, city, or county income taxes from employee earnings.

FYI

Each employee must have a social security number. Current law ensures that most infants who are at least one year old by the end of a tax year will have a social security number. Therefore, most employees will have received their social security number as a child. Employees without social security numbers can apply for a number at the nearest Social Security office.

LEGAL ISSUES IN ACCOUNTING

DISSOLVING A PARTNERSHIP

Under the Uniform Partnership Act (UPA), any change in the membership of a partnership causes a *dissolution.* Members may decide to dissolve a partnership for several reasons: (1) One or more of the partners wants to discontinue doing business. (2) The partners need more capital and agree to admit an additional partner. (3) The partners may disagree on how to operate the business. (4) The partnership agreement may call for the partnership to be dissolved on a specific date.

When a partnership is dissolved, legal requirements must be met and correct accounting procedures followed. The terms of the dissolution may be set forth in the partnership agreement. Any such terms must be followed. If no partnership agreement was created, the UPA or laws of the state will govern its dissolution.

Noncash assets are usually sold, and the available cash is used to pay creditors. Any remaining cash is distributed to the partners. Each partner receives the balance of his or her capital account.

The UPA calls the process of finishing up the firm's business, paying off creditors, and dividing remaining assets *winding up* the partnership. When the winding up process has been completed, the partnership is *terminated.*

EMPLOYEE'S WITHHOLDING ALLOWANCE CERTIFICATE

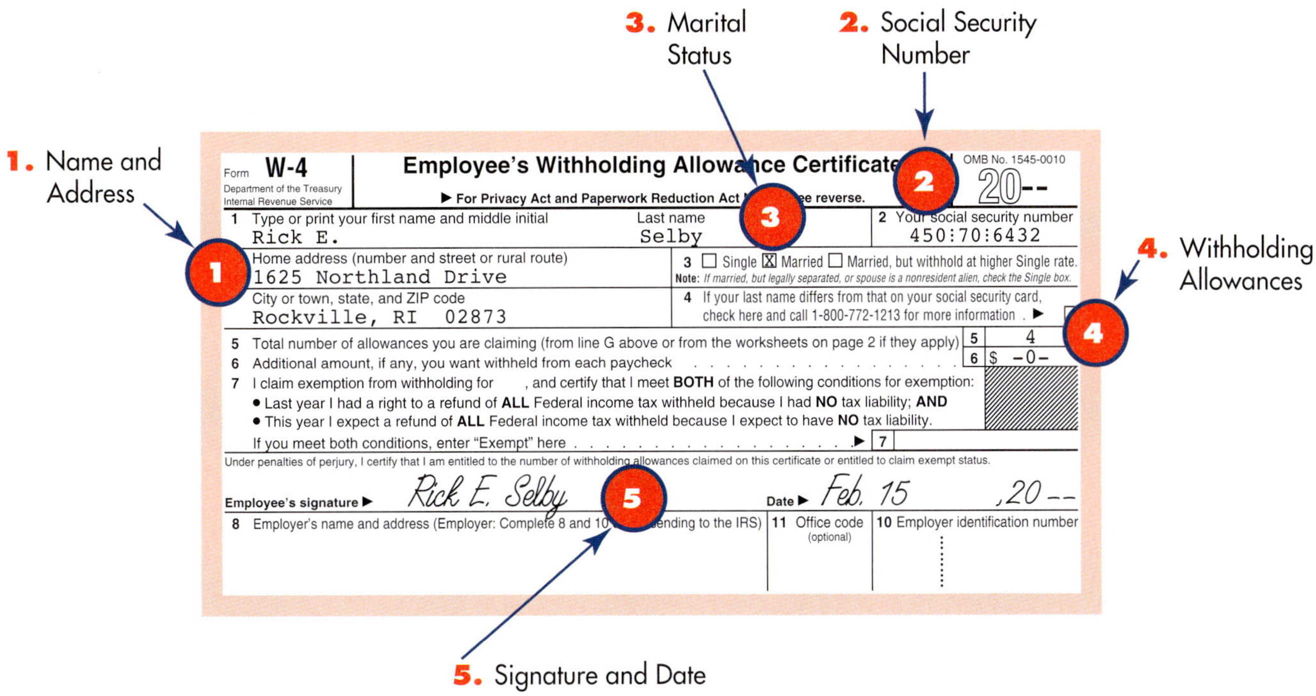

Form W-4 Department of the Treasury Internal Revenue Service

Employee's Withholding Allowance Certificate

▶ For Privacy Act and Paperwork Reduction Act Notice, see reverse.

OMB No. 1545-0010 20--

1 Type or print your first name and middle initial: Rick E. Last name: Selby

2 Your social security number: 450:70:6432

Home address (number and street or rural route): 1625 Northland Drive

3 ☐ Single ☒ Married ☐ Married, but withhold at higher Single rate.

Note: If married, but legally separated, or spouse is a nonresident alien, check the Single box.

City or town, state, and ZIP code: Rockville, RI 02873

4 If your last name differs from that on your social security card, check here and call 1-800-772-1213 for more information . ▶ ☐

5 Total number of allowances you are claiming (from line G above or from the worksheets on page 2 if they apply) 5 4

6 Additional amount, if any, you want withheld from each paycheck . . . 6 $ -0-

7 I claim exemption from withholding for , and certify that I meet **BOTH** of the following conditions for exemption:

- Last year I had a right to a refund of **ALL** Federal income tax withheld because I had **NO** tax liability; **AND**
- This year I expect a refund of **ALL** Federal income tax withheld because I expect to have **NO** tax liability.

If you meet both conditions, enter "Exempt" here . . . ▶ 7

Under penalties of perjury, I certify that I am entitled to the number of withholding allowances claimed on this certificate or entitled to claim exempt status.

Employee's signature ▶ Rick E. Selby Date ▶ Feb. 15 , 20--

8 Employer's name and address (Employer: Complete 8 and 10 only if sending to the IRS) | 9 Office code (optional) | 10 Employer identification number

The information used to determine the amount of income tax withheld is identified on Form W-4, Employee's Withholding Allowance Certificate. A deduction from total earnings for each person legally supported by a taxpayer, including the employee, is called a **withholding allowance.** Employers are required to have on file a current Form W-4 for all employees. The amount of income tax withheld is based on employee marital status and number of withholding allowances. A married employee will have less income tax withheld than a single employee with the same total earnings. The larger the number of withholding allowances claimed, the smaller the amount of income tax withheld.

Most employees are required to have federal income taxes withheld from their salaries. An exemption from withholding is available for certain low-income and part-time employees. The employee must meet the requirements listed in item 7 of the Form W-4. However, individuals cannot claim exemption from withholding if (1) their income exceeds $700 and includes unearned income such as interest and dividends and (2) another person can claim them as a dependent on their tax return.

The Form W-4 shown was the form in use when this textbook was prepared. Employers must be aware of changes in tax laws and forms. If Form W-4 is changed, an employer must obtain a new W-4 from each employee.

STEPS: Preparing an Employee's Withholding Allowance Certificate

1. Write the employee's name and address.
2. Write the employee's social security number.
3. Check appropriate marital status block. Mr. Selby checked the married box for item 3 of the Form W-4.
4. Write the total number of withholding allowances claimed. Mr. Selby claimed four withholding allowances, one each for himself, his wife, and his two children.
5. Employee signs and dates the Form W-4.

SEMIMONTHLY PAYROLL PERIOD — SINGLE PERSONS

And the wages are–		And the number of withholding allowances claimed is–										
At least	But less than	0	1	2	3	4	5	6	7	8	9	10
		The amount of income tax to be withheld shall be–										
$0	$115	0	0	0	0	0	0	0	0	0	0	0
115	120	1	0	0	0	0	0	0	0	0	0	0
120	125	2	0	0	0	0	0	0	0	0	0	0
125	130	3	0	0	0	0	0	0	0	0	0	0
130	135	3	0	0	0	0	0	0	0	0	0	0
640	660	81	64	48	31	15	0	0	0	0	0	0
660	680	84	67	51	34	18	1	0	0	0	0	0
680	700	87	70	54	37	21	4	0	0	0	0	0
700	720	90	73	57	40	24	7	0	0	0	0	0
720	740	93	76	60	43	27	10	0	0	0	0	0
740	760	96	79	63	46	30	13	0	0	0	0	0
760	780	99	82	66	49	33	16	0	0	0	0	0
780	800	102	85	69	52	36	19	3	0	0	0	0
800	820	106	88	72	55	39	22	6	0	0	0	0
820	840	108	91	75	58	42	25	9	0	0	0	0
840	860	111	94	78	61	45	28	12	0	0	0	0
860	880	114	97	81	64	48	31	15	0	0	0	0
880	900	117	100	84	67	51	34	18	1	0	0	0
900	920	120	103	87	70	54	37	21	4	0	0	0
920	940	123	106	90	73	57	40	24	7	0	0	0
940	960	126	109	93	76	60	43	27	10	0	0	0
960	980	129	112	96	79	63	46	30	13	0	0	0
980	1,000	132	115	99	82	66	49	33	16	0	0	0
1,000	1,020	135	118	102	85	69	52	36	19	2	0	0
1,020	1,040	138	121	105	88	72	55	39	22	5	0	0
1,040	1,060	141	124	108	91	75	58	42	25	8	0	0
1,060	1,080	144	127	111	94	78	61	45	28	11	0	0
1,080	1,100	147	130	114	97	81	64	48	31	14	0	0
1,100	1,120	153	133	117	100	84	67	51	34	17	1	0
1,120	1,140	158	136	120	103	87	70	54	37	20	4	0
1,140	1,160	164	139	123	106	90	73	57	40	23	7	0
1,160	1,180	169	142	126	109	93	76	60	43	26	10	0
1,180	1,200	175	145	129	112	96	79	63	46	29	13	0
1,200	1,220	181	150	132	115	99	82	66	49	32	16	0
1,220	1,240	186	155	135	118	102	85	69	52	35	19	2
1,240	1,260	192	161	138	121	105	88	72	55	38	22	5
1,260	1,280	197	166	141	124	108	91	75	58	41	25	8
1,280	1,300	203	172	144	127	111	94	78	61	44	28	11
1,300	1,320	209	178	147	130	114	97	81	64	47	31	14
1,320	1,340	214	183	152	133	117	100	84	67	50	34	17
1,340	1,360	220	189	158	136	120	103	87	70	53	37	20
1,360	1,380	225	194	164	139	123	106	90	73	56	40	23
1,380	1,400	231	200	169	142	126	109	93	76	59	43	26
1,400	1,420	237	206	175	145	129	112	96	79	62	46	29
1,420	1,440	242	211	180	149	132	115	99	82	65	49	32

The amount of federal income tax withheld from each employee's total earnings is determined from withholding tables prepared by the Internal Revenue Service. These withholding tables are revised each year and are available from the Internal Revenue Service in Circular E, Employer's Tax Guide. The withholding tables shown in this chapter are those available when this textbook was prepared.

Tables are prepared for various payroll periods—monthly, semimonthly, biweekly, weekly, and daily. Single persons are taxed at different levels of income than married persons. Therefore, one table is available for single persons and another table is available for married persons for each pay period.

Omni Import's pay period is semimonthly, so Omni uses the semimonthly witholding tables.

EMPLOYEE'S INCOME TAX WITHHOLDING—MARRIED PERSONS

1. Select the appropriate table.

SEMIMONTHLY PAYROLL PERIOD — MARRIED PERSONS

(For Wages Paid in)

And the wages are–		And the number of withholding allowances claimed is–										
At least	But less than	0	1	2	3	4	5	6	7	8	9	10
		The amount of income tax to be withheld shall be–										
520	540	39	23	6	0	0	0	0	0	0	0	0
540	560	42	26	9	0	0	0	0	0	0	0	0
560	580	45	29	12	0	0	0	0	0	0	0	0
580	600	48	32	15	0	0	0	0	0	0	0	0
600	620	51	35	18	2	0	0	0	0	0	0	0
620	640	54	38	21	5	0	0	0	0	0	0	0
640	660	57	41	24	8	0	0	0	0	0	0	0
660	680	60	44	27	11	0	0	0	0	0	0	0
680	700	63	47	30	14	0	0	0	0	0	0	0
700	720	66	50	33	17	0	0	0	0	0	0	0
720	740	69	53	36	20	3	0	0	0	0	0	0
740	760	72	56	39	23	6	0	0	0	0	0	0
760	780	75	59	42	26	9	0	0	0	0	0	0
780	800	78	62	45	29	12	0	0	0	0	0	0
800	820	81	65	48	32	15	0	0	0	0	0	0
820	840	84	68	51	35	18	1	0	0	0	0	0
840	860	87	71	54	38	21	4	0	0	0	0	0
860	880	90	74	57	41	24	7	0	0	0	0	0
880	900	93	77	60	44	27	10	0	0	0	0	0
900	920	96	80	63	47	30	13	0	0	0	0	0
920	940	99	83	66	50	33	16	0	0	0	0	0
940	960	102	86	69	53	36	19	3	0	0	0	0
960	980	105	89	72	56	39	22	6	0	0	0	0
980	1,000	108	92	75	59	42	25	9	0	0	0	0
1,000	1,020	111	95	78	62	45	28	12	0	0	0	0
1,020	1,040	114	98	81	65	48	31	15	0	0	0	0
1,040	1,060	117	101	84	68	51	34	18	1	0	0	0
1,060	1,080	120	104	87	71	54	37	21	4	0	0	0
1,080	1,100	123	107	90	74	57	40	24	7	0	0	0
1,100	1,120	126	110	93	77	60	43	27	10	0	0	0
1,120	1,140	129	113	96	80	63	46	30	13	0	0	0
1,140	1,160	132	116	99	83	66	49	33	16	0	0	0
1,160	1,180	135	119	102	86	69	52	36	19	3	0	0
1,180	1,200	138	122	105	89	72	55	39	22	6	0	0
1,200	1,220	141	125	108	92	75	58	42	25	9	0	0
1,220	1,240	144	128	111	95	78	61	45	28	12	0	0
1,240	1,260	147	131	114	98	81	64	48	31	15	0	0
1,260	1,280	150	134	117	101	84	67	51	34	18	1	0
1,280	1,300	153	147	120	104	87	40	54	37	21	4	0
1,300	1,320	156	140	123	107	90	43	57	40	24	7	0
1,320	1,340	159	143	126	110	93	46	60	43	27	10	0
1,340	1,360	162	146	129	113	96	49	63	46	30	13	0
1,360	1,380	165	149	132	116	99	82	66	49	33	16	0
1,380	1,400	168	152	135	119	102	85	69	52	36	19	3
1,400	1,420	171	155	138	122	105	88	72	55	39	22	6
1,420	1,440	174	158	141	125	108	91	75	58	42	25	9
1,440	1,460	177	161	144	128	111	94	78	61	45	28	12
1,460	1,480	180	164	147	131	114	97	91	64	48	31	15
1,480	1,500	183	167	150	134	117	100	94	67	51	34	18
1,500	1,520	186	170	153	137	120	103	97	70	54	37	21
1,520	1,540	189	173	156	140	123	106	90	73	57	40	24
1,540	1,560	192	176	159	143	126	109	93	76	60	43	27
1,560	1,580	195	179	162	146	129	112	96	79	63	46	30
1,580	1,600	198	182	165	149	132	115	99	82	66	49	33
1,600	1,620	201	185	168	152	135	118	102	85	69	52	36

2. Locate employee's total earnings.

3. Follow selected wages line across to column headed by number of withholding allowances.

STEPS: Determining an employee's income tax withholding

1. Select the appropriate table. Semimonthly Payroll Period—Married Persons is selected to determine income tax withholding for employee Rick E. Selby.
2. Locate employee's total earnings between the appropriate lines of the At Least and But Less Than columns. Mr. Selby's total earnings for the pay period ended December 15, 20—, are $1,137.00. Locate the line At Least $1,120.00 But Less Than $1,140.00.
3. Follow the selected wages line across to the column headed by the employee's number of withholding allowances. The amount listed at the intersection of the wages line and number of withholding allowances is the employee's amount of income tax withholding. Mr. Selby's federal income tax withholding, with total earnings of $1,137.00 and withholding allowances of four, is $63.00 for the semimonthly pay period ended December 15, 20—.

EMPLOYEE SOCIAL SECURITY AND MEDICARE TAX

The Federal Insurance Contributions Act (FICA) provides for a federal system of old-age, survivors, disability, and hospital insurance. A federal tax paid for old-age, survivors, and disability insurance is called **social security tax.** A federal tax paid for hospital insurance is called **Medicare tax.** Each of these taxes is accounted for and reported separately.

Social security and Medicare taxes are paid by both employees and employer. Employers are required to withhold and deposit employees' part of the taxes and pay a matching amount of these taxes.

Social security tax is calculated on employee earnings up to a maximum paid in a calendar year. The maximum amount of earnings on which a tax is calculated is called a **tax base.** Congress sets the tax base and the tax rates for social security tax. An act of Congress can change the tax base and tax rate at any time. The social security tax rate and base used in this text are 6.5% of earnings up to a maximum of $65,400.00 in each calendar year.

Between January 1 and December 15, Mr. Selby's earnings are less than the social security tax base. Therefore, Mr. Selby's social security tax deduction for the semimonthly pay period ended December 15, 20—, is calculated as shown.

Total Earnings	×	Social Security Tax Rate	=	Social Security Tax Deduction
$1,137.00	×	6.5%	–	$73.91

Medicare does not have a tax base. Therefore, Medicare tax is calculated on total employee earnings. The Medicare tax rate used in this text is 1.5% of total employee earnings.

Rick E. Selby's Medicare tax deduction for the semimonthly pay period ended December 15, 20—, is calculated as shown.

Total Earnings	×	Medicare Tax Rate	=	Medicare Tax Deduction
$1,137.00	×	1.5%	=	$17.06

FYI

Accounting procedures are the same regardless of changes in the tax base and tax rate. The social security tax rate and the tax base shown above are assumed for all payroll calculations in this textbook.

REMEMBER

When an employee's earnings exceed the tax base, no more social security tax is deducted.

TERMS REVIEW

payroll taxes
withholding allowance
social security tax
Medicare tax
tax base

AUDIT YOUR UNDERSTANDING

1. Where does an employer get the information used to determine the amount of federal income tax to withhold from employees' earnings?
2. Employee federal income tax withholdings are based on what two factors?
3. Does the employer or employee pay social security tax and Medicare tax?

WORK TOGETHER

Determining payroll tax withholding

Information taken from a semimonthly payroll is given in the *Working Papers.* Your instructor will guide you through the following examples.

4. For each employee, determine the federal income tax that must be withheld. Use the tax withholding tables shown on pages 310–311.
5. Calculate the amount of social security tax and Medicare tax that must be withheld for each employee. Use a social security tax rate of 6.5% and a Medicare tax rate of 1.5%. None of the employees has accumulated earnings greater than the tax base.

ON YOUR OWN

Determining payroll tax withholding

Information taken from a semimonthly payroll is given in the *Working Papers.* Work these problems independently.

6. For each employee, determine the federal income tax that must be withheld. Use the tax withholding tables on pages 310–311.
7. Calculate the amount of social security tax and Medicare tax that must be withheld for each employee. Use a social security tax rate of 6.5% and a Medicare tax rate of 1.5%. None of the employees has accumulated earnings greater than the tax base.

13-3 Preparing Payroll Records

PAYROLL REGISTER

1. Pay Period Date
2. Payment Date
3. Employee Personal Data
4. Earnings
5. Federal Income Tax
6. Social Security Tax
7. Medicare Tax
8. Health Insurance
9. Other Deductions
10. Total Deductions
11. Net Pay
12. Total, Prove, and Rule
13. Check Numb

SEMIMONTHLY PERIOD ENDED *December 15, 20--* PAYROLL REGISTER DATE OF PAYMENT *December 15, 20--*

	EMPL. NO.	EMPLOYEE'S NAME	MARITAL STATUS	NO. OF ALLOWANCES	EARNINGS 1 REGULAR	2 OVERTIME	3 TOTAL	DEDUCTIONS 4 FEDERAL INCOME TAX	5 SOC. SEC. TAX	6 MEDICARE TAX	7 HEALTH INSURANCE	8 OTHER	9 TOTAL	10 NET PAY	CHECK NO.	
1	1	*Aranda, Susan A.*	M	2	968 00		968 00	72 00	62 92	14 52	45 60	B 10 00	205 04	762 96	482	1
2	5	*Drew, Paul S.*	S	1	105 00		105 00		6 83	1 58			8 41	96 59	483	2
3	4	*Hakala, Erik D.*	M	1	598 40	[illegible]	608 60	[illegible]	[illegible]	[illegible]	[illegible]	[illegible]	122 09	486 51	484	3
4	6	*Mendel, Ann M.*	S	1	78 75	[illegible]	78 75	[illegible]	[illegible]	[illegible]	[illegible]	[illegible]	6 30	72 45	485	4
5	3	*Selby, Rick E.*	M	4	1,056 00	81 00	1,137 00	63 00	73 91	17 06	60 00	UW 10 00	233 97	903 03	486	5
6	2	*Young, Justin L.*	S	1	906 40		906 40	103 00	58 92	13 60	38 40	B 15 00 UW 10 00	238 92	667 48	487	6
7		*Totals*			3,712 55	91 20	3,803 75	273 00	247 26	57 07	182 40	B 35 00 UW 20 00	814 73	2,989 02		7
8																8
9																9

A business form used to record payroll information is called a **payroll register.** A payroll register summarizes the payroll for one pay period and shows total earnings, payroll withholdings, and net pay of all employees. Omni prepares a separate payroll register for each semimonthly payroll.

STEPS Preparing a payroll register

1. Enter the last date of the semimonthly payroll period, *December 15, 20—*, at the top of the payroll register.
2. Enter the date of payment, *December 15, 20—*, also at the top of the payroll register.
3. For each employee, enter employee number, name, marital status, and number of allowances. This information is taken from personnel records. Entries for Rick E. Selby are on line 5 of the register.
4. Enter regular earnings, overtime earnings, and total earnings for each employee in columns 1, 2, and 3 of the payroll register. This information is taken from each employee's time card.
5. Enter in column 4 the federal income tax withheld from each employee. Mr. Selby's federal tax withholding is *$63.00.*

6. Enter in column 5 of the payroll register the social security tax withheld from each employee. Mr. Selby's social security tax deduction, *$73.91*, is recorded in column 5 of the payroll register. Mr. Selby's total earnings for the year have not exceeded the social security tax base, so his total earnings for the pay period are taxed.
7. Enter in column 6 the Medicare tax withheld from each employee. Mr. Selby's Medicare tax deduction is *$17.06*.
8. Enter in column 7 the health insurance premium deductions. Full-time employees of Omni Import participate in a group health insurance plan to take advantage of lower group rates. Mr. Selby's semimonthly health insurance premium is *$60.00*. Premiums are set by the insurance company and are usually based on the employee marital status and whether coverage is for an individual or a family. Some health insurance premiums may be based on the number of individuals covered.
9. Enter in column 8 all other employee payroll deductions. The Other column is used to record voluntary deductions requested by an employee. Entries are identified by code letters. Omni uses the letter *B* to identify amounts withheld for buying U.S. Savings Bonds. *UW* is used to identify amounts withheld for employee contributions to United Way. Mr. Selby has authorized Omni to withhold *$10.00* each pay period to buy U.S. Savings Bonds for him. Mr. Selby has also authorized that *$10.00* be withheld as a contribution to the United Way.
10. After all deductions are entered in the payroll register, add all the deduction amounts for each employee and enter the totals in column 9. Mr. Selby's total deductions, *$233.97*, are calculated as shown.

Federal Income Tax	+	Social Security Tax	+	Medicare Tax	+	Health Insurance	+	Other	=	Total Deductions
$63.00	+	$73.91	+	$17.06	+	$60.00	+	$20.00	=	$233.97

11. Determine the net pay for each employee. The total earnings paid to an employee after payroll taxes and other deductions is called **net pay.** Subtract the total deductions, column 9, from total earnings, column 3, to determine net pay. Enter net pay in column 10. Mr. Selby's net pay, *$903.03*, is calculated as shown.

Total Earnings	–	Total Deductions	=	Net Pay
$1,137.00	–	$233.97	=	$903.03

12. Total, prove, and rule the payroll register. Total each amount column. Subtract the Total Deductions column from the Total Earnings column. The result should equal the total of the Net Pay column. If the totals do not agree, the errors must be found and corrected. Proving the accuracy of Omni's payroll register for pay period ended December 15, 20—, is shown.

Total Earnings	–	Total Deductions	=	Net Pay
$3,803.75	–	$814.73	=	$2,989.02

The net pay, *$2,989.02*, is the same as the total of the Net Pay column. The payroll register is proved. After the payroll register is proved, rule double lines below all amount column totals to show the totals have been verified as correct.

13. Payroll checks are written after payroll calculations are verified and a partner approves the payroll. Write the payroll check numbers in the Check No. column.

EMPLOYEE EARNINGS RECORDS

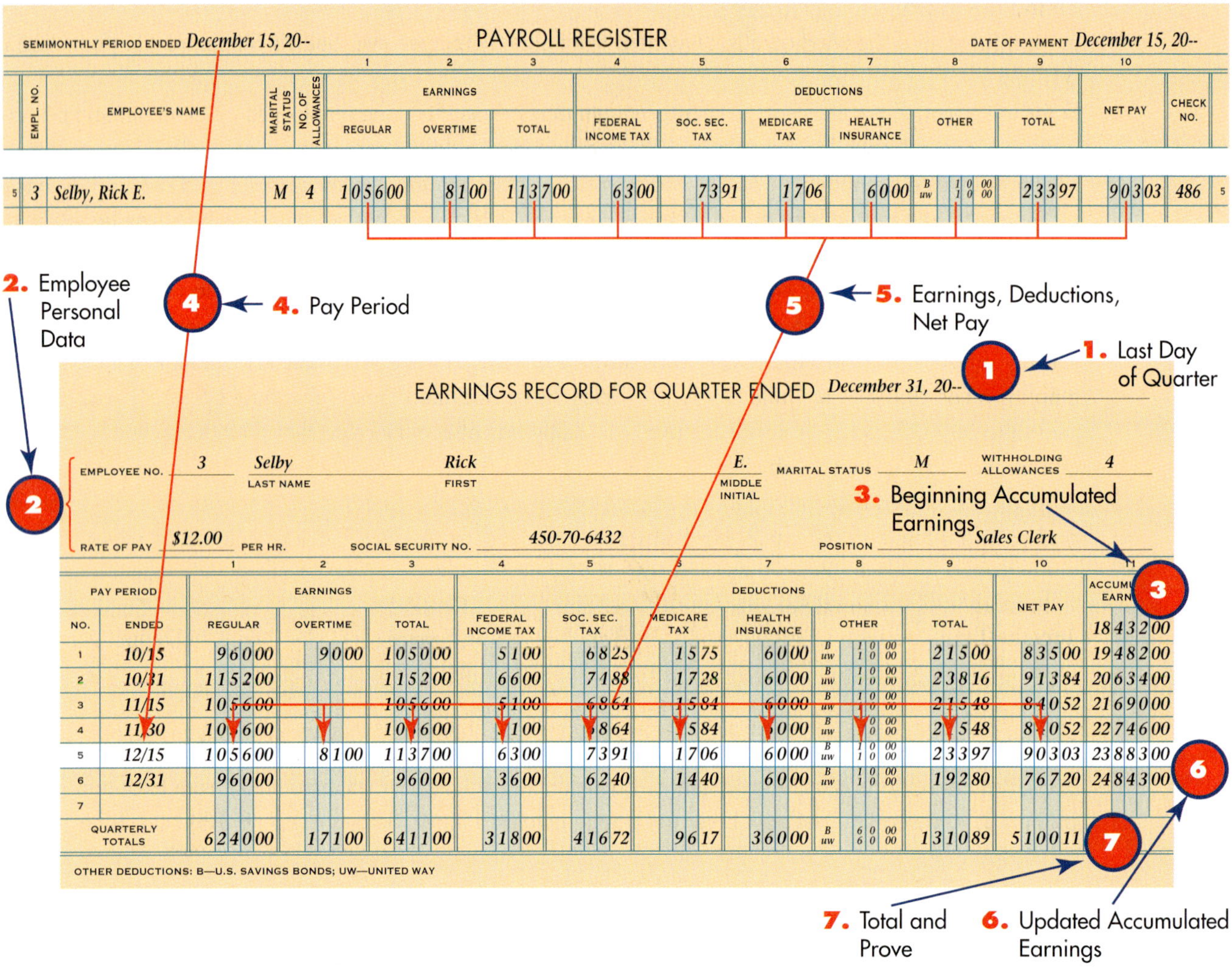

PAYROLL REGISTER

SEMIMONTHLY PERIOD ENDED *December 15, 20--* — DATE OF PAYMENT *December 15, 20--*

	EMPL. NO.	EMPLOYEE'S NAME	MARITAL STATUS	NO. OF ALLOWANCES	EARNINGS 1 REGULAR	2 OVERTIME	3 TOTAL	DEDUCTIONS 4 FEDERAL INCOME TAX	5 SOC. SEC. TAX	6 MEDICARE TAX	7 HEALTH INSURANCE	8 OTHER	9 TOTAL	10 NET PAY	CHECK NO.	
5	3	Selby, Rick E.	M	4	1,056.00	81.00	1,137.00	63.00	73.91	17.06	60.00	B 1.00 UW 1.00	233.97	903.03	486	5

EARNINGS RECORD FOR QUARTER ENDED *December 31, 20--*

EMPLOYEE NO. *3* — LAST NAME *Selby* — FIRST *Rick* — MIDDLE INITIAL *E.* — MARITAL STATUS *M* — WITHHOLDING ALLOWANCES *4*

RATE OF PAY *$12.00* PER HR. — SOCIAL SECURITY NO. *450-70-6432* — POSITION *Sales Clerk*

PAY PERIOD NO.	ENDED	EARNINGS 1 REGULAR	2 OVERTIME	3 TOTAL	DEDUCTIONS 4 FEDERAL INCOME TAX	5 SOC. SEC. TAX	6 MEDICARE TAX	7 HEALTH INSURANCE	8 OTHER	9 TOTAL	10 NET PAY	11 ACCUMULATED EARNINGS
												18,432.00
1	10/15	960.00	90.00	1,050.00	51.00	68.25	15.75	60.00	B 1.00 UW 1.00	215.00	835.00	19,482.00
2	10/31	1,152.00		1,152.00	66.00	71.88	17.28	60.00	B 1.00 UW 1.00	238.16	913.84	20,634.00
3	11/15	1,056.00		1,056.00	51.00	68.64	15.84	60.00	B 1.00 UW 1.00	215.48	840.52	21,690.00
4	11/30	1,0[illegible]6.00		1,0[illegible]6.00	[illegible]1.00	[illegible]8.64	[illegible]5.84	[illegible]0.00	B [illegible] UW [illegible]	2[illegible]5.48	8[illegible]0.52	22,746.00
5	12/15	1,056.00	81.00	1,137.00	63.00	73.91	17.06	60.00	B 1.00 UW 1.00	233.97	903.03	23,883.00
6	12/31	960.00		960.00	36.00	62.40	14.40	60.00	B 1.00 UW 1.00	192.80	767.20	24,843.00
7												
QUARTERLY TOTALS		6,240.00	171.00	6,411.00	318.00	416.72	96.17	360.00	B 6.00 UW 6.00	1,310.89	5,100.11	

OTHER DEDUCTIONS: B—U.S. SAVINGS BONDS; UW—UNITED WAY

A business must send a quarterly report to federal and state governments showing employee taxable earnings and taxes withheld from employee earnings. Detailed information about each employee's earnings is summarized in a single record for each employee. A business form used to record details affecting payments made to an employee is called an **employee earnings record.** An employee's earnings and deductions for each pay period are summarized on one line of the employee earnings record. A new earnings record is prepared for each employee each quarter. Rick E. Selby's earnings record for the fourth quarter is shown.

STEPS

Preparing an employee earnings record

1. Enter the last day of the yearly quarter, *December 31, 20—*, at the top of the earnings record.
2. Enter the employee's number, name, marital status, withholding allowances, hourly rate, social security number, and position in the provided space. This information is taken from the employee's personnel records.
3. Enter the fiscal year's accumulated earnings for the beginning of the current quarter. This information is taken from the ending accumulated earnings for the previous quarter. Mr. Selby's accumulated earnings for the first three quarters ended September 30 are *$18,432.00*. The Accumulated Earnings column of the employee earnings record shows the accumulated earnings since the beginning of the fiscal year.
4. Enter the last date of the pay period being recorded.
5. Enter the earnings, deductions, and net pay in the columns of the employee earnings record. This information is taken from the current pay period's payroll register.
6. Add the current pay period's total earnings to the previous period's accumulated earnings. Mr. Selby's accumulated earnings as of December 15 are calculated as shown.

Accumulated Earnings as of December 1	+	Total Earnings for Pay Period Ended December 15	=	Accumulated Earnings as of December 15
$22,746.00	+	$1,137.00	=	$23,883.00

The Accumulated Earnings column shows the total earnings for Mr. Selby since the first of the year. The amounts in the Accumulated Earnings column supply an up-to-date reference for an employee's year-to-date earnings. When employee earnings reach the tax base, certain payroll taxes do not apply. For example, social security taxes are paid only on a specified amount of earnings.

7. At the end of each quarter, total and prove the earnings record for each employee. Calculate quarterly totals for each amount column. Subtract the Total Deductions column from the Total Earnings column. The result should equal the total of the Net Pay column. If the totals do not agree, the errors must be found and corrected. Proving the accuracy of Mr. Selby's fourth quarterly totals is shown.

Total Earnings	−	Total Deductions	=	Net Pay
$6,411.00	−	$1,310.89	=	$5,100.11

The net pay, *$5,100.11*, is compared to the total of the Net Pay column. The earnings record is proved because these amounts are equal. These totals are needed to prepare required government reports.

REMEMBER

Total earnings, not net pay, are added to the previous accumulated earnings amount on the earnings record.

Terms Review

payroll register
net pay
employee earnings record

Audit Your Understanding

1. What does the payroll register summarize?
2. How is net pay calculated?
3. Why do companies complete employee earnings records?

Work Together

Preparing payroll records

Selected payroll data for Antique Shop are provided in a payroll register in the *Working Papers.* Your instructor will guide you through the following examples.

4. Complete the payroll register entries for Judy Hensley and Mike McCune for the semimonthly pay period ended July 15, 20—. Use the tax withholding tables shown on pages 310–311. The tax rate for social security tax is 6.5% and for Medicare tax, 1.5%. Neither employee has reached the tax base. For each employee, withhold $60.00 for health insurance and $15.00 for U.S. Savings bonds, per pay period.
5. Total all the amount columns of the payroll register. Prove the payroll register.
6. Prepare a quarterly earnings record for Ms. Hensley for the quarter ended September 30, 20—, and enter the July 15 payroll information. Ms. Hensley's employee number is 5; rate of pay is $13.00; social security number is 543-69-0123; position is sales clerk. Accumulated earnings at the end of the second quarter are $13,520.00. Save your work to complete Work Together on page 321.

On Your Own

Preparing payroll records

Selected payroll data for The Sign Store are provided in a payroll register in the *Working Papers.* Work these problems independently.

7. Complete the payroll register entries for Gary Eubanks and Ellen Park for the semimonthly pay period ended July 15, 20—. Use the tax withholding tables shown on page 310–311. The tax rate for social security tax is 6.5%, and for Medicare tax, 1.5%. For each employee, withhold $50.00 for health insurance and $10.00 for United Way, per pay period. For Mr. Eubanks also withhold $10.00 for U.S. Savings Bonds per pay period.
8. Total all the amount columns of the payroll register. Prove the payroll register.
9. Prepare a quarterly earnings record for Mr. Eubanks for the quarter ended September 30, 20—, and enter the July 15 payroll information. Mr. Eubanks's employee number is 8; rate of pay is $12.80; social security number is 345-68-9876; position is sales clerk. Accumulated earnings at the end of the second quarter are $13,312.00. Save your work to complete On Your Own on page 321.

13-4 Preparing Payroll Checks

PAYROLL BANK ACCOUNT

1. Prepare the check stub.

2. Prepare the check.

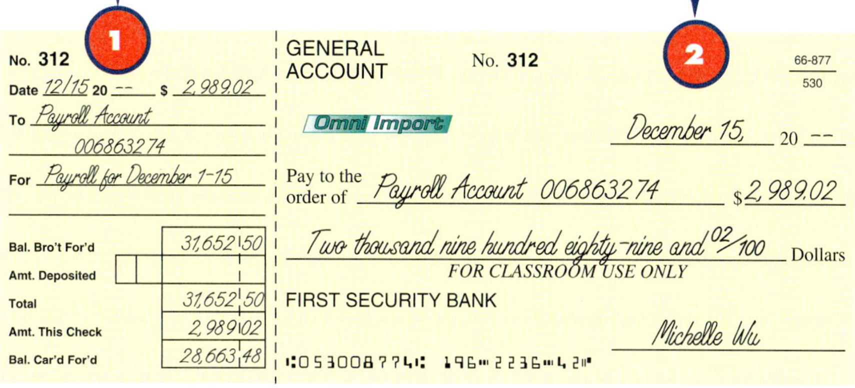
No. 312
Date 12/15 20 -- $ 2,989.02
To Payroll Account 006863274
For Payroll for December 1-15

Bal. Bro't For'd	31,652	50
Amt. Deposited		
Total	31,652	50
Amt. This Check	2,989	02
Bal. Car'd For'd	28,663	48

GENERAL ACCOUNT No. 312 66-877/530

Omni Import December 15, 20 --

Pay to the order of Payroll Account 006863274 $2,989.02

Two thousand nine hundred eighty-nine and 02/100 Dollars

FOR CLASSROOM USE ONLY

FIRST SECURITY BANK

Michelle Wu

⑆053008774⑆ 196⑈2236⑈4 2⑈

Omni Import pays its employees with checks written on a special payroll checking account. A check for the total net pay is written on Omni's general checking account. The check is deposited in the payroll checking account.

A separate checking account for payroll checks helps to protect and control payroll payments. The exact amount needed to pay the payroll is deposited in the special payroll checking account. If amounts on checks are altered or unauthorized payroll checks are prepared, the amount in the special payroll account would be insufficient to cover all the checks. Thus, the bank and Omni would be alerted quickly to an unauthorized payroll check. Also, since payroll checks are drawn on the separate account, any balance in this account will correspond to the sum of outstanding payroll checks.

STEPS

Preparing a check for total net pay

1. Prepare the check stub. The date of the check is *12/15*. The amount, *$2,989.02*, is the total of the Net Pay column of the payroll register. The check is payable to *Payroll Account 006863274*, Omni's special payroll checking account. The payment is for the payroll period from December 1 to 15. Calculate and record the new general checking account balance.
2. Prepare the check from the information on the check stub. Omni's check is drawn on the company's general account and is signed by partner Michelle Wu.

REMEMBER

Using a separate checking account for payroll checks provides internal control and helps to prevent fraud.

EMPLOYEE'S PAYROLL CHECK

1. Enter on check stub information from payroll register.

2. Prepare employee's payroll check for net amount of earnings.

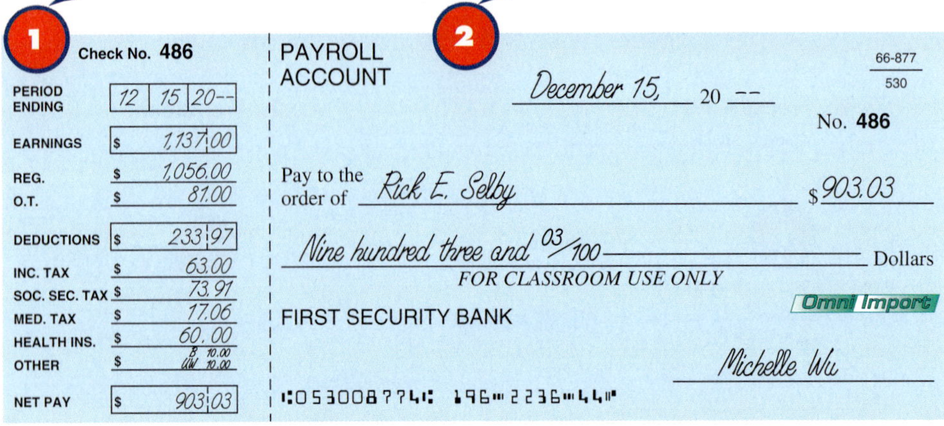

The information used to prepare payroll checks is taken from a payroll register. A special payroll check form is used that has a detachable stub for recording earnings and amounts deducted. Employees keep the stubs for a record of deductions and cash received.

STEPS: Preparing an employee's payroll check

1. Prepare the check stub of each employee's payroll check. Enter information from the payroll register.
2. Prepare each employee's payroll check payable for the amount of net pay for the pay period. Rick E. Selby's net pay for the pay period ended December 15, 20—, is $903.03.

ELECTRONIC FUNDS TRANSFER

A computerized cash payments system that uses electronic impulses to transfer funds is known as electronic funds transfer (EFT). Some businesses deposit employee net pay directly to each employee bank account by using EFT. When EFT is used, the bank's computer deducts the amount of net pay from the business's bank account and adds the amount to each employee bank account. The payroll must still be calculated, but individual checks are not written and do not have to be distributed. Under this system, each employee receives a statement of earnings and deductions similar to the detachable stub on a payroll check.

AUDIT YOUR UNDERSTANDING

1. Why does Omni Import have a separate checking account for payroll checks?
2. What is the source of the information that is recorded on each employee's payroll check stub?
3. How do payroll procedures differ for an employee who requests that her pay be deposited through electronic funds transfer?

WORK TOGETHER

Preparing payroll checks

Use the payroll register from Work Together on page 318. In the *Working Papers* are three blank checks: one General Account check and two Payroll Account checks. Your instructor will guide you through the following examples.

4. Prepare Antique Shop's General Account check for the pay period ended July 15, 20—. The payment date is July 15. Balance brought forward from the previous check is $16,542.00. The Payroll Account number is 0639583. Sign your name as a partner of Antique Shop.
5. For the pay period ended July 15, 20—, prepare payroll checks for Judy Hensley and Mike McCune. The payment date is July 15. Sign your name as a partner of Antique Shop. Record the two payroll check numbers in the payroll register.

ON YOUR OWN

Preparing payroll checks

Use the payroll register from On Your Own on page 318. In the *Working Papers* are three blank checks: one General Account check and two Payroll Account checks. Work these problems independently.

6. Prepare The Sign Shop's General Account check for the pay period ended July 15, 20—. The payment date is July 15. Balance carried forward from the previous check is $13,597.00. The Payroll Account number is 983-5839. Sign your name as a partner of The Sign Shop.
7. For the pay period ended July 15, 20—, prepare payroll checks for Gary Eubanks and Ellen Park. The payment date is July 15. Sign your name as a partner of The Sign Shop. Record the two payroll checks in the payroll register.

CHAPTER 13 SUMMARY

After completing this chapter, you can

1. Define important accounting terms related to payroll records.
2. Identify accounting practices related to payroll records.
3. Complete a payroll time card.
4. Calculate payroll taxes.
5. Complete a payroll register and an employee earnings record.
6. Prepare payroll checks.

EXPLORE ACCOUNTING

EMPLOYEE VS. INDEPENDENT CONTRACTOR

A business sometimes contracts with individuals to perform specified services for the business. Determining whether such an individual is an employee or a self-employed independent contractor is an important issue.

If the person is found to be an employee, the employer must withhold and submit employee income tax, social security tax, and Medicare tax to the Internal Revenue Service (IRS). The employer must pay an equal amount of social security and Medicare tax. Also, the employer will pay unemployment taxes (discussed in Chapter 14) and be subject to various employer reporting requirements.

A person who is found to be a self-employed independent contractor must pay an amount of social security and Medicare tax that is equivalent to both the employer and employee taxes.

If an employer incorrectly treats an employee as a self-employed independent contractor, the penalties can be severe. Therefore, it is important to a business to make an accurate determination of the status of all individuals performing work for the business.

The IRS has provided guidelines to help businesses make the distinction. Every individual who performs services subject to the will and control of an employer both as to what shall be done and how it shall be done, is considered an employee for withholding purposes. The major determining factor is whether the employer has the legal right to control both the method and result of the services. If the business has the right to control *only* the result of the service performed and *not* the means and methods of accomplishing the result, the individual is probably a self-employed independent contractor.

Research: Review federal tax publications or interview local businesses on the issues below. Then prepare a written or oral report to present to your class. (1) Why is it important to determine an individual's status? What is at stake for the individual, the employer, and the IRS? (2) What are the advantages and disadvantages of determining an individual to be an employee or independent contractor—to the individual? to the employer? to the IRS?

13-1 APPLICATION PROBLEM
Preparing payroll time cards

Employee time cards are given in the *Working Papers.*

Instructions:

1. Calculate the regular, overtime, and total hours worked by each employee. Any hours over the regular 8-hour day are considered overtime. Record the hours on the time cards.
2. Determine the regular, overtime, and total earnings for each employee. The overtime rate is $1\frac{1}{2}$ times the regular rate. Complete the time cards.

13-2 APPLICATION PROBLEM
Determining payroll tax withholding

Information taken from the semimonthly payroll register is given in the *Working Papers.*

Instructions:

1. Determine the federal income tax that must be withheld for each of the eight employees. Use the tax withholding tables shown on pages 310–311.
2. Calculate the amount of social security tax and Medicare tax that must be withheld for each employee using 6.5% and 1.5% tax rates, respectively. None of the eight employees has accumulated earnings greater than the tax base.

13-3 APPLICATION PROBLEM
Preparing a payroll register

The information for the semimonthly pay period October 1–15 of the current year is given in the *Working Papers.*

Instructions:

Complete a payroll register. The date of payment is October 15. Use the tax withholding tables shown on pages 310–311 for the income tax withholding for each employee. Calculate social security and Medicare taxes withholding using 6.5% and 1.5% tax rates, respectively. None of the employee accumulated earnings has exceeded the social security tax base.

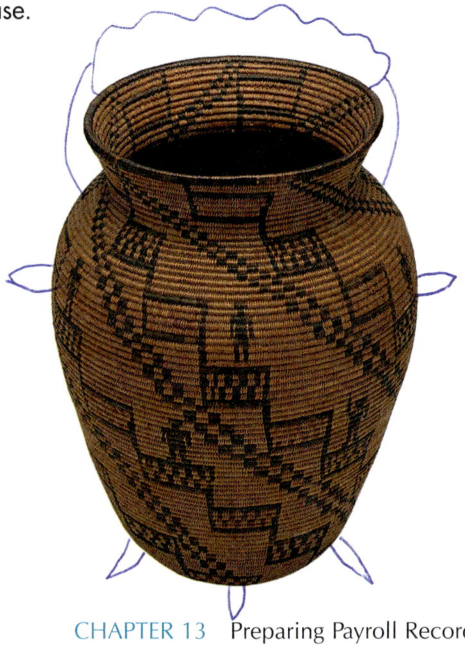

13-4 APPLICATION PROBLEM
Preparing an employee earnings record

Grady R. Hurley's earnings for the six semimonthly pay periods in July, August, and September of the current year are given in the *Working Papers.* Deductions and net pay have been completed for July and August.

The following additional data about Grady R. Hurley are needed to complete the employee earnings record.

1. Employee number: 28
2. Marital status: married
3. Withholding allowances: 2
4. Rate of pay: regular, $15.00
5. Social security number: 462-81-5823
6. Position: service manager
7. Accumulated earnings for the end of second quarter: $15,750.00
8. Deductions from total earnings:
   a. Health insurance: $60.00 each semimonthly pay period
   b. U. S. Savings Bonds: $10.00 each semimonthly pay period
   c. Federal income tax: determined each pay period by using the withholding tables on pages 310–311.
   d. Social security taxes: 6.5% of total earnings each pay period
   e. Medicare taxes: 1.5% of total earnings each pay period

Instructions:

1. Calculate and record the accumulated earnings for the July and August pay periods.
2. Complete the earnings record for the pay periods ended September 15 and September 30.
3. Total all amount columns on the earnings record.
4. Verify the accuracy of the completed employee earnings record. The Quarter Total for Regular and Overtime Earnings should equal the Quarter Total for Net Pay plus Total Deductions. The Quarter Total for Total Earnings should equal the end-of-quarter Accumulated Earnings minus the beginning-of-quarter Accumulated Earnings.

13-5 APPLICATION PROBLEM
Preparing payroll checks

Royal Appliances' net payroll for the semimonthly pay period ended May 15, 20—, is $7,498.80. Payroll checks are prepared May 15, 20—. Blank checks are provided in the *Working Papers.*

Instructions:

1. Prepare a General Account check for the total amount of the net pay. Make the check payable to Payroll Account 018-65-4237, and sign your name as partner of Royal Appliances. The beginning check stub balance is $10,138.95.
2. Prepare payroll checks for two employees of Royal Appliances. Payroll information for the two employees is as follows. Sign your name as a partner of Royal Appliances.
   a. Wanda M. Curtis
      Check No. 823
      Regular Earnings $740.00
      Overtime Earnings 40.00

Deductions:

Federal Income Tax	$ 85.00
Social Security Tax	50.70
Medicare Tax	11.70
Net Pay	632.60

b. Kevin R. Hayes
Check No. 827

Regular Earnings	$920.00
Overtime Earnings	30.00
Deductions:	
Federal Income Tax	$ 69.00
Social Security	61.75
Medicare Tax	14.25
Health Insurance	60.00
Net Pay	745.00

13-6 MASTERY PROBLEM
Preparing a semimonthly payroll

The following information is for the semimonthly pay period May 1-15 of the current year. Forms are given in the *Working Papers.*

EMPL. NO.	EMPLOYEE'S NAME	MARITAL STATUS	NO. OF ALLOWANCES	EARNINGS		DEDUCTIONS	
				REGULAR	OVERTIME	HEALTH INSURANCE	SAVINGS BONDS
3	*Baird, Panette L.*	M	2	721 60	18 45	42 00	20 00
6	*Carmichael, Gary R.*	S	1	809 60	27 60		
8	*Fields, Margo S.*	M	3	880 00	15 00	54 00	10 00
1	*Hahn, Todd M.*	M	2	792 00	47 25	42 00	10 00
5	*Liu, Jin C.*	S	1	941 60			
9	*Pruitt, Wilma C.*	M	2	862 40	102 90	42 00	20 00
10	*Roth, Thomas B.*	S	2	756 80	19 35	42 00	20 00
2	*Sevilla, Jose C.*	M	4	862 40		62 00	
4	*Taylor, Cindy J.*	S	1	897 60	45 90		
7	*Wylie, Howard K.*	S	1	660 00			30 00

Instructions:

1. Prepare a payroll register. The date of payment is May 15. Use the income tax withholding tables shown on pages 310–311 to find the income tax withholding for each employee. Calculate social security and Medicare tax withholdings using 6.5% and 1.5% tax rates, respectively. None of the employee accumulated earnings has exceeded the social security tax base.
2. Prepare a check for the total amount of the net pay. Make the check payable to Payroll Account 156-42-8796, and sign your name as a partner of Rainbo Company. The beginning check stub balance is $14,344.60.
3. Prepare payroll checks for Todd M. Hahn, Check No. 528, and Cindy J. Taylor, Check No. 533. Sign your name as a partner of Rainbo Company. Record the two payroll check numbers in the payroll register.

13-7 CHALLENGE PROBLEM
Calculating piecework wages

Production workers in factories are frequently paid on the basis of the number of units they produce. This payroll method is referred to as the piecework incentive wage plan. Most piecework incentive wage plans include a guaranteed hourly rate to employees regardless of the number of units they produce. This guaranteed hourly rate is referred to as the base rate.

Time and motion study engineers usually determine the standard time required for producing a single unit. Assume, for example, that time studies determine that one-third of an hour is the standard time required to produce a unit. Then the standard rate for an 8-hour day would be 24 units (8 hours divided by $\frac{1}{3}$ hour = 24 units per day). If a worker's daily base pay is \$96.00, the incentive rate per unit is \$4.00 (\$96.00 divided by 24 units = \$4.00 per unit). Therefore, the worker who produces 24 or fewer units per day is paid the base pay, \$96.00. However, each worker is paid an additional \$4.00 for each unit over 24 produced each day.

Premier Woodworks Company has eight employees in production departments that are paid on a piecework incentive wage plan. The following standard and incentive wage rates are listed by department.

Department	Standard Production per Employee	Incentive Rate per Unit
Cutting	30 units per day	\$3.50
Assembly	20 units per day	\$6.20
Finishing	40 units per day	\$2.70

A payroll register is given in the *Working Papers*. Each employee worked eight hours a day during the semimonthly pay period, June 1–15. Payroll records for June 1–15 are summarized in the following table.

Employee		Marital Status	No. of Allowances	Guaranteed Daily Rate	Units Produced per Day Pay Period June 1–15									
No.	Name				2	3	4	5	6	9	10	11	12	13
	Cutting Department													
C2	Martinez, Luis L.	S	1	\$105.00	29	32	31	34	28	27	30	32	36	26
C4	Price, Nancy C.	M	1	\$105.00	32	31	28	29	27	29	31	32	27	28
C8	King, Debra S.	M	2	\$105.00	31	28	27	24	31	33	32	29	30	29
	Assembly Department													
A1	Heath, Scott R.	S	1	\$124.00	20	21	19	19	18	18	19	21	20	21
A6	Nowlin, Daniel W.	M	3	\$124.00	25	21	17	18	19	21	20	20	21	18
A7	Scofield, Martha A.	S	1	\$124.00	22	24	25	21	20	19	23	21	18	17
	Finishing Department													
F5	Isaacs, Julie M.	M	2	\$108.00	41	40	38	39	42	43	41	40	38	37
F3	Stewart, Gary W.	M	2	\$108.00	37	37	38	38	39	38	40	41	41	42

Instructions:

Prepare a payroll register. The earnings column Incentive is used instead of Overtime. The date of payment is June 15. Use the income tax withholding tables shown on pages 310–311. Calculate the employee social security and Medicare tax withholdings using 6.5% and 1.5% tax rates, respectively. None of the employees has health insurance or other deductions.

INTERNET ACTIVITY

Point your browser to

http://accounting.swpco.com

Choose **First-Year Course**, choose **Activities**, and complete the activity for Chapter 13.

Applied Communication

The employees of Kaden Company currently use time cards and a time clock to record their arrival and departure times. Management plans to replace the time clock with a device that reads a magnetic strip on the back of each employee's name badge. The badge is scanned by a reader in the same manner that credit cards are scanned. Because the badge reader is connected to a computer, the information is recorded directly to a computer file. Thus, the new system will enable management to make daily analyses of employee hours and productivity. This information should allow managers to make more timely decisions and increase profits.

Instructions: Assume you work in the payroll department for Kaden Company. Write a memo to the employees informing them of the new system. Because some employees may not be happy with this new system, be sure to include reasons why the policy is being implemented.

Cases for Critical Thinking

Case 1 Sullivan Lumber currently requires each employee to inform the accounting clerk of the total hours worked each day during the pay period. The total number of hours worked by all employees has been steadily increasing during the prior pay periods. The new store manager has suggested that a time clock be installed to record arrival and departure times. The accounting clerk believes the current system is satisfactory. Do you agree with the new manager or the accounting clerk? Explain your response.

Case 2 A banker has recommended that Mueller Construction Company open a second checking account. The company would write payroll checks on the new checking account. The company's 50 employees are currently paid with checks written on its general checking account. Do you agree with the banker's recommendation? Explain the reason for your decision.

AUTOMATED ACCOUNTING

AUTOMATED PAYROLL ACCOUNTING

In an automated payroll system, the computer is used to maintain the employee database, to record payroll transactions at the end of each pay period, to calculate withholding taxes, and to create all the related journal entries. The employee database identifies each employee by employee number. Other data required for each employee includes the employee's name, social security number, marital status, number of withholding allowances, pay rate, and voluntary deductions. Employee accounts may be added, changed, or deleted from the accounting system.

Maintaining Employees

Since payroll data is used to calculate income taxes, the payroll system must contain accurate, up-to-date data for each employee. Maintenance is required to:

1. Add new employees.
2. Remove employees who no longer work for the company.
3. Record changes in employee information, including changes in marital status, number of withholding allowances, pay rate, and voluntary deductions.

To perform employee maintenance in *Automated Accounting 7.0* or higher:

1. Click the Accounts toolbar button.
2. Click the Employees tab.
3. To add a new employee:
   - Enter the sequential employee number.
   - Enter information in all the data fields, including name, address, social security number, and marital status.
   - Press Enter or click Add Employee.
4. To change or delete data for a current employee:
   - Select the employee by clicking the grid cell containing the data you wish to change.
   - Enter the correct data.
   - Click the Change Employee button, or click the Delete button to remove the employee from the database. (Employees with cumulative earnings may be deleted only after the end of the calendar year.)

Entering Payroll Transactions

1. Click the Other toolbar button.
2. Click the Payroll tab.
3. Enter the date of the check.
4. Select the employee from the employee drop-down list.
5. Verify that the check number displayed is correct, or key the correct number.
6. For salaried employees, the salary amount will be automatically displayed. For hourly employees, enter the regular and overtime hours worked during the current payroll period.
7. Click the Calculate Taxes button to direct the software to calculate the employee taxes.
8. Enter the employee's voluntary deductions.
9. Click OK to generate and display the payroll check.
10. Click the Close button to dismiss the check and continue, or click Print to print the check.

Automating Application Problem 13-5: Preparing payroll checks

Instructions:

1. Load *Automated Accounting 7.0* or higher software.
2. Select database F13-1 from the appropriate directory/folder.
3. Select File from the menu bar and choose the Save As menu command. Key the path to the drive and directory that contains your data files. Save the database with a file name of XXX131 (where XXX are your initials).
4. Access Problem Instructions through the Help menu. Read the Problem Instructions screen.
5. Key the data listed on pages 324–325.
6. Exit the *Automated Accounting* software.

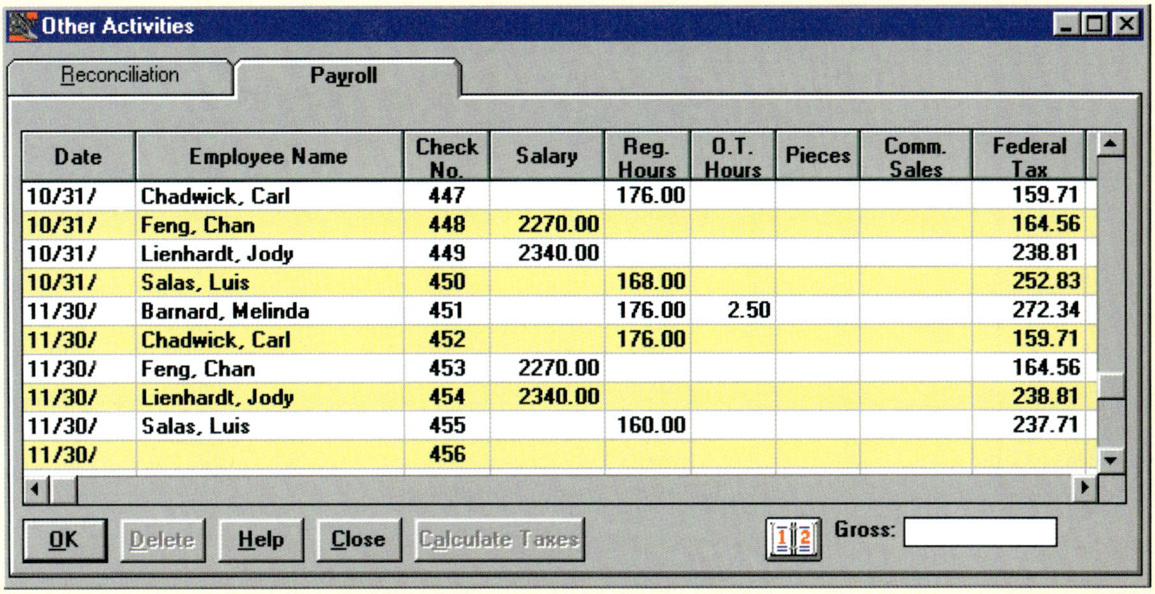

Other Activities

Reconciliation | Payroll

Date	Employee Name	Check No.	Salary	Reg. Hours	O.T. Hours	Pieces	Comm. Sales	Federal Tax
10/31/	Chadwick, Carl	447		176.00				159.71
10/31/	Feng, Chan	448	2270.00					164.56
10/31/	Lienhardt, Jody	449	2340.00					238.81
10/31/	Salas, Luis	450		168.00				252.83
11/30/	Barnard, Melinda	451		176.00	2.50			272.34
11/30/	Chadwick, Carl	452		176.00				159.71
11/30/	Feng, Chan	453	2270.00					164.56
11/30/	Lienhardt, Jody	454	2340.00					238.81
11/30/	Salas, Luis	455		160.00				237.71
11/30/		456						

OK | Delete | Help | Close | Calculate Taxes | Gross:

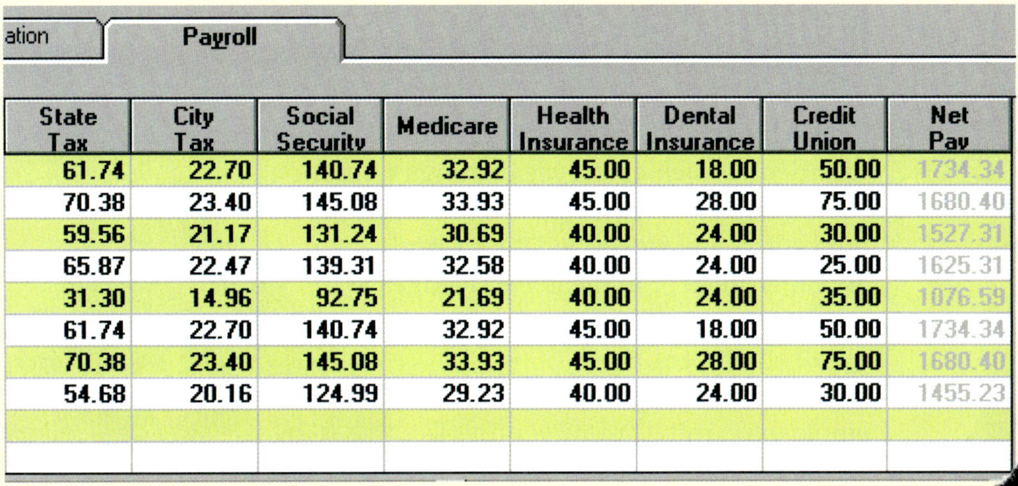

ation | Payroll

State Tax	City Tax	Social Security	Medicare	Health Insurance	Dental Insurance	Credit Union	Net Pay
61.74	22.70	140.74	32.92	45.00	18.00	50.00	1734.34
70.38	23.40	145.08	33.93	45.00	28.00	75.00	1680.40
59.56	21.17	131.24	30.69	40.00	24.00	30.00	1527.31
65.87	22.47	139.31	32.58	40.00	24.00	25.00	1625.31
31.30	14.96	92.75	21.69	40.00	24.00	35.00	1076.59
61.74	22.70	140.74	32.92	45.00	18.00	50.00	1734.34
70.38	23.40	145.08	33.93	45.00	28.00	75.00	1680.40
54.68	20.16	124.99	29.23	40.00	24.00	30.00	1455.23

14 Payroll Accounting, Taxes, and Reports

AFTER STUDYING CHAPTER 14, YOU WILL BE ABLE TO:

1. Define accounting terms related to payroll accounting, taxes, and reports.
2. Identify accounting concepts and practices related to payroll accounting, taxes, and reports.
3. Analyze payroll transactions and record a payroll.
4. Record employer payroll taxes.
5. Prepare selected payroll tax reports.
6. Pay and record withholding and payroll taxes.

TERMS PREVIEW

federal unemployment tax

state unemployment tax

DIFFERENT FORMS OF PAYROLL INFORMATION

Payroll information for each pay period is recorded in a payroll register. Each pay period the payroll information for each employee is also recorded on each employee earnings record. Separate payroll accounts for each employee are not kept in the general ledger. Instead, accounts are kept in the general ledger to summarize total earnings and deductions for all employees.

The payroll register and employee earnings records provide all the payroll information needed to prepare a payroll and payroll tax reports. Journal entries are made to record the payment of the payroll and the employer payroll taxes. In addition, various quarterly and annual payroll tax reports are required to report the payment of payroll taxes.

ACCOUNTING IN YOUR CAREER

HOW MUCH DO EMPLOYEES REALLY COST?

Walter Johnson, staff accountant for VideoPlus Company, is meeting with the two partners to discuss how they will begin making plans for next year's operations. Deborah Stricklin and Paul Kassem, partners, like to have their management strategy planned before meeting with the department managers to prepare the next year's budget.

Deborah begins the meeting with the statement, "Walter, we're about to plan the budget for next year, and we need your help."

"That's right, Walter," continues Paul. "You've been in these budget meetings before. Every time we ask for increases in sales, all the managers ask for more employees. That seems to be their answer to everything. They never talk about economizing on costs, or finding more efficient ways to operate. How can we get them to realize that new employees are not always the solution?"

"Deborah, Paul," answers Walter, "you're right. I've been in those meetings, and you've described what goes on pretty accurately. I wonder if it would help to show the managers how much a new employee really costs."

"I'm not sure I know what you're getting at, Walter," responds Paul.

"Well, I think most of the managers look only at salary costs. They forget all the other payroll costs, such as taxes and benefits, not to mention the cost of training a new employee."

Deborah and Paul like this analysis and ask Walter to work up some estimates and make a presentation at the first budget meeting next week.

Critical Thinking:

1. Where could Walter Johnson find a record of all salary and benefit costs paid for all employees in a year?
2. How could Walter quickly calculate the average annual salary of a VideoPlus employee?
3. How should Walter use the information in the ledger accounts for Employee Income Tax Payable, Social Security Tax Payable, and Medicare Tax Payable?

14-1 Recording a Payroll

PAYROLL REGISTER

SEMIMONTHLY PERIOD ENDED *December 15, 20--* — PAYROLL REGISTER — DATE OF PAYMENT *December 15, 20--*

	EMPL. NO.	EMPLOYEE'S NAME	MARITAL STATUS	NO. OF ALLOWANCES	1 EARNINGS REGULAR	2 EARNINGS OVERTIME	3 EARNINGS TOTAL	4 DEDUCTIONS FEDERAL INCOME TAX	5 DEDUCTIONS SOC. SEC. TAX	6 DEDUCTIONS MEDICARE TAX	7 DEDUCTIONS HEALTH INSURANCE	8 DEDUCTIONS OTHER	9 DEDUCTIONS TOTAL	10 NET PAY	CHECK NO.	
1	1	*Aranda, Susan A.*	M	2	968 00		968 00	72 00	62 92	14 52	45 60	B 10 00	205 04	762 96	482	1
2	5	*Drew, Paul S.*	S	1	105 00		105 00		6 83	1 58			8 41	96 59	483	2
3	4	*Hakala, Erik D.*	M	1	598 40	10 20	608 60	35 00	39 56	9 13	38 40		122 09	486 51	484	3
4	6	*Mendel, Ann M.*	S	1	78 75		78 75		5 12	1 18			6 30	72 45	485	4
5	3	*Selby, Rick E.*	M	4	1056 00	81 00	1137 00	63 00	73 91	17 06	60 00	B 10 00 UW 10 00	233 97	903 03	486	5
6	2	*Young, Justin L.*	S	1	906 40		906 40	103 00	58 92	13 60	38 40	B 15 00 UW 10 00	238 92	667 48	487	6
7		*Totals*			3712 55	91 20	3803 75	273 00	247 26	57 07	182 40	B 35 00 UW 20 00	814 73	2989 02		7
8																8
9																9

The column totals of a payroll register provide the debit and credit amounts needed to journalize a payroll.

As you will learn in this chapter, the payroll journal entry is based on the totals of the Earnings Total column, each deduction column, and the Net Pay column. The totals of the Earnings Regular, Earnings Overtime, and Deductions Total columns are not used to journalize the payroll.

TECHNOLOGY FOR BUSINESS

How Smart Are Your Cards?

Americans use lots of cards—library cards, credit cards, ATM cards, insurance cards. When you use them, do you ever think that cards may be smart?

A *smart card* looks like a plastic credit card, but it has a microprocessor, or computer chip, planted inside. Depending on the intended use, these chip cards can be really smart.

One type of smart card is called a *stored value card.* Generally you purchase a stored value card through a vending machine. You insert cash, a credit card, or a debit card to buy the stored value card. Each time you use it, the card deducts the amount of your purchase from its stored value.

While smart cards are relatively new in the U. S., other countries are using them for more complex reasons. For example, Spain has issued 500,000 identification cards, with stored fingerprints for verification, that give access to medical benefits.

Just how smart do you think cards will be in the future?

ANALYZING PAYMENT OF A PAYROLL

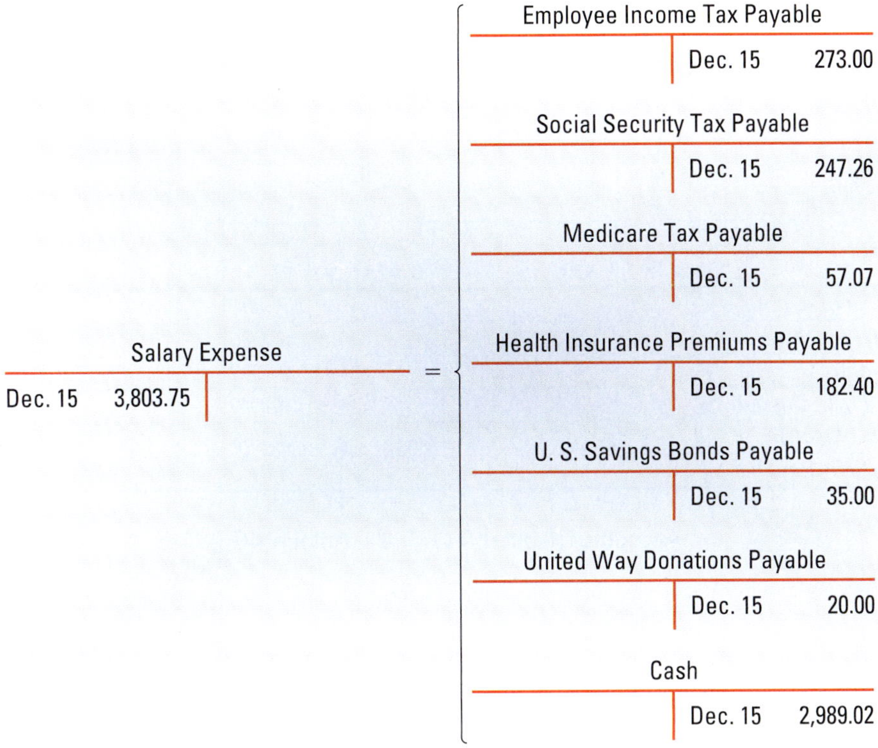

Data about Omni Import's semimonthly pay period ended December 15, obtained from the payroll register, is summarized in the T accounts.

The Total Earnings column total, $3,803.75, is the salary expense for the period. Salary Expense is debited for this amount.

The Federal Income Tax column total, $273.00, is the amount withheld from employee salaries for federal income tax. The amount withheld is a liability of the business until the taxes are sent to the federal government. Employee Income Tax Payable is credited for $273.00 to record this liability.

The Social Security Tax column total, $247.26, is the amount withheld for social security tax. The amount is a liability of the business until the tax is paid to the government. Social Security Tax Payable is credited for $247.26.

The Medicare Tax column total, $57.07, is the amount withheld for Medicare tax. The amount is a liability of the business until the tax is paid to the government. Medicare Tax Payable is credited for $57.07.

The Health Insurance column total, $182.40, is the amount withheld for health insurance premiums. The amount is a liability of the business until the premiums are paid to the insurance company. Health Insurance Premiums Payable is credited for $182.40 to record this liability.

Two types of Other deductions are recorded in Omni's payroll register. The $35.00 Other column total identified with the letter *B* is withheld to buy savings bonds for employees. The $20.00 total identified with the letters *UW* is withheld for employee United Way pledges. Until these amounts have been paid by the employer, they are liabilities of the business. U.S. Savings Bonds Payable is credited for $35.00. United Way Donations Payable is credited for $20.00.

The Net Pay column total, $2,989.02, is the net amount paid to employees. Cash is credited for $2,989.02. A check for the total net pay amount, $2,989.02, is written on Omni's general checking account and is deposited in a special payroll checking account. Individual payroll checks are then written on the special payroll checking account.

JOURNALIZING PAYMENT OF A PAYROLL

1. Date 2. Account Debited 3. Check Number 4. Amount Debited 5. Amount Paid to Employees

PAGE 24 — JOURNAL — PAGE 24

	DATE		ACCOUNT TITLE	DOC. NO.	POST. REF.	GENERAL DEBIT (1)	GENERAL CREDIT (2)	CASH DEBIT (10)	CASH CREDIT (11)	
21		15	Salary Expense	C312		3803 75			2989 02	21
22			Employee Income Tax Payable				273 00			22
23			Social Security Tax Payable				247 26			23
24			Medicare Tax Payable				57 07			24
25			Health Insurance Prem. Payable				182 40			25
26			U. S. Savings Bonds Payable				35 00			26
27			United Way Donations Payable				20 00			27

6. Accounts Credited 7. Amounts Credited

Omni Import journalized the company's payroll for the semimonthly period ended December 15, 20—.

December 15. Paid cash for semimonthly payroll, $2,989.02 (total payroll, $3,803.75, less deductions: employee income tax, $273.00; social security tax, $247.26; Medicare tax, $57.07; health insurance premiums, $182.40; U.S. Savings Bonds, $35.00; United Way donations, $20.00). Check No. 312.

Amounts recorded in the General columns of a journal are posted individually to general ledger accounts. The credit to Cash, $2,989.02, is not posted separately to the cash account. The amount is included in the journal's Cash Credit column total that is posted at the end of the month. The same procedures are followed to post this journal entry to the appropriate accounts as were described in Chapter 12.

STEPS: Journalizing payment of a payroll

1. Write the date, *15,* in the Date column.
2. Write the title of the account debited, *Salary Expense,* in the Account Title column.
3. Write the check number, *C312,* in the Doc. No. column.
4. Write the amount debited to Salary Expense, *$3,803.75,* in the General Debit column.
5. On the same line, write the total amount paid to employees, *$2,989.02,* in the Cash Credit column.
6. On the next six lines, write the titles of the accounts credited, *Employee Income Tax Payable, Social Security Tax Payable, Medicare Tax Payable, Health Insurance Premiums Payable, U.S. Savings Bonds Payable,* and *United Way Donations Payable,* in the Account Title column.
7. On the same six lines, write the amounts credited to the corresponding liability accounts, *$273.00, $247.26, $57.07, $182.40, $35.00,* and *$20.00,* in the General Credit column.

REMEMBER

Total Earnings is the debit amount for Salary Expense. Net Pay is the credit amount for cash.

AUDIT YOUR UNDERSTANDING

1. What account title is used to journalize the Total Earnings column of the payroll register?
2. What account title is used to journalize the Federal Income Tax column of the payroll register?
3. What account title is used to journalize the Social Security Tax column of the payroll register?
4. What account title is used to journalize the Medicare Tax column of the payroll register?

WORK TOGETHER

Recording a payroll

Metro Company's payroll register has the following totals for the semimonthly pay period, July 1–15 of the current year.

T accounts and a journal page are provided in the *Working Papers.* Your instructor will guide you through the following examples.

Total Earnings	Federal Income Tax Withheld	Social Security Tax Withheld	Medicare Tax Withheld
$12,600.00	$1,386.00	$819.00	$189.00

5. Use the T accounts provided to analyze Metro's July 1–15 payroll.
6. Journalize the payment of Metro's July 1–15 payroll on page 15 of the journal. The payroll was paid by Check No. 455 on July 15 of the current year.

ON YOUR OWN

Recording a payroll

Metro Company's payroll register has the following totals for the semimonthly pay period, July 16–31 of the current year.

T accounts and a journal page are provided in the *Working Papers.* Work independently to complete these problems.

Total Earnings	Federal Income Tax Withheld	Social Security Tax Withheld	Medicare Tax Withheld
$12,950.00	$1,424.50	$841.75	$194.25

7. Use the T accounts provided to analyze Metro's July 16–31 payroll.
8. Journalize the payment of Metro's July 16–31 payroll on page 16 of a journal. The payroll was paid by Check No. 483 on July 31 of the current year.

14-2 Recording Employer Payroll Taxes

CALCULATING EMPLOYER PAYROLL TAXES

Employers must pay to the government the taxes withheld from employee earnings. Omni Import has withheld federal income tax, social security tax, and Medicare tax from employee salaries. The amounts withheld are liabilities to the business until they are actually paid to the government. In addition, employers must pay several of their own payroll taxes. Employer payroll taxes are business expenses.

Most employers must pay four separate payroll taxes. These taxes are (1) employer social security tax, (2) Medicare tax, (3) federal unemployment tax, and (4) state unemployment tax. Employer payroll taxes expense is based on a percentage of employee earnings.

Employer Social Security and Medicare Taxes

The social security and Medicare taxes are the only payroll taxes paid by *both* the employees and the employer. Omni withheld $247.26 in social security tax and $57.07 in Medicare tax from employee wages for the pay period ended December 15. Omni owes the same amount of social security and Medicare taxes as the amount withheld from employees. Therefore, Omni's social security and Medicare taxes for the pay period ended December 15 are also $247.26 and $57.07 respectively.

Congress sets the social security and Medicare tax rates for employees and employers. Periodically, Congress may change the tax rates and tax base. The social security tax rate and base used in this text are 6.5% of earnings up to a maximum of $65,400.00 in each calendar year. Medicare does not have a tax base. Therefore, Medicare tax is calculated on total employee earnings. The Medicare tax rate used in this text is 1.5% of total employee earnings.

REMEMBER

Employers must pay four taxes on employee earnings—social security tax, Medicare tax, federal unemployment tax, and state unemployment tax.

UNEMPLOYMENT TAXABLE EARNINGS

OMNI IMPORT
Taxable Earnings
for December 15, 20—, Pay Period

	Accumulated Earnings as of Nov. 30, 20--	Total Earnings for Dec. 15, 20-- Pay Period	Unemployment Taxable Earnings
Aranda, Susan A.	$21,115.00	$ 968.00	—
Drew, Paul S.	2,595.25	105.00	$105.00
Hakala, Erik D.	13,518.00	608.60	—
Mendel, Ann M.	2,030.00	78.75	78.75
Selby, Rick E.	22,746.00	1,137.00	—
Young, Justin L.	19,816.00	906.40	—
			$183.75

1. Enter accumulated earnings and total earnings for each employee.

2. Enter unemployment taxable earnings.

3. Total the unemployment taxable earnings column.

Federal unemployment insurance laws require that employers pay taxes for unemployment compensation. These tax funds are used to pay workers benefits for limited periods of unemployment and to administer the unemployment compensation program.

The total earnings subject to unemployment tax is referred to as unemployment taxable earnings. The unemployment tax is applied to the first $7,000.00 earned by each employee for each calendar year. The amount of unemployment taxable earnings for Omni's pay period ended December 15, 20—, is shown in the illustration.

STEPS: Calculating unemployment taxable earnings

1. For each employee, enter accumulated earnings as of November 30 and total earnings for the December 15 pay period. These amounts are taken from each employee earnings record. Rick E. Selby's accumulated earnings as of November 30, *$22,746.00*, are recorded in the first column. His total earnings for the December 15 pay period, *$1,137.00*, are recorded in the second column.
2. Enter unemployment taxable earnings for the pay period in the Unemployment Taxable Earnings column for employees whose accumulated earnings are less than $7,000.00. The November 30 accumulated earnings for Paul S. Drew, *$2,595.25*, are less than $7,000.00. Therefore, his total earnings for the December 15 pay period, *$105.00*, are subject to unemployment tax and are recorded in the Unemployment Taxable Earnings column. Since the accumulated earnings for Mr. Selby are greater than $7,000.00, none of his current earnings are subject to unemployment tax. Thus, the amount of unemployment taxable earnings recorded in the third column is zero, which is represented by a dash.
3. Total the Unemployment Taxable Earnings column. This total amount, *$183.75*, is used to calculate the unemployment tax.

UNEMPLOYMENT TAXES

Omni Import pays two unemployment taxes, federal unemployment tax and state unemployment tax.

Federal Unemployment Tax

A federal tax used for state and federal administrative expenses of the unemployment program is called **federal unemployment tax.** The federal unemployment tax is 6.2% of the first $7,000.00 earned by each employee. An employer generally can deduct from federal unemployment payments the amounts paid to state unemployment funds. This deduction cannot be more than 5.4% of taxable earnings. The effective federal unemployment tax rate in most states is, therefore, 0.8% on the first $7,000.00 earned by each employee. (Federal, 6.2% − deductible for state, 5.4% = 0.8%.) All of the unemployment tax on the first $7,000.00 of salary is paid by the employer.

Omni's federal unemployment tax for the pay period ended December 15, 20—, is calculated as shown.

Unemployment Taxable Earnings	×	Federal Unemployment Tax Rate	=	Federal Unemployment Tax
$183.75	×	0.8%	=	$1.47

State Unemployment Tax

A state tax used to pay benefits to unemployed workers is called **state unemployment tax.** The Social Security Act specifies certain standards for unemployment compensation laws. Therefore, a high degree of uniformity exists in state unemployment laws. However, details of state unemployment laws do differ. Because of these differences, employers must know the requirements of the states in which they operate.

Most states require that employers pay unemployment tax of 5.4% on the first $7,000.00 earned by each employee. The unemployment taxable earnings used to calculate the federal unemployment tax are also used to calculate the state unemployment tax. Omni's state unemployment tax for the pay period ended December 15, 20—, is calculated as shown.

Unemployment Taxable Earnings	×	State Unemployment Tax Rate	=	State Unemployment Tax
$183.75	×	5.4%	=	$9.92

JOURNALIZING EMPLOYER PAYROLL TAXES

1. Date **2.** Account Debited **3.** Memorandum Number **4.** Amount Debited

PAGE 24 JOURNAL PAGE 24

	DATE		ACCOUNT TITLE	DOC. NO.	POST. REF.	GENERAL DEBIT (1)	GENERAL CREDIT (2)	CASH DEBIT (10)	CASH CREDIT (11)	
28		15	*Payroll Taxes Expense*	*M63*		315 72				28
29			*Social Security Tax Payable*				247 26			29
30			*Medicare Tax Payable*				57 07			30
31			*Unemployment Tax Payable—Federal*				1 47			31
32			*Unemployment Tax Payable—State*				9 92			32

5. Accounts Credited **6.** Amounts Credited

Employer payroll taxes are paid to the government at a later date. However, the liability is incurred when salaries are paid. Therefore, the transaction to record employer payroll taxes expense is journalized on the same date the payroll is journalized. The salary expense and the employer payroll taxes expense are, therefore, both recorded in the same accounting period.

December 15. Recorded employer payroll taxes expense, $315.72, for the semimonthly pay period ended December 15. Taxes owed are: social security tax, $247.26; Medicare tax, $57.07; federal unemployment tax, $1.47; state unemployment tax, $9.92. Memorandum No. 63.

Payroll Taxes Expense is debited for $315.72 to show the increase in the balance of this expense account. Four liability accounts are credited to show the increase in payroll tax liabilities.

Payroll Taxes Expense	
315.72	

Social Security Tax Payable	
	247.26

Medicare Tax Payable	
	57.07

Unemployment Tax Payable—Federal	
	1.47

Unemployment Tax Payable—State	
	9.92

Amounts recorded in the General columns of the journal are posted individually to general ledger accounts. The same procedures are followed to post this journal entry to the appropriate accounts as were described in Chapter 12.

STEPS Journalizing employer payroll taxes

1. Write the date, *15,* in the Date column.
2. Write the title of the expense account debited, *Payroll Taxes Expense,* in the Account Title column.
3. Write the memorandum number, *M63,* in the Doc. No. column.
4. Write the debit amount, *$315.72,* in the General Debit column.
5. Write the titles of the liability accounts credited, *Social Security Tax Payable, Medicare Tax Payable, Unemployment Tax Payable—Federal,* and *Unemployment Tax Payable—State,* on the next four lines of the Account Title column.
6. Write the credit amounts, *$247.26, $57.07, $1.47,* and *$9.92,* respectively, in the General Credit column.

TERMS REVIEW

federal unemployment tax

state unemployment tax

AUDIT YOUR UNDERSTANDING

1. What is the tax rate Omni Import must pay on employees for each of the following taxes: social security, Medicare, federal unemployment, and state unemployment?
2. What is the amount of each employee's earnings that is subject to federal and state unemployment taxes at Omni Import?

WORK TOGETHER

Recording employer payroll taxes

Payroll information taken from employee earnings records is given below. A form and journal page are provided in the *Working Papers.* Your instructor will guide you through the following examples.

Employee Name	Accumulated Earnings, April 30	Total Earnings for May 1–15 Pay Period
Beltran, Tamela C.	$5,100.00	$637.50
Cintron, Irma V.	7,350.00	920.00

3. Calculate the amount of earnings subject to unemployment taxes. Unemployment taxes are owed on the first $7,000.00 of earnings for each employee.
4. Calculate the amount of employer payroll taxes owed for the May 1–15 pay period. Use the employer payroll tax rates shown in this chapter.
5. Journalize the employer's payroll taxes for the May 1–15 pay period on May 15 of the current year. Use journal page 10 and Memorandum No. 46.

ON YOUR OWN

Recording employer payroll taxes

Payroll information taken from employee earnings records is given below. A form and journal page are provided in the *Working Papers.* Work independently to complete these problems.

Employee Name	Accumulated Earnings, May 31	Total Earnings for June 1–15 Pay Period
Cowaski, Renee Y.	$ 5,730.00	$ 720.00
LeCrone, Mark J.	10,500.00	1,320.00

6. Calculate the amount of earnings subject to unemployment taxes. Unemployment taxes are owed on the first $7,000.00 of earnings for each employee.
7. Calculate the amount of employer payroll taxes owed for the June 1–15 pay period. Use the employer payroll tax rates shown in this chapter.
8. Journalize the employer's payroll taxes for the June 1–15 pay period on June 15 of the current year. Use journal page 12 and Memorandum No. 52.

14-3 Reporting Withholding and Payroll Taxes

EMPLOYER ANNUAL REPORT TO EMPLOYEES OF TAXES WITHHELD

a Control number	22222	Void ☐	For OfficialUse Only ▶ OMB No. 1545-0008	

b Employer's identification number 31-0429632	**1** Wages, tips, other compensation 24,843.00	**2** Federal income tax withheld 1,152.00
c Employer's name, address, and ZIP code Omni Import 1374 Parklane Ashton, RI 02805	**3** Social security wages 24,843.00	**4** Social security tax withheld 1,614.80
	5 Medicare wages and tips 24,843.00	**6** Medicare tax withheld 372.65
	7 Social security tips	**8** Allocated tips
d Employee's social security number 450-70-6432	**9** Advanced EIC payment	**10** Dependent care benefits
e Employee's name (first, middle initial, last) Rick E. Selby	**11** Nonqualified plans	**12** Benefits included in box 1
1625 Northland Drive Ashton, RI 02805	**13** See Instrs. for box 13	**14** Other
f Employee's address and ZIP code	**15** Statutory employee ☐ Deceased ☐ Pension plan ☐ Legal rep. ☐ Hshld. emp. ☐ Subtotal ☐ Deferred compensation ☐	

16 State	Employer's state I.D. No.	17 State wages, tips, etc.	18 State income tax	19 Locality name	20 Local wages, tips, etc.	21 Local income tax

39-1754529 Department of the Treasury—Internal Revenue Service
For Paperwork Reduction Act Notice, see separate instructions.

Form **W-2 Wage and Tax Statement 20—**

Copy A For Social Security Administration

Each employer who withholds income tax, social security tax, and Medicare tax from employee earnings must furnish each employee with an annual report of these withholdings. The report shows total year's earnings and the amounts withheld for taxes for an employee. These amounts are obtained from the employee earnings records. The report is prepared on the Internal Revenue Service Form W-2, Wage and Tax Statement. The Form W-2 prepared by Omni Import for Rick E. Selby is shown.

Employers are required to furnish Form W-2 to each employee by January 31 of the next year. If an employee ends employment before December 31, Form W-2 must be furnished within 30 days of the last date of employment.

Four copies (A to D) of Form W-2 are prepared for each employee. Copies B and C are given to the employee. The employee attaches Copy B to a personal federal income tax return and keeps Copy C for a personal record. The employer sends Copy A to the Social Security Administration and keeps Copy D for the business's records.

Businesses in states with state income tax must prepare additional copies of Form W-2. The employee attaches the additional copy to the personal state income tax return.

EMPLOYER'S QUARTERLY FEDERAL TAX RETURN

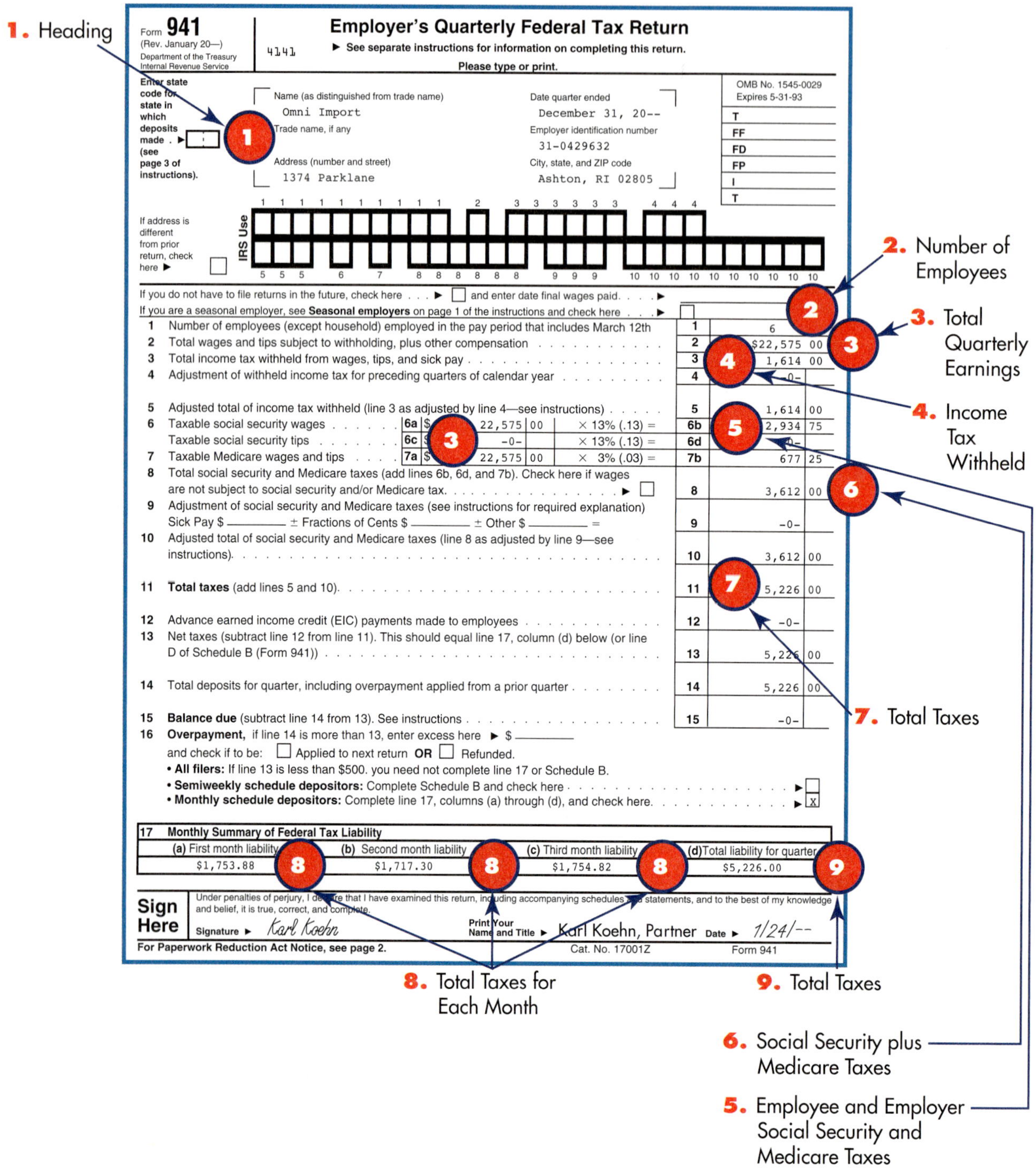

Form **941** (Rev. January 20—) Department of the Treasury Internal Revenue Service 4141

Employer's Quarterly Federal Tax Return

▶ See separate instructions for information on completing this return.

Please type or print.

Enter state code for state in which deposits made . ▶ (see page 3 of instructions).

Name (as distinguished from trade name)	Omni Import	Date quarter ended	December 31, 20--
Trade name, if any		Employer identification number	31-0429632
Address (number and street)	1374 Parklane	City, state, and ZIP code	Ashton, RI 02805

OMB No. 1545-0029 Expires 5-31-93

T / FF / FD / FP / I / T

If address is different from prior return, check here ▶ ☐ IRS Use

If you do not have to file returns in the future, check here . . . ▶ ☐ and enter date final wages paid. . . . ▶

If you are a seasonal employer, see **Seasonal employers** on page 1 of the instructions and check here . . . ▶ ☐

1	Number of employees (except household) employed in the pay period that includes March 12th	1	6
2	Total wages and tips subject to withholding, plus other compensation	2	$22,575 00
3	Total income tax withheld from wages, tips, and sick pay	3	1,614 00
4	Adjustment of withheld income tax for preceding quarters of calendar year	4	-0-
5	Adjusted total of income tax withheld (line 3 as adjusted by line 4—see instructions)	5	1,614 00
6	Taxable social security wages . . . 6a $ 22,575 00 × 13% (.13) =	6b	2,934 75
	Taxable social security tips . . . 6c $ -0- × 13% (.13) =	6d	-0-
7	Taxable Medicare wages and tips . . . 7a $ 22,575 00 × 3% (.03) =	7b	677 25
8	Total social security and Medicare taxes (add lines 6b, 6d, and 7b). Check here if wages are not subject to social security and/or Medicare tax. ▶ ☐	8	3,612 00
9	Adjustment of social security and Medicare taxes (see instructions for required explanation) Sick Pay $ ___ ± Fractions of Cents $ ___ ± Other $ ___ =	9	-0-
10	Adjusted total of social security and Medicare taxes (line 8 as adjusted by line 9—see instructions).	10	3,612 00
11	**Total taxes** (add lines 5 and 10).	11	5,226 00
12	Advance earned income credit (EIC) payments made to employees	12	-0-
13	Net taxes (subtract line 12 from line 11). This should equal line 17, column (d) below (or line D of Schedule B (Form 941))	13	5,226 00
14	Total deposits for quarter, including overpayment applied from a prior quarter	14	5,226 00
15	**Balance due** (subtract line 14 from 13). See instructions	15	-0-
16	**Overpayment,** if line 14 is more than 13, enter excess here ▶ $ ___ and check if to be: ☐ Applied to next return **OR** ☐ Refunded.		

- **All filers:** If line 13 is less than $500. you need not complete line 17 or Schedule B.
- **Semiweekly schedule depositors:** Complete Schedule B and check here ▶ ☐
- **Monthly schedule depositors:** Complete line 17, columns (a) through (d), and check here. ▶ ☒

17 Monthly Summary of Federal Tax Liability

(a) First month liability	(b) Second month liability	(c) Third month liability	(d) Total liability for quarter
$1,753.88	$1,717.30	$1,754.82	$5,226.00

Sign Here Under penalties of perjury, I declare that I have examined this return, including accompanying schedules and statements, and to the best of my knowledge and belief, it is true, correct, and complete.

Signature ▶ *Karl Koehn* Print Your Name and Title ▶ Karl Koehn, Partner Date ▶ 1/24/--

For Paperwork Reduction Act Notice, see page 2. Cat. No. 17001Z Form 941

PREPARING EMPLOYER'S QUARTERLY FEDERAL TAX RETURN

Each employer is required by law to periodically report the payroll taxes withheld from employee salaries and the employer payroll taxes due the government. Some reports are submitted quarterly and others, annually.

Each employer must file a quarterly federal tax return showing the federal income tax, social security tax, and Medicare tax due the government. This information is submitted on Form 941, Employer's Quarterly Federal Tax Return. Form 941 is filed before the last day of the month following the end of a quarter. Omni Import's Form 941 for the quarter ended December 31 is shown on the previous page. The information needed to prepare Form 941 is obtained from employee earnings records.

STEPS Preparing an employer's quarterly federal tax return

1. Enter company name, address, employer identification number, date quarter ended, and state code in the heading section of Form 941.
2. Enter number of employees, *6,* on line 1 of Form 941.
3. Enter total quarterly earnings, *$22,575.00,* on line 2. This amount is the sum of the fourth quarter total earnings of all employees. Total earnings, *$22,575.00,* is also recorded on lines 6a and 7a.
4. Enter the income tax withheld, *$1,614.00,* on line 3. The amount is the total of the fourth quarter federal income tax withheld from all employees. The same amount is entered on line 5.
5. Enter the quarterly employee and employer social security taxes, *$2,934.75,* and Medicare taxes, *$677.25,* on lines 6b and 7b, respectively. The taxes due are calculated as shown.

	Total Earnings	×	Tax Rate	=	Tax
Social Security	$22,575.00	×	13%	=	$2,934.75
Medicare	$22,575.00	×	3%	=	$ 677.25

The 13% tax rate is the sum of the *employee* 6.5% and the *employer* 6.5% social security tax rates. The 3% tax rate is the sum of the *employee* 1.5% and the *employer* 1.5% Medicare tax rates.

6. Enter the total social security tax plus Medicare tax, *$3,612.00* ($2,934.75 + $677.25 = $3,612.00), on line 8. Since Omni has no adjustment to its taxes, the total is also entered on line 10.
7. Enter the total taxes, *$5,226.00,* on lines 11 and 13. Omni is required to pay the federal government the sum of the social security tax, Medicare tax, and federal income tax withheld.
8. Enter on lines 17a, 17b, and 17c the total amounts of employee income tax withheld and employee and employer social security and Medicare taxes for each month of the quarter. For the month of December, the amount of taxes owed is calculated as shown and recorded on line 17c.

	Federal Income Tax Withheld	+	Employee Social Security and Medicare Tax	+	Employer Social Security and Medicare Tax	=	Federal Tax Liability
Dec. 1–15	$273.00	+	$304.33	+	$304.33	=	$ 881.66
Dec. 16–31	$269.00	+	$302.08	+	$302.08	=	$ 873.16
Totals	$542.00	+	$606.41	+	$606.41	=	$1,754.82

9. Enter the total quarterly withholding and payroll taxes, *$5,226.00,* on line 17d. This total is the sum of the three monthly totals reported on line 17 ($1,753.88 + $1,717.30 + $1,754.82 = $5,226.00).

DO NOT STAPLE

a Control number	33333	For Official Use Only ► OMB No. 1545-0008

b Kind of Payer ► 941 [X] Military [ ] 943 [ ] CT-1 [ ] Hshld. [ ] Medicare govt. emp. [ ]	1 Wages, tips, other compensation 89,400.00	2 Federal income tax withheld 6,416.00
	3 Social security wages 89,400.00	4 Social security tax withheld 5,811.00
c Total number of statements / d Establishment number	5 Medicare wages and tips 89,400.00	6 Medicare tax withheld 1,341.00
e Employer's identification number 31-0429632	7 Social security tips	8 Allocated tips
f Employer's name Omni Import	9 Advance EIC payments	10 Dependent care benefits
1374 Parklane Ashton, RI 02805	11 Nonqualified plans	12 Deferred compensation
	13 Adjusted total social security wages and tips 89,400.00	
g Employer's address and ZIP code	14 Adjusted total Medicare wages and tips 89,400.00	
h Other EIN used this year	15 Income tax withheld by third-party payer	
i Employer's state I.D. No.		

Under penalties of perjury, I declare that I have examined this return and accompanying documents, and, to the best of my knowledge and belief, they are true, correct, and complete.

Signature ► *Karl Koehn* Title ► *Partner* Date ► *2/27/--*

Telephone number *(401) 555-9368*

Form **W-3 Transmittal of Income and Tax Statements 20—** Department of the Treasury Internal Revenue Service

Form W-3, Transmittal of Wage and Tax Statements, is sent to the Social Security Administration by February 28 each year. Form W-3 reports the previous year's earnings and payroll taxes withheld for all employees. Attached to Form W-3 is Copy A of each employee Form W-2. Employers with more than 250 employees must send the information to the Internal Revenue Service in computer files rather than the actual Forms W-2 and W-3.

At the end of a calendar year, employers must also report to the federal and state governments a summary of all earnings paid to employees during the twelve months.

Global Perspective

International Quality Standards

The quality of products is a major concern for industry, especially when trading those products among nations. In order for some products to be used in other nations, they must be standardized. In this sense, a *standard* is a technical specification or other precise criteria used consistently in the production of a product.

Companies who intend to sell their products globally must produce them in compliance with the standards set for the industry. International standardization has been established for many fields, including information processing and communications, textiles, packaging, energy production, shipbuilding, and banking and financial services. Standardization will continue to grow in importance for all sectors of business activity.

AUDIT YOUR UNDERSTANDING

1. When must employers furnish a W-2 statement to their employees?
2. What taxes are included in the quarterly federal tax return filed by the employer?

WORK TOGETHER

Reporting withholding and payroll taxes

A Form 941, Employer's Quarterly Federal Tax Return, is given in the *Working Papers*. Your instructor will guide you through the following example. The following data is for Digital Supplies.

Date Paid	Total Earnings	Federal Income Tax Withheld	Employee Social Security Tax Withheld	Employee Medicare Tax Withheld
Jan. 31	$10,440.00	$1,148.00	$678.60	$156.60
Feb. 28	10,950.00	1,204.00	711.75	164.25
Mar. 31	12,600.00	1,386.00	819.00	189.00

a. Company address: 625 Sandpiper Street, Ormond Beach, Florida 32074-4060
b. Employer identification number: 70-7818356
c. Number of employees: 6

3. Prepare a Form 941 for Digital Supplies for the first quarter of the current year. Use the preparation date of April 24. Sign your name as a partner of the company.

ON YOUR OWN

Reporting withholding and payroll taxes

A Form 941, Employer's Quarterly Federal Tax Return, is given in the *Working Papers*. Work independently to complete this problem. The following data is for Digital Supplies. Company address, employer identification number, and number of employees are the same as in Work Together.

Date Paid	Total Earnings	Federal Income Tax Withheld	Employee Social Security Tax Withheld	Employee Medicare Tax Withheld
Apr. 30	$11,600.00	$1,276.00	$754.00	$174.00
May 31	12,160.00	1,338.00	790.40	182.40
June 30	13,986.00	1,538.00	909.09	209.79

4. Prepare a Form 941 for Digital Supplies for the second quarter of the current year. Use the preparation date of July 22. Sign your name as a partner of the company.

14-4 Paying Withholding and Payroll Taxes

PAYING THE LIABILITY FOR EMPLOYEE INCOME TAX, SOCIAL SECURITY TAX, AND MEDICARE TAX

Employers must pay to the federal, state, and local governments all payroll taxes withheld from employee earnings as well as the employer payroll taxes. The frequency of payments is determined by the amount owed.

Frequency and method of payment of withheld employees' federal income tax, social security tax, and Medicare tax plus employer's social security tax and Medicare tax is determined by the total amount of tax paid each year. If the total amount paid in the previous four quarters is $50,000.00 or less, a business is classified as a monthly schedule depositor. A monthly schedule depositor must pay the total amount due to an authorized financial institution by the 15th day of the following month accompanied by Form 8109, Federal Tax Deposit Coupon. A semiweekly schedule depositor must deposit amounts accumulated on salary payments made on Saturday, Sunday, Monday, or Tuesday by the following Friday. For salary payments made on Wednesday, Thursday, or Friday, payment must be made by the following Wednesday. Payment must be made through an authorized agent to the Internal Revenue Service by Electronic Federal Tax Payment System (EFTPS).

There are two exceptions to the standard tax payment schedules: (1) If less than $500.00 tax liability is accumulated during a three-month quarter, the deposit may be paid at the end of the month following the end of the quarter. (2) If a tax liability of $100,000.00 or more is accumulated on any day, the amount must be deposited on the next banking day.

Omni Import is classified as a monthly depositor. So the payroll taxes are deposited with a local authorized financial institution by the 15th day of the following month accompanied by Form 8109.

FYI

Methods of paying payroll taxes described in this chapter were in effect when this textbook was written. Businesses with payroll tax liabilities of more than $20,000.00 in 1997 were required to pay electronically using the Electronic Federal Tax Payment System by 1999. There will probably be a time when all businesses will be required to pay payroll taxes electronically.

REMEMBER

For monthly schedule depositor businesses, a deposit coupon, Form 8109, must accompany payment of employee income tax, social security, and Medicare tax to the federal government. For semiweekly schedule depositor businesses, payment must be made electronically through an automated clearing agent.

FORM 8109, FEDERAL DEPOSIT COUPON

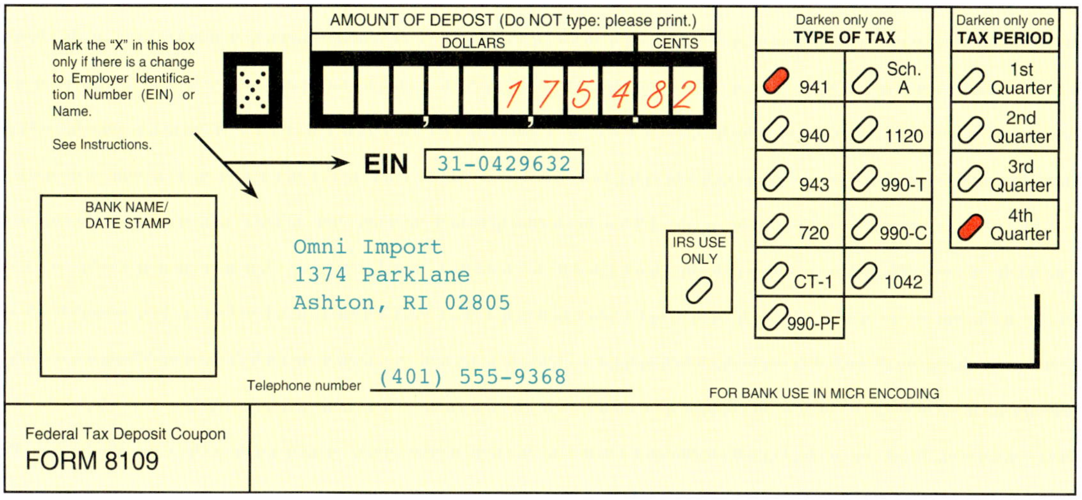

Mark the "X" in this box only if there is a change to Employer Identification Number (EIN) or Name.

See Instructions.

AMOUNT OF DEPOSIT (Do NOT type: please print.)

DOLLARS	CENTS
1,754	82

EIN 31-0429632

BANK NAME/ DATE STAMP

Omni Import
1374 Parklane
Ashton, RI 02805

Telephone number (401) 555-9368

IRS USE ONLY

Darken only one TYPE OF TAX: 941 (darkened), Sch. A, 940, 1120, 943, 990-T, 720, 990-C, CT-1, 1042, 990-PF

Darken only one TAX PERIOD: 1st Quarter, 2nd Quarter, 3rd Quarter, 4th Quarter (darkened)

FOR BANK USE IN MICR ENCODING

Federal Tax Deposit Coupon
FORM 8109

In December, Omni Import withheld $542.00 from employee salaries for federal income taxes. The December liability for social security tax is $985.40 and for Medicare tax is $227.42. These amounts include both the employer share and the amounts withheld from employees. Omni's federal tax payment, $1,754.82, is sent January 15 to an authorized bank with Form 8109 as shown.

The type of tax—federal income, social security, and Medicare taxes—is identified by marking the 941 circle. These taxes are reported to the government using Form 941. The calendar quarter is identified on the right side of the form.

FYI

Tax rates change periodically. Always check the most current tax information before calculating an amount for any tax.

REMEMBER

Social security tax and Medicare tax are the only payroll taxes paid by both the employer and employee. A business pays the same amount of social security tax and Medicare tax as the amount withheld from employees.

JOURNALIZING PAYMENT OF LIABILITY FOR EMPLOYEE INCOME TAX, SOCIAL SECURITY TAX, AND MEDICARE TAX

PAGE 27 JOURNAL PAGE 27

	DATE	ACCOUNT TITLE	DOC. NO.	POST. REF.	1 GENERAL DEBIT	2 GENERAL CREDIT	10 CASH DEBIT	11 CASH CREDIT	
25	15	*Employee Income Tax Payable*	C330		542 00			1 754 82	25
26		*Social Security Tax Payable*			985 40				26
27		*Medicare Tax Payable*			227 42				27

1. Date **2.** Accounts Debited **3.** Check Number **4.** Debit Amounts **5.** Credit Amount

January 15. Paid cash for liability for employee income tax, $542.00; social security tax, $985.40; and Medicare tax, $227.42; total, $1,754.82. Check No. 330.

The balances of the liability accounts are reduced by this transaction. Therefore, Employee Income Tax Payable is debited for $542.00. Social Security Tax Payable is debited for $985.40. Medicare Tax Payable is debited for $227.42. The balance of Cash is decreased by a credit for the total payment, $1,754.82.

Employee Income Tax Payable	
542.00	

Social Security Tax Payable	
985.40	

Medicare Tax Payable	
227.42	

Cash	
	1,754.82

FYI

Semimonthly pay periods are paid twice a month. Biweekly pay periods are paid every two weeks.

STEPS

Journalizing a payment of liability for employee income tax, social security tax, and Medicare tax

1. Write the date, *15,* in the Date column.
2. Write the titles of the three accounts debited, *Employee Income Tax Payable, Social Security Tax Payable,* and *Medicare Tax Payable,* in the Account Title column.
3. Write the check number, *C330,* in the Doc. No. column.
4. Write the three debit amounts, *$542.00, $985.40,* and *$227.42,* in the General Debit column.
5. Write the amount of the credit to Cash, *$1,754.82,* in the Cash Credit column.

PAYING THE LIABILITY FOR FEDERAL UNEMPLOYMENT TAX

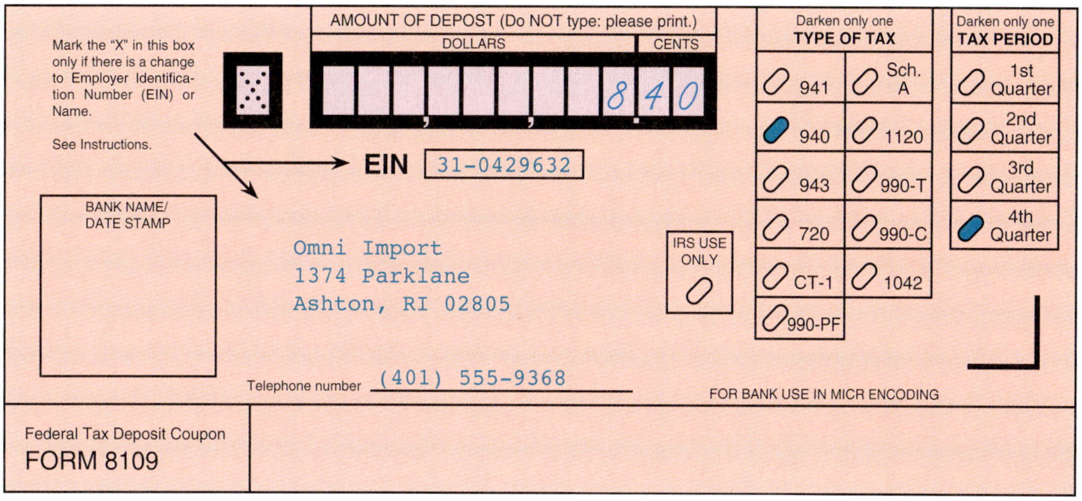

Mark the "X" in this box only if there is a change to Employer Identification Number (EIN) or Name.

See Instructions.

AMOUNT OF DEPOST (Do NOT type: please print.)

DOLLARS	CENTS
8	40

EIN 31-0429632

BANK NAME/ DATE STAMP

Omni Import
1374 Parklane
Ashton, RI 02805

Telephone number (401) 555-9368

IRS USE ONLY

Darken only one TYPE OF TAX: 941, Sch. A, 940 (marked), 1120, 943, 990-T, 720, 990-C, CT-1, 1042, 990-PF

Darken only one TAX PERIOD: 1st Quarter, 2nd Quarter, 3rd Quarter, 4th Quarter (marked)

FOR BANK USE IN MICR ENCODING

Federal Tax Deposit Coupon
FORM 8109

Federal unemployment insurance is paid by the end of the month following each quarter if the liability amount is more than $100. However, all unemployment tax liabilities outstanding at the end of a calendar year should be paid. Federal unemployment tax is paid to the federal government by sending the check to an authorized bank. The payment for federal unemployment tax is similar to the one required for income tax, social security tax, and Medicare tax. Form 8109, Federal Tax Deposit Coupon accompanies the unemployment tax payment. A payment is made each quarter that the liability exceeds $100.00, but no report is due until the end of the year.

Omni's federal unemployment tax liability at the end of December 31 is $8.40. Omni's Form 8109 for the fourth quarter is shown.

The type of tax, federal unemployment tax, is identified by marking the 940 circle since this tax is reported to the government using Form 940. The calendar quarter is identified on the right side of the form.

JOURNALIZING PAYMENT OF LIABILITY FOR FEDERAL UNEMPLOYMENT TAX

PAGE *28* JOURNAL PAGE *28*

	DATE	ACCOUNT TITLE	DOC. NO.	POST. REF.	GENERAL DEBIT (1)	GENERAL CREDIT (2)	CASH DEBIT (10)	CASH CREDIT (11)	
27	*31*	*Unemployment Tax Payable—Federal*	*C343*		*8 40*			*8 40*	27
28									28

1. Date **2.** Account Debited **3.** Check Number **4.** Debit Amount **5.** Credit Amount

January 31. Paid cash for federal unemployment tax liability for quarter ended December 31, $8.40. Check No. 343.

Unemployment Tax Payable—Federal	
8.40	

Cash	
	8.40

The balance of the liability account is reduced by this transaction. Therefore, Unemployment Tax Payable—Federal is debited for $8.40. The balance of the asset account, Cash, is decreased by a credit for the payment, $8.40.

STEPS: Journalizing a payment of liability for federal unemployment tax

1. Write the date, *31*, in the Date column.
2. Write the title of the account debited, *Unemployment Tax Payable—Federal*, in the Account Title column.
3. Write the check number, *C343*, in the Doc. No. column.
4. Write the debit amount, *$8.40*, in the General Debit column.
5. Write the amount of the credit to Cash, *$8.40*, in the Cash Credit column.

JOURNALIZING PAYMENT OF LIABILITY FOR STATE UNEMPLOYMENT TAX

PAGE *28* JOURNAL PAGE *28*

	DATE	ACCOUNT TITLE	DOC. NO.	POST. REF.	GENERAL DEBIT (1)	GENERAL CREDIT (2)	CASH DEBIT (10)	CASH CREDIT (11)	
28	*31*	*Unemployment Tax Payable—State*	*C344*		*56 70*			*56 70*	27
									28

2. Account Debited **3.** Check Number **4.** Debit Amount **5.** Credit Amount

...quirements for reporting and paying ...ployment taxes vary. In general, ...re required to pay the state ...ent tax during the month following ...r quarter.

January 31. Paid cash for state unemployment tax liability for quarter ended December 31, $56.70. Check No. 344.

AUDIT YOUR UNDERSTANDING

1. For a monthly schedule depositor, when are payroll taxes paid to the federal government?
2. What are two different uses for Form 8109?

WORK TOGETHER

Paying withholding and payroll taxes

A journal page is provided in the *Working Papers.* Your instructor will guide you through the following examples. The following payroll data is for Digital Supplies for the monthly pay period ended March 31 of the current year.

Date Paid	Federal Income Tax Withheld	Employee Social Security Tax Withheld	Employee Medicare Tax Withheld
Mar. 31	$1,386.00	$819.00	$189.00

Credit balances on March 31 for the unemployment tax accounts for the first quarter are as follows: Unemployment Tax Payable—Federal, $100.80; Unemployment Tax Payable—State, $680.40. Digital Supplies pays both unemployment taxes each quarter, regardless of the amount owed.

3. Prepare a journal entry for payment of the withheld taxes. Digital Supplies is classified as a monthly schedule depositor. Date journal page 14 on the day taxes are due to the federal government. Check No. 383.
4. Prepare journal entries for payment of the federal and state unemployment taxes liability. State taxes are due on the same day as federal taxes. Check Nos. 401 and 402.

ON YOUR OWN

Paying withholding and payroll taxes

A journal page is provided in the *Working Papers.* Work independently to complete these problems. The following payroll data is for Digital Supplies for the monthly pay period ended June 30 of the current year.

Date Paid	Federal Income Tax Withheld	Employee Social Security Tax Withheld	Employee Medicare Tax Withheld
June 30	$1,538.00	$909.09	$209.79

Credit balances on June 30 for the unemployment tax accounts for the second quarter are as follows: Unemployment Tax Payable—Federal, $108.48; Unemployment Tax Payable—State, $732.24. Digital Supplies pays both unemployment taxes each quarter, regardless of the amount owed.

5. Prepare a journal entry for payment of the withheld taxes. Date journal page 18 on the day taxes are due to the federal government. Check No. 496.
6. Prepare journal entries for payment of the federal and state unemployment taxes liability. State taxes are due on the same day as federal taxes. Check Nos. 515 and 516.

CHAPTER 14 SUMMARY

After completing this chapter, you can

1. Define important accounting terms related to payroll accounting, taxes, and reports.
2. Identify accounting concepts and practices related to payroll accounting, taxes, and reports.
3. Analyze payroll transactions and record a payroll.
4. Record employer payroll taxes.
5. Prepare selected payroll tax reports.
6. Pay and record withholding and payroll taxes.

EXPLORE ACCOUNTING

NET INCOME VS. TAXABLE INCOME

Financial statements should provide important information that is accurate, reliable, comparable, and consistent. Over the years, a set of principles and concepts for maintaining accounting records and preparing financial statements has been developed. These guidelines are known as Generally Accepted Accounting Principles (GAAP). Most businesses use GAAP in preparing their financial statements and determining their net income.

The Internal Revenue Service (IRS) is responsible for collecting money to operate the federal government. Federal income taxes are calculated as a percentage of business or individual income. To accomplish its task, the IRS prepares Internal Revenue Service Regulations.

The objectives of the accounting profession and business community, however, are not necessarily the same as those of the federal government and the IRS. For example, a GAAP concept, Matching Expenses with Revenue, requires that the cost of business equipment be allocated over the usable life of the equipment. However, to encourage businesses to replace equipment more rapidly, IRS Regulations may permit the cost of equipment to be allocated more rapidly. Thus, in a certain year the expense for allocating cost would be greater for tax purposes than for financial reporting purposes. These types of differences create different amounts reported as net income for financial reporting purposes and for tax reporting purposes.

Thus, most businesses follow GAAP in preparing their financial statements but must follow IRS Regulations in preparing their tax returns. As a result, net income on financial statements generally differs from taxable income reported on tax returns.

Research: Examine several company annual reports. Study the financial statements and the notes connected with those statements. Is there any information indicating a difference between net income reported on the financial statements and taxable income for tax purposes? What are they, if any?

14-1 APPLICATION PROBLEM
Recording a payroll

Dana's payroll register has the following totals for two semimonthly pay periods, July 1–15 and July 16–31 of the current year.

Period	Total Earnings	Deductions					Net Pay
		Federal Income Tax	Social Security Tax	Medicare Tax	Other	Total	
July 1–15.	$6,970.00	$766.00	$453.05	$104.55	B $180.00	$1,503.60	$5,466.40
July 16–31	6,040.00	664.00	392.60	90.60	B 150.00	1,297.20	4,742.80
Other Deductions: B—U.S. Savings Bonds							

Instructions:

Journalize payment of the two payrolls on page 15 of the journal given in the *Working Papers*. The first payroll was paid by Check No. 547 on July 15 of the current year. The second payroll was paid by Check No. 568 on July 31 of the current year.

14-2 APPLICATION PROBLEM
Recording employer payroll taxes

Malone's selected payroll information for the two semimonthly pay periods, April 1–15 and April 16–30 of the current year, are given. Forms and a journal are given in the *Working Papers*.

Employee Name	Accumulated Earnings, March 31	Total Earnings for April 1–15 Pay Period	Total Earnings for April 16–30 Pay Period
Bolser, Frank T.	$4,860.00	$ 810.00	$ 795.00
Denham, Beth R.	5,670.00	945.00	980.00
Harjo, Teresa S.	7,500.00	1,250.00	1,250.00
Knutzen, John L.	3,720.00	620.00	635.00
Prescott, Laura F.	4,560.00	760.00	740.00
Schmidt, Ian T.	6,900.00	1,150.00	1,125.00

Employer payroll tax rates are as follows: social security, 6.5%; Medicare, 1.5%; federal unemployment, 0.8%; state unemployment, 5.4%. Unemployment taxes are owed on the first $7,000.00 of earnings for each employee.

Instructions:

1. Calculate the amount of earnings subject to unemployment taxes for the April 1–15 pay period.
2. Calculate the employer payroll tax amounts for the April 1–15 pay period.
3. Journalize the employer payroll taxes on page 16 of a journal. Use the date of April 15 of the current year. The source document is Memorandum No. 69.
4. Calculate the employer payroll taxes for the April 16–30 pay period. Calculate April 15 accumulated earnings by adding total earnings for the April 1–15 pay period to the March 31 accumulated earnings.
5. Journalize the employer payroll taxes on page 16 of a journal. Use the date of April 30 of the current year. The source document is Memorandum No. 76.

14-3 APPLICATION PROBLEM
Reporting withholding and payroll taxes

The following payroll data is for Eagle Toys for the second quarter of the current year.

Date Paid	Total Earnings	Federal Income Tax Withheld	Employee Social Security Tax Withheld	Employee Medicare Tax Withheld
Apr. 30	$ 9,166.00	$1,008.00	$595.79	$137.49
May 31	10,224.00	1,125.00	664.56	153.36
June 30	9,872.00	1,086.00	641.68	148.08

Additional data:

1. Company address: 784 MacDonald Street, Mesa, AZ 85201
2. Employer identification number: 80-7818356
3. Number of employees: 5
4. Federal tax payments have been made on May 15, June 15, and July 15.

Instructions:

Prepare the Form 941, Employer's Quarterly Federal Tax Return, given in the *Working Papers*. Use the date July 21. Sign your name as a partner of the company.

14-4 APPLICATION PROBLEM
Paying withholding and payroll taxes

The following payroll data is for Zimmerman Company for the first quarter of the current year.

Period	Total Earnings	Federal Income Tax Withheld
March	$17,552.00	$1,728.00
First Quarter	$52,210.00	—

In addition, total earnings are subject to 6.5% employee and 6.5% employer social security tax, plus 1.5% employee and 1.5% employer Medicare tax. The federal unemployment tax rate is 0.8% and the state unemployment tax rate is 5.4% of total earnings. No total earnings have exceeded the tax base for calculating unemployment taxes.

Instructions:

1. Calculate the appropriate liability amount of social security and Medicare taxes for March. Journalize the payment of the withheld taxes on page 8 of the journal given in the *Working Papers*. The taxes were paid by Check No. 813 on April 15 of the current year.
2. Calculate the appropriate federal unemployment tax liability for the first quarter. Journalize payment of this liability in the journal. The tax was paid by Check No. 830 on April 30 of the current year.
3. Calculate the appropriate state unemployment tax liability for the first quarter. Journalize payment of this liability in the journal. The tax was paid by Check No. 831 on April 30 of the current year.

14-5 MASTERY PROBLEM
Journalizing payroll transactions

Travis Athletics completed payroll transactions during the period April 1 to May 15 of the current year. Payroll tax rates are as follows: social security, 6.5%; Medicare, 1.5%; federal unemployment, 0.8%; state unemployment, 5.4%. The company buys savings bonds for employees as accumulated withholdings reach the necessary amount to purchase a bond. No total earnings have exceeded the tax base for calculating unemployment taxes.

Instructions:

1. Journalize the following transactions on page 12 of the journal given in the *Working Papers*. Source documents are abbreviated as follows: check, C, and memorandum, M.

Transactions:

Apr. 15. Paid cash for liability for employee income tax, $948.00; social security tax, $1,120.60; and Medicare tax, $258.60; total, $2,327.20. C331.

15. Paid cash for semimonthly payroll, $3,618.20 (total payroll, $4,560.00, less deductions: employee income tax, $502.00; social security tax, $296.40; Medicare tax, $68.40; U.S. Savings Bonds, $75.00). C332.

15. Recorded employer payroll taxes expense. M22.

15. Paid cash for U.S. Savings Bonds for employees, $375.00. C333.

30. Paid cash for semimonthly payroll, $3,733.84 (total payroll, $4,702.00, less deductions: employee income tax, $517.00; social security tax, $305.63; Medicare tax, $70.53; U.S. Savings Bonds, $75.00). C351.

30. Recorded employer payroll taxes expense. M26.

30. Paid cash for federal unemployment tax liability for quarter ended March 31, $214.89. C352.

30. Paid cash for state unemployment tax liability for quarter ended March 31, $1,450.51. C353.

2. Prove and rule journal page 12.
3. Journalize the following transactions on page 13 of the journal.

Transactions:

May 15. Paid cash for liability for employee income tax, $1,019.00; social security tax, $1,204.06; and Medicare tax, $277.86; total, $2,500.92. C380.

15. Paid cash for semimonthly payroll, $3,491.75 (total payroll, $4,403.00, less deductions: employee income tax, $484.00; social security tax, $286.20; Medicare tax, $66.05; U.S. Savings Bonds, $75.00). C381.

15. Recorded employer payroll taxes expense. M33.

4. Prove and rule journal page 13.

14-6 CHALLENGE PROBLEM
Journalizing and posting payroll transactions

Dozier Spring Water completed payroll transactions during the period January 1 to April 30 of the current year. Payroll tax rates are as follows: social security, 6.5%; Medicare, 1.5%; federal unemployment, 0.8%; and state unemployment, 5.4%. The company buys savings bonds for employees as the accumulated withholdings reach the necessary amount to purchase a bond. No total earnings have exceeded the tax base for calculating unemployment taxes.

The balances in the general ledger as of January 1 of the current year are recorded in the *Working Papers*.

Chart of Accounts

Account Number	Account Title
2120	Employee Income Tax Payable
2130	Social Security Tax Payable
2140	Medicare Tax Payable

Account Number	Account Title
2150	Unemployment Tax Payable—Federal
2160	Unemployment Tax Payable—State
2180	U.S. Savings Bonds Payable
6150	Payroll Taxes Expense
6170	Salary Expense

Instructions:

1. Journalize the following transactions on page 1 of the journal given in the *Working Papers*. Source documents are abbreviated as follows: check, C, and memorandum, M.

Transactions:

Jan. 2. Wrote a check for 12 U.S. Savings Bonds at $25.00 each for employees. C163.
15. Paid the December liability for employee income tax, social security tax, and Medicare tax. C172.
31. Wrote a check for federal unemployment tax liability for quarter ended December 31. C178.
31. Wrote a check for state unemployment tax liability for quarter ended December 31. C179.
31. Paid January payroll, $9,524.44 (total payroll, $11,882.00, less deductions: employee income tax, $1,307.00; social security tax, $772.33; Medicare tax, $178.23; U.S. Savings Bonds, $100.00). C184.
31. Recorded employer payroll taxes expense. M98.
Posting. Post the items that are to be posted individually.

Feb. 15. Wrote a check for January liability for employee income tax and for social security tax and Medicare tax. C190.
28. Paid February payroll, $9,650.03 (total payroll, $12,037.00, less deductions: employee income tax, $1,324.00; social security tax, $782.41; Medicare tax, $180.56; U.S. Savings Bonds, $100.00). C200.
28. Recorded employer payroll taxes expense. M107.
Posting. Post the items that are to be posted individually.

2. Prove and rule journal page 1. Carry the column totals forward to page 2 of the journal.
3. Journalize the following transactions on page 2 of the journal.

Transactions:

Mar. 15. Wrote a check for February liability for employee income tax, social security tax, and Medicare tax. C205.
31. Paid March payroll, $10,138.80 (total payroll, $12,640.00, less deductions: employee income tax, $1,390.00; social security tax, $821.60; Medicare tax, $189.60; U.S. Savings Bonds, $100.00). C226.
31. Recorded employer payroll taxes expense. M116.
Posting. Post the items that are to be posted individually.

Apr. 1. Paid cash for 12 U.S. Savings Bonds at $25.00 each for employees. C227.
15. Wrote a check for March liability for employee income tax, social security tax, and Medicare tax. C238.
30. Wrote a check for federal unemployment tax liability for quarter ended March 31. C244.
30. Wrote a check for state unemployment tax liability for quarter ended March 31. C245.
Posting. Post the items that are to be posted individually.

4. Prove and rule journal page 2.

INTERNET ACTIVITY

Point your browser to

http://accounting.swpco.com

Choose **First-Year Course**, choose **Activities**, and complete the activity for Chapter 14.

Applied Communication

As a worker, you will receive a paycheck. In addition, you will be required to pay certain federal and state taxes, including social security tax and Medicare tax. These taxes will be withheld from your paycheck.

Instructions: Look up the Social Security Act in an encyclopedia or other reference work in your library or on the Internet. Find out why social security was created, who the U.S. president was at the time, and the purpose of social security. Write a one- or two-paragraph history of social security. Use clear, descriptive sentences.

Cases for Critical Thinking

Case 1 The partners of Myers and Woods have decided to hire a sales manager. They agree that the business can afford to pay the manager a salary of only $30,000.00. The accounting assistant informs the partners that hiring the manager will cost the business more than the $30,000.00 salary. Do you agree with the accounting assistant? Explain your response.

Case 2 Penner Manufacturing had a total salary expense for the month of November of $60,000.00. Jerry Cruz, accounting clerk, calculated the November employer social security and Medicare taxes as $4,800.00 ($60,000.00 x 8%). Jean Edens, accountant, stated that the social security and Medicare taxes withheld from employee earnings were $4,275.00. What is the most likely reason for the difference between Mr. Cruz's and Ms. Edens's calculations for social security and Medicare taxes? Explain.

Case 3 One of the unwritten rules of business is that payroll information is private and confidential. People usually do not want their coworkers to know how much they are paid. This common business practice presents a challenge for employees responsible for payroll accounting. Payroll workers handle many different types of data. The payroll department records personal information about employees, such as addresses and social security numbers, and verifies and totals time cards. In addition, each pay period payroll accountants calculate each employee's earnings, deductions, and net pay. Why is it important for payroll employees to be trustworthy and able to maintain confidentiality?

AUTOMATED ACCOUNTING

PAYROLL TAXES AND JOURNAL ENTRIES

In an automated payroll system, the computer is used to maintain the employee database, to record payroll transactions at the end of each pay period, and to display and print various payroll reports.

Generating Payroll Journal Entries

Automated Accounting 7.0 can generate the current payroll journal entry, including salary expenses; employee federal, state, and city taxes payable; social security and Medicare taxes payable; and all voluntary deductions.

1. Choose the Current Payroll Journal Entry menu item from the Options menu.
2. When the confirmation dialog box appears, click Yes.
3. Click the Post button.

Generating the Employer's Payroll Taxes Journal Entries

The employer's payroll taxes journal entry includes social security, Medicare, federal unemployment, and state unemployment taxes.

1. Choose the Employer's Payroll Taxes menu item from the Options menu.
2. When the confirmation dialog box appears, click Yes.
3. Click the Post button.

Generating Payroll Reports

1. Click the Reports toolbar button.
2. Choose the Payroll Reports option from the Select a Report Group list.

There are four types of payroll reports available:

1. *Employee List Report:* The report provides a complete listing of the employee payroll information.
2. *Payroll Report:* The report shows employee earnings and withholding information for the month, quarter, and year. Information is listed by employee and is summarized.
3. *Quarterly Report:* The report summarizes wages subject to social security and Medicare taxes. The information is listed by employee.
4. *W-2 Statements:* The report summarizes an employee's taxable wages and various withholdings for both the employee and the Internal Revenue Service.

Current Payroll Journal Entries

Acct. #	Account Title	Debit	Credit
6210	Sales Salary Expense	10522.03	
6170	Office Salary Expense	9320.88	
2140	Emp. Fed. Inc. Tax Pay.		2102.62
2150	Emp. State Inc. Tax Pay.		653.10
2160	Social Security Tax Pay.		1230.27
2170	Medicare Tax Payable		287.72
2155	Emp. City Inc. Tax Pay.		198.43
2200	Health Ins. Premiums Pay.		505.00
2210	Dental Ins. Premiums Pay.		203.00
2220	Credit Union Deduct. Pay.		1025.00
2130	Salaries Payable		13637.77

Post Cancel Help

AUTOMATED ACCOUNTING

After each payroll period, the appropriate reports may be generated as needed. The W-2 statement is generated only at the end of the calendar year.

AUTOMATING MASTERY PROBLEM 14-5: Journalizing payroll transactions

Instructions:

1. Load *Automated Accounting 7.0* or higher software.
2. Select database F14-1 from the appropriate directory/folder.
3. Select File from the menu bar and choose the Save As menu command. Key the path to the drive and directory that contains your data files. Save the database with a file name of XXX141 (where XXX are your initials).
4. Access Problem Instructions through the Help menu. Read the Problem Instructions screen.
5. Key the data listed on page 355.
6. Exit the *Automated Accounting* software.

AUTOMATING CHALLENGE PROBLEM 14-6: Journalizing and posting payroll transactions

Instructions:

1. Load *Automated Accounting 7.0* or higher software.
2. Select database F14-2 from the appropriate directory/folder.
3. Select File from the menu bar and choose the Save As menu command. Key the path to the drive and directory that contains your data files. Save the database with a file name of XXX142 (where XXX are your initials).
4. Access Problem Instructions through the Help menu. Read the Problem Instructions screen.
5. Key the data listed on page 356.
6. Exit the *Automated Accounting* software.

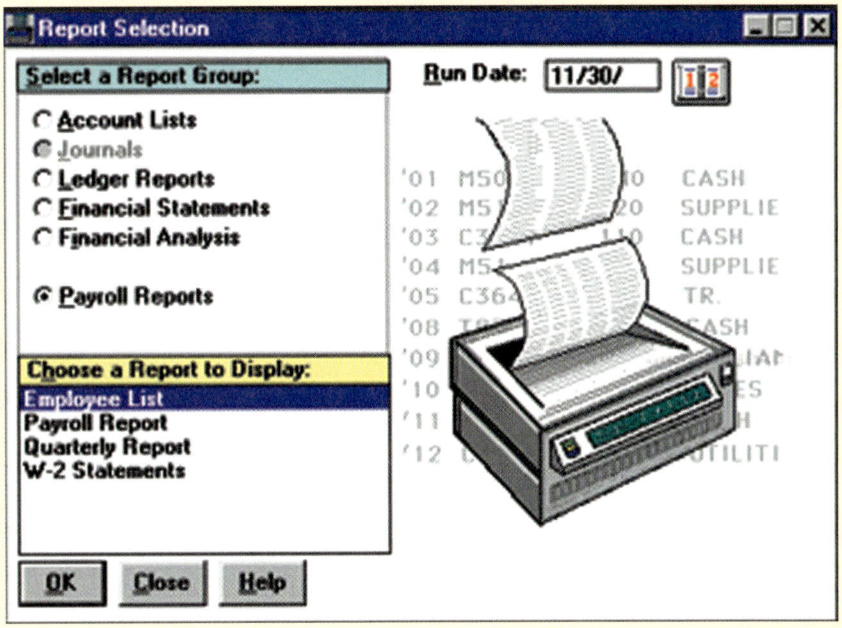

REINFORCEMENT ACTIVITY 2—PART A

An Accounting Cycle for a Partnership: Journalizing and Posting Transactions

Reinforcement Activity 2 reinforces learnings from Cycle 2, Chapters 10 through 17. Activities cover a complete accounting cycle for a merchandising business organized as a partnership. Reinforcement Activity 2 is a single problem divided into two parts. Part A includes learnings from Chapters 10 through 14. Part B includes learnings from Chapters 15 through 17.

The accounting work of a single merchandising business for the last month of a yearly fiscal period is used in this reinforcement activity. The records kept and reports prepared, however, illustrate the application of accounting concepts for all merchandising businesses.

CLEARVIEW OPTICAL

Ester Burks and Juan Ortiz, partners, own and operate ClearView Optical, a merchandising business. The business sells a complete line of fashion, sun, and sport eyewear. ClearView is located in a downtown shopping area and is open for business Monday through Saturday. A monthly rent is paid for the building and fixtures. ClearView accepts credit cards from customers.

CHART OF ACCOUNTS

ClearView Optical uses the chart of accounts shown on the next page.

JOURNAL AND LEDGERS

The journal and ledgers used by ClearView Optical are listed below. Models of the journal and ledgers are shown in the textbook chapters indicated.

Journal and Ledgers	Chapter
Expanded journal	11
Accounts payable ledger	12
Accounts receivable ledger	12
General ledger	12

CHART OF ACCOUNTS

Balance Sheet Accounts

(1000) ASSETS
1110 Cash
1120 Petty Cash
1130 Accounts Receivable
1140 Merchandise Inventory
1145 Supplies—Office
1150 Supplies—Store
1160 Prepaid Insurance

(2000) LIABILITIES
2110 Accounts Payable
2120 Employee Income Tax Payable
2130 Social Security Tax Payable
2135 Medicare Tax Payable
2140 Sales Tax Payable
2150 Unemployment Tax Payable—Federal
2160 Unemployment Tax Payable—State
2170 Health Insurance Premiums Payable
2180 U.S. Savings Bonds Payable
2190 United Way Donations Payable

(3000) OWNER'S EQUITY
3110 Ester Burks, Capital
3120 Ester Burks, Drawing
3130 Juan Ortiz, Capital
3140 Juan Ortiz, Drawing
3150 Income Summary

Income Statement Accounts

(4000) OPERATING REVENUE
4110 Sales

(5000) COST OF MERCHANDISE
5110 Purchases

(6000) OPERATING EXPENSES
6110 Advertising Expense
6120 Credit Card Fee Expense
6130 Insurance Expense
6140 Miscellaneous Expense
6150 Payroll Taxes Expense
6160 Rent Expense
6170 Salary Expense
6175 Supplies Expense—Office
6180 Supplies Expense—Store
6190 Utilities Expense

SUBSIDIARY LEDGERS

Accounts Receivable Ledger

110 Doritha Busch
120 Linda Cortez
130 Dallas Giles
140 Kristin Jung
150 Jack O'Brien
160 Don Teal

Accounts Payable Ledger

210 ABC Optical Co.
220 Central Office Supply
230 Eyecare Optical
240 Optical Mart
250 Solar Optical
260 Zen Supply

RECORDING TRANSACTIONS

The December 1 account balances for the general and subsidiary ledgers are given in the *Working Papers*.

Instructions:

1. Journalize the following transactions on page 23 of a journal. A 6% sales tax has been added to each sale. Source documents are abbreviated as follows: check, C; memorandum, M; purchase invoice, P; receipt, R; sales invoice, S; cash register tape, T.

Dec. 1. Paid cash for rent, $1,200.00. C372.
1. Ester Burks, partner, withdrew cash for personal use, $1,500.00. C373.
1. Juan Ortiz, partner, withdrew cash, for personal use, $1,500.00. C374.
2. Paid cash for electric bill, $346.20. C375.
2. Received cash on account from Linda Cortez, $413.40, covering S64. R92.
3. Paid cash for miscellaneous expense, $72.00. C376.
3. Paid cash on account to Solar Optical, $580.00, covering P73. C377.
4. Sold merchandise on account to Doritha Busch, $450.00, plus sales tax, $27.00; total, $477.00. S67.
5. Recorded cash and credit card sales, $5,796.00, plus sales tax, $347.76; total, $6,143.76. T5.

Posting. Post the items that are to be posted individually.

7. Sold merchandise on account to Dallas Giles, $462.00, plus sales tax, $27.72; total, $489.72. S68.
7. Received cash on account from Don Teal, $432.48, covering S65. R93.
8. Bought office supplies on account from Central Office Supply, $351.60. M43.
9. Purchased merchandise on account from Optical Mart, $1,350.00. P77.
9. Bought store supplies on account from Zen Supply, $330.00. M44.
10. Ester Burks, partner, withdrew merchandise for personal use, $300.00. M45.
10. Paid cash for office supplies, $174.00. C378.
11. Paid cash on account to Eyecare Optical, $1,170.00, covering P74. C379.
11. Purchased merchandise on account from Solar Optical, $1,032.00. P78.
12. Paid cash for store supplies, $264.00. C380.
12. Recorded cash and credit card sales, $7,125.00, plus sales tax, $427.50; total, $7,552.50. T12.

Posting. Post the items that are to be posted individually.

14. Juan Ortiz, partner, withdrew merchandise for personal use, $390.00. M46.
14. Purchased merchandise on account from Eyecare Optical, $3,276.00. P79.
14. Sold merchandise on account to Jack O'Brien, $170.00, plus sales tax, $10.20; total, $180.20. S69.
14. Paid cash for advertising, $415.00. C381.
15. Paid cash on account to ABC Optical Co., $1,272.00, covering P75. C382.
15. Received cash on account from Kristin Jung, $821.50, covering S66. R94.
15. Sold merchandise on account to Linda Cortez, $490.00, plus sales tax, $29.40; total, $519.40. S70.
15. Paid cash for liability for employee income tax, $342.00, social security tax, $767.00, and Medicare tax, $177.00; total, $1,286.00. C383.

Posting. Post the items that are to be posted individually.

2. Prove and rule page 23 of the journal.

3. Carry the column totals forward to page 24 of the journal.

4. Journalize the following transactions on page 24 of the journal.

Dec. 15. Paid cash for semimonthly payroll, $2,303.60 (total payroll, $2,930.00, less deductions: employee income tax, $162.00; social security tax, $190.45; Medicare tax, $43.95; health insurance, $170.00; U.S. Savings Bonds, $30.00; United Way donations, $30.00). C384.

15. Recorded employer payroll taxes, $259.20, for the semimonthly pay period ended December 15. Taxes owed are: social security tax, $190.45; Medicare tax, $43.95; federal unemployment tax, $3.20; and state unemployment tax, $21.60. M47.

19. Recorded cash and credit card sales, $6,925.00, plus sales tax, $415.50; total, $7,340.50. T19.

23. Paid cash on account to Optical Mart, $2,200.00, covering P76. C385.

26. Recorded cash and credit card sales, $6,980.00, plus sales tax, $418.80; total, $7,398.80. T26.

Posting. Post the items that are to be posted individually.

ClearView Optical's bank charges a fee for handling the collection of credit card sales deposited during the month. The credit card fee is deducted from ClearView Optical's bank account. The amount is then shown on the bank statement. The credit card fee is recorded in the journal as a reduction in cash.

Dec. 28. Recorded credit card fee expense, $342.00. M48. (Debit Credit Card Fee Expense; credit Cash.)

30. Purchased merchandise on account from ABC Optical Co., $1,940.00. P80.

31. Paid cash to replenish the petty cash fund, $364.00: office supplies, $75.00; store supplies, $70.00; advertising, $104.00; miscellaneous, $115.00. C386.

31. Paid cash for semimonthly payroll, $2,451.40 (total payroll, $3,120.00, less deductions: employee income tax, $189.00; social security tax, $202.80; Medicare tax, $46.80; health insurance, $170.00; U.S. Savings Bonds, $30.00; United Way donations, $30.00). C387.

31. Recorded employer payroll taxes, $274.40, for the semimonthly pay period ended December 31. Taxes owed are: social security tax, $202.80: Medicare tax, $46.80; federal unemployment tax, $3.20; and state unemployment tax, $21.60. M49.

31. Recorded cash and credit card sales, $3,890.00, plus sales tax, $233.40; total, $4,123.40. T31.

Posting. Post the items that are to be posted individually.

5. Total page 24 of the journal. Prove the equality of debits and credits.
6. Prove cash. The balance on the next unused check stub is $40,126.14.
7. Rule the journal.
8. Post the totals of the special columns of the journal.
9. Prepare a schedule of accounts payable and a schedule of accounts receivable. Prove the accuracy of the subsidiary ledgers by comparing the schedule totals with the balances of the controlling accounts in the general ledger. If the totals are not the same, find and correct the errors.

The ledgers used in Reinforcement Activity 2—Part A are needed to complete Reinforcement Activity 2—Part B.

15 Work Sheet for a Merchandising Business

AFTER STUDYING CHAPTER 15, YOU WILL BE ABLE TO:

1. Define accounting terms related to a work sheet for a merchandising business.
2. Identify accounting concepts and practices related to a work sheet for a merchandising business.
3. Begin a work sheet for a merchandising business.
4. Plan adjustments on a work sheet for a merchandising business.
5. Complete a work sheet for a merchandising business.

TERMS PREVIEW

inventory

merchandise inventory

FINANCIAL INFORMATION

Management decisions about future business operations are often based on financial information. This information shows whether a profit is being made or a loss is being incurred. Profit or loss information helps an owner or manager determine future changes. Financial information is also needed to prepare required tax reports. A business summarizes financial information at least once each fiscal period. Omni Import uses a one-year fiscal period that begins on January 1 and ends on December 31. Therefore, Omni Import summarizes its financial information on December 31 of each year.

LEGAL ISSUES IN ACCOUNTING

LIMITED LIABILITY PARTNERSHIPS

A new form of partnership in the U.S. is called a *limited liability partnership (LLP).* The LLP tries to combine the advantages of the partnership and the corporation, while avoiding their disadvantages. At least two members, or partners, are necessary.

The primary advantage of the LLP is that it does not pay separate income tax. LLP partners allocate profits and losses among themselves, according to the partnership agreement.

All members in the LLP have "limited" liability for the debts of the business. This means that none of the personal assets of the members are subject to the claims of business creditors.

The LLP follows partnership rules for dissolution. If one member drops out, all others must formally agree to continue the business.

Many major accounting firms have changed to the LLP form of business organization in an effort to limit the costs associated with malpractice liability.

ACCOUNTING IN YOUR CAREER

DISCOVERING THE TRUTH ABOUT WORK SHEETS

Cheryl Wendling is a junior accountant at a large accounting firm. She specializes in financial analysis, has recently passed the CPA examination, and is working toward becoming a full partner in the firm. The firm expects all its partners to participate in community service, so Cheryl volunteers her time talking with students enrolled in accounting courses at local high schools and colleges.

Cheryl recently admitted to one of her friends that at first she thought this volunteer work was just another hoop to jump through to earn her partnership. But after a few classroom visits, she discovered that she genuinely liked sharing her knowledge and experience, and she now believes she may have inspired a few students to pursue accounting careers.

Today Cheryl is visiting with Mr. Stern's Accounting I class at Lamont High School. The students have just finished a unit on work sheets for partnerships and are eager to discuss work sheets with her. Cheryl likes to begin with a dramatic statement that grabs the students' attention. So today she says, "I'm going to tell you three lies about work sheets. Then I want you to tell me what's wrong with my statements." She gives a big grin and then says, "If you get these three right, then I'll tell you how to succeed in the field of accounting."

Critical Thinking:

1. Cheryl's first statement is: *A 10-column work sheet is always better than an 8-column work sheet.* When might an 8-column work sheet be preferable to a 10-column work sheet?
2. The second statement is: *The trial balance totals prove that all the work in the general ledger is correct.* What kinds of errors are not detected by a trial balance?
3. The third statement is: *All the account balances in the Income Statement and Balance Sheet columns are the amounts that will appear on the income statement and balance sheet.* What account would be an exception to this statement and why?

15-1 Beginning an 8-Column Work Sheet for a Merchandising Business

TRANSFERRING GENERAL LEDGER ACCOUNT BALANCES TO A WORK SHEET

ACCOUNT *Cash* ACCOUNT NO. *1110*

DATE		ITEM	POST. REF.	DEBIT	CREDIT	BALANCE DEBIT	BALANCE CREDIT
20-- Dec.	1	Balance	✓			28 260 00	
	31		25	37 180 80		65 440 80	
	31		25		36 360 52	29 080 28	

ACCOUNT *Sales* ACCOUNT NO. *4110*

DATE		ITEM	POST. REF.	DEBIT	CREDIT	BALANCE DEBIT	BALANCE CREDIT
20-- Dec.	1	Balance	✓				387 919 20
	31		25		35 200 80		423 120 00

A columnar accounting form on which the financial information needed to prepare financial statements is summarized is known as a work sheet. A work sheet is used to plan adjustments and sort financial statement information. A work sheet may be prepared whenever a business wishes to summarize and report financial information. A work sheet is always prepared at the end of each fiscal period because financial statements are prepared at the end of each fiscal period. *(CONCEPT: Accounting Period Cycle)* Omni Import prepares a work sheet and financial statements annually. To begin a work sheet, Omni completes the Trial Balance columns. Two selected general ledger accounts are shown in the illustration.

RECORDING A TRIAL BALANCE ON A WORK SHEET

Omni Import
Work Sheet
For Year Ended December 31, 20--

	ACCOUNT TITLE	1 TRIAL BALANCE DEBIT	2 TRIAL BALANCE CREDIT
1	Cash	29,080.28	
2	Petty Cash	300.00	
3	Accounts Receivable	11,198.40	
4	Merchandise Inventory	270,480.00	
5	Supplies—Office	6,480.00	
6	Supplies—Store	6,944.00	
7	Prepaid Insurance	5,800.00	
8	Accounts Payable		12,542.38
9	Employee Income Tax Payable		542.00
10	Social Security Tax Payable		985.40
11	Medicare Tax Payable		227.42
12	Sales Tax Payable		2,112.05
13	Unemployment Tax Payable—Federal		8.40
14	Unemployment Tax Payable—State		56.70
15	Health Insurance Premiums Payable		1,008.00
16	U.S. Savings Bonds Payable		60.00
17	United Way Donations Payable		72.00
18	Karl Koehn, Capital		136,750.00
19	Karl Koehn, Drawing	29,100.00	
20	Michelle Wu, Capital		136,552.48
21	Michelle Wu, Drawing	28,800.00	
22	Income Summary		
23	Sales		423,120.00
24	Purchases	189,960.00	
25	Advertising Expense	6,600.00	
26	Credit Card Fee Expense	3,385.00	
27	Insurance Expense		
28	Miscellaneous Expense	2,584.15	
29	Payroll Taxes Expense	9,105.00	
30	Rent Expense	21,000.00	
31	Salary Expense	89,400.00	
32	Supplies Expense—Office		
33	Supplies Expense—Store		
34	Utilities Expense	3,820.00	
35		714,036.83	714,036.83

1. Account Titles

2. Account Balances

3. Total and rule the Debit and Credit columns.

STEPS Recording a trial balance on a work sheet

1. Write the title of each general ledger account in the work sheet's Account Title column in the same order they appear in the general ledger. All accounts are listed regardless of whether there is a balance or not. Listing all accounts reduces the possibility of overlooking an account that needs to be brought up to date.
2. Write the balance of each account in the appropriate work sheet's Trial Balance Debit or Credit column. The amounts are taken from the general ledger accounts.
3. Total, prove, and rule the Trial Balance Debit and Credit columns of the work sheet.

PLANNING ADJUSTMENTS ON A WORK SHEET

After posting is completed at the end of a fiscal period, some general ledger accounts, such as the two supplies accounts and the prepaid insurance account, are not up to date. Adjustments for supplies and prepaid insurance are described in Chapter 7. In addition to supplies and prepaid insurance, Omni Import needs to adjust the merchandise inventory account. Changes recorded on a work sheet to update general ledger accounts at the end of a fiscal period are known as adjustments.

Adjustments are planned in the Adjustments columns of a work sheet. Adjustments recorded on a work sheet are for planning purposes only. The general ledger account balances are not changed until entries are journalized and posted. Journal entries made to bring general ledger accounts up to date are known as adjusting entries.

The amount of goods on hand is called an **inventory.** The amount of goods on hand for sale to customers is called **merchandise inventory.** The general ledger account in which merchandise inventory is recorded is titled Merchandise Inventory. Merchandise Inventory is an asset account with a normal debit balance.

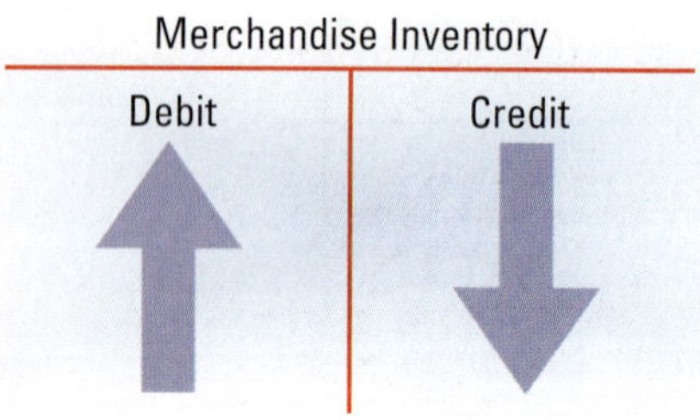

Omni Import's merchandise inventory account on January 1, the beginning of the fiscal year, has a debit balance of $270,480.00.

Merchandise Inventory		
Jan. 1 Bal.	270,480.00	

The balance of the merchandise inventory account on December 31, the end of the fiscal year, is the same amount, $270,480.00. The January 1 and December 31 balances are the same because no entries have been made in the account during the fiscal year. The changes in inventory resulting from purchases and sales transactions have not been recorded in the merchandise inventory account.

During a fiscal period, the amount of merchandise on hand increases each time merchandise is purchased. However, all purchases are recorded in the purchases account. The amount of merchandise on hand decreases each time merchandise is sold. However, all sales are recorded in the sales account. This procedure makes it easier to determine the total purchases and sales during a fiscal period. The merchandise inventory account balance, therefore, must be adjusted to reflect the changes resulting from purchases and sales during a fiscal period.

ANALYZING A MERCHANDISE INVENTORY ADJUSTMENT

The two accounts used to adjust the merchandise inventory are Merchandise Inventory and Income Summary. The T accounts show the merchandise inventory and income summary accounts before the merchandise inventory adjustment is made.

BEFORE ADJUSTMENT

Income Summary

Merchandise Inventory

Jan. 1 Bal.	270,480.00		

Before the adjustment, the merchandise inventory account has a January 1 debit balance of $270,480.00. The merchandise inventory account balance, however, is not up to date. The actual count of merchandise on December 31 shows that the inventory is valued at $254,640.00. Therefore, the merchandise inventory account balance must be adjusted to show the current value of merchandise on hand.

Most accounts needing adjustment at the end of a fiscal period have a related temporary account. For example, when the account Supplies is adjusted, Supplies Expense is the related expense account, a temporary account. Merchandise Inventory, however, does not have a related expense account. Therefore, Income Summary, a temporary account, is used to adjust the merchandise inventory account at the end of a fiscal period.

Four questions are asked in analyzing the adjustment for merchandise inventory.

1. **What is the balance of Merchandise Inventory?** *$270,480.00*
2. **What should the balance be for this account?** *$254,640.00*
3. **What must be done to correct the account balance?** *Decrease $15,840.00*
4. **What adjustment is made?**
   Debit Income Summary, *$15,840.00*
   Credit Merchandise Inventory, *$15,840.00*

The merchandise inventory adjustment is shown in the T accounts.

AFTER ADJUSTMENT

Income Summary

Adj. (a)	15,840.00		

Merchandise Inventory

Jan. 1 Bal.	270,480.00	Adj. (a)	15,840.00
(New Bal.	*254,640.00)*		

Income Summary is debited and Merchandise Inventory is credited for $15,840.00. The beginning debit balance of Merchandise Inventory, $270,480.00, *minus* the adjustment credit amount, $15,840.00, *equals* the ending debit balance of Merchandise Inventory, $254,640.00.

REMEMBER

When an account that requires adjusting does not have a related expense account, the temporary account Income Summary is used.

RECORDING A MERCHANDISE INVENTORY ADJUSTMENT

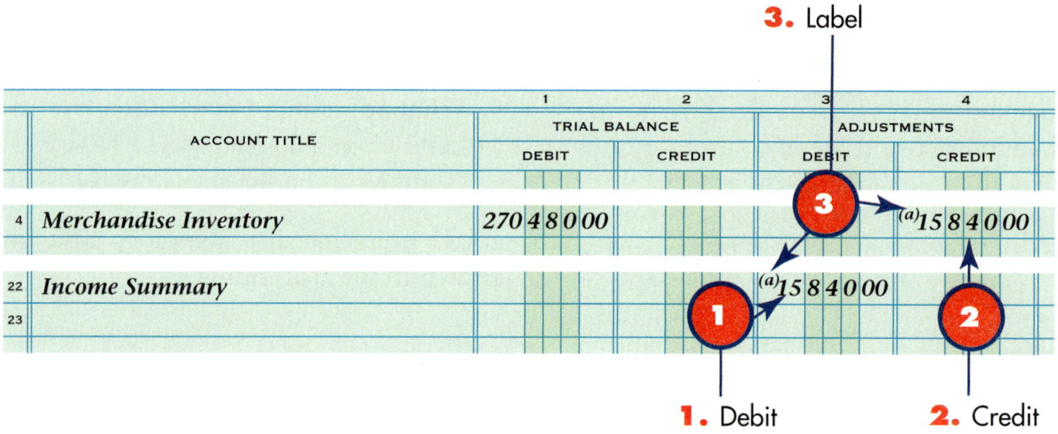

STEPS: Recording a merchandise inventory adjustment on a work sheet

1. Write the debit amount, *$15,840.00,* in the Adjustments Debit column on the line with the account title Income Summary.
2. Write the credit amount, *$15,840.00,* in the Adjustments Credit column on the line with the account title Merchandise Inventory.
3. Label the two parts of this adjustment with the small letter *a* in parentheses, *(a).*

ANALYZING AN ADJUSTMENT WHEN ENDING MERCHANDISE INVENTORY IS GREATER THAN BEGINNING MERCHANDISE INVENTORY

If the amount of merchandise inventory on hand is greater than the January 1 balance of Merchandise Inventory, opposite entries would be made—debit Merchandise Inventory and credit Income Summary. For example, Venable Company's merchandise inventory account on January 1 has a debit balance of $294,700.00. The count of merchandise on December 31 shows that the inventory is valued at $298,900.00. The merchandise on hand is $4,200.00 *greater* than the January 1 balance of Merchandise Inventory.

Four questions are asked in analyzing the adjustment for merchandise inventory.

1. **What is the balance of Merchandise Inventory?** *$294,700.00*
2. **What should the balance be for this account?** *$298,900.00*
3. **What must be done to correct the account balance?** *Increase $4,200.00*
4. **What adjustment is made?**

Debit Merchandise Inventory, *$4,200.00*
Credit Income Summary, *$4,200.00*

The merchandise inventory adjustment is shown in the T accounts.

AFTER ADJUSTMENT

Merchandise Inventory

Jan. 1 Bal.	294,700.00		
Adj. (a)	4,200.00		
(New Bal.	*298,900.00)*		

Income Summary

		Adj. (a)	4,200.00

Merchandise Inventory is debited and Income Summary is credited for $4,200.00. The beginning debit balance of Merchandise Inventory, $294,700.00, *plus* the adjustment debit amount, $4,200.00, *equals* the ending debit balance of Merchandise Inventory, $298,900.00.

TERMS REVIEW

inventory

merchandise inventory

AUDIT YOUR UNDERSTANDING

1. In what order should general ledger accounts be listed on a work sheet?
2. What accounts are used for the adjustment for merchandise inventory?

WORK TOGETHER

Beginning an 8-column work sheet for a merchandising business

A work sheet for Paradise Company is given in the *Working Papers.* The company's general ledger account balances on December 31 of the current year, after all transactions have been posted, are listed below. Your instructor will guide you through the following examples.

Cash	$ 26,424.00	
Petty Cash	300.00	
Accounts Receivable	10,693.00	
Merchandise Inventory	254,244.00	
Supplies—Office	6,091.00	
Supplies—Store	6,516.00	
Prepaid Insurance	5,540.00	
Accounts Payable		$ 10,740.00
Sales Tax Payable		1,985.00
Jean Brower, Capital		117,875.00
Jean Brower, Drawing	20,530.00	
Dale Edson, Capital		118,520.00
Dale Edson, Drawing	20,980.00	
Income Summary		
Sales		316,440.00
Purchases	178,560.00	
Advertising Expense	6,200.00	
Credit Card Fee Expense	3,264.00	
Insurance Expense		
Miscellaneous Expense	2,470.00	
Rent Expense	20,160.00	
Supplies Expense—Office		
Supplies Expense—Store		
Utilities Expense	3,588.00	

3. Enter the trial balance on the work sheet.
4. Total, prove, and rule the trial balance.
5. From a physical count of merchandise inventory, the December 31 balance is determined to be $239,354.00. Analyze the merchandise inventory adjustment and enter the adjustment on the work sheet. Save your work to complete Work Together on page 377.

ON YOUR OWN

Beginning an 8-column work sheet for a merchandising business

A work sheet for Mueller Company is given in the *Working Papers.* The company's general ledger account balances on December 31 of the current year, after all transactions have been posted, are listed below. Work these problems independently.

Cash	$ 27,210.00	
Petty Cash	500.00	
Accounts Receivable	12,475.00	
Merchandise Inventory	296,620.00	
Supplies—Office	7,106.00	
Supplies—Store	7,602.00	
Prepaid Insurance	6,480.00	
Accounts Payable		$ 12,530.00
Sales Tax Payable		2,315.00
Harry Glover, Capital		134,550.00
Harry Glover, Drawing	23,950.00	
Laura Montez, Capital		138,270.00
Laura Montez, Drawing	24,475.00	
Income Summary		
Sales		369,180.00
Purchases	208,320.00	
Advertising Expense	7,240.00	
Credit Card Fee Expense	3,808.00	
Insurance Expense		
Miscellaneous Expense	2,873.00	
Rent Expense	24,000.00	
Supplies Expense—Office		
Supplies Expense—Store		
Utilities Expense	4,186.00	

6. Enter the trial balance on the work sheet.

7. Total, prove, and rule the trial balance.

8. From a physical count of merchandise inventory, the December 31 balance is determined to be $279,247.00. Analyze the merchandise inventory adjustment and enter the adjustment on the work sheet. Save your work to complete On Your Own on page 377.

15-2 Analyzing and Recording Work Sheet Adjustments

ANALYZING A SUPPLIES ADJUSTMENT

Omni Import uses office and store supplies in the daily operation of the business. The amount of supplies *not used* during a fiscal period represents an asset. The amount of supplies *used* during a fiscal period represents an expense. Accurate financial reporting includes recording expenses in the fiscal period in which the expenses contribute to earning revenue. *(CONCEPT: Matching Expenses with Revenue)*

The account balance for Supplies—Office, $6,480.00, includes two items: (1) the account balance on January 1 and (2) the cost of office supplies bought during the year. The account balance does not reflect the value of any office supplies *used* during the year (an expense). Therefore, the office supplies account balance must be adjusted to show the value of office supplies on hand on December 31. The amount of supplies on hand on December 31 is determined by counting the supplies on hand and calculating the value.

The two accounts used to adjust office supplies are Supplies—Office and Supplies Expense—Office. Before the adjustment, the office supplies account has a December 31 debit balance of $6,480.00. However, office supplies have been used throughout the fiscal period. These changes in office supplies were not recorded in the office supplies account. Therefore, the office supplies account balance is not up to date.

BEFORE ADJUSTMENT

Supplies Expense—Office

Supplies—Office

Dec. 31 Bal.	6,480.00		

The actual count of office supplies on December 31 shows that the value of the inventory is $1,750.00. The office supplies account balance must be adjusted to show the current value of the office supplies inventory.

Four questions are asked in analyzing the adjustment for office supplies inventory.

1. **What is the balance of Supplies—Office?** *$6,480.00*
2. **What should the balance be for this account?** *$1,750.00*
3. **What must be done to correct the account balance?** *Decrease $4,730.00*
4. **What adjustment is made?**
   Debit Supplies Expense—Office, *$4,730.00*
   Credit Supplies—Office, *$4,730.00*

The office supplies inventory adjustment is shown in the T accounts.

AFTER ADJUSTMENT

Supplies Expense—Office

Adj. (b)	4,730.00		

Supplies—Office

Dec. 31 Bal.	6,480.00	Adj. (b)	4,730.00
(New Bal.	*1,750.00)*		

Supplies Expense—Office is debited and Supplies—Office is credited for $4,730.00. The beginning debit balance of Supplies—Office, $6,480.00, *minus* the adjustment credit amount, $4,730.00, *equals* the ending debit balance of Supplies—Office, $1,750.00.

FYI

In automated accounting, adjustments are prepared from the trial balance. The software automatically generates the financial statements with no need for a work sheet.

RECORDING SUPPLIES ADJUSTMENTS

3. Labels **2.** Credits

		1	2	3	4
	ACCOUNT TITLE	TRIAL BALANCE		ADJUSTMENTS	
		DEBIT	CREDIT	DEBIT	CREDIT
5	*Supplies—Office*	6480 00			(b) 4730 00
6	*Supplies—Store*	6944 00			(c) 3910 00
32	*Supplies Expense—Office*			(b) 4730 00	
33	*Supplies Expense—Store*			(c) 3910 00	
34					
35					
36					
37					
38					

1. Debits

Omni Import makes a similar adjustment for store supplies. The steps in recording the *two* supplies inventory adjustments are the same as those described for Encore Music in Chapter 7. The *two* supplies inventory adjustments are shown in the Adjustments columns of the work sheet above. The adjustment for Supplies—Office is labeled *(b)* and is shown on lines 5 and 32. The adjustment for Supplies—Store is labeled *(c)* and is shown on lines 6 and 33.

STEPS

Recording supplies adjustments on a work sheet

1. Write the debit amounts in the Adjustments Debit column on the lines with the appropriate account titles: *$4,730.00* with Supplies Expense—Office and *$3,910.00* with Supplies Expense—Store.
2. Write the credit amounts in the Adjustments Credit column on the lines with the appropriate account titles: *$4,730.00* with Supplies—Office and *$3,910.00* with Supplies—Store.
3. Label the two parts of the Supplies—Office adjustment with a small letter *b* in parentheses, *(b)*. Label the two parts of the Supplies—Store adjustment with a small letter *c* in parentheses, *(c)*.

REMEMBER

The adjustment for supplies is the amount of supplies used.

ANALYZING A PREPAID INSURANCE ADJUSTMENT

Payment for insurance protection is paid in advance. The value of prepaid insurance *not expired* during a fiscal period is an asset. The value of prepaid insurance *expired* during a fiscal period is an expense.

The account balance for Prepaid Insurance, $5,800.00, includes two items: (1) the account balance on January 1 and (2) the cost of insurance premiums paid during the year. The account balance does not reflect the value of the insurance expired during the year (an expense). Therefore, the prepaid insurance account balance must be adjusted to bring the balance up to date. *(CONCEPT: Matching Expenses with Revenue)*

The two accounts used to adjust the prepaid insurance account are Prepaid Insurance and Insurance Expense. Before the adjustment, the prepaid insurance account has a December 31 debit balance of $5,800.00. The account balance, however, is not up to date. The value of the prepaid insurance *not expired* is determined to be $2,630.00. The prepaid insurance account balance must be adjusted to show its current value.

BEFORE ADJUSTMENT

Insurance Expense

Prepaid Insurance

Dec. 31 Bal.	5,800.00		

Four questions are asked in analyzing the adjustment for prepaid insurance.

1. **What is the balance of Prepaid Insurance?** *$5,800.00*
2. **What should the balance be for this account?** *$2,630.00*
3. **What must be done to correct the account balance?** *Decrease $3,170.00*
4. **What adjustment is made?**
   Debit Insurance Expense, *$3,170.00*
   Credit Prepaid Insurance, *$3,170.00*

The prepaid insurance adjustment is shown in the T accounts.

AFTER ADJUSTMENT

Insurance Expense

Adj. (d)	3,170.00		

Prepaid Insurance

Dec. 31 Bal.	5,800.00	Adj. (d)	3,170.00
(New Bal.	*2,630.00)*		

Insurance Expense is debited and Prepaid Insurance is credited for $3,170.00. The beginning debit balance of Prepaid Insurance, $5,800.00, *minus* the adjustment credit amount, $3,170.00, *equals* the ending debit balance of Prepaid Insurance, $2,630.00.

FYI

Companies with more complicated businesses and charts of accounts will need to make more adjustments than companies with less complicated businesses and charts of accounts.

RECORDING A PREPAID INSURANCE ADJUSTMENT

	ACCOUNT TITLE	TRIAL BALANCE DEBIT (1)	TRIAL BALANCE CREDIT (2)	ADJUSTMENTS DEBIT (3)	ADJUSTMENTS CREDIT (4)
7	*Prepaid Insurance*	5 800 00			(d) 3 170 00
27	*Insurance Expense*			(d) 3 170 00	
28					
29					
30					

1. Debit

2. Credit

3. Labels

The steps in recording the prepaid insurance adjustment on a work sheet are the same as those followed by Encore Music in Chapter 7.

The adjustment for Prepaid Insurance is labeled *(d)* and is shown in the Adjustments columns on lines 7 and 27 of the work sheet above.

ACCOUNTING AT WORK

GLENDA COUSINS

Glenda Cousins is the branch manager of Star Bank's Over-the-Rhine branch in Cincinnati, Ohio. She began her career with Star Bank as a teller and worked her way through several different positions to reach her current job. She was first promoted from teller to loan and documentation processor. In this job she was responsible for inputting information about certificates of deposit (CDs) and commercial notes. She then worked as a customer service representative, selling new accounts and CDs.

As an assistant manager, she gained supervisory experience and took part in the management of a branch office. She also was the branch manager's backup. Then finally she had her own branch to manage. When asked how she was able to consistently rise in the organization, Glenda said, "It took hard work and a positive attitude. I had to remain positive even when others were promoted to positions I felt I deserved."

Glenda advises that "students who hope to enter the banking industry at the teller level need a customer service orientation. You will learn the bank's products and must be able to refer customers to the different services offered by the bank. Another good skill for a prospective teller is experience in dealing with cash. You can usually obtain this experience in a retail environment as a sales associate."

Glenda recommends that students determine one or two career fields and then focus on a career choice. This focus will guide your decisions about education and the courses you enroll in. She says that her two years of high school accounting well prepared her for her entry into banking. The knowledge of debits and credits gave her an understanding that other bank employees lacked.

AUDIT YOUR UNDERSTANDING

1. What accounts are used for the adjustment to office supplies?
2. What accounts are used for the adjustment to prepaid insurance?

WORK TOGETHER

Analyzing and recording adjustments on a work sheet for a merchandising business

Use the work sheet from Work Together on page 371. Your instructor will guide you through the following examples.

3. From a physical count of the following, December 31 balances are determined to be:

Supplies—Office	$1,646.00
Supplies—Store	2,838.00
Prepaid Insurance	2,540.00

Analyze adjustments that need to be made for the accounts above and enter the adjustments on the work sheet.

4. Total, prove, and rule the Adjustments columns. Save your work to complete Work Together on page 384.

ON YOUR OWN

Analyzing and recording adjustments on a work sheet for a merchandising business

Use the work sheet from On Your Own on page 372. Work these problems independently.

5. From a physical count of the following, December 31 balances are determined to be:

Supplies—Office	$1,920.00
Supplies—Store	3,310.00
Prepaid Insurance	2,940.00

Analyze adjustments that need to be made for the accounts above and enter the adjustments on the work sheet.

6. Total, prove, and rule the Adjustments columns. Save your work to complete On Your Own on page 384.

15-3 Completing Work Sheets

COMPLETING AN 8-COLUMN WORK SHEET

1. Extend balance sheet items to Balance Sheet columns.

2. Extend income statement items to Income Statement columns.

	ACCOUNT TITLE	1 TRIAL BALANCE DEBIT	2 TRIAL BALANCE CREDIT	3 ADJUSTMENTS DEBIT	4 ADJUSTMENTS CREDIT	5 INCOME STATEMENT DEBIT	6 INCOME STATEMENT CREDIT	7 BALANCE SHEET DEBIT	8 BALANCE SHEET CREDIT	
1	*Cash*	29080 28						29080 28		1
2	*Petty Cash*	300 00						300 00		2
3	*Accounts Receivable*	11198 40						11198 40		3
4	*Merchandise Inventory*	270480 00			(a) 15840 00			254640 00		4
5	*Supplies—Office*	6480 00			(b) 4730 00			1750 00		5
6	*Supplies—Store*	6944 00			(c) 3910 00			3034 00		6
7	*Prepaid Insurance*	5800 00			(d) 3170 00			2630 00		7
8	*Accounts Payable*		12542 38						12542 38	8
18	*Karl Koehn, Capital*		136750 00						136750 00	18
19	*Karl Koehn, Drawing*	29100 00						29100 00		19
20	*Michelle Wu, Capital*		136552 48						136552 48	20
21	*Michelle Wu, Drawing*	28800 00						28800 00		21
22	*Income Summary*			(a) 15840 00		15840 00				22
23	*Sales*		423120 00				423120 00			23
24	*Purchases*	189960 00				189960 00				24
32	*Supplies Exp.—Office*			(b) 4730 00		4730 00				32
33	*Supplies Exp.—Store*			(c) 3910 00		3910 00				33
34	*Utilities Expense*	3820 00				3820 00				34
35		714036 83	714036 83	27650 00	27650 00	353504 15	423120 00	360532 68	290916 83	35
36	*Net Income*					69615 85			69615 85	36
37						423120 00	423120 00	360532 68	360532 68	37
38										38

3. Total Income Statement and Balance Sheet columns.

4. Calculate net income or net loss.

5. Extend net income or net loss to Balance Sheet Debit or Credit column.

6. Total Income Statement and Balance Sheet columns.

7. Check that totals are in balance.

Omni Import follows the same procedures for completing a work sheet as described for Encore Music in Chapter 7, with the exception of the income summary account. Encore Music sells a service, not merchandise. Therefore, Encore Music has no amount recorded in the income summary account, a related account used to adjust Merchandise Inventory. Omni Import sells merchandise. Therefore, the income summary account is used as the related account to adjust Merchandise Inventory. The merchandise inventory adjustment reflects the increases and decreases in the amount of goods on hand resulting from purchases and sales. Therefore, the amount recorded in Income Summary is extended to the work sheet's Income Statement Debit or Credit column. An Income Summary debit amount is extended to the Income Statement Debit column. An Income Summary credit amount is extended to the Income Statement Credit column.

Omni Import's completed work sheet for the year ended December 31, 20—, is shown on the following two pages.

STEPS: Completing an 8-column work sheet for a merchandising business

1. Extend balance sheet items to the work sheet's Balance Sheet columns.
2. Extend income statement items, including Income Summary, to the work sheet's Income Statement columns.
3. Subtotal the Income Statement and Balance Sheet columns.
4. Calculate the net income or net loss. If the Income Statement Credit column total (revenue) is larger than the Debit column total (costs and expenses), a net income has occurred. If the Income Statement Debit column total (costs and expenses) is larger than the Credit column total (revenue), a net loss has occurred. Omni Import's net income is calculated as shown below.

Income Statement Credit Column Total	–	Income Statement Debit Column Total	=	Net Income
$423,120.00	–	$353,504.15	=	$69,615.85

5. Extend the amount of net income or net loss to the Balance Sheet Debit or Credit column. When a net income occurs, the net income amount is extended to the Balance Sheet Credit amount column, as shown on line 36. When a net loss occurs, the net loss amount is extended to the Balance Sheet Debit amount column.
6. Total the four Income Statement and Balance Sheet amount columns.
7. Check that the totals for each pair of columns are in balance. As shown on line 37, the totals for the Income Statement columns, *$423,120.00,* are the same. The totals for the Balance Sheet columns, *$360,532.68,* are also the same. Omni Import's work sheet is in balance.

A COMPLETED 8-COLUMN WORK SHEET FOR A MERCHANDISING BUSINESS

Omni Import
Work Sheet
For Year Ended December 31, 20--

	ACCOUNT TITLE	1 TRIAL BALANCE DEBIT	2 TRIAL BALANCE CREDIT	3 ADJUSTMENTS DEBIT	4 ADJUSTMENTS CREDIT	5 INCOME STATEMENT DEBIT	6 INCOME STATEMENT CREDIT	7 BALANCE SHEET DEBIT	8 BALANCE SHEET CREDIT	
1	Cash	29 080 28						29 080 28		1
2	Petty Cash	300 00						300 00		2
3	Accounts Receivable	11 198 40						11 198 40		3
4	Merchandise Inventory	270 480 00			(a) 15 840 00			254 640 00		4
5	Supplies—Office	6 480 00			(b) 4 730 00			1 750 00		5
6	Supplies—Store	6 944 00			(c) 3 910 00			3 034 00		6
7	Prepaid Insurance	5 800 00			(d) 3 170 00			2 630 00		7
8	Accounts Payable		12 542 38						12 542 38	8
9	Employee Income Tax Payable		542 00						542 00	9
10	Social Security Tax Payable		985 40						985 40	10
11	Medicare Tax Payable		227 42						227 42	11
12	Sales Tax Payable		2 112 05						2 112 05	12
13	Unemployment Tax Payable—Federal		8 40						8 40	13
14	Unemployment Tax Payable—State		56 70						56 70	14
15	Health Insurance Premiums Payable		1 008 00						1 008 00	15
16	U.S. Savings Bonds Payable		60 00						60 00	16
17	United Way Donations Payable		72 00						72 00	17
18	Karl Koehn, Capital		136 750 00						136 750 00	18
19	Karl Koehn, Drawing	29 100 00						29 100 00		19
20	Michelle Wu, Capital		136 552 48						136 552 48	20
21	Michelle Wu, Drawing	28 800 00						28 800 00		21

	Account Title	Trial Balance Debit	Trial Balance Credit	Adjustments Debit	Adjustments Credit	Income Statement Debit	Income Statement Credit	Balance Sheet Debit	Balance Sheet Credit	
22	Income Summary			(a) 15840 00		15840 00				22
23	Sales		423120 00				423120 00			23
24	Purchases	189960 00				189960 00				24
25	Advertising Expense	6600 00				6600 00				25
26	Credit Card Fee Expense	3385 00				3385 00				26
27	Insurance Expense			(d) 3170 00		3170 00				27
28	Miscellaneous Expense	2584 15				2584 15				28
29	Payroll Taxes Expense	9105 00				9105 00				29
30	Rent Expense	21000 00				21000 00				30
31	Salary Expense	89400 00				89400 00				31
32	Supplies Expense—Office			(b) 4730 00		4730 00				32
33	Supplies Expense—Store			(c) 3910 00		3910 00				33
34	Utilities Expense	3820 00				3820 00				34
35		714036 83	714036 83	27650 00	27650 00	353504 15	423120 00	360532 68	290916 83	35
36	Net Income					69615 85			69615 85	36
37						423120 00	423120 00	360532 68	360532 68	37
38										38
39										39
40										40
41										41
42										42
43										43
44										44
45										45
46										46
47										47

A 10-COLUMN WORK SHEET FOR A MERCHANDISING BUSINESS (LEFT PAGE)

1. Trial Balance

2. Adjustments

Omni Import
Work Sheet
For Year Ended December 31, 20--

	ACCOUNT TITLE	1 TRIAL BALANCE DEBIT	2 TRIAL BALANCE CREDIT	3 ADJUSTMENTS DEBIT	4 ADJUSTMENTS CREDIT	
1	*Cash*	29 080 28				1
2	*Petty Cash*	300 00				2
3	*Accounts Receivable*	11 198 40				3
4	*Merchandise Inventory*	270 480 00			(a) 15 840 00	4
5	*Supplies—Office*	6 480 00			(b) 4 730 00	5
6	*Supplies—Store*	6 944 00			(c) 3 910 00	6
7	*Prepaid Insurance*	5 800 00			(d) 3 170 00	7
8	*Accounts Payable*		12 542 38			8
9	*Employee Income Tax Payable*		542 00			9
29	*Payroll Taxes Expense*	9 105 00				29
30	*Rent Expense*	21 000 00				30
31	*Salary Expense*	89 400 00				31
32	*Supplies Expense—Office*			(b) 4 730 00		32
33	*Supplies Expense—Store*			(c) 3 910 00		33
34	*Utilities Expense*	3 820 00				34
35		714 036 83	714 036 83	27 650 00	27 650 00	35
36	*Net Income*					36
37						37
38						38

Some large merchandising businesses *with many accounts to be adjusted* at the end of a fiscal period may use a 10-column work sheet. A 10-column work sheet includes an additional pair of amount columns titled Adjusted Trial Balance.

STEPS: Completing a 10-column work sheet

1. Record the trial balance on the work sheet.
2. Plan the adjustments on the work sheet.
3. Extend the balances in the Trial Balance Debit and Credit columns to the Adjusted Trial Balance Debit and Credit columns. Calculate up-to-date adjusted balances for all accounts affected by adjustments.
4. Total, prove, and rule the Adjusted Trial Balance Debit and Credit columns.
5. Extend the amounts in the Adjusted Trial Balance Debit and Credit columns to the appropriate Income Statement and Balance Sheet columns.
6. Total, prove, and rule the Income Statement and Balance Sheet columns in the same way as on an 8-column work sheet.

A 10-COLUMN WORK SHEET FOR A MERCHANDISING BUSINESS (RIGHT PAGE)

3. Adjusted Trial Balance

5. Extend Amounts

4. Total, Prove, and Rule

6. Total, Prove, and Rule

	5	6	7	8	9	10	
	ADJUSTED TRIAL BALANCE		INCOME STATEMENT		BALANCE SHEET		
	DEBIT	CREDIT	DEBIT	CREDIT	DEBIT	CREDIT	
1	29080 28				29080 28		1
2	300 00				300 00		2
3	11198 40				11198 40		3
4	254640 00				254640 00		4
5	1750 00				1750 00		5
6	3034 00				3034 00		6
7	2630 00				2630 00		7
8		125422 38				125422 38	8
9		542 00				542 00	9
29	9105 00		9105 00				29
30	21000 00		21000 00				30
31	89400 00		89400 00				31
32	4730 00		4730 00				32
33	3910 00		3910 00				33
34	3820 00		3820 00				34
35	714036 83	714036 83	353504 15	423120 00	360532 68	290916 83	35
36			69615 85			69615 85	36
37			423120 00	423120 00	360532 68	360532 68	37
38							38

Any business with adjustments to make at the end of a fiscal period could use either an 8-column or a 10-column work sheet. However, completing two extra amount columns when most of the account balances *are not* adjusted requires extra time and work. Account balances not adjusted must be extended from the Trial Balance columns to the Adjusted Trial Balance columns; whereas, with an 8-column work sheet, account balances *not* adjusted are extended directly to the Balance Sheet or Income Statement columns. Omni Import prefers to use an 8-column work sheet because only four adjustments are needed at the end of each fiscal period.

REMEMBER

A 10-column work sheet is often used by large merchandising companies with many accounts to be adjusted.

AUDIT YOUR UNDERSTANDING

1. In what column is the Income Summary amount extended?
2. When does a net loss appear on a work sheet?
3. To which Balance Sheet column is a net loss amount extended?
4. What extra step is required when a 10-column work sheet is prepared instead of an 8-column work sheet?

WORK TOGETHER

Completing an 8-column work sheet for a merchandising business

Use the Paradise Company work sheet from Work Together on page 377. Your instructor will guide you through the following examples.

5. Extend balance sheet items to the work sheet's Balance Sheet columns.
6. Extend income statement items, including Income Summary, to the work sheet's Income Statement columns.
7. Subtotal the Income Statement and Balance Sheet columns.
8. Calculate the net income or net loss.
9. Extend the amount of net income or net loss to the Balance Sheet Debit or Credit column.
10. Total the four Income Statement and Balance Sheet amount columns.
11. Check that the totals for each pair of columns are in balance.

ON YOUR OWN

Completing an 8-column work sheet for a merchandising business

Use the Mueller Company work sheet from On Your Own on page 377. Work these problems independently.

12. Extend balance sheet items to the work sheet's Balance Sheet columns.
13. Extend income statement items, including Income Summary, to the work sheet's Income Statement columns.
14. Subtotal the Income Statement and Balance Sheet columns.
15. Calculate the net income or net loss.
16. Extend the amount of net income or net loss to the Balance Sheet Debit or Credit column.
17. Total the four Income Statement and Balance Sheet amount columns.
18. Check that the totals for each pair of columns are in balance.

CHAPTER 15 SUMMARY

After completing this chapter, you can

1. Define important accounting terms related to a work sheet for a merchandising business.
2. Identify accounting concepts and practices related to a work sheet for a merchandising business.
3. Begin a work sheet for a merchandising business.
4. Plan adjustments on a work sheet for a merchandising business.
5. Complete a work sheet for a merchandising business.

EXPLORE ACCOUNTING

ACCOUNTING SYSTEMS DESIGN

An important role of accountants is to prepare financial statements for businesses. In addition, many accountants design accounting systems used to prepare the various financial reports important to successful business operations.

An accounting system should be designed to meet the needs of the business it serves. Factors to consider are size of the company, number of facility locations, geographic area of operations (local, statewide, national, international), number of employees, and type of organization (service, merchandising, manufacturing). Also to be considered are the intended uses of the information: traditional financial statements (income statement, balance sheet, cash flow statement), income tax information, management decision information, management control information, and product pricing information.

An accounting system is built around a chart of accounts, which provides the organizational system around which information will be collected, filed, and made available for various types of financial reports.

A small business owned and operated by one person may not need detailed information. However, as a business grows in size and complexity, more detailed information is required. Large international businesses need very complex accounting systems with hundreds of accounts to furnish management with the information needed to make decisions and the data for various reports required by governments and other agencies. As businesses grow, accountants constantly look for ways to provide better information. Thus, accountants play a key role in the successful growth of a business.

Activity: Assume Omni Import has made the decision to change from a merchandising business to a manufacturing business. It will import fine yarns and cloth from Europe and Asia. From these imported materials, it will manufacture various items of clothing. As the accountant, how would you recommend the chart of accounts be modified to meet the changing needs of the company?

15-1 APPLICATION PROBLEM

Beginning an 8-column work sheet for a merchandising business

A work sheet for Drake Park Supply Company is given in the *Working Papers*. The company's general ledger account balances on December 31 of the current year, after all transactions have been posted, are listed below.

Cash	$ 29,066.00	
Petty Cash	330.00	
Accounts Receivable	11,762.00	
Merchandise Inventory	279,668.00	
Supplies—Office	6,700.00	
Supplies—Store	7,168.00	
Prepaid Insurance	6,094.00	
Accounts Payable		$ 11,814.00
Sales Tax Payable		2,184.00
Tracey Johnson, Capital		129,663.00
Tracey Johnson, Drawing	22,583.00	
Bill Fujiwara, Capital		130,394.00
Bill Fujiwara, Drawing	23,078.00	
Income Summary		
Sales		348,084.00
Purchases	196,416.00	
Advertising Expense	6,820.00	
Credit Card Fee Expense	3,590.00	
Insurance Expense		
Miscellaneous Expense	2,717.00	
Rent Expense	22,200.00	
Supplies Expense—Office		
Supplies Expense—Store		
Utilities Expense	3,947.00	

Instructions:

1. Enter Drake Park Supply Company's general ledger accounts and balances in the appropriate columns of the work sheet.
2. Total, prove, and rule the trial balance.
3. From a physical count of merchandise inventory, the December 31 balance is determined to be $263,289.00. Analyze the merchandise inventory adjustment and enter the adjustment on the work sheet.

15-2 APPLICATION PROBLEM

Analyzing and recording adjustments on a work sheet

The following chart contains adjustment information related to the preparation of work sheets for three businesses. A form for analyzing transactions is given in the *Working Papers*.

Business	Account Title and Balance		End-of-Fiscal-Period Information	
A	1. Merchandise Inventory	$177,600.00	Merchandise inventory	$160,800.00
	2. Supplies—Office	6,900.00	Office supplies inventory	5,040.00
	3. Supplies—Store	5,905.00	Store supplies inventory	4,610.00
	4. Prepaid Insurance	2,230.00	Value of prepaid insurance	1,490.00
B	1. Merchandise Inventory	$218,400.00	Merchandise inventory	$199,200.00
	2. Supplies—Office	5,620.00	Office supplies inventory	4,150.00
	3. Supplies—Store	7,110.00	Store supplies inventory	5,185.00
	4. Prepaid Insurance	3,025.00	Value of prepaid insurance	1,510.00
C	1. Merchandise Inventory	$199,800.00	Merchandise inventory	$213,600.00
	2. Supplies—Office	6,550.00	Office supplies inventory	5,425.00
	3. Supplies—Store	7,175.00	Store supplies inventory	5,950.00
	4. Prepaid Insurance	2,590.00	Value of prepaid insurance	1,295.00

Instructions:

For each business, analyze the adjustments for merchandise inventory, office supplies inventory, store supplies inventory, and prepaid insurance. List the accounts affected and the amounts for each of the adjustments. List the account titles in Column 3 and the amounts in either Column 4 or 5. Adjustment 1 for Business A is given as an example in the *Working Papers.*

15-3 APPLICATION PROBLEM
Completing an 8-column work sheet for a merchandising business

Lotus Gallery's partially completed work sheet is given in the *Working Papers.*

Instructions:

1. Extend the balance sheet items to the Balance Sheet columns of the work sheet.
2. Extend the income statement items to the Income Statement columns of the work sheet.
3. Subtotal the Income Statement and Balance Sheet columns.
4. Calculate and record the net income or net loss.
5. Extend the amount of net income or net loss to the Balance Sheet Debit or Credit column.
6. Total and rule the Income Statement and Balance Sheet columns.

15-4 MASTERY PROBLEM
Preparing an 8-column work sheet for a merchandising business

Seidler Supply's trial balance as of December 31 of the current year is recorded on a work sheet in the *Working Papers.*

Instructions:

1. Analyze the following adjustment information and record the adjustments on the work sheet.

End-of-Fiscal-Period Information

Merchandise inventory	$250,320.00
Office supplies inventory	2,226.00
Store supplies inventory	2,825.00
Value of prepaid insurance	1,890.00

2. Complete the work sheet.

15-5 CHALLENGE PROBLEM
Preparing a 10-column work sheet for a merchandising business

K.B. Cycle Shop's trial balance as of December 31 of the current year is recorded on a work sheet in the *Working Papers.*

Instructions:

1. Use the following adjustment information. Complete the 10-column work sheet.

End-of-Fiscal-Period Information

Merchandise inventory	$308,055.00
Office supplies inventory	3,240.00
Store supplies inventory	3,290.00
Value of prepaid insurance	1,980.00

2. Compare and contrast the advantages and disadvantages of 8-column and 10-column work sheets.

INTERNET ACTIVITY

Point your browser to
http://accounting.swpco.com
Choose **First-Year Course**, choose **Activities**, and complete the activity for Chapter 15.

Applied Communication

Sometimes a credit customer does not pay off the amount due on an account receivable by the deadline specified in the terms of the sale on account. In this situation, a business wants to (1) receive the amount owed and (2) preserve a long-term relationship so there can be repeated sales to that customer.

Instructions: Write a first-notice letter to a customer who has not yet paid an amount due. Balance your business's need to receive payment with the desire to keep the customer's goodwill now and in the future. Use a supportive opening and closing.

Cases for Critical Thinking

Case 1 After completing a work sheet, Park's Boutique finds that garment bags still in boxes were overlooked in calculating the supplies inventory. The value of the garment bags overlooked is $60.00. Jerry Park suggests that the accountant not worry because the oversight does not have any effect on balancing the Income Statement and Balance Sheet columns of the work sheet. Mr. Park says that the oversight will be corrected when the store supplies are counted at the end of the next fiscal period. The accountant recommends that the work sheet be redone to reflect the recalculated supplies inventory. Do you agree with Mr. Park or the accountant? Explain your answer.

Case 2 High Five Sports Equipment paid $1,800.00 for a one-year fire insurance policy. The company prepares an income statement and balance sheet every three months. However, the accountant prepares a prepaid insurance adjustment only at the end of the year. Wanda Fielder, one of the partners in the business, thinks the prepaid insurance should be adjusted every three months. Who is correct? Why?

AUTOMATED ACCOUNTING

UNDERSTANDING GRAPHS

Charts and graphs provide a picture of numeric data. Computer presentations and printed reports frequently include charts and graphs. Charts and graphs do not replace the numeric data, but they do help explain the data. To be effective, charts and graphs should be clearly labeled. Charts and graphs are commonly used to track sales goals, monitor expenses, identify trends, and make forecasts.

Graphs and charts effectively communicate summary data such as component percentages. Different styles of graphs are used to display different types of financial information. A pie graph is used to illustrate parts of a whole. For example, a pie graph could be used to show cost of goods sold, operating expenses, and net income as percentages of net sales. Bar graphs are used to show the relative size of related items, such as expenses. Line graphs are used to illustrate trends, such as net sales or net income over a period of years.

Many accounting software packages are capable of producing charts and graphs from data contained within their files. *Automated Accounting 7.0* can generate two- and three-dimensional pie and bar charts and line graphs from data found on the:

- Balance sheet.
- Income statement.
- Sales report.
- Expense distribution report.
- Actual versus budget comparison report.

To prepare a graph based on financial data:

1. Choose the Graph Selection menu item from the Reports menu or click the Graphs toolbar button.
2. When the Graph Selection dialog box appears, select an option from the Data to Graph list.
3. Select an option from the Type of Graph list. (Menu items may be unavailable for charts and graphs that are inappropriate for some reports.) (In *Automated Accounting 8.0*, graphs are selected from the Graph selection window. The types of graphs available depend on the types of company and available data.)
4. Click the OK button to produce the graph.

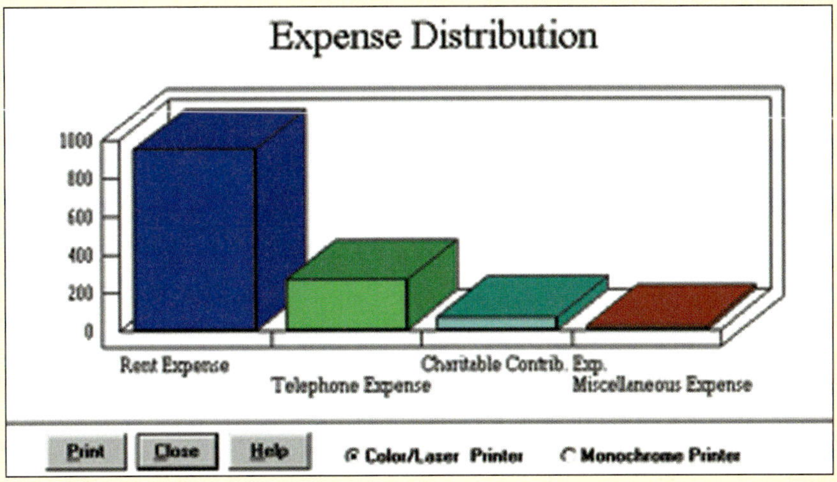

16 Financial Statements for a Partnership

AFTER STUDYING CHAPTER 16, YOU WILL BE ABLE TO:

1. Define accounting terms related to financial statements for a merchandising business organized as a partnership.
2. Identify accounting concepts and practices related to financial statements for a merchandising business organized as a partnership.
3. Prepare an income statement for a merchandising business organized as a partnership.
4. Analyze an income statement using component percentages for a merchandising business organized as a partnership.
5. Prepare a distribution of net income statement and an owners' equity statement for a merchandising business organized as a partnership.
6. Prepare a balance sheet for a merchandising business organized as a partnership.

TERMS PREVIEW

cost of merchandise sold

gross profit on sales

distribution of net income statement

owners' equity statement

supporting schedule

USES OF FINANCIAL STATEMENTS

Financial statements provide the primary source of information needed by owners and managers to make decisions on the future activity of a business. All financial information must be reported in order to make sound business decisions. The financial statements should provide information about a business's financial condition, changes in this financial condition, and the progress of operations. *(CONCEPT: Adequate Disclosure)*

Comparing financial condition and progress for more than one fiscal period also helps owners and managers make sound business decisions. Therefore, financial information must be reported the same way from one fiscal period to the next. *(CONCEPT: Consistent Reporting)*

A business organized as a partnership prepares four financial statements to report financial progress and condition. A partnership prepares an income statement and a balance sheet similar to those used by a proprietorship. A partnership also prepares two additional financial statements. One statement reports the distribution of net income or net loss for each partner. The other statement reports the changes in owners' equity for the fiscal period.

ACCOUNTING IN YOUR CAREER

SUPERSTAR PARTNERSHIP

Huston's is a new restaurant in town, owned by Marcus Huston. Marcus has a degree in business but has opened his own restaurant to combine his culinary skills with his business training. The restaurant business is very competitive, and Marcus spends up to $5,000 per month on advertising and promotion costs to attract customers. Huston's is beginning to become a well-known downtown restaurant and Marcus is earning a good living, but he has the space and the ambition to make the restaurant even more successful. He's been looking for something dramatic to draw media attention to his restaurant.

Drew Taylor is a popular professional football player in town. He is a solid player on the championship team and is also well-liked and respected by people who live in the area. Drew has approached Marcus, an old college friend, with the idea of forming a partnership to run Huston's. Both Drew and Marcus believe that Drew's fame and popularity could be the dramatic turn that would make the business soar.

Marcus is tempted. So he consults with his accountant and attorney for advice.

Critical Thinking:

1. The accountant advises against forming the partnership unless Drew Taylor invests a substantial amount of cash to buy his share of the business. What is the advantage of this plan?
2. The accountant suggests that there might be more advantages in just paying Drew for the use of his name for advertising purposes. Why would the accountant make this recommendation?
3. The accountant tells Marcus that if he pursues the partnership, he must be sure to have a written agreement that specifies the responsibilities of each partner and the distribution of earnings. Do you think this is necessary when friends go into business together?

16-1 Income Statement

INCOME STATEMENT INFORMATION ON A WORK SHEET

Omni Import
Work Sheet
For Year Ended December 31, 20--

	ACCOUNT TITLE	1 TRIAL BALANCE DEBIT	2 TRIAL BALANCE CREDIT	3 ADJUSTMENTS DEBIT	4 ADJUSTMENTS CREDIT	5 INCOME STATEMENT DEBIT	6 INCOME STATEMENT CREDIT	7 BALANCE SHEET DEBIT	8 BALANCE SHEET CREDIT	
4	*Merchandise Inventory*	270 480 00			(a) 15 840 00			254 640 00		4
23	*Sales*		423 120 00				423 120 00			23
24	*Purchases*	189 960 00				189 960 00				24
25	*Advertising Expense*	6 600 00				6 600 00				25
26	*Credit Card Fee Expense*	3 385 00				3 385 00				26
27	*Insurance Expense*			(d) 3 170 00		3 170 00				27
28	*Miscellaneous Expense*	2 584 15				2 584 15				28
29	*Payroll Taxes Expense*	9 105 00				9 105 00				29
30	*Rent Expense*	21 000 00				21 000 00				30
31	*Salary Expense*	89 400 00				89 400 00				31
32	*Supplies Expense—Office*			(b) 4 730 00		4 730 00				32
33	*Supplies Expense—Store*			(c) 3 910 00		3 910 00				33
34	*Utilities Expense*	3 820 00				3 820 00				34
35		714 036 83	714 036 83	27 650 00	27 650 00	353 504 15	423 120 00	360 532 68	290 916 83	35
36	*Net Income*					69 615 85			69 615 85	36
37						423 120 00	423 120 00	360 532 68	360 532 68	37
38										38
39										39
40										40
41										41
42										42

An income statement is used to report a business's financial progress. Merchandising businesses report revenue, cost of merchandise sold, gross profit on sales, expenses, and net income or loss. Current and previous income statements can be compared to determine the reasons for increases or decreases in net income. This comparison is helpful in making management decisions about future operations.

Information from a completed work sheet is used to prepare an income statement.

The income statement of a merchandising business has three main sections: (1) revenue section, (2) cost of merchandise sold section, and (3) expenses section. The total original price of all merchandise sold during a fiscal period is called the **cost of merchandise sold.** *(CONCEPT: Historical Cost)* Cost of merchandise sold is sometimes known as cost of goods sold or cost of sales. Omni uses eight steps in preparing an income statement. The steps are described on the following three pages.

FIRST TWO SECTIONS OF AN INCOME STATEMENT FOR A MERCHANDISING BUSINESS

1. Heading

2. Revenue Section

3. Cost of Merchandise Sold Section

Omni Import
Income Statement
For Year Ended December 31, 20--

			% OF SALES
Revenue:			
Sales		423,120.00	
Cost of Merchandise Sold:			
Merchandise Inventory, January 1, 20--	270,480.00		
Purchases	189,960.00		
Total Cost of Mdse. Available for Sale	460,440.00		
Less Mdse. Inventory, December 31, 20--	254,640.00		
Cost of Merchandise Sold		205,800.00	

STEPS: Preparing an income statement

1. Write the income statement heading on three lines.

2. Prepare the revenue section. Use information from the Income Statement Credit column of the work sheet.

a. Write the name of this section, *Revenue:*, at the extreme left of the wide column on the first line.

b. Write the title of the revenue account, *Sales,* on the next line, indented about one centimeter.

c. Write the balance of the sales account, *$423,120.00,* in the second amount column. For Omni Import, this amount is also the total of the revenue section.

3. Prepare the cost of merchandise sold section.

a. Write the name of this section, *Cost of Merchandise Sold:*, at the extreme left of the wide column.

b. Indent about one centimeter on the next line, and write the items needed to calculate cost of merchandise sold. Write the amount of each item in the first amount column.

Beginning merchandise inventory, January 1 ...... (Debit balance of Merchandise Inventory in the Trial Balance Debit column of the work sheet.)	$ 270,480.00
Plus purchases made during the fiscal period ...... (Debit balance of Purchases in the Income Statement Debit column of the work sheet.)	+189,960.00
Equals total cost of merchandise available for sale during the fiscal period.	$ 460,440.00
Less ending merchandise inventory, December 31 (Debit balance of Merchandise Inventory in the Balance Sheet Debit column of the work sheet.)	−254,640.00
Equals cost of merchandise sold during the fiscal period	$ 205,800.00

c. Indent about one centimeter on the next line, and write *Cost of Merchandise Sold.* Write the cost of merchandise sold amount, *$205,800.00,* in the second amount column.

COMPLETING AN INCOME STATEMENT FOR A MERCHANDISING BUSINESS

8. Component Percentages

4. Gross Profit on Sales

5. Expenses Section

6. Net Income

7. Double Lines

Omni Import Income Statement For Year Ended December 31, 20--			
			% OF SALES
Revenue:			
Sales		423,120.00	100.0
Cost of Merchandise Sold:			
Merchandise Inventory, January 1, 20--	270,480.00		
Purchases	189,960.00		
Total Cost of Mdse. Available for Sale	460,440.00		
Less Mdse. Inventory, December 31, 20--	254,640.00		
Cost of Merchandise Sold		205,800.00	48.6
Gross Profit on Sales		217,320.00	51.4
Expenses:			
Advertising Expense	6,600.00		
Credit Card Fee Expense	3,385.00		
Insurance Expense	3,170.00		
Miscellaneous Expense	2,584.15		
Payroll Taxes Expense	9,105.00		
Rent Expense	21,000.00		
Salary Expense	89,400.00		
Supplies Expense—Office	4,730.00		
Supplies Expense—Store	3,910.00		
Utilities Expense	3,820.00		
Total Expenses		147,704.15	34.9
Net Income		69,615.85	16.5

STEPS

Preparing an income statement *(continued)*

4. Calculate the gross profit on sales. The revenue remaining after cost of merchandise sold has been deducted is called **gross profit on sales.**

a. Write *Gross Profit on Sales* on the next line at the extreme left of the wide column.

b. Write the gross profit on sales amount, *$217,320.00*, in the second amount column. (Total revenue, $423,120.00, *less* cost of merchandise sold, $205,800.00, *equals* gross profit on sales, $217,320.00.)

5. Prepare the expenses section. Use the information from the Income Statement Debit column of the work sheet.

a. Write the name of this section, *Expenses:*, at the extreme left of the wide column.

b. On the next line, indented about one centimeter, list the expense account titles, one per line, in the order in which they appear on the work sheet.

c. Write the amount of each expense account balance in the first amount column.

d. Indent about one centimeter, and write *Total Expenses* on the next line in the wide column below the last expense account title.

e. Total the individual expense amounts and write the total, *$147,704.15,* in the second amount column on the total line.

6. Calculate the net income.

a. Write *Net Income* on the next line at the extreme left of the wide column.

b. Write the net income amount, *$69,615.85,* in the second amount column on the net income line. (Gross profit on sales, $217,320.00, *less* total expenses, $147,704.15, *equals* net income, $69,615.85.)

c. Verify accuracy by comparing the amount of net income calculated on the income statement, $69,615.85, with the amount on the work sheet, $69,615.85. The two amounts must be the same.

7. Rule double lines across both amount columns to show that the income statement has been verified as correct.

8. Calculate the component percentages. The percentage relationship between one financial statement item and the total that includes that item is known as a component percentage. On the income statement, sales includes four components: cost of merchandise sold, gross profit on sales, total expenses, and net income.

a. Calculate the component percentages by dividing the amount of each component by the amount of sales.

Cost of Merchandise Sold	÷	**Sales**	=	**Cost of Merchandise Sold Component Percentage**
$205,800.00	÷	$423,120.00	=	48.6%
Gross Profit on Sales	÷	**Sales**	=	**Gross Profit on Sales Component Percentage**
$217,320.00	÷	$423,120.00	=	51.4%
Total Expenses	÷	**Sales**	=	**Total Expenses Component Percentage**
$147,704.15	÷	$423,120.00	=	34.9%
Net Income	÷	**Sales**	=	**Net Income Component Percentage**
$69,615.85	÷	$423,120.00	=	16.5%

b. Write each component percentage in the % of Sales column. The use of the component percentages is described later in this chapter.

REMEMBER

Amounts are listed in the first amount column of the financial statement and totaled in the second column. These are amount columns, not debit and credit columns.

TERMS REVIEW

cost of merchandise sold

gross profit on sales

2398

AUDIT YOUR UNDERSTANDING

1. What is the major difference between the income statement for a merchandising business and a service business?
2. How is the cost of merchandise sold calculated?
3. How can the amount of net income calculated on the income statement be verified?

WORK TOGETHER

Preparing an income statement for a merchandising business

A to Z Auto Parts' work sheet for the year ended December 31 of the current year is given in the *Working Papers.* Your instructor will guide you through the following examples.

4. Prepare an income statement.
5. Calculate and record on the income statement the following component percentages: (a) cost of merchandise sold, (b) gross profit on sales, (c) total expenses, and (d) net income or loss. Round percentage calculations to the nearest 0.1%. Save your work to complete Work Together on page 401 and page 407.

ON YOUR OWN

Preparing an income statement for a merchandising business

Electron Games' work sheet for the year ended December 31 of the current year is given in the *Working Papers.* Work independently to complete these problems.

6. Prepare an income statement.
7. Calculate and record on the income statement the following component percentages: (a) cost of merchandise sold, (b) gross profit on sales, (c) total expenses, and (d) net income or loss. Round percentage calculations to the nearest 0.1%. Save your work to complete On Your Own on page 401 and page 407.

16-2 Component Percentages

ANALYZING AN INCOME STATEMENT SHOWING A NET INCOME

For Omni Import, a merchandising business, every sales dollar reported on the income statement includes four components: (1) cost of merchandise sold, (2) gross profit on sales, (3) total expenses, and (4) net income. To help make decisions about future operations, Omni analyzes relationships between these four income statement components and sales. Omni calculates a component percentage for each of the four components. The relationship between each component and sales is shown in a separate column on the income statement.

ACCEPTABLE COMPONENT PERCENTAGES

	Acceptable Industry Standards	Omni Import Component Percentages
Sales	100%	100.0%
Cost of merchandise sold	not more than 50.0%	48.6%
Gross profit on sales	not less than 50.0%	51.4%
Total expenses	not more than 35.0%	34.9%
Net income	not less than 15.0%	16.5%

For a component percentage to be useful, a business must know acceptable percentages. This information is determined by making comparisons with prior fiscal periods as well as with industry standards that are published by industry organizations. Based on these sources, Omni Import determines acceptable component percentages. Each percentage represents the amount of each sales dollar that is considered acceptable. For example, Omni Import determines that no more than 50 cents, or 50.0%, of each sales dollar should be devoted to cost of merchandise sold.

FYI

Unacceptable component percentages serve as a warning that management action is necessary. Calculating and reporting component percentages is an example of how accounting information can help management planning and decision making. Well-run businesses greatly value the information provided from accounting records.

ANALYSIS OF COMPONENT PERCENTAGES

Omni compares four of its component percentages to its acceptable component percentages. The four component percentages are for cost of merchandise sold, gross profit on sales, total expenses, and net income.

Cost of Merchandise Sold Component Percentage

The cost of merchandise sold is a major cost and must be kept as low as possible. Analysis of Omni Import's component percentages shows that the cost of merchandise sold is 48.6% of sales.

The component percentage for cost of merchandise sold, 48.6%, is *less than* the maximum acceptable percentage, 50.0%. Therefore, Omni Import's component percentage for cost of merchandise sold is considered acceptable.

Gross Profit on Sales Component Percentage

Gross profit must be large enough to cover total expenses and the desired amount of net income. Acceptable industry standards show that at least 50 cents, or 50.0%, of each sales dollar should result in gross profit. Omni Import's component percentage for gross profit on sales is 51.4%.

The component percentage for gross profit on sales, 51.4%, is *not less than* the minimum acceptable percentage, 50.0%. Therefore, Omni Import's component percentage for gross profit on sales is considered acceptable.

Total Expenses Component Percentage

Total expenses must be less than gross profit on sales to provide a desirable net income. Acceptable industry standards show that no more than 35 cents, or 35.0%, of each sales dollar should be devoted to total expenses. Omni Import's component percentage for total expenses is 34.9%.

The component percentage for total expenses, 34.9%, is *not more than* the maximum acceptable percentage, 35.0%. Therefore, Omni Import's component percentage for total expenses is considered acceptable.

Net Income Component Percentage

The component percentage for net income shows the progress being made by a business. Acceptable industry standards show that at least 15 cents, or 15.0%, of each sales dollar should result in net income. Omni Import's component percentage for net income is 16.5%.

The component percentage for net income, 16.5%, is *not less than* the minimum acceptable percentage, 15.0%. Therefore, Omni Import's component percentage for net income is considered acceptable.

F.Y.I.

A partnership is a traditional and very common form of business organization. The Revised Uniform Partnership Act is a law that governs partnerships in most states. Employees responsible for accounting records should be aware of the laws that apply to business operations.

ANALYZING AN INCOME STATEMENT SHOWING A NET LOSS

Cloth Circuit Income Statement For Year Ended December 31, 20--			% OF SALES
Revenue:			
Sales		270,480.00	100.0
Cost of Merchandise Sold:			
Merchandise Inventory, January 1, 20--	291,840.00		
Purchases	166,680.00		
Total Cost of Mdse. Available for Sale	458,520.00		
Less Mdse. Inventory, December 31, 20--	310,910.00		
Cost of Merchandise Sold		147,610.00	54.6
Gross Profit on Sales		122,870.00	45.4
Expenses:			
Advertising Expense	6,240.00		
Credit Card Fee Expense	3,744.00		
Insurance Expense	1,260.00		
Miscellaneous Expense	2,868.00		
Payroll Taxes Expense	7,615.00		
Rent Expense	17,280.00		
Salary Expense	74,770.00		
Supplies Expense—Office	5,544.00		
Supplies Expense—Store	5,136.00		
Utilities Expense	4,093.00		
Total Expenses		128,550.00	47.5
Net Loss		(5,680.00)	(2.1)

When a business's total expenses are greater than the gross profit on sales, the difference is known as a net loss. For example, the income statement above shows a net loss of $5,680.00 for the fiscal period.

Total expenses, $128,550.00, *less* gross profit on sales, $122,870.00, *equals* net loss, $5,680.00. The net loss amount, $5,680.00, is written in parentheses in the second amount column on the line with the words *Net Loss.* An amount written in parentheses on a financial statement indicates a negative amount.

Cloth Circuit uses the same acceptable component percentages as Omni Import. Analysis of the income statement indicates unacceptable component percentages: (1) The component percentage for cost of merchandise sold, 54.6%, is *more than* the maximum acceptable component percentage, 50.0%. (2) The component percentage for gross profit on sales, 45.4%, is *less than* the minimum acceptable component percentage, 50.0%. (3) The component percentage for total expenses, 47.5%, is *more than* the maximum acceptable component percentage, 35.0%. (4) Because a net loss occurred, the component percentage for net income, (2.1%), means that Cloth Circuit lost 2.1 cents on each sales dollar. The net loss amount, $5,680.00, is considered unacceptable.

REMEMBER

Negative amounts are written in parentheses.

ACTIONS TO CORRECT UNACCEPTABLE COMPONENT PERCENTAGES

The goal of any business is to earn an acceptable net income. When component percentages are not acceptable, regardless of whether a net income or net loss occurred, management action is necessary.

Unacceptable Component Percentage for Gross Profit on Sales

The component percentage for gross profit on sales is directly related to sales revenue and cost of merchandise sold. An unacceptable component percentage for gross profit on sales requires one of three actions: (1) increase sales revenue, (2) decrease cost of merchandise sold, or (3) increase sales revenue and also decrease cost of merchandise sold.

Increasing sales revenue while keeping the cost of merchandise sold the same will increase gross profit on sales. To increase sales revenue, management may consider increasing the markup on merchandise purchased for sale. However, a business must be cautious on the amount of the markup increase. If the increase in markup is too large, a decrease in sales revenue could occur for two reasons: (1) the sales price is beyond what customers are willing to pay or (2) the sales price is higher than what competing businesses charge for the same merchandise.

Decreasing the cost of merchandise sold while keeping the sales revenue the same will also increase gross profit on sales. To decrease cost of merchandise sold, management should review purchasing practices. For example, would purchasing merchandise in larger quantities or from other vendors result in a lower cost?

Combining a small increase in sales revenue and a small decrease in the cost of merchandise sold may also result in an acceptable component percentage for gross profit on sales.

Unacceptable Component Percentage for Total Expenses

Each expense account balance must be reviewed to determine if major increases have occurred. This review should include comparisons with prior fiscal periods as well as with industry standards. Actions must then be taken to reduce any expenses for which major increases have occurred or that are beyond industry standards.

Unacceptable Component Percentage for Net Income

If the component percentages for cost of merchandise sold, gross profit on sales, and total expenses are brought within acceptable ranges, net income will also be acceptable.

AUDIT YOUR UNDERSTANDING

1. For a merchandising business, every sales dollar includes what four components?
2. How does a company determine acceptable component percentages?
3. What is the result if total expenses are greater than gross profit on sales?

WORK TOGETHER

Analyzing component percentages

Use the income statement for A to Z Auto Parts from Work Together on page 396. A form for completing these problems is given in the *Working Papers.* Your instructor will guide you through the following examples.

4. A to Z Auto Parts determines that no more than 63 cents, or 63.0%, of each sales dollar should be devoted to cost of merchandise sold. Compare the actual component percentage for cost of merchandise sold to the acceptable percentage. Indicate if the actual component percentage is acceptable or unacceptable. If it is unacceptable, suggest an action that corrects it.
5. Acceptable auto parts industry standards show that at least 37 cents, or 37.0%, of each sales dollar should result in gross profit. For A to Z Auto Parts, compare the actual component percentage for gross profit on sales to the acceptable percentage. Indicate if the actual component percentage is acceptable or unacceptable. If it is unacceptable, suggest an action that corrects it.

ON YOUR OWN

Analyzing component percentages

Use the income statement for Electron Games from On Your Own on page 396. A form for completing these problems is given in the *Working Papers.* Work independently to complete these problems.

6. Acceptable game industry standards show that no more than 13 cents, or 13.0%, of each sales dollar should be devoted to total expenses. For Electron Games, compare the actual component percentage for total expenses to the acceptable percentage. Indicate if the actual component percentage is acceptable or unacceptable. If it is unacceptable, suggest an action that corrects it.
7. Acceptable game industry standards show that at least 25 cents, or 25.0%, of each sales dollar should result in net income. For Electron Games, compare the actual component percentage for net income to the acceptable percentage. Indicate if the actual component percentage is acceptable or unacceptable. If it is unacceptable, suggest an action that corrects it.

16-3 Distribution of Net Income and Owners' Equity Statements

PREPARING A DISTRIBUTION OF NET INCOME STATEMENT

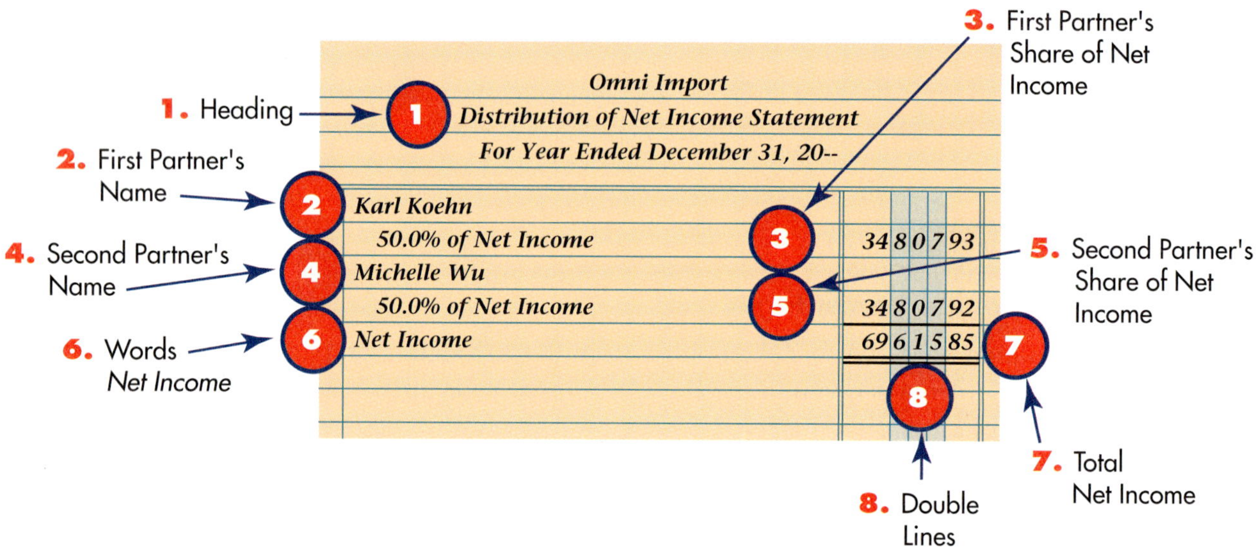

A partnership's net income or net loss may be divided in any way agreed upon by the partners in their partnership agreement. Karl Koehn and Michelle Wu, partners in Omni Import, agreed to share net income or net loss equally.

A partnership distribution of net income or net loss is usually shown on a separate financial statement. A partnership financial statement showing net income or loss distribution to partners is called a **distribution of net income statement.**

The net income, $69,615.85, from Omni Import's income statement is used to prepare the distribution of net income statement.

STEPS: Preparing a distribution of net income statement

1. Write the heading of the distribution of net income statement on three lines.
2. Write one partner's name, *Karl Koehn,* on the first line at the extreme left of the wide column.
3. Indent about one centimeter on the next line, and write Karl Koehn's share of net income as a percentage, *50.0% of Net Income.* Write Mr. Koehn's share of net income, *$34,807.93* (50.0% × $69,615.85), in the amount column on the same line. The last time net income was an odd number, Ms. Wu received the extra penny. For the current year, therefore, Mr. Koehn receives the extra penny.
4. Write the other partner's name, *Michelle Wu,* on the next line at the extreme left of the wide column.
5. Indent about one centimeter on the next line, and write Michelle Wu's share of net income as a percentage, *50.0% of Net Income.* Write Ms. Wu's share of net income, *$34,807.92* (50.0% × $69,615.85), in the amount column on the same line.
6. Write *Net Income* on the next line at the extreme left of the wide column.
7. Add the distribution of net income for Karl Koehn, *$34,807.93,* and for Michelle Wu, *$34,807.92.* Write the total amount, *$69,615.85,* in the amount column. Verify accuracy by comparing the total amount, $69,615.85, with the net income reported on the income statement, $69,615.85. The two amounts must be the same.
8. Rule double lines across the amount column to show that the distribution of net income statement has been verified as correct.

DISTRIBUTION OF NET INCOME STATEMENT WITH UNEQUAL DISTRIBUTION OF EARNINGS

Custom Cabinets	
Distribution of Net Income Statement	
For Year Ended December 31, 20--	
Beth Castillo	
60.0% of Net Income	48960 00
Jana Kenyon	
40.0% of Net Income	32640 00
Net Income	81600 00

Regardless of how earnings are shared, the steps in preparing a distribution of net income statement are the same. The only difference is the description of how the earnings are to be shared by the partners.

Beth Castillo and Jana Kenyon are partners in a business. Because Ms. Castillo spends more time in the business than Ms. Kenyon, the partners agree to share net income or loss unequally. Ms. Castillo gets 60.0% of net income or loss. Ms. Kenyon gets 40.0% of net income or loss. With a net income of $81,600.00, Ms. Castillo receives 60.0%, or $48,960.00. Ms. Kenyon receives 40.0%, or $32,640.00.

CULTURAL DIVERSITY

BUSINESS CULTURE AND ACCOUNTANCY IN RUSSIA

The changeover of Russia's economy from socialism to *free enterprise* is strongly influencing Russian business culture. Employees, who for generations have depended on the government to fulfill their needs, now have the opportunity to get ahead individually.

Russian business culture—the way Russians do business—is changing gradually. An example of this change can be seen in the accounting profession.

In the emerging Russian market economy, the person performing the role of accountant is called an "economist." These employees have a degree in "economics" and years of experience. Employees performing the role of "bookkeeper" have lower status and lower pay. The chief bookkeeper, however, has a prominent position because of his or her responsibility for the accuracy of financial statements.

The accounting profession in Russia is devising a regulatory framework based upon similar frameworks in existing market economies. Regulations are being written that include precise definitions for accounting terms. Regulations on the qualifications of auditors also are being developed.

PARTNERS' CAPITAL AND DRAWING ACCOUNTS

ACCOUNT *Karl Koehn, Capital* ACCOUNT NO. *3110*

DATE		ITEM	POST. REF.	DEBIT	CREDIT	BALANCE DEBIT	BALANCE CREDIT
20-- Jan.	1	Balance	✓				136,750.00

ACCOUNT *Karl Koehn, Drawing* ACCOUNT NO. *3120*

DATE		ITEM	POST. REF.	DEBIT	CREDIT	BALANCE DEBIT	BALANCE CREDIT
20-- Dec.	1	Balance	✓			26,700.00	
	5		24	1,200.00		27,900.00	
	20		25	1,200.00		29,100.00	

ACCOUNT *Michelle Wu, Capital* ACCOUNT NO. *3130*

DATE		ITEM	POST. REF.	DEBIT	CREDIT	BALANCE DEBIT	BALANCE CREDIT
20-- Jan.	1	Balance	✓				136,552.48

ACCOUNT *Michelle Wu, Drawing* ACCOUNT NO. *3140*

DATE		ITEM	POST. REF.	DEBIT	CREDIT	BALANCE DEBIT	BALANCE CREDIT
20-- Dec.	1	Balance	✓			26,400.00	
	5		24	1,200.00		27,600.00	
	20		25	1,200.00		28,800.00	

The amount of net income earned is important to business owners. Owners are also interested in changes that occur in owners' equity during a fiscal period. A financial statement that summarizes the changes in owners' equity during a fiscal period is called an **owners' equity statement.** Business owners can review an owners' equity statement to determine if owners' equity is increasing or decreasing and what is causing the change. Three factors can change owners' equity: (1) additional investments, (2) withdrawals, and (3) net income or net loss.

An owners' equity statement shows information about changes during a fiscal period in each partner's capital. Information needed to prepare an owners' equity statement is obtained from the distribution of net income statement and the general ledger capital and drawing accounts. The distribution of net income statement shows each partner's share of net income or net loss. Three kinds of information are obtained from each partner's capital and drawing account: (1) beginning capital amount, (2) any additional investments made during the fiscal period, and (3) each partner's withdrawal of assets during the fiscal period.

OWNERS' EQUITY STATEMENT

1. Heading
2. First Partner's Name
3. First Partner's Ending Capital
4. Second Partner's Name
5. Second Partner's Ending Capital
6. Total Owners' Equity
7. Double Lines

Omni Import
Owners' Equity Statement
For Year Ended December 31, 20--

Karl Koehn			
Capital, January 1, 20--		136 750 00	
Share of Net Income	34 807 93		
Less Withdrawals	29 100 00		
Net Increase in Capital		5 707 93	
Capital, December 31, 20--			142 457 93
Michelle Wu			
Capital, January 1, 20--		136 552 48	
Share of Net Income	34 807 92		
Less Withdrawals	28 800 00		
Net Increase in Capital		6 007 92	
Capital, December 31, 20--			142 560 40
Total Owners' Equity, December 31, 20--			285 018 33

Neither Karl Koehn nor Michelle Wu invested any additional capital during the year ended December 31. The beginning and ending capital balances, therefore, are the same as recorded in the accounts on January 1. Both partners withdrew cash and merchandise during the year ended December 31. Some businesses include the owners' equity statement information as part of the balance sheet. An example of this method of reporting changes in owner's equity is shown in Chapter 8.

STEPS: Preparing an owners' equity statement

1. Write the heading of the owners' equity statement on three lines.
2. Write the name *Karl Koehn* on the first line at the extreme left of the wide column.
3. Calculate the net increase in capital and ending capital amount for Karl Koehn.
   a. Indent about one centimeter on the next line, and write *Capital, January 1, 20—*. Write the amount *$136,750.00* in the second amount column. (This amount is obtained from the capital account.)
   b. Indent about one centimeter on the next line, and write *Share of Net Income*. Write the amount *$34,807.93* in the first amount column. (This amount is obtained from the distribution of net income statement.)
   c. Indent about one centimeter on the next line, and write *Less Withdrawals*. Write the amount *$29,100.00* in the first amount column. (This amount is obtained from the drawing account.)
   d. Indent about one centimeter on the next line, and write *Net Increase in Capital*. Write the amount *$5,707.93* in the second amount column. ($34,807.93 – $29,100.00 = $5,707.93.)
   e. Indent about one centimeter on the next line, and write *Capital, December 31, 20—*. Write the amount *$142,457.93* in the third amount column. ($136,750.00 + $5,707.93 = $142,457.93.)
4. Write the name *Michelle Wu* on the next line at the extreme left of the wide column.
5. Calculate the net increase in capital and ending capital amount for Michelle Wu. Follow Step 3.
6. Write *Total Owners' Equity, December 31, 20—* on the next line at the extreme left of the wide column. Write the amount *$285,018.33* in the third amount column.
7. Rule double lines across the three amount columns to show that the totals have been verified as correct.

OWNERS' EQUITY STATEMENT WITH AN ADDITIONAL INVESTMENT AND A NET LOSS

Cloth Circuit
Owners' Equity Statement
For Year Ended December 31, 20--

Mark Gavin			
Capital, January 1, 20--	125 200 00		
Plus Additional Investment	12 000 00		
Total		137 200 00	
Share of Net Loss	2 840 00		
Plus Withdrawals	17 760 00		
Net Decrease in Capital		20 600 00	
Capital, December 31, 20--			116 600 00
Judy Oliver			
Capital, January 1, 20--	123 400 00		
Plus Additional Investment	12 000 00		
Total		135 400 00	
Share of Net Loss	2 840 00		
Plus Withdrawals	18 120 00		
Net Decrease in Capital		20 960 00	
Capital, December 31, 20--			114 440 00
Total Owners' Equity, December 31, 20--			231 040 00

On December 31 the capital accounts of Mark Gavin and Judy Oliver showed additional investments of $12,000.00 each. Also, the income statement for their company, Cloth Circuit, showed a net loss of $5,680.00. The partners agreed to share net income or net loss equally. The owners' equity statement above shows the net loss as a deduction from the owners' capital.

FYI

Partnerships must file tax returns with the IRS to report how income was divided among the partners.

TERMS REVIEW

distribution of net income statement

owners' equity statement

AUDIT YOUR UNDERSTANDING

1. What information used to prepare an owners' equity statement is obtained from the distribution of net income statement?
2. What information used to prepare an owners' equity statement is obtained from the partners' capital and drawing accounts?
3. What is the procedure for calculating an owner's end-of-year capital?

WORK TOGETHER

Preparing distribution of net income and owners' equity statements

Use the A to Z Auto Parts work sheet and income statement from Work Together on page 396. Forms for completing these problems are given in the *Working Papers.* Your instructor will guide you through the following examples.

4. Prepare a distribution of net income statement for A to Z Auto Parts. Net income or loss is to be shared equally.
5. Using the balances of the general ledger capital and drawing accounts from the work sheet, prepare an owners' equity statement for A to Z Auto Parts. No additional investments were made. Save your work to complete Work Together on page 412.

ON YOUR OWN

Preparing distribution of net income and owners' equity statements

Use the Electron Games work sheet and income statement from On Your Own on page 396. Forms for completing these problems are given in the *Working Papers.* Work independently to complete these problems.

6. Prepare a distribution of net income statement for Electron Games. Net income or loss is to be shared equally.
7. Using the balances of the general ledger capital and drawing accounts from the work sheet, prepare an owners' equity statement for Electron Games. No additional investments were made. Save your work to complete On Your Own on page 412.

16-4 Balance Sheet

BALANCE SHEET INFORMATION ON A WORK SHEET

Omni Import
Work Sheet
For Year Ended December 31, 20--

		1	2	3	4	5	6	7	8	
	ACCOUNT TITLE	TRIAL BALANCE		ADJUSTMENTS		INCOME STATEMENT		BALANCE SHEET		
		DEBIT	CREDIT	DEBIT	CREDIT	DEBIT	CREDIT	DEBIT	CREDIT	
1	*Cash*	29,080.28						29,080.28		1
2	*Petty Cash*	300.00						300.00		2
3	*Accounts Receivable*	11,198.40						11,198.40		3
4	*Merchandise Inventory*	270,480.00			(a) 15,840.00			254,640.00		4
5	*Supplies—Office*	6,480.00			(b) 4,730.00			1,750.00		5
6	*Supplies—Store*	6,944.00			(c) 3,910.00			3,034.00		6
7	*Prepaid Insurance*	5,800.00			(d) 3,170.00			2,630.00		7
8	*Accounts Payable*		12,542.38						12,542.38	8
9	*Employee Income Tax Pay.*		542.00						542.00	9
10	*Social Sec. Tax Payable*		985.40						985.40	10
11	*Medicare Tax Payable*		227.42						227.42	11
12	*Sales Tax Payable*		2,112.05						2,112.05	12
13	*Unemploy. Tax Pay.—Fed.*		8.40						8.40	13
14	*Unemploy. Tax Pay.—State*		56.70						56.70	14
15	*Health Ins. Premiums Pay.*		1,008.00						1,008.00	15
16	*U.S. Savings Bonds Pay.*		60.00						60.00	16
17	*United Way Donations Pay.*		72.00						72.00	17

Some management decisions can best be made after owners have determined the amount of assets, liabilities, and owners' equity. Owners could obtain some of the information needed by inspecting general ledger accounts. The information needed might also be found on a work sheet. However, the information is easier to use when organized and reported on a balance sheet.

A balance sheet reports a business's financial condition on a specific date. A balance sheet may be prepared in account form or report form. As described in Chapter 8, Encore Music uses the account form. Omni Import uses the report form.

The information used to prepare a balance sheet is obtained from two sources: (1) the Balance Sheet columns of a work sheet and (2) the owners' equity statement.

REMEMBER

A balance sheet reports a business's financial condition on a specific date.

FIRST TWO SECTIONS OF A BALANCE SHEET FOR A MERCHANDISING BUSINESS

1. Heading
2. Assets Section
3. Liabilities Section

Omni Import Balance Sheet December 31, 20--		
Assets		
Cash	29,080.28	
Petty Cash	300.00	
Accounts Receivable	11,198.40	
Merchandise Inventory	254,640.00	
Supplies—Office	1,750.00	
Supplies—Store	3,034.00	
Prepaid Insurance	2,630.00	
Total Assets		302,632.68
Liabilities		
Accounts Payable	12,542.38	
Employee Income Tax Payable	542.00	
Social Security Tax Payable	985.40	
Medicare Tax Payable	227.42	
Sales Tax Payable	2,112.05	
Unemployment Tax Payable—Federal	8.40	
Unemployment Tax Payable—State	56.70	
Health Insurance Premiums Payable	1,008.00	
U.S. Savings Bonds Payable	60.00	
United Way Donations Payable	72.00	
Total Liabilities		17,614.35

Omni Import prepares a balance sheet for the end-of-fiscal date, December 31. Omni uses the seven steps described below and on the following page to prepare a balance sheet.

STEPS: Preparing a balance sheet

1. Write the balance sheet heading on three lines.

2. Prepare the assets section of the balance sheet. Use information from the work sheet.
   a. Write the section title, *Assets,* on the first line in the middle of the wide column.
   b. Beginning on the next line, at the extreme left of the wide column, write the asset account titles in the order in which they appear on the work sheet.
   c. Write the balance of each asset account in the first amount column.
   d. Write *Total Assets* on the next line below the last asset account title.
   e. Write the amount of total assets, *$302,632.68,* on the same line in the second amount column.

3. Prepare the liabilities section of the balance sheet. Use information from the work sheet.
   a. Write the section title, *Liabilities,* on the next line in the middle of the wide column.
   b. Beginning on the next line, at the extreme left of the wide column, write the liability account titles in the order in which they appear on the work sheet.
   c. Write the balance of each liability account in the first amount column.
   d. Write *Total Liabilities* on the next line below the last liability account title.
   e. Write the total liabilities, *$17,614.35,* on the same line in the second amount column.

COMPLETING A BALANCE SHEET FOR A MERCHANDISNG BUSINESS

Omni Import Balance Sheet December 31, 20--		
Assets		
Cash	29,080.28	
Petty Cash	300.00	
Accounts Receivable	11,198.40	
Merchandise Inventory	254,640.00	
Supplies—Office	1,750.00	
Supplies—Store	3,034.00	
Prepaid Insurance	2,630.00	
Total Assets		302,632.68
Liabilities		
Accounts Payable	12,542.38	
Employee Income Tax Payable	542.00	
Social Security Tax Payable	985.40	
Medicare Tax Payable	227.42	
Sales Tax Payable	2,112.05	
Unemployment Tax Payable—Federal	8.40	
Unemployment Tax Payable—State	56.70	
Health Insurance Premiums Payable	1,008.00	
U.S. Savings Bonds Payable	60.00	
United Way Donations Payable	72.00	
Total Liabilities		17,614.35
Owners' Equity		
Karl Koehn, Capital	**142,457.93**	
Michelle Wu, Capital	**142,560.40**	
Total Owners' Equity		**285,018.33**
Total Liabilities and Owners' Equity		**302,632.68**

6. Verify Accuracy

4. Owners' Equity Section **5.** Total of Liabilities and Owners' Equity Sections **7.** Double Lines

STEPS Preparing a balance sheet *(continued)*

4. Prepare the owners' equity section of the balance sheet. Use information from the owners' equity statement.
  a. Write the section title, *Owners' Equity,* on the next line in the middle of the wide column.
  b. Write the account title, *Karl Koehn, Capital,* on the next line at the extreme left of the wide column.
  c. On the same line, write the amount of current capital, *$142,457.93,* in the first amount column.
  d. Write the account title, *Michelle Wu, Capital,* on the next line at the extreme left of the wide column.
  e. On the same line, write the amount of current capital, *$142,560.40,* in the first amount column.
  f. Write *Total Owners' Equity* on the next line at the extreme left of the wide column.
  g. Write the total amount, *$285,018.33,* on the same line in the second amount column.

5. Total the liabilities and owners' equity sections of the balance sheet.
  a. Write *Total Liabilities and Owners' Equity* on the next line at the extreme left of the wide column.
  b. Write the total amount, *$302,632.68,* on the same line in the second amount column.

6. Verify accuracy by comparing the total amount of assets and the total amount of liabilities and owners' equity. These two amounts must be the same. The two amounts, *$302,632.68,* are the same.

7. Rule double lines across both amount columns below Total Assets and below Total Liabilities and Owners' Equity. These two sets of double lines show that the amounts have been verified as correct.

SUPPORTING SCHEDULES FOR A BALANCE SHEET

A report prepared to give details about an item on a principal financial statement is called a **supporting schedule.** A supporting schedule is sometimes referred to as a supplementary report or an exhibit.

Omni Import prepares two supporting schedules to accompany the balance sheet. The supporting schedules are a schedule of accounts payable and a schedule of accounts receivable. A balance sheet shows only the accounts payable total amount. The account balance for each vendor is not shown. When detailed information is needed, a supporting schedule of accounts payable is prepared showing the balance for each vendor. A balance sheet also shows only the accounts receivable total amount. When information about the account balance for each customer is needed, a supporting schedule of accounts receivable is prepared. Omni Import's supporting schedules on December 31 are similar to the supporting schedules for November 30 shown in Chapter 12.

PROFESSIONAL BUSINESS ETHICS

TECHNOLOGY TEMPTATIONS

Along with many benefits, technology also presents us with new temptations. Technology allows us to access information for many legitimate reasons, but it can also create ethical dilemmas. What do you think about the situations presented below?

Instructions

Use the three-step checklist to help determine whether or not each of the following situations demonstrates ethical behavior.

Situation 1. Jack Azerrad collects overdue accounts for a large credit card company. He has access to records of all transactions for any customer. Jack sometimes looks up the records of famous people. He checks to see where they use their credit cards and how much money they spend. He sometimes tells his friends about the buying habits of entertainers and politicians.

Situation 2. Madilyn Hodges works for a not-for-profit organization. Recently, she found a list of computer passwords near a photocopier. She started using these passwords to look at other employees' e-mail files.

Situation 3. Elena Marquez is studying to be an accountant. While in college she works as a sales clerk in a bookstore. Occasionally, the scanner is unable to read a bar code on a customer's selection, and the clerk must enter the code using the keypad. Elena sometimes makes mistakes when she enters the code. As long as the customer does not object, Elena thinks it's unnecessary to correct her mistakes.

Situation 4. Andrew Kwan works for a mortgage company. As part of his job, he checks credit histories of loan applicants. He requests information from a company that specializes in providing credit checks. Mike Buckley, one of Andrew's friends, wanted to see what kind of information was included in his own credit history. He asked Andrew to request a credit check. Andrew made the request and passed the information on to Mike.

TERM REVIEW

supporting schedule

AUDIT YOUR UNDERSTANDING

1. What does a balance sheet report?
2. In what two forms may a balance sheet be prepared?
3. Where is the information found to prepare a balance sheet?
4. What are two supporting schedules that might accompany a balance sheet?

WORK TOGETHER

Preparing a balance sheet for a partnership

Use the A to Z Auto Parts work sheet from Work Together on page 407 and the owners' equity statement from Work Together on page 407. A form for completing this problem is given in the *Working Papers*. Your instructor will guide you through the following example.

5. Prepare a balance sheet in report form for A to Z Auto Parts.

ON YOUR OWN

Preparing a balance sheet for a partnership

Use the Electron Games work sheet from On Your Own on page 407 and the owners' equity statement from On Your Own on page 407. A form for completing this problem is given in the *Working Papers*. Work independently to complete this problem.

6. Prepare a balance sheet in report form for Electron Games.

CHAPTER 16 SUMMARY

After completing this chapter, you can

1. Define accounting terms related to financial statements for a merchandising business organized as a partnership.
2. Identify accounting concepts and practices related to financial statements for a merchandising business organized as a partnership.
3. Prepare an income statement for a merchandising business organized as a partnership.
4. Analyze an income statement using component percentages for a merchandising business organized as a partnership.
5. Prepare a distribution of net income statement and an owners' equity statement for a merchandising business organized as a partnership.
6. Prepare a balance sheet for a merchandising business organized as a partnership.

EXPLORE ACCOUNTING

ALTERNATIVE FISCAL YEARS

Most small companies use a fiscal year that is the same as the calendar year, January 1 to December 31. However, there may be several reasons why a different fiscal period would be beneficial. If the calendar year end comes in the middle of a high sales period, a fiscal year ending at this time can be more difficult. All employees are extremely busy with sales and shipping. Because of this activity, accurately identifying sales, inventory, and accounts receivable is more difficult. If the calendar year end comes just before the high sales period begins, an analysis of the company's financial condition will not be as favorable. The company may have borrowed money to buy a high level of inventory, so the company has higher debt and high inventory levels. Therefore, some companies choose to use a *natural business year* as the fiscal year, as discussed in Chapter 7.

FanciFoods is a partnership that makes and sells decorative cakes, cookies, and candies. Approximately 90% of its sales are made between November 1 and February 15—or the three holidays of Thanksgiving, Christmas, and Valentine's Day. The company spends six months—May to November—preparing for its heavy sales period. The company has selected April 1 to March 31 as its fiscal year. By March 31, inventory is low, most accounts receivable have been collected, and the company has not yet replaced inventory to begin preparing for the next season. Thus, this is an ideal time to end the fiscal period. Inventory is easier to count, the level of accounts receivable is lower, and more employees are available to help with the closing activities.

Research: What other types of companies may find it beneficial to use a fiscal year different from the calendar year? What would be the ideal fiscal period for these companies? You may wish to find a local business that has a fiscal period different from the calendar year. If so, determine the reasons for selecting the fiscal period it now uses.

16-1 APPLICATION PROBLEM

Preparing an income statement for a merchandising business

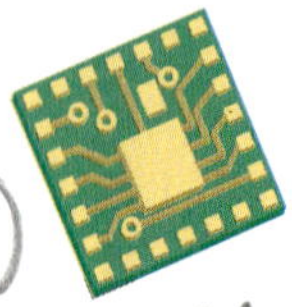

Flower Mart's partial work sheet for the year ended December 31 of the current year is given in the *Working Papers*.

Instructions:

1. Prepare an income statement.
2. Calculate and record on the income statement the following component percentages: (a) cost of merchandise sold, (b) gross profit on sales, (c) total expenses, and (d) net income or loss. Round percentage calculations to the nearest 0.1%.

16-2 APPLICATION PROBLEM

Analyzing component percentages

The income statement for Carol and Teresa's Historic Door Supply Co. and a form for completing this problem are given in the *Working Papers*.

Instructions:

1. Carol and Teresa's Historic Door Supply determines that no more than 47.5 cents, or 47.5%, of each sales dollar should be devoted to cost of merchandise sold. Compare the actual component percentage for cost of merchandise sold to the acceptable percentage. Indicate if the actual component percentage is acceptable or unacceptable. If it is unacceptable, suggest a possible action to correct the unacceptable component percentage.
2. Acceptable door supply industry standards show that at least 52.5 cents, or 52.5%, of each sales dollar should result in gross profit. For Carol and Teresa's Historic Door Supply, compare the actual component percentage for gross profit on sales to the acceptable percentage. Indicate if the actual component percentage is acceptable or unacceptable. If it is unacceptable, suggest a possible action different from the suggestion in Instruction 1 to correct the unacceptable component percentage.
3. Acceptable door supply industry standards show that no more than 29 cents, or 29.0%, of each sales dollar should be devoted to total expenses. For Carol and Teresa's Historic Door Supply, compare the actual component percentage for total expenses to the acceptable percentage. Indicate if the actual component percentage is acceptable or unacceptable. If it is unacceptable, suggest a possible action to correct the unacceptable component percentage.
4. Acceptable door supply industry standards show that at least 23.5 cents, or 23.5%, of each sales dollar should result in net income. For Carol and Teresa's Historic Door Supply, compare the actual component percentage for net income to the acceptable percentage. Indicate if the actual component percentage is acceptable or unacceptable. If it is unacceptable, suggest a possible action different from any already suggested to correct the unacceptable component percentage.

APPLICATION PROBLEM

Preparing distribution of net income and owners' equity statements (net income)

Janet Kelly and Paul Sharp are partners in a merchandising business, Kelly Appliances. Forms for completing this problem are given in the *Working Papers.* The following information was taken from the records on December 31 of the current year.

Partner	Balance of Capital Account January 1	Balance of Drawing Account	Distribution of Net Income
Kelly	$159,000.00	$17,550.00	60.0%
Sharp	$142,600.00	$18,800.00	40.0%

Instructions:

1. On December 31, the partnership had a net income of $83,260.00. Prepare a distribution of net income statement for the partnership.
2. Prepare an owners' equity statement for Kelly Appliances. No additional investments were made.

16-4

APPLICATION PROBLEM

Preparing an owners' equity statement (net loss)

Judy Fulton and Lee Terry are partners in a merchandising business, Elegant Cosmetics. Forms for completing this problem are given in the *Working Papers.* The following information was taken from the records on December 31 of the current year.

Partner	Balance of Capital Account January 1	Balance of Drawing Account	Distribution of Net Loss
Fulton	$124,300.00	$13,950.00	$3,750.00
Terry	$118,000.00	$14,900.00	$3,750.00

Instructions:

Prepare an owners' equity statement for Elegant Cosmetics. Additional investments made during the year: Judy Fulton, $12,000.00; Lee Terry, $10,000.00.

16-5

APPLICATION PROBLEM

Preparing a balance sheet for a partnership

Athletic Supply's partial work sheet for the year ended December 31 of the current year is given in the *Working Papers.* A form for completing this problem is also given in the *Working Papers.*

Instructions:

Prepare a balance sheet in report form. December 31 capital balances for partners are as follows: Glenda Tyler, $145,480.00; Ashley Winn, $144,260.00.

16-6

MASTERY PROBLEM

Preparing financial statements

Central Electronics prepared the following work sheet for the year ended December 31 of the current year. Forms for completing this problem are given in the *Working Papers*.

Central Electronics
Work Sheet
For Year Ended December 31, 20--

		1	2	3	4	5	6	7	8
	ACCOUNT TITLE	TRIAL BALANCE		ADJUSTMENTS		INCOME STATEMENT		BALANCE SHEET	
		DEBIT	CREDIT	DEBIT	CREDIT	DEBIT	CREDIT	DEBIT	CREDIT
1	Cash	33,110.00						33,110.00	
2	Petty Cash	500.00						500.00	
3	Accounts Receivable	14,760.00						14,760.00	
4	Merchandise Inventory	334,190.00			(a) 16,685.00			317,505.00	
5	Supplies—Office	6,180.00			(b) 3,865.00			2,315.00	
6	Supplies—Store	6,720.00			(c) 4,280.00			2,440.00	
7	Prepaid Insurance	5,920.00			(d) 3,380.00			2,540.00	
8	Accounts Payable		10,500.00						10,500.00
9	Sales Tax Payable		1,230.00						1,230.00
10	Irene Greer, Capital		164,400.00						164,400.00
11	Irene Greer, Drawing	21,750.00						21,750.00	
12	Gayle Stewart, Capital		157,990.00						157,990.00
13	Gayle Stewart, Drawing	21,100.00						21,100.00	
14	Income Summary			(a) 16,685.00		16,685.00			
15	Sales		295,900.00				295,900.00		
16	Purchases	148,670.00				148,670.00			
17	Advertising Expense	6,420.00				6,420.00			
18	Credit Card Fee Expense	2,715.00				2,715.00			
19	Insurance Expense			(d) 3,380.00		3,380.00			
20	Miscellaneous Expense	3,040.00				3,040.00			
21	Rent Expense	22,080.00				22,080.00			
22	Supplies Expense—Office			(b) 3,865.00		3,865.00			
23	Supplies Expense—Store			(c) 4,280.00		4,280.00			
24	Utilities Expense	2,865.00				2,865.00			
25		630,020.00	630,020.00	28,210.00	28,210.00	214,000.00	295,900.00	416,020.00	334,120.00
26	Net Income					81,900.00			81,900.00
27						295,900.00	295,900.00	416,020.00	416,020.00
28									

Instructions:

1. Prepare an income statement. Calculate and record the following component percentages: (a) cost of merchandise sold, (b) gross profit on sales, (c) total expenses, and (d) net income or loss. Round percentage calculations to the nearest 0.1%.
2. Prepare a distribution of net income statement. Net income or loss is to be shared equally.
3. Prepare an owners' equity statement. No additional investments were made.
4. Prepare a balance sheet in report form.

16-7 CHALLENGE PROBLEM
Preparing financial statements (unequal distribution of net income; additional investment)

Central Electronics' work sheet is shown in Mastery Problem 16-6. Assume the facts given here for distribution of net income. Forms for completing this problem are given in the *Working Papers*.

Instructions:

1. Prepare a distribution of net income statement. The net income is to be shared as follows: Irene Greer, 8% of January 1 capital, $15,000.00 salary, 60% of remainder; Gayle Stewart, 8% of January 1 capital, $12,000.00 salary, 40% of remainder. Ms. Stewart made an additional investment during the year. Her January 1 capital was $139,990.00.
2. Prepare an owners' equity statement. Ms. Stewart made an additional investment of $18,000.00 during the year. She had January 1 capital of $139,990.00.

INTERNET ACTIVITY

Point your browser to

http://accounting.swpco.com

Choose **First-Year Course**, choose **Activities**, and complete the activity for Chapter 16.

Applied Communication

A long written report should contain numerous headings. A heading enables the reader to focus on the primary idea of the next section. An outline is a special document that lists only the headings of a report. By reviewing an outline before and after reading a report, the reader can gain a better understanding of the relationship among the topics being presented.

Each chapter of this textbook is similar to a long report. Headings are used to separate and emphasize major concepts.

Instructions: Prepare an outline of this chapter.

Cases for Critical Thinking

Case 1 Christy Burch and Myung Lim, partners, compared their current income statement with their income statement of a year ago. They noted that sales were 12.0% higher than a year ago. They also noted that the total expenses were 20.0% higher than a year ago. What type of analysis should be done to determine whether the increase in expenses is justified?

Case 2 Rena Jacques and George Nadler are partners in a paint and decorating store. The store operates on a yearly fiscal period. At the end of each year, an accountant is hired to prepare financial statements. At the end of each month during the year, Ms. Jacques prepares a work sheet. The work sheet is prepared to determine if the business made or lost money that month. The accountant suggests that monthly financial statements also be prepared. Ms. Jacques believes, however, that the monthly work sheet is sufficient to determine how the business is doing. Do you agree with Ms. Jacques or the accountant? Why?

AUTOMATED ACCOUNTING

GENERATING AUTOMATED FINANCIAL STATEMENTS

Financial information needed by managers and owners of a business to make decisions is recorded in the journals and the ledgers. While this information may be helpful in analyzing the activity in a particular account, it is too detailed to be useful in decision making. When information from the ledgers is summarized and organized, the reports that are prepared are referred to as financial statements. The most commonly presented financial statements for a business organized as a partnership are the balance sheet and the income statement.

To display financial statements:

1. Click the Reports toolbar button, or choose the Report Selection menu item from the Reports menu.
2. When the Report Selection dialog appears, choose the Financial Statements option from the Select a Report Group list.
3. Choose the financial statement report you would like to display from the Choose a Report to Display list.
4. Click the OK button.

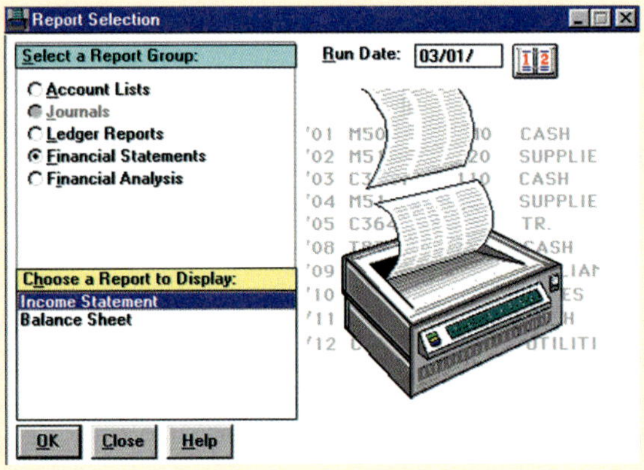

The up-to-date account balances stored by the software are used to calculate and display the current financial statements.

Income Statement

An income statement shows the revenue and expenses for a fiscal period. Merchandising businesses report revenue, cost of merchandise sold, gross profit on sales, expenses, and net income or loss. The software will display net income or loss (the difference between revenues earned and expenses incurred) in one of two formats:

1. *Report by Fiscal Period:* This format shows the profitability of the business from the beginning of the fiscal year to the date the income statement is displayed.
2. *Report by Month and Year:* This format includes columns for the current month and for the year to date.

A component percentage is included for each dollar amount. A component percentage shows the percentage relationship between one financial statement item and the total that includes that item. Component percentages calculated on the income statement show the relationship of items to total sales.

Balance Sheet

The balance sheet reports assets, liabilities, and owners' equity on a specific date, usually the end of the fiscal period. It is used to help evaluate the financial strength of the business. The owners' equity section of the balance sheet for a partnership shows the capital and drawing accounts for each partner. Net income is also included in the owners' equity section.

AUTOMATED ACCOUNTING

AUTOMATING APPLICATION PROBLEM 16-1: Preparing an income statement for a merchandising business

Instructions:

1. Load *Automated Accounting 7.0* or higher software.
2. Select database F16-1 from the appropriate folder/directory.
3. Select File from the menu bar and choose the Save As menu command. Key the path to the drive and directory that contains your data files. Save the database with a file name of XXX161 (where XXX are your initials).
4. Access Problem Instructions through the Help menu. Read the Problem Instructions screen.
5. Exit the *Automated Accounting* software.

AUTOMATING MASTERY PROBLEM 16-6: Preparing financial statements

Instructions:

1. Load *Automated Accounting 7.0* or higher software.
2. Select database F16-2 from the appropriate folder/directory.
3. Select File from the menu bar and choose the Save As menu command. Key the path to the drive and directory that contains your data files. Save the database with a file name of XXX162 (where XXX are your initials).
4. Access Problem Instructions through the Help menu. Read the Problem Instructions screen.
5. Exit the *Automated Accounting* software.

Central Electronics
Balance Sheet
12/31/--

Assets		
Cash	33110.00	
Petty Cash	500.00	
Accounts Receivable	14760.00	
Merchandise Inventory	317505.00	
Supplies—Office	2315.00	
Supplies—Store	2440.00	
Prepaid Insurance	2540.00	
Total Assets		373170.00
Liabilities		
Accounts Payable	10500.00	
Sales Tax Payable	1230.00	
Total Liabilities		11730.00
Owners' Equity		
Irene Greer Capital	164400.00	
Irene Greer Drawing	-21750.00	
Gayle Stewart Capital	157990.00	
Gayle Stewart Drawing	-21100.00	
Net Income	81900.00	
Total Owners' Equity		361440.00
Total Liabilities & Equity		373170.00

17 Recording Adjusting and Closing Entries for a Partnership

AFTER STUDYING CHAPTER 17, YOU WILL BE ABLE TO:

1. Identify accounting concepts and practices related to adjusting and closing entries for a merchandising business organized as a partnership.
2. Record adjusting entries.
3. Record closing entries for income statement accounts.
4. Record closing entries for net income or loss and partners' drawing accounts.
5. Prepare a post-closing trial balance.

JOURNAL ENTRIES AT THE END OF A FISCAL PERIOD

General ledger account balances are changed only by posting journal entries. Two types of journal entries change general ledger account balances at the end of a fiscal period: (1) Adjusting entries bring general ledger account balances up to date. (2) Closing entries prepare temporary accounts for the next fiscal period. *(CONCEPT: Matching Expenses with Revenue)*

GLOBAL PERSPECTIVE

INTERNATIONAL BUSINESS TRANSACTIONS

Any commercial transaction that occurs within the U.S. may also take place in international commerce. An example is the *international sale of goods.*

An international sale of goods usually requires the services of two banks, one in the seller's country and one in the buyer's country. To pay for the goods, the transfer of funds is done through a *letter of credit.*

Suppose a U.S. retailer purchases goods from a company in Korea. The U.S. retailer goes to a U.S. bank to obtain a letter of credit, naming the Korean seller as beneficiary of the letter. The U.S. bank's *correspondent* or *advising bank* in Korea notifies the seller that this has been done. The Korean seller may then draw drafts (orders for payment) on the American buyer's credit. The letter of credit ensures that the issuer will pay those drafts.

International sales are further discussed in Chapter 19.

ACCOUNTING IN YOUR CAREER

FREQUENT FINANCIAL STATEMENTS

Lionel Franklin and Talesia Patton are partners in GreenGrounds, a new company that sells lawn mowers, tractors, tillers, shredders, and other farm and garden machines. While the merchandise inventory has a large dollar value, only a small number of machines is kept in stock at any one time. Talesia, who has a university business degree and sales experience, does most of the sales work for the company. Lionel, who has a business education background from his high school and community college courses, runs the office and does the daily accounting work for the business. A CPA firm handles the annual financial statements and tax reporting for a fee.

The partners agree that annual financial statements do not provide enough timely information to make good business decisions. Therefore, Lionel is exploring the procedures for preparing monthly statements. Lionel is concerned about having to prepare closing entries each month because of the amount of time it would take. But he schedules a meeting with Angela Grady, the accountant assigned to his account, for advice on doing this work himself.

Angela agrees that monthly statements would be an excellent management tool for the partners and suggests that the most difficult part of preparing monthly statements would be determining the beginning and ending merchandise inventory figures. She says there are several methods for estimating these values, but since they have good records on what items are in stock at any one moment, they will probably not even have to rely on estimates. She also says that Lionel will not have to prepare closing entries each month, but that the information he needs for monthly statements can be obtained from the general ledger.

Critical Thinking:

1. If closing entries are recorded only at the end of the year, what kind of calculations will have to be made with the general ledger revenue and expense account balances to prepare an income statement for a single month?
2. Will the monthly balance sheet require the same kind of calculations as the income statement?

17-1 Recording Adjusting Entries

ADJUSTING ENTRIES RECORDED IN A JOURNAL

2. Date **1.** Heading **3.** Account Debited **4.** Debit **6.** Credit **5.** Account Credited

PAGE *26* JOURNAL

	DATE		ACCOUNT TITLE	DOC. NO.	POST. REF.	1 GENERAL DEBIT	2 GENERAL CREDIT	3 ACCOUNTS RECEIVABLE DEBIT	4 ACCOUNTS RECEIVABLE CREDIT	
1			*Adjusting Entries*							1
2	*20– Dec.*	*31*	*Income Summary*			*15 840 00*				2
3			*Merchandise Inventory*				*15 840 00*			3
4		*31*	*Supplies Expense—Office*			*4 730 00*				4
5			*Supplies—Office*				*4 730 00*			5
6		*31*	*Supplies Expense—Store*			*3 910 00*				6
7			*Supplies—Store*				*3 910 00*			7
8		*31*	*Insurance Expense*			*3 170 00*				8
9			*Prepaid Insurance*				*3 170 00*			9
10										10
11										11
12										12
13										13
14										14

Adjusting entries are recorded on the next journal page following the page on which the last daily transaction for the month is recorded.

The adjusting entries are entered in the General Debit and Credit columns of a journal.

STEPS

Recording adjusting entries in a journal

1. Write the heading, *Adjusting Entries,* in the middle of the journal's Account Title column. This heading explains all of the adjusting entries that follow. Therefore, indicating a source document is unnecessary. The first adjusting entry is recorded on the first two lines below the heading.
2. For the first adjusting entry identified by the letter *(a)* in the work sheet Adjustments columns, write the date, *Dec. 31, 20—,* in the Date column. The partial work sheet is shown on the following page.
3. Write the title of the account debited in the Account Title column.
4. Write the debit adjustment amount in the General Debit column.
5. Write the title of the account credited in the Account Title column.
6. Write the credit adjustment amount in the General Credit column.

Repeat Steps 2 through 6 for each of the additional adjusting entries.

REMEMBER

Remember to start a new journal page for adjusting entries.

PARTIAL WORK SHEET SHOWING ADJUSTMENTS

	ACCOUNT TITLE	1 TRIAL BALANCE DEBIT	2 TRIAL BALANCE CREDIT	3 ADJUSTMENTS DEBIT	4 ADJUSTMENTS CREDIT
4	*Merchandise Inventory*	270 480 00			(a) 15 840 00
5	*Supplies—Office*	6 480 00			(b) 4 730 00
6	*Supplies—Store*	6 944 00			(c) 3 910 00
7	*Prepaid Insurance*	5 800 00			(d) 3 170 00
22	*Income Summary*			(a) 15 840 00	
27	*Insurance Expense*			(d) 3 170 00	
32	*Supplies Expense—Office*			(b) 4 730 00	
33	*Supplies Expense—Store*			(c) 3 910 00	
34					

Information needed for journalizing the adjusting entries shown on the previous page is taken from the Adjustments columns of a work sheet.

ADJUSTING ENTRY FOR MERCHANDISE INVENTORY

The debit and credit parts of the merchandise inventory adjustment are identified on the work sheet by the letter *(a)*. The merchandise inventory adjustment includes a debit to Income Summary and a credit to Merchandise Inventory of $15,840.00. Omni Import's adjusting entry for merchandise inventory is shown on lines 2 and 3 of the journal.

The effect of posting the adjusting entry for merchandise inventory is shown in the T accounts.

Income Summary

Adj. (a)	15,840.00		

Merchandise Inventory

Bal.	270,480.00	Adj. (a)	15,840.00
(New Bal.	*254,640.00)*		

FYI

A document that describes a business idea and how the business will operate is known as a business plan. When creating a partnership, the partners should write a business plan to outline the purposes and goals of the business.

ADDITIONAL ADJUSTING ENTRIES

Omni Import also makes adjusting entries for office supplies, store supplies, and prepaid insurance.

Adjusting Entry for Office Supplies Inventory

The debit and credit parts of the office supplies adjustment are identified on the work sheet by the letter *(b)*. The office supplies inventory adjustment includes a debit to Supplies Expense—Office and a credit to Supplies—Office of $4,730.00. Omni Import's adjusting entry for office supplies inventory is shown on lines 4 and 5 of the journal.

The effect of posting the adjusting entry for office supplies inventory is shown in the T accounts.

Supplies Expense—Office			
Adj. (b)	4,730.00		

Supplies—Office			
Bal.	6,480.00	Adj. (b)	4,730.00
(New Bal.	*1,750.00)*		

Adjusting Entry for Store Supplies Inventory

The debit and credit parts of the store supplies adjustment are identified on the work sheet by the letter *(c)*. The store supplies inventory adjustment includes a debit to Supplies Expense—Store and a credit to Supplies—Store of $3,910.00. Omni Import's adjusting entry for store supplies inventory is shown on lines 6 and 7 of the journal.

The effect of posting the adjusting entry for store supplies inventory is shown in the T accounts.

Supplies Expense—Store			
Adj. (c)	3,910.00		

Supplies—Store			
Bal.	6,944.00	Adj. (c)	3,910.00
(New Bal.	*3,034.00)*		

Adjusting Entry for Prepaid Insurance

The debit and credit parts of the prepaid insurance adjustment are identified on the work sheet by the letter *(d)*. The prepaid insurance adjustment includes a debit to Insurance Expense and a credit to Prepaid Insurance of $3,170.00. Omni Import's adjusting entry for prepaid insurance is shown on lines 8 and 9 of the journal.

The effect of posting the adjusting entry for prepaid insurance is shown in the T accounts.

Insurance Expense			
Adj. (d)	3,170.00		

Prepaid Insurance			
Bal.	5,800.00	Adj. (d)	3,170.00
(New Bal.	*2,630.00)*		

SMALL BUSINESS SPOTLIGHT

Buying a franchise is a popular way to start a small business. Franchises are particularly appealing to people with less experience because the failure rate is much lower than that of other new businesses. Advantages of purchasing a franchise include the franchise's proven reputation, established customers, and time-tested business procedures. Disadvantages include the franchisee's sometimes limited control over the new business and the relatively high initial fees attached to the purchase of a franchise.

AUDIT YOUR UNDERSTANDING

1. What accounts are increased from zero balances after adjusting entries for prepaid insurance and merchandise inventory are journalized and posted?
2. When adjusting entries are journalized, why is no source document recorded?
3. What adjusting entry is recorded for a merchandising business that is not recorded for a service business?

WORK TOGETHER

Journalizing adjusting entries

The following information is related to adjustments needed at the end of a fiscal period for a partnership.

	Work Sheet	Adjustment Information	
Account Title	Trial Balance	Ending Inventories	Ending Value
Merchandise Inventory	$446,200.00	$419,750.00	
Supplies—Office	5,440.00	3,350.00	
Supplies—Store	6,020.00	3,990.00	
Prepaid Insurance	3,860.00		$970.00

Your instructor will guide you through the following example.

4. Record the appropriate adjusting entries on page 12 of a journal provided in the *Working Papers*. Use December 31 of the current year as the date.

ON YOUR OWN

Journalizing adjusting entries

The following information is related to adjustments needed at the end of a fiscal period for a partnership.

	Work Sheet	Adjustment Information	
Account Title	Trial Balance	Ending Inventories	Ending Value
Merchandise Inventory	$328,800.00	$343,200.00	
Supplies—Office	4,340.00	2,210.00	
Supplies—Store	4,740.00	2,530.00	
Prepaid Insurance	3,420.00		$680.00

Work independently to complete this problem.

5. Record the appropriate adjusting entries on page 15 of a journal provided in the *Working Papers*. Use December 31 of the current year as the date.

17-2 Recording Closing Entries for Income Statement Accounts

THE INCOME SUMMARY ACCOUNT

At the end of a fiscal period, the temporary accounts are closed to prepare the general ledger for the next fiscal period. *(CONCEPT: Matching Expenses with Revenue)* To close a temporary account, an amount equal to its balance is recorded on the side opposite the balance. Omni Import records the four kinds of closing entries listed below. The first two kinds of closing entries are discussed in this lesson. The remaining two kinds of closing entries are discussed in the following lesson.

1. An entry to close income statement accounts with credit balances.
2. An entry to close income statement accounts with debit balances.
3. An entry to record net income or loss and close the income summary account.
4. Entries to close the partners' drawing accounts.

Amounts needed for the closing entries are obtained from the Income Statement and Balance Sheet columns of the work sheet and from the distribution of net income statement. Closing entries are recorded in the General Debit and Credit columns of a journal.

Chapter 9 discusses the difference between permanent accounts and temporary accounts. Permanent accounts, also referred to as real accounts, include the asset and liability accounts as well as the owners' capital accounts. The ending account balances of permanent accounts for one fiscal period are the beginning account balances for the next fiscal period. Temporary accounts, also referred to as nominal accounts, include the revenue, cost, expense, and owners' drawing accounts.

Another temporary account is used to summarize the closing entries for revenue, cost, and expenses. The account is titled Income Summary because it is used to summarize information about net income. Income Summary is used only at the end of a fiscal period to help prepare other accounts for a new fiscal period.

The income summary account is unique because it does not have a normal balance side. The balance of this account is determined by the amounts posted to the account at the end of a fiscal period. When revenue is greater than total expenses, resulting in a net income, the income summary account has a credit balance, as shown in the T account.

Income Summary	
Debit Total expenses	Credit Revenue (greater than expenses) (Credit balance is the net income.)

REMEMBER

The income summary account is used only at the end of the fiscal period to help prepare other accounts for a new fiscal period.

CLOSING ENTRY FOR AN INCOME STATEMENT ACCOUNT WITH A CREDIT BALANCE

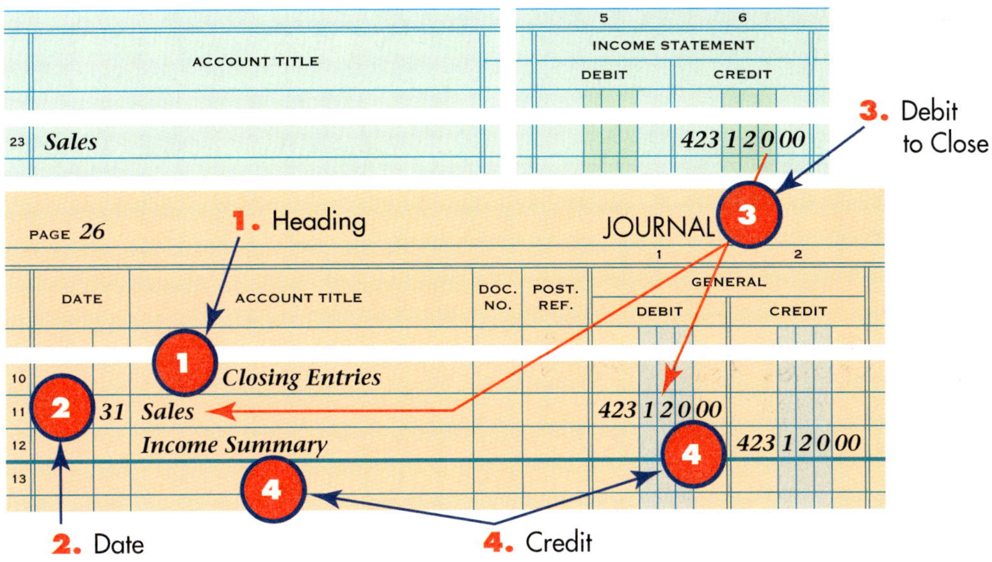

Omni Import's work sheet has one income statement account with a credit balance, Sales. This revenue account has a normal credit balance at the end of a fiscal period. This credit balance must be reduced to zero to prepare the account for the next fiscal period. *(CONCEPT: Matching Expenses with Revenue)*

To reduce the balance to zero, Sales is debited for the amount of the balance, $423,120.00. Income Summary is credited for $423,120.00 so that debits equal credits in this entry. The effect of this closing entry on the general ledger accounts is shown in the T accounts.

The balance of Sales is now zero, and the account is ready for the next fiscal period.

Sales

Closing	423,120.00	Bal.	423,120.00
		(New Bal. zero)	

Income Summary

Adj. (mdse. inv.)	15,840.00	Closing (revenue)	423,120.00

STEPS: Closing an income statement account with a credit balance

1. Write the heading, *Closing Entries,* in the middle of the journal's Account Title column following the last adjusting entry. This heading explains all of the closing entries that follow. Therefore, indicating a source document is unnecessary. The first closing entry is recorded on the first two lines below the heading.
2. Write the date, *31,* in the Date column.
3. Write the account debited, *Sales,* in the Account Title column. Write the account balance, *$423,120.00,* in the General Debit column.
4. Write the account credited, *Income Summary,* in the Account Title column. Write the amount, *$423,120.00,* in the General Credit column.

CLOSING ENTRY FOR INCOME STATEMENT ACCOUNTS WITH DEBIT BALANCES

	ACCOUNT TITLE	5 INCOME STATEMENT DEBIT	6 INCOME STATEMENT CREDIT
22	*Income Summary*	15840 00	
23	*Sales*		423120 00
24	*Purchases*	189960 00	
25	*Advertising Expense*	6600 00	
26	*Credit Card Fee Expense*	3385 00	
27	*Insurance Expense*	3170 00	
28	*Miscellaneous Expense*	2584 15	
29	*Payroll Taxes Expense*	9105 00	
30	*Rent Expense*	21000 00	
31	*Salary Expense*	89400 00	
32	*Supplies Expense—Office*	4730 00	
33	*Supplies Expense—Store*	3910 00	
34	*Utilities Expense*	3820 00	

1. Date **2.** Account Debited **4.** Debit Total **3.** Credits to Close

JOURNAL PAGE *26*

	DATE	ACCOUNT TITLE	DOC. NO.	POST. REF.	1 GENERAL DEBIT	2 GENERAL CREDIT
13	31	*Income Summary*			337664 15	
14		*Purchases*				189960 00
15		*Advertising Expense*				6600 00
16		*Credit Card Fee Expense*				3385 00
17		*Insurance Expense*				3170 00
18		*Miscellaneous Expense*				2584 15
19		*Payroll Taxes Expense*				9105 00
20		*Rent Expense*				21000 00
21		*Salary Expense*				89400 00
22		*Supplies Expense—Office*				4730 00
23		*Supplies Expense—Store*				3910 00
24		*Utilities Expense*				3820 00

Omni Import's work sheet has eleven income statement accounts with debit balances—the cost account, Purchases, and the ten expense accounts. These debit balances must be reduced to zero to prepare the accounts for the next fiscal period. *(CONCEPT: Matching Expenses with Revenue)* To reduce the balances to zero, the cost and expense accounts are credited for the amount of their balances. Income Summary is debited.

Income Summary has a debit balance shown on the work sheet. However, Income Summary is not closed as part of this closing entry. Instead, the account is closed with the third closing entry when net income is recorded.

STEPS: Closing income statement accounts with debit balances

1. Write the date, *31,* in the Date column.
2. Write the title of the account debited, *Income Summary,* in the Account Title column. The debit to Income Summary is not entered in the amount column until all cost and expense balances have been journalized and the total amount calculated.
3. Write the account title of each cost and expense account in the Account Title column. Write the balance of each cost and expense account in the General Credit column.
4. Add the credit amounts for this entry. Write the total of the cost and expense accounts, *$337,664.15,* in the General Debit column on the same line as the account title Income Summary.

SUMMARY OF CLOSING ENTRY FOR INCOME STATEMENT ACCOUNTS WITH DEBIT BALANCES

Income Summary

Adj. (mdse. inv.)	15,840.00	Closing (revenue)	423,120.00
Closing (cost and expenses)	337,664.15	*(New Bal.*	*69,615.85)*

Purchases

Bal.	189,960.00	Closing	189,960.00
(New Bal. zero)			

Rent Expense

Bal.	21,000.00	Closing	21,000.00
(New Bal. zero)			

Advertising Expense

Bal.	6,600.00	Closing	6,600.00
(New Bal. zero)			

Salary Expense

Bal.	89,400.00	Closing	89,400.00
(New Bal. zero)			

Credit Card Fee Expense

Bal.	3,385.00	Closing	3,385.00
(New Bal. zero)			

Supplies Expense—Office

Bal.	4,730.00	Closing	4,730.00
(New Bal. zero)			

Insurance Expense

Bal.	3,170.00	Closing	3,170.00
(New Bal. zero)			

Supplies Expense—Store

Bal.	3,910.00	Closing	3,910.00
(New Bal. zero)			

Miscellaneous Expense

Bal.	2,584.15	Closing	2,584.15
(New Bal. zero)			

Utilities Expense

Bal.	3,820.00	Closing	3,820.00
(New Bal. zero)			

Payroll Taxes Expense

Bal.	9,105.00	Closing	9,105.00
(New Bal. zero)			

The effect of this closing entry on the general ledger accounts is shown in the T accounts.

The cost account, Purchases, and the expense accounts are now closed and have zero balances. Income Summary has three amounts: (1) a debit of $15,840.00, the amount of the merchandise inventory adjustment; (2) a credit of $423,120.00, the amount of the entry to close the revenue account; and (3) a debit of $337,664.15, the total amount of the entry to close the cost and expense accounts. The balance of Income Summary is the net income for the fiscal period, $69,615.85.

AUDIT YOUR UNDERSTANDING

1. Where is the information obtained for journalizing closing entries for revenue, cost, and expenses?
2. What is the name of the temporary account that is used to summarize the closing entries for revenue, cost, and expenses?

WORK TOGETHER

Journalizing closing entries for income statement accounts

A partial work sheet of Fairbanks Auto Supply for the year ended December 31 of the current year is given in the *Working Papers*. Also given is a journal. Your instructor will guide you through the following example.

3. Record the following closing entries on page 12 of the journal. Save your work to complete Work Together on page 434.
   a. Close the income statement account with a credit balance.
   b. Close the income statement accounts with debit balances.

ON YOUR OWN

Journalizing closing entries for income statement accounts

A partial work sheet of Custom Aquarium for the year ended December 31 of the current year is given in the *Working Papers*. Also given is a journal. Work this problem independently.

4. Record the following closing entries on page 15 of the journal. Save your work to complete On Your Own on page 434.
   a. Close the income statement account with a credit balance.
   b. Close the income statement accounts with debit balances.

17-3 Recording Additional Closing Entries

CLOSING ENTRY TO RECORD NET INCOME OR LOSS AND CLOSE THE INCOME SUMMARY ACCOUNT

Omni Import
Distribution of Net Income Statement
For Year Ended December 31, 20--

Karl Koehn	
50% of Net Income	34 807 93
Michelle Wu	
50% of Net Income	34 807 92
Net Income	69 615 85

PAGE 26 JOURNAL

	DATE	ACCOUNT TITLE	DOC. NO.	POST. REF.	GENERAL DEBIT (1)	GENERAL CREDIT (2)
25	31	*Income Summary*			69 615 85	
26		*Karl Koehn, Capital*				34 807 93
27		*Michelle Wu, Capital*				34 807 92

1. Date
2. Account Debited
3. Debit to Close
4. Accounts Credited
5. Credits to Record Net Income

Net income increases the partners' equity and therefore must be credited to the partners' capital accounts. The share of the net income to be recorded for each partner is shown on the distribution of net income statement. The balance of the temporary account Income Summary must be reduced to zero to prepare the account for the next fiscal period. The effect of this closing entry on the general ledger accounts is shown in the T accounts.

If there is a net loss, partners' capital accounts are debited for their share of the net loss. Income Summary is credited for the total net loss.

Income Summary

Debit		Credit	
Adj. (mdse. inv.)	15,840.00	Closing (revenue)	423,120.00
Closing (cost and expenses)	337,664.15		
Closing (net income)	69,615.85	*(New Bal. zero)*	

Karl Koehn, Capital

Debit		Credit	
		Bal.	136,750.00
		Closing (net income)	34,807.93

Michelle Wu, Capital

Debit		Credit	
		Bal.	136,552.48
		Closing (net income)	34,807.92

STEPS: Closing the income summary account to record net income or loss

1. Write the date, *31,* in the Date column.
2. Write the title of the account debited, *Income Summary,* in the Account Title column.
3. Write the debit amount, *$69,615.85,* in the General Debit column. This is the amount of net income.
4. Write the titles of the two partners' capital accounts on the next two lines in the Account Title column.
5. Write the credit amounts, *$34,807.93* and *$34,807.92,* in the General Credit column.

CLOSING ENTRIES FOR THE PARTNERS' DRAWING ACCOUNTS

	ACCOUNT TITLE	7 BALANCE SHEET DEBIT	8 BALANCE SHEET CREDIT	
18	Karl Koehn, Capital		136 750 00	18
19	Karl Koehn, Drawing	29 100 00		19
20	Michelle Wu, Capital		136 552 48	20
21	Michelle Wu, Drawing	28 800 00		21

JOURNAL — PAGE 26

	DATE	ACCOUNT TITLE	DOC. NO.	POST. REF.	GENERAL 1 DEBIT	GENERAL 2 CREDIT
28	31	Karl Koehn, Capital			29 100 00	
29		Karl Koehn, Drawing				29 100 00
30	31	Michelle Wu, Capital			28 800 00	
31		Michelle Wu, Drawing				28 800 00
32						
33						

1. Date
2. Account Debited
3. Debit Amount
4. Account Credited
5. Credit to Close

As discussed in Chapter 9, the drawing accounts are not closed through Income Summary. The drawing account balances are closed directly to the partners' capital accounts.

The effect of these closing entries on the general ledger accounts is shown in the T accounts. After the closing entry for the partners' drawing accounts, the balances of the partners' capital accounts are the same as reported in the owners' equity section of the balance sheet.

Karl Koehn, Capital

Debit		Credit	
Closing (drawing)	29,100.00	Bal.	136,750.00
		Closing (net income)	34,807.93
		(New Bal.	*142,457.93)*

Michelle Wu, Capital

Debit		Credit	
Closing (drawing)	28,800.00	Bal.	136,552.48
		Closing (net income)	34,807.92
		(New Bal.	*142,560.40)*

Karl Koehn, Drawing

Debit		Credit	
Bal.	29,100.00	Closing	29,100.00
(New Bal. zero)			

Michelle Wu, Drawing

Debit		Credit	
Bal.	28,800.00	Closing	28,800.00
(New Bal. zero)			

STEPS

Closing the partners' drawing accounts

1. Write the date, *31,* in the Date column.
2. Write the title of the account debited, *Karl Koehn, Capital,* in the Account Title column.
3. Write the debit amount, *$29,100.00,* in the General Debit column.
4. Write the title of the account credited, *Karl Koehn, Drawing,* in the Account Title column.
5. Write the credit amount, *$29,100.00,* in the General Credit column.

Repeat Steps 1 through 5 to close the second partner's drawing account.

COMPLETED CLOSING ENTRIES FOR A PARTNERSHIP RECORDED IN A JOURNAL

PAGE *26* JOURNAL

	DATE	ACCOUNT TITLE	DOC. NO.	POST. REF.	1 GENERAL DEBIT	2 GENERAL CREDIT	3 ACCOUNTS RECEIVABLE DEBIT	4 ACCOUNTS RECEIVABLE CREDIT	
10		*Closing Entries*							10
11	*31*	*Sales*			*423120 00*				11
12		*Income Summary*				*423120 00*			12
13	*31*	*Income Summary*			*337664 15*				13
14		*Purchases*				*189960 00*			14
15		*Advertising Expense*				*6600 00*			15
16		*Credit Card Fee Expense*				*3385 00*			16
17		*Insurance Expense*				*3170 00*			17
18		*Miscellaneous Expense*				*2584 15*			18
19		*Payroll Taxes Expense*				*9105 00*			19
20		*Rent Expense*				*21000 00*			20
21		*Salary Expense*				*89400 00*			21
22		*Supplies Expense—Office*				*4730 00*			22
23		*Supplies Expense—Store*				*3910 00*			23
24		*Utilities Expense*				*3820 00*			24
25	*31*	*Income Summary*			*69615 85*				25
26		*Karl Koehn, Capital*				*34807 93*			26
27		*Michelle Wu, Capital*				*34807 92*			27
28	*31*	*Karl Koehn, Capital*			*29100 00*				28
29		*Karl Koehn, Drawing*				*29100 00*			29
30	*31*	*Michelle Wu, Capital*			*28800 00*				30
31		*Michelle Wu, Drawing*				*28800 00*			31

Omni Import's journal appears as shown above, after all closing entries have been recorded.

The next step would be to post the adjusting and closing entries to the general ledger.

AUDIT YOUR UNDERSTANDING

1. Where is the information obtained for journalizing closing entries for net income or loss and partners' drawing accounts?
2. How is a temporary account closed?

WORK TOGETHER

Journalizing additional closing entries

Use the journal from Work Together on page 430. Given in the *Working Papers* are a partial work sheet and a distribution of net income statement for the year ended December 31 of the current year. Your instructor will guide you through the following example.

3. Record the following closing entries on page 12 of the journal.
   a. Close the income summary account and record the net income.
   b. Close the partners' drawing accounts.

ON YOUR OWN

Journalizing additional closing entries

Use the journal from On Your Own on page 430. Given in the *Working Papers* are a partial work sheet and a distribution of net income statement for the year ended December 31 of the current year. Work this problem independently.

4. Record the following closing entries on page 15 of the journal.
   a. Close the income summary account and record the net income.
   b. Close the partners' drawing accounts.

17-4 Preparing a Post-Closing Trial Balance

COMPLETED GENERAL LEDGER AFTER ADJUSTING AND CLOSING ENTRIES ARE POSTED

ACCOUNT *Cash* — **ACCOUNT NO.** *1110*

DATE		ITEM	POST. REF.	DEBIT	CREDIT	BALANCE DEBIT	BALANCE CREDIT
20-- Dec.	31	Balance	✓			29,080.28	

ACCOUNT *Petty Cash* — **ACCOUNT NO.** *1120*

DATE		ITEM	POST. REF.	DEBIT	CREDIT	BALANCE DEBIT	BALANCE CREDIT
20-- Dec.	31	Balance	✓			300.00	

ACCOUNT *Accounts Receivable* — **ACCOUNT NO.** *1130*

DATE		ITEM	POST. REF.	DEBIT	CREDIT	BALANCE DEBIT	BALANCE CREDIT
20-- Dec.	31	Balance	✓			11,198.40	

ACCOUNT *Merchandise Inventory* — **ACCOUNT NO.** *1140*

DATE		ITEM	POST. REF.	DEBIT	CREDIT	BALANCE DEBIT	BALANCE CREDIT
20-- Jan.	1	Balance	✓			270,480.00	
Dec.	31		26		15,840.00	254,640.00	

ACCOUNT *Supplies—Office* — **ACCOUNT NO.** *1145*

DATE		ITEM	POST. REF.	DEBIT	CREDIT	BALANCE DEBIT	BALANCE CREDIT
20-- Dec.	31	Balance	✓			6,480.00	
	31		26		4,730.00	1,750.00	

ACCOUNT *Supplies—Store* — **ACCOUNT NO.** *1150*

DATE		ITEM	POST. REF.	DEBIT	CREDIT	BALANCE DEBIT	BALANCE CREDIT
20-- Dec.	31	Balance	✓			6,944.00	
	31		26		3,910.00	3,034.00	

ACCOUNT *Prepaid Insurance* — **ACCOUNT NO.** *1160*

DATE		ITEM	POST. REF.	DEBIT	CREDIT	BALANCE DEBIT	BALANCE CREDIT
20-- Dec.	31	Balance	✓			5,800.00	
	31		26		3,170.00	2,630.00	

ACCOUNT *Accounts Payable* — **ACCOUNT NO.** *2110*

DATE		ITEM	POST. REF.	DEBIT	CREDIT	BALANCE DEBIT	BALANCE CREDIT
20-- Dec.	31	Balance	✓				12,542.38

ACCOUNT *Employee Income Tax Payable* — **ACCOUNT NO.** *2120*

DATE		ITEM	POST. REF.	DEBIT	CREDIT	BALANCE DEBIT	BALANCE CREDIT
20-- Dec.	31	Balance	✓				542.00

ACCOUNT *Social Security Tax Payable* — **ACCOUNT NO.** *2130*

DATE		ITEM	POST. REF.	DEBIT	CREDIT	BALANCE DEBIT	BALANCE CREDIT
20-- Dec.	31	Balance	✓				985.40

ACCOUNT *Medicare Tax Payable* — **ACCOUNT NO.** *2135*

DATE		ITEM	POST. REF.	DEBIT	CREDIT	BALANCE DEBIT	BALANCE CREDIT
20-- Dec.	31		✓				227.42

ACCOUNT *Sales Tax Payable* — **ACCOUNT NO.** *2140*

DATE		ITEM	POST. REF.	DEBIT	CREDIT	BALANCE DEBIT	BALANCE CREDIT
20-- Dec.	31	Balance	✓				2,112.05

ACCOUNT *Unemployment Tax Payable—Federal* — **ACCOUNT NO.** *2150*

DATE		ITEM	POST. REF.	DEBIT	CREDIT	BALANCE DEBIT	BALANCE CREDIT
20-- Dec.	31	Balance	✓				8.40

ACCOUNT *Unemployment Tax Payable—State* — **ACCOUNT NO.** *2160*

DATE		ITEM	POST. REF.	DEBIT	CREDIT	BALANCE DEBIT	BALANCE CREDIT
20-- Dec.	31	Balance	✓				56.70

ACCOUNT *Health Insurance Premiums Payable* — **ACCOUNT NO.** *2170*

DATE		ITEM	POST. REF.	DEBIT	CREDIT	BALANCE DEBIT	BALANCE CREDIT
20-- Dec.	31	Balance	✓				1,008.00

ACCOUNT *U.S. Savings Bonds Payable* — **ACCOUNT NO.** *2180*

DATE		ITEM	POST. REF.	DEBIT	CREDIT	BALANCE DEBIT	BALANCE CREDIT
20-- Dec.	31	Balance	✓				60.00

ACCOUNT *United Way Donations Payable* — **ACCOUNT NO.** *2190*

DATE		ITEM	POST. REF.	DEBIT	CREDIT	BALANCE DEBIT	BALANCE CREDIT
20-- Dec.	31	Balance	✓				72.00

Omni Import's completed general ledger after adjusting and closing entries are posted is shown above and on the following page.

Balance sheet accounts (asset, liability, and capital accounts) have up-to-date balances to begin the new fiscal period.

Income statement accounts (revenue, cost, and expense accounts) have zero balances to begin the new fiscal period. *(CONCEPT: Matching Expenses with Revenue)*

ACCOUNT Karl Koehn, Capital ACCOUNT NO. 3110

DATE		ITEM	POST. REF.	DEBIT	CREDIT	BALANCE DEBIT	BALANCE CREDIT
20-- Dec.	31	Balance	✓				136 750 00
	31		26		34 807 93		171 557 93
	31		26	29 100 00			142 457 93

ACCOUNT Karl Koehn, Drawing ACCOUNT NO. 3120

DATE		ITEM	POST. REF.	DEBIT	CREDIT	BALANCE DEBIT	BALANCE CREDIT
20-- Dec.	31	Balance	✓			29 100 00	
	31		26		29 100 00	—	—

ACCOUNT Michelle Wu, Capital ACCOUNT NO. 3130

DATE		ITEM	POST. REF.	DEBIT	CREDIT	BALANCE DEBIT	BALANCE CREDIT
20-- Dec.	31	Balance	✓				136 552 48
	31		26		34 807 92		171 360 40
	31		26	28 800 00			142 560 40

ACCOUNT Michelle Wu, Drawing ACCOUNT NO. 3140

DATE		ITEM	POST. REF.	DEBIT	CREDIT	BALANCE DEBIT	BALANCE CREDIT
20-- Dec.	31	Balance	✓			28 800 00	
	31		26		28 800 00	—	—

ACCOUNT Income Summary ACCOUNT NO. 3150

DATE		ITEM	POST. REF.	DEBIT	CREDIT	BALANCE DEBIT	BALANCE CREDIT
20-- Dec.	31		26	15 840 00		15 840 00	
	31		26		423 120 00		407 280 00
	31		26	337 664 15			69 615 85
	31		26	69 615 85		—	—

ACCOUNT Sales ACCOUNT NO. 4110

DATE		ITEM	POST. REF.	DEBIT	CREDIT	BALANCE DEBIT	BALANCE CREDIT
20-- Dec.	31	Balance	✓				423 120 00
	31		26	423 120 00		—	—

ACCOUNT Purchases ACCOUNT NO. 5110

DATE		ITEM	POST. REF.	DEBIT	CREDIT	BALANCE DEBIT	BALANCE CREDIT
20-- Dec.	31	Balance	✓			189 960 00	
	31		26		189 960 00	—	—

ACCOUNT Advertising Expense ACCOUNT NO. 6110

DATE		ITEM	POST. REF.	DEBIT	CREDIT	BALANCE DEBIT	BALANCE CREDIT
20-- Dec.	31	Balance	✓			6 600 00	
	31		26		6 600 00	—	—

ACCOUNT Credit Card Fee Expense ACCOUNT NO. 6120

DATE		ITEM	POST. REF.	DEBIT	CREDIT	BALANCE DEBIT	BALANCE CREDIT
20-- Dec.	31	Balance	✓			3 385 00	
	31		26		3 385 00	—	—

ACCOUNT Insurance Expense ACCOUNT NO. 6130

DATE		ITEM	POST. REF.	DEBIT	CREDIT	BALANCE DEBIT	BALANCE CREDIT
20-- Dec.	31		26	3 170 00		3 170 00	
	31		26		3 170 00	—	—

ACCOUNT Miscellaneous Expense ACCOUNT NO. 6140

DATE		ITEM	POST. REF.	DEBIT	CREDIT	BALANCE DEBIT	BALANCE CREDIT
20-- Dec.	31	Balance	✓			2 584 15	
	31		26		2 584 15	—	—

ACCOUNT Payroll Taxes Expense ACCOUNT NO. 6150

DATE		ITEM	POST. REF.	DEBIT	CREDIT	BALANCE DEBIT	BALANCE CREDIT
20-- Dec.	31	Balance	✓			9 105 00	
	31		26		9 105 00	—	—

ACCOUNT Rent Expense ACCOUNT NO. 6160

DATE		ITEM	POST. REF.	DEBIT	CREDIT	BALANCE DEBIT	BALANCE CREDIT
20-- Dec.	31	Balance	✓			21 000 00	
	31		26		21 000 00	—	—

ACCOUNT Salary Expense ACCOUNT NO. 6170

DATE		ITEM	POST. REF.	DEBIT	CREDIT	BALANCE DEBIT	BALANCE CREDIT
20-- Dec.	31	Balance	✓			89 400 00	
	31		26		89 400 00	—	—

ACCOUNT Supplies Expense—Office ACCOUNT NO. 6175

DATE		ITEM	POST. REF.	DEBIT	CREDIT	BALANCE DEBIT	BALANCE CREDIT
20-- Dec.	31		26	4 730 00		4 730 00	
	31		26		4 730 00	—	—

ACCOUNT Supplies Expense—Store ACCOUNT NO. 6180

DATE		ITEM	POST. REF.	DEBIT	CREDIT	BALANCE DEBIT	BALANCE CREDIT
20-- Dec.	31		26	3 910 00		3 910 00	
	31		26		3 910 00	—	—

ACCOUNT Utilities Expense ACCOUNT NO. 6190

DATE		ITEM	POST. REF.	DEBIT	CREDIT	BALANCE DEBIT	BALANCE CREDIT
20-- Dec.	31	Balance	✓			3 820 00	
	31		26		3 820 00	—	—

Completed General Ledger after Adjusting and Closing Entries Are Posted *(concluded)*

POST-CLOSING TRIAL BALANCE

1. Heading
2. Accounts That Have Balances
3. Debit Balances
4. Credit Balances
5. Word *Totals*
6. Total Debits
7. Total Credits
8. Verify Equality of Totals
9. Double Lines

Omni Import
Post-Closing Trial Balance
December 31, 20--

ACCOUNT TITLE	DEBIT	CREDIT
Cash	29080 28	
Petty Cash	300 00	
Accounts Receivable	11198 40	
Merchandise Inventory	254640 00	
Supplies—Office	1750 00	
Supplies—Store	3034 00	
Prepaid Insurance	2630 00	
Accounts Payable		12542 38
Employee Income Tax Payable		542 00
Social Security Tax Payable		985 40
Medicare Tax Payable		227 42
Sales Tax Payable		2112 05
Unemployment Tax Payable—Federal		8 40
Unemployment Tax Payable—State		56 70
Health Insurance Premiums Payable		1008 00
U.S. Savings Bonds Payable		60 00
United Way Donations Payable		72 00
Karl Koehn, Capital		142457 93
Michelle Wu, Capital		142560 40
Totals	302632 68	302632 68

A post-closing trial balance is prepared to prove the equality of debits and credits in the general ledger. Account balances on the post-closing trial balance agree with the balances on the balance sheet shown in Chapter 16. Because the post-closing trial balance debit and credit totals are the same, the equality of debits and credits in the general ledger is proved. The general ledger is ready for the next fiscal period. *(CONCEPT: Accounting Period Cycle)*

STEPS Preparing a post-closing trial balance

1. Write the post-closing trial balance heading on three lines.
2. List all general ledger accounts that have balances in the Account Title column. Accounts are listed in the same order as they appear in the general ledger. Accounts with zero balances are not listed.
3. Write the balance of each asset account in the Debit column.
4. Write the balance of each liability and capital account in the Credit column.
5. Write the word *Totals* on the next line below the last account title.
6. Total the amounts in the Debit column and write the amount, *$302,632.68,* on the Totals line.
7. Total the amounts in the Credit column and write the amount, *$302,632.68,* on the Totals line.
8. Verify equality by comparing the Debit column total with the Credit column total. The two amounts, $302,632.68, are the same. The equality of debits and credits is proved.
9. Rule double lines below both Debit and Credit total amounts.

ACCOUNTING CYCLE FOR A MERCHANDISING BUSINESS ORGANIZED AS A PARTNERSHIP

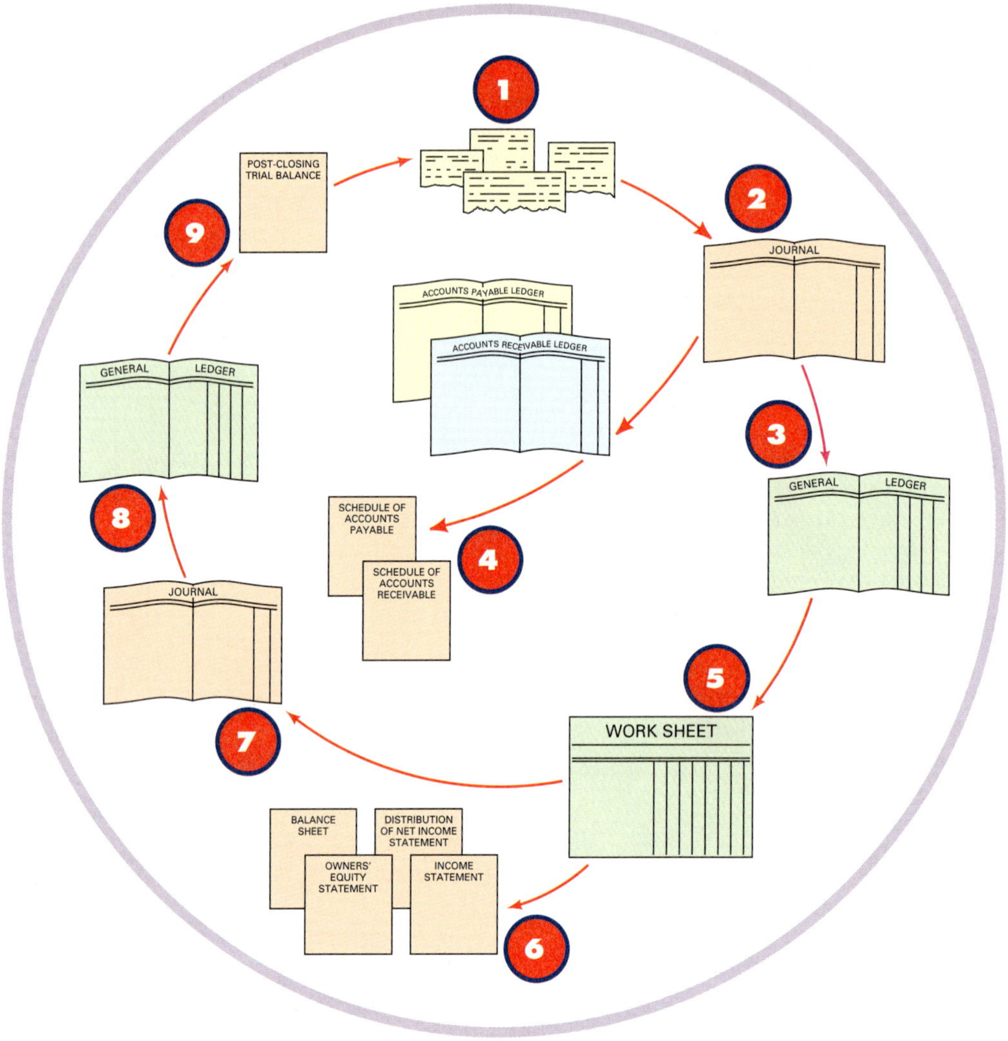

Service and merchandising businesses use a similar accounting cycle. The accounting cycles are also similar for a proprietorship and a partnership. Variations occur when subsidiary ledgers are used. Variations also occur in preparing financial statements.

STEPS

Accounting cycle for a merchandising business

1. Source documents are checked for accuracy, and transactions are analyzed into debit and credit parts.
2. Transactions, from information on source documents, are recorded in a journal.
3. Journal entries are posted to the accounts payable ledger, the accounts receivable ledger, and the general ledger.
4. Schedules of accounts payable and accounts receivable are prepared from the subsidiary ledgers.
5. A work sheet, including a trial balance, is prepared from the general ledger.
6. Financial statements are prepared from the work sheet.
7. Adjusting and closing entries are journalized from the work sheet.
8. Adjusting and closing entries are posted to the general ledger.
9. A post-closing trial balance of the general ledger is prepared.

AUDIT YOUR UNDERSTANDING

1. Which accounts are listed on a post-closing trial balance?
2. What is the purpose of preparing a post-closing trial balance?
3. In what order should accounts be listed on a post-closing trial balance?

WORK TOGETHER

Preparing a post-closing trial balance

For the current year, the December 31 balances for Visual Art Center's balance sheet accounts after adjusting and closing entries have been posted are given below.

Account	Balance	Account	Balance
Cash	$ 21,810.20	Accounts Payable	$ 11,676.50
Petty Cash	350.00	Sales Tax Payable	1,584.00
Accounts Receivable	8,398.80	Jane Cole, Capital	107,050.50
Merchandise Inventory	190,980.00	Jane Cole, Drawing	—
Supplies—Office	1,314.00	Gary Klein, Capital	106,790.00
Supplies—Store	2,268.00	Gary Klein, Drawing	—
Prepaid Insurance	1,980.00		

Your instructor will guide you through the following example.

4. Prepare a post-closing trial balance on the form provided in the *Working Papers.*

ON YOUR OWN

Preparing a post-closing trial balance

For the current year, the December 31 balances for Jan's Pastry Boutique's balance sheet accounts after adjusting and closing entries have been posted are given below.

Account	Balance	Account	Balance
Cash	$ 23,021.89	Accounts Payable	$ 12,255.25
Petty Cash	300.00	Sales Tax Payable	1,672.00
Accounts Receivable	8,865.40	Jan Dyer, Capital	112,998.27
Merchandise Inventory	201,590.00	Jan Dyer, Drawing	—
Supplies—Office	1,387.00	Becky Myers, Capital	112,722.77
Supplies—Store	2,394.00	Becky Myers, Drawing	—
Prepaid Insurance	2,090.00		

Work independently to complete this problem.

5. Prepare a post-closing trial balance on the form provided in the *Working Papers.*

CHAPTER 17 SUMMARY

After completing this chapter, you can

1. Identify accounting concepts and practices related to adjusting and closing entries for a merchandising business organized as a partnership.
2. Record adjusting entries.
3. Record closing entries for income statement accounts.
4. Record closing entries for net income or loss and partners' drawing accounts.
5. Prepare a post-closing trial balance.

EXPLORE ACCOUNTING

THE PERPETUAL INVENTORY METHOD

Many companies use one of two merchandise inventory methods to account for their cost of merchandise sold. (Inventory counting methods are fully discussed in Chapter 22.) A merchandise inventory determined by counting, weighing, or measuring items of merchandise on hand is known as *periodic inventory.*

The disadvantage of this method is that the business does not know the cost of merchandise sold until the merchandise inventory has been counted at the end of the fiscal period and costs calculated.

An inventory method that provides more timely cost information is the *perpetual inventory method*, which is determined by keeping a continuous record of increases, decreases, and balance on hand. When perpetual inventory is used, both sales and cost of merchandise sold are recorded at the time of sale. Assume All Sports Shop purchases 10 soccer balls, Item 929, for $13.00 each. Further assume the store sells two of these soccer balls for $25.00 each. The journal entries for the purchase and sale are shown below.

When the perpetual inventory method is used, the purchases account is not used. When merchandise is purchased, it is added to the merchandise inventory account. Two entries are made each time a sale is made—one for the sale at the selling price and one for the cost at the cost of merchandise sold. An additional account is used, Cost of Merchandise Sold. The cost is recorded in this account at the time of the sale.

The advantage of this inventory method is that the cost of merchandise sold can be determined at any time by reviewing the cost of merchandise sold account. However, the disadvantage is that the number of entries is doubled and the information needed to keep current records of the merchandise inventory is much more complex.

Activity: All Sports Shop purchased 5 sets of golf clubs, Item No. 389, for $140.00 each. One set of clubs, Item No. 389, was sold for $250.00. Using the perpetual inventory method, prepare the journal entries to record the purchase of the clubs and to record the sale of one set of clubs.

Purchase:	Merchandise Inventory (Item 929) (10 @ $13.00)	130.00	
	Cash		130.00
Sale:	Cash (2 @ $25.00)	50.00	
	Sales		50.00
	Cost of Merchandise Sold (2 @ $13.00)	26.00	
	Merchandise Inventory (Item 929)		26.00

17-1 APPLICATION PROBLEM
Journalizing adjusting entries

The following information is related to adjustments needed at the end of a fiscal period for a partnership.

		Adjustment Information	
Account Title	**Work Sheet Trial Balance**	**Ending Inventories**	**Ending Value**
Merchandise Inventory	$265,000.00	$347,500.00	
Supplies—Office	5,600.00	2,810.00	
Supplies—Store	5,160.00	2,900.00	
Prepaid Insurance	4,000.00		$1,000.00

Instructions:

Record the appropriate adjusting entries on page 12 of the journal provided in the *Working Papers*. Use December 31 of the current year as the date.

17-2 APPLICATION PROBLEM
Journalizing closing entries for income statement accounts

The following information is from the work sheet of Aladdin Cycle Shop for December 31 of the current year.

	ACCOUNT TITLE	5 INCOME STATEMENT DEBIT	6 INCOME STATEMENT CREDIT
15	*Sales*		278 500 00
16	*Purchases*	141 600 00	
17	*Advertising Expense*	4 880 00	
18	*Credit Card Fee Expense*	3 200 00	
19	*Insurance Expense*	3 780 00	
20	*Miscellaneous Expense*	2 070 00	
21	*Rent Expense*	21 600 00	
22	*Supplies Expense—Office*	4 470 00	
23	*Supplies Expense—Store*	4 680 00	
24	*Utilities Expense*	4 410 00	

Instructions:

Prepare the following closing entries on page 14 of the journal provided in the *Working Papers*. Save your work to complete Application Problem 17-3.

1. Close the income statement account with a credit balance.
2. Close the income statement accounts with debit balances.

17-3 APPLICATION PROBLEM
Journalizing additional closing entries

For Aladdin Cycle Shop on December 31 of the current year, the following information is from the work sheet and the distribution of net income statement. Use the journal from Application Problem 17-2.

	ACCOUNT TITLE	5 INCOME STATEMENT DEBIT	6 INCOME STATEMENT CREDIT	7 BALANCE SHEET DEBIT	8 BALANCE SHEET CREDIT	
10	*Sue Ogden, Capital*				223 000 00	10
11	*Sue Ogden, Drawing*			26 500 00		11
12	*Todd Marquez, Capital*				231 000 00	12
13	*Todd Marquez, Drawing*			26 800 00		13
14	*Income Summary*	18 000 00				14

Aladdin Cycle Shop
Distribution of Net Income Statement
For Year Ended December 31, 20--

Sue Ogden	
50% of Net Income	34 905 00
Todd Marquez	
50% of Net Income	34 905 00
Net Income	69 810 00

Instructions:

Prepare the following closing entries on page 14 of the journal.

1. Close the income summary account and record the net income.
2. Close the partners' drawing accounts.

17-4 APPLICATION PROBLEM
Preparing a post-closing trial balance

For the current year, the December 31 balances for Lawn and Garden Center's balance sheet accounts after adjusting and closing entries have been posted are given.

Account	Balance	Account	Balance
Cash	$ 26,656.93	Accounts Payable	$ 11,744.13
Petty Cash	500.00	Sales Tax Payable	1,936.00
Accounts Receivable	10,265.20	Rob Gresham, Capital	132,030.00
Merchandise Inventory	233,420.00	Rob Gresham, Drawing	—
Supplies—Office	1,606.00	Jose Zavala, Capital	131,710.00
Supplies—Store	2,552.00	Jose Zavala, Drawing	—
Prepaid Insurance	2,420.00		

Instructions:

Prepare a post-closing trial balance on the form provided in the *Working Papers*.

17-5 APPLICATION PROBLEM

Journalizing and posting adjusting and closing entries; preparing a post-closing trial balance

Use the following partial work sheet of Custom Marble Company for the year ended December 31 of the current year. The general ledger accounts and their balances as well as forms for completing this problem are in the *Working Papers*.

		3	4	5	6
		ADJUSTMENTS		INCOME STATEMENT	
	ACCOUNT TITLE	DEBIT	CREDIT	DEBIT	CREDIT
4	*Merchandise Inventory*		(a) 15,600.00		
5	*Supplies—Office*		(b) 2,568.00		
6	*Supplies—Store*		(c) 2,940.00		
7	*Prepaid Insurance*		(d) 3,168.00		
22	*Income Summary*	(a) 15,600.00		15,600.00	
23	*Sales*				275,060.00
24	*Purchases*			151,740.00	
25	*Advertising Expense*			5,664.00	
26	*Credit Card Fee Expense*			3,912.00	
27	*Insurance Expense*	(d) 3,168.00		3,168.00	
28	*Miscellaneous Expense*			2,316.00	
29	*Payroll Taxes Expense*			6,917.00	
30	*Rent Expense*			18,720.00	
31	*Salary Expense*			68,150.00	
32	*Supplies Expense—Office*	(b) 2,568.00		2,568.00	
33	*Supplies Expense—Store*	(c) 2,940.00		2,940.00	
34	*Utilities Expense*			3,528.00	
35		24,276.00	24,276.00	285,223.00	275,060.00
36	*Net Loss*				10,163.00
37				285,223.00	285,223.00
38					

Instructions:

1. Use page 24 of a journal. Journalize the adjusting entries using information from the partial work sheet.
2. Post the adjusting entries.
3. Continue using page 24 of the journal. Journalize the closing entries using information from the work sheet. The distribution of net income statement shows equal distribution of the net loss. The partners' drawing accounts show the following debit balances in the work sheet's Balance Sheet Debit column: Emma Bose, Drawing, $18,225.00; Kris Manuel, Drawing, $18,400.00.
4. Post the closing entries.
5. Prepare a post-closing trial balance.

17-6 MASTERY PROBLEM

Journalizing and posting adjusting and closing entries; preparing a post-closing trial balance

Use the following partial work sheet of Deco Paint Supplies for the year ended December 31 of the current year. The general ledger accounts and their balances as well as forms for completing this problem are in the *Working Papers*.

		3	4	5	6
	ACCOUNT TITLE	ADJUSTMENTS		INCOME STATEMENT	
		DEBIT	CREDIT	DEBIT	CREDIT
4	*Merchandise Inventory*		(a) 15000 00		
5	*Supplies—Office*		(b) 2916 00		
6	*Supplies—Store*		(c) 2724 00		
7	*Prepaid Insurance*		(d) 2736 00		
22	*Income Summary*	(a) 15000 00		15000 00	
23	*Sales*				374500 00
24	*Purchases*			156540 00	
25	*Advertising Expense*			6216 00	
26	*Credit Card Fee Expense*			4104 00	
27	*Insurance Expense*	(d) 2736 00		2736 00	
28	*Miscellaneous Expense*			2472 00	
29	*Payroll Taxes Expense*			7230 00	
30	*Rent Expense*			18000 00	
31	*Salary Expense*			71240 00	
32	*Supplies Expense—Office*	(b) 2916 00		2916 00	
33	*Supplies Expense—Store*	(c) 2724 00		2724 00	
34	*Utilities Expense*			3456 00	
35		23376 00	23376 00	292634 00	374500 00
36	*Net Income*			81866 00	
37				374500 00	374500 00
38					

Instructions:

1. Use page 25 of a journal. Journalize the adjusting entries using information from the partial work sheet.
2. Post the adjusting entries.
3. Continue using page 25 of the journal. Journalize the closing entries using information from the work sheet. The distribution of net income statement shows equal distribution of earnings. The partners' drawing accounts show the following debit balances in the work sheet's Balance Sheet Debit column: Anna Cao, Drawing, $22,800.00; Inez O'Neal, Drawing, $23,400.00.
4. Post the closing entries.
5. Prepare a post-closing trial balance.

17-7 CHALLENGE PROBLEM
Completing end-of-fiscal-period work

Lighting Solutions' trial balance is recorded on a 10-column work sheet in the *Working Papers*. The general ledger accounts and their balances as well as forms for completing this problem are also given.

Instructions:

1. Use the following adjustment information. Complete the 10-column work sheet.

Adjustment Information, December 31	
Merchandise inventory	$235,380.00
Office supplies inventory	3,030.00
Store supplies inventory	2,656.00
Value of prepaid insurance	2,530.00

2. Prepare an income statement from the information on the work sheet. Calculate and record the following component percentages: (a) cost of merchandise sold, (b) gross profit on sales, (c) total expenses, and (d) net income or loss. Round percentage calculations to the nearest 0.1%.
3. Prepare a distribution of net income statement. Net income or loss is to be shared equally.
4. Prepare an owners' equity statement. No additional investments were made.
5. Prepare a balance sheet in report form.
6. Use page 24 of a journal. Journalize the adjusting entries.
7. Post the adjusting entries.
8. Continue using page 24 of the journal. Journalize the closing entries.
9. Post the closing entries.
10. Prepare a post-closing trial balance.

Inventory auditing challenges

For most businesses, merchandise inventory is a major portion of the business's assets. Therefore, reporting an accurate amount on the financial statements is important to accurate financial reporting. Whether a member of the business's accounting staff or an outside auditor audits the merchandise inventory of the business, determining an accurate count of the merchandise inventory is very important. Different types of merchandise present different kinds of challenges for the auditor.

a. **Actual count, common costs:** A sports store has 50 tennis rackets, all the same model. The rackets should be counted and multiplied times the cost per racket to determine the inventory value.

b. **Actual count, unique costs:** An automobile dealer has 60 new automobiles. Since each automobile probably has a unique and significant cost, the cost of each automobile should be totaled to determine the inventory value.

c. **Sampling:** A hardware store has many machine bolts. Since the value of each is low and there are many items, a small quantity may be counted or weighed. Then estimate the total cost based on the sample size or weight.

d. **Measuring/calculating:** An oil company stores crude oil in large tanks. The depth of the oil in the tank can be measured with a measuring rod, then the circumference of the tank can be measured. The total volume of crude oil can be calculated, then divided by the volume of one barrel of crude oil to determine the total barrels. This number can then be multiplied by the cost per barrel of crude oil.

(Continued on next page)

11. How would you determine the value of the following inventory items?
    a. Grain in a grain elevator.
    b. Lumber in a lumber yard.
    c. Diamond rings in a jewelry store.
    d. Nails in a home improvement store.

INTERNET ACTIVITY

Point your browser to

http://accounting.swpco.com

Choose **First-Year Course**, choose **Activities**, and complete the activity for Chapter 17.

Applied Communication

Public speakers are judged by the ability of the audience to remember important points of their presentation. Effective public speakers use a variety of techniques to encourage the audience to listen to their message.

Instructions: Contact an instructor in your school or a local businessperson you have heard speak at school or community functions. Ask the person to describe the techniques used to help the audience listen and remember the message. Write a short report summarizing these techniques. Be prepared to present your report orally in class.

Cases for Critical Thinking

Case 1 Western Boot Warehouse's Trial Balance Debit column of the work sheet shows a debit balance of $3,000.00 for the office supplies account. The ending office supplies inventory is determined to be $2,200.00. The accounting clerk journalized the following adjusting entry: debit Supplies Expense—Office, $2,200.00; credit Supplies—Office, $2,200.00. Alice Hummell, partner, discussed the entry with the accounting clerk and suggested that the adjusting entry should have been for $800.00 instead of $2,200.00. The clerk indicated that there is no problem because the amounts will be adjusted again at the end of the next fiscal period. Do you agree with Ms. Hummell or the accounting clerk? Explain your answer.

Case 2 Two businesses have been using different accounting practices. One business first closes the income summary account to record the net income in the capital accounts and then closes the drawing accounts. The other business first closes the drawing accounts and then closes the income summary account to record the net income in the capital accounts. Which practice is correct? Explain.

AUTOMATED ACCOUNTING

END-OF-FISCAL-PERIOD WORK FOR A PARTNERSHIP

When a transaction affects more than one accounting period, an adjusting entry may be needed to match revenues and expenses with the appropriate accounting period. To complete the accounting cycle, adjusting entries are recorded in the computer and verified for accuracy. The financial statements are generated, and then the software generates and posts the closing entries.

Adjusting Entries

Changes in inventory resulting from purchases and sales transactions are not reflected in the merchandise inventory account. Therefore, this account balance must be adjusted to reflect the changes. Two accounts are used to adjust the merchandise inventory account balance: Merchandise Inventory and Income Summary. The asset account is increased (debited) or decreased (credited) to reflect the current balance, and the opposite entry is made in the income summary account. For other asset accounts, such as Supplies and Insurance, the adjustment is made to the related expense account.

Closing Entries

In an automated accounting system, closing entries are generated and posted by the software. *Automated Accounting 7.0* automatically prepares all closing entries when income or loss is distributed equally among the partners.

If the partnership has an unequal distribution of income or loss, only the entries to close the revenue and expense accounts will be automatically prepared. Two additional closing entries must be manually entered: (1) To distribute the net income or loss. This entry transfers the balance in Income Summary to the partners' capital accounts using the distribution method defined in the partnership agreement. (2) To close the drawing accounts.

1. Choose Generate Closing Journal Entries from the Options menu.
2. Click Yes to generate the closing entries.
3. The general journal will appear, containing the journal entries.
4. Click the Post button.
5. Display a post-closing trial balance report.
   a. Click on the Reports toolbar button, or choose the Report Selection menu item from the Reports menu.
   b. Select the Ledger Reports option button from the Select a Report Group list.
   c. Choose Trial Balance from the Choose a Report to Display list.

AUTOMATING APPLICATION PROBLEM 17-5: Journalizing and posting adjusting and closing entries; preparing a post-closing trial balance

Instructions:

1. Load *Automated Accounting 7.0* or higher software.
2. Select database F17-1 from the appropriate directory/folder.
3. Select File from the menu bar and choose the Save As menu command. Key the path to the drive and directory that contains your data files. Save the database with a file name of XXX171 (where XXX are your initials).
4. Access Problem Instructions through the Help menu. Read the Problem Instructions screen.
5. Key the adjusting entries from the work sheet on page 443.
6. Exit the *Automated Accounting* software.

AUTOMATING MASTERY PROBLEM 17-6: Journalizing and posting adjusting and closing entries; preparing a post-closing trial balance

Instructions:

1. Load *Automated Accounting 7.0* or higher software.
2. Select database F17-2 from the appropriate directory/folder.
3. Select File from the menu bar and choose the Save As menu command. Key the path to the drive and directory that contains your data files. Save the database with a file name of XXX172 (where XXX are your initials).
4. Access Problem Instructions through the Help menu. Read the Problem Instructions screen.
5. Key the adjusting entries from the work sheet on page 444.
6. Exit the *Automated Accounting* software.

REINFORCEMENT ACTIVITY 2—PART B

An Accounting Cycle for a Partnership: End-of-Fiscal-Period Work

The ledgers used in Reinforcement Activity 2—Part A are needed to complete Reinforcement Activity 2—Part B.

Reinforcement Activity 2—Part B includes those accounting activities needed to complete the accounting cycle of ClearView Optical.

END-OF-FISCAL-PERIOD WORK

Instructions:

10. Prepare a trial balance on a work sheet. Use December 31 of the current year as the date.
11. Complete the work sheet using the following adjustment information:

Adjustment Information, Account Balances on December 31

Merchandise inventory	$243,800.00
Office supplies inventory	2,840.00
Store supplies inventory	3,890.00
Value of prepaid insurance	310.00

12. Prepare an income statement. Figure and record the following component percentages: (a) cost of merchandise sold, (b) gross profit on sales, (c) total expenses, and (d) net income or loss. Round percentage calculations to the nearest 0.1%
13. Prepare a distribution of net income statement. Net income or loss is to be shared equally.
14. Prepare an owners' equity statement. No additional investments were made.
15. Prepare a balance sheet in report form.
16. Use page 25 of a journal. Journalize and post the adjusting entries.
17. Continue using page 25 of the journal. Journalize and post the closing entries.
18. Prepare a post-closing trial balance.

The following activities are included in Fitness Junction's simulation:

1. Recording transactions in a journal from source documents.
2. Posting items to be posted individually to a general ledger and subsidiary ledger.
3. Recording a payroll in a payroll register. Updating the employee earnings record. Recording payroll journal entries.
4. Posting column totals to a general ledger.
5. Preparing schedules of accounts receivable and accounts payable from subsidiary ledgers.
6. Preparing a trial balance on a work sheet.
7. Planning adjustments and completing a work sheet.
8. Preparing financial statements.
9. Journalizing and posting adjusting entries.
10. Journalizing and posting closing entries.
11. Preparing a post-closing trial balance.

This simulation covers the realistic transactions completed by Fitness Junction, a merchandising business organized as a partnership. The business, located in Raleigh, North Carolina, sells all kinds of athletic equipment—from in-house spas and weight bars to trampolines and multi-station weight machines. Transactions are recorded in a journal similar to the one used by Omni Import in Cycle 2. The activities included in the accounting cycle for Fitness Junction are listed at the left.

This real-life business simulation comes with source documents. It is available in manual and in automated versions, for use with *Automated Accounting* software.

ACCOUNTING CONCEPTS

The following accounting concepts and their definitions are provided in this appendix for ready reference.

ACCOUNTING CONCEPTS

Accounting personnel are guided in their work by generally accepted accounting concepts. Ten commonly accepted accounting concepts are described in this appendix. Each concept is fully explained in the text the first time an application of the concept is described. Throughout the textbook, each time a concept application occurs, a concept reference is given, such as *(CONCEPT: Business Entity)*.

1. ACCOUNTING PERIOD CYCLE [Chapter 7]
Changes in financial information are reported for a specific period of time in the form of financial statements.

2. ADEQUATE DISCLOSURE [Chapter 8]
Financial statements contain all information necessary to understand a business's financial condition.

3. BUSINESS ENTITY [Chapter 1]
Financial information is recorded and reported separately from the owner's personal financial information.

4. CONSISTENT REPORTING [Chapter 7]
The same accounting procedures are followed in the same way in each accounting period.

5. GOING CONCERN [Chapter 1]
Financial statements are prepared with the expectation that a business will remain in operation indefinitely.

6. HISTORICAL COST [Chapter 10]
The actual amount paid for merchandise or other items bought is recorded.

7. MATCHING EXPENSES WITH REVENUE [Chapter 7]
Revenue from business activities and expenses associated with earning that revenue are recorded in the same accounting period.

8. OBJECTIVE EVIDENCE [Chapter 4]
A source document is prepared for each transaction.

9. REALIZATION OF REVENUE [Chapter 11]
Revenue is recorded at the time goods or services are sold.

10. UNIT OF MEASUREMENT [Chapter 1]
Business transactions are stated in numbers that have common values; that is, using a common unit of measurement.

USING A CALCULATOR AND COMPUTER KEYPAD

KINDS OF CALCULATORS

Many different models of calculators, both desktop and hand held, are available. All calculators have their own features and particular placement of operating keys. Therefore, it is necessary to refer to the operator's manual for specific instructions and locations of the operating keys for the calculator being used. A typical keyboard of a desktop calculator is shown in the illustration.

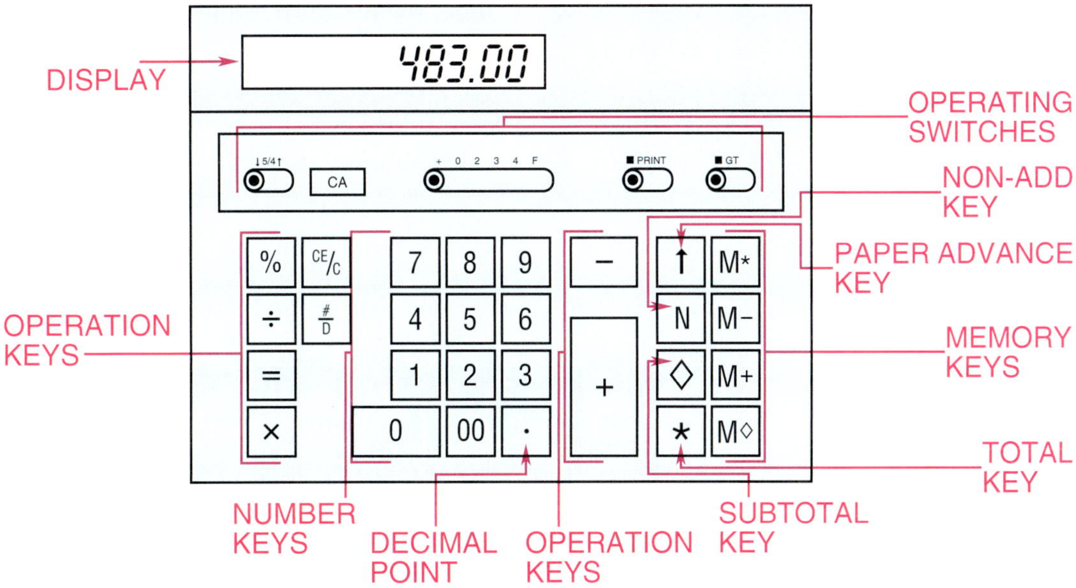

DESKTOP CALCULATOR SETTINGS

Several operating switches on a desktop calculator must be engaged before the calculator will produce the desired results.

The *decimal selector* sets the appropriate decimal places necessary for the numbers that will be entered. For example, if the decimal selector is set at 2, both the numbers entered and the answer will have two decimal places. If the decimal selector is set at F, the calculator automatically sets the decimal places. The F setting allows the answer to be unrounded and carried out to the maximum number of decimal places possible.

The *decimal rounding selector* rounds the answers. The down arrow position will drop any digits beyond the last digit desired. The up arrow position will drop any digits beyond the last digit desired and round the last digit up. In the 5/4 position, the calculator rounds the last desired digit up only when the following digit is 5 or greater. If the following digit is less than 5, the last desired digit remains unchanged.

The *GT* or *grand total switch* in the on position accumulates totals.

KINDS OF COMPUTER KEYBOARDS

The computer has a keypad on the right side of the keyboard called the *numeric keypad*. Even though several styles of keyboards for the IBM® and compatible computers are found, there are two basic layouts for the numeric keypad. The standard layout and enhanced layout are shown in the illustration. On the standard keyboard the directional arrow keys are found on the number keys. To use the numbers, press the key called *Num Lock*. (This key is found above the "7" key.) When the *Num Lock* is turned on, numbers are entered when the keys on the keypad are pressed. When the Num Lock is off, the arrow, Home, Page Up, Page Down, End, Insert, and Delete keys can be used.

The enhanced keyboards have the arrow keys and the other directional keys mentioned above to the left of the numeric keypad. When using the keypad on an enhanced keyboard, Num Lock can remain on.

The asterisk (*) performs a different function on the computer than the calculator. The asterisk on the calculator is used for the total while the computer uses it for multiplication.

Another difference is the division key. The computer key is the forward slash key (/). The calculator key uses the division key (÷).

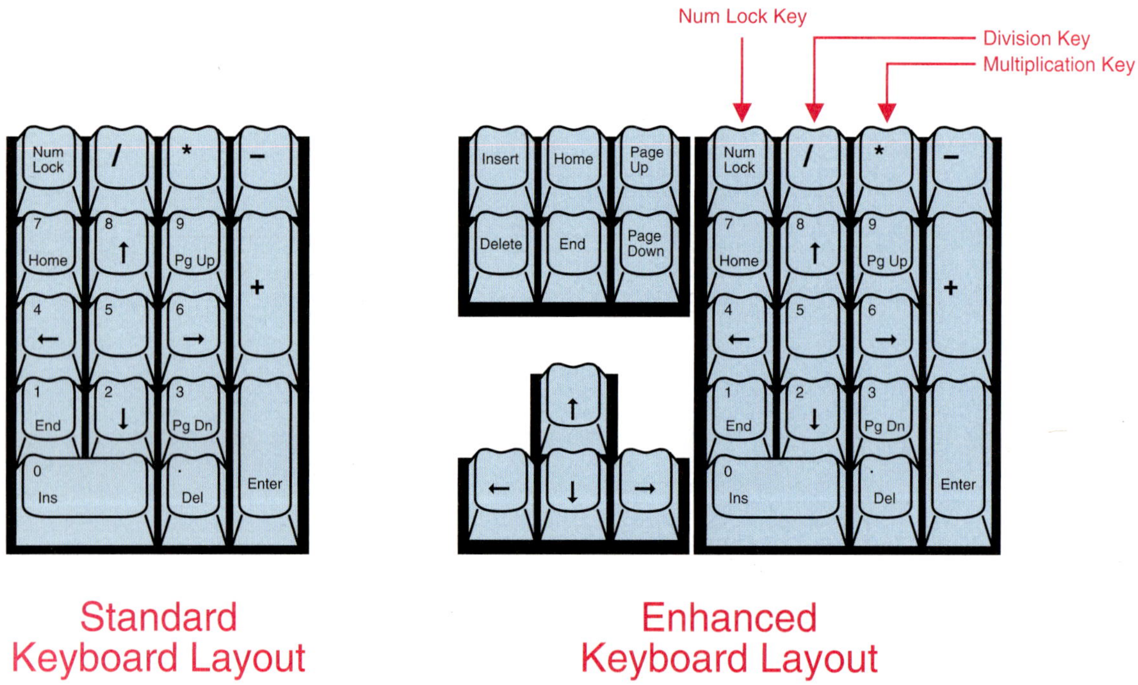

TEN-KEY TOUCH SYSTEM

Striking the numbers 0 to 9 on a calculator or numeric keypad without looking at the keyboard is called the *touch system*. Using the touch system develops both speed and accuracy.

The 4, 5, and 6 keys are called the *home row*. If the right hand is used for the keyboard, the index finger is placed on the 4 key, the middle finger on the 5 key, and the ring finger on the 6 key. If the left hand is used, the ring finger is placed on the 4 key, the middle finger on the 5 key, and the index finger on the 6 key.

Place the fingers on the home row keys. Curve the fingers and keep the wrist straight. These keys may feel slightly concaved or the 5 key may have a raised dot. The differences in the home row allow the operator to recognize the home row by touch rather than by sight.

Maintain the position of the fingers on the home row. The finger used to strike the 4 key will also strike the 7 key and the 1 key. Stretch the finger up to reach the 7; then stretch the finger down to reach the 1 key. Visualize the position of these keys.

Again, place the fingers on the home row. Stretch the finger that strikes the 5 key up to reach the 8 key, then down to reach the 2 key. Likewise, stretch the finger that strikes the 6 key up to strike the 9 and down to strike the 3 key. This same finger will stretch down again to hit the decimal point.

If the right hand is used, the thumb will be used to strike the 0 and 00 keys and the little finger to strike the addition key. If the left hand is used, the little finger will be used to strike the 0 and 00 keys and the thumb to strike the addition key.

HAND-HELD CALCULATORS

Hand-held calculators are slightly different from desktop calculators, not only in their size and features but also in their operation. Refer to the operator's manual for specific instructions for the calculator being used.

On a hand-held calculator, the numeric keys are usually very close together. In addition, the keys do not respond to touch as easily as on a desktop calculator. Therefore, the touch system is usually not used on a hand-held calculator.

PERFORMING MATHEMATICAL OPERATIONS ON DESKTOP CALCULATORS

Mathematical operations can be performed on a calculator both quickly and efficiently. The basic operations of addition, subtraction, multiplication, and division are used frequently on a calculator.

Addition

Each number to be added is called an *addend*. The answer to an addition problem is called the *sum*.

Addition is performed by entering an addend and striking the addition key (+). All numbers are entered on a calculator in the exact order they are given. To enter the number 4,455.65, strike the 4, 4, 5, 5, decimal, 6, and 5 keys in that order, and then strike the addition key. Commas are not entered. Continue in this manner until all addends have been entered. To obtain the sum, strike the total key on the calculator.

Subtraction

The top number or first number of a subtraction problem is called the *minuend*. The number to be subtracted from the minuend is called the *subtrahend*. The answer to a subtraction problem is called the *difference*.

Subtraction is performed by first entering the minuend and striking the addition key (+). The subtrahend is then entered, followed by the minus key (−), followed by the total key.

Multiplication

The number to be multiplied is called the *multiplicand*. The number of times the multiplicand will be multiplied is called the *multiplier*. The answer to a multiplication problem is called the *product*.

Multiplication is performed by entering

the multiplicand and striking the multiplication key (×). The multiplier is then entered, followed by the equals key (=). The calculator will automatically multiply and give the product.

Division

The number to be divided is called the *dividend*. The number the dividend will be divided by is called the *divisor*. The answer to a division problem is called the *quotient*.

Division is performed by entering the dividend and striking the division key (÷). The divisor is then entered, followed by the equals key (=). The calculator will automatically divide and give the quotient.

Correcting Errors

If an error is made while using a calculator, several methods of correction may be used. If an incorrect number has been entered and the addition key or equals key has not yet been struck, strike the clear entry (CE) key one time. This key will clear only the last number that was entered. However, if the clear entry key is depressed more than one time, the entire problem will be cleared on some calculators. If an incorrect number has been entered and the addition key has been struck, strike the minus key one time only. This will automatically subtract the last number added, thus removing it from the total.

HAND-HELD CALCULATORS PERFORMING MATHEMATICAL OPERATIONS ON COMPUTERS

On a computer keypad or a hand-held calculator, addition is performed in much the same way as on a desktop calculator. However, after the + key is depressed, the display usually shows the accumulated total. Therefore, the total key is not found. Some computer programs will not calculate the total until Enter is pressed.

Subtraction is performed differently on many computer keypads and hand-held calculators. The minuend is usually entered, followed by the minus (−) key. Then the subtrahend is entered. Pressing either the + key or the = key will display the difference. Some computer programs will not calculate the difference until Enter is pressed.

Multiplication and division are performed the same way on a computer keypad and hand-held calculator as on a desktop calculator. Keep in mind that computers use the * for multiplication and / for division.

SAFETY CONCERNS

Whenever electrical equipment such as a calculator or computer is being operated in a classroom or office, several safety rules apply. These rules protect the operator of the equipment, other persons in the environment, and the equipment itself.

1. Do not unplug equipment by pulling on the electrical cord. Instead, grasp the plug at the outlet and remove it.
2. Do not stretch electrical cords across an aisle where someone might trip over them.
3. Avoid food and beverages near the equipment where a spill might result in an electrical short.
4. Do not attempt to remove the cover of a calculator, computer, or keyboard for any reason while the power is turned on.
5. Do not attempt to repair equipment while it is plugged in.
6. Always turn the power off or unplug equipment when finished using it.

CALCULATION DRILLS

Instructions for Desktop Calculators

Complete each drill using the touch method. Set the decimal selector at the setting indicated in each drill. Compare the answer on the calculator to the answer in the book. If the two are the same, progress to the next problem. It is not necessary to enter 00 in the cents column if the decimal selector is set at 0-F. However, digits other than zeros in the cents column must be entered preceded by a decimal point.

Instructions for Computer Keypads

Complete each drill using the touch method. There is no decimal selector on computer keypads. Set the number of decimal places as directed in the instructions for the computer program. In spreadsheets, for example, use the formatting options to set the number of decimal places. When the drill indicates "F" for floating, leave the computer application in its default format. Compare the answer on the computer monitor to the answer in the book. If the two are the same, progress to the next problem. It is not necessary to enter 00 in the cents column. However, digits other than zeros in the cents column must be entered preceded by a decimal point.

DRILL D-1 Performing addition using the home row keys
Decimal Selector—2

4.00	44.00	444.00	4,444.00	44,444.00
5.00	55.00	555.00	5,555.00	55,555.00
6.00	66.00	666.00	6,666.00	66,666.00
5.00	45.00	455.00	4,455.00	44,556.00
4.00	46.00	466.00	4,466.00	44,565.00
5.00	54.00	544.00	5,544.00	55,446.00
6.00	56.00	566.00	5,566.00	55,664.00
5.00	65.00	655.00	6,655.00	66,554.00
4.00	64.00	644.00	6,644.00	66,555.00
5.00	66.00	654.00	6,545.00	65,465.00
49.00	561.00	5,649.00	56,540.00	565,470.00

DRILL D-2 Performing addition using the 0, 1, 4, and 7 keys
Decimal Selector—2

4.00	11.00	444.00	4,440.00	44,000.00
7.00	44.00	777.00	7,770.00	77,000.00
4.00	74.00	111.00	1,110.00	11,000.00
1.00	71.00	741.00	4,400.00	41,000.00
4.00	70.00	740.00	1,100.00	71,000.00
7.00	10.00	101.00	4,007.00	10,000.00
4.00	14.00	140.00	7,001.00	10,100.00
1.00	17.00	701.00	1,007.00	40,100.00
4.00	40.00	700.00	1,004.00	70,100.00
7.00	77.00	407.00	7,700.00	74,100.00
43.00	428.00	4,862.00	39,539.00	448,400.00

DRILL D-3 Performing addition using the 2, 5, and 8 keys
Decimal Selector—2

5.00	58.00	588.00	8,888.00	88,855.00
8.00	52.00	522.00	5,555.00	88,822.00
5.00	85.00	888.00	2,222.00	88,852.00
2.00	52.00	222.00	8,525.00	88,222.00
5.00	25.00	258.00	2,585.00	85,258.00
8.00	58.00	852.00	8,258.00	22,255.00
5.00	82.00	225.00	8,585.00	22,288.00
2.00	28.00	885.00	5,258.00	22,258.00
5.00	88.00	882.00	2,852.00	22,888.00
8.00	22.00	228.00	2,288.00	25,852.00
53.00	550.00	5,550.00	55,016.00	555,550.00

DRILL D-4 Performing addition using the 3, 6, 9, and decimal point keys
Decimal Selector—2

6.00	66.66	666.66	6,666.99	66,699.33
9.00	99.99	999.99	9,999.66	99,966.66
6.00	33.33	333.33	3,333.99	33,366.33
3.00	33.66	666.99	3,366.99	36,963.36
6.36	33.99	999.66	6,699.33	69,636.36
3.36	99.66	333.66	9,966.33	33,333.66
9.36	99.33	696.36	9,636.69	66,666.99
9.63	33.36	369.63	3,696.36	99,999.33
6.33	33.69	336.69	6,963.99	96,369.63
9.93	69.63	963.36	6,699.33	36,963.36
68.97	603.30	6,366.33	67,029.66	639,965.01

DRILL D-5 Performing subtraction using all number keys
Decimal Selector—F

456.73	789.01	741.00	852.55	987.98
−123.21	−456.00	−258.10	−369.88	−102.55
333.52	333.01	482.90	482.67	885.43

DRILL D-6 Performing multiplication using all number keys
Decimal Selector—F

654.05	975.01	487.10	123.56	803.75
× 12.66	× 27.19	× 30.21	× 50.09	× 1.45
8,280.273	26,510.5219	14,715.291	6,189.1204	1,165.4375

DRILL D-7 Performing division using all number keys
Decimal Selector—F

900.56	÷	450.28	=	2.
500.25	÷	100.05	=	5.
135.66	÷	6.65	=	20.4
269.155	÷	105.55	=	2.550023685*
985.66	÷	22.66	=	43.49779346*

**Number of decimal places may vary due to machine capacity.*

RECYCLING PROBLEM 1-1

Determining how transactions change an accounting equation and preparing a balance sheet

Alston Eubanks is starting Reef Divers, a scuba diving service. Reef Divers uses the accounts shown in the following accounting equation. Use the form given in the *Recycling Problem Working Papers* to complete this problem.

	Assets					=	Liabilities	+	Owner's Equity
Trans. No.	Cash	+	Supplies	+	Prepaid Insurance	=	Accts. Pay.— Divers Supply	+	Alston Eubanks, Capital
New Bal. 1.	0 +1,700		0		0		0		0 +1,700
New Bal. 2.	*1,700*		*0*		*0*		*0*		*1,700*

Transactions:

1. Received cash from owner as an investment, $1,700.00.
2. Bought supplies on account from Divers Supply, $800.00.
3. Paid cash for insurance, $175.00.
4. Paid cash for supplies, $230.00.
5. Received cash from owner as an investment, $400.00.
6. Paid cash on account to Divers Supply, $500.00.

Instructions:

1. For each transaction, complete the following. Transaction 1 is given as an example.
   a. Analyze the transaction to determine which accounts in the accounting equation are affected.
   b. Write the amount in the appropriate columns, using a plus (+) if the account increases or a minus (−) if the account decreases.
   c. Calculate the new balance for each account in the accounting equation.
   d. Before going on to the next transaction, determine that the accounting equation is still in balance.
2. Using the final balances in the accounting equation, prepare a balance sheet for Reef Divers. Use November 30 of the current year as the date of the balance sheet.

RECYCLING PROBLEM 2-1

Determining how transactions change an accounting equation and preparing a balance sheet

Alston Eubanks operates a scuba diving business called Reef Divers. Reef Divers uses the accounts shown in the following accounting equation. Use the form given in the *Recycling Problem Working Papers* to complete this problem.

Trans. No.	Assets				= Liabilities	+ Owner's Equity
	Cash +	Accts. Rec.— Club Scuba +	Supplies +	Prepaid Insurance =	Accts. Pay.— Divers Supply +	Alston Eubanks, Capital
Beg. Bal. 1.	1,195 *−150*	—0—	1,030	175	300	2,100 *−150 (expense)*
New Bal. 2.	*1,045*	*—0—*	*1,030*	*175*	*300*	*1,950*

Transactions:

1. Paid cash for telephone bill, $150.00.
2. Received cash from owner as an investment, $200.00.
3. Paid cash for rent, $400.00.
4. Received cash from sales, $550.00.
5. Bought supplies on account from Divers Supply, $220.00.
6. Sold services on account to Club Scuba, $300.00.
7. Paid cash for supplies, $300.00.
8. Paid cash for advertising, $550.00.
9. Received cash on account from Club Scuba, $200.00.
10. Paid cash on account to Divers Supply, $300.00.
11. Paid cash for insurance, $175.00.
12. Received cash from sales, $1,900.00.
13. Paid cash to owner for personal use, $1,000.00.

Instructions:

1. For each transaction, complete the following. Transaction 1 is given as an example.
   a. Analyze the transaction to determine which accounts in the accounting equation are affected.
   b. Write the amount in the appropriate columns, using a plus (+) if the account increases or a minus (−) if the account decreases.
   c. For transactions that change owner's equity, write in parentheses a description of the transaction to the right of the amount.
   d. Calculate the new balance for each account in the accounting equation.
   e. Before going on to the next transaction, determine that the accounting equation is still in balance.
2. Using the final balances in the accounting equation, prepare a balance sheet for Reef Divers. Use the date December 31 of the current year.

RECYCLING PROBLEM 3-1

Analyzing transactions into debit and credit parts

Harrison Ennis owns a business called Cayman Copies. Cayman Copies uses the following accounts:

Cash
Accounts Receivable—Coral Supply Company
Accounts Receivable—Coconut Inn
Supplies
Prepaid Insurance
Accounts Payable—Palms Paper
Accounts Payable—Pappagallo Company
Harrison Ennis, Capital
Harrison Ennis, Drawing
Sales
Advertising Expense
Miscellaneous Expense
Rent Expense
Repair Expense
Utilities Expense

Instructions:

Use the forms given in the *Recycling Problem Working Papers.*

1. Prepare a T account for each account.
2. Analyze each transaction into its debit and credit parts. Write the debit and credit amounts in the proper T accounts to show how each transaction changes account balances. Write the date of the transaction in parentheses before each amount.

Transactions:

July 1. Received cash from owner as an investment, $6,000.00.
2. Paid cash for supplies, $120.00.
4. Paid cash for rent, $400.00.
4. Received cash from sales, $700.00.
5. Paid cash for repairs, $20.00.
8. Sold services on account to Coral Supply Co., $400.00.
9. Bought supplies on account from Pappagallo Co., $1,000.00.
10. Paid cash for insurance, $200.00.
11. Received cash from owner as an investment, $1,800.00.
11. Received cash from sales, $600.00.
12. Bought supplies on account from Palms Paper, $100.00.
13. Received cash on account from Coral Supply Co., $250.00.
15. Paid cash for miscellaneous expense, $10.00.
16. Paid cash on account to Pappagallo Co., $100.00.
22. Paid cash for electric bill (utilities expense), $70.00.
23. Paid cash for advertising, $60.00.
25. Sold services on account to Coconut Inn, $440.00.
26. Paid cash to owner for personal use, $1,200.00.
30. Received cash on account from Coconut Inn, $200.00.

RECYCLING PROBLEM 4-1

Journalizing transactions and proving and ruling a journal

Merilda Bodden owns a service business called Bodden Express, which uses the following accounts:

Cash	Accts. Pay.—Bahling Supplies	Sales	Repair Expense
Supplies	Accts. Pay.—Kirk Company	Advertising Expense	Utilities Expense
Prepaid Insurance	Merilda Bodden, Capital	Miscellaneous Expense	
Accts. Rec.—Leta Scott	Merilda Bodden, Drawing	Rent Expense	

Transactions: Aug.
1. Received cash from owner as an investment, $8,750.00. R1.
2. Paid cash for rent, $200.00. C1.
3. Paid cash for supplies, $600.00. C2.
4. Bought supplies on account from Bahling Supplies, $1,000.00. M1.
5. Paid cash for insurance, $2,250.00. C3.
8. Paid cash on account to Bahling Supplies, $750.00. C4.
8. Received cash from sales, $375.00. T8.
8. Sold services on account to Leta Scott, $100.00. S1.
9. Paid cash for electric bill, $30.00. C5.
10. Paid cash for miscellaneous expense, $9.00. C6.
10. Received cash from sales, $375.00. T10.
11. Paid cash for repairs, $50.00. C7.
11. Received cash from sales, $425.00. T11.
12. Received cash from sales, $350.00. T12.
15. Paid cash to owner for personal use, $175.00. C8.
15. Received cash from sales, $375.00. T15.
16. Paid cash for supplies, $750.00. C9.
17. Received cash on account from Leta Scott, $100.00. R2.
17. Bought supplies on account from Kirk Company, $375.00. M2.
17. Received cash from sales, $300.00. T17.
18. Received cash from sales, $400.00. T18.
19. Received cash from sales, $375.00. T19.
22. Bought supplies on account from Kirk Company, $40.00. M3.
22. Received cash from sales, $350.00. T22.
23. Paid cash for advertising, $65.00. C10.
23. Sold services on account to Leta Scott, $325.00. S2.
24. Paid cash for telephone bill, $30.00. C11.
24. Received cash from sales, $300.00. T24.
25. Received cash from sales, $275.00. T25.
26. Paid cash for supplies, $35.00. C12.
26. Received cash from sales, $300.00. T26.
29. Received cash on account from Leta Scott, $325.00. R3.
30. Paid cash to owner for personal use, $160.00. C13.
30. Received cash from sales, $400.00. T30.

Instructions:

1. Use page 1 of the journal given in the *Recycling Problem Working Papers.* Journalize the transactions for August 1 through August 19 of the current year. Source documents are abbreviated as follows: check, C; memorandum, M; receipt, R; sales invoice, S; calculator tape, T.
2. Prove and rule page 1 of the journal. Carry the column totals forward to page 2 of the journal.
3. Use page 2 of the journal to journalize the transactions for the remainder of August.
4. Prove page 2 of the journal.
5. Prove cash. The beginning cash balance on August 1 is zero. The balance on the next unused check stub is $8,671.00.
6. Rule page 2 of the journal.

RECYCLING PROBLEM 5-1

Journalizing transactions and posting to a general ledger

Janet Porter owns a service business called Porter's Parties. Porter's Parties' general ledger accounts are given in the *Recycling Problem Working Papers*.

Transactions:

Aug. 1. Received cash from owner as an investment, $8,500.00. R1.
3. Paid cash for rent, $500.00. C1.
5. Sold services on account to Nicholas Calendo, $250.00. S1.
6. Received cash from sales, $830.00. T6.
9. Paid cash for miscellaneous expense, $15.00. C2.
11. Paid cash for supplies, $230.00. C3.
13. Bought supplies on account from Jordan Supplies, $700.00. M1.
13. Received cash from sales, $650.00. T13.
16. Paid cash for electric bill, $95.00. C4.
18. Paid cash on account to Jordan Supplies, $400.00. C5.
20. Paid cash for advertising, $55.00. C6.
20. Received cash on account from Nicholas Calendo, $150.00. R2.
25. Paid cash for supplies, $50.00. C7.
27. Paid cash for supplies, $75.00. C8.
27. Received cash from sales, $1,200.00. T27.
30. Paid cash to owner for personal use, $450.00. C9.
30. Received cash from sales, $780.00. T30.

Instructions:

1. Open an account for Utilities Expense. Use the 3-digit numbering system described in the chapter.
2. Journalize the transactions completed during August of the current year. Use page 1 of a journal. Source documents are abbreviated as follows: check, C; memorandum, M; receipt, R; sales invoice, S; calculator tape, T.
3. Prove the journal.
4. Prove cash. The beginning cash balance on August 1 is zero. The balance on the next unused check stub is $10,240.00.
5. Rule the journal.
6. Post from the journal to the general ledger.

RECYCLING PROBLEM 6-1

Reconciling a bank statement; journalizing a bank service charge, a dishonored check, and petty cash transactions

Emil Ibraham owns a business called Fast Print. Selected general ledger accounts are given below. Forms are given in the *Recycling Problem Working Papers.*

110 Cash	140 Prepaid Insurance	535 Repair Expense
115 Petty Cash	320 Emil Ibraham, Drawing	540 Supplies Expense
120 Accts. Rec.—Angus Restaurant	520 Miscellaneous Expense	550 Utilities Expense
130 Supplies	530 Rent Expense	

Instructions:

1. Journalize the following transactions completed during May of the current year. Use page 12 of a journal. Source documents are abbreviated as follows: check, C; memorandum, M.

Transactions:

May 21. Paid cash to establish a petty cash fund, $100.00. C61.
24. Paid cash for repairs, $115.00. C62.
26. Paid cash for supplies, $20.00. C63.
27. Received notice from the bank of a dishonored check from Angus Restaurant, $45.00, plus $20.00 fee; total, $65.00. M22.
28. Paid cash for miscellaneous expense, $24.00. C64.
31. Paid cash to owner for personal use, $200.00. C65.
31. Paid cash to replenish the petty cash fund, $65.00: supplies, $55.00; miscellaneous expense, $10.00. C66.

2. On May 31 of the current year, Fast Print received a bank statement dated May 30. Prepare a bank statement reconciliation. Use May 31 of the current year as the date. The following information is obtained from the May 30 bank statement and from the records of the business.

Bank statement balance	$1,486.00
Bank service charge	25.00
Outstanding deposit, May 31	340.00
Outstanding checks, Nos. 65 and 66	
Checkbook balance on Check Stub No. 67	$1,586.00

3. Continue using the journal and journalize the following transaction.

Transaction:

May 31. Received bank statement showing May bank service charge, $25.00. M23.

RECYCLING PROBLEM 7-1

Completing a work sheet

On February 28 of the current year, Chisholm Hair Care has the following general ledger accounts and balances. The business uses a monthly fiscal period.

Account Titles	Account Balances Debit	Credit
Cash	$1,609.00	
Petty Cash	300.00	
Accounts Receivable—Margo Angelo	581.00	
Supplies	795.00	
Prepaid Insurance	1,100.00	
Accounts Payable—Virginia Supplies		$ 450.00
Montana Freemantle, Capital		3,550.00
Montana Freemantle, Drawing	300.00	
Income Summary		
Sales		3,000.00
Advertising Expense	525.00	
Insurance Expense		
Miscellaneous Expense	250.00	
Rent Expense	1,100.00	
Supplies Expense		
Utilities Expense	440.00	

Instructions:

1. Prepare the heading and trial balance on the work sheet given in the *Recycling Problem Working Papers*. Total and rule the Trial Balance columns.
2. Analyze the following adjustment information into debit and credit parts. Record the adjustments on the work sheet.

Adjustment Information, February 28	
Supplies inventory	$ 250.00
Value of prepaid insurance	1,000.00

3. Total and rule the Adjustments columns.
4. Extend the up-to-date balances to the Balance Sheet or Income Statement columns.
5. Rule a single line across the Income Statement and Balance Sheet columns. Total each column. Calculate and record the net income or net loss. Label the amount in the Account Title column.
6. Total and rule the Income Statement and Balance Sheet columns.

RECYCLING PROBLEM 8-1

Preparing financial statements

The following information is obtained from the work sheet of Robbie's Rugcare for the month ended August 31 of the current year. Forms are given in the *Recycling Problem Working Papers.*

		5	6	7	8	
		INCOME STATEMENT		BALANCE SHEET		
	ACCOUNT TITLE	DEBIT	CREDIT	DEBIT	CREDIT	
1	*Cash*			8752 00		1
2	*Accounts Receivable—Crystal Thompson*			200 00		2
3	*Accounts Receivable—Robert Boje*			175 00		3
4	*Supplies*			400 00		4
5	*Prepaid Insurance*			220 00		5
6	*Accounts Payable—Daniel Supplies*				442 00	6
7	*Accounts Payable—Irene's Irons*				676 00	7
8	*Roberta Greenstein, Capital*				7951 00	8
9	*Roberta Greenstein, Drawing*			1800 00		9
10	*Income Summary*					10
11	*Sales*		5707 00			11
12	*Advertising Expense*	900 00				12
13	*Insurance Expense*	20 00				13
14	*Miscellaneous Expense*	267 00				14
15	*Supplies Expense*	500 00				15
16	*Utilities Expense*	1542 00				16
17		3229 00	5707 00	11547 00	9069 00	17
18	*Net Income*	2478 00			2478 00	18
19		5707 00	5707 00	11547 00	11547 00	19
20						20

Instructions:

1. Prepare an income statement for the month ended August 31 of the current year.
2. Calculate and record the component percentages for total expenses and net income. Round percentage calculations to the nearest 0.1%.
3. Prepare a balance sheet for August 31 of the current year.

RECYCLING PROBLEM 9-1

Journalizing adjusting and closing entries

The following information is obtained from the partial work sheet of Robbie's Rugcare for the month ended August 31 of the current year.

		3	4	5	6	7	8	
		ADJUSTMENTS		INCOME STATEMENT		BALANCE SHEET		
	ACCOUNT TITLE	DEBIT	CREDIT	DEBIT	CREDIT	DEBIT	CREDIT	
1	*Cash*					8752 00		1
2	*Accts. Rec.—Crystal Thompson*					200 00		2
3	*Accts. Rec.—Robert Boje*					175 00		3
4	*Supplies*		(a) 500 00			400 00		4
5	*Prepaid Insurance*		(b) 20 00			220 00		5
6	*Accts. Pay.—Daniel Supplies*						442 00	6
7	*Accts. Pay.—Irene's Irons*						676 00	7
8	*Roberta Greenstein, Capital*						7951 00	8
9	*Roberta Greenstein, Drawing*					1800 00		9
10	*Income Summary*							10
11	*Sales*				5707 00			11
12	*Advertising Expense*			900 00				12
13	*Insurance Expense*	(b) 20 00		20 00				13
14	*Miscellaneour Expense*			267 00				14
15	*Supplies Expense*	(a) 500 00		500 00				15
16	*Utilities Expense*			1542 00				16
17		520 00	520 00	3229 00	5707 00	11547 00	9069 00	17
18	*Net Income*			2478 00			2478 00	18
19				5707 00	5707 00	11547 00	11547 00	19
20								20

Instructions:

1. Use page 16 of the journal given in the *Recycling Problem Working Papers.* Journalize the adjusting entries.
2. Continue to use page 16 of the journal. Journalize the closing entries.

RECYCLING PROBLEM 10-1

Journalizing purchases, cash payments, and other transactions

Judy Daily and Donald Steele, partners, own a bookstore.

Instructions:

Journalize the following transactions completed during September of the current year. Use page 20 of the journal given in the *Recycling Problem Working Papers*. Source documents are abbreviated as follows: check, C; memorandum, M; purchase invoice, P.

Transactions:

Sept. 1. Paid cash for monthly rent, $800.00. C405.
2. Purchased merchandise for cash, $200.00. C406.
3. Purchased merchandise on account from Bookmaster, Inc., $900.00. P91.
6. Paid cash for office supplies, $75.00. C407.
7. Bought store supplies on account from Deluxe Display, $240.00. M53.
9. Paid cash on account to National Press, $600.00, covering P89. C408.
12. Purchased merchandise on account from Classic Books, $1,500.00. P92.
13. Paid cash for advertising, $75.00. C409.
18. Paid cash on account to Bookmaster, Inc., $900.00, covering P91. C410.
24. Donald Steele, partner, withdrew merchandise for personal use, $100.00. M54.
30. Judy Daily, partner, withdrew cash for personal use, $1,000.00. C411.
30. Donald Steele, partner, withdrew cash for personal use, $900.00. C412.
30. Paid cash to replenish the petty cash fund, $210.00: office supplies, $29.00; store supplies, $36.00; advertising, $90.00; miscellaneous, $55.00. C413.

RECYCLING PROBLEM 11-1

Journalizing sales and cash receipts transactions; proving and ruling a journal

Olga Flores and James Lazarus, partners, own Outdoor Living, a hunting and fishing equipment store.

Partial journal page 17 and page 18 for Outdoor Living are given in the *Recycling Problem Working Papers*.

Instructions:

1. September 23 column totals to be carried forward have been entered on line 32 of journal page 17. Prove the equality of debits and credits and rule the column totals of journal page 17.
2. Record the totals brought forward from journal page 17 to line 1 of page 18 of the journal. Prove the equality of debits and credits again. Use the current year.
3. Journalize the following transactions completed during the remainder of September on journal page 18. Sales tax rate is 6%. Source documents are abbreviated as follows: receipt, R; sales invoice, S; cash register tape, T.

Transactions:

Sept. 23. Received cash on account from Timothy Cole, $82.68, covering S69. R100.
24. Sold merchandise on account to Doretha Hunt, $160.00, plus sales tax, $9.60; total, $169.60. S74.
25. Received cash on account from Valerie Seeley, $110.24, covering S70. R101.
26. Recorded cash and credit card sales, $3,372.00, plus sales tax, $202.32; total, $3,574.32. T26.
29. Sold merchandise on account to Anthony Zolte, $230.00, plus sales tax, $13.80; total, $243.80. S75.
30. Recorded cash and credit card sales, $1,387.00, plus sales tax, $83.22; total, $1,470.22. T30.

4. Total the journal. Prove the equality of debits and credits.
5. Rule the journal.

RECYCLING PROBLEM 12-1

Posting to ledgers from a journal

The journal and ledgers for Custom Boots are given in the *Recycling Problem Working Papers.*

Instructions:

1. Post the separate items recorded in the following columns of the journal: (a) General Debit and Credit. (b) Accounts Receivable Debit and Credit. (c) Accounts Payable Debit and Credit.
2. Post the totals of the special columns of the journal.
3. Using the current year, prepare a schedule of accounts payable and a schedule of accounts receivable. Prove the accuracy of the subsidiary ledgers by comparing the schedule totals with the balances of the controlling accounts in the general ledger. If the totals are not the same, find and correct the errors.

RECYCLING PROBLEM 13-1

Preparing a semimonthly payroll

The following information is for the semimonthly pay period May 1–15 of the current year. Forms are given in the *Recycling Problem Working Papers.*

EMPL. NO.	EMPLOYEE'S NAME	MARITAL STATUS	NO. OF ALLOWANCES	EARNINGS		DEDUCTIONS
				REGULAR	OVERTIME	HEALTH INSURANCE
3	Boyd, Bruce E.	S	2	836 00	57 00	35 00
4	Gomez, Patti H.	M	3	739 20		45 00
7	Logan, Curt M.	S	1	880 00		
1	Payne, Myrna L.	S	1	774 40	13 20	
5	Sharp, Don E.	M	2	765 60		35 00
6	Terry, Daphne I.	M	3	809 60		45 00
8	Walsh, Linda P.	M	2	915 20	62 40	35 00

Instructions:

1. Prepare a payroll register. The date of payment is May 15. Use the federal income tax withholding tables shown on pages 310–311 to find the income tax withholding for each employee. Calculate social security and Medicare tax withholdings using 6.5% and 1.5% tax rates, respectively. None of the employee accumulated earnings has exceeded the social security tax base.
2. Prepare a check for the total amount of the net pay. Make the check payable to Payroll Account 982-561-4732, and sign your name as a partner of McKinley Company. The beginning check stub balance is $11,530.50.
3. Prepare payroll checks for Curt M. Logan, Check No. 286, and Daphne I. Terry, Check No. 289. Sign your name as a partner of McKinley Company. Record the two payroll check numbers in the payroll register.

RECYCLING PROBLEM 14-1

Journalizing payroll taxes

Folger Manufacturing completed payroll transactions during the period January 31 to April 30 of the current year. Payroll tax rates are as follows: social security, 6.5%; Medicare, 1.5%; federal unemployment, 0.8%; and state unemployment, 5.4%. No total earnings have exceeded the tax base for calculating unemployment taxes.

Instructions:

1. Journalize the following transactions on page 3 of the journal given in the *Recycling Problem Working Papers*. Source documents are abbreviated as follows: check, C, and memorandum, M.

Transactions:

Jan. 31. Paid cash for monthly payroll, $4,876.40 (total payroll, $6,020.00, less deductions: employee income tax, $662.00; social security tax, $391.30; Medicare tax, $90.30). C217.

31. Recorded employer payroll taxes expense. M54.

Feb. 15. Paid cash for liability for employee income tax, $662.00; social security tax, $782.60; and Medicare tax, $180.60; total, $1,625.20. C242.

28. Paid cash for monthly payroll, $4,907.36 (total payroll, $6,058.00, less deductions: employee income tax, $666.00; social security tax, $393.77; Medicare tax, $90.87). C285.

28. Recorded employer payroll taxes expense. M59.

Mar. 15. Paid cash for liability for employee income tax, $666.00; social security tax, $787.54; and Medicare tax, $181.74; total, $1,635.28. C310.

31. Paid cash for monthly payroll, $5,171.28 (total payroll, $6,384.00, less deductions: employee income tax, $702.00; social security tax, $414.96; Medicare tax, $95.76). C330.

2. Prove and rule journal page 3. Carry the column totals forward to page 4 of the journal.
3. Journalize the following transactions on page 4 of the journal.

Transactions:

Mar. 31. Recorded employer payroll taxes expense. M64.

Apr. 15. Paid cash for liability for employee income tax, $702.00; social security tax, $829.92; and Medicare tax, $191.52; total, $1,723.44. C351.

30. Paid cash for federal unemployment tax liability for quarter ended March 31, $147.69. C372.

30. Paid cash for state unemployment tax liability for quarter ended March 31, $996.95. C373.

4. Prove and rule journal page 4.

RECYCLING PROBLEM 15-1

Preparing an 8-column work sheet for a merchandising business

Jolson Music's trial balance as of December 31 of the current year is recorded on a work sheet in the *Recycling Problem Working Papers.*

Instructions:

1. Analyze the following adjustment information and record the adjustments on the work sheet.

End-of-Fiscal-Period Information	
Merchandise inventory	$262,520.00
Office supplies inventory	2,630.00
Store supplies inventory	2,645.00
Value of prepaid insurance	2,150.00

2. Complete the work sheet.

RECYCLING PROBLEM 16-1

Preparing financial statements

Mat's Antiques prepared the following work sheet for the year ended December 31 of the current year. Forms are given in the *Recycling Problem Working Papers.*

Mat's Antiques
Work Sheet
For Year Ended December 31, 20--

		1	2	3	4	5	6	7	8	
	ACCOUNT TITLE	TRIAL BALANCE		ADJUSTMENTS		INCOME STATEMENT		BALANCE SHEET		
		DEBIT	CREDIT	DEBIT	CREDIT	DEBIT	CREDIT	DEBIT	CREDIT	
1	*Cash*	22,300.00						22,300.00		1
2	*Petty Cash*	300.00						300.00		2
3	*Accounts Receivable*	10,270.00						10,270.00		3
4	*Merchandise Inventory*	295,780.00			(a) 12,200.00			283,580.00		4
5	*Supplies—Office*	5,890.00			(b) 3,730.00			2,160.00		5
6	*Supplies—Store*	5,610.00			(c) 3,920.00			1,690.00		6
7	*Prepaid Insurance*	5,550.00			(d) 3,450.00			2,100.00		7
8	*Accounts Payable*		9,610.00						9,610.00	8
9	*Sales Tax Payable*		1,130.00						1,130.00	9
10	*Mathew Logan, Capital*		135,400.00						135,400.00	10
11	*Mathew Logan, Drawing*	18,220.00						18,220.00		11
12	*Jerry Hill, Capital*		133,270.00						133,270.00	12
13	*Jerry Hill, Drawing*	18,320.00						18,320.00		13
14	*Income Summary*			(a) 12,200.00		12,200.00				14
15	*Sales*		270,800.00				270,800.00			15
16	*Purchases*	132,440.00				132,440.00				16
17	*Advertising Expense*	6,210.00				6,210.00				17
18	*Credit Card Fee Expense*	2,660.00				2,660.00				18
19	*Insurance Expense*			(d) 3,450.00		3,450.00				19
20	*Miscellaneous Expense*	2,860.00				2,860.00				20
21	*Rent Expense*	21,000.00				21,000.00				21
22	*Supplies Expense—Office*			(b) 3,730.00		3,730.00				22
23	*Supplies Expense—Store*			(c) 3,920.00		3,920.00				23
24	*Utilities Expense*	2,800.00				2,800.00				24
25		550,210.00	550,210.00	23,300.00	23,300.00	191,270.00	270,800.00	358,940.00	279,410.00	25
26	*Net Income*					79,530.00			79,530.00	26
27						270,800.00	270,800.00	358,940.00	358,940.00	27
28										28

Instructions:

1. Prepare an income statement. Calculate and record the following component percentages: (a) cost of merchandise sold, (b) gross profit on sales, (c) total expenses, and (d) net income or loss. Round percentage calculations to the nearest 0.1%.
2. Prepare a distribution of net income statement. Net income or loss is to be shared equally.
3. Prepare an owners' equity statement. No additional investments were made.
4. Prepare a balance sheet in report form.

RECYCLING PROBLEM 17-1

Journalizing adjusting and closing entries

Use the following partial work sheet of Let's Go Camping for the year ended December 31 of the current year.

	ACCOUNT TITLE	3 ADJUSTMENTS DEBIT	4 ADJUSTMENTS CREDIT	5 INCOME STATEMENT DEBIT	6 INCOME STATEMENT CREDIT
4	*Merchandise Inventory*		(a) 11,810.00		
5	*Supplies—Office*		(b) 3,012.00		
6	*Supplies—Store*		(c) 3,156.00		
7	*Prepaid Insurance*		(d) 3,096.00		
22	*Income Summary*	(a) 11,810.00		11,810.00	
23	*Sales*				357,600.00
24	*Purchases*			149,220.00	
25	*Advertising Expense*			5,736.00	
26	*Credit Card Fee Expense*			4,776.00	
27	*Insurance Expense*	(d) 3,096.00		3,096.00	
28	*Miscellaneous Expense*			2,568.00	
29	*Payroll Taxes Expense*			7,176.00	
30	*Rent Expense*			15,840.00	
31	*Salary Expense*			70,700.00	
32	*Supplies Expense—Office*	(b) 3,012.00		3,012.00	
33	*Supplies Expense—Store*	(c) 3,156.00		3,156.00	
34	*Utilities Expense*			3,310.00	
35		21,074.00	21,074.00	280,400.00	357,600.00
36	*Net Income*			77,200.00	
37				357,600.00	357,600.00
38					

Instructions:

1. Use page 25 of the journal given in the *Recycling Problem Working Papers.* Journalize the adjusting entries using information from the partial work sheet.
2. Continue using page 25 of the journal. Journalize the closing entries using information from the work sheet. The distribution of net income statement shows equal distribution of earnings. The partners' drawing accounts show the following debit balances in the work sheet's Balance Sheet Debit column: Tom Hill, Drawing, $22,170.00; Vern Teel, Drawing, $22,680.00.

ANSWERS TO AUDIT YOUR UNDERSTANDING

Chapter 1, Page 8

1. Planning, recording, analyzing, and interpreting financial information.
2. Answers will vary but should involve businesses that perform activities for a fee.
3. A business owned by one person.
4. Assets = Liabilities + Owner's Equity.

Chapter 1, Page 12

1. The right side must be increased.
2. If one account is increased, another account on the same side of the equation must be decreased by the same amount.
3. Buying items and paying for them at a future date.

Chapter 1, Page 15

1. Assets, liabilities, and owner's equity.
2. Assets.
3. Liabilities and owner's equity.
4. Find the errors before completing any more work.

Chapter 2, Page 29

1. Increased.
2. Increased
3. Decreased.

Chapter 2, Page 31

1. The name of the business, the name of the report, and the date of the report.
2. Assets.
3. Liabilities and owner's equity.

Chapter 3, Page 44

1. Assets = Liabilities + Owner's Equity (T-account: Assets on the left side; Liabilities + Owner's Equity on the right side)
2. (1) Account balances increase on the normal balance side of an account. (2) Account balances decrease on the side opposite the normal balance side of an account.

Chapter 3, Page 50

1. (1) Which accounts are affected?
   (2) How is each account classified?
   (3) How is each classification changed?
   (4) How is each amount entered in the accounts?
2. Supplies and Cash.

Chapter 3, Page 56

1. Cash and Sales.
2. Accounts Receivable and Sales.
3. Owner's drawing account and Cash.
4. Credit.
5. Debit.

Chapter 4, Page 71

1. By date.
2. Source documents are one way to verify the accuracy of a specific journal entry.
3. Date, debit, credit, and source document.

Chapter 4, Page 75

1. General Debit and Cash Credit.
2. General Debit and General Credit.
3. General Debit and Cash Credit.

Chapter 4, Page 81

1. Cash Debit and Sales Credit.

2. General Debit and Sales Credit.

3. General Debit and Cash Credit.

4. Cash Debit and General Credit.

5. General Debit and Cash Credit.

Chapter 4, Page 87

1. (1) Add each of the amount columns. (2) Add the debit column totals, and then add the credit column totals. (3) Verify that the total debits and total credits are equal.

2. Cash on hand at the beginning of the month, plus total cash received, less total cash paid.

3. (1) Rule a single line across all amount columns directly below the last entry to indicate that the columns are to be added. (2) On the next line, write the date in the Date column. (3) Write the word *Totals* in the Account Title column. (4) Write each column total below the single line. (5) Rule double lines below the column totals across all amount columns. The double lines mean that the totals have been verified as correct.

Chapter 5, Page 102

1. The first digit indicates in which general ledger division the account is located. The second and third digits indicate the location of the account within that division.

2. (1) Write the account title in the heading. (2) Write the account number in the heading.

Chapter 5, Page 106

1. (1) Write the date in the Date column of the account. (2) Write the journal page number in the Post. Ref. column of the account. (3) Write the amount in the Debit or Credit column. (4) Calculate and write the new account balance in the Balance Debit or Balance Credit column. (5) Write the account number in the Post. Ref. column of the journal.

2. No. Each separate amount in the General Debit and General Credit columns of a journal is posted to the account written in the Account Title column.

Chapter 5, Page 111

1. Special amount columns.

2. Whenever the debits in an account exceed the credits.

3. Whenever the credits in an account exceed the debits.

Chapter 5, Page 117

1. A journal entry made to correct an error in the ledger.

2. When a transaction has been improperly journalized and posted to the ledger.

3. To show the increase in this expense account.

4. To show the decrease in this expense account.

Chapter 6, Page 130

1. Blank endorsement, special endorsement, and restrictive endorsement.

2. (1) Write the amount of the check after the dollar sign at the top of the stub. (2) Write the date of the check on the Date line. (3) Write to whom the check is to be paid on the To line. (4) Record the purpose of the check on the For line. (5) Write the amount of the check after the words *Amt. This Check*. (6) Calculate the new checking balance and record it in the amount column on the last line of the stub.

3. (1) Write the date. (2) Write to whom the check is to be paid following the words

Pay to the order of. (3) Write the amount in figures following the dollar sign. (4) Write the amount in words on the line with the word *Dollars*. (5) Write the purpose of the check on the line labeled For. (6) Sign the check.

Chapter 6, Page 135

1. (1) A service charge may not have been recorded in the depositor's business records. (2) Outstanding deposits may be recorded in the depositor's records but not on a bank statement. (3) Outstanding checks may be recorded in the depositor's records but not on a bank statement. (4) A depositor may have made a math or recording error.
2. An outstanding check.

Chapter 6, Page 140

1. (1) The check appears to be altered. (2) The signature on the check does not match the signature on the signature card. (3) The amounts written in figures and in words do not agree. (4) The check is postdated. (5) The person who wrote the check has stopped payment on it. (6) The account of the person who wrote the check has insufficient funds to pay the check.
2. Cash.
3. Cash.

Chapter 6, Page 144

1. For making small cash payments.
2. The check issued to replenish petty cash is a credit to Cash and does not affect Petty Cash.

Chapter 7, Page 158

1. Name of the business, name of report, and date of report.
2. All general ledger accounts are listed in the Trial Balance columns of a work sheet, even if some accounts do not have balances.

Chapter 7, Page 164

1. An expense should be reported in the same fiscal period that it is used to produce revenue.
2. (1) What is the balance of the account? (2) What should the balance be for this account? (3) What must be done to correct the account balance? (4) What adjustment is made?

Chapter 7, Page 169

1. Asset, liability, and owner's equity accounts.
2. Revenue and expense accounts.
3. Income Statement Debit and Balance Sheet Credit columns.
4. Income Statement Credit and Balance Sheet Debit columns.

Chapter 7, Page 173

1. Subtract the smaller total from the larger total to find the difference.
2. The difference between two column totals can be divided evenly by 9.
3. A slide.

Chapter 8, Page 186

1. Heading, revenue, expenses, and net income or net loss.
2. Total Expenses *divided by* Total Sales *equals* Total Expenses Component Percentage.
3. Net Income *divided by* Total Sales *equals* Net Income Component Percentage.

Chapter 8, Page 191

1. Heading, assets, liabilities, and owner's equity.
2. Capital Account Balance *plus* Net Income

minus Drawing Account Balance *equals* Current Capital.

Chapter 9, Page 202

1. To update general ledger accounts.
2. Adjustments column of the work sheet.
3. Supplies Expense and Insurance Expense.

Chapter 9, Page 209

1. Beginning balances.
2. Changes in the owner's capital for a single fiscal period.
3. (1) An entry to close income statement accounts with credit balances. (2) An entry to close income statement accounts with debit balances. (3) An entry to record net income or net loss and close the income summary account. (4) An entry to close the owner's drawing account.

Chapter 9, Page 215

1. To assure a reader that a balance has not been omitted.
2. Only those with balances (permanent accounts).
3. Because they are closed and have zero balances.

Chapter 10, Page 232

1. Businesses often require the skills or capital of more than one person.
2. The selling of merchandise rather than a service.
3. Columns for the recording of frequently occurring transactions related to the purchasing and selling of merchandise.

Chapter 10, Page 237

1. Purchases Debit column and Accounts Payable Credit column.
2. Supplies—Store and the vendor name.

Chapter 10, Page 243

1. Accounts Payable Debit column and Cash Credit column.
2. Advertising Expense.
3. For making change at the cash register and for making small cash payments.
4. The partner's drawing account.
5. General Debit column and General Credit column.

Chapter 11, Page 259

1. A merchandising business sells merchandise; a service business sells services.
2. As a percentage of sales.
3. The amount of sales tax collected is a business liability until paid to the government.
4. *Realization of Revenue.*
5. Accounts Receivable.

Chapter 11, Page 266

1. To show the equality of debits and credits.
2. Whenever a journal page is filled and always at the end of a month.
3. To show that the totals have been verified as correct.
4. Cash on hand at the beginning of the month, *plus* total cash received during the month, *less* total cash paid during the month, *equals* cash balance on hand at the end of the month. Cash is proved if the balance on the next unused check stub is the same as the cash proof.

Chapter 12, Page 279

1. An account in a general ledger that summarizes all accounts in a subsidiary ledger.
2. The balance of a controlling account

equals the total of all account balances in its related subsidiary ledger.

3. Debit, Credit, Balance Debit, and Balance Credit.

4. (1) A check mark is placed in parentheses below the General Debit and General Credit column totals to indicate that the two column totals are not posted. (2) The general ledger account number of the account listed in the column heading is written in parentheses below the special amount column totals to show that the totals are posted.

Chapter 12, Page 285

1. Credit balance. Because accounts payable are liabilities and liabilities have normal credit balances.

2. By writing the vendor name and vendor number on the heading of the ledger account.

3. (1) Write the date in the Date column of the account. (2) Write the journal page number in the Post. Ref. column of the account. (3) Write the credit amount in the Credit column of the account. (4) Add the amount in the Credit column to the previous balance in the Credit Balance column. Write the new account balance in the Credit Balance column. (5) Write the vendor number in the Post. Ref. column of the journal. The vendor number shows that the posting for this entry is complete.

Chapter 12, Page 291

1. Accounts receivable are assets, and assets have normal debit balances.

2. (1) Write the date in the Date column of the account. (2) Write the journal page number in the Post. Ref. column of the account. (3) Write the debit amount in the Debit column of the account. (4) Add the amount in the Debit column to the previous balance in the Debit Balance column. Write the new account balance in the Debit Balance column. (5) Write the vendor number in the Post. Ref. column of the journal. The vendor number shows that the posting for this entry is complete.

Chapter 12, Page 294

1. Posting must be accurate to assure correct account balances.

2. A controlling account balance in a general ledger must equal the sum of all account balances in a subsidiary ledger.

3. Vendor accounts.

4. The accounts receivable ledger is proved.

Chapter 13, Page 307

1. The total amount earned by all employees for a pay period.

2. $3\frac{1}{2}$ hours.

3. Overtime earnings × the overtime rate.

4. $440.00.

Chapter 13, Page 313

1. Form W-4, Employee's Withholding Allowance Certificate.

2. Employee marital status and number of withholding allowances.

3. Both the employee and the employer.

Chapter 13, Page 318

1. The payroll register summarizes the payroll for one pay period and shows total earnings, payroll withholdings, and net pay of all employees.

2. By subtracting total deductions from total earnings.

3. Because a business must send a quarterly report to federal and state governments showing employee taxable earnings and taxes withheld from employee earnings.

Chapter 13, Page 321

1. To help protect and control payroll payments.
2. The payroll register.
3. Individual checks are not written and do not have to be distributed.

Chapter 14, Page 335

1. Salary Expense.
2. Employee Income Tax Payable.
3. Social Security Tax Payable.
4. Medicare Tax Payable.

Chapter 14, Page 340

1. Social security: 6.5% of earnings up to a maximum of $65,400.00 in each calendar year; Medicare: 1.5% of total employee earnings; federal unemployment: 0.8% of the first $7,000.00 earned by each employee; state unemployment: 5.4% on the first $7,000.00 earned by each employee.
2. The first $7,000.00.

Chapter 14, Page 345

1. By January 31.
2. Federal income tax, social security tax, and Medicare tax.

Chapter 14, Page 351

1. By the 15th day of the following month.
2. For paying payroll taxes and for paying federal unemployment tax.

Chapter 15, Page 371

1. In the same order they appear in the general ledger.
2. Merchandise Inventory and Income Summary.

Chapter 15, Page 377

1. Supplies—Office and Supplies Expense—Office.
2. Prepaid Insurance and Insurance Expense.

Chapter 15, Page 384

1. Income Statement Debit or Credit column.
2. When the Income Statement Debit column total (costs and expenses) is larger than the Credit column total (revenue).
3. Balance Sheet Debit.
4. Trial balance amounts after adjustments are extended to the Adjusted Trial Balance columns, and the Adjusted Trial Balance columns are proved before extending amounts to the Income Statement and Balance Sheet columns.

Chapter 16, Page 396

1. The cost of merchandise sold section.
2. Beginning merchandise inventory, *plus* purchases, *equals* total cost of merchandise available for sale, *less* ending merchandise inventory, *equals* cost of merchandise sold.
3. By comparing it with the amount calculated on the work sheet.

Chapter 16, Page 401

1. (1) Cost of merchandise sold, (2) gross profit on sales, (3) total expenses, and (4) net income.
2. By making comparisons with prior fiscal periods as well as with industry standards that are published by industry organizations.
3. Net loss.

Chapter 16, Page 407

1. Each partner's share of net income or loss.
2. (1) Beginning capital, (2) additional investments, and (3) each partner's withdrawal of assets.

3. The January 1 capital, *plus* the net increase in capital, *equals* the December 31 capital.

Chapter 16, Page 412

1. A business's financial condition on a specific date.
2. In account form or report form.
3. The Balance Sheet columns of a work sheet and the owner's equity statement.
4. A schedule of accounts payable and a schedule of accounts receivable.

Chapter 17, Page 425

1. Insurance Expense and Income Summary.
2. Because the explanation "Adjusting Entries" is recorded in the Account Title column to explain all of the adjusting entries that follow.
3. Adjusting entry for merchandising inventory.

Chapter 17, Page 430

1. Income Statement and Balance Sheet columns of the work sheet and the distribution of net income statement.
2. Income Summary.

Chapter 17, Page 434

1. The distribution of net income statement and the Balance Sheet columns of the work sheet.
2. An amount equal to its balance is recorded on the side opposite the balance.

Chapter 17, Page 439

1. General ledger accounts with balances.
2. To prove the equality of debits and credits in the general ledger.
3. In the same order as they appear in the general ledger.

A

Account a record summarizing all the information pertaining to a single item in the accounting equation. (p. 9)

Account balance the amount in an account. (p. 9)

Account number the number assigned to an account. (p. 99)

Account title the name given to an account. (p. 9)

Accounting planning, recording, analyzing, and interpreting financial information. (p. 4)

Accounting cycle the series of accounting activities included in recording financial information for a fiscal period. (p. 214)

Accounting equation an equation showing the relationship among assets, liabilities, and owner's equity. (p. 7)

Accounting period see *fiscal period.*

Accounting records organized summaries of a business's financial activities. (p. 4)

Accounting system a planned process for providing financial information that will be useful to management. (p. 4)

Accounts payable ledger a subsidiary ledger containing only accounts for vendors from whom items are purchased or bought on account. (p. 274)

Accounts receivable ledger a subsidiary ledger containing only accounts for charge customers. (p. 274)

Adjusting entries journal entries recorded to update general ledger accounts at the end of a fiscal period. (p. 198)

Adjustments changes recorded on a work sheet to update general ledger accounts at the end of a fiscal period. (p. 160)

Asset anything of value that is owned. (p. 7)

B

Balance sheet a financial statement that reports assets, liabilities, and owner's equity on a specific date. (p. 13)

Bank statement a report of deposits, withdrawals, and bank balances sent to a depositor by a bank. (p. 131)

Blank endorsement an endorsement consisting only of the endorser's signature. (p. 127)

C

Capital the account used to summarize the owner's equity in a business. (p. 9)

Cash sale a sale in which cash is received for the total amount of the sale at the time of the transaction. (p. 254)

Charge sale see *sale on account.*

Chart of accounts a list of accounts used by a business. (p. 45)

Check a business form ordering a bank to pay cash from a bank account. (p. 67)

Checking account a bank account from which payments can be ordered by a depositor. (p. 126)

Closing entries journal entries used to prepare temporary accounts for a new fiscal period. (p. 203)

Component percentage the percentage relationship between one financial statement item and the total that includes that item. (p. 184)

Controlling account an account in a general ledger that summarizes all accounts in a subsidiary ledger. (p. 274)

Correcting entry a journal entry made to correct an error in the ledger. (p. 116)

Cost of goods sold see *cost of merchandise sold.*

Cost of merchandise the price a business pays for goods it purchases to sell. (p. 230)

Cost of merchandise sold the total original price of all merchandise sold during a fiscal period. (p. 392)

Credit an amount recorded on the right side of a T account. (p. 42)

Credit card sale a sale in which a credit card is used for the total amount of the sale at the time of the transaction. (p. 254)

Glossary

Customer a person or business to whom merchandise or services are sold. (p. 252)

D

Debit an amount recorded on the left side of a T account. (p. 42)

Debit card a bank card that, when making purchases, automatically deducts the amount of the purchase from the checking account of the cardholder. (p. 139)

Dishonored check a check that a bank refuses to pay. (p. 136)

Distribution of net income statement a partnership financial statement showing net income or loss distribution to partners. (p. 402)

Double-entry accounting the recording of debit and credit parts of a transaction. (p. 66)

E

Electronic funds transfer a computerized cash payments system that uses electronic impulses to transfer funds. (p. 138)

Employee earnings record a business form used to record details affecting payments made to an employee. (p. 316)

Endorsement a signature or stamp on the back of a check transferring ownership. (p. 127)

Endorsement in full see *special endorsement.*

Entry information for each transaction recorded in a journal. (p. 66)

Equities financial rights to the assets of a business. (p. 7)

Exhibit see *supporting schedule.*

Expense a decrease in owner's equity resulting from the operation of a business. (p. 27)

F

Federal unemployment tax a federal tax used for state and federal administrative expenses of the unemployment program. (p. 338)

File maintenance the procedure for arranging accounts in a general ledger, assigning account numbers, and keeping records current. (p. 100)

Fiscal period the length of time for which a business summarizes and reports financial information. (p. 156)

G

General amount column a journal amount column that is not headed with an account title. (p. 66)

General ledger a ledger that contains all accounts needed to prepare financial statements. (p. 99)

Gross earnings see *total earnings.*

Gross pay see *total earnings.*

Gross profit on sales the revenue remaining after cost of merchandise sold has been deducted. (p. 394)

I

Income statement a financial statement showing the revenue and expenses for a fiscal period. (p. 166)

Inventory the amount of goods on hand. (p. 368)

Invoice a form describing the goods or services sold, the quantity, and the price. (p. 67)

J

Journal a form for recording transactions in chronological order. (p. 64)

Journalizing recording transactions in a journal. (p. 64)

L

Ledger a group of accounts. (p. 99)

Liability an amount owed by a business (p. 7)

M

Markup the amount added to the cost of merchandise to establish the selling price. (p. 230)

Medicare tax a federal tax paid for hospital insurance. (p. 312)

Memorandum a form on which a brief message is written describing a transaction. (p. 68)

Merchandise goods that a merchandising business purchases to sell. (p. 228)

Merchandise inventory the amount of goods on hand for sale to customers. (p. 368)

Merchandising business a business that purchases and sells goods. (p. 228)

N

Net income the difference between total revenue and total expenses when total revenue is greater. (p. 167)

Net loss the difference between total revenue and total expenses when total expenses is greater. (p. 168)

Net pay the total earnings paid to an employee after payroll taxes and other deductions. (p. 315)

Nominal account see *temporary accounts.*

Normal balance the side of the account that is increased. (p. 42)

O

Opening an account writing an account title and number on the heading of an account. (p. 101)

Owner's equity the amount remaining after the value of all liabilities is subtracted from the value of all assets. (p. 7)

Owners' equity statement a financial statement that summarizes the changes in owners' equity during a fiscal period. (p. 404)

P

Partner each member of a partnership. (p. 226)

Partnership a business in which two or more persons combine their assets and skills. (p. 226)

Pay period the period covered by a salary payment. (p. 302)

Payroll the total amount earned by all employees for a pay period. (p. 302)

Payroll register a business form used to record payroll information. (p. 314)

Payroll taxes taxes based on the payroll of a business. (p. 308)

Permanent accounts accounts used to accumulate information from one fiscal period to the next. (p. 203)

Petty cash an amount of cash kept on hand and used for making small payments. (p. 141)

Petty cash slip a form showing proof of a petty cash payment. (p. 142)

Post-closing trial balance a trial balance prepared after the closing entries are posted. (p. 213)

Postdated check a check with a future date on it. (p. 128)

Posting transferring information from a journal entry to a ledger account. (p. 103)

Proprietorship a business owned by one person. (p. 6)

Proving cash determining that the amount of cash agrees with the accounting records. (p. 85)

Purchase invoice an invoice used as a source document for recording a purchase on account transaction. (p. 233)

R

Real accounts see *permanent accounts.*

Receipt a business form giving written acknowledgement for cash received. (p. 68)

Restrictive endorsement an endorsement restricting further transfer of a check's ownership. (p. 127)

Retail merchandising business a merchandising business that sells to those who use or consume the goods. (p. 228)

Revenue an increase in owner's equity resulting from the operation of a business. (p. 26)

S

Salary the money paid for employee services. (p. 302)

Sale on account a sale for which cash will be received at a later date. (p. 26)

Sales invoice an invoice used as a source document for recording a sale on account. (p. 67)

Sales slip see *sales invoice.*

Sales tax a tax on a sale of merchandise or services. (p. 252)

Schedule of accounts payable a listing of vendor accounts, account balances, and total amount due all vendors. (p. 292)

Schedule of accounts receivable a listing of customer accounts, account balances, and total amount due from all customers. (p. 293)

Service business a business that performs an activity for a fee. (p. 6)

Social security tax a federal tax paid for old-age, survivors, and disability insurance. (p. 312)

Sole proprietorship see *proprietorship.*

Source document a business paper from which information is obtained for a journal entry. (p. 66)

Special amount column a journal amount column headed with an account title. (p. 66)

Special endorsement an endorsement indicating a new owner of a check. (p. 127)

State unemployment tax a state tax used to pay benefits to unemployed workers. (p. 338)

Subsidiary ledger a ledger that is summarized in a single general ledger account. (p. 274)

Supplementary report see *supporting schedule.*

Supporting schedule a report prepared to give details about an item on a principal financial statement. (p. 411)

T

T account an accounting device used to analyze transactions. (p. 42)

Tax base the maximum amount of earnings on which a tax is calculated. (p. 312)

Temporary accounts accounts used to accumulate information until it is transferred to the owner's capital account. (p. 203)

Terms of sale an agreement between a buyer and a seller about payment for merchandise. (p. 233)

Total earnings the total pay due for a pay period before deductions. (p. 306)

Transaction a business activity that changes assets, liabilities, or owner's equity. (p. 9)

Trial balance a proof of the equality of debits and credits in a general ledger. (p. 157)

V

Vendor a business from which merchandise is purchased or supplies or other assets are bought. (p. 230)

W

Wholesale merchandising business a business that buys and resells merchandise to retail merchandising businesses. (p. 228)

Withdrawals assets taken out of a business for the owner's personal use. (p. 28)

Withholding allowance a deduction from total earnings for each person legally supported by a taxpayer, including the employee. (p. 309)

Work sheet a columnar accounting form used to summarize the general ledger information needed to prepare financial statements. (p. 156)

Index

A

Index

Index

D

E

Index

H

I

J

O

P

Index

U

V

W

Y

Index

Photo Credits

FRONT MATTER
p. vi: © Gibson Guitar Corp.; p. vii: West Music Company; p. viii: © Image Club Graphics; p. ix: © Image Club Graphics; p. xv: © Steve Skjold/PhotoEdit

CHAPTER 1
p. 5: © Greg Grosse; p. 6: © Greg Grosse; p. 10: ESP Guitar Company; p. 13: Violin made by Charles J. Rufino—Photo: Giovanni Rufino

CHAPTER 2
p. 25: © Greg Grosse; p. 33: Folkcraft Instruments, Winsted, CT; p. 34: West Music Company

CHAPTER 3
p. 41: © Greg Grosse; p. 47: West Music Company; p. 52: Photo courtesy of Gemeinhardt Co., Inc.

CHAPTER 4
p. 65: © Greg Grosse; p. 67: © Gibson Guitar Corp.; p. 85: West Music Company; p. 95: Copyright © 2000, Gateway 2000, Inc. Reproduced with permission. All rights reserved.

CHAPTER 5
p. 96: West Music Company; p. 97: © Greg Grosse; p. 98: ESP Guitar Company

CHAPTER 6
p. 125: © Greg Grosse/Location courtesy of CINTEL Federal Credit Union, Cincinnati, Ohio; p. 153: West Music Company

CHAPTER 7
p. 155: © Greg Grosse; p. 177: Oscar Schmidt, Division of Washburn International

CHAPTER 8
p. 181: © Greg Grosse

CHAPTER 9
p. 199: © Greg Grosse; p. 204: West Music Company

CHAPTER 10
p. 226: The Nature Company; p. 227: © Jeff Greenberg/Photo Researchers; p. 228: © Greg Grosse; p. 229: © Image Club Graphics; p. 231: The Bombay Company; p. 236: © Image Club Graphics

CHAPTER 11
p. 253: © Greg Grosse; p. 256: © Image Club Graphics; p. 258: The Nature Company; p. 261: © Image Club Graphics; p. 262: © Image Club Graphics; p. 265: The Nature Company

CHAPTER 12
p. 275: Image Copyright © PhotoDisc, Inc.; p. 277: The Nature Company; p. 280: © Image Club Graphics; p. 282: The Nature Company; p. 287: © Image Club Graphics; p. 289: © Image Club Graphics; p. 292: © Image Club Graphics; p. 300: The Nature Company

CHAPTER 13
p. 303: © Greg Grosse; p. 304: © P. & R. Manley/SuperStock; p. 320: © Chris Marona/Photo Researchers; p. 323: © Lois Ellen Frank/Westlight

Photo Credits

CHAPTER 14

p. 330: © Bruce Forster/Tony Stone Images; p. 331: © Greg Grosse/Location courtesy of Quality Central Hotel & Suites, Cincinnati, Ohio; p. 336: © John Elk/Stock, Boston; p. 338: © R. A. Clevenger/Westlight; p. 347: © Richard Pasley/Stock, Boston; p. 349: © R. Ian Lloyd/Westlight

CHAPTER 15

p. 365: © Greg Grosse/Location courtesy of St. Xavier High School, Cincinnati, Ohio; p. 368: © Lawrence Migdale/Stock, Boston; p. 369: Photo courtesy of Pier 1 Imports; p. 375: © John Eastcott/Yva Momatiuk/Photo Researchers; p. 376: © Fred M. Middendorf; p. 379: © Mark Adams/Westlight

CHAPTER 16

p. 391: © Ian O'Leary/Tony Stone Images; p. 398: © Bob Daemmrich/Stock, Boston; p. 400: The Nature Company; p. 406: The Nature Company

CHAPTER 17

p. 421: © Tom McCarthy/PhotoEdit; p. 423: The Bombay Company; p. 429: Photo courtesy of Pier 1 Imports; p. 433: Photo courtesy of Pier 1 Imports